Nepal

Bradley Mayhew
Joe Bindloss, Stan Armington

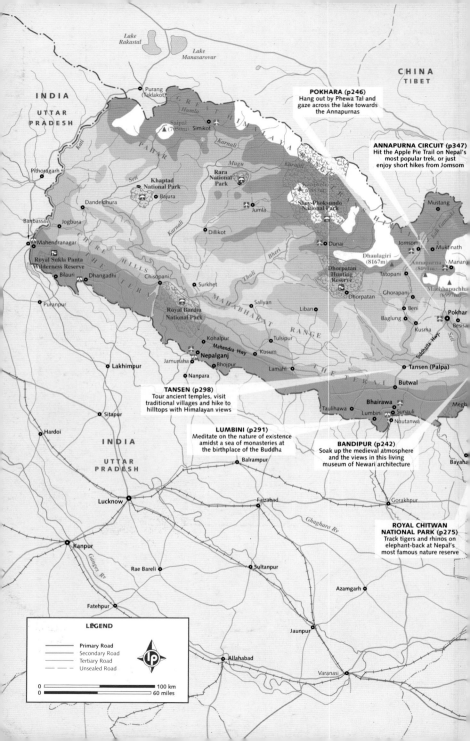

CHINA
TIBET

INDIA
UTTAR
PRADESH

Lake
Rakastal

Lake
Manasarovar

Purang
(Taklakot)

Saipal
(7035m) Simikot

Pithoragarh

Khaptad
National
Park Bajura

Rara
National
Park

Mugu

Jumla

Shey-Phoksundo
National Park

Mustang

Banbassa
Jogbura

Mahendranagar

**Royal Sukla Panta
Wilderness Reserve**

Bilauri Dhangadhi

Chisopani

Dilikot

Dunai

Jomsom Muktinath

Dhaulagiri
(8167m)

Annapurna
(8091m) Manang

Dandeldhura

Puranpur

**Royal Bardia
National Park**

Surkhet

Sallyan

Dhorpatan
Hunting
Reserve

Tatopani

Ghorapani

Machhapuchhare
(6997m)

Dhorpatan

Beni

Baglung

Liban

Kusma

Pokhara

Besisa

POKHARA (p246)
Hang out by Phewa Tal and
gaze across the lake towards
the Annapurnas

ANNAPURNA CIRCUIT (p347)
Hit the Apple Pie Trail on Nepal's
most popular trek, or just
enjoy short hikes from Jomsom

Lakhimpur

Jamunaha

Kohalpur

Nepalganj

Bhojpur

Nanpara

Mahendra Hwy

Kusum

Tulsipur

Lamahi

Butwal

Tansen (Palpa)

Megh

Sitapur

TANSEN (p298)
Tour ancient temples, visit
traditional villages and hike to
hilltops with Himalayan views

Taulihawa

Bhairawa

Lumbini Sunauli

Nautanwa

Bayaha

INDIA
UTTAR
PRADESH

Hardoi

LUMBINI (p291)
Meditate on the nature of existence
amidst a sea of monasteries at
the birthplace of the Buddha

BANDIPUR (p242)
Soak up the medieval atmosphere
and the views in this living
museum of Newari architecture

Balrampur

Lucknow

Faizabad

Gorakhpur

Ghaghara Rv

**ROYAL CHITWAN
NATIONAL PARK (p275)**
Track tigers and rhinos on
elephant-back at Nepal's
most famous nature reserve

Kanpur

Ganges Rv

Rae Bareli

Sultanpur

Azamgarh

Fatehpur

Jaunpur

LEGEND

—— Primary Road
—— Secondary Road
—— Tertiary Road
- - - Unsealed Road

Allahabad

Varanasi

0 ————————— 100 km
0 ————————— 60 miles

ELEVATION

6000m
4000m
2000m
1000m
500m
0

CHINA
TIBET

LANGTANG NATIONAL PARK (p341)
Get to the mountains quickly on the nearest trek to Kathmandu

RAFTING & CANYONING (p78)
Raft down the Bhote Kosi river or abseil down a thundering waterfall for the ultimate white-water rush

MOUNTAIN FLIGHTS (p384)
Hitch a ride into the heavens, so close you can almost touch the Himalaya

KATHMANDU (p108)
Immerse yourself in one of world's most fascinating and tourist-friendly cities

EVEREST REGION (p334)
Take it slowly up the classic trek to Everest Base Camp and the gorgeous Gokyo Valley

PATAN (p184)
Prepare for temple overload, with some of the finest Newari architecture in Nepal

BHAKTAPUR (p196)
Stroll along traffic-free backstreets and witness the unchanging rituals of Newari life

KOSHI TAPPU WILDLIFE RESERVE (p316)
Escape to this water world of thatched villages and rice paddies where bird species outnumber tourists 400:1

JANAKPUR (p312)
Join the other pilgrims to this ancient Hindu centre, scene of the famous Hindu epic the Ramayana

Destination Nepal

Draped along the greatest heights of the Himalaya, the kingdom of Nepal is where the ice-cold of the mountains meets the steamy heat of the Indian plains. It's a land of yaks and yetis, stupas and Sherpas, some of the best trekking on earth and the closest thing that backpackers have to Disneyland.

The Himalaya's most sophisticated urban cultures took shape here, in the three great minikingdoms of the Kathmandu Valley – Kathmandu, Patan and Bhaktapur – home to a world-class artistic and architectural heritage.

Behind the palaces and pagodas of the Kathmandu Valley rises the 'Abode of Snows' (Himalaya in Sanskrit), a magnet for trekkers and mountaineers the world over. Only in Nepal can you trek for weeks without the need even for a tent. No longer does your name have to be Tenzing or Hillary to set foot in Everest Base Camp.

Out of the mountains, get your adrenaline kick from world-class white-water rafting, kayaking and mountain biking, or from the spine-tingling sight of your first tiger or rhino in Royal Chitwan National Park.

Nepal is not just a bungee-jumping, apple-pie eating Shangri-la. It's also one of the poorest countries on earth. However, many visitors, drawn to Nepal by the promise of adventure, leave equally enchanted by the friendliness and openness of the Nepali people.

From the natural rhythm you ease into on a trek to the rhythm of a tabla drum at one of Kathmandu's palace restaurants, Nepal is an amazingly diverse country that offers something for everyone. One journey through this land is rarely enough. The first thing many people do after a visit is start planning the next one.

GARETH MCCORMA

People

STAN ARMINGTON

Share a laugh with the porters on market day at Namche Bazaar (p337)

BILL WASSMAN

Come face-to-face with the traditional cultures of Nepal (p42)

RYAN FOX

See thangkas (Tibetan religious paintings; p155) being created in Kathmandu

OTHER HIGHLIGHTS

- Get to know your Sherpa lodge owners, porters and mountain guides in the Khumbu region (p334)
- Mingle with the locals in the traditional Newari village of Bandipur (p242)

Potter about the action at Potter's Square (p197), Bhaktapur

ANDERS BLOMQVIST

Trekking & Hiking

Marvel at majestic Mt Everest (p34)

Walk through the rice fields of the Kali Gandaki valley on the Annapurna Circuit (p347)

OTHER HIGHLIGHTS

- Beat the crowds on a week-long teahouse trek in the Langtang Valley (p341)
- Experience spectacular scenery and meet the friendly locals on the Jomson Trek (p345)

Appreciate some of the world's greatest scenery on the Everest Base Camp trek (p334)

Mountain Views

ANTHONY PLUMMER

Witness Nepal's dawn spectacle with sunrise from Poon Hill (p268)

STAN ARMINGTON

Stand in awe of Machhapuchhare
(p250) or 'Fish Tail' mountain

OTHER HIGHLIGHTS

- Blow US$100 on a mountain flight (p384) and enjoy eye-level views of the world's greatest peaks, with a gin and tonic in your hand
- Savour the views of the Annapurnas and Machhapuchhare from languid Phewa Tal (p250)

View the arid landscapes of the Mustang Valley (p69)

BILL WASSMAN

Durbar Squares

See Vatsala Durga Temple (p200) in Bhaktapur's Durbar Square at night, without the crowds

RYAN FOX

ANDERS BLOMQ

Dive through the Buddhist courtyards of Patan and end up in Nepal's finest Durbar Square (p186)

RICHARD I'ANSON

Admire the neoclassical splendour of Gaddhi Baithak (p120) in Durbar Square, Kathmandu

OTHER HIGHLIGHTS

- Take a couple of hours to savour Patan's museum (p189), one of the best in the subcontinent
- Get lost in the medieval backstreets of Bhaktapur (p196), the Kathmandu Valley's most intact Newari town
- Clamber up the stepped temples to take in the pagodas and palaces of Kathmandu's majestic Durbar Square (p114)

Temples & Pilgrimages

Visit Swayambhunath temple (p162), the Kathmandu Valley's famous monkey temple

Meditate on the example of the Buddha at his birthplace in Lumbini (p291)

OTHER HIGHLIGHTS

- Join the Hindu pilgrimage at Janakpur, the birthplace of Rama (p312)
- Witness hundreds of devotees bathe in the icy waters of the Kali Gandaki during Magh Sankranti in Ridi Bazaar (p301)
- Follow the pilgrims on their clockwise circuit of Pharping (p218), a thriving Newari village

Follow Tibetan exiles on their daily devotions around Bodhnath stupa (p170), Kathmandu

Outdoor Activities

Be escorted by a rhino on an elephant safari in Royal Chitwan National Park (p275)

Take a relaxing break from the white water on a
Karnali River rafting trip (p98)

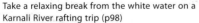

OTHER HIGHLIGHTS

- Abseil down a waterfall near the Tibetan border during a two-day canyoning course (p78)
- Go bird-watching in Koshi Tappu Wildlife Reserve (p316), where birds outnumber humans 400 to one
- Go mountain biking along the Scar Rd from Kathmandu (p83)

Contents

Regional Map Contents

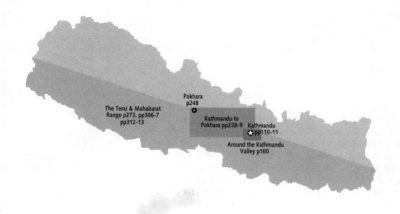

Pokhara
p248

The Terai & Mahabarat
Range p273, pp306-7
pp312-13

Kathmandu to
Pokhara pp238-9   Kathmandu
pp110-11

Around the Kathmandu
Valley p160

The Authors

BRADLEY MAYHEW
Coordinating Author, Kathmandu, Around Kathmandu Valley

Drawn to big snowy mountains and Tibetan Buddhist communities like a moth to a flame, Bradley has been travelling to Nepal for a decade now, often en route to and from Tibet. He owes over 80% of his CD collection to Thamel's music shops. British born, Bradley currently lives under the big skies of Montana.

He is the coauthor of Lonely Planet guides to *Tibet, Central Asia,* and *China* among others. He has lectured on Central Asia at the Royal Geographic Society. Bradley also wrote the front chapters and Directory and Transport.

My Favourite Trip

The best part of this research trip was my three-week trek around the Everest region (p334). The crowds came as a bit of a shock, as did the bakeries and bookstores of bustling Namche Bazaar (p337), but by staying at smaller lodges, in between the main halts, it's surprisingly easy to lose the Gore-Tex crowd. My favourite part was the Gokyo Valley (p339); second favourite was watching people see Cho La (p339) for the first time – everyone without exception responding with a squint and an appalled look on their faces. *'Up there?! You've got to be ****ing kidding me!!'*. Priceless.

The worst part of the trip was arriving back in the thick, syrupy air of noisy, polluted Kathmandu (p108) – am I really the only person who gets low-altitude sickness?

JOE BINDLOSS
Kathmandu to Pokhara, Pokhara, Terai & Mahabharat

Joe has been coming to Nepal for more than a decade, lured here by the sense of peace and quiet, both inner and outer. He was born in Cyprus, grew up in England and has since lived and worked in various countries, though he currently calls London home. He first developed a severe case of wanderlust on family trips through Europe in the old VW Kombi. A degree in biology eliminated science from his future choice of careers, and Joe moved through a string of occupations before finally settling on journalism. Joe's big area for Lonely Planet is India, but he has also contributed to more than 20 Lonely Planet guidebooks covering Southeast Asia, Africa, Europe and Australia.

My Favourite Trip

Taking the slow local bus from Kathmandu to Pokhara and overnighting in a village guest house in Bandipur (p242), followed by a dawn walk up to Thani Mai (p244) for a prebreakfast view of the Himalaya. Then riding on the bus roof from Dumre to Pokhara (p245), with Mt Machhapuchhare looming overhead like a beacon. In Pokhara (p246), I always make space for a two-inch–thick steak and a stroll up to the World Peace Pagoda (p255). Hiring motorcycles is an essential part of any trip and the hair-raising ride from Pokhara down to Tansen (p298) is one of the best in the country. Then back to Kathmandu for a final circumnavigation of Bodhnath (p169). *Fait accompli.*

CONTRIBUTING AUTHORS

Stan Armington wrote the Trekking chapter for this edition of Nepal. He has been organising and leading treks in Nepal since 1971. A graduate engineer, he has also worked for the US National Park service in the Yellowstone National and Olympic Parks, and served as a guide on Mt Hood in Oregon. He was one of Lonely Planet's first authors. His guide *Trekking in the Nepal Himalaya,* first published in 1979, won the 2002 PATA Gold Award for its eighth edition.

Stan lives in Kathmandu and is the director of the American Himalayan Foundation, a fellow of the Royal Geographical Society and the Explorers Club, and a member of the American Alpine Club and the Alpine Stomach Club.

LONELY PLANET AUTHORS

Why is our travel information the best in the world? It's simple: our authors are independent, dedicated travellers. They don't research using just the Internet or phone, and they don't take freebies in exchange for positive coverage. They travel widely, to all the popular spots and off the beaten track. They personally visit thousands of hotels, restaurants, cafés, bars, galleries, palaces, museums and more – and they take pride in getting all the details right, and telling it how it is. For more, see the authors section on www.lonelyplanet.com.

Getting Started

In many ways, Nepal is a dream destination. Travel can be as cheap as you want, but all the comforts are there for when you want to spend a little more and there's not much advanced required. Pick up a visa on arrival and just rock up to Thamel to join a rafting trip leaving the next day. Still, spending some time leafing through this book and browsing the web will guarantee you don't miss any of the fantastic things on offer and ensure you are on top of the frequently changing security situation (see opposite for more information).

WHEN TO GO

Nepal has a typical monsoonal, two-season year. The dry season runs from October to May and there's the wet (monsoon) season from June to September. Autumn (September to November) and spring (March to May) bring almost perfect weather and are definitely the best times to come to Nepal. For more on the best months for trekking see p324.

See climate charts (p357) for more information.

October to November, the start of the dry season, is in many ways the absolute best time. With the monsoon only recently finished, the countryside is green and lush, the air is sparkling clean and the Himalayan views are near perfect. Furthermore, the weather is still balmy. There are some important and colourful festivals to enjoy, though the Dasain festival in October can be disruptive if you are on a tight schedule (see p367). For obvious reasons this is also the high tourist season but in recent years, due to the political problems, even Nepal's 'high season' has been pretty quiet.

In December and January the climate and visibility are still good, though it can get very cold at high altitudes. Heading for the Everest Base Camp at this time of year can be a real feat of endurance and the Annapurna Circuit is often closed by snow on the Thorung La. Down in Kathmandu, the cheaper hotels – where there is no heating – are chilly in the mornings and evenings. Tourists start to leave Kathmandu in December like flocks of migratory birds, headed for the warmer climes of India or Thailand. October to February are considered the best times to visit the Terai and Royal Chitwan National Park.

February to April, the tail end of the dry season, is the second-best time to visit. The weather gets warmer so high-altitude treks are not as arduous. Visibility is not as good as earlier in the dry season, but Nepal's wonderful rhododendrons and other flowers are in Technicolor bloom.

May and early June are not the best times to visit as it is extremely hot and dusty, with temperatures often above 30°C, and the coming monsoon seems to hang over you like a threat.

Mid-June to September, when the monsoon finally arrives, is the least popular time to visit Nepal. Although it doesn't rain all day it usually rains every day, and the trails and roads are muddy and plagued by leeches; the Himalaya disappear behind rain clouds; most rivers are too high to raft; and landslides often hold up transport. The latter part of the monsoon (August and September) is a time of festivals, which will certainly enliven a visit to Kathmandu, and this is also the best time to visit neighbouring Tibet.

Because of its lower altitude, Pokhara is warmer and more pleasant than Kathmandu during winter, but hotter before the monsoon and wetter during it.

DON'T LEAVE HOME WITHOUT...

▪ Checking the security situation – see p359

▪ A face mask against Kathmandu's air pollution, especially if you have a respiratory problem or plan to ride a bike

▪ Sunglasses, a hat and high-factor sunscreen

▪ Hiking shoes – fine for light trekking and one of the few things you can't rent or buy in Kathmandu

▪ A fleece if visiting Pokhara, Kathmandu and the Terai between October and March

▪ A down sleeping bag, fleece hat and down vest or coat if visiting the mountains, even in summer

▪ Earplugs, a padlock, a torch (flashlight) for trekking and power cuts, insect repellent for Royal Chitwan National Park or other places in the Terai, tampons

▪ An umbrella, raincoat and antileech oil for monsoon travel

▪ Swimming costume for rafting, kayaking, canyoning, elephant-washing (yes, elephant washing – see p280), and, well, swimming

---

IS IT SAFE?

The seven-year Maoist 'people's war' has cost nearly 12,000 Nepali lives so far (for reasons behind the violence see p36). That said, the Maoists are more of a threat to the tourist industry as a whole, rather than to individual tourists, who have never been specifically targeted.

In March 2002 the Maoists chief ideologue, Dr Baburam Bhattarai, published an 'open letter to foreign tourists'. In it he stated that the Maoists welcomed tourism and tourists, but he also warned that 'the unassuming traveller can be caught between the crossfire of the contending armies'.

Maoist violence is generally concentrated in rural areas not frequented by tourists and is normally focussed against police stations, communications towers and other government infrastructure. Public buses carrying army personnel, even off-duty army personnel, have been targets, adding to the already significant danger of travelling by bus in Nepal, see p385 for more information.

In general the heavy army presence in the Kathmandu Valley means that it has been little affected. That said, minor bombs were detonated in 2004 in areas of Kathmandu, Pokhara and Patan frequented by tourists, including two top-end hotels. In June 2005, Maoists blew up a bus travelling between Madi and Narayangarh killing 40 people. The only tourists so far injured by the Maoists, as far as we know, were two Russian mountaineers, whose vehicle was attacked by grenades while travelling the road to the Tibetan border in April 2005 in defiance of a Maoist blockade.

Blockades, curfews, and strikes have affected all areas of Nepal, especially Kathmandu, which has come under a few dawn to dusk curfews in 2006. See p360 for advice on dealing with strikes and demonstrations. Another indirect risk comes from the general lawlessness created by the struggle.

Trekkers in the far west and east of the country and the Jiri to Lukla trek have had 'donations' extorted from them by Maoists, though they have received a receipt and some have even enjoyed the interaction, keeping their Maoists receipts as a souvenir. Others have had cameras stolen by hoodlums (*kaobadhi* in Nepali) pretending to be Maoists (*maobadhi*). Even Michael Palin came up against some Maoists during the filming of his *Himalaya* BBC documentary. As demands for money get higher so the potential for violence increases (some Israeli groups have already started fighting back!). If threatened, you'd be wise to pay up and then get a receipt. See the boxed text, p324 for more on trekking in Maoist areas.

Various governments offer advice on the areas they deem unsafe; most of these are remote and in midwestern Nepal. The Maoists are strongest in rural areas in the southwest, Dolpo, the mid-east (east of the Kathmandu Valley and Arniko Hwy to Tibet) and far east. At the time of research, the Kathmandu Valley, Pokhara, Chitwan, Langtang, Mustang and the Everest area north of Lukla were largely unaffected. The Annapurna region is considered fairly safe, though there have been some incidents along the southern half of the circuit, specifically around Beni, Gorepani and Ghandruk. The Mahendra Hwy in the Terai is normally unaffected, except for the occasional tedious checkpoint, though you should avoid night-time travel along this road. The Dolpo, Jumla, Jiri and Kanchenjunga trekking regions have largely been off limits in recent years. The US pulled all of its Peace Corps volunteers out of the country in September 2004.

Nepal is not the war zone portrayed by the foreign press and Maoist activity does not directly target tourists or tourist vehicles, but there's always the danger of being caught in the wrong place at the wrong time. Your best way of keeping out of trouble is to keep yourself aware of the situation.

- Follow the news on the ground through Nepalese news website such as www.kantipuronline.com, www.thehimalayantimes.com, www.nepal news.com, www.gorkhapatra.org.np, www.nepalitimes.com and www .nepalnews.net.
- Check out the 'Is Nepal Safe?' posts on the Thorn Tree forum (www .lonelyplanet.com), at www.trekinfo.com and at http://isnepalsafe .blogspot.com.
- The UN in Nepal has an excellent up-to-date security page at www .un.org.np/security.php, which includes a useful map of recent security incidents.
- Before travelling, always check the government travel advisories listed in the boxed text 'Government Travel Advice' on p360.
- Most travel warnings focus on administrative districts, which aren't shown on many maps – for an administrative map of Nepal go to www .ncthakur.itgo.com/map04.htm.

COSTS & MONEY

If you stay in budget accommodation and survive on a predominantly Nepali diet you could live in Nepal for US$5 to US$7 a day. On an independent 'village inn' or 'teahouse' trek your living costs are likely to be around that level.

If you stay in comfortable, upper budget or lower midrange hotels, sit down to eat in popular tourist-oriented restaurants, rent bicycles and take taxis from time to time your living costs could be around US$14 to US$20 a day. Move to a midrange hotel, hire a car between towns and spend much time rafting or on an organised trek and you are looking at US$40 to US$50 per day. The tourist centres of Kathmandu and Pokhara seem to suck money out of you by osmosis, primarily because there are so many ways to spend it. Kathmandu's Thamel district is aiming itself more at the upper budget range these days.

The current slump in tourism has resulted in widespread discounting and the rates at midrange hotels in particular are currently a steal (see p356).

Most hotels and restaurants in the mid to upper ranges charge 13% VAT on top of published prices.

HOW MUCH?

Budget hotel US$5-10

Midrange hotel US$20-60

Rafting trip per day US$35

Trekking porter per day US$7-10

Internet in Kathmandu per hour Rs 20-40

LONELY PLANET INDEX

Litre of petrol/gas Rs 67

Litre of bottled water Rs 10-15

Bottle of Tuborg Beer (in a restaurant) Rs 140-170

Souvenir T-shirt Rs 400

Plate of momos (steamed dumplings) Rs 20-40

TOP TENS

Festivals

- Magh Sankranti, Devghat (January; p363)
- Losar, all Tibetan areas (February; p364)
- Maha Shivaratri, Pashupatinath (February/March; p364)
- Balkumari Jatra, Thimi (mid-April; p209)
- Bisket Jatra chariot festival, Bhaktapur (mid-April; p203)
- Rato Machhendranath Festival, Patan (April/May; p191)
- Indra Jatra chariot festival, Kathmandu (August/September; p134)
- Dasain, nationwide (September/October; p365)
- Tihar/Deepawali, nationwide (October/November; p366)
- Mani Rimdu, Tengboche (November; p366)

Adventures

- Raft the scenic Sun Kosi (p98), the perfect combination of white water, scenic villages and quiet evenings
- Hike the Tamang Heritage Trail near the Tibetan border (p235)
- Track rhinos on elephant-back at Royal Chitwan National Park (p281)
- Trek along a classic teahouse trek, like the Annapurna Circuit (p347) or the Everest Base Camp treks (p334)
- Climb to the top of Island Peak, one of Nepal's trekking peaks (p100)
- Throw yourself off Asia's highest bungee jump (p77) at Bhote Kosi
- Mountain bike through untouched villages and trails (p83)
- Abseil down waterfalls on a canyoning trip near the Tibetan border (p78)
- Soar with the eagles while paragliding or even perhaps parahawking over picturesque Phewa Tal (p79)
- Beat the crowds and do a teahouse trek in the Langtang region (p341)

Top 10 Books for Reading in the Mountains

- *Annapurna* by Maurice Herzog – a mountaineering classic from 1950
- *Into Thin Air* by Jon Krakauer – an emotionally gripping story of the disastrous Everest expeditions of 1996
- *The Ascent of Rum Doodle* by WE Bowman – a highly enjoyable spoof of these often all-too-serious tomes
- *Chomolungma Sings the Blues: Travels Around Everest* by Ed Douglas – see p22
- *The Snow Leopard* by Peter Matthiessen – see p22
- *Himalayan Traders* by Von Fürer-Haimendorf – see p43
- *High Religion* by Sherry Ortner – see p43
- *Everest* by Walt Unsworth – the ultimate Everest reference
- *Tenzing Norgay and the Sherpas of Everest* by Tashi Tenzing – Everest and climbing from the Sherpa perspective
- *Nepal Himalaya* by WH Tillman – delightful wit from the 1950s

TRAVEL LITERATURE

The Snow Leopard by Peter Matthiessen is, on one level, an account of a trek to Dolpo in the west of Nepal, keeping an eye open for snow leopards on the way. On another level, however, this moving and beautiful book pursues the 'big questions' of spirituality, nature and Buddhism, with the Himalaya as a constant background. This is one of our favourite books.

Chomolungma Sings the Blues: Travels Around Everest, by Ed Douglas, is an interesting portrait of the communities that live in the shadow of Everest and how they continue to deal with the social and environmental problems brought by trekkers and mountaineers attracted to the world's most enigmatic peak. A 'state of the mountain' address, it's a good alternative to the blinding testosterone of most climbing books.

To the Navel of the World, by Peter Somerville-Large, is an amusing account of a saunter around Nepal and Tibet. The author does some deep-winter trekking in the Solu Khumbu region and up to the Everest Base Camp. His encounters with tourism in remote locations are very funny.

Shopping for Buddhas, by Jeff Greenwald, is a wry, astute book about the author's travels in Nepal, motivated by the obsessive and metaphorical pursuit of a perfect statue of the Buddha. Greenwald's earlier book *Mr Raja's Neighbourhood* is also worth a read.

Travelers' Tales Nepal, edited by Rajendra Khadka, is an anthology of 37 interesting stories from a variety of writers, including Peter Matthiessen.

Video Night in Kathmandu, by Pico Iyer, gallivants all around Asia, but the single chapter on Nepal has some astute and amusing observations on the collision between Nepali tradition and Western culture.

The Waiting Land: A Spell in Nepal, by Dervla Murphy, is an interesting account of a visit to Nepal at a time when great changes were at hand. The author tells of her time spent in a Tibetan refugee camp near Pokhara, and of her travels in the Langtang region.

Travels in Nepal, by Charlie Pye-Smith, is a travel account with an interesting theme; the author travelled Nepal studying the impacts and benefits of foreign aid to the country, and his conclusions are incisive and thought-provoking, though a little dated now.

Beyond the Clouds: Journeys in Search of the Himalayan Kings, by Jonathan Gregson, is a portrait of the royal kings of the Himalaya, including the kings of Nepal and Mustang, as well as Bhutan and Sikkim.

Mustang: A Lost Tibetan Kingdom, by Michael Peissel, is a wonderful travelogue describing the famous explorer's 1964 trek to Lo Manthang, as one of the first Westerners to enter the remote Tibetan kingdom.

You can find all of the books listed in this chapter in Kathmandu.

The Tutor of History, by Manjushree Thapa, is a Nepali novel written in English, set in the backdrop of political campaigning in a small town in Nepal on the eve of the Maoist rebellion

INTERNET RESOURCES

Explore Nepal (www.explorenepal.com) A good gateway information site with many links set up by category. Also try www.nepalhomepage.com or www.nepaltourism.info.

Lonely Planet (www.lonelyplanet.com) Get advice on the security situation from other travellers on the Thorn Tree, check out the Nepal web links and book accommodation online.

Ministry of Tourism (www.tourism.gov.np) Tourism information and news, plus climbing and trekking regulations.

Nepal Tourism Board (www.welcomenepal.com) The official site with tourism news, a rundown of the country's sights and some glossy photos.

Trekinfo.Com (www.trekinfo.com) You guessed it – all the trekking information about the region that you'll need to get started, plus a good forum board.

Visit Nepal (www.visitnepal.com) A comprehensive site with detailed information for travellers and many links to organisations and companies within the country.

Yeti Zone (www.yetizone.com) An excellent day-by-day description of the big treks.

Itineraries

CLASSIC ROUTES

THE KATHMANDU VALLEY

One Week / Kathmandu to Kathmandu

With a week you could get to grips with the cultural highlights of the Kathmandu Valley, though you'd have to prise yourself away from Thamel's culinary delights first. Take the **walking tour** (p129) south from Thamel to the impressive Malla architecture of **Durbar Sq** (p114).

On day two, walk to the Monkey Temple of **Swayambhunath** (p162) and then visit the quirky **National Museum** (p162).

A day trip to the impressive **Patan** (p186) is a must. Top off your trilogy of former royal kingdoms with a full day visit to medieval **Bhaktapur** (p199), where you should seriously consider overnighting.

Next get your Himalayan kick from the dawn views at **Nagarkot** (p223) or **Dhulikhel** (p227) before returning to Kathmandu the next morning.

Burn off all that Thamel comfort food by mountain biking out to the sacred Hindu and Buddhist sites around **Pharping** (p218), or to the traditional Newari village **Bungamati**, p220).

Finally, head to the Hindu temples of **Pashupatinath** (p166) before continuing on foot to the Tibetan community at **Bodhnath** (p169). Lastly return to Kathmandu for some serious **shopping** (p153) in Thamel.

Surprisingly few visitors discover the impressive sites of the Kathmandu Valley. From the squares in Patan and Bhaktapur to the stupas of Swayambhunath and Bodhnath, these world-class sites should not be missed.

FROM BUDDHA TO BOUDHA   Two Weeks / Lumbini to Bodhnath

Kick off at **Lumbini** (p291), the birthplace of the Buddha, just 22km from the border town of Bhairawa. The site is spread out, so hire a bike to get between temples in this Buddhist United Nations, overnight and then spend the next day detouring out to the archaeological site of **Tilaurakot** (p297) or riding/hiking out to surrounding Tharu villages.

From Lumbini make a beeline for **Royal Chitwan National Park** (p275) for a two- or three-day stay. Take a bath with an elephant and learn the easy way which Nepali animals gave us the English word 'mugger'. Track rhinos and tigers on an elephant-back safari and for a truly memorable experience, spend the night atop a wildlife viewing tower, in the nearby Kumrose community forest, surrounded by the roars and hoots of the jungle.

From Chitwan take the day-long tourist bus to Pokhara or Kathmandu. In **Pokhara** (p255), hike up to the World Peace Pagoda, sign up for a tandem **paraglide** (p79) or just stare mesmerised at the near-perfect views of Annapurna and Machhapuchhare mirrored in lovely Phewa Tal.

Kathmandu will easily keep you busy for four days (see Kathmandu Valley itinerary, p23). Check out the elephant Kama sutra carvings at **Bhaktapur**, gain a deeper understanding of Buddhist art at **Patan Museum** (p189) and enjoy the views over the city at dusk from **Swayambhunath** (p162).

Try to fit in a couple of days to try some **canyoning** (p78), **rafting** (p95) or **kayaking** (p92) at **The Last Resort** (p233) or **Borderlands**, (p233), half a day's drive from Kathmandu, up near the Tibetan border.

On your last day head out to **Bodhnath** (p169) to take in a taste of Tibet. Make thanks for your successful journey at one of the Tibetan monasteries and follow the Tibetan exiles around the stupa as the sun sets.

Taking in a great combination of historical and natural sights, artistic treasures and religious centres, this great overland route mixes one part meditation with two parts adrenaline.

CHINA
TIBET

Pokhara

KATHMANDU;
Swayambhunath;
Bodhnath

Bhaktapur

Lumbini

Royal Chitwan
National Park

INDIA

MOUNTAIN & VALLEY   One Month / Kathmandu to Kathmandu

One month is a perfect amount of time to get a good feel for Nepal. The **Kathmandu Valley** is really worth a week (see The Kathmandu Valley itinerary p23) but to truly experience Nepal and its people you have to do it on foot, along some of the world's most scenic trails.

The circular nature of the 17- to 19-day **Annapurna Circuit** (p347) gives you a nice sense of completion, takes you over the high Thorung La into the Trans-Himalaya around Jomsom and offers excellent quality lodges. It's not called the 'Apple Pie Trail' for nothing!

The **Everest Base Camp trek** (p334) costs a bit more because most people fly in and out of Lukla (US$180 return), but it offers an insight into Sherpa culture and the kind of outrageous high altitude scenery normally reserved for mountaineers, plus the strangely irresistible draw of the world's highest peak. Even better, add on a side trip to the spectacular **Gokyo Valley** (p339) for a total trek of around 21 days. It's a good idea to book your Lukla flights before you arrive in Nepal.

If you are flying back from Lukla or Jomsom, it's wise to leave yourself a few days buffer at the end of the trip in case flights are cancelled due to bad weather. Do your Kathmandu sightseeing *after* the trek, not before.

An alternative is to do a shorter trek, such as the **Langtang** (p341) or **Jomsom** (p345) trek, and then slot in a few days at **Royal Chitwan National Park** (p275). Other shorter trek options include flying to Jomsom for a few days of day hikes, or flying to Lukla for seven to nine days' of walking to monasteries around **Namche Bazaar** (p339).

Get fit on this classic combination of teahouse trek and the wonders of the Kathmandu Valley. Don't rush these treks, as you need time to acclimatise to the high altitudes.

ROADS LESS TRAVELLED

THE CENTRAL LOOP

Lose the crowds with this central loop through the Nepali heartland to experience both Pahari (hill) and Terai culture. There's great hiking here, as opposed to the multiday trekking of the mountain further north. Discover Nepal's undiscovered gems.

From Kathmandu follow the rushing Trisuli River east along the Prithvi Hwy. Take the **Manakamana** (p237) cable car up to watch the hilltop blood sacrifices to the goddess Kali (and perhaps spend the night). One option is to kick off the trip with a **rafting trip**, (p95), great fun in September.

Next stop is **Bandipur** (p242), a little-visited gem of a village with a cohesive culture and traditional Newari architecture. From here, continue to **Pokhara** (p246) for some mountain views, good food, some R&R and a trip out to Begnas Tal.

When you want to lose the traffic again, bus south along the winding Siddhartha Hwy through the hills to charming **Tansen** (p298), the site for some great day hikes, including to the serene palace of **Ranighat** (p301).

Continue south to the main highway at Butwal and change buses south to Bhairawa and on to peaceful **Lumbini** (p291), which is worth a full day (see From Buddha to Boudha, p24).

Next comes **Royal Chitwan National Park** (p275), and some superb wildlife spotting (see From Buddha to Boudha, p24). For something a bit different, try out the new **hike and homestay programme** (p288) in the hills north of the park.

From the Terai we suggest continuing east to Hetauda to take the snaking Tribhuvan Hwy up to **Daman** (p305), to savour the spectacular dawn views of the Himalaya. Head back down to **Kathmandu Valley** (p159).

TAILORED TRIPS

UNESCO WORLD HERITAGE SITES

The entire Kathmandu Valley is a World Heritage Site made up of seven individual sites. Most impressive are the valley's three Durbar Squares, at **Kathmandu** (p114), **Patan** (p186) and **Bhaktapur** (p199). Of these, Patan's is the most impressive, Kathmandu's is the busiest and Bhaktapur's is the quietest.

The Buddhist stupas of **Swayambhunath** (p162) and **Bodhnath** (p169) have been attracting pilgrims for over 1000 years and both are heritage sites. The Hindu complex at **Pashupatinath** (p166), by the sacred and filthy Bagmati River, is the holiest Hindu site in Nepal. Finally, the **Changu Naryan Temple** (p210) is an open-air museum of priceless stone sculpture, a few kilometres outside Bhaktapur.

The only other cultural heritage site is the Buddha's birthplace at **Lumbini** (p291), now an archaeological and Buddhist peace park.

Nepal has two natural World Heritage sites, the high altitude scenery of **Sagarmartha National Park** (p334), centred around the world's highest mountain, and the steamy tiger-inhabited jungles of **Royal Chitwan National Park** (p275), one of the subcontinent's best places to spot one-horned rhinos and Bengal tigers.

BACK TO NATURE

The bulk of Nepal's visitors are drawn to the scenic wonders of its mountains and jungles.

Royal Chitwan National Park (p275) is the most popular place for wildlife watching, either on elephant-back, on foot or in a 4WD.

Royal Bardia National Park (p308) sees far fewer visitors (check the security situation here), which makes it an even quieter spot to view rhinos, tigers, sarus cranes and gharials.

Nepal's birding paradise is the **Koshi Tappu Wildlife Reserve** (p316), where bird species outnumber humans 400:1 on the floodplains and grasslands of the Sapt Kosi river.

One of the best ways to experience Nepal's wilderness is on a multiday rafting trip down the **Sun Kosi** (p98) or **Karnali** (p98) rivers. The riverside camps, total lack of roads and expedition camaraderie make these two of the world's best rafting trips.

For a quick break from Kathmandu, head up to **Borderlands** (p233) or **The Last Resort** (p233), two relaxing riverside camps, far from the bustle of the capital, near the Tibetan border.

Our vote for the best mountain views is the **Gokyo Valley** (p334), but if you don't have time for a long trek try **Daman** (p305) or **Nagarkot** (p223), where you can enjoy breakfast in bed while eyeing an unbroken chain of Himalayan peaks.

Snapshot

Nepal has been on a real rollercoaster ride over the last couple of years. The capital has been the scene of curfews, mass demonstrations, clouds of tear gas, the surge of people power and finally, jubilation in the streets. As the dust settled, the world watched its only Hindu kingdom turn its back on its autocratic king and turn itself into a secular state, ending powers enjoyed by the Shah kings for over 230 years. It's been quite a year...

The process started against the backdrop of the brutal, decade-long conflict between the Maoist and the King that continued through 2005 without sign of resolution, despite the loss of 13,000 lives. Development stalled, tourism was down and large parts of the country were paralysed.

On 1 February 2005 the King of Nepal dismissed the government, assumed executive control and declared a three-month long state of emergency. The palace introduced a news blackout on military action in the countryside and placed a ban on public assemblies in central Kathmandu. News editors were arrested and intimidated.

In May 2005 10,000 protestors took to the streets of Kathmandu demanding a return to democracy. The Maoists and seven main political parties joined in a loose alliance, further pressuring King Gyanendra.

Things came to a head in April 2006 when, after days of mass demonstrations, curfews and the deaths of 16 protestors, the King finally agreed to restore democracy. Jubilation erupted in Kathmandu. Two weeks later parliament stripped the king of his immunity from prosecution and taxation and his position as head of the army. It assumed the power to set the king's budget and even to choose the next heir (a clear jab at the unpopular Prince Paras). The word 'Royal' was whitewashed from government and army signboards across the country and the king awoke to find himself a figurehead. Suddenly Nepal seems a different country, even to Nepalis, and a new mood of optimism is tangible across the country.

Serious problems remain, however. The sustained political chaos has led tourism, a major foreign currency earner and employer of 200,000 Nepalis, to collapse and the development challenges facing Nepal remain immense. After 40 years and over US$4 billion in aid (60% of its development budget), Nepal remains one of the world's poorest countries, with seven million Nepalis lacking adequate food or basic health and education. Nepal has one of the lowest health spending levels and the third highest infant mortality rate in the world. Political violence, extortion, executions, abductions and food shortages have led to the internal displacement of up to 200,000 Nepalis, many of whom continue to stream into the Kathmandu Valley, placing strain on an already shaky infrastructure.

But there is good news for the optimists out there. The number of people in Nepal living under the poverty line has dropped by 11% (over 2.5 million people) in the last decade, thanks largely to the US$650 million a year sent home by Nepalis working abroad. Today there are over 40,000 schools in Nepal and the potential for hydro-electricity remains huge.

A dozen corrupt and ineffectual governments have squandered Nepal's development over the last 15 years, setting a precedent that does not bode well for the future. Moreover, the Maoist problem remains and life for most Nepalis is unlikely to improve until a peaceful solution is resolved.

Nepal's politicians have resolutely failed Nepal in the past. The popular revolution of May 2006 has handed them a second chance and Nepal's people are watching them closely to deliver this time.

FAST FACTS

Population (2005): 26.3 million

Surface Area: 147,181 sq km – just larger than Greece

Human Development Index: 136, out of 177 countries (2005)

Life expectancy: 61 years

Literacy rate: male 63%, female 28% (average 49%)

Gross National Income(GNI): US$240 per capita

Doctors per 100,000 people: 5 (606 in Italy)

Proportion of seats in parliament held by women: 6%

Percentage of Nepalis who live on less than US$2 per day: 82%

Average age: 20

History

The history of Nepal began in, and centres on, the Kathmandu Valley. Over the centuries Nepal's boundaries have extended to include huge tracts of neighbouring India, and contracted to little more than the Kathmandu Valley and a handful of nearby city-states. Though it has ancient roots, the modern state of Nepal emerged only in the 18th century.

Squeezed between the Tibetan plateau and the plains of the subcontinent – the modern-day giants of China and India – Nepal has long prospered from its location as a resting place for traders, travellers and pilgrims. A cultural mixing pot, it has bridged cultures and absorbed elements of its neighbours, yet retained a unique character. After travelling through India for a while, many travellers notice both the similarities and differences. 'Same, same', they say, '…but different'.

THE KIRATIS & BUDDHIST BEGINNINGS

Nepal's recorded history kicks off with the Hindu Kiratis. Arriving from the east around the 7th or 8th century BC, these Mongoloid people are the first known rulers of the Kathmandu Valley. King Yalambar (the first of their 29 kings) is mentioned in the Mahabharata, the Hindu epic, but little more is known about them.

In the 6th century BC, Prince Siddhartha Gautama was born into the Sakya royal family of Kapilavastu, near Lumbini, later embarking on a path of meditation and thought that led him to enlightenment as the Buddha. The religion that grew up around him continues to shape the face of Asia.

Around the 2nd century BC, the great Indian Buddhist emperor Ashoka (c 272–236 BC) visited Lumbini and erected a pillar at the birthplace of the Buddha. Popular legend recounts how he then visited

A History of Nepal by John Whelpton is one of the few available titles covering Nepal's history. It concentrates on the last 250 years and is good at explaining not only political events but also changes in real people's lives throughout the period. It's available inside Nepal at a discounted price.

WARNING ABOUT FACTS & FIGURES

References for anything in Nepal are often inconsistent. For example, we've seen several different figures for the amount of square kilometres Nepal occupies. When temples were built is also a matter of speculation: some sources give a date of construction for a certain temple and the period of reign for the king who built it, and the two only sometimes coincide.

Many temples in Nepal have alternative names. For example, Vishnu Temple in Patan's Durbar Square is referred to as Jagannarayan or Charnarayan Temple. Where possible we have provided alternative names that are commonly used.

Further confusion results from different systems of transliteration from Sanskrit – the letter 'h', or the use of the double 'hh' appears in some systems, but does not appear in others, so you may see Manjushri and Manjusri, Machhendranath and Machendranath. This difference only occurs during translation – the Nepali script is always consistent. The letters 'b' and 'v' are also used interchangeably in different systems – Shiva's fearsome manifestation is Bhairab or Bhairav; Vishnu is often written as Bishnu; and the Nepali word for the Tibetan thunderbolt symbol can be a *bajra* or a *vajra*.

Finally, texts differ in their use of the words Nepali and Nepalese. In this book we use Nepali for the language and for other terms relating to the country and the people.

TIMELINE	100,000 BC	c 563–483 BC
	Kathmandu Valley formed, as the former lake bed dries	Life of Siddhartha Gautama, the Buddha

the Kathmandu Valley and erected four stupas (pagodas) around Patan, but there is no evidence that he actually made it there in person. In either event, his Mauryan empire (321–184 BC) played a major role in popularising Buddhism in the region, a role continued by the north Indian Buddhist Kushan empire (1st to 3rd centuries AD).

Over the centuries Buddhism gradually lost ground to a resurgent Hinduism and by the time the Chinese Buddhist pilgrims Fa Xian (Fa Hsien) and Xuan Zang (Hsuan Tsang) passed through the region in the 5th and 7th centuries the site of Lumbini was already in ruins.

LICCHAVIS, THAKURIS, THEN DARKNESS

Buddhism faded and Hinduism reasserted itself with the arrival from northern India of the Licchavis. In AD 300 they overthrew the Kiratis, who resettled in the east and are the ancestors of today's Rai and Limbu people.

Between the 4th and 8th centuries, the Licchavis ushered in a golden age of cultural brilliance. The *chaityas* (stupas) and monuments of this era can still be seen at the Changu Narayan Temple (p210), north of Bhaktapur, and in the backstreets of Kathmandu's old town. Their strategic position allowed them to prosper from trade between India and China. It's believed that the original stupas at Chabahil, Bodhnath and Swayambhunath date from the Licchavi era.

Amsuvarman, the first Thakuri king, came to power in 602, succeeding his Licchavi father-in-law. He consolidated his power to the north and south by marrying his sister to an Indian prince and his daughter Bhrikuti to the great Tibetan king Songsten Gompo. Together with the Gompo's Chinese wife Wencheng, Bhrikuti managed to convert the king to Buddhism around 640, changing the face of both Tibet and, later, Nepal.

From the late 7th century until the 13th century Nepal slipped into its 'dark ages', of which little is known. Tibet invaded in 705 and Kashmir invaded in 782. The Kathmandu Valley's strategic location, however, ensured the kingdom's growth and survival. King Gunakamadeva is credited with founding Kantipur, today's Kathmandu, around the 10th century. During the 9th century a new lunar calendar was introduced, one that is still used by Newars to this day.

THE GOLDEN AGE OF THE MALLAS

The first of the Malla kings came to power in the Kathmandu Valley around 1200. The Mallas (literally 'wrestlers' in Sanskrit) had been forced out of India and their name can be found in the Mahabharata and in Buddhist literature. This period was a golden one that stretched over 550 years, though it was peppered with fighting over the valuable trade routes to Tibet.

The first Malla rulers had to cope with several disasters. A huge earthquake in 1255 killed around one-third of Nepal's population. A devastating Muslim invasion by Sultan Shams-ud-din of Bengal less than a century later left plundered Hindu and Buddhist shrines in its wake, though the invasion did not leave a lasting cultural effect here (unlike in the Kashmir Valley which remains Muslim to this day). In India the damage was more widespread and many Hindus were driven into the hills and mountains of Nepal, where they established small Rajput principalities.

Nepal's founding father, Prithvi Narayan Shah, referred to Nepal as 'a yam between two boulders' – namely China and India – a metaphor that is as true geologically as it is historically.

You can visit the archaeological site of Kapilavastu, where Siddhartha Gautama (the Buddha) lived for first 29 years of his life, at Tilaurakot (p297).

Apart from this, the earlier Malla years (1220–1482) were largely stable, reaching a high point under the third Malla dynasty of Jayashithi Malla (r 1382–1395), who united the valley and codified its laws, including the caste system. The mid-13th century saw the de facto rule of Queen Devaladevi, the most powerful woman in Nepal's history.

After the death of Jayashithi Malla's grandson Yaksha Malla in 1482, the Kathmandu Valley was divided up among his sons into the three kingdoms of Bhaktapur (Bhadgaon), Kathmandu (Kantipur) and Patan (Lalitpur). They proceeded to fight with each other over the right to control the rich trading routes with Tibet.

The rest of what we today call Nepal consisted of a fragmented patchwork of almost 50 independent states, from Palpa to Jumla, and the semi-independent states of Banepa and Pharping, most of them minting their own coins and maintaining standing armies.

One of the most important of these was the Nepali-speaking Khasa empire (Western Mallas), based in the far west in the Karnali basin around Sinja and Jumla. The kingdom peaked in the 13th and 14th centuries, only to fragment in the 15th century. Its lasting contribution was the Nepali language that is spoken today as the unifying national language.

Nepal's most profound export was perhaps its architecture; in the 13th century the Nepali architect Arniko travelled to Lhasa and the Mongol capital in Beijing, bringing with him the design of the pagoda, thus changing the face of religious temples across Asia.

The rivalry between the three kingdoms of the Kathmandu Valley found its expression in the arts and culture, which flourished in the competitive climate. The outstanding collections of exquisite temples and buildings in each city's Durbar Square are testament to the huge amounts of money spent by the rulers to outdo each other.

The building boom was financed by trade, in everything from musk and wool to salt, Chinese silk and even yak tails. The Kathmandu Valley stood at the departure point for two separate routes into Tibet, via Banepa to the northeast and via Rasuwa and the Kyirong Valley near Langtang in the northwest. Traders would cross the jungle-infested Terai during winter to avoid the virulent malaria and then wait in Kathmandu for the mountain passes to open later that summer. Kathmandu grew rich and its rulers converted their wealth into gilded pagodas and ornately carved royal palaces. In the mid-17th century Nepal gained the right to mint Tibet's coins using Tibetan silver, further enriching the kingdom's coffers.

In Kathmandu King Pratap Malla (1641–74) oversaw that city's cultural highpoint with the construction of the Hanuman Dhoka Palace, the Rani Pokhari pond and the first of several subsequent pillars that featured a statue of the king facing the protective Temple of Taleju, who the Mallas had by that point adopted as their protective deity. The mid-17th century also saw a highpoint of building in Patan.

Around 1750 King Jaya Prakash Malla built Kathmandu's Kumari Temple. Not long afterwards came the Nyatapola Temple in Bhakatapur, the literal highpoint of pagoda-style architecture in Nepal.

The Malla era shaped the religious as well as artistic landscape, introducing the dramatic chariot festivals of Indra Jatra and Machhendranath. The Malla kings shored up their position by claiming to be reincarnations of the

Nepal's flag is totally unique, consisting of two overlapping red triangles, bearing a white moon and a white 12-pointed sun (the first mythological kings of Nepal are said to be descendents of the sun and moon).

AD 464

Nepal's earliest surviving inscription is carved into the beautiful Changu Narayan Temple in the Kathmandu Valley

879

Start of Newari calendar

Hindu god Vishnu and establishing the cult of the *kumari*, a living goddess whose role it was to bless the Malla's rule during an annual celebration.

The cosmopolitan Mallas also absorbed foreign influences. The Indian Mughal court influenced Malla dress and painting, presented the Nepalis with firearms and introduced the system of land grants for military service, a system which would have a profound effect in later years. Persian terminology was introduced to the court administration and in 1729 the three kingdoms sent presents to the Qing court in Beijing, which from then on viewed Nepal as a tributary state. In the early 18th century Capuchin missionaries passed through Nepal to Tibet, giving the West its first descriptions of exotic Kathmandu.

But change didn't only come from abroad. A storm was brewing inside Nepal, just 100km to the east of Kathmandu.

UNIFICATION UNDER THE SHAHS

It took more than a quarter of a century of conquest and consolidation, but by 1768 Prithvi Narayan Shah, ruler of the tiny hilltop kingdom of Gorkha (halfway between Pokhara and Kathmandu), stood poised on the edge of the Kathmandu Valley, about to realise his dream of a unified Nepal.

Visit the birthplace and launching pad of Nepal's unifier Narayan Prithvi Shah at Gorkha (p239).

Prithvi Narayan had taken the strategic hilltop fort of Nuwakot in 1744 and had blockaded the valley, after fighting off reinforcements from the British East India Company. In 1768 Shah took Kathmandu, sneaking in while everyone was drunk during the Indra Jatra festival. A year later he took Kirtipur, finally, after three lengthy failed attempts. In terrible retribution his troops hacked 120 pounds of noses and lips off Kirtipur's residents; unsurprisingly, resistance throughout the valley quickly crumbled. In 1769 he advanced on the three Malla kings, who were quivering in Bhaktapur, ending the Malla rule and unifying Nepal.

Shah moved his capital from Gorkha to Kathmandu, establishing the Shah dynasty, which rules to this day, with its roots in the Rajput kings of Chittor. Shah died just six years later in Nuwakot but is revered to this day as the founder of the nation.

Shah had built his empire on conquest and his insatiable army needed ever more booty and land to keep it satisfied. Within six years the Gurkhas had conquered eastern Nepal and Sikkim. The expansion then turned westwards into Kumaon and Garhwal, only halted on the borders of the Punjab by the armies of the powerful one-eyed ruler Ranjit Singh.

The kingdom's power continued to grow until a 1792 clash with the Chinese in Tibet led to an ignominious defeat, during which Chinese troops advanced down the Kyirong Valley to within 35km of Kathmandu. As part of the ensuing treaty the Nepalis had to cease their attacks on Tibet and pay tribute to the Chinese emperor in Beijing; the payments continued until 1912.

The expanding Nepali boundaries, by this time stretching all the way from Kashmir to Sikkim, eventually put it on a collision course with the world's most powerful empire, the British Raj. Despite early treaties with the British, disputes over the Terai led to the first Anglo-Nepali war, which the British won after a two-year fight. The British were so impressed by their enemy that they decided to incorporate Gurkha mercenaries into their own army.

1349	1428–82
Muslim armies of Sultan Shams-ud-Din plunder the Kathmandu Valley, looting Swayambhunath	Rule of Yaksha Malla, high point of Malla kings

The 1816 Sugauli treaty called a halt to Nepal's expansion and laid down its modern boundaries. Nepal lost Sikkim, Kumaon, Garhwal and much of the Terai, though some of this land was restored to Nepal in 1858 in return for support given to the British during the Indian Mutiny (Indian War of Independence). A British resident was sent to Kathmandu to keep an eye on things but the Raj knew that it would be too difficult to colonise the impossible hill terrain, preferring to keep Nepal as a buffer state. Nepalis to this day are proud that their country was never colonised by the British, unlike the neighbouring hill states of India.

Following its humiliating defeat, Nepal cut itself off from all foreign contact from 1816 until 1951. The British residents in Kathmandu were the only Westerners to set eyes on Nepal for more than a century.

On the cultural front, temple construction continued impressively, though perhaps of more import to ordinary people was the introduction, via India, of chillis, potatoes, tobacco and other New World crops.

The Shah rulers, meanwhile, swung from ineffectual to seriously deranged. At one point the kingdom was governed by a twelve-year-old female regent, in charge of a nine-year-old king! One particularly sadistic ruler, Crown Prince Surendra, expanded the horizons of human suffering by ordering subjects to jump down wells or ride off cliffs, just to see whether they would die.

THE RANOCRACY

The death of Prithvi Narayan Shah in 1775 set in motion a string of succession struggles, infighting, assassinations, feuding and intrigue that culminated in the Kot Massacre in 1846. This bloody night was engineered by the young Chhetri noble, Jung Bahadur; it catapulted his family into power and sidelined the Shah dynasty.

Ambitious and ruthless, Jung Bahadur organised (with the queen's consent) for his soldiers to massacre several hundred of the most important men in the kingdom – noblemen, soldiers and courtiers – while they were assembled in the Kot courtyard adjoining Kathmandu's Durbar Square. He then exiled 6000 members of their families to prevent revenge attacks.

Jung Bahadur took the title of Prime Minister and changed his family name to the more prestigious Rana. He later extended his title to maharajah (king) and decreed it hereditary. The Ranas became a second 'royal family' within the kingdom and held the reins of power – the Shah kings became listless figureheads, requiring permission even to leave their palace.

The hereditary family of Rana prime ministers held power for more than a century, eventually intermarrying with the Shahs. Development in Nepal stagnated, although the country did manage to preserve its independence. Only on rare occasions were visitors allowed into Nepal.

Jung Bahadur Rana travelled to Europe in 1850, attended the opera and the races at Epsom, and brought back a taste for neoclassical architecture, examples of which can be seen in Kathmandu today. To the Ranas' credit, *sati* (the Hindu practice of casting a widow on her husband's funeral pyre) was abolished in 1920, 60,000 slaves were released from bondage and a school and a college were established in Kathmandu. But while the Ranas and their relations lived lives of opulent luxury, the peasants in the hills were locked in a medieval existence.

Jung Bahadur Rana broke a religious taboo by becoming the first Nepali ruler to cross the *kalo pani* (black water, or ocean) and thus temporarily losing his caste, when he travelled to Europe in 1850.

1480

Kathmandu splits into the three kingdoms of Kathmandu, Patan and Bhaktapur

1531–34

Sherpas settle in the Solu Khumbu region from Eastern Tibet

Modernisation began to dawn on Kathmandu with the opening of the Bir Hospital, Nepal's first, in 1889, the first piped water system, limited electricity and the construction of the huge Singha Durbar palace. In 1923 Britain formally acknowledged Nepal's independence and in 1930 the kingdom of Gorkha was renamed the kingdom of Nepal, reflecting a growing sense of national consciousness.

The arrival of the Indian railway line at the Nepali border greatly aided the transportation of goods but sounded a death knell for the caravan trade that bartered Nepali grain and rice for Tibetan salt. The transborder trade suffered another setback when the British opened a second, more direct trade route with Tibet through Sikkim's Chumbi Valley (the real nail in the coffin came in 1966, when the Chinese closed the border to local trade).

Elsewhere in the region dramatic changes were taking place. The Nepalis supplied logistical help during Britain's invasion of Tibet in 1903, and over 300,000 Nepalis fought in WWI and WWII, garnering a total of 13 Victoria Crosses – Britain's highest military honour – for their efforts.

After WWII, India gained its independence and the communist revolution took place in China. Tibetan refugees fled into Nepal in the first of several waves when the new People's Republic of China tightened its grip on Tibet, and Nepal became a buffer zone between the two rival Asian giants. At the same time King Tribhuvan, forgotten in his palace, was being primed to overthrow the Ranas.

The first cars were transported to the Kathmandu Valley in parts, on the backs of porters, before there were even any roads or petrol in the kingdom.

THE LURE OF MT EVEREST

During the 1920s and '30s, reaching the top of Mt Everest came to dominate the Western imagination. Apart from the difficulties inherent in reaching such heights, the political constraints further upped the ante. Nepal continued to be totally isolated, and all attempts on Everest had to be made from the Tibetan side.

British assaults were made in 1921, 1922 and 1924. The 1922 expedition used oxygen to reach 8326m, while the 1924 expedition fell just 300m short of the top, reaching 8572m without the use of oxygen. Apart from numerous climbers and support staff, the 1924 expedition utilised at least 350 porters. Such massive numbers of porters and support staff set a pattern that was to continue until recent years.

The discovery in 1999 of the body of British climber George Mallory, frozen near the summit, was a new chapter in one of the enduring mysteries of mountaineering history. In 1924, Mallory and his climbing partner, Andrew Irvine, disappeared within sight of the top. Did they reach the summit? No-one can be sure. However, Mallory did leave behind his famous explanation of mountaineering: when asked why he was climbing Mt Everest, he said 'Because it's there'.

Further expeditions followed through the 1920s and '30s, but no real progress was made, although the 8000m level was achieved a number of times. Maurice Wilson added his name to the Everest legend, and to the Everest death roll, when he died during a bizarre solo attempt on the mountain in 1934.

In 1951, a climber who would soon become very famous took part in an exploratory expedition to the mountain – the climber was New Zealander Edmund Hillary. Another name, soon to be equally famous, appeared on the list of climbers on the Swiss Everest expedition of 1952 when Sherpa climber Norgay Tenzing reached 7500m. The conquest of Everest finally took place in 1953 when the British team led by John Hunt put those two climbers, Tenzing and Hillary, atop the world's highest peak.

| 20,000 die of plague in the Kathmandu Valley | Nepal unified under Prithvi Narayan Shah (1723–1775) to form the Shah dynasty – Kathmandu becomes the capital |

RESTORATION OF THE SHAHS

In late 1950 King Tribhuvan was driving himself to a hunting trip at Nagarjun when he suddenly swerved James-Bond-style into the expecting Indian embassy, claimed political immunity and was flown to India. Meanwhile, the recently formed Nepali Congress party, led by BP Koirala, managed to take most of the Terai by force from the Ranas and established a provisional government that ruled from the border town of Birganj. India exerted its considerable influence and negotiated a solution to Nepal's turmoil, and King Tribhuvan returned in glory to Nepal in 1951 to set up a new government composed of demoted Ranas and members of the Nepali Congress party.

Although Nepal gradually reopened its long-closed doors and established relations with other nations, dreams of a new democratic system were not permanently realised. Tribhuvan died in 1955 and was succeeded by his cautious son Mahendra. A new constitution provided for a parliamentary system of government and in 1959 Nepal held its first general election. The Nepali Congress party won a clear victory and BP Koirala became the new prime minister. In late 1960, however, the king decided the government wasn't to his taste after all, had the cabinet arrested and swapped his ceremonial role for real control (much as King Gyanendra would do 46 years later).

In 1962 Mahendra decided that a partyless, indirect *panchayat* (council) system of government was more appropriate to Nepal. The real power remained with the king, who chose 16 members of the 35-member National Panchayat, and appointed the prime minister and his cabinet. Political parties were banned.

Mahendra died in 1972 and was succeeded by his 27-year-old British-educated son Birendra. Nepal's hippy community was unceremoniously booted out of the country when visa laws were tightened in the run-up to Birendra's coronation in 1975. Simmering discontent with corruption, the slow rate of development and the rising cost of living erupted into violent riots in Kathmandu in 1979. King Birendra announced a referendum to choose between the *panchayat* system and one that would permit political parties to operate. The result was 55% to 45% in favour of the *panchayat* system; democracy had been outvoted.

Nepal's military and police apparatus were among the least publicly accountable in the world and strict censorship was enforced. Mass arrests, torture and beatings of suspected activists are well documented, and the leaders of the main opposition, the Nepali Congress, spent the years between 1960 and 1990 in and out of prison.

During this time there were impressive movements towards development, namely in education and road construction, with the number of schools increasing from 300 in 1950 to over 40,000 by 2000. But the relentless population growth (Nepal's population grew from 8.4 million in 1954 to 26 million in 2004) cancelled out many of these advances, turning Nepal from an exporter to a net importer of food within a generation. It is also widely accepted that a huge portion of foreign aid was routinely creamed off into royal and ministerial accounts.

During this time over one million hill people moved to the Terai in search of land and several million crossed the border to seek work in

1814–16	1846
Anglo-Nepalese War, Nepal's modern boundaries established	Kot Massacre ushers in the Rana era (1846–1951)

India (Nepalis are able to cross the border and work freely in India), creating a major population shift in favour of the now malaria-free Terai.

PEOPLE POWER

In 1989, as communist states across Europe crumbled and pro democracy demonstrations occupied China's Tiananmen Square, Nepali opposition parties formed a coalition to fight for a multiparty democracy with the king as constitutional head; the upsurge of protest was called the Jana Andolan, or People's Movement.

In early 1990 the government responded to a nonviolent gathering of over 200,000 people with bullets, tear gas and thousands of arrests. After several months of intermittent rioting, curfews, a successful strike, and pressure from various foreign-aid donors, the government was forced to back down. The people's victory did not come cheaply; it is estimated that more than 300 people lost their lives.

On 9 April King Birendra announced he was lifting the ban on political parties. On 16 April he asked the opposition to lead an interim government, and announced his readiness to accept the role of constitutional monarch. Nepal was a democracy.

DEMOCRACY & THE MAOIST UPRISING

In May 1991, 20 parties contested a general election for a 205-seat parliament. The Nepali Congress won power with around 38% of the vote. The Communist Party of Nepal-Unified Marxist-Leninist (CPN-UML) won 28%, and the next largest party, the United People's Front, 5%.

In the years immediately following the election, the political atmosphere remained uneasy. In April 1992 a general strike degenerated into street violence between protesters and police, and resulted in a number of deaths.

In late 1994 the Nepali Congress government, led by GP Koirala (brother of BP Koirala) called a midterm election. No party won a clear mandate, and a coalition formed between the CPN-UML and the third major party, the Rastriya Prajatantra Party (RPP), the old *panchayats*, with the support of the Nepali Congress. This was one of the few times in the world that a communist government had come to power by popular vote.

Political stability did not last long, and the late 1990s were littered with dozens of broken coalitions, dissolved governments and sacked politicians.

In 1996 the Maoists (of the Communist Party of Nepal), fed up with government corruption, the failure of democracy to deliver improvements to the people, and the dissolution of the Communist government, declared a 'people's war'. The insurgency began in the poor regions of the far west and gathered momentum, but was generally ignored by the politicians. The repercussions of this nonchalance finally came to a head in November 2001 when the Maoists broke their ceasefire and an army barracks was attacked west of Kathmandu. After a decade of democracy it seemed increasing numbers of people, particularly young Nepalis and those living in the countryside, were utterly disillusioned.

When Nepal's present King Gyanendra was crowned in 2001 he may well have experienced a feeling of dèja vu – he had already been crowned once before, aged three, and ruled as king for three months, after his grandfather Tribhuvan fled to India. He had to wait half a century to be crowned king for the second time.

For background on the Maoist rebellion try *Himalayan People's War: Nepal's Maoist Rebellion*, edited by Michael Hutt.

1934	1951–55
Massive earthquake destroys much of the Kathmandu Valley, killing 7000	Rule of King Tribhuvan

PEOPLE'S WAR

Since 13 February 1996, the Communist Party of Nepal (Maoist) has been waging a People's War against the Nepali state in the hills of Nepal. Formed in 1995 after innumerable splits in the country's communist movement, the extremist party advocates the establishment of a communist republic in place of the existing constitutional Hindu monarchy.

The 'war' itself started after the Maoists presented the then prime minister with a 40-point charter of demands that ranged from favourable state policies towards backward communities to an assertive Nepali identity, an end to public schools and better governance.

With an ideology owing more to Peru's Shining Path than Chairman Mao (China disowns the group), the two main leaders are the shadowy Chairman Pashpa Kumar Dahal, better known as Prachanda ('the Fierce'), and Dr Baburam Bhattarai; they are both high-caste intellectuals.

The initial Maoist forces were armed with little more than ancient muskets and *khukuris* (traditional knives) but they quickly obtained guns looted from police stations, home-made explosives and automatic weapons, all bankrolled by robbery and extortion and helped by an open border with India. After labelling Nepal's Maoists a terrorist group, the USA handed over millions of dollars to Kathmandu to help fight its own version of the 'war on terror'.

Initial army heavy-handedness only succeeded in alienating the local people. Political disenfranchisement, rural poverty, resentment against the caste system, issues of land reform and a lack of faith in squabbling and self-interested politicians has swelled the ranks of the Maoists, who now number between 10,000 to 15,000 fighters, with a further militia of 50,000. The Maoist heartland is the Rolpa region of midwestern Nepal, but attacks have occurred in almost every one of Nepal's 75 districts, including Kathmandu. Maoists effectively control around 40% of the country, including two protected areas in the far west.

Recent moves seem to suggest that the Maoist leadership is moving towards a political role, with an alliance with the seven main political parties. The Maoists have suggested UN mediation to end the dispute, a plan the government has rejected.

ROYAL TROUBLES

On 1 June 2001 the Nepali psyche was dealt a huge blow when Crown Prince Dipendra gunned down almost every member of the royal family during a get-together in Kathmandu (see the boxed text, p38). A monarch who had steered the country through some extraordinarily difficult times was gone. When the shock of this loss subsided the uncertainty of what lay ahead hit home.

The beginning of the 21st century saw the political situation in the country turn from bad to worse. Prime ministers were sacked and replaced in 2000, 2001, 2002, 2003, 2004 and 2005, making a total of nine governments in 10 years. The fragile position of Nepali politicians is well illustrated by Sher Bahadur Deuba, who was appointed prime minister for the second time in 2001, before being dismissed in 2002, reinstated in 2004, sacked again in 2005, thrown in jail on corruption charges and then released! Against such a background, modern politics in Nepal has become more about personal enrichment than public service.

Several Maoist truces, notably in 2003 and 2005, offered some respite, though these reflected as much a need to regroup and rearm as they did any move towards a lasting peace. By 2005 nearly 13,000 people, including many civilians, had been killed in the insurgency, more than half of them since the army joined the struggle in 2001. Amnesty International

1953	**1955–72**
Everest summited by Edmund Hillary and Tenzing Norgay on the 29 May	Rule of King Mahendra

accused both sides of horrific human-rights abuses, including executions, abductions, torture and child conscription.

The Maoist insurgency has, ironically, only worsened the plight of the rural poor by diverting much-needed government funds away from development and causing aid programmes to suspend activity due to security concerns. Until there is real social change and economic development in the countryside, the frustrations fuelling Nepal's current insurgency look set only to continue.

Nepal's 12-year experiment with democracy faced a major setback in October 2002 when the sour-faced King Gyanendra, frustrated with the political stalemate and the continued delay in holding national elections, dissolved the government. Gyanendra again dissolved the government in February 2005, amid a state of emergency, promising a return to democracy within three years. The controversial king has not been helped by his dissolute son (and heir) Paras, who has allegedly been involved in several drunken hit-and-run car accidents, one of which killed a popular Nepali singer.

Entry into the World Trade Organisation in 2004 and the creation of the regional South Asian free trade agreement in 2006 may offer some long-term economic advances but the country remains deeply dependent

Massacre at the Palace: The Doomed Royal Dynasty of Nepal, by Jonathan Gregson, takes a wider look at Nepal's royal family and reveals that assassination and murder have been part of royal life for centuries; it also examines the recent massacre in gripping detail. Sometimes published as *Blood Against the Snows.*

THE ROYAL MASSACRE – FOR THE LOVE OF A WOMAN?

It was meant to be a pleasant family gathering at Narayanhiti Royal Palace but the night of 1 June 2001 turned into one of Nepal's greatest tragedies.

That night, in a hail of bullets, 10 members of Nepal's royal family including King Birendra and Queen Aishwarya were gunned down by a deranged, drunken Crown Prince Dipendra, who eventually turned a weapon on himself. Dipendra did not die straight away and, ironically, despite being in a coma, was pronounced the king of Nepal. His rule ended two days later, when he too was declared dead. The real motive behind the massacre will never be known, but many believe Dipendra's murderous drug-fuelled rage was prompted by his parents' disapproval of the woman he wanted to marry.

The object of his love was Devyani Rana, a beautiful aristocrat. The pair had often been seen together in public. However, the king and queen had allegedly told him that were he to ever marry Devyani, he would be stripped of his title and money and the crown would go to his younger brother Nirajan.

In the days that followed the massacre, a tide of emotions washed over the Nepali people – shock, grief, horror, disbelief and denial. A 13-day period of mourning was declared and in Kathmandu impromptu shrines were set up for people to pray for their king and queen. About 400 shaven-headed men roamed the streets around the palace on motorbikes, carrying pictures of the monarch. Half a million stunned Nepalis lined the streets during the funeral procession. All over the city, barbers were shaving the heads of other men, a mark of grief in Hindu tradition.

The initial disbelief and shock gave way to suspicion and a host of conspiracy theories, many concerning the new king, Gyanendra (who was in Pokhara at the time of the massacre), and his son Paras (who emerged unscathed from the attack). None of this was helped by an official enquiry which initially suggested that the automatic weapon had been discharged *by accident* (killing nine people!), or the fact that the victims were quickly cremated without full post mortems. Other theories included that old chestnut, a CIA or Indian secret-service plot. Doubtless the truth will never be known.

1959	1972–2001
Nepal's first general elections	Rule of King Birendra

A ROYAL PAIN IN THE ARSE

At the time of going to press Nepal was in the process of removing references to the royal family from many official titles. You can expect some of the names in this book to change over time, including references to the Kingdom of Nepal and anything with royal in it, perhaps even including Royal Nepal Airlines.

on foreign aid, which makes up 25% of the state budget and over two-thirds of Nepal's total development budget. The aid industry has come under increased criticism for failing to generate the economic and social development that had been expected. Recent years have seen a move away from the megaprojects of the 1960s and '70s to smaller-scale community cooperation and microfinancing.

Everything changed in April 2006, when parlimentary democracy was grudgingly restored by the king, following days of mass demonstrations, curfews and the deaths of 16 protestors. The next month the newly restored parliament reduced the king to a figurehead, ending powers the royal Shah lineage had enjoyed for over 200 years. A new chapter in Nepal's political history looks set to unfold.

Fatalism & Development – Nepal's Struggle for Modernization, by Nepali anthropologist Dor Bahadur Bista, is an often-controversial analysis of Nepali society and its dynamics.

The Culture

THE NATIONAL PSYCHE

Nepal's location between India and Tibet, the diversity of its ethnic groups, its isolating geography and myriad languages have resulted in a complex pattern of customs and beliefs that make it hard to generalise about a 'Nepali people'.

Perhaps the dominant cultural concepts are those of caste and status, both of which contribute to a strictly defined system of hierarchy and deference. Caste determines not only a person's status, but also their career and marriage partner, how that person interacts with other Nepalis and how others react back. This system of hierarchy extends even to the family, where everyone has a clearly defined rank. The Nepali language has half a dozen words for 'you', each of which conveys varying shades of respect.

When it comes to their religious beliefs, Nepalis are admirably flexible, pragmatic and, above all, tolerant – there is almost no religious tension in Nepal. Nepalis are generally good humoured and patient, quick to smile and slow to anger, though they have a reputation as fierce fighters (witness the famous Gurkha forces).

The Nepali view of the world is dominated by puja; prayer and ritual and a knowledge that the gods are not remote, abstract concepts but living, present beings, who can influence human affairs in very direct ways. Nepalis perceive the divine everywhere, from the *namaste* greeting that literally means 'I greet the divine inside of you', to the spirits and gods present in trees, sacred river confluences *(dhoban)* and mountain peaks.

The notions of karma and caste, when combined a tangled bureaucracy and deep-rooted corruption, tend to create an endemic sense of fatalism in Nepal. Confronted with problems, many Nepalis will simply respond with a shrug of the shoulders and the phrase *khe garne?* ('what is there to do?'), which Westerners often find frustrating.

TRADITIONAL LIFESTYLE

The cornerstones of Nepali life are the demands (and rewards) of one's family, ethnic group and caste. To break these time-honoured traditions is to risk being ostracised from one's family and community. While

Contemporary Issues and Modern Nepal, edited by Kanak Mani Dixit and Shastri Ramachadaran, is a collection of essays examining education, development and the Maoist movement in Nepal between 1990 and 2001.

PUJA & SACRIFICE

Every morning Hindu women all over Nepal can be seen walking through the streets carrying a plate, usually copper, filled with an assortment of goodies. These women are not delivering breakfast but are taking part in an important daily ritual called puja. The plate might contain flower petals, rice, yogurt, fruit or sweets, and it is an offering to the gods made at the local temple. Each of the items is sprinkled onto a temple deity in a set order and a bell is rung to let the gods know an offering is being made. Once an offering is made it is transformed into a sacred object and a small portion (referred to as *prasad*) is returned to the giver as a blessing from the deity. Upon returning home from her morning trip, the woman will give a small portion of the blessed offerings to each member of the household.

Marigolds and sweets don't cut it with Nepal's more terrifying gods, notably Kali and Bhairab, who require a little extra appeasement in the form of bloody animal sacrifices. You can witness the gory executions, from chickens to water buffalo, at Dakshinkali (p219) in the Kathmandu Valley and the Kalika Mandir at Gorkha (p239), or during the annual Dasain festival, when these temples are literally awash with blood offerings.

NEPALI NAMES

You can tell a lot about a Nepali from their name, including often their caste, profession, ethnic group and where they live. 'Gurung' and 'Sherpa' are ethnic groups as well as surnames. The surname Bista or Pant indicates that the person is a Brahman, originally from western Nepal; Devkota indicates an eastern origin. Thapa, Pande and Bhasnet are names related to the former Rana ruling family. Shrestha is a high-caste Newari name. The initials KC often stand for Khatri Chhetri, a mixed-caste name. The surname 'Kami' is the Nepali equivalent of 'Smith'.

Sherpa names even reveal which day of the week the person was born – Dawa (Monday), Mingmar (Tuesday), Lhakpa (Wednesday), Phurbu (Thursday), Pasang (Friday), Pemba (Saturday) and Nyima (Sunday).

young Nepali people, especially in urban areas, are increasingly influenced by Western values and lifestyle, the vast majority of people live by traditional customs and principles. The biggest modernising influences are probably satellite TV, roads and tourism, in that order.

In most ethnic groups, joint and extended families live in the same house, even in Kathmandu. In some smaller villages extended families make up the entire community. Traditional family life has been dislocated by the large numbers (literally millions) of Nepali men forced to seek work away from home, whether in Kathmandu or the Terai, or abroad in India, Malaysia or the Gulf States.

Arranged marriages remain the norm in Nepali Hindu society and are generally between members of the same caste or ethnic group, although there are a growing number of 'love marriages'. Child marriages have been illegal since 1963 and today the average age of marriage for girls is just under 19 years old. Family connections generated by marriage are as much a social contract as a personal affair, and most families take the advice of matchmakers and astrologers when making such an important decision.

In the far western hills, the system of polyandry (one woman married to two brothers) developed over time in response to the limited amounts of land and the annual trading trips that required husbands to leave their families for months at a time. The practice kept population levels down and stopped family land being broken up between brothers. All children born into the family are considered the elder brother's. In recent years the system has started to break down.

To decide not to have children is almost unheard of and a Nepali woman will generally pity you if you are childless. Having a son is a particularly important achievement, especially for Hindu families, where some religious rites (such as lighting the funeral pyre to ensure a peaceful passage into the next life) can only be performed by the eldest son. Girls are regarded by many groups as a financial burden whose honour needs to be protected until she is married off, often at considerable cost.

Children stay at school for up to 12 years; 70 per cent of children will begin school but only seven per cent will reach their 10th school year, when they sit their School Leaving Certificate (SLC) board examination. Many villages only have a primary school, which means children either have to walk long distances each day or board in a bigger town to attend secondary school. The ratio of boys to girls at both primary and secondary schools is almost 2:1 in favour of boys.

Despite what you may see in Kathmandu and Pokhara, Nepal is overwhelmingly rural and poor. Farming is still the main occupation, and debt is a factor in most people's lives. Large areas of land are still owned by zamindars (absent landlords) and up to 50% of a landless farmer's

Up to half a million Nepali men seek seasonal work in Indian cities; in 2005 they sent home US$650 million last year to one-third of Nepali families.

The website www.mountainvoices.org/nepal.asp has an interesting collection of interviews with Nepali mountain folk on a wide variety of topics.

MOVING TIGERS

Nepal's national board game is *bagh chal,* which literally means 'move *(chal)* the tigers *(bagh)'.* The game is played on a lined board with 25 intersecting points. One player has four tigers, the other has 20 goats, and the aim is for the tiger player to 'eat' five goats by jumping over them before the goat player can encircle the tigers and prevent them moving. You can buy attractive brass *bagh chal* sets in Kathmandu and in Patan where they are made.

Nepal's other popular game is *carom,* which looks like 'finger snooker', using discs which glide over a chalked-up board to pot other discs into the corner pockets.

---

production will go to the landowner as rent. The World Bank estimates that 30% of Nepalis live below the poverty line.

Rice is grown up to 2000m; corn, wheat and millet up to 2800m; then barley, buckwheat and potatoes, up to altitudes of 4000m. Fields of yellow-flowering mustard are planted for making cooking oil, and soya beans, lentils, chilli peppers and sesame are grown on the berms dividing plots.

Older people are respected members of the community and are cared for by their children. Old age is a time for relaxation, prayer and meditation. The dead are generally cremated and the deceased's sons will shave their heads and wear white for an entire year following the death.

For a guide to some cultural Dos and Don'ts in Nepal see p62.

POPULATION

Nepal had just over 23 million people at the last census (2001) and this number is increasing at the rapid rate of 2.45% annually. Over 1.5 million people live in the Kathmandu Valley, 700,000 of them in Kathmandu. Nepal remains predominantly rural; 85% of people live in the countryside. Over 50% of Nepal's population live in the flat fertile lands of the Terai and the population here is increasing rapidly.

There are around 130,000 refugees, some Tibetan, but most expelled from Bhutan, kept in camps in the far east of the country.

People of Nepal by Dor Bahadur Bista describes the many and diverse ethnic groupings found in the country.

MULTICULTURALISM

The human geography of Nepal is a remarkable mosaic of peoples who have not so much assimilated as learned to coexist. Kathmandu is the best place to see diverse ethnic groups, including Limbu, Rai, Newar, Sherpa, Tamang and Gurung.

Simplistically, Nepal is the meeting place of the Indo-Aryan people of India and the Mongoloid peoples of the Himalaya. There are three main cultural zones running east to west: the north including the high Himalaya; the middle hills; and the Terai. Each group has adapted its lifestyle and farming practices to its environment but, thanks largely to Nepal's tortured topography has retained its own traditions. Social taboos, especially among caste Hindus, have meant limited mixing between groups.

Nepal's diverse ethnic groups speak somewhere between 24 and 100 different languages and dialects depending on how finely the distinctions are made. Nepali functions as the unifying language.

According to the 2001 census, Nepal's population is made up of the following groups: Chhetri 15.5%, Brahman-Hill 12.5%, Magar 7%, Tharu 6.6%, Tamang 5.5%, Newar 5.4%, Muslim 4.2%, Kami 3.9%, Yadav 3.9%, other 32.7%, unspecified 2.8%

Himalayan Zone

The hardy Mongoloid peoples who inhabit the high Himalaya are known in Nepal as Bhotiyas, a slightly derogatory term among caste Hindus. Each group remains distinct but their languages are all Tibetan-based and, with a few exceptions, they are Tibetan Buddhists.

The Bhotiyas are named after the region they come from by adding the suffix *pa* to their name. These include the Sherpas (literally 'easterners') of the Everest region and the Lhopa (literally 'southerners') of the Mustang region.

The difficulty of farming and herding at high altitude drives these people to lower elevations during winter, either to graze their animals or to trade in India and the Terai.

THAKALIS

Originating along the Kali Gandaki Valley in central Nepal, the Thakalis have emerged as the entrepreneurs of Nepal. They once played an important part in the salt trade between the subcontinent and Tibet, and today they are active in many areas of commercial life. Originally Buddhist, many pragmatic Thakalis have now adopted Hinduism. Most Thakalis have small farms, but travellers will regularly meet them in their adopted roles as hoteliers, especially on the Jomsom trek.

TAMANGS

The Tamangs make up one of largest groups in the country. They live mainly in the hills north of Kathmandu and have a noticeably strong Tibetan influence, from their monasteries, known as *ghyang,* to the *mani* walls that mark the entrance to Tamang villages.

According to some accounts, the Tamang's ancestors were horse traders and cavalrymen from an invading Tibetan army who settled in Nepal. They are well known for their independence and suspicion of authority, probably caused by the fact that in the 19th century they were relegated to a low status and seriously exploited, with much of their land distributed to Bahuns and Chhetris. As bonded labour they were dependent on menial work such as labouring and portering. Many of the 'Tibetan' souvenirs, carpets and thangka (religious paintings on cotton) you see in Kathmandu are made by Tamangs.

TIBETANS

About 12,000 of the 120,000 Tibetans in exile around the world live in Nepal. The heavy hand of the Chinese during the 1950s and the flight of the Dalai Lama in 1959 gave rise to waves of refugees who settled mainly in Kathmandu or Pokhara.

Although their numbers are small, Tibetans have a high profile, partly because of the important role they play in tourism. Many hotels and restaurants in Kathmandu are owned or operated by Tibetans. They are also responsible for the extraordinary success of the Tibetan carpet industry.

Tibetans are devout Buddhists and their arrival in the valley has rejuvenated a number of important religious sites, most notably the stupas at Swayambhunath (p162) and Bodhnath (p169). A number of large, new monasteries have been established in recent years.

SHERPAS

The Sherpas who live high in the mountains of eastern and central Nepal are probably the best-known Nepali ethnic group. These nomadic Tibetan herders moved to the Solu Khumbu region of Nepal 500 years ago from Eastern Tibet, bringing with them their Tibetan Buddhist religion and building the beautiful gompas (monasteries) that dot the steep hillsides. They are strongly associated with the Khumbu region around Mt Everest, although only 3000 of the total 35,000 Sherpas actually live in the Khumbu; the rest live in the lower valleys of the Solu region.

The Oscar-nominated, Nepali-French film *Caravan,* directed by Eric Valli, features magnificent footage of the Upper Dolpo district of western Nepal as it tells the tale of yak caravaners during a change of generations. It was renamed for distribution abroad as *Himalaya.*

Changes in trading patterns and cultures among Nepal's Himalayan people are examined in *Himalayan Traders,* by Von Fürer-Haimendorf.

Despite associations in the West, Sherpas actually do very little portering, focusing mostly on high-altitude expedition work. Most of the porters you meet on the trails are Tamang, Rai or other groups.

Tourism stepped in after the collapse of trade with Tibet in 1959, following the Chinese invasion of Tibet, and these days the Sherpa name is synonymous with mountaineering and trekking. Potatoes were introduced to the region in the late 19th century and are now the main Sherpa crop. Sherpas are famously hard drinkers.

Midlands Zone

The middle hills of Nepal are the best places to witness village life at its most rustic. In the east are the Kirati, who are divided into the Rai and Limbu groups. The Newari people dominate the central hills around the Kathmandu Valley, while the Magars and Gurungs inhabit the hills of the Kali Gandaki northeast of Pokhara.

Moving west, the Bahun and Chhetri are the dominant groups, although the lines between castes have become blurred over time.

RAIS & LIMBUS

The Rais and Limbus are thought to have ruled the Kathmandu Valley in the 7th century BC until they were defeated around AD 300. They then moved into the steep hill country of eastern Nepal, from the Arun Valley to the Sikkim border, where many remain today. Others have moved to the Terai or India as economic migrants. Many Rai work as porters in the middle hills.

The Kirati are easily distinguishable by their Mongolian features. They are of Tibeto-Burmese descent, and their traditional religion is distinct from either Buddhism or Hinduism, although the latter is exerting a growing influence. Himalayan hunter-warriors, they are still excellent soldiers and are well represented in the Gurkha regiments.

Many of the men still carry a large *khukuri* (curved knife) tucked into their belt and wear a *topi* (Nepali hat). Some communities in upper Arun live in bamboo houses.

NEWARS

The Newars of the Kathmandu Valley number about 1.1 million and make up 6% of the population. Their language, Newari, is distinct from Tibetan, Nepali or Hindi, and is one of the world's most difficult languages to learn. The Newars are excellent farmers and merchants, as well as skilled artists; the Kathmandu Valley is filled with spectacular examples of their artistic work.

Their origins are shrouded in mystery: most Newars have Mongoloid and Caucasian physical characteristics. It is generally accepted that the Newars' ancestors were of varied ethnicity, and all settled the valley – possibly originating with the Kiratis, or an even earlier group.

Newars lead a communal way of life and have developed several unique customs including the worship of the *kumari*, a girl worshipped as a living god, and the annual chariot festivals that provide the high point of the valley's cultural life. Living so close to the centre of power has also meant there are many Newars in the bureaucracies of Kathmandu.

Newari men wear *surwal* (trousers with a baggy seat that are tighter around the calves, like jodhpurs), a *daura* (thigh-length double-breasted shirt), a vest or coat and the traditional *topi* hat. Newari castes include the Sakyas (priests), Tamrakar (metal casters) and the Jyapu (farmers). Jyapu women wear a black sari with a red border, while the men often wear the traditional trousers and shirt with a long piece of cotton wrapped around the waist.

See the boxed text, opposite for more on this group.

High Religion, by Sherry B Ortner, is probably the best introduction to Sherpa history, culture, religion and traditional society, though it's a bit dated (written in 1989). Also worth looking for is *Sherpa of the Khumbu* by Barbara Brower.

Sherpas: Reflections on Change in Himalayan Nepal by James F Fisher offers a 1990 anthropological snapshot of how tourism and modernisation has affected Sherpa religious and cultural life. Fisher worked with Edmund Hilary in the Khumbu in the 1960s, bringing the first schools and airstrip to the region.

For information on Buddhist Newari art check out the website of the Huntington Archives of Newari Art at http://ka ladarshan.arts.ohio-state .edu/Nepal/nepal.html.

NEWARI RITES OF PASSAGE

Newari children undergo a number of *samskara* (rites of passage) as they grow up, many of which are shared by other Nepali Hindus. The *namakarana* (naming rite) is performed by the priests and chief of the clan, and the family astrologer gives the child its public and secret name. The next rite is the *machajanko* or *pasni* (rice feeding), which celebrates the child's presence on earth and wishes them a smooth life. Next for boys comes the *busakha*, performed between the ages of three and seven, when the head is shaved, leaving just a small tuft, known as a *tupi*. This is followed by the fixing of a *kaitapuja* (loincloth), which marks a commitment by the boy to bachelorhood and self-control. Girls undergo *Ihi* (a symbolic marriage to Vishnu) between the ages of five and 11, and at this time she begins to wear a thick cotton thread. The *Ihi samskara* venerates chastity and guarantees the girl a choice of husband. This is followed by a *barha* (menarche rite), which protects the girl's virginity and safeguards against passion.

Weddings are usually negotiated through a *lami* (mediator), and take place at times deemed auspicious by the family astrologer. The bride is taken in a noisy procession to the groom's house where she is received with an oil lamp and the key to the house. The *chipka thiyeke samskara* involves the serving of 84 (!) traditional dishes and is a symbol of the couple's union.

The first *janko* (old-age *samskara*) takes place at 77 years, seven months and seven days, the second at 83 years, four months and four days and the third at 99 years, nine months and nine days. The final *samskara* is *sithan* (cremation), which marks the body's move to its final destination.

GURUNGS

The Gurungs, a Tibeto-Burmese people, live mainly in the central midlands, from Gorkha and Baglung to Manang and the southern slopes of the Annapurnas, around Pokhara. One of the biggest Gurung settlements is Ghandruk, with its sweeping views of the Annapurnas and Machhapuchhare. The Gurungs have made up large numbers of the Gurkha regiments, and army incomes have contributed greatly to the economy of their region. Gurung women wear nose rings, known as *phuli,* and coral necklaces.

The Gurungs (who call themselves Tamu, or highlanders) originally migrated from western Tibet, bringing with them their animist Bön faith. One distinctive aspect of village life is the *rodi,* a cross between a town hall and a youth centre, where teenagers hang out and cooperative village tasks are planned.

The Blue Space (www .thebluespace.com) operates nine-day trekking trips in early August and December to watch the famous Gurung honey hunters of central Nepal.

MAGARS

The Magars, a large group (around 8% of the total population), are a Tibeto-Burmese people who live in many parts of the midlands zone of western and central Nepal. With such a large physical spread there are considerable regional variations.

The Magars are also excellent soldiers and fought with Prithvi Narayan Shah to help unify Nepal. Their kingdom of Palpa (based at Tansen) was one of the last to be incorporated into the unified Nepal. They make up the biggest numbers of Gurkhas, and army salaries have greatly improved Magar living standards.

The Magars generally live in two-storey, rectangular or square thatched houses washed in red clay. They have been heavily influenced by Hinduism, and in terms of religion, farming practices, housing and dress, they are hard to distinguish from Chhetris.

Tamu Kohibo Museum in Pokhara (p252) is dedicated to the culture and customs of the Gurung people.

BAHUNS & CHHETRIS

The Hindu caste groups of Bahuns and Chhetris are dominant in the middle hills, making up 30% of the country's population.

Even though the caste system was formally 'abolished' in 1963 these two groups remain the top cats of the caste hierarchy. Although there is no formal relationship in Hinduism between caste and ethnicity, Nepal's Bahuns and Chhetris (Brahmin priests and Kshatriya warriors respectively) are considered ethnic groups as well as the two highest castes.

Bahuns and Chhetris played an important role in the court and armies of Prithvi Narayan Shah, and after unification they were rewarded with tracts of land. Their language, Khas Kura, then became the national language of Nepal, and their high-caste position was religiously, culturally and legally enforced. Ever since, Bahuns and Chhetris have dominated the government in Kathmandu, making up over 80% of the civil service.

Outside the Kathmandu Valley, the majority of Bahuns and Chhetris are simple peasant farmers, indistinguishable in most respects from their neighbours. Many had roles as tax collectors under the Shah and Rana regimes, and to this day many are moneylenders with a great deal of power.

The Bahuns tend to be more caste-conscious and orthodox than other Nepali Hindus, which sometimes leads to difficulties in relationships with 'untouchable' Westerners. Many are vegetarians and do not drink alcohol; marriages are arranged within the caste.

Bahun and Chhetri men can be recognised by their sacred thread – the *janai*, which they wear over the right shoulder and under the right arm – which is changed once a year during the Janai Purnima festival (see p363).

Terai Zone

Until the eradication of malaria in the 1950s, the only people to live in the valleys of the Inner Terai, and along much of the length of the Terai proper, were Tharus and a few small associated groups, who enjoyed a natural immunity to the disease. Since the Terai was opened for development, it has also been settled by large numbers of people from the midlands – every group is represented and more than 50% of Nepali people live in the region.

A number of large groups straddle the India–Nepal border. In the eastern Terai, Mithila people dominate; in the central Terai, there are many Bhojpuri-speaking people; and in the western Terai, Abadhi-speaking people are significant. All are basically cultures of the Gangetic plain, and Hindu caste structure is strictly upheld.

THARUS

One of the most visible groups is the Tharus, who are thought to be the earliest inhabitants of the Terai (and they're even thought to be immune to malaria). About one million Tharu speakers inhabit the length of the Terai, including the Inner Terai around Chitwan, although they mainly live in the west. Caste-like distinctions exist between different Tharu groups or tribes. Most have Mongoloid physical features.

Nobody is sure where they came from, although some believe they are the descendants of the Rajputs (from Rajasthan), who sent their women and children away to escape Mughal invaders in the 16th century. Others believe they are descended from the royal Sakya clan, the Buddha's family, although they are not Buddhist. Tharu clans have traditionally lived in thatched huts with wattle walls, or in traditional long houses. Their beliefs are largely animistic, involving the worship of forest spirits and ancestral deities, but they are being increasingly influenced by Hinduism.

Nepal – the Kingdom in the Himalaya, by Toni Hagen, is one of the most complete studies of Nepal's people, geography and geology. Hagen has travelled extensively throughout Nepal since the 1950s, and the book reflects his intimate knowledge of the country.

More recently, the Tharus were exploited by zamindars (landlords), and many Tharus fell into debt and entered into bonded labour. In 2000 the *kamaiyas* (bonded labourers) were freed by government legislation, but little has been done to help these now landless and workless people. Consequently, in most Terai towns in western Nepal you will see squatter settlements of former *kamaiyas*.

MEDIA

The introduction of private FM radio stations following the introduction of multiparty democracy in 1990 revolutionised the Nepal media, breaking the monopoly enjoyed by Radio Nepal since the 1950s.

These stations have come under particular pressure since King Gyanendra seized power in 2005. The palace banned FM stations from presenting news stories or criticising the king, a move that led to 1000 journalists losing their jobs. The most popular station, Kantipur FM, was shut down by the government for a while in 2005. There are three private TV stations, including Kantipur TV and Channel Nepal.

RELIGION

From the simple early morning puja (worship; see the boxed text, p40) of a Kathmandu housewife at a local Hindu temple to the chanting of Buddhist monks in a village monastery, religion is a cornerstone of Nepali life. In Nepal, Hinduism and Buddhism have mingled wonderfully into a complex, syncretic blend. Nowhere is this more evident than in Kathmandu where Tibetan Buddhists and Nepali Hindus often worship at the same temples.

The Buddha was born in Nepal over 25 centuries ago but the Buddhist religion first arrived in the country later, around 250 BC. It is said to have been introduced by the great Indian Buddhist emperor, Ashoka. Buddhism eventually lost ground to Hinduism, although the Tantric form of Tibetan Buddhism made its way full circle back into Nepal in the 8th century AD. Today Buddhism is practised mainly by the people of the high Himalaya, such as the Sherpas and Tamangs, and by Tibetan refugees.

Officially Nepal is a Hindu country but in practice the blending of Hindu and Buddhist beliefs and deities, and the subsequent overlaying onto both of Tantric aspects make it hard to separate the religions. Perhaps because of this there is little religious tension in Nepal, and religion plays almost no part in politics.

Take the concepts of Hinduism and Buddhism, add some Indian and Tibetan influence and blend this with elements of animism, faith healing and a pinch of Tantric practice, and you get a taste of Nepal's fabulous spiritual stew.

One thing you'll quickly learn as you travel through Nepal is that it is fruitless to look for rational responses and distinctions in questions of Nepali faith.

Hinduism

Hinduism is a polytheistic religion that has its origins in the Aryan tribes of Central India about 3500 years ago.

Hindus believe in a cycle of life, death and rebirth with the aim being to achieve *moksha* (release) from this cycle. With each rebirth you can move closer to or further from eventual *moksha;* the deciding factor is karma, which is literally a law of cause and effect. Bad actions during your life result in bad karma, which ends in a lower reincarnation. Conversely, if your deeds and actions have been good you will reincarnate on a higher level and be a step closer to eventual freedom from rebirth. Buddhism later adapted this concept into one of its core principles.

Hinduism has a number of holy books, the most important being the four Vedas, the 'divine knowledge' that is the foundation of Hindu philosophy. The Upanishads are contained within the Vedas and delve into the metaphysical nature of the universe and soul. The Mahabharata is an epic 220,000-line poem that contains the story of Rama. The famous Hindu epic, the Ramayana, is based on this.

In 2005, for the third year in a row, more journalists were arrested in Nepal than in any other country. Reporters Sans Frontiers described Nepal's media in 2005 as the world's most censored.

According to the 2001 census 81% of Nepalis describe themselves as Hindu, 11% as Buddhist, 4% Muslim and 4% other religions (including Christianity).

The Hindu religion has three basic practices. These are puja (worship; see the boxed text, p40), the cremation of the dead, and the rules and regulations of the caste system.

There are four main castes: the Brahmin (Brahman), or priest caste; the Kshatriya (*Chhetri* in Nepali), or soldiers and governors; the Vaisyas, or tradespeople and farmers; and the Sudras, or menial workers and craftspeople. These castes are then subdivided, although this is not taken to the same extreme in Nepal as it is in India. Beneath all the castes are the Harijans, or untouchables, the lowest, casteless class for whom the most menial and degrading tasks are reserved.

Despite common misconceptions, it is possible to become a Hindu, although Hinduism itself is not a proselytising religion. Once you are a Hindu you cannot change your caste – you're born into it and are stuck with your lot in life for the rest of that lifetime.

HINDU GODS

Westerners often have trouble getting to grips with Hinduism principally because of its vast pantheon of gods. The best way to look upon the dozens of different Hindu gods is simply as pictorial representations of the many attributes of the divine. The one omnipresent god usually has three physical representations: Brahma the creator, Vishnu the preserver and Shiva the destroyer and reproducer.

Most temples are dedicated to one or another of these gods, but most Hindus profess to be either Vaishnavites (followers of Vishnu) or Shaivites (followers of Shiva). A variety of lesser gods and goddesses also crowd the scene. The cow is, of course, the holy animal of Hinduism, and killing a cow in Nepal brings a jail term.

The oldest deities are the elemental Indo-European Vedic gods, such as Indra (the god of war, storms and rain), Suriya (the sun), Chandra (the moon) and Agni (fire). Added to this is a range of ancient local mountain spirits, which Hinduism quickly co-opted. The Annapurna and the Ganesh Himal massifs are named after Hindu deities, and Gauri Shankar and Mt Kailash in Tibet are said to be the residences of Shiva and Parvati.

The definitions that follow include the most interesting and most frequently encountered 'big names', plus associated consorts, vehicles and religious terminology.

Shiva

As creator and destroyer, Shiva is probably the most important god in Nepal – so it's important to keep on his good side! Shiva is often represented by the phallic lingam, symbolic of his creative role. His vehicle is the bull Nandi, which you'll often see outside Shiva temples. The symbol most often seen in Shiva's hand is the trident.

INCARNATIONS, MANIFESTATIONS, ASPECTS & VEHICLES

There's a subtle difference between these three concepts. Vishnu has incarnations – 10 of them in all. They include Narsingha the man-lion, Krishna the cowherd and Buddha. Shiva, on the other hand, may be the god of 1000 names, but these are manifestations – what he shows himself as – not incarnations. When you start to look at the Buddhist 'gods' their various appearances are aspects rather than incarnations or manifestations.

Each god also has an associated animal known as the 'vehicle' (*vahana*) on which they ride, as well as a consort with certain attributes and abilities. You can normally pick out which god is represented by identifying either the vehicle or the symbols held in the god's hand.

SHAKTI

As well as being the name of one of Shiva's consorts, *shakti* in general is a deity's creative or reproductive energy, which often manifests in their female consorts. A Hindu god's *shakti* is far more than just a companion. A *shakti* often symbolises certain parts of a god's personality, so while Shiva is the god of both creation and destruction, it is often his *shakti*, Parvati, manifesting as Kali or Durga, who handles the destructive business and demands the blood sacrifices.

Shiva is also known as Nataraja, the cosmic dancer whose dance shook the cosmos and created the world. Shiva's home is Mt Kailash in the Himalaya, and he's supposed to be keen on smoking hashish.

In the Kathmandu Valley Shiva is most popularly worshipped as Pashupati, the lord of the beasts. As the keeper of all living things, Pashupati is Shiva in a good mood. The temple of Pashupatinath outside Kathmandu (p166) is the most important Hindu temple in the country.

Shiva appears as bushy-eyebrowed Bhairab when he is in his fearful or 'terrific' manifestation. Bhairab can appear in 64 different ways, but none of them is pretty. Typical of Tantric deities, he has multiple arms, each clutching a weapon; he dances on a corpse and wears a headdress of skulls and earrings of snakes. More skulls dangle from his belt, and his staring eyes and bared fangs complete the picture. Usually Bhairab is black, carries a cup made from a human skull and is attended by a dog. The gruesome figure of Bhairab near the Hanuman Dhoka palace entrance in Kathmandu is a good example of this fearsome god at his worst. Bhairab's female counterparts are the Joginis, wrathful goddesses whose shrines can be found near Sankhu in the eastern end of the Kathmandu Valley, at Guhyeshwari near Pashupatinath, and at Pharping.

Outside of the Kathmandu Valley, Shiva is most commonly worshipped as Mahadeva (Great God), the supreme deity.

Vishnu

Vishnu is the preserver in Hindu belief, although in Nepal (where he often appears as Narayan) he also plays a role in the creation of the universe. Narayan is the reclining Vishnu, sleeping on the cosmic ocean, and from his navel appears Brahma, who creates the universe. The King of Nepal enjoys added legitimacy because he is considered an incarnation of Vishnu.

Vishnu has four arms and can often be identified by the symbols he holds: the conch shell or *sankha*, the disclike weapon known as a *chakra*, the sticklike weapon known as a *gada*, and a lotus flower or *padma*. Vishnu's vehicle is the faithful man-bird Garuda, and a winged Garuda will often be seen kneeling reverently in front of a Vishnu temple. Garuda has an intense hatred of snakes and is often seen destroying them. Vishnu's *shakti* is Lakshmi, the goddess of wealth and prosperity, whose vehicle is a tortoise.

Vishnu has 10 incarnations, starting with Matsya, the fish. Then he appeared as Kurma, the tortoise on which the universe is built. Number three was his boar incarnation as Varaha, who bravely destroyed a demon who would have drowned the world. Vishnu was again in a demon-destroying mood in incarnation four as Narsingha (or Narsimha), half-man and half-lion (see p212 for an explanation of the legend behind this incarnation).

Still facing difficulties from demons, Vishnu's next incarnation was Vamana (or Vikrantha), the dwarf who reclaimed the world from the demon-king Bali. The dwarf politely asked the demon for a patch of ground upon which to meditate, saying that the patch need only be big enough that he, the dwarf, could walk across it in three paces. The demon agreed, only to see the dwarf swell into a giant who strode across the universe in three gigantic steps.

In his sixth incarnation Vishnu appeared as Parasurama, a warlike Brahman who proceeded to put the warrior-caste Chhetris in their place.

Incarnation seven was as Rama, the hero of the Ramayana who, with help from Hanuman the monkey god, rescued his beautiful wife Sita from the clutches of Rawana, evil king of Lanka. Sita is believed to have been born in Janakpur, and this is also where she and Rama married (see p312).

Incarnation eight was the gentle and much-loved Krishna, the fun-loving cowherd, who dallied with the *gopis* (milkmaids), danced, played his flute and still managed to remain devoted to his wife Radha.

For number nine Vishnu appeared as the teacher, the Buddha. Of course, Buddhists don't accept that the Buddha was just an incarnation of some other religion's god. But perhaps it was just a ploy to bring converts back into the fold.

Incarnation 10? Well, we haven't seen that one yet, but it will be as Kalki the destroyer, when Vishnu wields the sword that will destroy the world at the end of the Kaliyuga, the age we are currently in.

It is joked that Nepal has three main religions – Hinduism, Buddhism and Tourism.

Brahma

Despite his supreme position, Brahma appears much less often than Shiva or Vishnu. Like those gods, Brahma has four arms, but he also has four heads, to represent his all-seeing presence. The four Vedas (ancient orthodox Hindu scriptures) are supposed to have emanated from his mouths.

Parvati

Shiva's *shakti* (see the boxed text, p49) is Parvati the beautiful, and she is the dynamic element in their relationship. Just as Shiva is also known as Mahadeva, the Great God, so she is Mahadevi (or just Devi), the Great Goddess. Shiva is often symbolised by the phallic *lingam,* so his *shakti*'s symbol is the *yoni,* representing the female sex organ. Their relationship is a sexual one and it is often Parvati who is the energetic and dominant partner.

Shiva's *shakti* has as many forms as Shiva himself. She may be peaceful Parvati, Uma or Gauri, but she may also be fearsome Kali, the black goddess, or Durga, the terrible. In these terrific forms she holds a variety of weapons in her hands, struggles with demons and rides a lion or tiger. As skeletal Kali, she demands blood sacrifices and wears a garland of skulls.

Actress Uma Thurman is named after the beautiful Hindu goddess Uma, a manifestation of Parvati. Uma forms half of the Uma-Maheshwar image, a common representation of Shiva and Parvati.

Ganesh

With his elephant head, Ganesh is probably the most easily recognised and most popular of the gods. He is the god of prosperity and wisdom and there are thousands of Ganesh shrines and temples across Nepal. His parents are Shiva and Parvati, and he has his father's temper to thank for this elephant head. After a long trip, Shiva discovered Parvati in bed with a young man. Not pausing to think that their son might have grown up a little during his absence, Shiva lopped his head off! Parvati then forced him to bring his son back to life, but he could only do so by giving him the head of the first living thing he saw – which happened to be an elephant.

Chubby Ganesh has a super sweet tooth and is often depicted with his trunk in a mound of sweets and with one broken tusk; he broke it off and threw at the moon for making fun of his fatness.

Hanuman

The monkey god Hanuman is an important character from the Ramayana, who came to the aid of Rama to help defeat the evil Rawana and

---

TIKA

A visit to Nepal is not complete without being offered a *tika* by one of the many sadhus (Hindu holy men) that wander the streets, dusty, barefoot and carrying an alms bowl and walking staff. The ubiquitous *tika* is a symbol of blessing from the gods worn by both women and men. It can range from a small dot to a full-on mixture of yogurt, rice and *sindur* (a red powder) smeared on the forehead. The *tika* represents the all-seeing, all-knowing third eye, as well as being an important chakra (energy) point, and receiving this blessing is a common part of most Hindu ceremonies. It is an acknowledgment of a divine presence at the occasion and a sign of protection for those receiving it. Shops these days carry a huge range of tiny plastic *tikas*, known as *bindi*, that women have turned into an iconic fashion statement.

---

release Sita from his grasp. Hanuman's trustworthy and alert nature is commemorated by the many statues of Hanuman seen guarding palace entrances, most famously the Hanuman Dhoka, which lends its name to Kathmandu's old Royal Palace.

Hanuman also has an important medicinal connection in Nepal and other Hindu countries. The Ramayana recounts a legend of how Rama desperately needed a rare herb grown only in the Himalaya region, and sent Hanuman to procure it for him. Unfortunately, by the time he finally arrived in the mountains, Hanuman had forgotten which particular herb he had been asked to bring back to Rama, but he got around the problem by simply grabbing a whole mountain, confident that at least somewhere on the mountain would be the required plant.

Machhendranath

A strictly Nepali Hindu god, Machhendranath (also known as Bunga Dyo) has power over the rains and the monsoon and is regarded as protector of the Kathmandu Valley. It is typical of the intermingling of Hindu and Buddhist beliefs in Nepal that, in the Kathmandu Valley at least, Machhendranath has come to be thought of as an incarnation of Avalokiteshvara, the Bodhisattva of our era.

There are two forms of Machhendranath based on colour and features: Seto (White) Machhendranath of Kathmandu and Rato (Red) Machhendranath of Patan. Some scholars say that they are the same god, others say they are distinct.

Tara

The goddess Tara is another deity who appears in both the Hindu and Buddhist pantheons. There are 108 different Taras, but the best known are Green Tara and White Tara. Tara is generally depicted sitting with her right leg hanging down and her left hand in a *mudra* (hand gesture).

Saraswati

The goddess of learning and consort of Brahma, Saraswati rides upon a white swan and holds the stringed musical instrument known as a *veena*.

Buddhism

Strictly speaking, Buddhism is not a religion, as it is centred not on a god but on a system of philosophy and a code of morality. Buddhism was founded in northern India in about 500 BC when prince Siddhartha Gautama achieved enlightenment. According to some, Gautama Buddha was not the first Buddha but the fourth; nor is he expected to be the last 'enlightened one'.

The Buddha never wrote down his dharma (teachings), and a schism that developed later means that today there are two major Buddhist schools. The Theravada (Doctrine of the Elders), or Hinayana, holds that the path to nirvana is an individual pursuit. In contrast, the Mahayana school holds that the combined belief of its followers will eventually be great enough to encompass all of humanity and bear it to salvation. To some, the less austere and ascetic Mahayana school is considered a 'soft option'. Today it is practised mainly in Vietnam, Japan and China, while the Hinayana school is followed in Sri Lanka, Myanmar (Burma) and Thailand. There are still other, sometimes more esoteric, divisions of Buddhism, including the Tantric Buddhism of Tibet, which is the version found in Nepal.

The Buddha renounced material life to search for enlightenment but, unlike other prophets, found that starvation did not lead to discovery. He developed his rule of the 'middle way' (moderation in all things). The Buddha taught that all life is suffering, and that suffering comes from our sensual desires and the illusion of their importance. By following the 'eightfold path' these desires will be extinguished and a state of nirvana, where we are free from their delusions, will be reached. Following this process requires going through a series of rebirths until the goal is reached and no more rebirths into the world of suffering are necessary. The path that takes you through this cycle of births is karma, but this is not simply fate. Karma is a law of cause and effect; your actions in one life determine what you will have to go through in your next life.

The first images of the Buddha date from the 5th century AD, 1000 years after his death (stupas were the symbol of the faith previous to this). The Buddha didn't want idols made of himself but a pantheon of Buddhist gods grew up regardless, with strong iconographical influence from Hinduism. As in Hinduism, the many Buddhist deities reflect various aspects of the divine, here called 'Buddha-nature'. Multiple heads convey multiple personalities, *mudra*s (hand positions) convey coded messages, and everything from eyebrows to stances indicate the nature of the god.

There are many different types of Buddha images, though the most common are those of the past (Dipamkara), present (Sakyamuni) and future (Maitreya) Buddhas. Buddha is recognised by 32 physical marks, including a bump on the top of his head, his third eye and the images of the Wheel of Law on the soles of his feet. In his left hand he holds a begging bowl, and his right hand touches the earth in the witness *mudra*. He is often flanked by his two disciples.

Bodhisattvas are beings who have achieved enlightenment but decide to help everyone else gain enlightenment before entering nirvana. The Bodhisattva Manjushri has strong connections to the Kathmandu Valley. The Dalai Lama is considered a reincarnation of Avalokiteshvara (Chenresig in Tibetan), the Bodhisattva of Compassion. Tibetan Buddhism also has a whole host of fierce protector gods, called *dharmapalas*.

The pipal tree, under which the Buddha gained enlightenment, is also known by its Latin name, *ficus religious*.

If you are heading out on a trek (or flying on Royal Nepal!), bear in mind that according to Nepali superstition it's bad luck to start a journey on Tuesday or return on a Saturday.

TIBETAN BUDDHISM

There are four major schools of Tibetan (Vajrayana) Buddhism, all represented in the Kathmandu Valley: Nyingmapa, Kargyupa, Sakyapa and Gelugpa. The Nyingmapa order is the oldest and most dominant in the Nepal Himalaya. It origins come from the Indian sage Padmasambhava (or Guru Rinpoche), who is credited with the establishment of Buddhism in Tibet in the 8th century. (He is a common image in Nyingmapa monasteries and is recognisable by his *katvanga* staff of human heads and his fabulously curly moustache.) The Dalai Lama is the head of the Gelugpa school and the spiritual leader of Tibetan Buddhists.

In some texts the Gelugpa are known as the Yellow Hats, while the other schools are sometimes collectively identified as the Red Hats. Nepal has small pockets of Bön, Tibet's pre-Buddhist animist faith, now largely considered a fifth school of Tibetan Buddhism.

Islam

Nepal's small population of Muslims (about 4% of the total population) are mainly found close to the border with India, with a large population in Nepalganj.

The first Muslims, who were mostly Kashmiri traders, arrived in the Kathmandu Valley in the 15th century. A second group arrived in the 17th century from Northern India, and they primarily manufactured armaments for the small hill states.

The largest Muslim group are the Terai Muslims, many of whom still have strong ties with the Muslim communities in the Indian states of Bihar and Uttar Pradesh. Communal tension is a major problem in India, but Nepal's Hindu and Muslim communities coexist peacefully.

Shamanism

Shamanism in practised by many mountain peoples throughout the Himalaya and dates back some 50,000 years. Its ancient healing traditions are based on a cosmology that divides the world into three main levels: the Upper World where the sun, moon, stars, planets, deities and spirits important to the shaman's healing work abide; the Middle World of human life; and the Lower World, where powerful deities and spirits exist.

Faith healers protect against a wide range of spirits, including headless *mulkattas,* which have eyes in their chest and signify imminent death; the *pret,* ghosts of the recently deceased that loiter in crossroads; and *kichikinni,* the ghost of a beautiful and sexually insatiable siren who is recognisable by her sagging breasts and the fact that her feet are on backwards.

During ceremonies the shaman or faith healer *(jhankri)* uses techniques of drumming, divination, trances and sacrifices to invoke deities and spirits, which he or she wishes to assist in the ritual. The shaman essentially acts as a broker between the human and spirit worlds.

WOMEN IN NEPAL

Women have a hard time of it in Nepal. Female mortality rates are higher than men's, literacy rates are lower and women generally work harder and longer than men, for less reward. Women only truly gain status in traditional society when they bear their husband a son.

AIDS & PROSTITUTION IN NEPAL

HIV/AIDS has become a major problem in Nepal. There are an estimated 60,000 Nepalis infected with the virus, and more than 30,000 intravenous drug users in Nepal who are at risk of contracting the virus. A public education programme has been implemented, and along roadsides throughout the country you'll see billboards with pictures of cartoon condoms.

Although prostitution exists in Nepal, particularly in the border towns and along the main truck routes, it is virtually invisible to Western visitors. It is believed that over 100,000 Nepali women work in Indian brothels (7000 Nepali women are sold or trafficked into brothels every year), often in conditions resembling slavery, and over 30,000 of these women are estimated to be HIV positive. When obvious AIDS symptoms force these women out of work, some manage to return to Nepal. However, they are shunned by their families and there is virtually no assistance available to them or their children.

Nepali society is strongly patriarchal society, though this is less the case among Himalayan communities such as the Sherpa, where women often run the show (and the lodge). Boys are strongly favoured over girls, who are often the last to eat and the first to be pulled from school during financial difficulties.

Nepal legalised abortion in 2002. In 2005 landmark rulings gave women under the age of 35 the right for the first time to apply for a passport without their husband's or parent' permission, and safeguarded their right to inherited property. The rural custom of exiling women to cowsheds for four days during their period was only made illegal in 2005. A man may legally take a second wife if the first has not borne him a child after ten years.

On the death of her husband, a widow is often expected to marry the brother of the deceased and property is turned over to her sons, on whom she is then financially dependant. The traditional practice of *sati,* where a woman was expected to throw herself on her husband's funeral pyre, was outlawed in the 1920s.

The annual festival of Teej is the biggest festival for women, though ironically this honours their husbands. The activities include feasting, fasting, ritual bathing (in the red and gold saris they were married in) and ritual offerings.

> The lives and roles of Nepali women are examined in the insightful *The Violet Shyness of Their Eyes: Notes from Nepal* by Barbara J Scot and *Nepali Aama* by Broughton Coburn, which details the life of a remarkable Gurung woman.

ARTS

Wander around the towns of the Kathmandu Valley and you'll come across priceless woodcarvings and sculptures at every turn, in surprisingly accessible places. Nepal's artistic masterpieces are not hidden away in dusty museums but are part of a living culture, to be touched, worshipped, feared or ignored.

Architecture & Sculpture

The oldest architecture in the Kathmandu Valley has faded with history. Grassy mounds are all that remain of Patan's four Ashoka stupas, and the magnificent stupas of Swayambhunath and Bodhnath have been rebuilt many times over the centuries. Magnificent stonework is one of the lasting reminders of the Licchavi period (4th to 9th centuries AD) and you'll see beautiful pieces scattered around the temples of the Kathmandu Valley. The Licchavi sculptures at the temple of Changu Narayan near Bhaktapur (p210) are particularly good examples, as is the statue of Vishnu asleep on a bed of serpents at Budhanilkantha (p182).

> Before you start to visit the Kathmandu Valley's many temples, get a great overview on Buddhist and Nepali art at the Patan Museum (p189) and at Kathmandu's National Museum (p165), both of which explain the concepts behind Buddhist and Hindu art and iconography in an insightful and accessible way.

NEPAL'S STOLEN HERITAGE

In the last 20 years Nepal has seen a staggering amount of its artistic heritage spirited out of the country by art thieves – 120 statues were stolen in the 1980s alone. Much of the stolen art languishes in museums or private collections in European nations and in the United States, while in Nepal, remaining temple statues are, sadly, increasingly kept under lock and key.

One of the reasons that photography is banned in some temples in Nepal is that international thieves often use photos of temple images to publish underground 'shopping catalogues'. Pieces are then stolen to order, often with the aid of corrupt officials, to fetch high prices on the lucrative Himalayan art market. UN conventions against the trade exist but are weakly enforced.

Several catalogues of stolen Nepali art have been produced in an attempt to locate these treasures, and in 2000 and 2003 several pieces were returned to Kathmandu's National Museum, marking the slow return of Nepal's heritage to its rightful home. Most recently, in 2005, a Buddha statue stolen from Patan was returned after a dealer tried to sell it to an ethnographic museum in Austria for a cool US$200,000.

No wooden buildings and carvings are known to have survived from before the 12th century, although Newari craftsmen were responsible for parts of the Jokhang Temple in Lhasa, which still survive.

The famed artistic skills of the valley's Newar people reached their zenith under the Mallas, particularly between the 15th and 17th centuries. Squabbling and one-upmanship between the city-states of Kathmandu, Patan and Bhaktapur fuelled a competitive building boom as each tried to outdo the other with even more magnificent palaces and temples.

Their skills extended far beyond the woodwork for which they are so well known and included fine metalwork, terracotta, brickwork and stone sculptures. The finest metalwork includes the stunning images of the two Tara goddesses at Swayambhunath, and the Sun Dhoka (Golden Gate) in Bhaktapur.

Statues were created through two main techniques – the repoussé method of hammering thin sheets of metal and the 'lost wax' method. In the latter, the statue is carved in wax, this is then encased in clay and left to dry. The wax is then melted, metal is poured into the clay mould and the mould is then broken, leaving the finished statue.

The Nepali architect Arniko can be said to be the father of the Asian pagoda. It was his transplanting of the multiroofed Nepali pagoda design to the court of Kublai Khan in the late 13th century that kick-started the introduction and reinterpretation of the pagoda in China and eastern Asia.

The great age of Nepali architecture came to a dramatic end when Prithvi Narayan Shah invaded the valley in 1769. These days traditional building skills are still evidenced in the extensive restoration projects of the Hanuman Dhoka in Kathmandu and the Tachupal Tole buildings in Bhaktapur, which were completed in the 1970s. Today some young architects are attempting to incorporate traditional features into their buildings, particularly hotels.

Nepal by Michael Hutt is an excellent guide to the art and architecture of the Kathmandu Valley, it outlines the main forms of art and architecture, and describes specific sites within the valley, often with layout plans. It has great colour plates and black-and-white photos.

If you are interested in the architectural conservation of Kathmandu check out the website of the Kathmandu Valley Preservation Trust at www.kvptnepal.org.

NEWAR PAGODA TEMPLES

The distinctive Newar pagoda temples are a major feature of the Kathmandu Valley skyline, echoing, and possibly inspired by, the horizon's pyramid-shaped mountain peaks. While strictly speaking they are neither wholly Newari nor pagodas, the term has been widely adopted to describe the temples of the valley.

The temples are generally square in design, and may be either Hindu or Buddhist (or both, as is the nature of Nepali religion). On occasion temples are rectangular or octagonal; Krishna can occupy an octagonal temple, but Ganesh, Shiva and Vishnu can only inhabit square temples.

The major feature of the temples is the tiered roof, which may have one to five tiers, with two or three being the most common. In the Kathmandu Valley there are two temples with four roofs and another two with five (Kumbeshwar at Patan and Nyatapola at Bhaktapur). The sloping roofs are usually covered with distinctive *jhingati* (baked clay tiles), although richer temples will often have one roof of gilded copper. The bell-shaped *gajur* (pinnacle) is made of baked clay or gilded copper.

The temples are usually built on a stepped plinth, which may be as high as, or even higher than, the temple itself. In many cases the number of steps on the plinth corresponds with the number of roofs on the temple.

The temple building itself has just a small sanctum, known as a *garbhagriha* (literally 'womb room') housing the deity. Worshippers practise individually, with devotees standing outside the door to make their supplications. The only people permitted to actually enter the sanctum are *pujari* (temple priests).

Good News:
The Kathmandu has the world's densest collection of Unesco World Heritage Sites.

Bad News:
The valley was added to Unesco's List of World Heritage Sites in Danger in 2004.

Perhaps the most interesting feature of the temples is the detailed decoration, which is only evident close up. Under each roof there are often brass or other metal decorations, such as *kinkinimala* (rows of small bells) or embossed metal banners. The metal streamer that often hangs from above the uppermost roof to below the level of the lowest roof (such as on the Golden Temple in Patan) is called a *pataka*. Its function is to give the deity a means of descending to earth.

The other major decorative elements are the wooden *tundala* (struts) that support the roofs. The intricate carvings are usually of deities associated with the temple deity or of the *vahana* (deity's vehicle) but quite a few depict explicit sexual acts (see the boxed text, p118 for more on Nepali erotic art).

SHIKHARA TEMPLES

The second-most common temples are the *shikhara* temples, which have a heavy Indian influence. The temples are so named because their tapering tower resembles a *shikhara* (mountain peak, in Sanskrit). Although the style developed in India in the 6th century, it first appeared in Nepal in the late Licchavi period (9th century).

The main feature is the tapering, pyramidal tower, which is often surrounded by four similar but smaller towers, and these may be located on porches over the shrine's entrances. The Krishna Mandir and the octagonal Krishna Temple, both in Patan's Durbar Square, and the spire of the Mahabouddha Temple in Patan are all excellent examples.

In *Power Places of Kathmandu*, by Kevin Bubriski and Keith Dowman, Bubriski provides photos of the valley's most important sacred sites and temples, while noted Buddhist scholar Dowman provides the interesting text.

Painting

Chinese, Tibetan, Indian and Mughal influences can all be seen in Nepali painting styles. The earliest Newari paintings were illuminated manuscripts dating from the 11th century. Newari *paubha* paintings are iconic religious paintings similar to Tibetan thangkas. Notable to both is a lack of perspective, symbolic use of colour and strict iconographic rules.

Modern Nepali artists struggle to make a living, although there are a few galleries in Kathmandu that feature local artists. Some artists are fortunate enough to get a sponsored overseas exhibition or a posting at an art college outside the country to teach their skills. Commissioning a painting by a local artist is a way to support the arts and take home a unique souvenir of your trip.

The eastern Terai has its own distinct form of colourful mural painting called Mithila art – see the boxed text, p315.

Music & Dance

The cultural organisation Spiny Babbler (www .spinybabbler.org) has an online Nepali art museum and articles on Nepali art. It is named after Nepal's only endemic species of bird.

The last few years have seen a revival in Nepali music and songs, both folk and 'Nepali modern'. The staple Hindi film songs have been supplanted by a vibrant local music scene thanks to advances made in FM radio.

In the countryside most villagers supply their own entertainment. Dancing and traditional music enliven festivals and family celebrations, when villages erupt with the energetic sounds of *bansari* (flutes), *madal* drums and cymbals, or sway to the moving soulful sounds of devotional singing and the gentle twang of the four-stringed *sarangi*. Singing is one important way that girls and boys in the hills have to interact and flirt, showing their grace and wit through dances and improvised songs.

There are several musician castes, including the *gaine*, a dwindling caste of travelling minstrels, and *damai*, who often perform in wedding bands. Women generally do not perform music in public.

TIBETAN CARPETS

One of most amazing success stories of the last few decades is the local Tibetan carpet industry. Although carpet production has long been a cottage industry inside Tibet, in 1960 the Nepal International Tibetan Refugee Relief Committee, with the support of the Swiss government, began encouraging Tibetan refugees in Patan to make and sell carpets.

Tibetan and New Zealand wool is used to make the carpets. The exuberant colours and lively designs of traditional carpets have been toned down for the international market, but the old ways of producing carpets remain the same. The intricacies of the senna loop method are hard to pick out in the blur of hands that is usually seen at a carpet workshop; each thread is looped around a gauge rod that will determine the height of the carpet pile, then each row is hammered down and the loops of thread split to release the rod. To finish it off the pile is clipped to bring out the design.

The carpet industry has declined somewhat over recent years, largely because of negative publicity about the exploitative use of child labour and the use of carcinogenic dyes (practices that continue, despite being illegal). Still, today Nepal exports more than 244,000 sq metres of rugs (down from a peak of 300,000 sq metres in the 1990s), valued at around US$135 million. The industry accounts for around 50% of the country's exports of manufactured goods to countries other than India, and employs more than 250,000 workers directly, and up to a million indirectly.

Nepali dance styles are as numerous and varied as its ethnic groups. They range from the stick dances of the Tharu in the Terai and the quasi-linedancing style of the mountain Sherpas. Joining in with an enthusiastic group of porters from different parts of the country at the end of a trekking day is a great way to learn some of the moves. Masked dances are also common, from the Cham dances performed by Tibetan Buddhist monks to the masked Hindu dances of Nava Durga in Bhaktapur.

A good introduction to popular Nepali folk music is the trio (flute, sitar and tabla) of Sur Sudha, Nepal's de facto musical ambassadors, whose evocative recordings will take you back to the region long after you've tasted your last daal bhaat. Try their *Festivals of Nepal* and *Images of Nepal* recordings. You can listen to track excerpts at www.amazon.com, and check out the band at www.sursudha.com.

The folk song that you hear everywhere in Nepal (you'll know which one we mean when you get there) is *Resamm Phirri*.

> You can see 'for-tourist' versions of Nepal's major dances at Newari restaurants in Kathmandu and the New Himalchuli Cultural group (p152) in Kathmandu.

Film

The Nepali film industry has come a long way since the 1980s and early '90s, when only four or five films were produced annually. More recently the local film industry was making up to 70 films per year, although this bubble burst in 2001 when government-imposed curfews caused audience numbers to plummet and finances to dry up.

Recent scandal has both helped and rocked the industry. A Bollywood heart-throb's incendiary anti-Nepal comments in December 2000 prompted a violent backlash against Indian films. In 2002 the publication of paparazzi-style nude pictures of a famous Nepali film starlet led to her subsequent suicide.

According to John Whelpton in his *History of Nepal*, the first film showed in Kathmandu depicted the wedding of the Hindu god Ram. The audience threw petals and offerings at the screen as they would do at a temple or if the god himself were present.

Basantpur by Neer Shah, the coproducer of *Caravan*, is a recent Nepali film depicting the intrigues and conspiracies of life at the Rana court. It owes something to Bollywood 'masala movies' (a little bit of everything)

> Film South Asia is a biannual festival of South Asian documentaries (odd years) that alternates with the Kathmandu International Mountain Film Festival (even years). For details see www.himalassociation.org/fsa.

Himalayan Voices, by Michael Hutt, subtitled 'An Introduction to Modern Nepali Literature', includes work by contemporary poets and short-story writers.

and is based on a historical novel written nearly 60 years ago. Another Nepali film to look out for is *Mukundo* (Mask of Desire) directed by Tsering Rita Sherpa, which explores secular and spiritual desires in Kathmandu. Tulsi Ghimire is another popular Nepali director. Perhaps the best-known film shot in Nepal is Bernado Bertolucci's *Little Buddha*, which was partly filmed at Bhaktapur's Durbar Sq and the Gokarna Forest Reserve.

Literature

Nepal's literary history is brief, dating back to just the 19th century. The written language was little used before then, although religious verse, folklore, songs and translations of Sanskrit and Urdu dating back to the 13th century have been found.

Arresting God in Kathmandu, by Samrat Upadhyay, is an engaging, and readable series of short stories set in Kathmandu, by an author billed as the first Nepali writer writing in English (he's now living in the US). The follow-up novel *Guru of Love* is also recommended.

One of the first authors to establish Nepali as a literary language was Bhanubhakta Acharya (1814–68), who broke away from the influence of Indian literature and recorded the Ramayana in Nepali; this was not simply a translation but a 'Nepali-ised' version of the Hindu epic. Motiram Bhatta (1866–96) also played a major role in 19th-century literature, as did Lakshmi Prasad Devkota (1909–59) in the 20th century. Nepal's literary community has always struggled in a country where literacy levels are extremely low.

Today a vibrant and enthusiastic literary community exists, meeting in teashops, brew houses and bookstalls in Kathmandu and other urban centres. Funding comes from small prizes and writers' families – sales are often so low they barely cover the cost of the paper.

Responsible Tourism

Tourism, and trekking in particular, is having a great environmental and social impact in Nepal, (for more on responsible trekking see p330). The local communities in or around popular tourist routes have been hugely affected by tourism, for better and worse, usually without having any say in the matter.

It is an irony that we as travellers often inadvertently damage the very things we came to see: we crave to get off the beaten track and end up creating another beaten track; we want to experience traditional culture but don't want to lose our foreign comforts. We are often disappointed when traditional villages adopt modern housing, transport and dress – things we would not question in our own culture. These are among the many contradictions, inherent in travel, you will face when visiting Nepal.

A few tour operators, both abroad and in Nepal, are making conscious efforts to address problems associated with tourism, but it's slow going. The best companies are those that have a serious commitment to protecting the fragile ecosystems, and which direct at least some portion of profits back into local communities. Although these won't always be the cheapest trips, the extra money you spend is an important way to contribute to the future of the areas you visit.

Your very presence in Nepal will certainly have an effect – some people say an increasingly negative one. The challenge for you as a visitor to Nepal is to respect the rights and beliefs of the local people, and to minimise your impact – culturally and environmentally. The further you venture off the beaten track, the greater your responsibility as a visitor becomes. As the cliché goes, 'the Himalaya is there to change you, not for you to change the Himalaya'.

SUSTAINABLE TOURISM INITIATIVES

There are increasing numbers of good examples of how tourism can act as a force for positive change, merging tourism with community work.

As part of its **Tourism for Rural Poverty Alleviation Programme** (TRPAP; www .welcomenepal.com/trpap), the Nepal Tourism Board, with British and Dutch funding, has established several village tourism projects across Nepal, with the aim of bringing tourism money to communities not currently benefiting from tourist dollars. Profits from homestay accommodation, food sales and handicrafts are funnelled into village social funds. Projects include village walks in Lumbini, hikes and homestays in the hills north of Chitwan (see p288), and new trekking routes in the Langtang (see p235), Solu Khumbu, Dolpo and Kangchenjunga regions. For more details, you can download brochures and maps at the website or contact the Nepal Tourism Board's **Sustainable Tourism Unit** (☎ 01-4256909; info_trpap@ntb.org.np) in Kathmandu.

A similarly good village homestay programme operates in the Gurung village of Sirubari, about 30km from Pokhara (see p302).

Explore Nepal (Map p116; ☎ 01-4248942; www.xplorenepal.com.np; Kamaladi, Kathmandu) is a private Nepali company that operates a number of 'clean-up treks', where participants are involved in helping clean up villages along the trekking routes. The company's director was at the forefront of the campaign to have polluting three-wheeler Vikram tempos banned from the Kathmandu Valley. Its hotel, Kantipur Temple House (p135) in Kathmandu recycles its water and has banned plastic goods from the hotel.

You can download a free responsible tourism brochure from World Expeditions (www .worldexpeditions.net).

You can help reduce the growing mountains of waste plastic in village rubbish heaps by not buying unrecyclable bottles of mineral water; instead carry a water bottle and filter or treat the water with iodine. In Kathmandu and Pokhara refill it at KEEP offices (see p65) and on the Annapurna Circuit use the Safe Water Drinking Scheme (see p330).

Consider this: trekkers in Nepal leave behind an estimate 100 tonnes of unrecyclable water bottles every year.

The gorgeous **Dwarika's Hotel** (p144) in Kathmandu funds a large workshop where craftspeople patiently repair and restore fretwork windows and carvings that would otherwise almost certainly be lost in Kathmandu's rush to survive and modernise.

Community Action Treks (www.catreks.co.uk, www.cancharitytreks.co.uk) is the fundraising arm of **Community Action Nepal** (www.canepal.org.uk), an NGO run by British mountaineer Doug Scott. It runs three charity treks a year to the Everest region. **Porters Progress** (www.portersprogress.org) – see the boxed text, p327 – also runs an annual Everest trek to raise funds for its worthy organisation.

Himalayan Travel (☎ 01304-620880; www.himalayantravel.co.uk) runs treks to support the **Nepal Trust** (www.nepaltrust.org), an NGO that works on development and sustainable tourism projects in far western Nepal's remote and impoverished Humla district. It also runs one trek a year where the trekkers work on development initiatives – a 2005 group helped renovate Halji Gompa.

In a similar project, the US-based **Cultural Restoration Tourism Project** (CRTP; http://crtp.net) arranges volunteer treks to restore Chhairro Gompa in Mustang (www.chhairrogompa.org).

Sometimes contributing to a charity just involves kicking back in a good guesthouse. Nature's Grace Lodge (p258) in Pokhara is run by the **Child Welfare Scheme** (www.childwelfarescheme.org), which operates development programmes, a clinic and a vocational centre in the region. Administrative costs are directly covered by profits from the guesthouse.

Crooked Trails (www.crookedtrails.com) is a nonprofit US travel company that promotes community-based tourism and runs trips to Nepal, during which you get to work on community projects in the Terai and trek around Jomsom. Part of your trip fee goes to programmes that support the communities you are visiting.

Dolma Tours (www.dolmatours.com) runs 14-day trips to Briddim in the Langtang area, during which you get to know the local community, stay in village-owned lodges, learn the local language and take cookery classes. Part of the profits go into a village development and education fund. See the boxed text, p235 for more details on the area.

Several travel companies contribute to local development projects; **Spirit Adventures** (www.spiritadventures.com.au) funds a orphanage in Kathmandu and **Wilderness Travel** (www.wildernesstravel.com) provides half of the funds for a Sherpa dental clinic in the Khumbu. Ask what your preferred travel company does before handing over your cash.

> For more on the general issues behind responsible tourism, check out Tourism Concern (www.tourismconcern.org.uk) or Partners in Responsible Tourism (www.pirt.org).

> Pay a fair price for goods or services but don't get carried away. Haggling down the last Rs 10 like a terrier chewing on a toy will only result in hardship and disrespect; yet paying over the odds will drive up local inflation (especially for the next tourist).

ECONOMIC CHOICES

As the country's third-largest money earner and an employer of up to 250,000 Nepalis, tourism is vital to Nepal, but it often has a price. While visitors can instil local pride with their interest in Nepal's traditional arts and crafts, for example, the resulting souvenir trade often warps the very nature of these traditional crafts, robbing religious items like thangkas (Buddhist religious paintings) and Hindu statuary of their sacred significance.

Don't underestimate your power as an informed consumer. You can maximise the beneficial effects of your expenditure by frequenting locally owned restaurants and fair-trade craft stores, and by using environmentally aware trekking agencies. 'Ecotourism' in Nepal's national parks and conservation areas has encouraged local governments to make environmental protection a priority. Entry fees contribute to their preservation. Hiring a guide on a trek also helps; it adds to your safety and understanding and provides direct employment and infuses money into the hill economy. All good stuff!

Fair Trade

The principles of fair trade emphasise an exchange that benefits both parties, by supporting safe working environments, sustainable and traditional methods of production, profit sharing, supporting low-income groups and discouraging child labour.

A number of shops in Nepal specialise in handicrafts produced by low-income women. These are nonprofit development organisations and the money goes to the craftspeople in the form of fair wages (not charity). They also provide training, product development, and rehabilitation programmes. Your purchasing power can help low-income and low-status women and at the same time support traditional craft-making skills. Plus you walk away with some great souvenirs!

One of the best of these organisations is **Mahaguthi** (www.mahaguthi.org), which was established with the help of Oxfam. Its shops in Kathmandu and Patan sell a wide range of crafts that support programmes to rehabilitate destitute women and children. It works with 150 craft producers, encouraging micro-financing, entrepreneurship, social welfare programs and a revival of traditional crafts.

Sana Hastakala (www.sanahastakala.org) in Kathmandu, Dhankuta Sisters in Patan and Dhukuti in Patan and Pokhara (established with the help of UNICEF) are similar organisations based on the principles of fair trade. Dhukuti operates as a sales agent for the **Association of Craft Producers** (www.acp.org.np), an organisation that works with over 1000 low-income craft producers.

The Maheela shop is operated by the **Women's Foundation** (www.womenfoundation.org), which runs a shelter for women and children who have been victims of abuse, domestic violence, forced labour or trafficking, or have been displaced or widowed by fighting between Maoists and the Nepalese army. It offers training in handicraft production. You can sponsor children through the organisation and you'll receive regular updates on their progress.

> More information on fair trade can be found on the website of the Fair Trade Group Nepal (www.fairtradegroupnepal.org) or the International Federation of Alternative Trade (www.ifat.org).

Ethical Shopping

There is still a thriving trade in endangered animal furs and trophies in Nepal, despite the fact that this is officially prohibited.

Be aware that *shahtoosh* (or *shartoosh*) shawls are illegal both in Nepal and abroad. *Shahtoosh* comes from the wool of the protected *chiru*, or Tibetan antelope, which are killed for their superfine hair (a 2m shawl requires the death of three antelopes). *Shahtoosh* shawls are often referred to as 'ring shawls', as they are fine enough to pass through a finger ring, but this term is also used for perfectly legal pashmina (where the hair is merely sheared from a living mountain goat). If in doubt check with the dealer, though you can also tell by the price; *shahtoosh* is four or five times more expensive than pashmina (see p370).

> For details on fair-trade organisations and their crafts, see p153 and p194. See also the boxed text about the Janakpur Women's Development Centre, p315).

Begging

Begging is relatively common in Nepal, partly because both Hinduism and Buddhism encourage the giving of alms. This presents many visitors with a heart-rending moral dilemma. Should you give? Sometimes, especially if you've just spent Rs 500 on drinks, it seems grotesque to ignore someone who is genuinely in need. It is often worth checking to see how the local Nepalis react; if they give, it's a reasonably safe assumption that the beneficiary is genuine.

Around the main religious shrines, especially Pashupatinath, there are long lines of beggars. Pilgrims customarily give a coin to everyone in the line (there are special moneychangers nearby who will change notes for small-denomination coins). Sadhus (holy men) are another special case, and are usually completely dependent on alms. There are plenty of con artists among their ranks, but equally, plenty of genuine holy men.

In the countryside, visitors will quickly be discovered by small children who chant a mantra that sounds something like: 'bonbonpenonerupeeee?' Someone, somewhere, started giving children sweets, pens and money, and it sometimes seems that every child in Nepal now tries their luck. Don't encourage this behaviour. Most Nepalis find it offensive and demeaning (as do most visitors), and it encourages a whole range of unhealthy attitudes.

By presenting school books or teaching materials (such as exercise books, school text books and pens bought in Kathmandu bookshops) to teachers and village elders, you can contribute more to long-term progress than you would by giving a cash donation or passing out pens. Several organisations, including **READ Nepal** (www.readnepal.org) and **Room to Read** (www.roomtoread.org) work towards building and stocking libraries in Nepal.

Thamel attracts many of Kathmandu's estimated 1000-plus street kids. The lure of easy money attracts many kids onto the streets in the first place, and gives them a powerful incentive to remain. It's also a dog-eat-dog world: children seen receiving money may well be beaten up and have it stolen. By giving to beggars in Thamel you are in many ways encouraging a further influx of people into Kathmandu, where very few facilities exist for them. There are signs up around Thamel asking visitors not to do so. If you want to give money, several organisations operate child shelters, including **Child Welfare Scheme** (www.childwelfarescheme.org) in Pokhara and the UK-based **Street Children of Nepal Trust** (☎ 0117-9321156; www.streetchildrenofnepal.org). **APC Nepal** (☎ 01-4268299; www.pommecannelle.org) operates a home for street kids in Basantapur. Travellers can sponsor a kid for €20 per month or make a donation through Paypal.

Although the blind and people with leprosy are probably genuinely dependent on begging for their survival, long-term solutions are offered by organisations like Kathmandu's Leprosy Hospital and Tilganga Eye Centre. In association with The Fred Hollows Foundation and other partners, the **Tilganga Eye Centre** (www.tilganga.org) provides eye-care services to the poorest of Nepal's poor, often restoring people's sight with relatively simple treatments and surgical techniques. Many Australians will remember the late Professor Fred Hollows, who was instrumental in establishing the centre, which was opened in 1994. Both the Tilganga Eye Centre and **The Fred Hollows Foundation** (www.hollows.org) accept donations, as does the excellent **Himalayan Cataract Project** (www.cureblindness.org). A donation of as little as US$12 can restore someone's sight.

> If you have any clothes or medicines left at the end of your trip, don't haul them home. Instead donate them to Porter's Progress or the Porters Clothing Bank. Alternatively, contact them in advance and carry out clothing from your home country.

CULTURAL CONSIDERATIONS

An important dimension of responsible tourism is the manner and attitude that visitors assume towards local people. You'll get more out of your visit by learning about Nepali life and culture and by travelling with an open mind.

One of travel's great gifts is that it allows you to re-examine your own culture in a new light. Life for many is extremely hard, but despite the scarcity of material possessions, Nepal has many qualities that shame the 'developed' world.

Most Nepalis make allowances for the odd social gaffe, even if it does embarrass them, but they do appreciate it when a genuine effort is made to observe local customs. Following is a collection of simple suggestions that will help you to avoid offence.

Behaviour

Follow a Nepali proverb and 'Dress according to the land you are in' – shorts, Lycra and revealing clothes are unsuitable for women. Shorts are acceptable for men only when trekking; going without a shirt anywhere is not. Nudity is unacceptable anywhere.

Public displays of affection between men and women are frowned upon. Nepali men often walk around hand in hand, but this does not carry any sexual overtones.

Raising your voice or shouting show extremely bad manners and will not solve your problem, whatever it might be. Always try to remain cool, calm and collected.

Nepalis rarely shake hands, although among Nepali men with frequent Western connections it is becoming more accepted. The *namaste* greeting (placing your palms together in a prayer position) is a better choice. A sideways tilt or wobble of the head, accompanied by a slight shrug of the shoulders, conveys agreement in Nepal, not a 'no' (visitors from India will be used to this).

Never touch anything or point at anything with your feet, the 'lowest' part of the body. If you accidentally do this, apologise by touching your hand to the person's arm and then touching your own head. It's bad manners to step over someone's outstretched legs, so avoid doing that, and move your own legs when someone wants to pass. In contrast, the head is spiritually the 'highest' part of the body, so don't pat children on the head.

Other tips:

- When handing money to someone (or receiving) pass (or receive) with your right hand and touch your right elbow with your left hand, as a gesture of respect.
- When addressing someone, particularly elders, it's a good idea to add *-ji* at the end of the name (eg Danny-*ji*) to convey respect.
- Nepalis do not like to give negative answers or no answer at all. If you are given a wrong direction or told a place is much nearer than it turns out to be, it may be through fear of disappointing you.
- Fire is sacred, so do not throw rubbish or cigarette butts into it.
- Always remove your shoes before entering a Nepali home.

Visiting a Temple

Always walk clockwise around Buddhist stupas, *chörtens* and mani walls, and always remove your shoes before entering a Buddhist or Hindu temple or sanctuary. You may also have to remove any items made from leather, such as belts and bags. Many Hindu temples do not permit Westerners to enter, so respect this.

It's customary to give a *khata* (white scarf) to a lama when you are introduced. The scarves can easily be found in Tibetan shops. A small donation to a temple or monastery will always be appreciated.

Finally, a few other things to remember; don't step over a shrine or offering, don't smoke in a holy place and *definitely* don't urinate on a *chörten* (yes, we actually saw that one!).

Photography

Do not intrude with a camera, unless it is clearly OK with the people you are photographing. Ask before entering a temple compound whether it is permissible to enter and take photographs, and don't photograph cremations or people washing at riverbanks or wells.

Respect people's privacy; most Nepalis are very modest. Although people carry out many activities in public (they have no choice), it does

'If you are given a wrong direction or told a place is much nearer than it turns out to be, it may be through fear of disappointing you'

not follow that passers-by have the right to watch or take photographs. Riverbanks and village wells, for example, are often used to wash at, but the users expect consideration and privacy.

Religious ceremonies are also often private affairs, so first ask yourself whether it would be acceptable for a tourist to intrude and take photographs at a corresponding event in your home country – then get explicit permission from the senior participants. The behaviour of some photographers at places such as Pashupatinath (the most holy cremation site in Nepal) is shameful – imagine the outrage a busload of scantily clad, camera-toting tourists would create if they invaded a family funeral in the West.

VOLUNTEER WORK

Culture Shock! Nepal: A Guide to Customs & Etiquette by Jon Burbank is an insightful guide to Nepali culture and is perfect for anyone planning to work or volunteer in Nepal.

It's possible to get work as a volunteer, and this can be a rewarding experience and one which gives you the opportunity to put something back into the community. It's harder than you think to offer your services for free and most foreign organisations will charge you heftily for the privilege. Check out www.volunteernepal.org for volunteering tips and ideas.

The **International Mountain Explorers Connection** (IMEC; Map p136; www.mountainexplorers.org) publishes an annual Nepal Volunteer Handbook, which outlines the opportunities for volunteering in Nepal. It is available for US$10 from the IMEC office in Thamel or online to members.

Volunteer programmes have been scaled back in recent years due to Maoist activity in the rural areas that form the Maoist heartland. Contact the agencies below (a web search will bring up many more) to see what programmes they are running.

Child Environment Nepal (☎ 4352492; www.cennepal.org.np) Takes childcare volunteers in its orphanage at a cost of US$75 per week to cover board and lodging.

Educate the Children (www.etc-nepal.org) Three-month teaching stints in rural Nepal offered by this Nepali organisation. There's a US$100 placement fee and living costs of around US$30 per week.

Ford Foundation (☎ 01-4378864; www.fordnepal.org) Arranges volunteer work focusing on teaching and childcare, from two weeks upwards, accommodation arranged with host family.

Gift For Aid (Map p136; ☎ 01-4418100; www.giftforaid.org) Can help with placements in fields of teaching, health, occupational therapy and the environment. There's no placement charge and volunteers stay with local families.

Global Vision International (www.gvi.co.uk) British organisation that arranges four- to 12-week placements in is schools, orphanages and environmental work. Placements are pricey. If you are already in Kathmandu contact Tony Jones at Himalayan Encounters (see p90) about teaching positions in orphanages in Pokhara or Chitwan.

Global Volunteer Network (www.volunteer.org.nz/nepal) Healthcare, children education, environment, US$350 plus local fee, two months US$800.

Himalayan Healthcare (www.himalayan-healthcare.org) Doctors and healthcare professionals can volunteer at the organisation's clinic in Ilam, and they also run medical treks (around US$2000 for two weeks) when the security situation allows.

Himalayan Light Foundation (www.hlf.org.np) Minimum five-months commitment. US$150 administration fee.

Himshikhar Socio-Cultural Society (www.hopenhome.org) Nepali NGO, fees from US$250.

Info Nepal (☎ 01-4700210; www.infonepal.org/index.html) Wide variety of volunteering opportunities, costing around €600 for three months.

Insight Nepal (www.insightnepal.org.np) Pokhara-based programme that runs six-week/three-month volunteer programmes for US$480/840, which includes training, food, accommodation, trekking and a Chitwan safari excursion. A similar organisation is Cultural Destination Nepal (www.volunteernepal.org.np).

KEEP (www.keepnepal.org) Arranges rural volunteer work positions, preferably for a minimum two months, or you can offer to teach English to porters and guides in Kathmandu for a month in December/January and July/August. There's a US$50 placement fee. See p114 for details.

Know Nepal (www.knownepal.org) Mostly teaching, costs US$350/450 for three/five months.
Nepal Kingdom Foundation (www.nkf-mt.org.uk/nkf.htm) Project in Panglong, near the Tibetan border.
Prison Assist (info@panepal.org) Kathmandu-based organisation that looks after children whose parents are in prison. Contact Indira Rana Magar. No volunteering costs.
Rokpa (www.rokpa.org) Swiss-Tibetan organisation that takes general volunteers for a winter (mid-December to March) soup kitchen in Bodhnath and nurses for a medical tent.
Rural Community Development Programme (www.rcdpnepal.org/nepal) Costs around US$700/900 for one/two months.
Starchildren (☎ 071-3615245 in the Netherlands; www.starchildren.nl) Pokhara-based charity that works with children with HIV. No volunteering costs.
Vajrayana Centre (☎ 01-2074256; www.vajrayanana.org; vajrayana_centre@yahoo.com) Contact Tsewang Sherpa about teaching English to Tibetan refugees in Bodhnath.
Volunteer Nepal Himalaya (USA ☎ 303-998-0101; www.hec.org/volunteering/teaching.htm) Programme run by IMEC (see earlier) to teach English for three months in the Solu-Khumbu region. Costs include a US$1000 fee/donation, plus US$150 per month food and lodging.
Volunteer Work Opportunity Programs (VWOP; ☎ 01-4416614; vwop2000@hotmail.com) Nepali organisation that coordinates teaching, agricultural and environmental volunteers. There's a one-off administration fee of US$220.

Foreign-based organisations that arrange pricier volunteer placements in Nepal include:
Experiential Learning International (www.eliabroad.org)
Global Action Nepal (☎ 01403-864704; www.gannepal.org)
Global Crossroad (www.globalcrossroad.com)
I-to-I (www.i-to-i.com) UK (☎ 0870-333 2332); USA (☎ 800-985 4864)
Involvement Volunteers Association (☎ 03-9646 5504; www.volunteering.org.au)

USEFUL ORGANISATIONS

There are a number of organisations based in Nepal that are involved in grass-roots initiatives to minimise the impact of tourist; they include:
American Himalayan Foundation (USA ☎ 415-2887245; www.himalayan-foundation.org) Runs projects in Sherpa education, reforestation, assistance to elderly Tibetans in exile and restoration of monasteries in Mustang, Tengboche and Thamel.
Annapurna Conservation Area Project (ACAP; ☎ 01-4225393, ext 363; Tridevi Marg, Kathmandu; ☺ 9am-5pm, 9am-4pm winter) Nongovernmental, nonprofit organisation that exists to improve local standards of living, to protect the environment and to develop more sensitive forms of tourism. ACAP has started work on a number of projects, such as forestry nurseries, introducing wood-saving technologies (eg efficient stoves), banning fires altogether in certain areas, and building rubbish tips and latrines.
Gift for Aid (Map p136; ☎ 01-4418100; gift@infoclub.com.np, www.giftforaid.org; Thamel, Kathmandu) is a Dutch initiative that aims to connect foreign travellers with local small-scale tourism-funded development projects. It can often link visitors with volunteer opportunities. Pop into the office to view some local development projects and donate to your favourite project.
Himalayan Foundation for Integrated Development (www.himalayafoundation.org) Assists the Sherpa communities in the Khumbu with small-scale ecotourism and education projects.
International Mountain Explorers Connection (Map p136; ☎ 2081407; www.mountainexplorers.org; ☎ USA 303-9980101; Thamel, Kathmandu) Educates trekkers, offers English and first-aid training to porters and operates a clothing bank through the Porter Assistance Project. Travellers can volunteer to help teach porters English.
Kathmandu Environmental Education Project (KEEP; ☎ 01-4216775; www.keepnepal.org; ☺ 10am-5pm Sun-Fri; Thamel) KEEP offer tips on how you can lessen your environmental impact, offers clean water refills and also accepts donations of medical supplies and other equipment. See p114 for details; there's also an office in Pokhara.

If you have time it's well worth checking out the BBC video *Carrying the Burden,* which plays everyday except Saturday at 3.30pm (or on request) at Porters Progress in Kathmandu and Lukla, and daily at 2pm at the International Mountain Explorers Connection in Thamel (see Map p136).

Porters Progress (Map p136; ☎ 01-4410020; www.portersprogress.org; Thamel, Kathmandu) Campaigns for the ethical treatment of porters, porter safety and medical relief, and offers free English tuition and medical training to porters. It operates a clothes and kerosene stove bank in Lukla and currently has clothes for 700 porters.

Sagarmatha Pollution Control Committee (SPCC; spcc@mail.com.np) Works on waste reduction and recycling in the Khumbu region and helped banned glass bottles from the Everest region.

Environment

Nepal is blessed by, and is hostage to, its incredible environment. Its economy, history, culture, tourist attractions and development are all tied closely to its daunting mountains and valleys. Remote as they may seem, the Himalaya are not a wilderness Shangri-la – some 50 million people live in the Himalaya. Life here is, by necessity, in fine ecological balance, a balance that in places has been upset, most notably by tourism.

It's easy to fret about trail erosion, overgrazing, landslides and litter, but the reality in these awesome mountains is that the natural processes of the Himalaya have long dwarfed the impact of man. The question is for how long.

The Sanskrit word Himalaya means abode *(alaya)* of the snows *(himal)*. Pronounce it correctly as they do in the corridors of the Royal Geographical Society, with the emphasis on the second syllable – himaaarliya, darling...

THE LAND

Nepal may be a small country, but when it comes to height it is number one in the world. Mountains cover 64% of Nepal, providing huge challenges in a country where 80% of people live off the land. Nepal measures about 800km east–west and 230km at its widest point north–south, making a total area of around 147,181 sq km.

Within that small area, however, is the second-greatest range of altitude on earth – starting with the Terai, less than 100m above sea level, and finishing at the top of Mt Everest (8850m), the world's highest point. With this comes an incredible ecological diversity, where conditions change from tropical to arctic in a mere 160km. The overriding geographical feature is the Himalaya, born of a slow-motion continental crash of mind-boggling proportions.

Nepalis divide the year into six, not four, seasons: Basanta (spring), Grisma (pre-monsoon heat), Barkha (monsoon), Sharad (post-monsoon), Hemanta (autumn) and Sheet (winter).

Geology

About 60 million years ago, the Indo-Australian tectonic plate collided with the Eurasian continent. As the former was pushed under Eurasia, the Earth's crust buckled and folded and the Himalayas were born.

The upheaval of mountains caused the temporary obstruction of rivers that once flowed unimpeded from Eurasia to the sea. However, on the southern slopes of the young mountains, new rivers formed as trapped moist winds off the tropical sea rose and precipitated. As the mountains

---

HOW HIGH IS MT EVEREST?

Using triangulation from the plains of India, the Survey of India established the elevation of the top of Everest at 29,002ft (8839m). A century later, in 1954, the Survey of India revised the height to 29,028ft (8848m) using the unweighted mean of altitudes determined from 12 different survey stations around the mountain.

On 5 May 1999, scientists supported by the National Geographic Society and Boston's Museum of Science recorded GPS data on the top of Mt Everest for 50 minutes. Their measurements produced a revised elevation of 29,035ft (8850m). Nepal, however, continues to favour the 8848m elevation. As part of the same survey, GPS readings from the South Col indicated that the horizontal position of Everest is moving steadily and slightly northeastward at about 6cm a year.

Then in May 2005 a Chinese team made measurements from the summit using ice radars and GPS systems and eventually calculated a height of 8844.43m, accurate to 20cm. So is Everest shrinking? Not exactly; the Chinese claim that this is the most accurate measurement yet since it measures the height of the rock, without the accumulated 3.5m of ice and snow measured on the summit by other readings.

continued to rise and the gradient became steeper, both sets of rivers cut deeper into the soft, young terrain. When you look at Nepal's amazing mountain ranges and dividing gorges you are actually seeing what *isn't* there – the gap between the peaks eroded by rivers over millions of years. Rivers such as the Arun, Bhote Kosi and Humla, which rise in Tibet and breach the Himalaya, are actually older than the mountains themselves.

The mountain-building process continues today, not only displacing material laterally, but also sending the ranges even higher (about 1cm per year) and resulting in natural erosion, landslides, silt-laden rivers, rock faults and earthquakes. Nepal's terrain can be likened to a complex maze of ceilingless rooms.

One result of all this plate tectonics is that Nepal is in an active seismic zone. A huge earthquake in 1934 destroyed much of the country. A similar-sized quake would cause unimaginable damage to modern Kathmandu's densely-packed and poorly constructed buildings.

The Kali Gandaki valley between the Annapurna and Dhaulagiri massifs is considered the world's deepest gorge, with a vertical gain of 7km spaced between 20km.

Physiographic Regions

Nepal consists of several physiographic regions, or natural zones: the plains in the south, four mountain ranges, and the valleys lying between them. Most people live in the fertile lowlands or on the southern sunny slopes of the mountains where farming is easier and life less harsh.

THE TERAI & CHURE HILLS

Mt Everest's 'real' name is its Tibetan name, Chomolangma, which translates as 'Goddess Mother of the Universe'. The Nepali name is Sagarmartha, which is Sanskrit for 'Brow of the Ocean'.

The only truly flat land in Nepal is the Terai (sometimes written Tarai), a patchwork of paddy fields, mango groves, bamboo stands and thatched villages. Seen from the air, the monotonous expanse of the Gangetic plain extends up to 40km into Nepal before the land rears up an average 900m to form the Chure Hills (known in India as the Siwalik Hills), which runs the length of the country and is the first of the four mountain ranges. The range harbours the fossilised remains of many mammals no longer typical of Eurasia, and separates the Terai from the Inner Terai or the Dun.

MAHABHARAT RANGE

North of the Inner Terai, the next range of foothills is the Mahabharat Range, or the 'Middle Hills'. These vary between 1500m and 2700m in height, and though quite steep, are characterised by water-retentive soils that allow cultivation and extensive terracing. On the lower slopes, remnants of subtropical forests can be found. On the upper reaches, above cultivation, temperate elements begin. These mountains are cut by three major river systems: the Karnali, the Narayani and the Sapt Kosi.

The Terai makes up only 18% of Nepal's area but holds 50% of its population and 70% of its agricultural land.

PAHAR ZONE

Between the Mahabharat Range and the Himalaya lies a broad, extensively cultivated belt called the midlands, or the Pahar zone. This includes the fertile valleys (previously large lakes) of Kathmandu, Banepa and Pokhara, and supports nearly half of Nepal's population. Lying between 1000m and 2000m, subtropical and lower temperate forests (damaged by fuel and fodder gathering) are found here.

The stunningly located Pokhara area, right at the foot of the Annapurna massif, is unique because there is no formidable barrier directly to the south to block the path of spring and monsoon rain clouds. As a result Pokhara receives an exceptionally high level of rainfall, limiting cultivation to below 2000m.

At the other extreme, the Humla-Jumla area in the west is protected to the south by ranges over 4000m in height; these stop much of the region's monsoon moisture. The area is characterised by wide, uneroded valleys, snowless peaks and drier vegetation.

THE HIMALAYA

Nepal's borders contain about one-third of the total length of the Himalaya and include 10 of the world's 14 tallest mountains. These mountains are terraced and cultivated up to about 2700m, or to the level of cloud and mist. As a result, the high-temperate forest above this to the tree line is fairly well preserved.

The inner valleys are those cradled within the Himalayan ranges. The higher parts of these broad, glacier-worn valleys, which are found in the Everest, Langtang and upper Kali Gandaki areas, are not affected by the strong winds that desiccate the valley floors. The partial rainscreen of all these high valleys creates ecologies that are different again.

The Himalaya do not form an unbroken wall of peaks, but rather groups of massifs, or himal. The range is crossed by passes that have been used for centuries by Himalayan traders, migrating peoples and, most recently, Tibetan refugees.

THE TRANS-HIMALAYA

North of the Himalaya is a high desert region, similar to the Tibetan plateau. This area encompasses the arid valleys of Mustang, Manang and Dolpo, as well as the Tibetan marginals (the fourth range of mountains, which sweeps from central to northwestern Nepal, averaging less than 6000m in height). The trans-Himalaya is in the rainshadow area and receives significantly less precipitation than the southern slopes. Uneroded crags, spires and formations like crumbling fortresses are typical of this stark landscape.

WILDLIFE
Animals
BIRDS

More than 850 bird species are known in Nepal and, surprisingly considering the population and pollution, almost half of these can be spotted in the Kathmandu Valley. March to May is the main breeding season and so it's a great time to spot birds. Resident bird numbers are augmented by migratory species, which arrive in the Terai in spring (February and March) en route from Siberia. During this migration the bar-headed goose has been observed flying at altitudes near 8000m.

Eight species of stork have been identified along the watercourses of the Terai. Similar in appearance are the cranes, though these are not as well represented, save for the demoiselle cranes that fly down the Kali Gandaki and Dudh Kosi for the winter, before returning in spring to their Tibetan nesting grounds. The endangered sarus crane (found in Royal Bardia National Park) is particularly beautiful, with a dramatic red band around its eyes that makes it look like a cartoon bank robber. Around 30 sarus cranes live at the privately funded Lumbini Crane Sanctuary near Lumbini (p295).

Raptors or birds of prey of all sizes are found in the Himalaya, and are especially prevalent with the onset of winter. Raptors include the huge Himalayan griffon and lammergeier, both of which have a wingspan of nearly 3m. Vulture populations have plummeted across the Himalaya in recent years and of Nepal's nine species of vulture, three are now critically endangered.

There are six species of pheasant in Nepal, including the national bird, the *daphe,* or impeyan pheasant, the male of which has a plumage of iridescent colours. These birds are 'downhill fliers' – they do not fly, per

Saligrams (fossilised ammonites) are found throughout the Himalaya (and regarded as a symbol of Shiva), and seashell fossils have been even found halfway up Mt Everest, proof that the region used to lie beneath the ancient Tethys Sea.

The best places in Nepal for bird-watching are Koshi Tappu Wildlife Reserve (p316) and Royal Chitwan National Park (p275). The best spots in the Kathmandu Valley are Pulchowki, Nagarjun and Shivapuri National Park.

Nepal covers only 0.1% of the world's surface area but is home to nearly 10% of the world's species of birds, including 72 critically endangered species.

se, and must walk uphill! The cheer and koklas pheasants live west of the Kali Gandaki, while the kalij pheasant is common throughout Nepal.

Nepal hosts 17 species of cuckoo, whose arrival in March heralds the coming of spring. The Indian cuckoo is recognised by its '*kaphal pakyo*' call, which announces in Nepali that the fruit of the box myrtle is ripe. The common hawk cuckoo has a repetitious call that rises in a crescendo and sounds like 'brain fever' – or so it was described by British sahibs as they lay sweating with malarial fevers.

One of the most colourful, varied and vocal families is the timalids, or babblers and laughing thrushes, common from the tropical Terai to the upper temperate forest. They can often be identified by their raucous calls. The black-capped sibia with its constant prattle and ringing song is an integral part of the wet temperate forests. The spiny babbler is Nepal's only endemic species.

Above the tree line, two species of chough, congregating in large flocks in winter, are prevalent. Though the two species often overlap in range, the yellow-billed chough is found higher and is known to enter mountaineers' tents high on Everest.

Besides such families as kingfishers, bee-eaters, drongos, minivets, parakeets and sunbirds, there are a host of others including 30 species of flycatchers and nearly 60 species of thrushes and warblers.

Dark kites, hawklike birds with forked tails, are common over Kathmandu. At sunset loose groups of crows, mynahs, egrets and kites fly to their respective roosts.

In the Pokhara region, the Indian roller is conspicuous when it takes flight, flashing the iridescent turquoise on its wings. Otherwise, while perched, it appears as a plain brown bird. Local superstition has it that if someone about to embark on a journey sees a roller going their way it is a good omen.

MAMMALS

Due to habitat degeneration from both natural and human causes, opportunities for viewing mammals are usually restricted to national parks, reserves and western Nepal, where the population is sparse. Wildlife numbers have been thinned by poaching, whether for pelts or medicinal parts. Animals are also hunted because of the damage they inflict on crops and domestic animals.

At the top of the food chain is the royal Bengal tiger (*bagh* in Nepali), which is solitary and territorial. Males have territorial ranges that encompass those of two or three females and may span as much as 100 sq km. Royal Chitwan National Park in the Inner Terai and Royal Bardia National Park in the western Terai protect sufficient habitat to sustain viable breeding populations (Chitwan has 110 tigers, Bardia 22). For more on the signature species of Royal Chitwan National Park see the boxed text, p279.

The spotted leopard *(chituwa)* is an avid tree climber and, in general, more elusive than the tiger. Like the tiger, this nocturnal creature has been known to prefer human flesh when it has grown old or been maimed. Local people liken the spotted leopard to an evil spirit because its success at evading hunters suggests it can read minds.

The near-mythical snow leopard ('white leopard' in Nepali) is rarely spotted, partly because of its superb camouflage and partly because it inhabits some of the most remote and inhospitable high mountain terrain on earth, notably around Dolpo. Numbers are estimated at between 300 and 500, which makes up around 10% of the global population. Its territory depends upon the ranges of its main prey, ungulate (hoofed)

Bird Conservation Nepal (www.birdlifenepal.org) is an excellent Nepali organisation based in Kathmandu that organises bird-watching trips every other Saturday and publishes books, birding checklists and a good quarterly newsletter.

Birds of Nepal, by Robert Fleming Sr, Robert Fleming Jr and Lain Singh Bangdel, is a field guide to Nepal's many hundreds of birds. *Birds of Nepal* by Richard Grimmett and Carol Inskipp is a comprehensive paperback with line drawings.

The Bird Education Society (www.besnepal .org) offers an online and printed checklist of birds in Royal Chitwan National Park and runs birding trips from its office by the park.

herds. Packs of wolves compete directly and when territories overlap, the solitary snow leopard will be displaced.

The one-horned rhinoceros *(gaida)* is the largest of three Asian species and is a distinct genus from the two-horned African rhino. It has poor eyesight, and though it weighs up to two tonnes, it is amazingly quick-footed. Anyone who encounters a mother with its calf is likely to witness a charge, which is disconcertingly swift, even if you are on an elephant. The rhino inhabits the grasslands of the Inner Terai, specifically the Chitwan Valley (which has 372 rhinos), although it has also been reintroduced to Royal Bardia National Park and Royal Sukla Phanta Wildlife Reserve.

The Asian elephant *(hathi)* is genetically distinct from its African relative. The only wild elephants known to exist in Nepal are in the western part of the Terai and Chure hills, though individuals often range across the border from India. Elephants are known to maintain matriarchal societies, and females up to 60 years of age bear calves. Though elephants are able to reach 80 years of age, their life spans are determined by dentition. Molars are replaced as they wear down, but only up to six times. When the final set is worn, the animal dies of starvation.

There are several species of deer, but most are confined to the lowlands. The spotted deer is probably the most beautiful, while the sambar is the largest. The muntjac, or barking deer, which usually makes its presence known by its sharp, one-note alarm call, is found at altitudes up to 2400m, while the tiny musk deer (the male is hunted for its valuable musk pods) ranges even higher.

There are two primates: the rhesus macaque and the common langur *(bandar)*. The rhesus is earth-coloured, with a short tail and travels on the ground in a large, structured troop, unafraid of humans. The langur is arboreal, with a black face, grey fur, and long limbs and tail. Because of Hanuman, the monkey god in the Hindu epic the Ramayana, both species are considered holy and are well protected. The rhesus ranges from the Terai up to 2400m, while the langur goes up to 3600m.

Two even-toed ungulate mammals are found in the alpine regions. They are the Himalayan tahr, a near-true goat, and the blue sheep *(bharal)*, which is genetically stranded somewhere between the goat and the sheep. The male tahr with its flowing mane poses on the grassy slopes of inner valleys, while the blue sheep turns a bluish-grey in winter and is found in the trans-Himalayan region. Harder to spot is the nimble goral, which combines characteristics of both goats and antelope, and makes a sneezing noise when alarmed.

The Himalayan black bear is omnivorous and a bane to corn crops in the temperate forests. Though it rarely attacks humans, its poor eyesight may lead it to interpret a standing person as making a threatening gesture and to attack. Nepal's bears are known to roam in winter instead of hibernating.

The pika, or mouse hare, is the common guinea pig–like mammal of the inner valleys, often seen scurrying nervously between rocks. The marmot of western Nepal is a large rodent; it commonly dwells in the trans-Himalaya.

Noisy colonies of flying foxes or fruit bats have chosen the trees near the Royal Palace in Kathmandu and the chir pines at the entrance to Bhaktapur as their haunts. They are known to fly great distances at night to raid orchards. They have adequate eyesight for their feeding habits and do not require the sonar system of insectivorous bats.

Nepal's endangered river dolphin, on the other hand, is the only animal to have eyes but no lenses. It is therefore effectively blind, relying on sonar to find its way through muddy river courses.

A shocking survey in April 2005 revealed that the rhino population of Royal Chitwan National Park had declined by 182 animals, almost 30% of the population, since 2000. Of these, 94 animals were killed by poachers.

More than 30% of the world's total one-horned rhino population lives in Nepal's Royal Chitwan National Park.

Most of the yaks you see in Nepal are actually *dzo* or *dzopkyo*, male yak-cow hybrids; one reason being that yaks won't plough, but *dzo* will. And while we are at it, there's no such thing as 'yak' cheese or 'yak' butter – a female yak is actually called a *nak*.

REPTILES

The Terai is home to two indigenous species of crocodile: the gharial and the marsh mugger. The endangered gharial inhabits rivers, and is a prehistoric-looking fish-eating creature with bulging eyes and a long, narrow snout. The marsh mugger prefers stagnant water and is omnivorous, feeding on anything within reach. Because of the value of its hide and eggs, the gharial was hunted to the brink of extinction, but has increased in numbers since the establishment of a hatchery in Chitwan (now home to 25% of the world's gharial population).

Though venomous snakes such as cobras, vipers and kraits are present, the chance of encountering one is small. The majority of species are found in the Terai, though the mountain pit viper is known higher up, along with a few other nonvenomous species.

Plants

And the Wildest dreams of Kew are but the facts of Kathmandu

Rudyard Kipling

Nag is the Nepali name for both the cobra and the serpent spirits who live in the soil and control the rains.

There are 6500 known species of trees, shrubs and wildflowers in Nepal. The height of floral glory can be witnessed in March and April when Nepal's 30 species of rhododendrons (*lali gurans* in Nepali) burst into colour. The huge magnolias of the east with their showy white flowers on bare branches are also spectacular, as are Nepal's dozens of species of orchid.

In the postmonsoon season, the flowers of summer are all but gone. However, in the subtropical and lower temperate areas, some wildflowers that have survived environmental degradation aree pink luculia, mauve osbeckia and yellow St John's wort. Flowering cherry trees, and blue gentians in the temperate areas, add autumnal colours. Otherwise enjoy the autumn yellows of maples and ginger, and the reds of barberry shrubs.

Rhododendron arboreum, Nepal's national flower, reaches heights of 18m and ranges in colour from red to white, getting paler with altitude.

In the Kathmandu Valley, silky oak with its spring golden inflorescence, and bottlebrush and eucalyptus, are planted as ornamentals, along with cherry, poplar and jacaranda. Historically, the Nepalis have been avid gardeners of such exotics as hibiscus, camellia, cosmos, salvia and marigold.

Throughout Nepal the magnificent mushrooming canopies of banyan and pipal trees are unmistakable, usually found together atop a stone dais designed for accommodating porters' loads. The pipal tree has a special religious significance (the Buddha gained enlightenment under a pipal tree) and often shelters shrines or has threads wrapped around it.

Sal, a broad-leaved, semideciduous hardwood, dominates the low-lying tropical areas of the Terai. The leaves are used as disposable plates, and the wood is used for construction. There are also deciduous moist forests of acacia and rosewood here. Open areas of tall elephant grass (*phanta*) can grow to 2½ metres high and is used by local Tharu people for thatching.

Himalayan Flowers & Trees, by Dorothy Mierow and Tirtha Bahadur Shrestha, is the best available field guide to the plants of Nepal.

NATIONAL PARKS & CONSERVATION AREAS

Despite Nepal's small size and heavy demand for land, the Department of National Parks and Wildlife Conservation (www.dnpwc.gov.np) has managed to set aside an impressive 18% of its land for protection. There are nine national parks, three conservation areas, three wildlife reserves and one hunting reserve protecting every significant ecological system in the country. There is talk of creating a new national park in the Rolwaling region.

The first protected areas such as Sagarmartha were similar to the New Zealand park service (where the park has no inhabitants), imposed from above with little partnership with locals and initially, at least, without their cooperation. Recent initiatives concentrate on accommodating people and their needs, not evicting them. They promote sustainable development, the preservation of culture and work to balance conservation needs with resource development, including tourism. The Annapurna Conservation Area, for example, has 40,000 residents. Between 20% and 50% of park revenues are reserved for community-development projects.

NATIONAL PARKS & CONSERVATION AREAS

Name	Location	Features	Best time to visit	Entry fee (Rs)
Annapurna CA	north of Pokhara, west-central Nepal (p352)	most popular trekking area in Nepal, extremely diverse landscapes and cultural groups, high Annapurna peaks	Oct-Apr/May	2000
Dhorpatan HR	west-central Nepal	Nepal's only hunting reserve (access is difficult), blue sheep	Mar-Apr	500
Kangchenjunga CA	eastern Nepal	third-highest mountain in the world, 30 species of rhododendron, many endemic flower species, snow leopard	Mar-Apr, Oct-Nov	2000
Khaptad NP	far western Nepal	core area is important religious site	Mar-Apr,	1000
Koshi Tappu WR	eastern Nepal (p316)	grasslands, often flooded during monsoon, 440 species of birds, wild water buffalo	Oct-Nov, Oct-Apr	500
Langtang NP	north-central Nepal, on the Tibetan border (p341)	culturally diverse, varied topography, important location on migratory route for birds travelling between India and Tibet	Mar-Apr, Sept–mid-Dec	1000
Makalu-Barun NP	eastern Nepal, bordering Sagarmatha NP	rugged steep remote wilderness areas, rich diversity of plant and animal life	Oct-May	1000
Manaslu CA	west-central Nepal, bordering Annapurna CA	rugged terrain, 11 types of forest, snow leopard, musk deer	Oct-Nov, Mar-Apr	2000
Parsa WR	central Terai, east of Chitwan	sal forests, wild elephants, 300 species of birds, many snake species	Oct-Apr	500
Rara NP	northwest Nepal	Nepal's biggest lake, little visited, many migratory birds	Oct-Dec, Mar-May	1000
Royal Bardia NP	far western Terai (p308)	sal forest, tiger, one-horned rhinoceros, over 250 species of birds	Oct-early Apr	500
Royal Chitwan NP	central Terai (p275)	tropical and subtropical forests, rhinoceros, tiger, gharial crocodile, 540 species of birds, World Heritage site	Oct-Feb	500
Royal Sukla Phanta WR	southwestern Nepal (p310)	riverine flood plain, grasslands, endangered swamp deer, wild elephants	Oct-Apr	500
Sagarmatha (Everest) NP	mid-eastern Nepal (p334)	highest mountains on the planet, home of the Sherpa people, stunning monasteries, World Heritage site	Oct-May	1000
Shey Phoksundo NP	northwest Nepal	trans-Himalayan ecosystem, alpine flowers, high passes, snow leopard, musk deer	Jun-Sep	1000
Shivapuri NP	northern Kathmandu Valley (p183)	close to Kathmandu, many bird and butterfly species, good hiking and biking	Oct-May	250

NP = National Park CA = Conservation Area WR = Wildlife Reserve HR = Hunting Reserve

These core protected areas are then surrounded by a zone of community-owned forests, whose people have a stake in their continued existence.

Most people visit at least one of the Nepal's protected areas. In 2003 43,000 tourists visited the Annapurna Conservation Area, 35,000 visited Royal Chitwan National Park and 3100 visited Langtang. Only 290 people visited the wonderful Koshi Tappu Wildlife Reserve. Most other conservation areas are in hard-to-reach places, where roads are bad and transportation difficult, or in the Maoist-affected regions of the far west and east of the country.

The last few years have seen a shift in the management of protected areas from government to NGOs. The non governmental **King Mahendra Trust for Nature Conservation** (☎ 5526571; www.kmtnc.org.np) runs the ACAP and Manaslu Conservation Areas, as well as Patan Zoo, and is hoping to add management of the Rara, Shey Phoksundo and Shivapuri protected areas to its CV. The Mountain Institute has put forward proposals to run the Makalu-Barun and Kangchenjunga conservation areas.

> Bis Hajaar Tal (20,000 Lakes) in Royal Chitwan National Park (p275) and the Koshi Tappu Wildlife Reserve (p316) are both Ramsar sites, thus designated as wetlands of international importance.

ENVIRONMENTAL ISSUES

The ecology and environment of Nepal are fragile and a rapidly growing population is constantly putting more pressure on the land. Much of the land between the Himalaya and the Terai has been vigorously modified by humans to provide space for crops, animals and houses. Forests have been cleared, towns have grown and roads have eaten into valleys that were previously accessible only on foot. Shangri-la is now in danger of environmental collapse.

> The Heart of the Jungle, by KK Gurung, details the wildlife of Royal Chitwan National Park.

Population growth is the biggest issue facing the environment. More people need more land for agriculture, and trees continue to be cut down for housing and firewood. In places like the Annapurna Conservation Area, Kangchenjunga Conservation Area and Sagarmatha National Park efforts have been made to promote alternative fuels and support reforestation. Solar energy and biogas energy have great potential in Nepal, which also boasts the world's greatest hydroelectric potential.

Grazing animals and deforestation have meant that during each monsoon huge chunks of hillsides devoid of trees are washed away. These often-massive landslides leave gigantic scars and wash downriver valuable soil that is eventually dumped in the Bay of Bengal. In 2002 virtually the entire village of Khobang in eastern Nepal was washed away in a landslide.

Tourism has also brought environmental problems, either directly, with increasing litter, trail erosion and demand for fuel, or indirectly, as local wealth converts into unsustainably large herds, though the scope is still limited to a few regions.

> Nepal Nature (www .nepalnature.com) is a tour company run by Nepali conservationists and nature experts. It runs bird-watching tours to Shivapuri National park and crane sanctuaries around Lumbini and you can download birding checklists from its website. Nature Trail (www .naturetrail.com.np) also runs birding tours.

The return to the concept of community forests has been quite successful in Nepal. The forests buffer national parks like Royal Chitwan and provide local residents with economic alternatives to poaching and resource gathering in the main parks. For more on the concept see the boxed text, p275.

Air and water pollution in the Kathmandu Valley are severe, due partly to the uncontrolled population growth in the valley (currently 10% a year) and partly because of the closed bowl-like structure of the valley, where winter temperature inversion traps pollutants in the valley. In the dry season the holy Bagmati River is little more than a stinking, black stream of floating sewage.

The victims of Nepal's Maoist insurgency are not just human. The deteriorating security situation in many parks has led to a cut in the number of army checkposts, which in turn has spurred poachers. Nepal's rhino population of 600 fell by over 25% between 2000 and 2005. Snow-leopard bones and pelts were discovered in a hotel room in Thamel in 2004, hours before they were to be smuggled over the little-patrolled mountain passes into Tibet and China.

Global warming brings its own long-term challenges to the region. Edmund Hillary and environmental organisations want Mt Everest to be added to Unesco's list of threatened heritage sites, a move which would legally require international governments to cut emissions of greenhouse gases.

Warming has already caused glaciers to start to melt, creating dangerous levels in many of the region's 2300 glacial lakes. In 1985 a natural dam collapsed in the Khumbu, creating a flash flood that destroyed 16 bridges and killed 20 people. A breach in a larger lake, such as the Imja Glacier Lake in the Everest region's Chukhhung Valley, could create catastrophic flooding.

It is predicted that Himalayan glaciers will shrink by 20% by 2035. Eventually rivers will shrink too, affecting agriculture and river flows far downriver into India. Consider that the Ganges alone provides water for 25% of India's population and that 40% of the Ganges' water comes from Nepal (rising to 70% in the dry season) and it's easy to see how global warming quickly becomes a global problem.

Himal South Asia (www.himalmag.com) is a bimonthly magazine mainly devoted to development and environmental issues. It's an excellent publication with top-class contributors.

For more on Nepal's environment check out www.iucnnepal.org and www.wwfnepal.org.

Outdoor Activities

Nepal is possibly the world's greatest outdoors destination. The towering mountains famously offer some of the Himalaya's most awe-inspiring treks but also some spectacular mountain biking; and its mighty rivers fuel some of the best white-water rafting you'll find anywhere. An added bonus is that all this fun comes in at least half the price of places like the US or New Zealand. For an added thrill try bungee jumping 160m into a Himalayan gorge or abseiling *into* a thundering 45m waterfall. Oh, and did we mention that Pokhara is one of the best paragliding spots in the world? Pack a spare pair of underpants – you're going to need them.

HOW MUCH TIME DO YOU HAVE?

One day

- bungee jump at The Last Resort (opposite)
- paraglide at Sarangkot (p79)
- take a mountain flight (p384)
- mountain bike down the Scar Rd (p83)

Two days

- go canyoning at Borderlands or The Last Resort (p78)
- raft the Bhote Kosi or Trisuli River (p95)
- trek Nagarkot to Sundarijal (p224)

Three days

- mountain bike Kathmandu–Dhulikhel–Namobuddha–Lakuri Bhanjyang (p84)
- raft the Kali Gandaki (p97)

Four Days

- learn to kayak at a kayak clinic (p92)
- do a canyoning and Bhote Kosi rafting combo (p78)
- raft the Kali Gandaki or Marsyangdi (p95)
- take a Chitwan safari excursion from Kathmandu (p282)
- take on the Tatopani loop trek from Pokhara (p268)
- experience the views on the Annapurna Skyline Trek (Royal Trek) (p269)

Six days

- trek from Borderlands or The Last Resort (p233)

- hike the Tamang Heritage Trail near Langtang (p235)
- complete the Ghorapani to Ghandruk loop trek (p268)

Seven days

- fly in to Lukla then trek to Thami, Namche Bazaar and Tengboche on the Everest Base Camp trek (p334)

Eight days

- trek the Helambu trek (p339)

Nine days

- trek the Jomsom trek (p345)
- raft the Sun Kosi River (p98)

10 days

- complete the Langtang trek (p341)
- do a Karnali River trip (p98)

15 days

- trek up to Everest Base Camp with flights in and out of Lukla (p334)

18 days

- complete the Annapurna Circuit (p347)

21 days

- combine the Everest Base Camp and Gokyo trek (p334)

TOP 10 PLACES FOR DAY HIKES

The following locations are some of the most rewarding places for day hiking, as opposed to multiday trekking:

- Chitwan Hills – p288
- Bandipur – p244
- Tamang Heritage Trail, Langtang region – p235
- Kathmandu Valley – see 'Top Five Valley Hikes' p162
- Around Tansen – p301
- Tansen to Ranighat – p301
- Nagarkot – p224
- Shivapuri National Park – p183
- Pokhara's World Peace Pagoda – p255
- Around Pokhara (Rupa Tal, Begnas Tal & Sarangkot) – p265

TREKKING

Nepal is the world's greatest trekking destination, even (and perhaps especially) if the only camping you do at home is lip-synching to Kylie Minogue and Queen songs (we know you do it!). For an overview of the most popular multiday teahouse treks, see the Trekking chapter, p323.

Short Treks & Day Hikes

If you don't have time for a big trek, there are several shorter treks which give you a taste of life on Nepal's trails – see the boxed text opposite. In particular, there are several short treks from Pokhara in the southern foothills of the Annapurnas (see p268), or you could easily cobble together a trek of several days around the rim of the Kathmandu Valley (p162).

You can also throw in a couple of flights here and there to speed up the trekking process. As an example, fly in to Jomsom and take a few days to hike to surrounding villages of Muktinath, Kagbeni and Marpha before flying back to Pokhara for a four- or five-day trip.

There are also plenty of great day hikes around Nepal. We have detailed many of these throughout the text; see the boxed text to help locate these.

ADVENTURE SPORTS
Bungee Jumping

The 'ultimate bungee' straddles a mighty 160m drop into the gorge of the Bhote Kosi at The Last Resort, just 12km from the Tibetan border. It's one of the world's longest bungee jumps (higher than the highest bungee in New Zealand) and the roars and squeals of free falling tourists echo up and down the valley for miles.

The swing or bungee costs US$80 from Kathmandu (including return transport from Kathmandu and lunch) or US$65 if you are already up at The Last Resort. Extra jumps cost US$25, or add on a swing to a bungee for an extra US$40. Every fourth jump is free. For US$15 you can reveal your inner wisdom and travel up to watch someone else jump and enjoy the looks on everyone else's faces when they catch their first glimpse of how deep a 160m gorge really is. The price includes whatever lunch you can muster, wisely served up *after* the jump.

Visit the office of **The Last Resort** (Map p136; ☎ 01-4439525; www.tlrnepal.com) in Kathmandu for details of current packages. A two-day bungee and rafting

For information on some of the golfing opportunities in Nepal see p253.

As if the tallest bungee in Asia wasn't enough, the fiendish minds at the Last Resort have devised the 'swing', a stomach-loosening eight-second free fall, followed by a Tarzan-like swing and then three or four pendulum swings back up and then down the length of the gorge. We feel ill just writing about it.

ALL FOR THE SAKE OF RESEARCH *Bradley Mayhew*

'Its the most exciting thing you can do in a day from Kathmandu' was what Megh Ale told me when I mentioned I might try some canyoning up at the Borderlands Resort. Sure, I thought, it'll be fun but how exciting can a day trip from the capital really be?

The first day was pretty relaxed, meeting my fellow canyoners (experienced abseilers, just what the novice in me needed…), learning how to abseil down a large boulder (I had to stifle a yawn) and then some small cascades. This is nice, I thought, but not quite the underpant-soiling adrenalin Megh had promised me.

So the next day, as I stood astride a small stream and shuffled backwards towards a drop-off, it came as a bit of a shock to see the water fall away into vertical nothingness. It takes a certain leap of faith to trust all your weight to a harness but I eventually learned that the key to canyoning is to lean right back, with your weight all on the rope 'brake', in order to get your legs 90 degrees from the rock face. This stops your legs slipping quite so much on the mossy, water-polished rock face.

The challenge of the first drop was to avoid slipping into the waterfall just to the side. The second involved a backwards jump of about 5m into a churning pool of uncertain depth. It took several 'one, two, THREE!'s from the guides and some considerable swearing on my part before I let myself fall backwards into the narrow rock pool.

The scariest thing about the third descent was that I couldn't see the bottom of the drop (and there's nothing worse than the thousand-foot gorge of my imagination). After about 10m of descent, the rock overhang meant I had to lower myself down into mid-air, dangling like bait on hook.

That freaked me out a bit but it wasn't until the last fall, as I stood astride Big Jumbo (the name of the waterfall, unfortunately…) that the fear really hit me like, well, a 50-tonne waterfall. This was a 45m drop and when you are leaning back over the slippery lip of a waterfall, that's a BIG drop! Even the instructors were looking a bit nervous… There was no way out, no way back up the last waterfall. The only option was to go down Big Jumbo (again, the waterfall).

As I lowered myself down the cliff the angle between the rope and the waterfall began to narrow until there was only one harrowing choice; straddle the waterfall or enter it. Apparently there was one other option – slip on some wet moss, swing into the full force of the water and scream like a girl. I chose the latter. Actually, there was no chance of screaming because the full crashing force of the icy water made it hard to breath. I tried to keep calm and lower myself down the chute but at one point I remember thinking 'Holy Crap! This is too much pressure, I'm going to fall – and I don't even know how far it is!'.

After a serious pummelling, I felt a tug on the rope and swung out of the waterfall scrambling on the rock face like Buster Keaton in a wetsuit. I stood there shaking for a while, before lowering myself down the last 10m. '*Jesus!*' I shouted at the main guide. '*That was frickin' GREAT*!! Now *that* I can recommend in a guide book!'.

The things I do for you guys…

package with overnight accommodation and four meals and transport costs around US$130.

Canyoning

For details of accommodation at The Last Resort see p233.

This exciting sport is a wild combination of rappelling/abseiling, climbing, sliding and swimming that has been pioneered in the canyons and waterfalls near The Last Resort and Borderlands (see p233).

Both companies run two-day canyoning trips for about US$100, or you can combine two days of canyoning with a two-day Bhote Kosi rafting trip for US$190 to US$200. On day one you drive up from Kathmandu, have lunch, get some basic abseiling training and then practise on nearby cascades. Day two involves a trip out to more exciting falls, with a maximum abseil of up to 45m. Most canyons involve a short hike to get there.

The Last Resort uses Panglong canyon early in the season and to train novices. After December the action moves to higher and more exciting canyons such as Kanglang, Kahule and Bhukute (a 60m drop), once the water flow has subsided to safe levels. Canyoning is not possible during the monsoon.

Borderlands uses Old and New Jumbo canyons. Old Jumbo (also called Big Jumbo) is the more challenging of the two (only possible from late November) and involves a flying fox cable ride across the Bhote Kosi River and then a 30-minute walk up to the first of four waterfalls and a short water slide.

It's best to bring a pair of closed-toe shoes that can get wet as these are better than sandals. Hiking shoes, a water bottle and bathing suits are also required and a waterproof camera is a real bonus. After November, wetsuits are a must and are provided.

Paragliding

Pokhara is the place to head for if you want to hurl yourself off a cliff and glide in majestic silence above the Himalaya, either on a tandem paragliding flight or solo after a multiday course. November, December and January bring perfect flying conditions and stunning views of Phewa Tal and the Himalayan peaks that have inspired gliders to rank Sarangkot as one of the best paragliding spots in the world.

Sunrise Paragliding (www.nepal-paragliding.com; Pokhara ☎ 61-521174; UK ☎ 07879-424089) are the leading company. They offer short tandem flights (30 to 40 minutes, US$75) in the morning and late afternoon, longer distance flights (60 to 90 minutes, US$120) that take advantage of midday thermals and even multiday 'treks' that journey from valley to valley. For something a lot scarier try the 20-minute acrobatic tandem flights. If you want to learn to fly yourself, a 10-day paragliding course costs US$1250. Most flights start with a short jeep ride up to Sarangkot.

In conjunction with Sunrise, **Himalayan Frontiers** (www.himalayanfrontiers.co.uk) has pioneered parahawking, an intriguing mix of paragliding and hawking that uses trained steppe eagles and pariah kites to lead gliders to the best thermals, enabling them to glider higher and further. You can experience this glorious blending of man and nature on a 30-minute tandem flight. Both companies run a seven-day parahawking course from November to February for US$650. Glider and ultralight flights are also available. See p253 for details. Less brave souls can see the avian guides at their roost at Maya Devi Village on the northern shore of Phewa Tal (see p254).

Blue Sky Paragliding (☎ 61-534737; www.paragliding-nepal.com) is a new Nepali–Swiss operation. In Kathmandu you can contact them through the Hotel Northfield (p140).

Avia Club Nepal (☎ 61-540338; www.avianepal.21bc.net; Lakeside, Pokhara) operates microlight flights from Pokhara between October and May. The 15/30/60-minute flights cost US$65/112/198.

Rock Climbing

If you need to polish up or learn some climbing skills before heading off into the mountains, try the **Pasang Lhamu Climbing Wall** (Map pp110-11; ☎ 4370742; www.pasanglhamu.org; ⏰ 10am-5.30pm) on the outskirts of Kathmandu. A day's membership costs Rs 350 and equipment can be rented for Rs 100. Week-long climbing courses are available (Rs 4799). See p128 for details.

The **Shreeban Rock Climbing Nature Camp** (www.shreeban.com.np) in Dhading, on the road from Kathmandu to Pokhara, offers climbing on the roped rock wall behind its camp. See p237.

Check to see if Balloon Sunrise Nepal (www.balloon-sunrise-nepal.com.np) has resumed balloon flights (US$195) over the Kathmandu Valley. The views of the Himalaya and valley were incredible and the rice field landings usually attracted a huge, excited and curious crowd of local villagers.

For details on elephant-back jungle safaris in Royal Chitwan National Park see p281, in Royal Bardia National Park see p308 and in Koshi Tappu Wildlife Reserve see p317.

The Nepal Open Paragliding Championships are held every year over five days in January in Sarangkot and attract competitors from around the world.

The **Nepal Mountaineering Association** (Map p116; ☎ 4434525; www.nma.com.np; Naxal, Kathmandu) runs month-long climbing courses in Manang, on the Annapurna Circuit, every August/September. These are really aimed at Nepali guides but also accept foreigners for a fee of US$1000. They also run occasional rock climbing courses in Nagarjun.

For mountaineering and climbing on Nepal's trekking peaks see later in this chapter.

Marathons

As if a normal marathon wasn't enough, two marathons are held in the Everest region at an altitude of over 5000m. Participants get to enjoy a two-week acclimatisation trek to base camp, before running all the way back to Namche Bazaar in around five hours.

The annual **Tenzing Hillary Everest Marathon** (www.everestmarathon.com; registration fee US$250) on May 29th commemorates the first ascent of Mt Everest on May 29th 1953 with the world's highest marathon (42km). The similar **Everest Marathon** (www.everestmarathon.org.uk) is run every other November (next in 2007), to raise money for charities working in Nepal.

The **Toyota Kathmandu Marathon** (www.kathmandumarathon.org) is organised every 18 months (next is Oct 2006) in the Kathmandu Valley by the Scheer Memorial Hospital at Banepa to raise funds for charitable medical care in Nepal. A half-marathon and 5km race are also run.

If those don't sound challenging enough, go for psychological testing and then consider the annual **Annapurna Mandala Trail**, a nine-day, 340km foot race around the Annapurna Circuit from Besisahar, over the 5400m Thorung La and down the Kali Gandaki valley to Dhampus.

The even crazier **Himal Race**, a 955km, 22-day run from Annapurna to Everest Base Camps, is on hold, due to a temporary bout of sanity.

The Nepal branch of **Hash House Harriers** (www.aponarch.com/hhhh) meets for a run every Saturday afternoon. Check the website for details.

MOUNTAIN BIKING

Strong wheels, knobbly tyres, a soft padded seat and 17 more gears than the average Nepali bike – the mountain bike is an ideal, go anywhere, versatile machine for exploring Nepal. These attributes make it possible to escape sealed roads, and to ride tracks and ancient walking trails to remote, rarely visited areas of the country. Importantly, they allow independent travel – you can stop whenever you like – and they liberate you from crowded buses and claustrophobic taxis.

Nepal's tremendously diverse terrain and its many tracks and trails are ideal for mountain biking. In recent years, Nepal has rapidly gained recognition for the biking adventures it offers – from easy village trails in the Kathmandu Valley to challenging mountain roads that climb thousands of metres to reach spectacular viewpoints, followed by unforgettable, exhilarating descents. For the adventurous there are large areas of the country still to be explored by mountain bike.

The Kathmandu Valley offers the best and most consistent biking in Nepal, with a vast network of tracks, trails and back roads. A mountain bike really allows you to get off the beaten track and discover idyllic Newari villages that have preserved their traditional lifestyle. Even today, it's possible to cycle into villages in the Kathmandu Valley that have rarely seen a visitor on a foreign bicycle. Each year more roads are developing, opening trails to destinations that were previously accessible only on foot.

Many trails are narrow, century-old walkways that are not shown on maps, so you need a good sense of direction when venturing out without

---

Nepa Maps and Himalayan Maphouse (www.himalayan-maphouse.com) produce a fairly useful map to paragliding the Annapurna region.

Borderlands (p233) offer a day's tuition on fixed rope climbing at Nagarjun, just outside Kathmandu. The day costs US$35 per person and includes equipment, transport and tuition.

The Yak Attack is a planned nine-day, 300km mountain bike and foot race around the Annapurna Circuit, including over the 5416m Thorung La. It's due to kick off in March 2007 and the organisers hope to make it an annual event. The 13-day trip costs £1095; see www.e-w-c.co.uk for details.

a guide. To go unguided entails some risks, and you should learn a few important words of Nepali to assist in seeking directions. It's also important to know the name of the next village you wish to reach.

Transporting Your Bicycle

If you plan to do a mountain biking trip of more than a day or two it may be a good idea to bring your own bicycle from home. Your bicycle can be carried as part of your baggage allowance on international flights. You are required to deflate the tyres, turn the handlebars parallel with the frame and remove the pedals. Passage through Nepali customs is quite simple once you reassure airport officers that it is 'your' bicycle and it will also be returning with you, though this requirement is never enforced.

On most domestic flights, if you pack your bicycle correctly, removing wheels and pedals, it is possible to load it in the cargo hold. Check with the airline first.

Local buses are useful if you wish to avoid some of the routes that carry heavy traffic. You can place your bicycle on the roof for an additional charge (Rs 50 to Rs 100 depending on the length of the journey and the bus company). If you're lucky, rope may be available and the luggage boy will assist you. Make sure the bicycle is held securely to cope with the rough roads and that it's lying as flat as possible to prevent it catching low wires or tree branches. Unless you travel with foam padding it is hard to avoid the scratches to the frame. Supervise its loading and protect the rear derailleur from being damaged. Keep in mind that more baggage is likely to be loaded on top once you're inside. A lock and chain is also a wise investment.

Equipment

Most of the bicycles you can hire in Nepal are low-quality Indian so-called mountain bikes, not suitable for the rigours of trail riding. The better operators like Himalayan Mountain Bikes or Dawn Till Dusk rent high quality front shock, 18-gear mountain bikes for around Rs 700 per day, or Rs 500 per day for a week's hire. Cheaper companies offer battered front suspension bikes for Rs 450, with discounts for a week's hire. Nepal Mountain Bike Tours rents front suspension bikes for Rs 300 to 700 per day. The better rental shops can supply helmets and other equipment.

If you bring your own bicycle it is essential to bring tools and spare parts, as these are largely unavailable outside of Kathmandu. Established mountain bike tour operators have mechanics, workshops and a full range of bicycle tools at their offices in Kathmandu. Dawn Till Dusk also has a separate repair workshop near Kilroy's restaurant in Thamel – see map p136.

Although this is not a complete list, a few items that may be worth considering bringing with you include:

- bicycle bell
- cycling gloves, tops and padded shorts (or even your own seat)
- energy bars and electrolyte water additives
- fleece top for evenings and windbreaker
- helmet
- lightweight clothing (eg Coolmax or other wicking materials)
- medium-sized money bag for valuables
- minipump
- spare parts (including inner tubes)
- stiff-soled shoes that suit riding and walking
- sun protection and sunglasses
- water bottles or hydration system (eg CamelBak)
- face mask and gloves

The most detailed Kathmandu Valley map is commonly referred to as the 'German map' (also Schneider and Nelles Verlag), and is widely available in Kathmandu. The maps by Karto Atelier are also excellent.

Nepa Maps and Himalayan Maphouse (www .himalayan-maphouse .com) produce useful maps to *Mountain Biking the Kathmandu Valley* and *Biking around Annapurna*, though they aren't to be relied on completely.

Road Conditions

Traffic generally travels on the left-hand side, though it's not uncommon to find a vehicle approaching you head-on or even on the wrong side of the road. In practice, smaller vehicles give way to larger ones, and bicycles are definitely at the bottom of the hierarchy. Nepali roads carry a vast array of vehicles: buses, motorcycles, cars, trucks, tractors, holy cows, wheelbarrows, dogs, wandering children and chickens, all moving at different speeds and in different directions.

The centre of Kathmandu is a particularly unpleasant place to ride because of pollution, heavy traffic and the increasingly reckless behaviour of young motorcyclists.

Extreme care should be taken near villages as young children play on the trails and roads. The onus seems to fall on the approaching vehicle to avoid an incident. A good bicycle helmet is a sensible accessory, and you should ride with your fingers continually poised on the rear brake lever.

A few intrepid mountain bikers have taken bicycles into trekking areas hoping to find great riding but these areas are generally not suitable for mountain biking and you have to carry your bicycle for at least 80% of the time. Trails are unreliable, and are subject to frequent rock falls. In addition, there are always trekkers, porters and local people clogging up the trails. Sagarmatha National Park doesn't allow mountain bikes. Courtesy and care on the trails should be a high priority when biking.

Trail Etiquette

Arriving in a new country for a short time where social and cultural values are vastly different from those of your home country does not allow much time to gain an appreciation of these matters. So consider a few pointers to help you develop respect and understanding. For more information, see p62.

CLOTHING

Tight-fitting Lycra bicycle clothing might be functional, but is a shock to locals, who maintain a very modest approach to dressing. Such clothing is embarrassing and also offensive to Nepalis.

A simple way to overcome this is by wearing a pair of comfortable shorts and a T-shirt over your bicycle gear. This is especially applicable to female bicyclists, as women in Nepal generally dress conservatively.

> When it comes to caring for the environment, the guidelines that apply to trekkers also apply to mountain bikers. For more detailed information, see p330.

SAFETY

Trails are often filled with locals going about their daily work. A small bell attached to your handlebars and used as a warning of your approach, reducing your speed, and a friendly call or two of 'cycle ioh!' (cycle coming!) goes a long way in keeping everyone on the trails happy and safe. Children love the novelty of the bicycles, the fancy helmets, the colours and the strange clothing, and will come running from all directions to greet you. They also love to grab hold of the back of your bicycle and run with you. You need to maintain a watchful eye so no-one gets hurt.

Guided Tours

A small number of Nepali companies offer guided mountain-bike trips. They provide high-quality bicycles, local and Western guides, helmets and all the necessary equipment. There is usually a minimum of four bicyclists per trip, although for shorter tours two is often sufficient. For the shorter tours (two to three days) vehicle support is not required, while for longer tours vehicles are provided at an extra cost.

Tours range from US$25 to US$35 for a simple day trip, such as the loop routes north from Kathmandu to Tinpiple, Tokha and Budhanil-kantha; or south to the traditional village of Bungamati.

A downhill day trip with vehicle support costs around US$55 per person. Options include driving to Nagarkot and riding down to Sankhu and Bodhnath or Bhaktapur, or driving to Kakani and taking the Scar Rd down. Dawn Till Dusk offers exhilarating downhill runs from the top of Phulchowki and Nagarjun peaks.

Multiday trips around the Kathmandu Valley cost around US$45 per day without vehicle backup, or US$65 with vehicle support and range from two to 10 days. Prices include bike hire, a guide, hotel accommodation and meals. The following three-day routes rank among the most popular offerings:

- Budhanilkantha–Chisopani–Nagarkot and back
- Kathmandu to Chitwan via Daman and Hetauda; via the backroads west of Dakshinkali
- Bhaktapur–Dhulikhel–Namobuddha–Panauti
- Nagarkot–Dhulikhel–Panauti–Lakuri Bhanjyang–Sisneri

> The Trans Himalayan Mountain Bike Race is a 1000km annual race from Lhasa to Kathmandu – contact Himalayan Marathons (www.hima layanmarathons.com) for details.

TOUR COMPANIES

The following companies have good-quality imported mountain bikes that can also be hired independently of a tour. Any others fall a long way back in standards and safety.

Bike Nepal (Map p136; ☎ 01-4240633; www.bikenepal.com, Thamel, Kathmandu) Day trips US$25. Located next to Pumpernickel Bakery.

Dawn Till Dusk (Map p136; ☎ 01-4700286, 4215046; www.nepalbiking.com; JP School Rd, Thamel, Kathmandu) Contact Chhimi Gurung. Local tours, rentals and servicing at the Kathmandu Guest House office; longer tours and sales a five minute walk to the south in Thamel. Day trips US$35, multiday trips around US$45/65 without/with transport backup.

Himalayan Mountain Bikes (HMB; www.bikingnepal.com, www.bikeasia.info) Kathmandu (Map p136; ☎ 01-4212860; hmb@bikeasia.info); Pokhara (Map p248; ☎ 061-523240; Central Lakeside) Kathmandu Valley tours US$50 per day with accommodation but no transport. Full service & repairs, bike hire RS 700 per day.

Massif Mountain Bikes (Map p136; ☎ 01-4700468; www.massifmountainbike.com, www .mtbnepal.com; Thamel, Kathmandu) Bike hire Rs 600 per day, guide US$15 per day, day tour US$30. Acts as the Nepal representative of Unique Trails (www.uniquetrails.com). Located across from La Dolce Vita Restaurant.

Nepal Mountain Bike Tours (Map p136; ☎ 01-4701701; www.bikehimalayas.com) One-man-show run by Suresh Kumar Dulal. Day trips from US$25, bike rentals Rs 300 to Rs 700. Next to Green Hill Tours.

> For more ideas on biking routes around the Kathmandu Valley see p161.

Routes
THE SCAR ROAD FROM KATHMANDU
Distance 70km
Duration Six hours
Start/Finish Kathmandu
Brief description Fine views & a fun descent through a national park, after a tough initial climb of around 700m

> The Scar Rd is considered one of the Kathmandu Valley's classic mountain-bike adventures, offering a challenging ride for all levels of experience.

Leaving Kathmandu (elevation 1337m), head towards Balaju, on the Ring Rd 2km north of Thamel, and follow the sealed Trisuli Bazaar road towards Kakani, 23km away at an altitude of 2073m. You start to climb out of the valley as the road twists and turns past the **Nagarjun Forest Reserve** (see p182), which provides the road with a leafy canopy. Once you're through the initial pass and out of the valley, the road continues northwest and offers a view of endless terraced fields to your left. On reaching the summit of the ridge, take a turn right (at a clearly marked T-junction), instead of continuing down to Trisuli Bazaar. (If you go too far you reach a checkpoint just 100m beyond.) At this point magnificent views of the Ganesh Himal (*himal* means a range with permanent snow) provide the inspiration required to complete the remaining 4km of steep and deteriorating blacktop to the crown of the hill at **Kakani** (see p234), for a well-deserved rest.

After admiring the view from a road-side teashop, descend for just 30m beyond the gate and take the first left on to a 4WD track. This track will take you through the popular picnic grounds frequented on Saturday by Kathmandu locals. Continue through in an easterly direction towards Shivapuri. The track narrows after a few kilometres near a metal gate on your left. Through the gate, you are faced with some rough stone steps and then a 10-minute push/carry up and over the hilltop to an army checkpoint. Here it's necessary for foreigners to pay an entry fee of Rs 250 to the Shivapuri National Park. Exit the army camp, turning right where the Scar Rd is clearly visible in front of you. You are now positioned at the day's highest point – approximately 2200m.

Taking the right-hand track you start to descend dramatically along an extremely steep, rutted single trail with several water crossings. The trail is literally cut into the side of the hill, with sharp drops on the right that challenge a rider's skill and nerve. As you hurtle along, take time to admire the view of the sprawling Kathmandu Valley below – it's one of the best.

The trail widens, after one long gnarly climb before the saddle, then it's relatively flat through the protected Shivapuri watershed area. This beautiful mountain biking section lasts for nearly 25km before the trail descends into the valley down a 7km spiral on a gravel road. This joins a sealed road, to the relief of jarred wrists, at **Budhanilkantha** (see p182), where you can buy refreshments. Take a moment to see the Sleeping Vishnu just up on your left at the main intersection. From here the sealed road descends gently for the remaining 15km back into the bustle of Kathmandu.

KATHMANDU TO DHULIKHEL
Distance 90km
Duration Two days
Start/Finish Kathmandu
Brief description A circular route past a classic selection of the valley's cultural sights

This circular tour (see map p160) takes you along valley backroads to Dhulikhel on the first day (32km), and then to Namobuddha and back to Kathmandu via the busy Arniko Hwy (58km), or better the remote dirt road through the southern foothills (see 'The Back Door to Kathmandu' route).

From Thamel, head east out of town in the direction of **Pashupatinath** (see p166). Proceed along the northern fringe of the Pashupatinath complex, on the south side of the Bagmati River, and look for the road running off to the right near the northern end of the airport runway. From the northeast corner join the road running north–south and then the road running east to the town of Bhaktapur. This road runs parallel to the much busier Arniko Hwy and is a much better option to Bhaktapur, via the northern tip of Thimi.

You can also access this road from the Arniko Hwy; take a left off the main hwy, just pass the bridge over the Manohara River, onto a narrower sealed road that heads back towards the airport on its east side. At the next main intersection (1.8km on) is the turn right to **Bhaktapur** (see p196), 16km away.

You could spend time in this wonderfully preserved former kingdom, but if you intend to cycle straight through, you'll save yourself Rs 750 entry fee by taking the roads around the town, to the north and east. Make your way to the town's eastern gate, join a tarmac road and then bear southeast.

The asphalt ends and the road continues in the form of a compacted track towards the rural village of Nala, 9km away through a beautiful corner of the valley. The track climbs gradually to a minor pass and army checkpoint. A gentle 2km downhill gradient brings you past the Buddhist Karunamaya Temple (dedicated to Machhendranath) to rural **Nala**, with its pretty four-roofed Bhagwati Temple in the central square.

From Nala head right and continue for 3km to **Banepa** (see p227), riding through the old town before hitting the main Arniko Hwy. Turn left at the highway and continue along the sealed main road for a further 4km uphill to **Dhulikhel** (see p227). This completes the first day (32km).

Dhulikhel to Namobuddha & Kathmandu

The trail to **Namobuddha** is a popular detour from Dhulikhel, and offers superb trail riding with spectacular views of the Himalaya. See p230 for a description of the route.

From Panauti you join a sealed road that's a flat run along the valley to the main road at Banepa. From this point you can return to Kathmandu, 26km via the Arniko Hwy, or ride the 3.5km back to Dhulikhel. The loop from Dhulikhel via Namobuddha is 37km; if you return to Kathmandu it's a total run of 58km via Namobuddha. Alternatively, take the adventurous alternative route back to Kathmandu via Lakuri Bhanjyang (see below).

THE BACK DOOR TO KATHMANDU

Distance 30km
Duration Half day
Start Panauti
Finish Patan/Kathmandu
Brief description Remote mountain route with almost zero traffic

Don't let the heavenly first 4.5km of tarmac lull you into a false sense of security. The road soon deteriorates into 3km of dirt road to the village of Kushadevi, followed by 2.5km of bone-jarring stony track to Riyale. From here the valley really starts to close in and gets increasingly remote – this is definitely not the place to blow a tyre! It's amazing how remote the route is, considering it is so close to Kathmandu.

The next 8.5km is on smooth dirt road that switchbacks up the hillsides to the pass of **Lakuri Bhanjyang** (1960m). You may find some basic food stalls but the actual summit is currently occupied by the army. In the past, travel companies have set up tented camp accommodation near here but this depends on tourism numbers and the levels of army presence. Figure on two to three hours to here.

From here on it's all downhill. The first section drops down the back side of the hill, blocking the views, but you soon get great views of the Annapurna and Ganesh Himal massifs – particularly spectacular in sunset's pink glow.

A further 5km of descent, rough at times, brings you to the turnoff left to Sisneri and the first village on this side of the pass. Soon the asphalt kicks in again, shortly followed by the pleasant village of **Lubbhu**, with its impressive central three-tiered Mahalakshmi Mahadev Temple. Traffic levels pick up for the final 5km to the Kathmandu ring road near Patan; be prepared for the 'civilisation' to come as a bit of a shock after such a beautiful, peaceful ride.

This backroads track offers a great alternative return route to Kathmandu, bypassing the busy, dangerous and polluted main Arniko Hwy. It's a surprisingly remote route (see map p160), so make sure you take enough water, food and spare parts as there's nothing en route.

DHULIKHEL TO THE TIBETAN BORDER
Distance 83km one way
Duration Four days return
Start Dhulikhel
Finish Kodari
Brief description A long descent followed by a gradual climb alongside the white water of the Bhote Kosi to the border with Tibet

From Dhulikhel, it is possible to continue 83km along the Arniko Hwy to the Friendship Bridge that marks the Tibetan border at Kodari (1500m). This is a three- or (more likely) four-day return trip from Dhulikhel. Add it on to the previous itinerary for a great four- or five-day run from Kathmandu. See map p160 for details.

Dhulikhel to Lamosangu (49km)
From Dhulikhel you immediately begin an adrenaline-filled descent (almost 900m) into the Panchkhal Valley, on a slick sealed road, with majestic views of the Himalaya adding to a thrilling ride. A couple of short climbs interrupt the descent as you cycle to Dolalghat, on the Indrawati River, a popular starting point for Sun Kosi rafting trips (see p98 for more information). On the downhill watch for overtaking buses on the blind corners.

From Dolalghat (around 53km from Kathmandu) you cross the bridge over the Indrawati River and climb out of the Panchkhal Valley to join the Bhote Kosi, which you follow for the rest of the journey. Owing to landslide damage there is a mixture of surfaced and unsurfaced roads. Traffic can be quite heavy along this section. The road climbs at a gentle gradient as it follows the river.

A couple of kilometres past the turn-off to Jiri is Lamosangu, 27km from Dolalghat, where there are a couple of fish restaurants.

Accommodation options are at Barabise, Borderlands resort (a further 16km from Lamosangu, on a dirt road), and The Last Resort (4km further). See p232 for more on accommodation options in this area.

Lamosangu to Tatopani & Kodari (34km)
The next section of the ride continues for around 7km to Barabise, where the road changes into a compacted dirt track with a top layer of dust that is transformed into choking clouds when buses pass; in wet weather it all turns to mud. Care should be taken during heavy rains as this section of the road is particularly susceptible to landslides. The valley's sides begin to get steeper and it gradually changes into a beautiful gorge with spectacular waterfalls.

The track climbs practically the entire 23km to Tatopani and a further 4km to Kodari (p233), at the edge of the Friendship Bridge and the border with Tibet. The section of the ride that climbs from Tatopani to the Friendship Bridge is probably the most beautiful.

It should be possible to return as far as Borderlands the same day, taking advantage of a mainly downhill ride. Otherwise, you can stay in Tatopani and visit the hot springs there (see p233).

It may be possible (but dependent on border guards) for border junkies to cycle beyond the bridge and climb a rough, winding and steep track to the Chinese customs checkpoint (8km), just outside of Zhangmu (Nepali: Khasa), which is visible from the bridge.

Tatopani to Dhulikhel
The ride back to Dhulikhel is around 80km and includes the long climb out of Dolalghat, for which you should allow plenty of time. An option here is to jump on a local bus with your bicycle. Depending on how you feel after the climb, you can stay in Dhulikhel or complete the trip by returning the 32km to Kathmandu.

THE RAJPATH FROM KATHMANDU
Distance 150km
Duration Two days
Start Kathmandu
Finish Hetauda
Brief description Classic but gruelling on-road ride over a 2488m pass, culminating with incomparable Himalayan views at Daman. For a regional overview see the map pp312–13.

The ride begins on the Kathmandu–Pokhara (Prithvi) Hwy, which gives the only access to the valley. After leaving the valley, the highway descends to Naubise, at the bottom of the Mahesh Khola Valley, 27km from Kathmandu, where the Rajpath intersects with the Prithvi Hwy. Take the Rajpath, which forks to the left and is well signposted for Hetauda. Start a 35km climb to Tistung (2030m) past terraced fields, carved into steep hillsides. On reaching the pass at Tistung you descend for 7km into the beautiful Palung Valley before the final steep 9km climb to Daman, at a height of 2322m.

This day's ride (almost all climbing) takes between six and nine hours in the saddle. Thus, with an early start it is possible to stay in **Daman**, which will give you the thrill of waking up to the broadest Himalayan panorama Nepal has to offer (see p305). The following day the road climbs a further 3km to the top of the pass, at 2488m. At this point, you can savour the very real prospect of an exhilarating 2300m descent in 60km!

As you descend towards the Indian plains, laid out before you to the south, notice the contrast with the side you climbed, as the south side is lush and semitropical. With innumerable switchbacks and a bit of speed you should watch out for the occasional bus and truck looming around blind corners. The road eventually flattens out after the right turn to cross a newly constructed bridge and the first main river crossing. The rest of the journey is a gently undulating route alongside a river; a further 10km brings you to **Hetauda**. (See p304 for details on accommodation and the useful cyclists' notebooks in the Motel Avocado.) After a night's rest, you can continue along the Rajpath towards India or turn right at the statue of the king in the centre of town and head towards Royal Chitwan National Park.

HETAUDA TO NARAYANGARH & MUGLING

Distance 91km to Narayangarh, 105km via Sauraha
Duration One to 1½ days
Start Hetauda
Finish Narayangarh or Mugling
Brief description Tropical ride across the Terai plains, best during winter and combined with a visit to Chitwan.

This is vastly different riding from that of the other rides described in this chapter, and in the summer months (May to September) it can be a very hot and humid ride. From Hetauda, as you cycle along the flat, smooth road towards Narayangarh enjoying the lush subtropical scenery, watch for resort signposts on your left. Machan Wildlife Resort's (p285) turn-off is 40km from Hetauda, and the resort is reached after a further 4km of beautiful trail riding with three river crossings. Alternatively, a further 23km from the Machan turn-off brings you to the Chitwan Jungle Lodge (p285) turn-off. A further 14km brings you to Tadi Bazaar and the turn-off for Sauraha, reached by an interesting 6km-long 4WD track.

From Narayangarh (p273), on the banks of the Narayani River 20km from Sauraha, you can return to either Kathmandu or Pokhara via Mugling. Although some may say this section from Narayangarh to Mugling is best avoided on a bicycle because of heavy bus and truck traffic, it is nonetheless a very beautiful section of road to ride, and traffic during many times of the day can be light. The alternative is to catch a bus. If you're heading to Pokhara (96km) it may be a good idea to miss the busy highway between Mugling and Pokhara by catching a bus in Mugling (see p239). Here, the road is much improved and vehicles travel a lot faster in what are still quite dusty conditions.

The switchbacking Tribhuvan Hwy (or Rajpath as it is popularly known) was the first highway to connect Kathmandu with the rest of the world. Most traffic from the Terai and India uses the highway that runs to the west between Narayangarh (Narayanghat) and Mugling, which, although longer, is actually quicker, so traffic along the Rajpath is relatively light.

Hetauda is just to the east of Royal Chitwan National Park, which has a wide selection of accommodation, both in the park and in the town of Sauraha – see p283. You are prohibited from riding inside the park, but are allowed to ride directly to your resort.

For a map of the area around Royal Chitwan National Park see pp276–7.

KATHMANDU TO POKHARA VIA THE PRITHVI HIGHWAY
Distance 216km
Duration Two days
Start Kathmandu
Finish Pokhara
Brief description Riverside views, changing scenery and plenty of traffic separates Nepal's two tourist magnets.

A surprisingly large number of bicyclists show an interest in this ride, perhaps due to the riverside views, and the attractions at either end. You are almost guaranteed to see the remains of a truck or bus crash en route. The message is obvious – take care on this notorious stretch of road.

It's theoretically possible to make Pokhara in 12 to 14 hours of steady biking, but it's a much better idea to break the trip at the wonderful but little-visited sights of Bandipur and Gorkha, both of which are a short detour off the road and offer decent accommodation. For details of the sights along this road see the Kathmandu to Pokhara chapter, p236.

After leaving the valley on the Prithvi Hwy at Thankot, the highway descends to Naubise, at the bottom of the Mahesh Khola Valley, 27km from Kathmandu, where the Rajpath intersects with the Prithvi Hwy.

Following the thrilling, if not hair-raising, descent (watching for oil slicks after on-the-spot truck repairs), Mugling is about the halfway mark at 120km, four to five hours' ride from Kathmandu. There are also lots of simple food stops along the way at some very scenic spots.

From Mugling you keep to the right as you exit the town and within 300m you will cross the Trisuli River bridge. The second half of your journey to Pokhara is mostly uphill, but still offers some excellent downhills. From Mugling there's overall altitude gain of about 550m over 96km. Again there are numerous roadside cafés and food stops to keep the carbohydrates supplied. The final approach to Pokhara, with the Annapurnas as a backdrop, will pick you up after a long day of biking.

At Mugling you'll find plenty of food and accommodation (see p239), or break the trip at the idyllic River Side Springs Resort (p238), just before Mugling, at Kurintar.

POKHARA TO SARANGKOT & NAUDANDA
Distance 54km
Duration Seven hours, or an overnight trip
Start/Finish Pokhara
Brief description Work up a sweat to two of Pokhara's best Himalayan viewpoints, followed by a great downhill coast.

Leave early and ride along Lakeside (towards the mountains) to the last main intersection and sealed road. Turn right; this is the road that returns to central Pokhara. After 2km you turn left and continue straight on (north). This intersection is the zero km road marker. After a further 2km there is a smaller sealed road to the left, signposted as the road to Sarangkot.

This winds its way along a ridge into Sarangkot, providing outstanding views of the Himalaya, which seems close enough to reach out and touch. After 6km a few tea shops mark a welcome refreshment stop just where the stone steps mark the walking trail to the summit. From here it's a 4WD track that closely hugs the edge of the mountain overlooking Phewa Tal. Continue until you join a Y-intersection that doubles back sharply to the right and marks the final climb to Sarangkot Point. You can turn this ride into a relaxed overnight trip by staying in lodges here (see p266).

The ride to Sarangkot, visible directly north from Pokhara Lakeside, provides an excellent, challenging day trip. This is in fact the bicycle leg of the Annapurna Triathlon. For a map of the area see map p266.

From Sarangkot continue straight ahead, riding the narrower motorcycle trails leading to Kaski and Naudanda. After the Sarangkot turn-off the trail soon begins to climb to Kaski, towards the hill immediately in front of you. The section to Kaski takes around 30 to 60 minutes, and you may need to push your bicycle on the steeper section near the crown of the hill. Over the top you follow the trail through to Naudanda. You are now at around 1590m, having gained around 840m altitude from

Pokhara. The trail is rocky in parts and will test your equipment to the extreme, so do not consider riding this trail on a cheap hire bicycle.

From Naudanda it's a 32km downhill run to Pokhara along the smooth asphalt highway. This route starts with a twisting 6km descent into the Mardi Khola Valley then descends gently as it follows the river, allowing an enjoyable coast almost all the way back to Pokhara.

RAFTING & KAYAKING

Nepal has a reputation for being one of the best places in the world for rafting and kayaking, with outstanding river journeys ranging from steep, adrenaline-charged mountain streams to classic big-volume wilderness expeditions. Warm water, a subtropical climate (with no bugs!) and huge white sandy beaches that are ideal for camping just add to the appeal.

There has also been a continuous increase in the number of kayakers coming to Nepal and it is justifiably recognised as a mecca for paddlers. Several companies offer trips that cater specifically to kayakers, where you get to explore the river with rafts carrying all your gear and food, and often camp near choice play spots.

When to Go

The best times for rafting are September to early December, and March to early June. From early September to early October, and May to June, the rivers can be extremely high with monsoon runoff. Any expeditions attempted at this time require a very experienced rafting company with an intimate knowledge of the river and strong teams, as times of high flows are potentially the most dangerous times to be on a river.

From mid-October onwards is one of the most popular times to raft, with warm settled weather and exciting runs. In December many of the rivers become too cold to enjoy unless you have a wetsuit, and the days are short with the start of winter – the time to consider shorter trips. The summer season from March to early June has long hot days and lower water flows to begin with, which generally means the rapids are a grade lower than they are from September to November. The rivers rise again in May with the premonsoon storms and some snowmelt.

From June to August, the monsoon rains arrive. The rivers carry 10 times their low-water flows, and can flood with 60 to 80 times the low-water levels,

The view from the ridge at Naudanda is spectacularly beautiful. Dhaulagiri, Manaslu, the Annapurnas and Machhapuchhare create a classic Himalayan panorama, especially on a cool, clear morning. To the south you can look down over Pokhara and Phewa Tal.

The website www.raft nepal.org offers an excellent overview of rafting options across Nepal, as well as advice about other extreme sports.

THE FUTURE OF RIVER-RUNNING IN NEPAL

In the past 15 years, a number of rivers have stopped flowing freely because of construction of hydroelectric projects. Nepal sees hydro development as a means of stimulating economic growth. If this is done responsibly, with consensus among the river-running community and other concerned parties, then there will still be many world-class river runs but this is currently not happening. A new river project on the Marsyangdi – to take water out at Philesangu and drop it back in at Bhote Odar – has made the Marsyangdi a series of shorter sections. There are projects planned for the Karnali, Arun and Bhote Kosi Rivers.

The Nepal River Conservation Trust (NRCT) was formed by a group of concerned river guides in 1995 to raise awareness of the plight of Nepal's rivers, to lobby governments and to promote responsible use of rivers. The NRCT trains river guides in best environmental practice and organises river restoration projects. The NRCT organises the Bagmati River Festival from June to August (main events mid-August), which involves clean-up and environmental awareness campaigns, and rafting trips on the Bagmati from Sundarijal to Sankhamul. It also organises the Seti River festival in Pokhara (last week of September) and an annual Bhote Kosi festival in February. Contact the NRCT (☎ 01-4361995; www.nepalrivers.org.np; PO Box 12346 Kathmandu) for more information.

making most rivers insanely difficult. Only parts of the Seti and Trisuli are commercially run during the monsoon. River levels can fluctuate dramatically at any time, although as a general rule weather patterns in Nepal are quite stable.

What to Bring

If you go on an organised rafting trip all specialised equipment is supplied, as well as tents. Roll-top dry bags keep your gear dry even if the raft flips.

Usually you will only need light clothing, with a warmer change for nights. A swimsuit, a sunhat, sunscreen and light tennis shoes or sandals (that will stay on your feet) are all necessary, but can be bought in Kathmandu. Overnight trips require a sleeping bag, but these can easily be hired. In winter you will need thermal clothing.

Organised Trips

There are dozens of companies in Kathmandu claiming to be rafting and kayaking operators. A few are well-established companies with good reputations, and the rest are newer companies, often formed by guides breaking away and starting their own operations, and sometimes people with very little experience of rivers. Although these new companies can be enthusiastic and good, they can also be shoestring operations that may not have adequate equipment and staff. Most of the small travel agencies simply sell trips on commission; often they have no real idea about the details of what they are selling and are only interested in getting bums on seats.

If a group has recently returned from a trip, speak to its members. This will give you reliable information about the quality of equipment, the guides, the food and the transportation. Question the company about things such as how groups get to and from the river, the number of hours spent paddling or rowing, where the camps are set up, food provided (rafting promotes a very healthy appetite), who does the cooking and work around the camp, the cooking fuel used (wood isn't convenient or responsible), what happens to rubbish, hygiene precautions, and nighttime activities. Many companies have a photo file or video in their office, which can give you an impression of the equipment, safety and how trips are operated.

Check how many people have booked and paid for a trip, as well as the maximum number that will be taken.

The quality of the rafting equipment is another variable, and can make a huge difference to the comfort and safety of participants. Modern self-bailing rafts, good life jackets and helmets are essential. Check how old the equipment is (modern plastic and alloy paddles are preferable to locally made wooden ones, for example) and ask what first-aid gear, supplies, spare parts and repair equipment are carried.

If your time is limited you may choose to book a trip before you leave home, though all Kathmandu operators accept walk-in bookings. Shorter trips depart every few days but the recent downturn in tourism has led to a drop in the number of longer rafting trips, especially at the beginning and end of the season, so it's worth contacting a company in advance to see when they are planning a trip. The best companies will refer you to a friendly competitor if they don't have any suitable dates.

Rafting trips vary from quite luxurious trips where you are rowed down the river and staff do everything for you (pitch camp, cook and so on), to trips where you participate in the running of the expedition including pitching tents, loading the rafts and helping with the cooking.

Anyone who is seriously interested in rafting and kayaking should get hold of *White Water Nepal* by Peter Knowles, with David Allardice as the consultant on rafting. It has very detailed information on river trips, with 60 maps, river profiles and hydrographs, plus advice on equipment and health. It's possible to get copies of the book in Kathmandu, or check out www.riverspublishing.co.uk.

Nepa Maps and Himalayan Maphouse (www.himalayan-maphouse.com) produce fairly useful rafting maps to the Bhote Kosi, Sun Kosi and Trisuli.

The annual Himalayan Whitewater Challenge, or rodeo, is a kayaking competition that runs for three days in November on the Bhote Kosi.

Generally you'll be rafting for around five to six hours a day, you can expect to be running rapids about 30% of the time depending on the river. The first and last day will most likely be half days. Longer trips of a week or more will have one rest day when you can recover or explore the surroundings.

Trips range in price from US$30 to US$60 a day, and generally you get what you pay for. It is better to pay a bit more and have a good, safe trip than to save US$100 and have a lousy, dangerous trip. Bear in mind that trips in Nepal are generally less than half the cost of similar trips in the USA, so in relative terms all the prices are extremely reasonable. If you plan to do a more difficult trip it's particularly important to choose a company that has the experience, skills and equipment to run a safe and exciting expedition. As one rafting company says, 'saving you a little can cost you a lot'.

With the constant change in rafting companies it's difficult to make individual recommendations; the fact that a company is not recommended here does not necessarily mean it will not deliver an excellent trip. Nonetheless, the following companies have been recommended for their professionalism.

Drift Nepal (Map p136; ☎ 01-4700797; driftnepal@wlink.com.np) Contact Samir Thapa.

Equator Expeditions (Map p136; ☎ 01-4700782; www.equatorexpeditionsnepal.com, www.nepalgate.com; Thamel, Kathmandu) This company specialises in long participatory rafting and kayaking trips as well as kayak instruction.

Himalayan Encounters Kathmandu (Map p136; ☎ 01-4700426; raftnepal@himenco.wlink.com.np; Thamel, Kathmandu); Pokhara (Map p257; ☎ 061-520873) This company is associated with Encounter Overland, and has earned a solid reputation through many Trisuli and Sun Kosi trips. Their Trisuli trips stay at their lodge, the Old Inn in Bandipur (see p244).

Mountain River Rafting (Map p136; ☎ 01-4700770; www.raftnepal.com; Thamel, Kathmandu) 1st fl next to Nargila Restaurant and across from the Northfield Café.

Ultimate Descents Nepal (www.udnepal.com) Kathmandu (Map p136; ☎ 01-4701295); Pokhara (Map p257; ☎ 061-523240) Near Northfield Café. Specialises in long participatory rafting trips as well as kayak instruction and clinics on the Seti River.

Ultimate Rivers (Map p136; ☎ /fax 01-4700526; info@urnepal.wlink.com.np; www.ultimate asia.info; Thamel, Kathmandu) Ultimate Rivers is associated with the New Zealand company Ultimate Descents International (www.ultimatedescents.com) and specialises in participatory rafting and kayak instruction.

Safety

Safety is the most important part of any river trip. Safety is a combination of the right technical skills, teamwork, planning and local knowledge. Unfortunately, there are no minimum safety conditions enforced by any official body in Nepal. This makes it very important to choose a professional rafting and kayaking company.

www.raftingassociation.org.np is the website of the Nepal Association of Rafting Agents and has information on the annual Himalayan Whitewater Challenge, contact details of rafting companies and overviews of river routes.

Waterproof camera containers allow you to take photos all the way down the river – ask your company if they have any for rent or, better, bring your own.

Ganesh Kayak Shop in Pokhara is the only place to hire kayaks by the day – see p253.

RIVER GRADING SYSTEM

Rivers are graded for difficulty on an international scale from class I to VI, with class I defined as easy-moving water with few obstacles, and class VI as nearly impossible to negotiate and a hazard to life. Anyone who is in reasonable physical shape and isn't afraid of water can safely go on rivers graded class I to III. For more difficult and exciting class IV rivers, you should be active, confident in water, and have rafting experience. Class V is a very large step up from class IV; expect long continuous sections of powerful white water, strenuous paddling, steep constricted channels, powerful waves and the possibility of overturning a raft. Swimming in a class V rapid poses a significant risk.

RAFT NUMBERS

There should be a minimum of two rafts per trip. If anyone falls out of a raft the second raft can help with the rescue. In higher water, three rafts are safer than two. Many experts agree that one or two safety kayakers can replace the second raft, though the kayakers need to be white-water professionals with the training, skill and experience not only to run the most difficult rapids on the river, but also to be able to perform rescues in these rapids. Good safety kayakers are invaluable on steeper rivers where they can often get to swimmers in places no other craft could manage.

RAFT GUIDES

The most important aspects of rafting safety are both the skills and judgment of the raft guides and the teamwork of the group on the trip. If possible, speak with the guide who will lead the trip to get an impression of the people you will be spending time with and the type of trip they run. Ask them about their previous experience. Overseas experience or training allows the guides to keep up with the latest advances and safety training. Kayaking experience adds additional depth to a guide's skills.

All guides should have a current first-aid certificate and be trained in cardiopulmonary resuscitation. Reputable companies with reliable guides will seek international accreditation such as the Swiftwater Rescue Technician (SRT) qualification.

ON THE RIVER

Your guide should give you a comprehensive safety talk and paddle training before you launch off downstream. If you don't get this it is probably cause for concern.

- Listen to what your guide is telling you. Always wear your life jacket in rapids. Wear your helmet whenever your guide tells you, and make sure that both the helmet and jacket are properly adjusted and fitted.
- Keep your feet and arms inside the raft. If the raft hits a rock or wall and you are in the way, the best you'll escape with is a laceration.
- If you do swim in a rapid, get into the 'white-water swimming position'. You should be on your back, with your feet downstream and up where you can see them. Hold on to your paddle as this will make you more visible. Relax and breathe when you aren't going through waves. Then turn over and swim at the end of the rapid when the water becomes calmer. Self rescue is the best rescue.

Kayaking

The opportunities for kayak expeditions are exceptional. Apart from the rivers discussed later in this chapter, of note at the right flows are the Mardi Khola, Tamba Kosi, Karnali headwaters, Thuli Bheri, Balephi Khola and tributaries of the Tamur.

The upper Modhi Khola is also good for experienced kayakers. The side creek of the Bhurungdi Khola, by Birethani village, hides several waterfalls which are runable by experienced kayakers.

KAYAK CLINICS

Nepal is an ideal place to learn to kayak and several rafting companies offer learner kayak clinics. For the communication required to teach, the best instruction clinics tend to be staffed with both Western and Nepali instructors. Kayak clinics normally take about four days, which gives you time to get a good grounding in the basics of kayaking, safety and river dynamics.

Nepal is an ideal place to learn to kayak and several rafting companies offer learner kayak clinics

The clinics are a pretty laid-back intro to kayaking, with around four to six hours of paddling a day. On day one you'll learn self-rescue, T-rescue and Eskimo roll, which will help you to right yourself when you capsize. Day two sees you on the river, learning to ferry glide (cross the river), eddy in and eddy out (entering and leaving currents), brace and perfect your strokes. Day three is when you start really having fun on the river, running small (class II) rapids and journeying down the river, learning how to read the rapids. The key is to relaxed your upper body to move with the kayak, and not to panic underwater. Flexibility is a real plus. Expect one instructor for every three people.

Equator Expeditions and Ultimate Descents International (see rafting companies p90) operate clinics on the upper Sun Kosi. Equator runs the Sukute Beach Resort, just north of Sukute village at km 69/70. It's fairly comfortable but isn't as luxurious as Borderlands or The Last Resort, with squat toilets and cold showers. Still, it has a great spot on the river, with a private beach, a bar area with pool tables and a lovely stretch of river nearby. It also has a pool which is a real bonus when learning Eskimo rolls.

The Last Resort/Ultimate Descents International uses the Riverside Camp, between kilometre markers 83 and 84, which is a similarly basic camp, made up of dome tents. Both companies charge around US$160 for the four-day clinic, though Equator will drop this in low season to US$120 if you take the bus there and back. For both trips check what kind of transportation is included. You may find yourself flagging down local buses and putting your kayak on the roof for short rides after a trip down the river.

Other companies such as Ultimate Descents Nepal and Mountain River Rafting (see rafting companies p90) operate their four-day clinics on the gentle Seti River, for around US$200, from Pokhara to Pokhara. The first day's training takes place on Phewa Tal and the remaining 2½ days are on the Seti, with two nights' riverside camping. The kayak route follows the rafting route (see p96), putting in at Damauli and taking out at Ghaighat, at the junction with the Trisuli River. The advantage to learning on the Seti is that you get to journey down a real river, unlike the shorter runs of Bhote Kosi.

Kayak clinic accommodation is generally more basic than other trips so you should bring your own sleeping bag, towel, swimming costume, snacks and hot drinks. Nose plugs are useful for those practice Eskimo rolls.

The bulk of kayak clinics operate in October, November, April and May. December is quieter but there's a lot less sunlight to warm you up at the beginning and end of the day.

Nose plugs are useful for those practice Eskimo rolls.

TRANSPORTING YOUR OWN KAYAK

Most airlines will carry short kayaks on the same basis as surfboards or bicycles; there's no excess baggage charge, so long as you are within the weight limits. If you are a group, negotiate a deal at the time of booking. If there are only one or two of you, just turn up, put all your bulky light gear in the kayak, with heavy items in your carry-on luggage, and smile sweetly! If you phone the airline in advance they have to quote the rulebook and start talking air cargo, which is expensive.

Choosing a River

Before you decide on a river, you need to decide what it is that you want out of your trip. There are trips available from two to 12 days on different rivers, all offering dramatically different experiences.

First, don't believe that just because it's a river it's going to be wet 'n' wild. Some rivers, such as the Sun Kosi, which is a full-on white-water trip

RIVER TRIPS IN NEPAL

River	Trip duration (Days)	Cost	Transport	Season and grade	Add-ons
Bhote Kosi	2	US$60-80	3hr drive from Kathmandu	Oct-Dec III-V, Feb-May III-IV	canyoning and kayak clinics at Borderlands and The Last Resort
Trisuli	2	US$70-80	from Kathmandu or Pokhara	Jun-Aug III-IV, Sep-May III	Bandipur
Seti	3	US$120	from Pokhara	Jun-Aug IV, Sep-May II-III	kayak clinics are popular here
Kali Gandaki	3	US$80-120	from Pokhara	Sep-Nov III-IV+, Feb-May III-IV	Royal Chitwan NP
Marsyangdi	4	US$200-225	5hr drive from Kathmandu or Pokhara, then day-long trek	Oct-Dec IV-V, Feb-Apr IV+	
Sun Kosi	8-9	US$300-350	3hr from Kathmandu to start point; 16hr drive or flight back from Biratnagar	Sep-Nov III+ to V-, June III to V+	Koshi Tappu Wildlife Reserve, or continue on to Darjeeling in India
Karnali	10	US$350-400	16hr bus ride or flight, followed by 2-day trek	Sep-Nov III to V, Feb-May III to IV	Royal Bardia National Park
Tamur	11	US$550-650	flight/15-hour bus drive and three-day trek there; flight or 16 hour bus drive back	Oct-Dec III to IV, Mar-Apr III to IV+	The Hide Out

in September and October, are basically flat in the low water of early spring. On the flip side, early spring can be a superb time to raft rivers such as the Marsyangdi or Bhote Kosi, which would be suicidal during high flows. The Karnali is probably the only river that offers continually challenging white water at all flows, though during the high-water months of September and May it's significantly more challenging than in the low-water months.

Longer trips such as the Sun Kosi (in the autumn), the Karnali and the Tamur offer some real heart-thumping white water with the incredible journeying aspect of a long river trip. With more time on the river, things are more relaxed, relationships progress at a more natural pace, and memories become entrenched for a lifetime. Long after the white water has blurred into one white-knuckled thrill ride, the memories of a moonrise over the river and the friends you inevitably make will remain. River trips are much more than gravity powered roller coaster rides; they're liquid journeys traversed on very special highways. For many people they become a way of life.

If a long trip is simply impossible because of financial or time constraints, don't undervalue the shorter ones. Anyone who has ever taken a paddle-raft or kayak down the Bhote Kosi (at any flow) would be hard pressed to find anything better to do with two days in Nepal. There are also medium-length options that are perfect for people who want to experience a river journey but have limited time.

River Routes

This section describes the main commercially rafted rivers in Nepal. It is by no means a complete list, and private boaters who have the experience, equipment and desire to run their own expeditions are best advised to consult the aforementioned guidebook, *White Water Nepal*.

TRISULI
Distance 40km
Duration Two days
Start Baireni
Finish Multiple locations
Brief description Popular, a wild ride during the monsoon

With easy access just out of Kathmandu, the Trisuli is where many commercial trips operate. This is the cheapest trip available in Nepal – if you sign on to a US$15-a-day raft trip, this is where you'll end up.

What makes the Trisuli so cheap is also what makes it one of the least desirable rafting trips in the country. The easy access is provided by the Prithvi Hwy, which is the only highway connecting Kathmandu and India, and it runs right alongside the river. During most flows the rapids are straightforward and spread well apart. The large number of companies operating on the river drives the prices down, but it also detracts considerably from the experience of the trip. Beaches are often heavily used and abused, with garbage, toilet paper and fire pits well assimilated into the sand. This, combined with the noise and pollution of the highway, makes the Trisuli a less than ideal rafting experience.

It's not all bad news though. During the monsoon months the Trisuli changes character completely as huge runoffs make the river swell and shear like an immense ribbon of churning ocean. There are fewer companies running at this time of the year, and the garbage and excrement of the past season should by now be well on its way to Bangladesh as topsoil.

The best white water is found on the section between Baireni and Mugling, and trips on the Trisuli can be combined with trips to Pokhara or Chitwan.

BHOTE KOSI
Distance 10km
Duration Two days
Start Borderlands
Finish Lamosangu
Brief description Just three hours from Kathmandu, the Bhote Kosi is one of the best short raft trips to be found anywhere in the world

The Bhote Kosi is the steepest river rafted in Nepal – technical and totally committing. With a gradient of 80ft per mile (24m per 1.6km), it's a full eight times as steep as the Sun Kosi, which it feeds further downstream. The rapids are steep and continual class IV, with a lot of continual class III in between.

This river is one of the most fun things you can do right out of Kathmandu and a great way to get an adrenaline fix during the low-water months, but it should only be attempted with a company that has a lot of experience on the Bhote Kosi, and is running the absolute best guides, safety equipment and safety kayakers. The Great Wall rapid is normally portaged as it is simply too dangerous during normal flows. The river is more challenging in October, by November it has dropped to medium flows.

The normal run is from around 95km northeast of Kathmandu (north of Barabise) to the dam at Lamosangu. The river has been kayaked above this point, but a raft trip here would not be recreational. At high flows

You can get an idea of what you are in for by looking at the names of some of the rapids – Gerbil in the Plumbing, Frog in a Blender, Carnal Knowledge of a Deviant Nature, Exlax and Liquid Bliss!

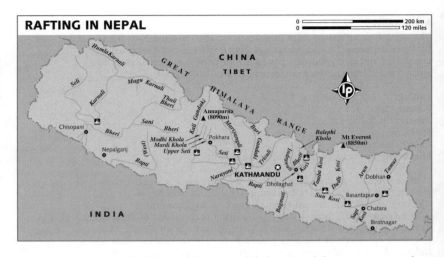

RAFTING IN NEPAL

several of the rapids become solid class V, and the consequences of any mistakes become serious.

Most trips are two days, but the first day consists largely of training in the calmer waters below the dam (from just above the turn-off to Jiri), with most of the rapids coming thick and furious further upstream on the second day, so if you are already up there then it can be done as a day trip.

Camping on the Bhote Kosi is limited, with few good beaches, so most groups stay at comfortable river camps like Borderlands and The Last Resort (see p233). Borderlands has the highest put-in point which gives you a little more rafting time.

Rafting the Bhote Kosi out of one of these camps means you get more river time and can relax at the end of the day in pristine surroundings and comfort. The environmental impact of trips is limited by staying at fixed camps, which also create local employment and business. They also offer other activities, so you can mix and match what you do.

SETI
Distance 32km
Duration Two days
Start Damauli
Finish Gaighat
Brief description Perfect for beginners, families and learner kayakers

Beware if you decide to try the upper section of the Seto River, as it disappears underground above Dule Gouda! Perhaps this is what they refer to as class VI…

The Seti is an excellent two-day trip in an isolated area, with beautiful jungle and plenty of easy rapids. Beware of companies who market this as a hot white-water trip. While it's a beautiful river valley well worth rafting, it's not a white-water bonanza.

This is the perfect river for a family trip or in which to learn to kayak (see above). The water is warm and the rapids are class II or II+. During the monsoon (June and August) the river changes gear and creates white water action up to class IV.

The logical starting point is Damauli on the Prithvi Hwy between Mugling and Pokhara. This would give you 32km of rafting to the confluence with the Trisuli River. From the take out at Gaighat it's just a one-hour drive to Royal Chitwan National Park.

KALI GANDAKI
Distance 90km
Duration Three days
Start Baglung
Finish Andhi Khola
Brief description Diverse trip down the holy river, through deep gorges and past waterfalls

The Kali Gandaki is an excellent alternative to the Trisuli, as there is no road alongside, and the scenery, villages, and temples all combine to make it a great trip.

The rapids on the Kali Gandaki are much more technical and continual than those on the Trisuli (at class III to IV depending on the flows), and in high water it's no place to be unless you are an accomplished kayaker experienced in avoiding big holes. At medium and lower flows, it's a fun and challenging river with rapids that will keep you busy for three days.

The Kali Gandaki is one of the holiest rivers in Nepal, and every river junction is dotted with cremation sites and above-ground burial mounds. If you've been wondering what's under that pile of rocks, we recommend against exploring. Because of the recent construction of a dam at the confluence with the Andhi Khola, what was once a four- to five-day trip has now become a three-day trip, starting at Baglung and taking out at the dam site. At very high flows it will probably be possible to run the full five-day trip to Ramdhighat by just portaging the dam site. This option would add some great white water and you could visit the fantastic derelict palace at Ranighat (see p301), which is slowly being restored.

If you can raft to Ramdhighat beside the Siddhartha Hwy between Pokhara and Sunauli, you could continue on to the confluence with the Trisuli at Devghat. This adds another 130km and three or four more days. The lower section below Ramdhighat doesn't have much white water, but it is seldom rafted and offers a very isolated area with lots of wildlife.

Kayakers have the option of descending the Modhi Khola on the first day to its confluence to the Kali Gandaki, to join up with the rafting group at the end of the first day.

MARSYANGDI
Distance 27km
Duration Four days (two days rafting)
Start Ngadi
Finish Phalesangu
Brief description Short but sweet white knuckle ride

The Marsyangdi is steeper and offers more continuous white water than most other rivers in Nepal; it's not called the 'Raging River' for nothing! A hydro project has severely affected this world-class rafting and kayaking river but it is still possible to have a two-day run on the rapids before reaching the dam.

The trip starts with a bus ride from Dumre to Besisahar. From here it is a beautiful trek up to the village of Ngadi, with great views of the Manaslu and the Annapurnas ahead of you the whole time.

From Ngadi downstream to the end of the trip at the dam side above Philesangu, it's pretty much solid white water. Rapids are steep, technical and consecutive, making the Marsyangdi a serious undertaking. Successful navigation of the Marsyangdi requires companies to have previous experience on the river and to use the best guides and equipment. Rafts must be self-bailing, and should be running with a minimum of weight and gear on board. Professional safety kayakers should be considered a standard safety measure on this river.

The dam on the Marsyangdi is due for completion in 2006, so check with rafting operators on current information on what itineraries they're running.

KARNALI
Distance 180km
Duration 10-11 days (seven days rafting)
Start Surkhet
Finish Chisopani
Brief description A wilderness trip in far western Nepal down Nepal's largest and longest river

The Karnali is a gem, combining a two-day trek with some of the prettiest canyons and jungle scenery in Nepal. Most experienced river people who have paddled the Karnali find it one of the best all-round river trips they've ever done. In high water, the Karnali is a serious commitment, combining *huge,* though fairly straightforward, rapids with a seriously remote location. At low water the Karnali is still a fantastic trip. The rapids become smaller when the river drops, but the steeper gradient and constricted channel keep it interesting.

Being the longest and largest river in all of Nepal, the Karnali drains a huge and well-developed catchment. Spring snowmelts can drive the river up dramatically in a matter of hours – as the river rises, the difficulty increases exponentially. The river flows through some steep and constricted canyons where the rapids are close together, giving little opportunity to correct for potential mistakes. Pick your company carefully.

The trip starts with a long, but interesting, two-day bus ride to the remote far west of Nepal. If you're allergic to bus rides, it's possible to fly to Nepalganj and cut the bus transport down to about four hours on the way over, and two hours on the way back. From the hill town of Surkhet a lovely two-day trek brings you to Sauli, from where it is a two-hour trek to the Karnali River. Once you start on the Karnali it's 180km to the next road access at Chisopani, on the northern border of the Royal Bardia National Park.

The river section takes about seven days, giving plenty of time to explore some of the side canyons and waterfalls that come into the river valley. Better-run trips also include a layover day, where the expedition stays at the same campsite for two nights. The combination of long bus rides and trekking puts some people off, but anyone who has ever done the trip raves about it. Finish with a visit to the Royal Bardia National Park at the end for what is an unbeatable combination.

SUN KOSI
Distance 270km
Duration Eight to nine days (seven days rafting)
Start Dolalghat
Finish Chatara
Brief description A self-sufficient expedition through central Nepal from the Himalaya to the Gangetic Plain

This is the longest river trip offered in Nepal, traversing 270km through the beautiful Mahabharat Range on its meandering way from the put-in at Dolalghat to the take-out at Chatara in the far east of the country. It's quite an experience to begin a river trip just three hours out of Kathmandu, barely 60km from the Tibetan border, and end the trip looking down the hot, dusty gun barrel of the north Indian plain just eight or nine days later. Because it's one of the easiest trips logistically, it's also one of the least expensive for the days you spend on a river.

The Sun Kosi (River of Gold) starts off fairly relaxed, with only class II and small class III rapids to warm up on during the first couple of days. Savvy guides will take this opportunity to get teams working together

> **THE HIDE OUT**
>
> If joining a rafting trip down the Sun Kosi consider a break at **The Hide Out** (Map p136; ☎ 01-4413209; www.nepalhideout.com), a tented camp along the lines of Borderlands or The Last Resort, way out in the remote eastern foothills of Kangchenjunga.
>
> Getting here involves a two- to three-day trek from the road head at Basantapur, or a 1½-hour walk from Taplejung, which has unreliable flights from Kathmandu. The camp is at the junction of the Tamur and Maiwa Kholas, near Dobhan.
>
> The resort runs a series of treks and cultural activities, including hikes to the impressive Sobwa Falls and Khamlung Peak, or a five-day trek to Pathibara Temple, plus a wide range of village visits and cultural programmes. See the website for details or contact Andy Coopland at info@nepalhideout.com.

with precision. The river volume increases with the air temperature as several major tributaries join the river and from the third day the rapids become more powerful and frequent. During high-water trips you may well find yourselves astonished at just how big a river wave can get.

While the lower sections of large-volume rivers are usually rather flat, the Sun Kosi reserves some of its biggest and best rapids for the last days, and the last section is nonstop class IV before a final quiet float down the Sapt Kosi. Some companies add on an extra day's rafting on the lower section of the Tamur, from Mulghat down.

At the right flow it's an incredible combination of white water, scenery, villages, and quiet and introspective evenings.

> Many rafters consider the Sun Kosi to be one of the world's 10 classic river journeys.

TAMUR
Distance 120km
Duration 11 days
Start Dobhan
Finish Chatara
Brief description Remote expedition in the foothills of Kangchenjunga in the far east of the country; includes a three-day trek.

Way out in the far east, this river combines one of the best short treks in Nepal with some really challenging white-water action. The logistics of this trip make it a real expedition, and while it is a little more complicated to run than many rivers in Nepal, the rewards are worth the effort.

First you have to get to Basantapur, a 15-hour drive from Kathmandu or a US$81 flight to Biratnagar and then a five-hour drive. Most expeditions begin with a stunning three- or four-day trek from Basantapur up over the Milke Danda Range, past the alpine lake of Gupha Pokhari to Dobhan. At Dobhan three tributaries of the Tamur join forces, combining the waters of the mountains to the north (including Kangchenjunga, the world's third largest mountain). The first 16km of rapids is intense, with rapid after rapid, and the white water just keeps coming through towering canyons until the big finale. The best time to raft is probably when flows are at medium, which is between mid-October and mid-November.

OTHER RIVERS
The **Upper Seti** just outside Pokhara makes an excellent half-day trip when it is at high flows. Trips operate in mid-September and October (grade III+) and cost US$35 return from Pokhara.

The new and exciting **Balephi Khola** (above the Bhote Kosi) is run by a few companies from Jalbire to its confluence with the upper Sun Kosi.

Ultimate Descents Nepal runs trips from mid-September to early November and in May, and charges US$90 for the two-day trip

The **Bheri**, which is in the west, is a great float trip with incredible jungle scenery and lots of wildlife. This is one of the best fishing rivers and can be combined with a visit to the Royal Bardia National Park.

The **Arun** from Tumlingtar makes an excellent three-day wilderness trip, although the logistics of getting to the starting point are pretty complicated.

CLIMBING & TREKKING PEAKS

Bivouacked somewhere between trekking and mountaineering are Nepal's 'trekking peaks'. The name 'trekking peak' can be quite deceiving; they vary in their level of difficulty but most include significant mountaineering challenges. They are the natural first step if you are interested in progressing from trekking and scrambling onto crampon and rope work.

Organised Climbs

Because of the bureaucracy involved (see 'Permits and Fees', opposite), it is easiest to use an adventure travel company to organise the climb, rather than do the running around yourself. Trip permit fees are included in all the prices listed in this section.

Equator Expeditions (see p91) is one company that organises mountaineering courses and ascents of Mera and Island Peaks in the Solu Khumbu region. If you sign up for a climb you can often get discounts on their other trips, such as a free two-day Bhote Kosi raft or US$50 off a kayak clinic.

Equator operates a six-day course and ascent of Island Peak, properly known as Imja Tse (6189m), from a base in Chhukung. After acclimatisation, training and a half-day hike to base camp, the peak is generally climbed in a single eight-hour day, departing early in the morning. It's physically demanding but not technically difficult – only the last section is on ice and snow. The north ridge offers a slightly more difficult route option. Trips run weekly in season (mid-October to mid-November, end March to May) and cost US$600.

The second most popular option is to Lobuche East (6119m), a more technically difficult ascent that requires two days' training. Climbers generally depart from a high camp at 1.30am and are back by noon. The six-day round trip from Dzonglha costs around US$600. Trips operate in November and from mid-April to mid-May.

Also in the Everest region, Mera Peak (6476m) involves more trekking than climbing, though it is the highest of the trekking peaks. It's a minimum 15-day trip from Lukla and involves trekking up to the 5415m Mera La, from where the climbing begins. Trips from Kathmandu cost from US$1300 to US$1800 and run in November, April and May. Don't confuse Mera Peak with Mehra Peak (Kongma Tse), further north.

Other possible trekking peak ascents in the Everest region include Phari Lapche (6017m or 6073m) Machhermo (6273m) and Kyozo/Kyajo Ri (6186m), all in the stunning Gokyo Valley.

For all of these trips you will need to hire your own plastic climbing boots and gaiters, either from Kathmandu or Namche Bazaar. Prices include permits, equipment, guides, tent accommodation and food. Expect a group size of around six to eight climbers.

In the Annapurna region, Pisang Peak (6091m) and Chulu East (6584m) are both five-day excursions from Manang; the former is more common, with an organised trip costing around US$1200. A few companies, such as the UK's **Himalayan Frontiers** (www.himalayanfrontiers.co.uk), run

Bill O'Connor's book *The Trekking Peaks of Nepal* gives a detailed description of the climb to each of the 18 traditional peaks plus the approach trek to the mountain. Equipment, applications, procedures and other matters are comprehensively covered but there's little information on the new 'A' trekking peaks.

climbing trips to Tharpu Chuli/Tent Peak (5663m) from Machhapuchhare Base Camp in the Annapurna Sanctuary.

Several companies, including Mountain Monarch run trekking peaks as part of a standard trek. In the Everest region this includes the Everest Base Camp trek and Island Peak (21 to 23 days, US$1500) or Lobuche East (25 days, US$1750). Pisang peak or Chulu West can be combined with the Annapurna Circuit trek (24 to 25 days, US$1650 to US$1700). Yala Peak (5500m) can be included as part of a 16-day Langtang trek (US$1140).

Trekking companies in Kathmandu that organise ascents of trekking peaks include:

Climb High Himalaya (☎ 01-4372874; www.climbhighhimalaya.com, Kathmandu)

Equator Expeditions (Map p136; ☎ 01-4700782; www.equatorexpeditionsnepal.com, www.nepalgate.com; Thamel, Kathmandu)

Himalayan Ecstasy (Map p136; ☎ 01-2012171; www.himalayanecstasy.com, Kathmandu) Offer Island and Lobuche peaks together in one trip for US$1000.

Mountain Monarch (☎ 01-4361668; www.mountainmonarch.com; Lazimpat, Kathmandu)

Nepal Mountain River (Map p136; ☎ 01-4700770; www.nepalmountain.com) Across from Northfield Café; generally a bit more expensive.

Permits & Fees

To arrange your own climbing trip, a permit is required from the **Nepal Mountaineering Association** (NMA; Map p116; ☎ 01-4434525; www.nma.com.np.; PO Box 1435, Nag Pokhari, Kathmandu). Permits must be applied for in advance and are only valid for one month, although weekly extensions are available for 25% of the total fee. All people ascending trekking peaks must be accompanied by a *sirdar* (leader) who is registered with the NMA.

Of the 33 'trekking peaks' the 15 'new' peaks designated in 2002 are classified as 'A' peaks, the original 18 (including all those above) are 'B' peaks. The fees for climbing trekking peaks depend on the group size and the classification. For group 'B' peaks the fees are: one to four people, US$350; five to eight people, US$350 for the group plus US$40 per person; nine to 12 people (the maximum group size), US$510 plus US$25 per person. For Group 'A' peaks the fees are: one to seven people, US$500; eight to 12 people, US$500 plus US$100 per person.

Food & Drink

Eating in Nepal is a mixed bag. The bad news is that generic Nepali food is distinctly dull (think rice and vegetables twice a day for the rest of your life). The good news is that, unless you're trekking off the beaten track, you probably won't spend much time eating it because you'll be too busy tucking into Tibetan, Mexican, Chinese, Japanese, Indian and pretty much anything else. And for when you want to remind yourself that you are in Nepal there are a fair number of places that serve up varied, spicy and interesting Newari dishes.

One of the most common highland foods is *dhedo*, a thick doughlike paste made from grain or millet flour.

STAPLES & SPECIALITIES

Most Hindu Nepalis are vegetarians, whether out of choice or necessity, and most of the time meals consist of a dish called *daal bhaat tarkari*, literally 'lentil soup', 'rice' and 'curried vegetables'. If you are lucky it will be spiced up with a bowl of *achar* (pickles) and maybe some chapati (unleavened Indian bread), *dahi* (curd or yoghurt) or *papad* (pappadam – crispy fried thin pancake). Only very occasionally does it come with *masu* (meat). The occasional *daal bhaat tarkari*, especially home cooked, can be just fine and it's perfect at the end of a long day trekking. Eaten day in and day out it can get very boring indeed. The most common vegetables are spinach, squash and potato.

Throughout the Indian subcontinent butter *(makan)* is clarified into ghee to make it last longer.

Newars in contrast are great meat eaters. *Buff* (water buffalo) is the meat of choice (cows, and thus beef, are sacred and never eaten) but goat is also common and Newars have a particular fondness for wild boar. Spices are heavily used in Newari food, especially chilli, though in general Nepali food is not as spicy as the rest of the Indian subcontinent. Many Newari dishes are only eaten at particular celebrations or family events and for these (and the best Newari food in general) you need to be invited to a Newari home. However, a few top-end restaurants in Kathmandu offer a good range of Newari cuisines (see p147). For a rundown of Newari dishes see p106.

Nepal is also one of the best places to try a range of Tibetan cuisine (it's certainly a lot better than in Tibet!), though most dishes are just variations on momos (dumplings; fried or steamed) or noodles (long or short) and end up tasting remarkably similar. See p107 for a rundown of dishes.

TRAVEL YOUR TASTEBUDS

Tongba is a Himalayan brew made by pouring (and periodically re-adding) boiling water to a bamboo tube of fermented millet. As with all fine beers, it's generally drunk through a straw.

We Dare You!

Very little is wasted when a beast is slaughtered, and in true Newari eateries you can find dishes made from just about every imaginable animal part or fluid – from stewed brains to boiled lungs and fried blood!

Our favourite dishes include *jan-la* (raw steak with the skin attached), *bul-la* (dregs of rice wine with diced spleen and pieces of bone swimming in it), *ti-syah* (fried spinal bone marrow) and the aptly named *swan-puka* (lung filled through the windpipe with spicy batter and then boiled, sliced and fried), topped off with some *cho-hi* (steamed blood pudding). Oh…my…God… Still hungry?

HOW TO MAKE NEPALI CHIYA

Heat three cups of milk in a saucepan, along with four cloves, four cardamom pods, four tea-spoons of sugar and two cinnamon sticks. Heat until it comes to the boil but be careful not to burn it. In a separate saucepan add three cups of boiling water to four teaspoons of black tea leaves. Let sit for three minutes. Strain hot milk into tea and gently heat for a couple of minutes but do not boil.

Desserts

Like their Indian neighbours, Nepalis enjoy a huge range of sticky sweets, mostly milk-based, of which the most visible are *barfi* (milk boiled down into a fudge), *rasbari* (milk balls – similar to Indian *rasgulla*), *lal mohan* (deep-fried milky dough balls), *kheer* (rice pudding) and *julebi* (orange, figure-of-eight deep-fried syrupy sweets).

Anyone who visits Bhaktapur should try the *juju dhau* (king of curds), a wonderfully creamy thick yogurt. *Sikarni* is a traditional dessert of yogurt flavoured with cinnamon and cardamom.

DRINKS
Nonalcoholic

In general *don't drink the water* (see p396). Most good restaurants do boil and filter their water, and tea is almost always safe. There are dozens of brands of cheap bottled water – some spring water, others just treated tap water – though prices rise rapidly in the countryside. You can be environmentally friendly and save some money by purifying your own water or refilling your water bottle from safe water sources.

Tea is the national drink and comes in two distinct types. Tourist restaurants generally serve up the world's weakest tea, often a totally ineffectual Mechi teabag dunked into a glass of hot milk. Proper Nepali *chiya* (sometimes called *masala* tea) is a far more satisfying brew, where the tea leaves are boiled up together with milk, sugar and spices. In Tibetan-influenced areas the drink of choice is black tea churned up with salt, soda and yak butter to produce a soupy consistency.

Lassi – a refreshing drink of curd (yoghurt) mixed with sugar and what may be untreated water (proceed with caution) – is a highlight of travelling in the subcontinent and comes in a range of sweet and salty flavours.

Alcoholic

Locally produced Nepali beer is pretty good, especially after a hard day's walking or bicycling around the valley. The best brands are Tuborg (Danish), Carlsberg (Danish) and San Miguel (Filipino), all brewed in Gorkha, though you can also get the odd imported Indian-bottled Kingfisher or can of Guinness. The best local beer is Everest Beer.

Chang, the popular Himalayan homebrew, is a mildly alcoholic concoction made from barley, millet or rice and what may be untreated water. It's found along many trekking routes and can be served hot or cold.

Harder spirits include arak, fermented from potatoes or grain, and *rakshi*, a Newari-style distilled rice wine that runs the gamut from smooth firewater to paint stripper. Kukhri Rum is probably the most famous locally bottled spirit.

Officially alcohol is not sold by retailers on the first two days and last two Saturdays of the Nepali month, but this rarely affects foreigners or restaurants.

Most Nepalis round off a meal with a *digestif* of *pan* (betel nut and leaf mixture). Those little spots of red on the pavement that look like little pools of blood are (generally) *pan*.

To eat daal bhaat the local way, pour the soupy daal onto the rice, mix it into balls with your fingers, add a bit of pickle and vegetable and shovel it into your mouth with your right hand.

CELEBRATIONS

At festival time, most Nepalis cram their annual meat intake into a couple of days. Feasts known as *bhoj* follow major sacrifices during Dasain and other dates.

Certain festivals are associated with specific foods. During the Janai Purnima festival, Newars make up batches of *kwati*, a soup made from up to a dozen types of sprouted beans. Most festival sites attract vendors selling sweets, snacks and fruit, some of which are used as offerings.

WHERE TO EAT & DRINK
Restaurants

In 1955 Kathmandu had only one restaurant. These days, Nepal's hundreds of backpacker restaurants offer some of the world's most varied menus. Travel outside of Kathmandu and Pokhara, however, and you'll quickly find yourself limited to chow mein and daal bhaat.

If you eat *daal bhaat tarkari*, most local restaurants (known as *bhojanalaya*) and roadside stalls will be able to find you some kind of spoon (*chamchah*), but the custom is to eat with your right hand. Daal bhaat is often served on a metal plate called a thali and is an all-you-can-eat deal. If a restaurant advertises a 'homepacking system', this means it can arrange takeaway.

In small local restaurants the cooking equipment is often limited to a couple of gas ring burners and a sweaty bloke with a wok, so if you and your five friends order six different dishes you can expect to be waiting for dinner when breakfast time rolls around the next day. In that situation it makes a lot of sense to order the same dish six times, preferably a few hours in advance. This will not only save time, but also cooking fuel, which is often firewood.

FARANGI FOOD

Although the real local food can be limited in its scope, Kathmandu's restaurants offer an amazing variety of dishes. In the days of 'Asia overlanding', when many travellers arrived in Kathmandu having made a long and often wearisome trip through Asia from Europe, Kathmandu's restaurants had a near mythic appeal.

These days, as most travellers jet straight in from abroad, the food doesn't seem quite so amazing, but restaurants in Kathmandu and Pokhara still give international cuisine a damn good try and they will attempt almost anything from Mexican tacos to Japanese sukiyaki.

This culinary creativity has resulted in a number of hybrid foods that form a unique Nepali 'tourist ghetto cuisine'. Chop suey, for example, comes American-style, with a sweet and sour-ish sauce over crispy noodles ('American chop suey' has a fried egg on top). 'Swiss *rosti*' is a dish of potatoes covered in cheese. Some dishes are obvious ('chicken chilli' is barbecued spicy chicken), others are far more cryptic ('chicken lollipop' is a plate of grilled chicken wings).

Quick Eats

Nepali towns have a wide range of snack foods, from bagels in tourist bakeries to grilled corn on the cob on the street corner. A couple of *samsa* (samosas) or *papad* make a great snack and Newari beer snacks are legendary – try a plate of *sekuwa* (spiced meat) next time you have a cold beer. Stalls everywhere offer a mix of dried peas, chickpeas and puffed rice, flavoured with onion, lemon and chilli. Rice-flour doughnuts called *sel* are also popular. A plate of momos makes a great light meal.

Garam masala (hot mix) is a standard mix of spices that includes cardamom, cloves, fenugreek, coriander, cinnamon, cumin, fennel and pepper. You can buy it premixed in supermarkets.

The Nepal Cookbook by the Association of Nepalis in the Americas is a good collection of home recipes. You can get it at www.amazon.com or in Kathmandu.

Food Nepal (www.food-nepal.com) offers an excellent introduction to Nepali food and ingredients, with recipes from mango lassi to chicken chilli.

DOS & DON'TS

■ Don't share food from your plate or another's and don't use your own fork or spoon to serve yourself food. Food becomes ritually polluted (*jhuto*) if touched by someone else's hand, plate or utensils.

■ When using water from a communal jug or cup don't touch it to your mouth, but rather pour it straight into your mouth without touching it (and without pouring it all over your shirt).

■ Don't use your left hand for eating or passing food to others. The left hand is used for washing yourself after defecating and so is considered unclean.

■ Do wait to be served.

■ Do leave your shoes outdoors when dining in someone's house.

■ Do wash your hands and mouth before dining.

■ Do ask for seconds when eating at someone's home.

HABITS & CUSTOMS

For a start, the Nepali eating schedule is quite different from that in the West. The morning usually begins with little more than a cup of sweet tea. The main meal is not taken until late morning. Dinner is eaten quite late, generally just before going to bed. In areas where there are few Western visitors, finding food is much simpler if you go along with this schedule.

Hindus have strict rules about keeping food and drink ritually pure and unpolluted. A high-caste Brahmin simply cannot eat food prepared by a lower-caste individual. Putting your used plate on a buffet table, for example, risks making all the food still on the table *jhuto* (polluted).

Plates and glasses must be purified by rinsing with water before they are considered clean. Any leftover food is considered polluted, as is anything that touches another's lips, especially if that person comes from another caste.

In general, when eating in a group, no-one gets up until everyone has finished their food. If for some reason you have to leave early, make your apologies with *bistaai khaanus*, or 'please eat slowly'.

> Nepali Hindus eat very little meat, so vegetarians and vegans won't have a problem finding food in Nepal. Nepal's Buddhist communities occasionally eat meat, as Buddhism doesn't forbid the eating of meat, just the killing of animals, a fine distinction...

COOKING COURSES

Trekkers Holiday Inn (☎ 01-4480334; www.4free.ch/nepal; Chuchepati) Based at the Hotel Samasara, midway between Kathmandu and Bodhnath, this Swiss-run centre offers a Nepali cookery course every Saturday afternoon for Rs 450, which includes the meal. See p357 for details on how to get there.
Via Via Café (Map p136; www.viaviacafé.com; Kathmandu) This Belgian-Nepali restaurant (see p149) runs weekly cookery courses (Rs 420).

EAT YOUR WORDS

For pronunciation guidelines and other general language phrases see p398.

Useful Phrases
I'm a vegetarian
ma sāhkāhari hun

> The Hindu caste system brings its own dietary restrictions – strict Brahmins, for example, do not eat chicken, buffalo, onion, tomatoes, mushrooms or eggs, or rice if it has been cooked by someone from another caste.

I don't like spicy food
ma piro khandina/piro nahahlnuhos

Can I have the bill?
bill pauna sakchhu?

Please bring me a spoon
malai chamchah lyaunuhos

Menu Decoder
NEPALI & NEWARI FOOD

Nepali uses different words for 'clean' *(saphaa)* and 'ritually clean' *(choko)*.

aloo tahmah	stewlike dish made from potatoes, bamboo shoots and beans
aloo tareko	fried potato with cumin, turmeric and chilli
bandhel tareko	fried wild boar (or pork) with onions, tomatoes and spices
chatamari	rice-flour pancake topped with meat and/or egg, sometimes over-optimistically called a 'Newari pizza'
choyla	roasted, diced *buff* (buffalo) meat, usually heavily spiced and eaten with *chura*
chura	beaten rice (think of flat Rice Bubbles!), served in place of rice
chyau ko tarkari	mushrooms with peas, tomatoes and spices
dayakula	meat curry
gundruk	traditional Nepali sour soup with dried vegetables
gurr	made from raw potatoes ground and mixed with spices and then grilled like a large pancake and eaten with cheese
kachila	raw *buff* mince mixed with oil, ginger and spices
khasi kho ledo	lamb curry
kwati	soup made from a dozen types of sprouted beans and eaten during festivals
mis mas tarkari	seasonal mixed vegetables
momoch	Newari version of Tibetan *momo*
samay baji	ritual feast of *chura, choyla,* boiled egg, black soybeans, diced ginger and lentil-flour pancake
sandeko	cold pickles
sekuwa	barbecued meat: *buff,* pork, fish or chicken
sikarni	sweet whipped yogurt dessert that may include nuts, cinnamon and dried fruit
sukuti	spicy nibble of dried roasted meat
tama	traditional Nepali soup made from dried bamboo shoots
tawkhaa	a jelly of curried meat, served cold
wo	lentil-flour pancake

The Nepali word to eat *(khanu)* also doubles as the verb 'to drink' and 'to smoke'.

TIBETAN DISHES

gacok	a hotpot extravaganza named for the pot it's cooked in, normally for a minimum of two or three people; order an hour or two in advance
kothey (kothe)	fried *momos*
momo	meat or vegetables wrapped in dough and steamed; typical Tibetan dish similar to Chinese dim sum or Italian ravioli
phing	glass noodles, vermicelli
pingtsey	wontons
richotse	momos in soup
sha-bhalay (sya-bhakley)	meat in a deep-fried pancake or pastie
shabrel	meat balls
talumein	egg noodle soup
thentuk	similar to *thugpa* but with noodle squares
thugpa	traditional thick Tibetan meat soup
tsampa	ground roasted barley, mixed with tea, water or milk and eaten dry either instead of rice or mixed with it; a staple dish in the hill country
tserel	vegetable balls

In rural areas Nepalis often greet each other with *khaanaa khaiyo?* – have you eaten yet?

INDIAN DISHES

bhaji	vegetable fritter
biryani	steamed rice with meat or vegetables

channa masala	chickpea curry
chicken tikka	skewered chunks of marinated chicken, often displayed with a noticeable lack of refrigeration in restaurant windows
korma	curry-like braised dish, often quite sweet
makani	any dish cooked with butter, often daal or chicken
malai kofta	vegetable dish of potato and nut dumplings in a rich gravy
matter paneer	unfermented cheese with peas
nan	baked bread
palak paneer	unfermented cheese with spinach in a gravy
pakora	fried vegetables in batter
pilau	rice cooked in stock and flavoured with spices
rogan josh	Kashmiri lamb curry
samosa	pyramid-shaped, deep-fried and potato-filled pasties

Food Glossary

alu	potato
badam	peanut
bhanta	eggplant
bhaat	cooked rice
dahi	yogurt
daal	lentils
dudh	milk
gobi	cauliflower
kerah	banana
kukhara	chicken
khasi	mutton
maachha	fish
masu	meat
murgh	chicken
phul	egg
ram toriya	okra (lady's finger)
roti	bread
sag	spinach
tarkari	vegetable

DRINKS

(chiso) biyar	(cold) beer
chini	sugar
chiya	tea
sodamah kagati	lemon soda
tato panimah kagati	hot lemon
umaahleko pani	boiled water

Kathmandu

For many people, stepping off a plane into Kathmandu is an exhilarating shock – the sights, sounds and smells can quickly lead to sensory overload. Whether it be buzzing around the crazy polluted traffic in a taxi, trundling down the narrow winding streets of the old town in a rickshaw, marvelling at Durbar Sq or dodging the tiger balm sellers and trekking touts in Thamel, Kathmandu can be an intoxicating, amazing and exhausting place.

As the largest (and pretty much the only) city in the country, Kathmandu also feels like another developing-world city rushing into a modern era of concrete and traffic pollution. Take a walk in the backstreets, however, and the capital's amazing cultural and artistic heritage reveals itself in hidden temples overflowing with marigolds, courtyards full of drying chillis and rice, and tiny hobbit-sized workshops largely unchanged since the Middle Ages.

Kathmandu has been a travellers mecca since the 1960s but these days you're less likely to see a tie-dyed hippy in search of enlightenment than a well-heeled Gore-Tex–clad tourist in search of a good espresso. With tourist numbers down and political tensions up, the last few years have been uncertain, yet residents have retained a good-humoured self-respect.

Kathmandu is well worth a week of your time, but it's too easy to spend too much time stuck in touristy Thamel. Enjoy the Internet cafés, the Western music and the lemon cheesecake, but make sure you also get out into the 'real Nepal', before your time runs out.

HIGHLIGHTS

- Stroll around Kathmandu's medieval-like **old town** (p131) and soak up its atmosphere
- Appreciate the amazing architectural monuments of **Durbar Square** (p114), an artistic and architectural tradition that rivals anything you'll find in the great cities of Europe
- Dine in one of the city's superb **Newari restaurants** (p147), with the accompaniment of traditional dances
- **Shop** (p153) till you drop in Thamel for cut-price CDs, books, backpacks, carpets and handicrafts
- Chill out in one of Thamel's rooftop garden **restaurants** (p145), with a good book and a slice of chocolate cake
- Take day trips out to the nearby Unesco World Heritage Sites of **Swayambhunath** (p162), **Pashupatinath** (p166), **Bodhnath** (p169) and **Patan** (p184)

Thamel ★
★ Old Town
★ Durbar Square

| ▪ AREA CODE: ☎ 01 | ▪ POPULATION: 740,000 | ▪ ELEVATION: 1337M |

KATHMANDU IN...

Two Days
Start off with the two-hour **walking tour** (p129) south from Thamel to Durbar Sq. Grab lunch overlooking Basantapur Sq or in nearby **Freak St** (p149) and then spend the afternoon taking in the grandeur of **Durbar Square** (p114). Finish the day with a cold beer and dinner in Thamel.
     Next day walk out to **Swayambhunath** (p162) in the morning and spend the afternoon **shopping** (p153) in Thamel. For your final meal splurge at one of the blowout Newari restaurants like **Bhojan Griha** or **Nepali Chulo** (see p147).

Four Days
If you have an extra couple of days, take a short taxi ride out to **Patan** (p184) for a full day exploring its **Durbar Square, Patan Museum** (the best in the country) and more fascinating backstreets.
     After an early lunch on day four, take a taxi to **Pashupatinath** (p166) and then make the short walk out to **Bodhnath** (p169) to soak up some Tibetan culture as the sun sets.
     If you are in town on Friday, splurge on the Friday barbeque at **Dwarika's** (p150).

One Week
With a week up your sleeve you can spend a day at **Bhaktapur** (p196). At the beginning of the week sign up for a two-day **rafting** (p89) or **canyoning** (p78) trip up at **Borderlands** or **The Last Resort**. When stress levels build, fit in some quiet time at the delightful **Garden of Dreams** (p126).
     Seven days gives you the chance to gorge on Thai (Krua Thai), Indian (Third Eye), Japanese (Koto), South Indian *dosas* (Dudh Sagar), yak steak (Everest Steak House), felafel (Nargila's) and maybe even some Nepali food! Don't get me started on lunch...

HISTORY

The history of Kathmandu is really a history of the Newar people, the main inhabitants of the Kathmandu Valley. While the documented history of the valley goes back to the Kiratis, around the 7th century BC, the foundation of Kathmandu itself dates from the 12th century AD, during the time of the Malla dynasty.

The original settlements, in what is the southern half of the old town, grew up around the trade route to Tibet and in early pilgrim resthouses such as the Kasthamandap, which later lent its name to the city.

Originally known as Kantipur, the city flourished during the Malla era, and the bulk of its superb temples, buildings and other monuments date from this time. Initially, Kathmandu was an independent city within the valley, but in the 14th century the valley was united under the rule of the Malla king of Bhaktapur. The 15th century saw division once more, this time into the three independent kingdoms of Kathmandu, Patan and Bhaktapur. Rivalry between the three city-states led to a series of wars that left each state weakened and

vulnerable to the 1768 invasion of the valley by Prithvi Narayan Shah.

The ensuing Shah dynasty unified Nepal and made the expanded city of Kathmandu its new capital – a position the city has held ever since.

ORIENTATION

The most interesting part of Kathmandu is the crowded backstreets of the rectangular-shaped old town. This is bordered to the north by the main tourist and backpacker district of Thamel (pronounced Tha-*MEL*) and to the east by the sprawling modern new town. Thamel is bursting with hundreds of hotels, restaurants, Internet cafés, travel agencies and shops that can be rivalled only by Bangkok's Khao San Rd.

In the centre of the old town is the historic Durbar Sq and Hanuman Dhoka (old Royal Palace). Freak St, the focus of Kathmandu's overland scene during the hippie era, runs south from here. Thamel is 15 or 20 minutes' walk north from Durbar Sq.

Running east from Durbar Sq is New Rd, constructed after the great earthquake of 1934, and one of the main shopping streets

KATHMANDU

KATHMANDU

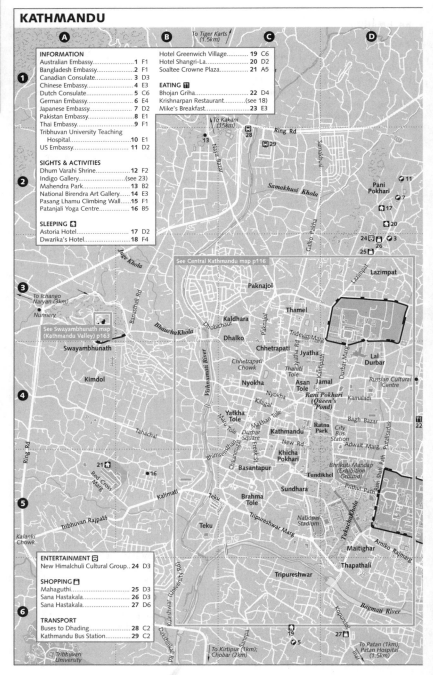

INFORMATION
Australian Embassy.....................1 F1
Bangladesh Embassy...................2 F1
Canadian Consulate....................3 D3
Chinese Embassy........................4 E3
Dutch Consulate.........................5 C6
German Embassy.........................6 E4
Japanese Embassy.......................7 D2
Pakistan Embassy........................8 E1
Thai Embassy..............................9 F1
Tribhuvan University Teaching
    Hospital................................10 E1
US Embassy...............................11 D2

SIGHTS & ACTIVITIES
Dhum Varahi Shrine..................12 F2
Indigo Gallery.........................(see 23)
Mahendra Park.........................13 B2
National Birendra Art Gallery.....14 E3
Pasang Lhamu Climbing Wall...15 F1
Patanjali Yoga Centre...............16 B5

SLEEPING
Astoria Hotel............................17 D2
Dwarika's Hotel........................18 F4

Hotel Greenwich Village............19 C6
Hotel Shangri-La.......................20 D2
Soaltee Crowne Plaza...............21 A5

EATING
Bhojan Griha.............................22 D4
Krishnarpan Restaurant...........(see 18)
Mike's Breakfast.......................23 E3

ENTERTAINMENT
New Himalchuli Cultural Group..24 D3

SHOPPING
Mahaguthi...............................25 D3
Sana Hastakala........................26 D3
Sana Hastakala........................27 D6

TRANSPORT
Buses to Dhading.....................28 C2
Kathmandu Bus Station.............29 C2

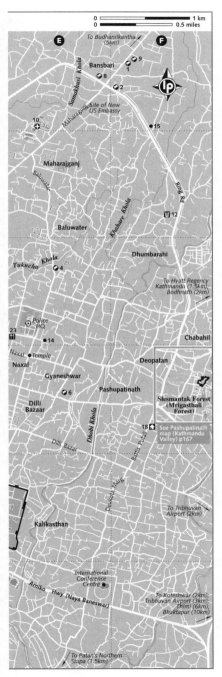

in town. At the eastern end are the offices of Royal Nepal Airlines (RNAC). South of the junction of New Rd and Kantipath is the main post office and Sundhara district, easily located by the minaret-like Bhimsen Tower.

The street known as Kantipath forms the boundary between the older and newer parts of the city. On the east side of Kantipath is a large, open parade ground known as Tundikhel, and on the eastern edge of this is the City (Ratna Park) bus station, for buses around the Kathmandu Valley.

North of the Tundikhel is Durbar Marg, a wide street flanked by airline offices, restaurants and expensive hotels, and at its northern end is the New Royal Palace. Further north are the embassy and NGO districts of Lazimpat and Maharajganj. To the south of town is Patan (see p184), an historically distinct city, which has now partially merged with Kathmandu's southern sprawl.

Both Kathmandu and Patan are encircled by the Ring Rd. On this road in the north of the city is the main Kathmandu bus station and on the eastern edge is Tribhuvan Airport.

Addresses

In old Kathmandu, streets are only named after their district, or *tole*. The names of these districts, squares, and other landmarks (perhaps a monastery or temple) form the closest thing to an address. For example, the address of everyone living within a 100m radius of Thahiti Tole is Thahiti Tole. 'Thamel' is now used to describe a sprawling area with at least a dozen roads and several hundred hotels and restaurants.

Outside the old town, the government made an arbitrary decision to name the main streets but most people (especially taxi drivers, who are often from outside the capital) have never heard of these newly created names.

Given this anarchic approach it is amazing that any mail gets delivered – it does, but slowly. Most businesses have post office boxes. If you're trying to find a particular house, shop or business, make sure you get detailed directions.

INFORMATION
Bookshops

Kathmandu has excellent bookshops with a great selection of Himalayan titles, including books that are not usually avail-able outside the country. Prices for new books are generally 30% cheaper than their home-market prices, and there are plenty of second-hand books for sale and trade. Most dealers will buy back books for 50% of what you paid.

Barnes & Noble Bookhouse (Map p136; Thamel)

Bookworld (Map p136; Tridevi Marg)

Mandala Bookpoint (Map p136; Kantipath) Excellent selection, with a good range in French and German.

Nepal Book Depot (Map p136; Thamel) Some of the best prices.

New Tibet Book Store (Map p136; ☎ 4415788; Tridevi Marg) The best collection of Tibet-related titles but few discounts.

Pilgrims Book House (Map p136; ☎ 4424942; www .pilgrimsbooks.com) A couple of doors north of the Kathmandu Guest House; the best in town and particularly strong on antiquarian travelogues, though it's pricier than the competition. There are a couple of smaller branches around town.

United Books (Map p136; Thamel) Well-chosen selection and sensible prices, run by Danish Lars.

Walden Book House (Map p136; Chhetrapati)

Cultural Centres

Alliance Française (Map p116; ☎ 4241163; www.alli ancefrancaise.org.np; Ganeshman Singh Path, Tripureshwar) French publications and French film screenings once a month, in southern Kathmandu.

British Council (Map p116; ☎ 4410798; www.british council.org/nepal; Lainchhaur; ☒ 8.30am-5.45pm Mon-Fri, 10am-4pm Sat) You'll have to become a member (Rs 800 per year, one photo and ID required) to use this library, but nostalgic Brits can get a cheap cup of tea at the attached Tibetan café and leaf through British newspapers.

Emergency

Ambulance service (☎ 4521048) Provided by Patan Hospital.

Fire Brigade (☎ 101, 4221177)

Police (Map p115; ☎ 100, 4223011; Durbar Sq)

Red Cross Ambulance (☎ 4228094)

Tourist Police Bhrikuti Mandap (☎ 4247041); Thamel (☎ 4700750) There's a tourist booth in Durbar Sq (see map p115).

Immigration Office/Visa Extensions

Central Immigration Office (Map p116; ☎ 4223590, 42236817; www.immi.gov.np; Bhrikuti Mandap; ☒ 10am-5pm Sun-Fri, 11am-4pm Sat & public holidays) next to the central Tourism Directorate, home of the Tourist Service Centre, this offers relatively painless visa extensions of 30 days.

Get a form, join the queue, supply one photo and then join a separate queue to pay the US$30 fee (in rupees). If you apply before 2pm you should get your passport back the same day at 3.30pm. See p375 for more on visa extensions.

Internet Access

Email is widely available in Thamel and elsewhere in Kathmandu. The best cyber-cafés have scanners and printers (Rs 10 per page) plus power backup. Connection speeds are generally fast and the rates are cheap, from Rs 15 per hour in a backstreet dive to Rs 40 at the more obvious locations such as Cybernet Cafe in central Thamel. For less than an hour's use you'll end up with a higher per-minute rate.

If you have your own laptop you can get free wireless Internet access during the day at the New Orleans Café (see p148).

Laundry

Several laundries across Thamel will ma-chine wash laundry for Rs 50 per kilo. Get it back the next day or pay double for a three-hour service. Amazingly, it all comes back smelling sweeter than you thought possible, even after a three-week trek.

Left Luggage

Any hotel will hold your luggage free of charge.

Libraries

Kaiser Library (Map p136; ☎ 4411318; Ministry of Education & Sports compound, cnr Kantipath & Tridevi Marg; ☒ 10am-5pm Sun-Thu, 10am-3pm Fri) Also known as the Kesar Library, this place is definitely worth a visit. The main reading room has antique globes, a stuffed tiger and suits of armour that you expect to spring to life at any moment. The library has a remarkable collection of antique travel books, with Nepal titles on the upper floor.

Media

Travellers' Nepal and *Nepal Traveller* are good-quality, free monthly magazines that cover a broad range of topics and have a section of practical information.

Thamel Time Out is the kind of flagrant copyright violation that is par for the course in Thamel but it has a map and some useful information.

You can find these magazines sporadi-cally at most hotels and restaurants.

Medical Services

Bir Hospital (Map p116; ☎ 4221119) Government hospital where terminally ill Nepalis come to die; not recommended.

CIWEC Clinic (Map p116; ☎ 4424111; www.ciwec-clinic .com; ☺ 9am–noon & 1–4pm Mon–Fri) Just across from the British Embassy, to the northeast of Thamel and used by many foreign residents. It has operated since 1982 and has developed an international reputation for research into travellers' medical problems. The clinic is staffed mostly by foreigners and a doctor is on call around the clock. A consultation costs around US$45. Credit cards are accepted and they are used to dealing with insurance claims.

CIWEC Dental Clinic (Map p116; ☎ 4440100; ciwec dental@subisu.net.np) US dentist on the top floor of CIWEC Clinic (see above). A consultation costs around US$35.

Nepal International Clinic (Map p116; ☎ 4434642, 4435357; www.nepalinternationalclinic.com; ☺ 9am–1pm & 2–5pm) Just south of the new Royal Palace, east of Thamel. It has an excellent reputation and is slightly cheaper than the CIWEC clinic. A consultation costs about US$40 (US$50 at weekends). Credit cards accepted.

NORVIC Hospital (Map p116; ☎ 4258554; www.norvic hospital; Thapathali) Private Nepali hospital with a good reputation for cardiology.

Patan Hospital (Map p184; ☎ 5522266) Probably the best hospital in the Kathmandu Valley, in the Lagankhel district of Patan. Partly staffed by Western missionaries.

Tribhuvan University Teaching Hospital (Map pp110–11; ☎ 4412808, 4412363; Maharagunj) Reasonably well equipped (and carrying a ventilator), northeast of the centre.

Money

It is worth checking banks' exchange rates and commission – both vary. There are also dozens of licensed moneychangers in Thamel. Their hours are longer than those of the banks (until 8pm, later if things are busy), and rates are pretty consistent, though slightly lower than the banks. See p368 for information on exchange rates, commissions and transfers.

Himalaya Bank (Map p136; ☎ 4250208; Tridevi Marg; ☺ 10am–7.30pm Sun–Fri) The most convenient bank for travellers staying in Thamel is this small branch, opposite the Three Goddesses (Tridevi) Temples. You can change cash (no commission) and travellers cheques (commission of 0.75%, minimum Rs 150), get cash advances on a Visa card and access their ATM here.

Nepal Bank Ltd (Map p116; ☎ 4221185; ☺ 7am–7pm) The main branch on Dharma Path near New Rd is handy if you're staying in Freak St; has long opening hours.

Sita World Travel (Map p136; ☎ 4248556; wu@sitanepal.com; www.sitanepal.com; ☺ 9am–6pm Sun–Fri, 9am–1pm Sat; Tridevi Marg) One of hundreds of local agents for Western Union money transfers and the closest to Thamel.

Standard Chartered Bank (Map p136; ☎ 4228474; Kantipath; ☺ 9.45am–7pm Sun–Thu, 9.45am–4.30pm Fri, 9.30am–12.30pm Sat & holidays) Has an ATM for credit-card withdrawals. It has a 1.5% charge (minimum Rs 200) for changing travellers cheques and Rs 200 per transaction for cash. There's no charge for a rupee cash advance on a credit card but you pay 2% to get the cash in US dollars. There are two more Standard Chartered ATMs in Thamel – opposite the Third Eye Restaurant and in the compound of the Kathmandu Guest House – and others on New Rd, Durbar Marg and a couple of other locations around Kathmandu.

Yeti Travels (Map p116; ☎ 4221234; yeti@vishnu.ccsl .com.np; ☺ 10am–4pm Mon–Fri) American Express (AmEx) agent, which has its office just off the southern end of Durbar Marg. It provides AmEx cash advances, purchase and encashment of travellers cheques, and client mail services.

Post

Most bookshops in Thamel, including Pilgrims Book House (opposite), sell stamps and deliver postcards to the post office, which is much easier than making a special trip to the post office yourself. Pilgrims charges a 10% commission for this service.

Everest Postal Care (Map p136; ☎ 4417913; Tridevi Marg; ☺ 9.30am–5.30pm Sun–Fri) Convenient private post office near Thamel, which posts letters and parcels at the same rates as the post office.

General post office (Map p116; Sundhara; ☺ 7am–6pm Sun–Thu, 7am–3pm Fri) Close to the Bhimsen Tower. Stalls in the courtyard sell air mail and padded envelopes. Poste restante is here. Get stamps at counter 10. You can post packages up to 2kg at counter 18; beyond that you need to go to the foreign post office.

Foreign post office (Map p116; Sundhara; ☺ 10am–5pm Sun–Fri) Parcels can be sent from here, in a separate building just north of the main post office. Parcels have to be examined and sealed by a customs officer and then packed in an approved manner. Start the process before 2pm.

Sending parcels from the foreign post office is something of a procedure, so if you're short of time you're best off using a cargo agency like **Diki Continental Exports** (Map p136; ☎ 4256919; JP School Rd, Thamel; www.dikiexports .com).

Courier agencies include:

DHL Kamaladi (Map p116; ☎ 4496248); Thamel (Map p136; ☎ 2012221; ☺ 11am–7pm Sun–Fri)

FedEx (Map p136; ☎ 4269248; www.fedex.com/np; Kantipath; ☺ 9am–6pm Sun–Fri, 9am–1pm Sat)

KATHMANDU

Telephone

You can make international telephone calls and send faxes from any of the dozens of 'communication centres' in Thamel and elsewhere throughout the city.

Many of the communication centres offer Internet phone calls. The cheapest places charge around Rs 20 per minute, with some places as low as Rs 10 per minute to the US. See p373 for more information.

Tourist Information

There are a number of good notice boards in Thamel that are worth checking for information on apartments, travel and trekking partners, courses and cultural events. The Kathmandu Guest House has a good notice board, as do the Pumpernickel Bakery and Fire & Ice Restaurant.

For Kathmandu-based offices that offer trekking-related information see p331.

Kathmandu Environmental Education Project (KEEP; Map p136; ☎ 4216775; www.keepnepal.org; ✆ 10am-5pm Sun-Fri) A good place for trekking reports, occasional lectures, a small collection of reference books, a café and a mineral-water refill service (Rs 10 per litre). They also sell biodegradable travel products such as anti-leech oil (Rs 80) and fair trade beeswax lip balm, as well as water purification tablets (Rs 500). Leave your shoes outside.

Tourist office (☎ 4470537) In the international terminal at the airport; usually dishes out a handy free map to arriving passengers who ask for it.

Tourist Service Centre (Map p116; ☎ 4256909, 24hr tourism hotline ☎ 4225709; Bhrikuti Mandap; ✆ 9am-1pm, 2-5pm Sun-Fri) On the eastern side of the Tundikhel parade ground, the center has a few brochures and maps but the location of the office is inconvenient.

Travel Agencies

Kathmandu has a great number of travel agencies, particularly along Durbar Marg, Kantipath and in Thamel. See p327 for details of local trekking agencies.

Wayfarers (Map p136; ☎ 4266010; www.wayfarers .com.np;Thamel; ✆ 9am-7pm Mon-Fri, 9am-5pm Sat & Sun) For straight-talking travel and ticketing (particularly international air tickets) this is the place. The staff also book domestic Indian air and train tickets and offer Kathmandu Valley walking trips (see p162).

DANGERS & ANNOYANCES

Kathmandu is frequently the focus of political demonstrations, strikes and even occasional curfews. These generally just affect transport but they can turn violent so are best avoided. *Bandh*s (strikes) paralyse the city every now and then, closing shops and shutting down transport. See p360.

The main annoyances in Thamel are the crazy motorcyclists and the limpet-like hash/tiger balm/chess set sellers.

For details of Thamel's gem scams see p360.

SIGHTS

Most of the interesting things to see in Kathmandu are clustered in the old part of town, focused around the majestic Durbar Sq and its surrounding backstreets.

Durbar Square

Kathmandu's **Durbar Square** (Map p115; admission foreigner/SAARC/Nepali Rs 200/25/free, no student tickets) was where the city's kings were once crowned and legitimised, and from where they ruled (*durbar* means 'palace'). As such, the square remains the traditional heart of the old town and Kathmandu's most spectacular legacy of traditional architecture, even thought the king no longer lives in the Hanuman Dhoka – the palace was moved north to Narayanhiti about a century ago.

It's easy to spend hours wandering around the square and watching the world go by from the terraced platforms of the towering Maju Deval; it's a wonderful way to get a feel for the city. Although most of the square dates from the 17th and 18th centuries (and many of the original buildings are much older), a great deal of damage was caused by the great earthquake of 1934 and many were rebuilt, not always in their original form. The entire square was designated a Unesco World Heritage Monument in 1979.

The Durbar Sq area is actually made up of three loosely linked squares. To the south is the open Basantapur Sq area, off which runs Freak St. The main Durbar Sq area, with its popular watch-the-world-go-by temples, is to the west. Running northeast is a second part of Durbar Sq, which contains the entrance to the Hanuman Dhoka and an assortment of temples. From this open area Makhan Tole, at one time the main road in Kathmandu and still the most interesting street to walk down, continues northeast.

A good place to start an exploration of the square is with what may well be the oldest building in the valley, the unprepossessing Kasthamandap.

INFORMATION

The entry ticket to Durbar Sq is valid only for the date stamped. If you want a longer duration you need to go to the **site office** (Map p115; ☎ 4268969; ⊙ 7am-7pm), on the south side of Basantapur Sq, to get a free visitor pass, which allows you access for as long as your visa is valid. You will need your passport and one photo and the process takes about two minutes. You generally need to show your ticket even if you are just transiting the square to New Rd or Freak St.

There is a toilet near the site office.

KASTHAMANDAP

Kathmandu owes its name to the **Kasthamandap** (Pavilion of Wood; Map p115). Although

its history is uncertain, local tradition says the three-roofed building was constructed around the 12th century from the wood of a single sal tree. It first served as a community centre where visitors gathered before major ceremonies (a *mandap* is a 16-pillared pilgrim shelter), but later it was converted to a temple dedicated to Gorakhnath, a 13th-century ascetic who was subsequently linked to the royal family. The last disciples were kicked out in the 1960s.

A central wooden enclosure houses the image of the god, which is noteworthy since Gorakhnath is mostly represented only by his footprints. In the corners of the building are four images of Ganesh. Hindu epics are illustrated around the corner platforms.

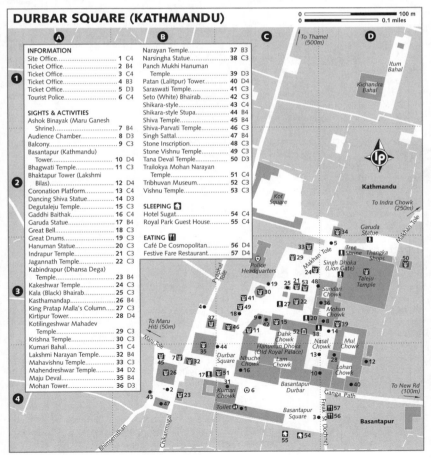

DURBAR SQUARE (KATHMANDU)

INFORMATION
Site Office................................. 1 C4
Ticket Office............................. 2 B4
Ticket Office............................. 3 C4
Ticket Office............................. 4 B3
Ticket Office............................. 5 D3
Tourist Police............................ 6 C4

SIGHTS & ACTIVITIES
Ashok Binayak (Maru Ganesh
Shrine)...................................... 7 B4
Audience Chamber.................... 8 D3
Balcony....................................... 9 C3
Basantapur (Kathmandu)
Tower... 10 D4
Bhagwati Temple..................... 11 C3
Bhaktapur Tower (Lakshmi
Bilas)... 12 D4
Coronation Platform................. 13 C4
Dancing Shiva Statue............... 14 C3
Degutaleju Temple.................... 15 C4
Gaddhi Baithak.......................... 16 C4
Garuda Statue............................ 17 B4
Great Bell.................................... 18 C3
Great Drums............................... 19 C3
Hanuman Statue........................ 20 C3
Indrapur Temple........................ 21 C3
Jagannath Temple..................... 22 C3
Kabindrapur (Dhansa Dega)
Temple.. 23 B4
Kakeshwar Temple.................... 24 C3
Kala (Black) Bhairab................. 25 C3
Kasthamandap........................... 26 B4
King Pratap Malla's Column..... 27 C3
Kirtipur Tower............................ 28 D4
Kotilingeshwar Mahadev
Temple.. 29 C3
Krishna Temple.......................... 30 C3
Kumari Bahal.............................. 31 C4
Lakshmi Narayan Temple......... 32 B4
Mahavishnu Temple.................. 33 C3
Mahendreshwar Temple........... 34 D2
Maju Deval................................. 35 B4
Mohan Tower............................. 36 D3

Narayan Temple........................ 37 B3
Narsingha Statue....................... 38 C3
Panch Mukhi Hanuman
Temple.. 39 D3
Patan (Lalitpur) Tower.............. 40 D4
Saraswati Temple...................... 41 C3
Seto (White) Bhairab................ 42 C3
Shikara-style.............................. 43 C4
Shikara-style Stupa................... 44 B4
Shiva Temple.............................. 45 B4
Shiva-Parvati Temple................ 46 C3
Singh Sattal................................ 47 B4
Stone Inscription....................... 48 C3
Stone Vishnu Temple................ 49 C3
Tana Deval Temple.................... 50 D3
Trailokya Mohan Narayan
Temple.. 51 C4
Tribhuvan Museum.................... 52 C4
Vishnu Temple........................... 53 C3

SLEEPING 🛏
Hotel Sugat................................ 54 C4
Royal Park Guest House........... 55 C4

EATING 🍴
Café De Cosmopolitan.............. 56 D4
Festive Fare Restaurant............ 57 D4

KATHMANDU

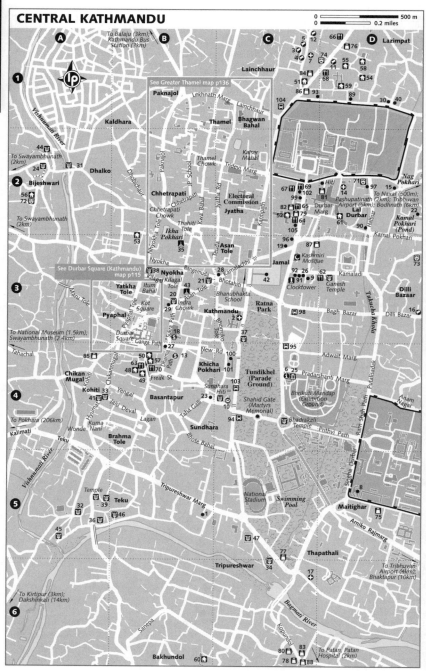

CENTRAL KATHMANDU

0 ———— 500 m
0 ———— 0.2 miles

To Balaju (3km);
Kathmandu Bus
Station (3km)

Lazimpat

Lainchhaur

Yashmandi River

To Swayambhunath
(2km)

Dhalko

Kaldhara

Paknajol

Lekhnath Marg

Lainchhaur

See Greater Thamel map p136

Thamel

Bhagwan
Bahal

Bijeshwari

Thamel
Chowk

Kaiser
Mahal

To Swayambhunath
(2km)

Chhetrapati

Paknajol

Chhetrapati
Chowk

Thamel
Chowk

Tridevi Marg

Electoral
Commission

Jyatha

Ikha
Pokhari

Thahiti
Tole

Asan
Tole

Nag
Pokhari

Hiti

Durbar
Marg

Lal
Durbar

Pashupatinath (2km); Tribhuvan
Airport (5km); Bodhnath (6km)

To Naxal (500m);

Kamal
Pokhari
(Pond)

Kamal Pokhari

Kashmiri
Mosque

Jamal

Nyokha

Bangemuda

Bhotahiti

Kamaladi

Dilli
Bazaar

See Durbar Square (Kathmandu)
map p115

Yatkha
Tole

Nyokha

Kilagal
Tole

Itum
Bahal

Asan Tole

Bhanubhakta
School

Ratna
Park

Ganesh
Temple

Clocktower

Dilli Bazar

Takucha Khola

Manu Tole

Pyaphal

Kot
Square

Indra
Chowk

Kathmandu

Bagh Bazar

To National Museum (1.5km);
Swayambhunath (2.4km)

Durbar
Square

Ganga Path

New Rd

Khicha
Pokhari

Tundikhel
(Parade
Ground)

Adwait Marg

Prashanti Marg

Tahachal

Chikan
Mugal

Freak St

Kohiti

Basantapur

Sundhara
Hiti

Shahid Gate
(Martyrs'
Memorial)

Bhrikuti Mandap
(Exhibition
Ground)

Bhadrakali
Temple

Prithvi Path

Ram Shah Path

Putalisadak

Anam
Nagar

To Pokhara (206km)

Yengal

Jaisi Deval

Kuma
Nani

Wonde

Lagan

Sundhara

Maitighar

Kalimati

Teku

Brahma
Tole

Vishnumati River

Bhote Bahal

Tripureshwar Marg

National
Stadium

Swimming
Pool

Amiko Rajmarg

Temple

Teku

Snega Durbar

To Kirtipur (3km);
Dakshinkali (14km)

Saneega

Tripureshwar

Thapathali

To Tribhuvan
Airport (4km);
Bhaktapur (10km)

Bagmati River

Kopundol

Bakhundol

To Patan; Patan
Hospital (2km)

The squat, medieval-looking building is especially busy in the early morning hours when the valley's vegetable sellers set up shop and porters sit awaiting customers.

Across the square is the **Kabindrapur Temple** (Map p115) or Dhansa Dega, an ornate 17th-century performance pavilion which houses the god of music.

ASHOK BINAYAK

On the northern side of Kasthamandap, at the top of Maru Tole, stands the tiny golden **Ashok Binayak** (Map p115), or Maru Ganesh Shrine. The small size of this shrine

belies its importance, as this is one of the four most important Ganesh shrines in the valley. Ganesh is a much-loved god and there is a constant stream of visitors, helping themselves to the self-serve *tika* dispenser and then ringing the bells at the back. A visit to this shrine is thought to ensure safety on a forthcoming journey so make an offering here if you are headed on a trek.

It's uncertain how old the temple is, although its gilded roof was added in the 19th century. Look for the golden shrew (Ganesh's vehicle) opposite the temple.

KATHMANDU

MARU TOLE

This *tole* leads you away from Durbar Sq down to the Vishnumati River, where a foot-bridge continues the pathway to Swayam-bhunath (see p165). This was a busy street in the hippy era, but the famous pastry shops that gave it the nickname 'Pie Alley' have long gone. Just 30m from Durbar Sq down Maru Tole is Maru Hiti, one of the finest sunken water conduits in the city.

MAJU DEVAL

A pleasant half hour can easily be spent sitting on the steps of this Shiva temple. In fact the nine-stage ochre platform of the **Maju Deval** (Map p115) is probably the most popular meeting place in the city. From here you can watch the constant activity of fruit and vegetable hawkers, the comings and goings of taxis and rickshaws, and the flute and other souvenir sellers importun-ing tourists. The large, triple-roofed temple has erotic carvings on its roof struts and of-fers great views over the square and across the roofs of the city. Marigold sellers set up shop on the ground level.

The temple dates from 1690 and was built by the mother of Bhaktapur's King Bhupat-indra Malla. The temple has a well-known Shiva lingam (phallic symbol) inside. At the bottom of the **temple** (Map p115) stairway on the east side is a small temple to Kam Dev, a 'companion' of Shiva. It was built in the Indian *shikhara* style, with a tall corn-coblike spire.

TRAILOKYA MOHAN NARAYAN TEMPLE

The other temple standing in the open area of the square is the smaller five-roofed **Trailokya Mohan Narayan** (1680; Map p115). It is easily identified as a temple to Narayan/Vishnu by the fine Garuda kneeling before it. This huge Garuda figure was a later ad-dition, erected by King Prithvibendra Mal-la's widow soon after his death. Look for the Vaishnavite images on the carved roof struts and the window screens with their decoratively carved medallions. Dances de-picting the 10 incarnations of Vishnu are performed on the platform to the east of the temple during the Indra Jatra festival.

SHIVA-PARVATI TEMPLE

From the steps of the Maju Deval you can look across to the **Shiva-Parvati Temple** (Map p115), where the much-photographed im-ages of Shiva and his consort look out from the upstairs window on the comings and goings below them. The temple was built in the late 1700s by Bahadur Shah, the son of Prithvi Narayan Shah. Although the temple is not very old by Kathmandu standards, it

---

EROTIC ART

The most interesting woodcarving on Nepali temples is on the roof struts, or *tunala,* and on many temples these carvings include erotic scenes. These scenes are rarely the central carving on the strut, they're usually the smaller carving at the bottom of the strut, like a footnote to the larger image. Nor are the carvings sensuous and finely sculptured like those at Khajuraho and Konark in India. In Nepal the figures are often smaller and cruder, even cartoonlike.

The themes have a Tantric element, a clear connection to the intermingling of Tibetan Bud-dhist and Hindu beliefs in Nepal, but their real purpose is unclear. Are they simply a celebration of an important part of the life cycle? Are they a more explicit reference to Shiva's and Parvati's creative roles than the enigmatic lingams and yonis scattered around so many temples? Or are they supposed to play some sort of protective role for the temple? It's popularly rumoured that the goddess of lightning is a shy virgin who wouldn't dream of striking a temple with such goings-on, although that's probably more a tourist-guide tale than anything else.

Whatever the reason for their existence, these Tantric elements can be found on temples throughout the valley. Some temples reveal just the odd sly image while others are covered in the stuff. The activities range from straightforward exhibitionism to scenes of couples engaged in impressively athletic acts of intercourse. More exotic carvings include medieval *ménages à trois,* scenes of oral or anal intercourse or couplings with demons or animals.

The temples with the more interesting erotic carvings include Kathmandu's Jagannath Temple, Basantapur Tower and Ram Chandra Temple; Patan's Jagannarayan Temple; and Bhaktapur's Erotic Elephants and Pashupatinath temples.

KUMARI DEVI

Not only does Nepal have countless gods, goddesses, deities, Bodhisattvas, Buddhas, avatars (in-carnations of deities) and manifestations – which are worshipped and revered as statues, images, paintings and symbols – but it also has a real living goddess. The Kumari Devi is a young girl who lives in the building known as the Kumari Bahal, right beside Kathmandu's Durbar Square.

The practice of having a living goddess probably came about during the reign of Jaya Prakash Malla, the last of the Malla kings of Kathmandu, whose reign abruptly ended with the conquest of the valley by Prithvi Narayan Shah in 1768. As usual in Nepal, where there is never one simple answer to any question, there are a number of legends about the Kumari.

One such legend relates that a paedophile Malla king had intercourse with a prepubescent girl. She died as a result of this and in penance he started the practice of venerating a young girl as a living goddess. Another tells of a Malla king who regularly played dice with the goddess Taleju, the protective deity of the valley. When he made an unseemly advance she threatened to withdraw her protection, but relented and promised to return in the form of a young girl. Yet another tells of a young girl who was possessed by the goddess Durga and banished from the kingdom. When the furious queen heard of this she ordered her husband to bring the young girl back and keep her as a real goddess.

Whatever the background, in reality there are a number of living goddesses around the Kath-mandu Valley, although the Kumari Devi, or Royal Kumari, of Kathmandu is the most important. The Kumari is selected from a particular caste of Newari gold- and silversmiths. Customarily, she is somewhere between four years old and puberty and must meet 32 strict physical require-ments ranging from the colour of her eyes and shape of her teeth to the sound of her voice. Her horoscope must also be appropriate, of course.

Once suitable candidates have been found they are gathered together in a darkened room where terrifying noises are made, while men dance by in horrific masks and 108 gruesome buffalo heads are on display. Naturally these goings-on are unlikely to frighten a real goddess, particularly one who is an incarnation of Durga, so the young girl who remains calm and collected throughout this ordeal is clearly the new Kumari. In a process similar to the selection of the Dalai Lama, the Kumari then chooses items of clothing and decoration worn by her predecessor as a final test.

Once chosen as the Kumari Devi, the young girl moves into the Kumari Bahal with her fam-ily and makes only a half-dozen ceremonial forays into the outside world each year. The most spectacular of these occasions is the September Indra Jatra festival, when she travels through the city on a huge temple chariot over a three-day period. During this festival the Kumari cus-tomarily blesses the king of Nepal.

The Kumari's reign ends with her first period, or any serious accidental loss of blood. Once this first sign of puberty is reached she reverts to the status of a normal mortal, and the search must start for a new Kumari. During her time as a goddess the Kumari is supported by the temple income and on retirement she is paid a handsome dowry. It is said that marrying an ex-Kumari is unlucky, but it's believed more likely that taking on a spoilt ex-goddess is likely to be too much hard work!

For an account of the life of a kumari, check out *From Goddess to Mortal,* the story of Rashmilla Shakya, Kathmandu's kumari between 1984 and 1991. It's available in Kathmandu bookstores.

stands on a two-stage platform, which may have been an open dancing stage hundreds of years earlier. A **Narayan (Vishnu) temple** (Map p115) stands to the west side.

KUMARI BAHAL

At the junction of Durbar and Basantapur Sqs is a red brick, three-storey building with some incredibly intricate carved windows. This is the **Kumari Bahal** (House of the Living Goddess; Map p115), home to the Kumari, the girl who is selected to be the town's living goddess until she reaches puberty and re-verts to being a normal mortal! (See above). The building, in the style of the Buddhist *viharas* (monastic abodes) of the valley, was built in 1757 by Jaya Prakash Malla.

Inside the building is the three-storey courtyard, or Kumari Chowk. It is enclosed by magnificently carved wooden balconies and windows, making it quite possibly the most beautiful courtyard in Nepal. Photographing the goddess is forbidden, but you are quite free to photograph the courtyard when she is not present. The Kumari went on strike in 2005, refusing to appear at her window for tourists, after authorities denied her guardians' request for a 10% cut of the square's entry fees!

The courtyard contains a miniature stupa carrying the symbols of Saraswati, the goddess of learning. Non-Hindus are not allowed to go beyond the courtyard.

The big gate to the right of the Kumari Bahal conceals the huge chariot that transports the Kumari around the city during the annual Indra Jatra festival (see p134). Look for the huge wooden runners in front of the Kumari Bahal that are used to transport the chariot. The wood is considered sacred. You can see part of the chariot from the top of the nearby Trailokya Mohan Narayan Temple steps.

GADDHI BAITHAK

The eastern side of Durbar Sq is closed off by this white neoclassical **building** (Map p115), With its imported European style, it was built as part of the palace in 1908 during the Rana period and makes a strange contrast to the traditional Nepali architecture that dominates the square. It is said to have been modelled on London's National Gallery.

BHAGWATI TEMPLE

Next to the Gaddhi Baithak, this triple-storey, triple-roofed **temple** (Map p115) is easily missed since it surmounts the building below it, which currently has thangka shops along its front. The best view of the temple and its golden roofs is probably from the Maju Deval, across the square. The temple was built by Jagat Jaya Malla and originally had an image of Narayan. This image was stolen in 1766, so when Prithvi Narayan Shah conquered the valley two years later he simply substituted it with an image of the goddess Bhagwati. In April each year the image of the goddess is conveyed to the village of Nuwakot, 65km to the north, then returned a few days later.

GREAT BELL

On your left as you leave the main square along Makhan Tole is the **Great Bell** (Map p115), el-

evated atop a white building erected by Rana Bahadur Shah (son of Prithvi Narayan Shah) in 1797. The bell's ring drives off evil spirits, but it is only rung during puja (worship) at the **Degutaleju Temple** (Map p115).

Across from the great bell is a very ornate corner **balcony** (Map p115), decorated in gorgeous copper and ivory, from where members of the royal court could view the festival action taking place in Durbar Sq.

KRISHNA TEMPLE

The history of the octagonal **Krishna Temple** (Map p115) is well documented. It was built in 1648 by Pratap Malla, perhaps as a response to Siddhinarsingh's magnificent Krishna Temple in Patan. Inside there are images of Krishna and two goddesses, which, according to a Sanskrit inscription, are modelled on the king and his two wives. The temple also has a Newari inscription, but this neglects to mention the king's little act of vanity. The temple is a favourite of sadhus (itinerant holy men) who pose (and expect to be paid) for photos here.

GREAT DRUMS & KOT SQUARE

Just beyond the temple are the **Great Drums** (Map p115), to which a goat and a buffalo must be sacrificed twice a year. In front of these is the police headquarters building (currently sandbagged against possible Maoist attacks). Beyond here is the closed-off Kot Sq, where Jung Bahadur Rana perpetrated the famous 1846 massacre that led to a hundred years of Rana rule (see p33). *Kot* means 'armoury' or 'fort'. During the Dasain festival each year, blood again flows in Kot Sq as hundreds of buffaloes and goats are sacrificed. Young soldiers are supposed to lop off each head with a single blow.

KING PRATAP MALLA'S COLUMN

Across from the Krishna Temple is a host of smaller temples and other structures, all standing on a slightly raised platform in front of the Hanuman Dhoka and the towering Taleju Temple behind. The square stone pillar, known as the Pratap Dhvaja, is topped by a **statue** (Map p115) of the famous King Pratap Malla (1641–74), seated with folded hands and surrounded by his two wives and his five (including an infant) sons. He looks towards his private prayer room on the 3rd floor of the Degutaleju

Temple. The column was erected in 1670 by Pratap Malla and preceded the similar columns in Patan and Bhaktapur.

This area and its monuments are usually covered in hundreds if not thousands of pigeons, and you can buy packets of grain to feed them.

SETO (WHITE) BHAIRAB

Seto (White) Bhairab's horrible face is hidden away behind a grille opposite King Pratap Malla's column. The huge **mask** (Map p115) dates from 1794, during the reign of Rana Bahadur Shah, the third Shah dynasty king. Each September during the Indra Jatra festival the gates are opened to reveal the mask for a few days. At that time the face is covered in flowers and rice and at the start of the festivities beer is poured through the horrific mouth, as crowds of men fight to get a drink of the blessed brew (see p134). At other times of the year you can peek through the lattice to see the mask, which is used as the symbol of Royal Nepal Airlines.

JAGANNATH TEMPLE

This **temple** (Map p115), noted for the erotic carvings on its roof struts, is the oldest structure in this part of the square. Pratap Malla claimed to have constructed the temple during his reign, but it may actually date back to 1563, during the rule of Mahendra Malla. The temple has a three-tiered platform and two storeys. There are three doors on each side of the temple, but only the centre door opens.

DEGUTALEJU TEMPLE

This triple-roofed **temple** (Map p115) is actually part of the Hanuman Dhoka, surmounting the buildings below it, but is most easily seen from outside the palace walls. Degutaleju is another manifestation of the Malla's personal goddess Taleju. This temple was built by Shiva Singh Malla.

KALA (BLACK) BHAIRAB

Behind the Jagannath Temple is the figure of **Kala (Black) Bhairab** (Map p115). Bhairab is Shiva in his most fearsome aspect, and this huge stone image of the terrifying Kala Bhairab has six arms, wears a garland of skulls and tramples a corpse, which is symbolic of human ignorance. The figure is said to have been brought here by Pratap Malla,

having been found in a field to the north of the city. The image was originally cut from a single stone, but the upper left-hand corner has since been repaired. It is said that telling a lie while standing before Kala Bhairab will bring instant death and it was once used as a form of trial by ordeal.

INDRAPUR TEMPLE

Immediately to the east of the horrific Bhairab stands the mysterious **Indrapur Temple** (Map p115). This puzzling temple may be of great antiquity but has been renovated recently and little is known of its history. Even the god to which it is dedicated is controversial – the lingam inside indicates that it is a Shiva temple but the Garuda image half-buried on the southern side indicates that it is dedicated to Vishnu. To compound the puzzle, however, the temple's name clearly indicates it is dedicated to Indra! The temple's unadorned design and plain roof struts together with the lack of an identifying *torana* (pediment above the temple doors) offer no further clues.

KAKESHWAR TEMPLE

This **temple** (Map p115) was originally built in 1681 but, like so many other structures, was rebuilt after it was badly damaged in the 1934 earthquake. It may have been considerably altered at that time as the temple is a strange combination of styles. It starts with a Newari style floor, above which is an Indian *shikhara*-style upper storey, topped by a spire shaped like a *kalasa* (water vase), indicative of a female deity.

STONE INSCRIPTION

On the outside of the palace wall, opposite the **Vishnu Temple** (Map p115), is a long, low **stone inscription** (Map p115) to the goddess Kalika written in 15 languages, including one word of French. King Pratap Malla, renowned for his linguistic abilities, set up this inscription in 1664 and a Nepali legend tell that milk will flow from the spout in the middle if somebody is able to decipher all 15 languages!

KOTILINGESHWAR MAHADEV TEMPLE

This early Malla **temple** (Map p115) dates from the reign of Mahendra Malla in the 16th century. The three-stage plinth is topped by a temple in the *gumbhaj* style, which basically means a square structure topped by a bell-shaped dome. The bull facing the temple on the west side indicates that it is a Shiva temple. Next door is the **Mahavishnu Temple** (Map p115), which was damaged in the 1934 earthquake.

MAHENDRESHWAR TEMPLE

At the extreme northern end of the square, this **temple** (Map p115) dates from 1561, during the reign of Mahendra Malla. The temple was restored in 1963 and is dedicated to Shiva. A small image of Shiva's bull Nandi fronts the temple and at the northeastern corner there is an image of Kam Dev. The temple has a wide, two-level plinth and a spire topped by a golden umbrella.

TALEJU TEMPLE

The square's most magnificent **temple** (Map p115) stands at its northeastern extremity but is not open to the public. Even for Hindus entry is restricted; they can only visit it briefly during the annual Dasain festival.

The Taleju Temple was built in 1564 by Mahendra Malla. Taleju Bhawani was originally a goddess from the south of India, but she became the titular deity, or royal goddess, of the Malla kings in the 14th century. Taleju temples were erected in her honour in Patan and Bhaktapur, as well as in Kathmandu.

The temple stands on a 12-stage plinth and reaches more than 35m high, dominating the Durbar Square area. The eighth stage of the plinth forms a wall around the temple, in front of which are 12 miniature temples. Four more miniature temples stand inside the wall, which has four beautifully carved wide gates. If entry to the temple were permitted it could be reached from within the Hanuman Dhoka or from the Singh Dhoka (Lion Gate) facing Durbar Sq.

TANA DEVAL TEMPLE & MAKHAN TOLE

Directly across from the Taleju Temple is a 10th-century kneeling **Garuda statue** (Map p115), facing a small Vishnu Temple.

To your right, in a walled courtyard just past the long row of stalls, is the **Tana Deval Temple**, with three carved doorways and multiple struts, the latter of which show the multi-armed Ashta Matrikas (Mother Goddesses). It's possible to enter the temple. Nearby shops sell brightly-coloured Tibetan thangkas.

Crowded and fascinating **Makhan Tole** (*makhan* is the Nepali word for butter, *tole* means street) starts from here and runs towards the busy marketplace of Indra Chowk (see p125). Makhan Tole was at one time the main street in Kathmandu and the start of the main caravan route to Tibet.

From here you can either head south to visit the Hanuman Dhoka or continue northeast up Makhan Tole back towards Thamel.

Hanuman Dhoka

The inner palace complex of the **Hanuman Dhoka** (Map p115; admission foreigner/SAARC Rs 250/25; 9.30am-5pm Tue-Sun Feb-Oct, 9.30am-3pm Tue-Sun Nov-Jan) was originally founded during the Licchavi period, but as it stands today most of it was constructed by King Pratap Malla in the 17th century. The royal palace was renovated many times in later years. The oldest parts are the smaller Sundari Chowk and Mohan Chowk at the northern part of the palace (both closed). The complex originally housed 35 courtyards and spread as far as New Rd but the 1934 earthquake reduced the palace to today's 10 chowks (courtyards). Cameras are allowed only in the courtyards, not inside the buildings of the complex.

Hanuman's very brave assistance to the noble Rama during the exciting events of the Ramayana has led to the monkey god's appearance guarding many important entrances. Here, cloaked in red and sheltered by an umbrella, a **Hanuman statue** (Map p115) marks the *dhoka* (entrance) to the Hanuman Dhoka and has even given the palace its name. The statue dates from 1672 and the god's face has long disappeared under a coating of orange paste applied by generations of faithful visitors.

Standards bearing the double-triangle flag of Nepal flank the statue, while on each side of the palace gate are stone lions, one ridden by Shiva, the other by his wife Parvati. Above the gate a brightly painted niche is illustrated with a central figure of a ferocious Tantric version of Krishna. On the left side is the gentler Hindu Krishna in his traditional blue colour accompanied by two of his comely *gopi* (milkmaids). On the other side are King Pratap Malla and his queen.

NASAL CHOWK

From the entrance gate of the Hanuman Dhoka you immediately enter its most famous chowk. Although the courtyard was constructed in the Malla period, many of the buildings around the square are later Rana constructions. During that time Nasal Chowk was used for coronations, a practice that continues to this day on the **coronation platform** (Map p115) in the centre of the courtyard (the current King Gyanendra was crowned here in 2001). The nine-storey **Basantapur (Kathmandu) Tower** (Map p115) looms over the southern end of the courtyard.

The rectangular courtyard is aligned north–south and the entrance is at the northwestern corner. Just by the entrance there is a surprisingly small but beautifully carved doorway, which once led to the Malla kings' private quarters.

Beyond the door is the large **Narsingha Statue** (Map p115), Vishnu in his man-lion incarnation, in the act of disembowelling a demon. The stone image was erected by Pratap Malla in 1673 and the inscription on the pedestal explains that he placed it here for fear that he had offended Vishnu by dancing in a Narsingha costume. The Kabindrapur Temple in Durbar Sq was built for the same reason.

Next is the **Audience Chamber** (Map p115) of the Malla kings. The open veranda houses the Malla throne and contains portraits of the Shah kings. Images of the present king and queen dominate the eastern wall.

PANCH MUKHI HANUMAN TEMPLE

At the northeastern corner of the Nasal Chowk stands the **Panch Mukhi Hanuman** (Map p115) with its five circular roofs. Each of the valley towns has a five-storey temple, although it is the great Nyatapola Temple of Bhaktapur that is by far the best known. Hanuman is worshipped in the temple in Kathmandu, but only the priests of the temple may enter it.

DANCING SHIVA STATUE

In Nepali *nasal* means 'dancing one', and Nasal Chowk takes its name from this Shiva **statue** (Map p115) hidden in the whitewashed chamber on the eastern side of the square.

TRIBHUVAN MUSEUM

The part of the palace west of Nasal Chowk, overlooking the main Durbar Sq area, was constructed by the Ranas in the middle to late part of the 19th century. Ironically, it

is now home to a **museum** (Map p115) that celebrates King Tribhuvan (ruled 1911–55) and his successful revolt against their regime, along with memorials to Kings Mahendra (1955–72) and Birendra (1972–2001).

Exhibits with names such as 'the Royal Babyhood' include some fascinating re-creations of the foppish king's bedroom and study, with genuine personal effects that give quite an eerie insight into his life. Some of the exhibits, like the king's favourite stuffed bird (looking a bit worse for wear these days!), his boxing gloves, the walking stick with a spring-loaded sword hidden inside and his dusty, drained aquarium, add some surreal moments. There are several magnificent thrones, plenty of hunting photos and the obligatory coin collection.

Halfway through the museum you descend before ascending the steep stairways of the nine-storey **Basantapur Tower**, which was extensively restored prior to King Birendra's coronation. There are superb views over the palace and the city from the top. The struts along the facade of the Basantapur Tower, particularly those facing out to Basantapur Sq, are decorated with erotic carvings.

It's hard not to rush through the second half of the museum, full of dull press clippings about the rather Peter Sellers–looking King Mahendra, before glossing over the massacre of King Birendra by his son in 2001 (see the boxed text, p38). The museum exits into Lohan Chowk.

LOHAN CHOWK

King Prithvi Narayan Shah was involved in the construction of the four red-coloured towers around the Lohan Chowk. The towers represent the four ancient cities of the valley, the towers include the Kathmandu or Basantapur Tower; the Kirtipur Tower; the Bhaktapur Tower or Lakshmi Bilas; and the Patan or Lalitpur Tower.

OTHER CHOWKS

The palace's other courtyards are currently closed to visitors, but you can get glimpses of them from the Tribhuvan Museum and they might reopen at a future date.

North of Lohan Chowk, **Mul Chowk** was completely dedicated to religious functions within the palace and is configured like a *vihara*, with a two-storey building surrounding the courtyard. Mul Chowk is dedicated to Taleju Bhawani, the royal goddess of the Mallas, and sacrifices are made to her in the centre of the courtyard during the Dasain festival. A smaller Taleju temple stands in the southern wing of the square and the image of the goddess is moved here from the main temple during the Dasain festival.

North of Nasal Chowk is **Mohan Chowk**, the residential courtyard of the Malla kings. It dates from 1649 and at one time a Malla king had to be born here to be eligible to wear the crown. (The last Malla king, Jaya Prakash Malla, had great difficulties during his reign, even though he was the legitimate heir, because he was born elsewhere.) The golden waterspout, known as Sundhara, in the centre of the courtyard delivers water from Budhanilkantha in the north of the valley. The Malla kings would ritually bathe here each morning.

North of Durbar Square

Hidden in the bustling and fascinating backstreets north of Durbar Sq is a dense sprinkling of colourful temples, courtyards and shrines. The best way to get a feel for this district is on the walking tour 'From Thamel to Durbar Square' (see p129).

KATHESIMBHU STUPA

The most popular Tibetan pilgrimage site in the old town is this lovely **stupa** (Map p116), a small copy dating from around 1650 of the great Swayambhunath complex. Just as at Swayambhunath, there is a two-storey pagoda to Harti, the goddess of smallpox, right behind the main stupa. The entrance is flanked by metal lions atop red ochre concrete pillars, just a couple of minutes' walk south of Thamel.

Various statues and a few smaller *chaityas* (small stupas) stand around the temple, including a fine standing Avalokiteshvara statue enclosed in a glass case and protective metal cage in the northeast corner. Avalokiteshvara carries a lotus flower in his left hand, and the Dhyani Buddha Amitabha is seen in the centre of his crown.

ASAN TOLE

From dawn until late the junction of **Asan Tole** (Map p116) is jammed with buyers, sellers and passers-by, making it the busiest square in the city. Every day, produce is carried to this popular marketplace from all over the valley so it is fitting that the three-storey **Annapurna Temple** (Map p116) is dedicated to the goddess of abundance, Annapurna is represented by a *purana* bowl full of grain. At most times, but especially Sundays, you'll see locals walk around the shrine, touch a coin to their heads, throw it into the temple and ring the bell above them.

Nearby the two-storey **Ganesh shrine** (Map p116) is coated in bathroom tiles. South is the Yita Chapal (Southern Pavilion) which was once used for festival dances (the dance platform out front is still visible). Cat Stevens wrote his hippie-era song *Kathmandu* in a smoky teahouse in Asan Tole.

On the western side of the square are spice shops. Near the centre of the square is a small **Narayan shrine** (Narayan is a form of Vishnu).

SETO MACHHENDRANATH TEMPLE (JAN BAHAL)

Southwest of Asan Tole, this **temple** (Map p116) attracts both Buddhists and Hindus – Buddhists consider Seto (White) Machhendranath to be a form of Avalokiteshvara, while to Hindus he is a rain-bringing incarnation of Shiva. The temple's age is not known but it was restored during the 17th century. The arched entrance to the temple is marked by a small Buddha figure on a high stone pillar in front of two metal lions.

In the courtyard there are lots of small shrines, *chaityas* and statues, including a mysteriously European-looking female figure surrounded by candles who faces the temple. It may well have been an import from Europe that has simply been accepted into the pantheon of gods. Facing the other way, just in front of the temple, are two graceful bronze figures of the Taras seated atop tall pillars. Buy some grain to feed the pigeons and boost your karma.

Inside the temple you can see the white-faced image of the god covered in flowers. The image is taken out during the Seto Machhendranath festival in March/April each year and paraded around the city in a chariot, see opposite. You can follow the interior path that circles the central building.

In the courtyard you may see men standing around holding what looks like a bizarre string instrument. This tool is used to separate and fluff up the downlike cotton padding that is sold in bulk nearby.

SETO MACHHENDRANATH FESTIVAL

Kathmandu's Seto (White) Machhendra-nath festival kicks off a month prior to the much larger and more important Rato (Red) Machhendranath festival in Patan (see p191). The festival starts with removing the image of Seto Machhendranath from the temple at Kel Tole and placing it on a towering and creaky wooden temple chariot known as a *rath*. For the next four evenings, the chariot proceeds slowly from one historic location to another, eventually arriving at Lagan in the south of Kathmandu's old town. There the image is taken down from the chariot and carried back to its starting point in a palanquin while the chariot is disassembled and put away until next year.

The string is plucked by a wooden double-headed implement that looks like a cross between a dumbbell and a rolling pin.

As you leave the temple, to the left you'll see the small, triple-roofed **Lunchun Lunbun Ajima**, a Tantric temple that's red-tiled around the lower level and has some erotic carvings at the base of the struts at the back.

INDRA CHOWK

The busy street of Makhan Tole spills into Indra Chowk, the courtyard named after the ancient Vedic deity, Indra. On the right of the square is the **Akash Bhairab Temple** (Map p116), or Bhairab of the Sky Temple. From the balcony four metal lions rear out over the street. The temple's entrance is at the right-hand side of the building, guarded by two more metal lions, but non-Hindus cannot enter. The silver image inside is visible through the open windows from out in the street, and during important festivals, particularly Indra Jatra (September), the image is displayed in the square. A large lingam (phallic symbol) is also erected in the centre of the square at that time.

In a small niche just to the left of the Akash Bhairab Temple is a very small but much-visited brass Ganesh shrine.

Indra Chowk is traditionally a centre for the sale of blankets and cloth, and there are often many merchants on the platforms of the **Mahadev Temple**. The next door **Shiva Temple** is a smaller and simplified version of Patan's Krishna Temple.

ITUM BAHAL

The long, rectangular courtyard of the **Itum Bahal** (Map p115) is the largest Buddhist *bahal* (courtyard) in the old town and remains a haven of tranquillity in the chaotic surroundings. A small, white-painted stupa stands in the centre of the courtyard. On the western side of the courtyard is the **Kichandra Bahal** (Map p115) or 'Keshchandra Paravarta Mahar Bihar', one of the oldest *bahals* in the city, dating from 1381. A *chaitya* in front of the entrance has been completely shattered by a bodhi tree, which has grown right up through its centre. In autumn and winter the square is decorated in ornate swirling patterns of drying grain.

Inside the Kichandra Bahal is a central pagoda-like sanctuary, and to the south is a small *chaitya* decorated with graceful standing Bodhisattvas. On the northern side of the courtyard are four brass plaques mounted on the upper-storey wall. The one on the extreme left shows a demon known as Guru Mapa taking a misbehaving child from a woman and stuffing it greedily into his mouth. Eventually the demon was bought off with the promise of an annual feast of buffalo meat, and the plaque to the right shows him sitting down and dipping into a pot of food. With such a clear message on juvenile misbehaviour it is fitting that the courtyard houses a primary school – right under the Guru Mapa plaques!

To this day, every year during the festival of Holi the inhabitants of Itum Bahal sacrifice a buffalo to Guru Mapa on the banks of the Vishnumati River, cook it in the afternoon in the courtyard and in the middle of the night carry it in huge cauldrons to a tree in the Tundikhel parade ground where the demon is said to live.

NARA DEVI TEMPLE

Halfway between Chhetrapati and Durbar Sq, the **Nara Devi Temple** (Map p116) is dedicated to Kali, Shiva's destructive consort. It's also known as the Seto Kali (White Kali) Temple.

Although the temple, with its three tiers, golden roof and red and white guardian lions, is quite old, some of the decorations are clearly more recent additions. It is said that Kali's powers protected the temple from the 1934 earthquake, which destroyed so many other temples in the

KATHMANDU

valley. A Malla king once stipulated that a dancing ceremony should be held for the goddess every 12 years, and dances are still performed on the small dance platform that is across the road from the temple.

THREE GODDESSES TEMPLES
Next to the modern Sanchaya Kosh Bhawan Shopping Centre in Thamel is the often ignored **Three Goddesses Temples** (Map p136). The street on which the temples are located is named Tridevi Marg – *tri* means 'three' and *devi* means 'goddesses'. The goddesses are Dakshinkali, Manakamana and Jawalamai, and the roof struts have some creative erotic carvings.

GARDEN OF DREAMS
Just two minutes' walk, but a million miles from Thamel is the beautifully restored Swapna Bagaicha, or **Garden of Dreams** (Map p136), one of the most serene and beautiful enclaves in Kathmandu.

Field marshal Kaiser Shamser, whose palace the gardens complement, built the Garden of Dreams in the 1920s after a visit to several Edwardian estates in England, using funds won from his father in an epic Rs 100,000 game of cowrie shells. The gardens and its pavilions suffered neglect to the point of collapse before they were lovingly brought back to life over a six-year period by the same team that created the Patan Museum.

There are dozens of gorgeous details in the garden, including the original gate, a marble inscription from Omar Khayam's rubaiyat, the new fountains and ponds, and a quirky 'hidden garden' to the south. Of the original four acres and six pavilions (named after the six Nepali seasons), only 1.2 acres and three pavilions remain.

A café is due to open in the Basanta (Spring) Pavilion and you can expect the gardens to be a prime site for cultural events and exhibitions.

RANI POKHARI
This large fenced **tank** (Map p116) is said to have been built by King Pratap Malla in 1667 to console his queen over the death of their son (who was trampled by an elephant). The pool (*pokhari* means pool or small lake) was apparently used during the Malla era for trials by ordeal and later became a favourite suicide spot.

Perhaps because of the high suicide rate, the gate to the tank and its central Shiva Temple is unlocked only one day each year, during the festival of Tihar. The footbridge over the nearby chowk has the best views of Rani Pokhari. The chowk has rather optimistically been declared a no-horn zone!

Across Kantipath is a long imposing building originally known as the Durbar School, which was the first school in Nepal (1854). It has since been renamed the Bhanubhakta School, after the Nepali poet of that name.

East of Durbar Square
MAHAKALA TEMPLE
On the eastern side of Kantipath, just north of New Rd, the **Mahakala Temple** (Map p116) was very badly damaged in the 1934 earthquake and is now of little architectural merit. If you can see inside the darkened shrine you may be able to make out the 1.5m-high figure of Mahakala, the 'Great Black One', a particularly ferocious form of Shiva.

ETHNOGRAPHIC MUSEUM
If you have some time to kill while waiting for your visa extension, pop into the next-door tourism service centre and its **Ethnographic Museum** (Map p116; admission Rs 25; 🕙 10am-4pm Tue-Sun; Bhrikuti Mandap), which has a vaguely interesting collection of puppets, costumes and traditional crafts. There are grand plans (but no money as yet) to build a huge new ethnographic museum complex south of Kirtipur in the southern Kathmandu Valley.

South of Durbar Square
JAISI DEVAL TEMPLE
The south of Kathmandu's old city was the heart of the ancient city in the Licchavi period (4th to 9th centuries) and its major temple is the tall, triple-roofed **Jaisi Deval Temple** (Map p116), built just two years before Durbar Sq's famous Maju Deval (which is one platform higher). It's a Shiva temple, as indicated by the bull on the first few steps and the mildly erotic carvings on some of the temple struts. Right across the road from the temple is a stone lingam rising a good 2m from a yoni (female equivalent of a phallic symbol). This is definitely a god-sized phallic symbol and a prayer here is said to aid fertility.

In its procession around the town during the Indra Jatra festival (see p134), the Kumari Devi's chariot pauses here. During its stop, dances are held on the small dance platform across the road from the temple.

Southwest of the temple, enter the courtyard of the **Ram Chandra Temple** (Map p116), named after Ram, incarnation of Vishnu and the hero of the Hindu epic the Ramayana. This small temple is notable for the tiny erotic scenes on its roof struts; it looks as if the carver set out to illustrate 16 different positions, starting with the missionary position, and just about made it before running out of ideas (there's one particularly ambitious, back-bending position). The north side of the courtyard is used as a cow stable, highlighting the wonderful mix of the sacred and profane in Nepal!

The temple is best visited as part of the walking tour 'South From Durbar Square' (see p131).

BHIMSEN TOWER (DHARAHARA)

Towering like a lighthouse over the old town, this white, minaret-like **tower** (Map p116; ☎ 4215616; admission foreigner/SAARC/Nepali Rs 299/49/49, over 65 & under five years free, no student tickets; ⏲ 8am-8pm), is a useful landmark near the post office. The views from 61.88m up – 213 steps above the city – are the best you can get. There is a small Shiva shrine right at the very top.

The tower was originally built in 1826 by the Rana prime minister, Bhimsen Thapa, as part of the city's first European-style palace. It was rebuilt after being severely damaged in the 1934 earthquake. The nearby Sundhara water tank lends its name to the district.

PACHALI BHAIRAB & THE SOUTHERN GHATS

The northern banks of the Bagmati River south of the old town are home to little visited temples and shrines, as well as the worst urban poverty in Kathmandu; rarely do such splendour and squalor sit so close.

Between Tripureshwar Marg and the Bagmati River at **Pachali Bhairab** (Map p116) a huge, ancient pipal tree forms a natural sanctuary for an image of Bhairab Pachali, surrounded by tridents (Pachali is a form of Shiva). To the side lies the brass body of Baital, one of Shiva's manifestations. Worshippers gather here on Tuesday and Saturday. It is particularly busy here during the festival of Pachali Bhairab Jatra (see p366).

From the temple you could explore the temples and ghats that line the holy, polluted, Bagmati River. Head south of Pachali Bhairab to the ghats on the riverbank to find a collection of lovely statuary. To the west is the Newari-style pagoda of the **Lakshmi Mishwar Mahadev** (Map p116); to the east is the interesting **Tin Deval Temple** (Map p116), easily recognisable by its three *shikari*-style spires. From here you can continue west along footpaths to cremation ghats and a temple at the holy junction of the Bagmati and Vishnumati Rivers; or east past some of Kathmandu's poorest and lowest caste communities to the triple-roofed **Tripureshwar Mahadev Temple** (Map p116). Further east is the Mughal-style **Kalmochan Temple** (Map p116) built in 1873.

Elsewhere
DHUM VARAHI SHRINE

In an unprepossessing schoolyard just inside Kathmandu's Ring Rd to the northeast

---

KATHMANDU ART

If you have a particular interest in Nepali art the following galleries might be worth visiting. Check the websites to see what's being exhibited.

Siddhartha Art Gallery (Map p116; ☎ 4218048; www.siddharthaartgallery.com; Babar Mahal Revisited; ⏲ 11am-6pm) The best in the city, with a wide range of top-notch exhibitions.

Park Gallery (Map p116; ☎ 4419353; www.parkgallery.com.np; Lazimpat; ⏲ 10am-6pm Sun-Fri) Smaller, with exhibits in its upper-floor space and prints and cards on the ground floor.

National Birendra Art Gallery (Map p116; ☎ 4411729; ⏲ 9am-5pm Sun-Fri; admission Rs 75) The offbeat location in a crumbling old Rana palace is probably more interesting than the dusty collection of Nepali oils and watercolours.

Indigo Gallery (Map pp110-11; ☎ 4424303; Naxal; ⏲ 7am-5pm) An upmarket gallery at Mike's Breakfast (see p150), set in a lovely old Rana building, with excellent exhibits of modern thangkas, photography and prints, most for sale at top-end prices.

of Kathmandu, a huge pipal tree encloses a small **shrine** (Map pp110–11) and a dramatic 5th-century sculpture of Vishnu as a wild boar with a human body, holding Prithvi, the earth goddess, on his left elbow.

The statue is one of the earliest depictions of an animal-human, created before iconographic rules were established, which perhaps contributes to the unusual sense of movement and vitality that the statue possesses. The statue shows Vishnu rescuing Prithvi from the clutches of a demon.

To get here head north along the Ring Rd from Pashupatinath and take a left about 200m north of the bridge over the Dhobi River. The statue lies 100m down the dirt track, in the grounds of the Shridhumrabarah Primary School.

ACTIVITIES

See p76 for the various rafting, canyoning, climbing and bungee-jumping trips that you can arrange from Kathmandu.

For golfing near the capital, see the Gokarna Forest Golf Resort on p213.

Pools & Fitness Centres

Generally, pools in the major hotels can be used by friends of hotel guests, or at some hotels by outsiders, for a charge. Yak & Yeti Hotel charges Rs 500 for a one-time use of its pools, plus Rs 500 for its health club.

The **Clark Hatch Fitness Center** (Map p116; ☎ 4411818) located at the Radisson charges Rs 780/910 weekdays/weekends for gym, pool and aerobics. **Club Oasis** (☎ 4491234; 7am-9.30pm) at the Hyatt Regency charges Rs 1000 for its gym, pool, sauna, steam and Jacuzzi, or Rs 534/350 adult/child for its pool (plus 13% tax).

The Park Village Hotel at Budhanilkantha, 15km north of Kathmandu (see p183), offers a nice half-day escape from busy Kathmandu. Access to its pool costs Rs 300, or choose a half-day spa package for Rs 2600.

A recommended health club for aerobic classes is **Banu's Total Fitness** (Map p116; ☎ 4434024; banu94@yahoo.com; Kamal Pokhari; 6am-9pm Sun-Fri, 7am-11am Sat), hidden down an alleyway southeast of the new Royal Palace. There are aerobic classes at 7am, 10.30am (women only) and 5.30pm and regular yoga lessons (Rs 1500 per month). A visit costs Rs 170 for nonmembers, or Rs 375 with cardio machines and sauna.

The **Self-Awakening Centre** (Map p116; ☎ 4256 618; Babar Mahal Revisited; closed Sat) offers classes in t'ai chi, yoga, transcendental meditation and anything else you can dream up. Yoga classes cost Rs 200 per hour, t'ai chi Rs 2800 per month.

Climbing

If you need to polish your climbing skills before heading to the mountains, try the **Pasang Lhamu Climbing Wall** (Map pp110-11; ☎ 4370 742; www.pasanglhamu.org; 10am-5.30pm) on the city's northeastern edge. A day's membership costs Rs 350 and equipment rental costs Rs 100. Week-long climbing courses and private tuition are available.

The wall is on the Ring Rd, near the Bangladesh embassy, and is part of the Pasang Lhamu Mountaineering Federation, named after the first Nepali woman to summit Everest, in 1993. A taxi here from central Kathmandu costs around Rs 150.

Karting

If negotiating Kathmandu's lunatic traffic isn't enough of a challenge for you, let off some steam at **Tiger Karts** (☎ 4361500; www.tiger karts.com.np; 10am-sunset; carting Rs 500/800/1200 for 5/10/15-min), out in the middle of nowhere, 3km north of the bus park, down a dirt road in Manamaiju.

WALKING TOURS

A stroll around Kathmandu's backstreets will lead the casual wanderer to many intriguing sights, especially in the crowded maze of streets and courtyards in the area north of Durbar Sq. There are temples, shrines and sculptures hidden away in the most unlikely of places. You can really appreciate Kathmandu's museumlike quality when you come across a 1000-year-old statue – something that would be a prized possession in many Western museums – being used as a plaything or a washing line.

Both of the walks will take you to a number of markets, temples, toles, bahals (courtyards), bahil (courtyard with accommodation) and chowks which remain the focus of traditional Nepali life.

The walks can be made as individual strolls or linked together into one longer walk. Walking Tour 1 gives you a taste of the crowded and fascinating shopping streets in the oldest part of Kathmandu

KATHMANDU

and takes you to some of the city's most important temples. Walking Tour 2 takes you to a lesser-known section of southern Kathmandu, without spectacular sites but where the everyday life of city dwellers goes on and tourists are fairly rare.

South from Thamel to Durbar Square

This walk is best made en route from Thamel to Durbar Sq, or vice versa. To get to Thahiti Tole, walk south from Thamel on the road from the main Thamel Chowk; the first square you come to is Thahiti.

Thahiti Tole wraps around a central **stupa (1)**, whose stone inscription indicates it was constructed in the 15th century. Legends relate that it was built over a pond plated

with gold and that the stupa served to keep thieves at bay. Or perhaps the pond was full of dangerous snakes and the stupa kept the snakes in their place – the legends vary!

Nateshwar Temple (2), on the northern side of the square, is dedicated to a form of Shiva that doubles as the local Newari god of music; the metal plates that surround the doors show creatures busily playing a variety of musical instruments.

WALK FACTS

Duration 2-2½ hours
Start Thahiti Tole
Finish Durbar Square

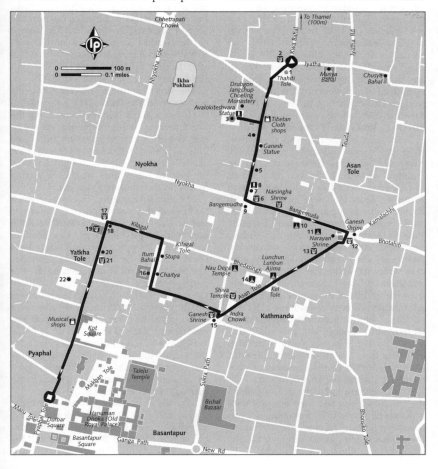

Take the road heading south past shops selling prayer flags and Buddhist cloth to the impressive **Kathesimbhu Stupa (3)**, just southwest of Thahiti Tole (see p124). There are lots of *malla* (prayer beads) stalls in the square, as well as a little teahouse/restaurant on the corner if energies are flagging (already?!).

A little further on your right, a single broken stone lion (his partner has disappeared) guards a passageway to the small enclosed courtyard of the **Nag Bahal (4)**, signed as the 'Ratna Mandal Mahabihar', with painted murals above the shrine.

Further down on the left, past a Ganesh statue, is a small recessed area and a dark grilled doorway marking a small but intricate central **stone relief (5)** dating from the 9th century. It shows Shiva sitting with Parvati on Mt Kailash, her hand resting proprietarily on his knee in the pose known as Uma Maheshwar. Various deities and creatures, including Shiva's bull Nandi, stand around them. The door is marked by an almost unrecognisable orange-coloured Ganesh head. Incidentally, the impressive wooden balcony across the road is said to have had the first glass windows in Kathmandu (it looks like it's the same glass!).

Continue south past a string of dentists' shops (the reason will soon become clear), advertised by signs showing a grinning mouthful of teeth. When you hit a square you'll see a small, double-roofed **Sikha Narayan Temple (6)**, easily identified by the kneeling Garuda figure facing and the modern clock on the wall. The temple houses a beautiful 10th- or 11th-century four-armed Vishnu figure that sadly isn't generally on display. The square also has a fine image of the goddess Saraswati playing her lute at the **Saraswati Shrine (7)**, with a Shiva shrine to the left.

In the middle of the nondescript northern frontage, directly beneath the 'Raj Dental Clinic' sign, is a standing **Buddha statue (8)** framed by modern blue and white tilework. The image is only about 60cm high but dates from the 5th or 6th century. It's a reminder of the casual treatment of what really is an incredible artistic treasure.

At the southern end of the area, just across the crossroads you will see a lump of **wood with coins (9)** into which thousands of coins have been nailed. The coins are offerings to the toothache god, which is represented by a tiny image in the ugly lump of wood. The

square at the junction is known as Bangemudha, which means 'Twisted Wood'.

Head east to the triple-roofed **Ugratara Temple (10)**, by a small square known as Nhhakantalla; a prayer at the shrine is said to work wonders for the eyes. Just further on your right you will pass the Krishna Music Emporium (maker and repairer of harmoniums), before spotting a grilled entrance that leads into **Haku Bahal (11)**. Look for the sign that advertises 'Opera Eye Wear'. This tiny *bahal* has a finely carved wooden window overlooking the courtyard.

You'll soon come to the bustling chowk of **Asan Tole** (see p124), old Kathmandu's busiest market junction and a fascinating area to explore. The diagonal southwest to northeast main road was for centuries the main commercial street in Kathmandu, and the start of the caravan route to Tibet. It was not replaced as Kathmandu's most important street until the construction of New Rd after the great earthquake of 1934. The main shrine here is the **Annapurna Temple (12)**.

The street continues southwest past the octagonal **Krishna Temple (13)**, jammed between brass shops. It looks decrepit, but the woodcarvings on this temple are very elaborate, depicting beaked monsters and a tiny Tibetan protector, holding a tiger on a chain like he's taking the dog for a walk. Look for the turn-of-the-century plaques depicting troops on the building to the left.

The next square is Kel Tole, where you'll find one of the most important and ornate temples in Kathmandu, the **Seto (White) Machhendranath Temple (14)**. See p124 for details.

The busy shopping street spills into **Indra Chowk**, marked by the stepped Mahadev Temple and **Akash Bhairab Temple (15)**. For more on these see p125. From the south of the square, wide Surkha Path leads to New Rd; the shops along this road sell consumer goods imported from Hong Kong and Singapore, and many of them end up in India.

Before you leave Indra Chowk, look for the market hidden in the alleyways to the east, crowded with stalls selling the glass bangles and beads that are so popular with married Nepali women.

Take the quiet alleyway west from Indra Chowk and after 200m or so look for a tiny entryway to the right, by a shrine and under the sign for 'Jenisha Beauty Parlour'. The entryway leads in to the long, rectangular courtyard of **Itum Bahal**, one of the oldest and largest *bahals* in the city, with some lovely architecture and stupas. See p125 for more on this and the **Kichandra Bahal (16)**.

Exit the courtyard at the north and turn left (west). On your right at the next junction is the **Nara Devi Temple (17)** – see p125 for details. Just to the south of the **dance platform (18)** is a small shop occupied by one of Kathmandu's many marching bands, mainly used for weddings – look for gleaming tubas, red uniforms and tuneless trumpeting. Also across the road is a three-roofed **Narsingha Temple (19)** but it's almost impossible to find through a maze of small courtyards (you can see the roof from the dance platform).

At the Nara Devi corner, turn left (south) for 30m and you soon come to a nondescript photocopy shop on your left with an utterly magnificent **wooden window (20)** above it. It has been called *deshay madu* in Nepali, which means 'there is not another one like it'. Next to the building, in a small courtyard, is the recently restored triple-roofed **Bhulukha Dega Temple (21)**, dedicated to Shiva.

Further south, on the right is the entrance to the **Yatkha Bahal (22)**, a huge open courtyard with a central unremarkable stupa. Directly behind it is an old building, whose upper storey is supported by four superb carved-wood struts. Dating from the 14th century, they are carved in the form of *yakshas* (attendant deities or nymphs), one of them gracefully balancing a baby on her hip. The struts were recently restored by the Department of Architecture, Unesco and the Kathmandu Valley Preservation Trust.

Back on the road, head south again, passed the music shops on the right, to Durbar Sq, your final destination for this walk.

South from Durbar Square

Starting from the Kasthamandap in Durbar Sq (see p114), a circular walk can be made to

WALK FACTS

Duration 45 minutes-1 hour
Start Durbar Square
Finish Durbar Square

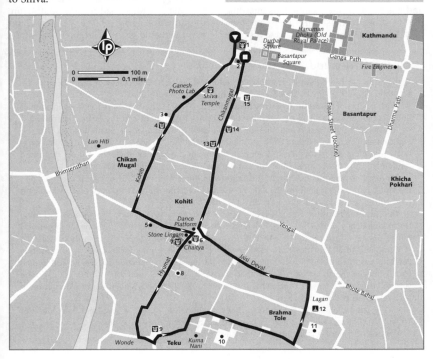

the older parts in the south of the city. This area is not as packed with historical interest as the walks north of Durbar Sq, but the streets are less crowded and you are far less likely to run into other tourists.

Starting from the **Kasthamandap (1)** in the southwestern corner of Durbar Sq, the road out of the square forks almost immediately around the **Singh Sattal (2)**, built with wood left over from the Kasthamandap Temple. The squat building has small shop stalls around the ground floor and golden-winged lions guarding each corner of the upper floor and is a popular place for *bhajan* (devotional music) in the mornings and evenings. The building was originally called the Silengu Sattal (a *sattal* is a pilgrim hostel) until the addition of the *singh* (guardian lions).

Take the road running diagonally to the right of this building, past a Shiva Temple, and you eventually come to the large tank-like **hiti (3)**, or water tank, where people will usually be washing clothes.

Immediately beyond is the highly decorated **Bhimsen Temple (4)**, which is fronted by a brass lion ducking under the electric wires and has white-painted snow lions guarding the two front corners. Bhimsen is supposed to watch over traders and artisans so it's quite

appropriate that the ground floor of this well-kept temple should be devoted to shop stalls. An image of Bhimsen used to be carried to Lhasa in Tibet every 12 years to protect those vital trade routes, until the route was closed by Chinese control and the flight of the Dalai Lama in 1959. There are some lovely *chaityas* here. Tourists are not allowed in the temple.

Continue south beyond the Bhimsen Temple then turn sharp left (uphill) where the road ends, passing the ornate **Kohiti water tank (5)** en route. At the top of the hill you'll come out by the tall, triple-roofed, 17th-century **Jaisi Deval Temple (6)**, which stands on a seven-level base. Nearby is the **Ram Chandra Temple (7)**. For more on both of these see p126.

There is a series of *bahals* on the next stretch of the walk, but most are of little interest apart from the small and very much lived-in courtyard of **Tukan Bahal (8)**. The Swayambhunath-style 14th-century stupa in the centre is surprisingly impressive.

The road continues with a few bends, then turns sharply left (east) at Wonde junction, which is marked by several temples, including a taller **shikhara temple (9)**. If you take the downhill road leading south from this junction (and off the Walking Tour map) you emerge onto Tripureshwar Marg,

QUIRKY KATHMANDU

Kathmandu has more than its fair share of quirk and, as with most places in the subcontinent, a 10-minute walk in any direction will throw up numerous curiosities.

The corridors of the **Natural History Museum** (see p164) are full of bizarre moth-eaten animals and jars that lie somewhere between a school science experiment and *The Texas Chainsaw Massacre*. The 20-ft python skin and nine-month old baby rhino in a jar are guaranteed to give you nightmares. The other exhibits are a bit slapdash, including the line of stuffed birds nailed carelessly to a bit of wood to indicate their distribution, or the big pile of elephant dung deposited randomly in the front corner. After all this fun the section on algae is a bit dull…

For items of personal quirkiness, the **Tribhuvan Museum** (see p123) offers up such gems as the king's parachuting uniform, the king's personal film projector and the king's personal walking stick with a spring-loaded sword inside – very '007'.

The National Museum (see p164) also houses more than its fair share of weirdness, including the mandible of a whale (?), a portrait of King Prithvi Narayan Shah giving everyone the finger, and a man poking a fox in the arse with a stick, the significance of which passed us by completely.

Compared to all this funkiness, Kathmandu's old town is pretty docile. Look for the antique **fire engines** (Map p116) hidden behind a grille just west of the junction of New Rd and Surkha Path, opposite the ticket office for Durbar Square. If you get a toothache during your trip, be sure to visit the old town's **toothache god** (see p130) – a raggedy old stump of wood covered with hundreds of nails and coins.

Finally, the Indian **snake charmers** who set up shop in front of the New Tibet Book Store on Tridevi Marg always raise a smile, as does the crazy sadhu, dressed as the god Hanuman in a very unrealistic monkey suit, who occasionally haunts Durbar Square.

from where you can continue to the Pachali Bhairab Temple (see p127).

Our walk continues past Brahma Tole to the **Musum Bahal (10)**, with its phallic-shaped Licchavi-style *chaityas,* an enclosed well and surrounding interconnecting *bahals.* Turn sharp left (north) at the next main junction and, after 25m, look out for the large, spacious **Ta Bahal (11)** with its many *chaityas,* down an alley on the right.

The road opens into an open square featuring the white 5m-high **Machhendranath Temple (12)**, as well as the occasional neighbourhood cricket match. During the annual Seto Machhendranath festival, the image of the god is transported here from the Seto Machhendranath Temple in Kel Tole (see p124). The final stage of the procession is to pull the god's chariot three times around the temple, after which the image is taken back to its starting point on a palanquin while the chariot is dismantled here.

Turn left out of Lagan and walk back to the tall Jaisi Deval Temple, then turn right (northeast) back towards Durbar Sq.

At the next crossroads the slender three-storey **Hari Shankar Temple (13)** stands to the left of the road.

Continue north past a **Vishnu (Narayan) Temple (14)** to a second Vishnu temple, the **Adko Narayan Temple (15)**. Although it's not all that large, it is one of the four most important Vishnu temples in Kathmandu. Twin feathered Garudas front the temple, while lions guard each corner. An ornately carved *path* (pilgrim's shelter) is on the street corner.

Beyond the temple you pass the Singh Sattal building again and arrive back at the starting point. Alternatively, head east through the backstreets for a reviving chocolate cake and milk tea at Freak Street's Snowman Restaurant (see p149).

KATHMANDU FOR CHILDREN
Pilgrims Bookstore in Kathmandu has a fine collection of kids' books, including colouring books. Away from the tourist areas highchairs are virtually nonexistent and finding nonspicy food children will eat may be more of a problem.

Kids will probably enjoy the zoo in nearby Patan (see p192) and older kids will get a thrill from spotting the monkeys at Swayambhunath.

DAY TRIPS FROM KATHMANDU

The great thing about Kathmandu is that there are so many fantastic sights just a couple of kilometres outside the city. You can check out any of the following sites and still be back in Thamel for the start of happy hour.

■ Bhaktapur – see p196

■ Patan – see p184

■ Bodhnath – see p169

■ Ichangu Narayan – see p165

■ Budhanilkantha – see p182

FESTIVALS & EVENTS
Kathmandu has many festivals, of which the most outrageous is probably Indra Jatra (see p134) in September, closely followed by the Seto Machhendranath chariot festival (see p124) in March/April, Dasain in October, and the Pachali Bhairab Jatra, also in October. See p363 for details.

The annual **Jazzmandu Festival** (www.kathmandujazzfestival.com) is a week-long programme of local and international jazz acts that plays in venues across town in November. Tickets cost around Rs 900. See the website for details.

SLEEPING
Kathmandu has a great range of places to stay, from luxurious international-style hotels to cheap and cheerful lodges, and almost all offer competitive prices.

Most of Kathmandu's accommodation offers some form of discount these days (see the boxed text, p356). Normal high-season rates are given here, followed where relevant by the amount of discount being offered on this rate at the time of high-season research. If you email a reservation in advance you probably won't get the largest discount but you should get a free airport pickup.

It's difficult to recommend hotels, especially in the budget and middle brackets, as rooms in each hotel can vary widely. Many of these hotels have additions to additions, and while some rooms may be very gloomy and run-down, others (generally the upper floors) might be bright and pleasant. A friendly crowd of travellers can also make all the difference. In general, roadside rooms

KATHMANDU'S INDRA JATRA FESTIVAL

Indra, the ancient Aryan god of rain, was once captured in the Kathmandu Valley while stealing a certain flower for his mother, Dagini. He was imprisoned until Dagini revealed his identity and his captors gladly released him. The festival celebrates this remarkable achievement (villagers don't capture a real god every day of the week). In return for his release Dagini promised to spread dew over the crops for the coming months and to take back with her to heaven all those who had died in the past year.

The Indra Jatra festival thus honours the recently deceased and pays homage to Indra and Dagini for the coming harvests. It begins when a huge, carefully selected pole, carried via the Tundikhel, is erected outside the Hanuman Dhoka in Kathmandu. At the same time images and representations of Indra, usually as a captive, are displayed and sacrifices of goats and roosters are made; the screened doors obscuring the horrific face of Seto (White) Bhairab are also opened and for the next three days his gruesome visage will stare out at the proceedings.

The day before all this activity, three golden temple chariots are assembled in Basantapur Sq, outside the home of the Kumari. In the afternoon, with the Durbar Square packed with colourful and cheerful crowds, two boys emerge from the Kumari's house. They play the roles of Ganesh and Bhairab and will each ride in a chariot as an attendant to the goddess. Finally, the Kumari herself appears either walking on a rolled-out carpet or carried by attendants so that her feet do not touch the ground.

The chariots move off and the Kumari is greeted from the balcony of the old palace by the king. The procession then continues out of Durbar Square towards Hanuman Dhoka where it stops out in front of the huge Seto Bhairab mask. The Kumari greets the image of Bhairab and then, with loud musical accompaniment, beer starts to pour from Bhairab's mouth! Getting a sip of this beer is guaranteed to bring good fortune, but one lucky individual will also get the small fish, which has been put to swim in the beer – this brings especially good luck (though probably not for the fish).

Numerous other processions also take place around the town until the final day when the great pole is lowered and carried down to the river.

are brighter but noisier than interior rooms and top-floor rooms are the best, as you stand a chance of getting a view and have easy access to the roof garden. Quite a few hotels bridge the budget and midrange categories by having a range of room standards – these places have been grouped according to their lowest price.

Intense competition between Kathmandu's enormous number of low-priced hostels means that you can find hot showers in even the cheapest places, although they are sometimes solar-heated and are only hot in the late afternoon.

Budget places generally don't have heating, so in winter you'll want the warmer south-facing rooms and garden access, as it's always pleasant to sit outside during the cool, but sunny, autumn and winter days.

Most budget and some midrange places are found in the bustling Thamel district. Midrange and top-end places are widely scattered around Kathmandu, some quite a way from the centre.

Some travellers base themselves further a field, outside Kathmandu in Patan or Bodhnath, to escape the traffic, pollution and commercialism of Thamel (see p172 and p193 for details) and this isn't a bad idea. For something quieter still, there is an increasing number of mostly top-end resorts around the Kathmandu Valley, which offer a peaceful rural atmosphere less than an hour from the centre of Kathmandu.

Thamel

For budget and midrange places the Thamel area is the main locale, and it is a bit of a tourist ghetto. It's a convenient and enjoyable area to stay for a short time, especially to meet fellow travellers or for a budget-priced apple crumble, but you are likely to tire of the place in a couple of days.

In an attempt to establish some order, we have somewhat arbitrarily divided the Greater Thamel area into: Thamel, around the two main intersections; Paknajol, to the north; Bhagwan Bahal, to the northeast;

Jyatha, to the southeast; and Chhetrapati, to the southwest.

BUDGET
Central Thamel
Kathmandu Guest House (Map p136; ☎ 4700800; www.ktmgh.com; s US$2-50, d US$4-60; ⛽) The KGH is a bit of an institution. It was the first hotel to open in Thamel and still serves as the central landmark – everything in Thamel is 'near the Kathmandu Guest House'. In strictly dollar terms you can get better rooms elsewhere, but most people enjoy the bustling atmosphere and it's often booked out weeks in advance during the high season. There's BBC TV in the foyer, a front wi-fi–enabled courtyard and a very pleasant rear garden that acts as a haven from the Thamel mayhem. Facilities include a mini-cinema and even a sauna – this is budget travel in the deluxe category!

The cheapest rooms without bathroom form part of the original 13-room guesthouse and really aren't up to much – you'll certainly get better-value rooms elsewhere – but at least the common showers are clean and hot. In the newer wing, the best-value rooms are probably the garden-facing rooms.

Hotel Horizon (Map p136; ☎ 4220904; www.visit nepal.com/hotelhorizon; s US$5-10, d US$8-15, deluxe s/d US$15/20) A good choice down an alley off the main street in southern Thamel, making it a quiet and central option. It has a range of rooms at reasonable prices, all with bathroom, most of which are bright and spacious, and there are some nice communal seating areas. The mid-priced (US$8) rooms are the best value; more than this and you are really just paying for a bathtub.

Hotel Potala (Map p136; ☎ 4700159; s/d/tr without bathroom from Rs 125/175/250) Bang in the beating heart of Thamel, this small Tibetan-run backpacker place is cheap and cheerful, though the rooms are dark and the hot water iffy. The rooftop and balconies overlook Thamel's main drag. Rooms facing inside are darker but much quieter; try for a room on the 5th floor. The deluxe rooms have better mattresses and are worth the extra Rs 25. It's down an alleyway near the Maya Cocktail Bar.

Marco Polo Guest House (Map p136; ☎ 4251914; marcopolo@wlink.com.np; d with/without bathroom Rs 420/200, deluxe Rs 560) The rather morose management adds to a certain boarding school feel here but it's a popular place with a convenient location on the eastern edge of Thamel, near traffic-soaked Tridevi Marg. The rooms at the top and back are surprisingly quiet and bright, especially the deluxe rooms; others are noisier and darker. There are no single prices.

Student Guest House (Map p136; ☎ 4251551; krishna@student.wlink.com.np; s/d with bathroom Rs 300/500; 🖳) Right next door to Marco Polo and a similar deal. It's quiet and clean but the

---

THE AUTHOR'S CHOICE

Hotel Ganesh Himal (Map p116; ☎ 4243819, 4263598; www.ganeshhimal.com; s/d budget US$7/9, s/d standard US$9/12, deluxe US$14/17, discounts of 15-20%) Our pick for comfort on a budget is this well-run and friendly place, a 10-minute walk southwest of Thamel – far enough to be out of range of the tiger balm salesmen but close enough to restaurants for dinner. The rooms are among the best value in Kathmandu, with endless hot water, satellite TV and lots of balcony and garden seating, plus a sunny rooftop. The deluxe rooms are more spacious, a little quieter and come with a bath tub. Here's a tip – bring earplugs, as the residential neighbourhood can be a bit noisy. Make a reservation and you'll get a free airport pickup.

Kantipur Temple House (Map p136; ☎ 4250131; www.kantipurtemplehouse.com; s/d US$50/60, deluxe US$70/90, discounts of 40-50%) Hidden down an alley on the edge of the old town, at the southern end of Jyatha, this boutique-style hotel has been built in old Newari-temple style with a fine attention to detail. The spacious rooms are tastefully decorated, with traditional carved wood and *dhaka* (hand-woven) cloth bedspreads, commissioned from local fair trade shops. This place is doing its best to be eco-friendly – guests are given cloth bags to use when shopping and bulk mineral water is available free of charge, so you don't need to buy plastic bottles. In fact there's no plastic anywhere in the hotel. The new block encircles a traditional courtyard and there's garden and rooftop seating. The old town location is close to almost anywhere in town, but taxi drivers might have a hard time finding it.

KATHMANDU

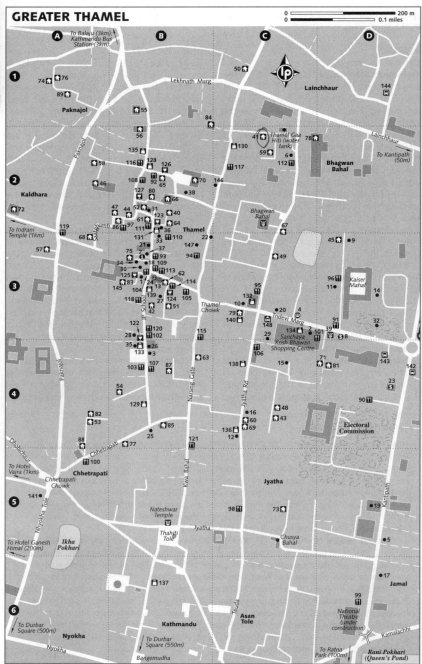

GREATER THAMEL

0 ——————— 200 m
0 ——————— 0.1 miles

To Balaju (3km);
Kathmandu Bus
Station (3km)

Lekhnath Marg

Lainchhaur

Lainchhaur

To Kantipath
(50m)

Paknajol

Thamel Gaa
Hiti (water
tank)

Bhagwan
Bhal

Kaldhara

Bhagwan
Bhal

To Indrani
Temple (1km)

Thamel

Kaiser
Mahal

Thamel
Chowk

Thamel
Chowk

Sanchaya
Kosh Bhawan
Shopping Centre

Electoral
Commission

Narsing Gate

Jyatha Rd

Kwa Bahal

Jyatha

Chusya
Bahal

To Hotel
Vajra (1km)

Chhetrapati

Chhetrapati
Chowk

To Hotel Ganesh
Himal (200m)

Ikha
Pokhari

Nateshwar
Temple

Thahiti
Tole

Jamal

To Durbar
Square (500m)

Nyokha

Nyokha

Kathmandu

To Durbar
Square (550m)

Asan
Tole

National
Theatre
(under
construction)

Kamalachhi

Bangemudha

To Ratna
Park (100m)

Rani Pokhari
(Queen's Pond)

Kantipath

buildings are so crammed in that there's little natural light and no views. The rooms out the back are much better and solo travellers can often get these double rooms for a single price, which is a good deal.

Hotel Red Planet (Map p136; ☎ 4700879; redplan et_thamel@hotmail.com; s/d from Rs 375/530, deluxe Rs 600/830, discounts of 15%) Tucked away by the bend in the road just north of Kathmandu Guest House, this is a good Thamel cheapie, and not too noisy, despite it's central location. Rooms are clean and good value with decent bathrooms; try to get a gardenside room with a balcony.

Acme Guest House (Map p136; ☎ 4700236; www .acmeguesthouse.com; s/d US$5-20/8-25, discounts of 30-40%) Next to the Hotel Red Planet, the rooms here are quite large and there is an open lawn area, which is something of a rarity in crowded Thamel. The rooms with balcony overlooking the lawn are the best value; those at the back can be dark.

Thorong Peak Guest House (Map p136; ☎ 4253458, fax 4251008; s/d/q without bathroom US$8/12/18, deluxe s/d US$14/18, discounts of 30%) A clean and well-looked after place, off the main street in a small cul de sac. Most rooms are light and airy and there are nice communal balconies and a rooftop terrace, though it's a little overpriced. It doesn't get much sunlight in winter.

There are dozens of other places, including the **Hotel Puskar** (Map p136; ☎ 4262956; s Rs 150-250, d Rs 250-450), with a wide range of rooms in various blocks (including some real stinkers with dark, sweaty bathrooms) and the very basic but cheap **Pheasant Lodge** (Map p136; ☎ 4417415; s/d without bathroom Rs 100/150), tucked around an alleyway south of the Kathmandu Guest House.

Paknajol

This area lies to the north of central Thamel and can be reached by continuing north from the Kathmandu Guest House, or by approaching from Lekhnath Marg.

Not far from the steep Paknajol intersection with Lekhnath Marg (northwest of Thamel) are a few pleasant guesthouses. They're away from traffic, a short walk from Thamel (but it could be a million miles), and they have beautiful views across the valley towards Balaju and Swayambhunath.

Tibet Peace Guest House (Map p136; ☎ 4381026; www.tibetpeace.com; s Rs 210-700, d Rs 210-1050) Friendly and family-run, this is a quiet and

mellow hangout, with a lovely garden, small restaurant with a wide range of herbal teas and BBC World in the foyer. There's a wide range of rooms in several buildings so have a dig around before committing.

Kathmandu Peace Guest House (Map p136; ☎ 43 80369; www.ktmpeaceguesthouse.com; s with/without bathroom US$8/5 d with/without bathroom US$12/6, s/d deluxe with bathroom US$12/16, discounts of 25%) Further along the road, this is a little more upmarket, offering rooms with satellite TV in either the slightly ramshackle old wing or the better new block sporting piney fresh furniture. There are fine views from the rooftop towards Nagarjun.

Kathmandu Garden House (Map p136; ☎ 4381 239; www.hotel-in-nepal.com; s with/without bathroom Rs 300-400/200 d with/without bathroom Rs 400-500/250) A small and intimate guest house that is cosy and deservedly popular. The upper floor doubles with hot-water shower are best but always seem to be occupied. The views from the roof are excellent and there are nice sitting areas and a lovely garden, where you can sit back and marvel at the staff cutting the grass by hand (literally!).

Hotel Encounter Nepal (Map p136; ☎ 4440534; www.encounternepal.com; old block s/d without bathroom US$3/5, s/d with bathroom from US$5/6, new block s/d US$8/15, deluxe $15/20; 🖳) A good-value place to the north of Thamel, in a more lived-in part of Kathmandu. The hotel consists of an old and new block separated by a garden. The best old block rooms are sunny, spacious and good value, and the spiffier new block has nice corner rooms with views over the valley, some with balcony. The only downer is that you take your life in your hands crossing diabolical Lekhnath Marg to get here.

Pilgrims Guest House (Map p136; ☎ 4440565; pil grimsghouse@yahoo.com; s/d without bathroom US$4/6, s/d with bathroom US$6-8/8-15; 🖳) The first thing that appeals about this secluded and well-managed place in northern Thamel is the outdoor garden restaurant and bar. The wide range of rooms fit most budgets, from top-floor rooms with a sofa and balcony, to the cheapest singles, which are little more than a box. It's a popular place so you may have to take what's available for the first night and then upgrade as rooms become available.

Hotel New Florid (Map p136; ☎ 4701055; www .hotelflorid.com.np; s/d without bathroom US$5/7, s/d with bathroom US$8/10) This is one of several small guesthouses just north of central Thamel, down a lane west of Advanced Photo Finisher. There is a pleasant garden at the rear and no buildings behind so there's a feeling of space that is often lacking in Thamel. The large doubles overlooking the garden are bright, spacious and best. Doubles overlooking the road are noisier but come with a common balcony. You'll need to negotiate a discount to get good value here.

Holy Lodge (Map p136; ☎ 4700265; holylodge@wlink .com.np; s/d from Rs 200/350, with bathroom up to Rs 500/700, deluxe Rs 700/1050) This place offers neat, clean rooms but there's a sad lack of garden, sitting areas or views, especially in the warrenlike back building, which has the cheaper rooms. Deluxe rooms on top of the back building have TV and AC.

Hotel Down Town (Map p136; ☎ 4700471; www .hoteldowntown-nepal.com; r with/without bathroom from Rs 350/250) One door down from Holy Lodge, this decent Thamel cheapie has a wide range of rooms, the best of which are clustered around the rooftop. There are a couple of nice communal sitting areas and balconies but no single room rates. The website makes it look much more glamorous than it actually is…

Prince Guest House (Map p136; ☎ 4700456; prince guesthouse@hotmail.com; s/d Rs 350/500) Across the road from Down Town, this is a very decent budget place, cheered up by potted plants and a pleasant rooftop. Rooms have hot water bathrooms and some have a TV. The upper floor rooms are much brighter.

Hotel Metropolitan Kantipur (Map p136; ☎ 4266 518; www.kantipurhotel.com; s/d from US$6/9, deluxe US$12/16, discounts of 10%) Just west of the Thamel action, this is a decent find, with a nice garden, a rooftop restaurant and friendly staff. Rooms are spacious, though levels of maintenance vary. There's even a small Kumari Temple in the corner of the grounds.

Via Via Café (Map p136; ☎ 4700184; www.viavia café.com; s/d without bathroom Rs 250/350) A Belgian-Nepali café with half a dozen pokey rooms in its century-old building. It's right on a major road junction so don't expect a lie-in in the mornings (staff even provide ear plugs!). It's a bit too jammed in for some but there are some nice touches like reading lights and it's also a sociable option, especially for a small group. Be sure to book in advance.

Hotel Shree Tibet (Map p136; ☎ 4419902; sri tibet@ccsl.com.np; s/d US$10/15, deluxe US$20, discounts of 20-30%) It's easy to miss this upper budget Tibetan-run place and most people do (it's often deserted). It's a clean and quiet place with cosy, clean rooms decorated with Tibetan prayer flags, although some rooms are dark and smallish due to the buildings being very close together. The bigger deluxe rooms are a better bet for doubles. The small restaurant serves decent Tibetan food.

Hotel Tashi Dhargey (Map p136; ☎ 4700030; www.hoteltashidhargey.com; s/d US$20/25, deluxe US45/40, discounts of 60-70%; 🖳) A pretty good upper budget choice in the heart of things, down a back alley with entrances on two different roads. It has a wide range of slightly old-fashioned but spacious rooms, the best of which are on the upper floors and on the sunny south side. Deluxe rooms come with air-con/heating and have a large bathroom and are good value at the discounted rate of US$10/12.

Another acceptable cheapie is the **Mustang Guest House** (Map p136; ☎ 4426053; chitaure@mos .com.np; s/d without bathroom Rs 130/180, s/d with bathroom Rs 200/250), tucked away down an inconspicuous laneway, with decent, quiet rooms but a dearth of natural light.

Bhagwan Bahal

This area to the northeast of Thamel takes its name from a Buddhist monastery. Some travellers like the area because it is quieter than Thamel proper, and has not yet been completely taken over by restaurants, souvenir shops and travel agencies.

Annapurna Guest House (Map p136; ☎ 4420159; www.annapurnaguesthouse.com; r US$4-6) Further north near the Hotel Norbu Linka; also known as Hotel Crown, this guest house is down a side alley. The rooms are smallish but clean and comfortable and most come with private bathroom.

Hotel Earth House (Map p136; ☎ 4418197; www .hotelearthhouse.com; s/d without bathroom Rs 150/250, s/d with bathroom Rs 200/300) The caged stairwells make this place feel a little institutional and the cheaper rooms ain't pretty. However, it does have friendly staff, a nice rooftop garden and a variety of rooms. The rooms at the back are best as they are quieter and brighter.

The nearby **Hotel Tokyo** (Map p136; ☎ 4424683; r without bathroom Rs 150, s/d with bathroom Rs 300/400) is a similar deal.

KATHMANDU

Chhetrapati

This area is named after the important five-way intersection (notable by its distinctive bandstand) to the southwest of Thamel. The further you get from Thamel, the more traditional the surroundings become.

Khangsar Guest House (Map p136; ☎ 4260788; www.khangsarguesthouse.com; s/d Rs 200/300) Friendly, central and good value, this is one of the best of the cheapies. Rooms come with an anorexically thin but clean bathroom with (generally) hot water, plus there's a Korean restaurant and a rooftop bar for cold beers under the stars. TV costs an extra Rs 50.

Hotel Hama (Map p136; ☎ 4251009; hama@info .com.np; s/d Rs 250/300, s/d cnr r Rs 600/700) The draws at this quiet place are the bright corner rooms, the sunny balconies, and the small garden in front of the hotel. Try not to get landed with one of the stuffy cheaper rooms, which aren't half as nice. It's right opposite the Tibet Guest House.

MIDRANGE
Central Thamel

Hotel Garuda (Map p136; ☎ 4700766; www.garuda -hotel.com; s/d US$10/15, standard US$15/20, deluxe US$25/30) The good news is that this busy place is bang in the centre of bustling Thamel, about 100m north of the Kathmandu Guest House. Unfortunately it's bang in the bustling centre of Thamel... Some rooms are dark and claustrophobic so look around. Budget rooms don't have the deluxe room's TV or balcony, but are quieter and better value. There are great views from the rooftop. There's a definite mountaineering connection going on here – there are lots of signed climbing photos on the walls and John Krakauer mentions staying here in his bestseller *Into Thin Air*.

Hotel Excelsior (Map p136; ☎ 4257748; www.ex celsiornepal.com; economical s/d US$10/14, standard US$20/28, deluxe US$32/40, discounts of 60%) The Excelsior isn't a bad central choice. The standard rooms are a bit musty but probably offer the best value. The small, stuffy 'economic' rooms are in a separate block across the road and smell like your granny's spare room. Best thing about staying here is the classy rooftop garden.

Hotel Northfield (Map p136; ☎ 4700078; www.ho telnorthfield.com; s/d US$8/12, standard US$20/25, deluxe US$25/35; 🛈) This new add-on to the popular Northfield Restaurant is right in the eye of the Thamel storm and doesn't do itself any favours by having noisy rooms on a bend in Thamel's main street. Still, it's well run and friendly and things quieten down at night.

Hotel Vaishali (Map p136; ☎ 4413968; www.hotel vaishali.com, www.vaishalihotel.com; s/d US$90/110, discounts of 40%; 🛈 🛈) From the marbly foyer to the pink rose décor, this hotel feels a bit out of out of place in the heart of budget Thamel. Rooms are spacious, clean and modern, if a little dull, with central air-con and satellite TV but they're let down a bit by the bathrooms. A bonus here in summer is the small outdoor swimming pool – like the hotel it's more functional than stylish.

Hotel Blue Horizon (Map p136; ☎ 4421971; www .hotelbluehorizon.com; Tridevi Marg; s US$8-30, d US$12-60, discounts of 30%; 🛈 🛈) There's a wide range of comfortable, bright modern rooms here but the best thing is the secluded location down an alleyway off Tridevi Marg. It's close to Thamel but it's also super easy for transport around the city, plus the location is quiet. The mid-priced corner rooms with a sofa are the best value and the top-priced suites are good for families.

The **Hotel Manang** (Map p136; ☎ 4410993; www .hotelmanang.com; s/d US$55/65, deluxe US$80/90, discounts of 30%; 🛈) and **Hotel Marshyangdi** (Map p136; ☎ 4700105; www.hotelmarshyangdi.com; s/d standard US$60/70, deluxe US$75/85, discounts of 66%) are similarly solid but dull modern three-star blocks in the north of Thamel. Beware the standard rooms at the latter as they have no natural light.

Paknajol

Hotel Courtyard (Map p136; ☎ 4700648; www.hotel courtyard.com; s/d US$45/60, ste US$90, discounts of 50%) For something a little more stylish, this is a good choice, particularly now that discounts make it a steal. Built in a traditional style with oil bricks and Newari-style carved wooden lintels, it's very insulated from the Thamel madness, there are nice sitting areas and the rooms are big enough to tango in. Front view rooms are a little pricier.

Hotel Tradition (Map p136; ☎ 4700217; www.ho teltradition.com; s/d standard US$30/40, deluxe US$55/65, discounts of 50%) At eight storeys, this is probably the tallest building in the area and a good choice. The rooms are comfortable and well furnished (though some are a bit small) and the views from the sixth-floor terrace restaurant are sensational. The hotel is located on the snaking side road known as Saatghumti, or 'Seven Bends'. Reservations are a good idea in high season.

International Guest House (Map p136; ☎ 4252 299; www.ighouse.com; s/d with bathroom from US$16/20, deluxe s/d US$20/25, superior US$25/30, monsoon discounts of 50%) Further west from the Hotel Tradition in an area known as Kaldhara, this is another nicely decorated place with traditional carved woodwork, lots of plants and terrace sitting areas, a spacious garden and one of the best rooftop views in the city. The deluxe rooms come with a garden view and are probably the best value; standard rooms vary and can be small and dark. This area is quieter and much less of a scene than Thamel but still close to plenty of restaurants. Keep an eye open for the stuffed yak…

Bhagwan Bahal

Hotel Norbu Linka (Map p136; ☎ 4410630; www.hotel norbulinka.com; s/d US$35/45, ste US$55-65, discounts of 60%) A modern, secluded place, down an alley opposite the interesting Thamel Gaa Hiti (water tank). The spacious modern rooms aren't as Tibetan as you'd think from the name but they are clean and comfortable and there are a couple of rooms on the rooftop garden area. The opulent suites are great for families and the restaurant is open 24 hours, so if you are jetlagged, with kids, look no further. Credit cards are accepted.

Jyatha

The neighbourhood southeast of Thamel is traditionally known as Jyatha, but the word is also used to describe the main north–south road that runs into the western end of Tridevi Marg.

Turn east a short way down Jyatha Rd, and a couple of twists and turns will bring you to a neat little cluster of modern guesthouses, whose central but quiet location feels a million miles from the Thamel hustle.

Mustang Holiday Inn (Map p136; ☎ 4249041; www.mustangholidayinn.com.np; s/d with bathroom US$15/20, s/d US$22/28, deluxe US$30/40, discounts of 50%) Really, how many times do you get to stay in a hotel owned by the king of a remote Himalayan kingdom? The clean, spacious and comfortable rooms are suitably decorated in Tibetan style with thangkas decked in *khata*s (silk scarfs) and some come with a balcony. It's quiet, great value, has a restau-rant, nice terraces and is owned by the King of Mustang! What's not to like?

Imperial Guest House (Map p136; ☎ 4249339; imperial_guesthouse@hotmail.com; s/d US$12/15, discounts of 70%) Across the road from Mustang Holiday Inn, this is a cheaper but good option, with a rooftop sitting area that overlooks a small shrine.

Hotel Dynasty (Map p136; ☎ 4263172; www.hotel dynasty.com.np; s/d without air-con US$40/50, deluxe with air-con US$50/60, super deluxe US$60/70, discounts of 50%; 🖳) Tucked away in a lane behind the Hotel Utse, this is a good midrange find frequented by small in-the-know tour groups. It's a modern, upmarket place that even has a lift! The rooms are a good size and come with TV and, in some cases, a balcony. The deluxe rooms are the best value.

Fuji Guest House (Map p136; ☎ 4250435; www.fuji guesthouse.com; s with/without bathroom US$10/6, d with/without bathroom US$15/10, s/d deluxe $US20/30, off-season discounts of 30%) Another well-run place in the same lane as the Hotel Dynasty. It's popular with Japanese travellers and is a little over-priced, but rooms are neat, quiet and spot-lessly clean, and the more expensive rooms have balconies, towels and bathtubs. The rooms with shared bathroom are a good deal. Super-deluxe rooms are under construction.

Hotel Utse (Map p136; ☎ 4228952; www.hotel utse.com; Jyatha Rd; s/d standard US$15/21, s/d deluxe US$19/25, s/d super deluxe US$24/30, discounts of 25%) This comfortable Tibetan hotel is owned by Ugen Tsering, one of the original Thamel tourism pioneers, with his long-running and popular Utse Restaurant. It's a well-run hotel, with a good rooftop area and foyer area. Deluxe rooms have nice Tibetan touches and satellite TV but the standard rooms probably offer best value. Super-deluxe rooms have air-con/heating. The roadside rooms are bright but noisy.

Hotel Norling (Map p136; ☎ 4240734; www.hotel norling.com; standard s/d US$10/16, deluxe d US$19-25, discounts of 45%) A thin slice of a hotel next door to the Hotel Utse that is a good-value option. Also Tibetan-run, it has small but neat rooms and a lush rooftop garden. The small single rooms are worth avoiding; deluxe rooms have a larger bathroom but that's the only difference.

Chhetrapati

Potala Guest House (Map p136; ☎ 4220467; www.potalaguesthouse.com; s US$10, d US$15-20, deluxe US$35, discounts of 30%) At the quiet southern end of Thamel is this large popular hotel. The garden is small but pleasant, with a lovely terrace and a rooftop garden. The quiet deluxe rooms, with air-con and wooden floors, are the best bet; the other rooms are older and much plainer, especially the singles.

Tibet Guest House (Map p136; ☎ 4251763; www.ti betguesthouse.com; s/d US$16/19, main block US$24/27, s/d deluxe US$32/35, s/d superior US$40/44, suite US$55/59, discounts of 40-50%) You can't go wrong at this well run and popular Manangi Hotel, so book in advance. All the rooms are well-maintained and comfortable; the deluxe rooms are much more spacious. There's a lovely breakfast patio and the superb views of Swayambhunath from the rooftop garden just cry out to be appreciated at sunset with a cold beer. The cheapest rooms, in a separate block across the street, aren't up to much.

Nirvana Garden Hotel (Map p136; ☎ 4256200; www.nirvanagarden.com; s/d US$25/30, s/d deluxe US$30/40, discounts of 30%) The relaxing garden here may not quite be nirvana but it is the nicest in Thamel and is a real oasis, making this hotel a very relaxing choice. The clean and fresh deluxe rooms with private balcony are the ones to opt for (ask for a garden view) and offer great midrange value. The standard rooms are much smaller.

Freak Street (Jochne) & Durbar Square
BUDGET

Although Freak St's glory days have passed, a few determined rock-bottom budget restaurants and lodges have clung on. Staying here offers two pluses – you won't find much cheaper, there are fewer crowds and you're right in the heart of the old city. On the

downside, the pickings are slimmer and the lodges generally grungier than in Thamel.

Hotel Sugat (Map p115; ☎ 4245824; maryman@mos .com.np; s/d without bathroom from Rs 110/300, with bathroom Rs 300/400) This is one of the better options in the area. The choice here is between the more expensive, nicer and more spacious rooms out back, which don't have views, or the darker, creakier and pokier front rooms, which offer views over Basantapur Sq. There's a fine rooftop area with great views.

Royal Park Guest House (Map p115; ☎ 4247487; www.royalparkguesthouse.com; r with/without bathroom Rs 400/200-300) Almost next door to Hotel Sugat, this is a similar deal; nice views over Basantapur Sq, shame about the headache-inducing carpet. Like the Sugat, you are really paying for the location more than the quality of the rooms. There's a nice rooftop restaurant. Before you get your hopes up, bear in mind that the rooms pictured on the website are from a totally different hotel!

Annapurna Lodge (Map p116; ☎ 4247684; s/d without bathroom Rs 150/200, s/d with bathroom Rs 200/275) Simple but well kept, cheerful and cosy, this is probably the best option in Freak St. The attached Diyalo Restaurant (p149) is a good place to eat and there are evening movies and a laundry service.

Century Lodge (Map p116; ☎ 4247641; www.cen turylodge.4t.com; s/d without bathroom Rs 175/275, s/d with bathroom Rs 300/350) One of Freak St's long-term survivors, this place treads a tightrope between atmospheric and dingy but remains fairly popular. The creaky old-wing rooms haven't changed since 1972 (be warned, neither have the mattresses); the new top-floor rooms are cleaner but disappointingly concrete. The nicest rooms

---

FREAK STREET – THE END OF THE ROAD

Running south from Basantapur Sq, Freak St dates from the overland days of the late 1960s and early 1970s, when it was one of the great gathering places on 'the road east'. In its hippy prime this was the place for cheap hotels (Rs 3 a room!), colourful restaurants, hash and 'pie' (pastry) shops, the sounds of Jimmy and Janis blasting from eight-track players and, of course, the weird and wonderful foreign 'freaks' who gave the street its name. Along with Bodhnath and Swayambhunath, Freak St was a magnet for those in search of spiritual enlightenment, freedom and cheap dope.

Times change and Freak St (better known these days by its real name, Jochne) is today only a pale shadow of its former funky self. While there are still cheap hotels and restaurants, it's the Thamel area in the north of the city that is the main gathering place for a new generation of travellers. However, for those people who find Thamel too commercialised, Freak St retains a faint echo of those mellower days.

come with a balcony. There's a small library for book rental and some garden seating. Water supplies can be problematic.

Monumental Paradise (Map p116; ☎ 4240876; mparadise52@hotmail.com s/d with bathroom Rs 250/400) A newish place that's a lot more modern than the rest of Freak St. Rooms are clean and fresh, if devoid of charm, though the upper floor back rooms come with a private balcony. There's a good rooftop bar and restaurant and one suite (Rs 600) in the crow's nest has its own balcony and hammock!

Asia Holiday Lodge (Map p116; ☎ 4246579, asia _holiday62@yahoo.com s/d 200/300) Being colour blind is a definite advantage when faced with the snot-green walls and Day-Glo pink bedspreads of this modern place, but if you can get over the appalling décor it's not all that bad. It's impossible to see how the towel-sized bathrooms could physically be any smaller.

Central Kathmandu

Most of the following hotels are within walking distance of Durbar Marg and the Thamel area.

TOP END

Malla Hotel (Map p136; ☎ 4418385; mallahtgrp@mos .com.np; s/d US$130/156, s/d club deluxe US$150/182, discounts of 50%; ☒ ☒) On the northeastern edge of Thamel, west of the new Royal Palace, but still only a five-minute walk to all the Thamel restaurants, the Malla is solid four-star comfort. The slightly anaemic rooms enjoy either pool or garden views. There's a good swimming pool and, best of all, a superb garden, complete with a mini-stupa and even a peacock enclosure.

Shanker Hotel (Map p116; ☎ 4410151; www.shan kerhotel.com.np; s/d US$90/105, discounts of 30%; ☒) There's nowhere in town quite like this former Rana palace – the kind of place where you expect some whiskered old Rana prince to come shuffling around one of the wooden corridors. The rooms are quirky (some are split level) but for real grandeur you'll have to track down the dining halls and Durbar Hall conference space. The façade's palatial white columns of whipped cream look onto a huge front garden and swimming pool.

Yak & Yeti Hotel (Map p116; ☎ 4248999; www.yak andyeti.com; Newari Wing d US$185, Durbar Wing d US$205, discounts of 30-50%; ☒) This hotel is probably

the best-known in Nepal, due to its connections with the near-legendary Boris Lissanevitch, its original owner. The oldest section of the hotel is part of the Lal Durbar, a Rana palace, which houses the restaurants and casino; these retain traces of an overblown but spectacular Rana-baroque décor. The actual rooms are in two modern wings; the Newari Wing is the older of the two and the rooms incorporate Newari woodcarvings and local textiles without being kitsch. Businesspeople will find an executive floor and a well-equipped business centre. There's also a beautiful garden, two pools, tennis courts and a fitness centre.

Hotel de l'Annapurna (Map p116; ☎ 4221711; www.annapurna.com.np; s/d standard US$140/150, s/d superior US$180/190, discounts of 50%; ☒) Just off Durbar Marg, this is one of Kathmandu's longest-established hotels and is starting to show its age. Its central location on Durbar Marg is convenient, and apart from the usual five-star facilities, it has a casino and the largest hotel swimming pool in Kathmandu. If business is lax you should get a plush deluxe room for the price of a standard room. Look for the copy of the old town's Annapurna Temple in the foyer.

Lazimpat

North of Central Kathmandu is the Lazimpat embassy area. The options in this area are popular with nongovernment organisation (NGO) staff, repeat visitors and business people.

MIDRANGE

Hotel Ambassador (Map p116; ☎ 4410432; ambas sador@ambassador.com.np; s/d economy US$12/15, s/d standard US$20/25, s/d deluxe US$30/35, discounts of 20%; ☒ ☒) A solid rather than stylish choice, with a good restaurant and a small garden; it is on a noisy intersection so try to get a garden-facing, not road-facing room. The wooden-floored rooms are a little bit old-fashioned and can be dim. It's within walking distance of Thamel and Durbar Marg. The hotel's owners also run The Tea House in Nagarkot (see p227).

Hotel Tibet (Map p116; ☎ 4429085; www.hotel -tibet.com; s/d US$70/80, discounts of 40%; ☒) Tibetophiles and tour groups headed to or from Tibet like this recommended midrange choice, run by a friendly Tibetan family. The quiet and comfortable 55 rooms come with TV and private bathroom. There's also a great rooftop terrace, a garden and even a meditation chapel. It's just in front of the Radisson Hotel.

Hotel Manaslu (Map p116; ☎ 4410071; www.hotel manaslu.com; s/d standard US$28/32, s/d deluxe US$40/45, discounts of 25%; 🖳 🖳) Just beyond Hotel Tibet, this is a very nice modern hotel with a pleasant garden area and a pool fed by Newari-style fountains. The glorious carved windows in the restaurant were brought in from Bhaktapur. For some reason the standard rooms are brighter and have better views than the pricier deluxe rooms. The slightly inconvenient location explains the bargain rates.

Astoria Hotel (Map pp110–11; ☎ 4436180; www .astoria-hotel.com; s/d US$28/35, s/d deluxe US$50/60, discounts of 30–50%; 🖳) Further north along Lazimpat, signposted down a secluded alley to the side of the Hotel Shangri-La, is this excellent find. This hotel is tucked away and has pleasant gardens with a vegetable patch, which supplies the swish French restaurant with organic produce. The light and airy rooms are spotlessly clean, and have TV, carpet and nice home touches. The spacious standard rooms are in the block out back; deluxe rooms are bigger and come with air-con.

TOP END

Radisson Hotel (Map p116; ☎ 4423888; www.radisson .com/kathmandu.ne; standard/deluxe US$175/185, discounts of 30%; 🖳) North of the city in the Lazimpat embassy area, the Radisson is modern, well maintained and pleasantly decorated, with excellent facilities, including a 6th-floor pool with great views and a good gym operated by Clark Hatch. Rooms come with nice touches such as coffeemakers and data ports for laptop computers.

Hotel Shangri-La (Map pp110–11; ☎ 4412999; www .hotelshangrila.com; s/d superior US$120/130, s/d executive US$150/160, discounts of 35%; 🖳) This hotel is currently being renovated to bring it up to five stars, with a new casino, bar and fitness centre. Until then, the superior rooms are looking pretty tired, so ask for a free upgrade to the much nicer executive wing. The real draw, though, is the relaxing garden and twice-weekly barbeques (Rs 500).

Elsewhere
MIDRANGE
Hotel Vajra (Map p116; ☎ 4271545; www.hotelvajra .com; s/d without bathroom US$14/16, s/d with bathroom

from US$33/38, new wing rooms s/d from US$53/61, discounts of 30–40%) Across the Vishnumati River in the Bijeshwari district, this is one of Kathmandu's most interesting hotels in any price category. The complex feels more like a retreat than a hotel, with an art gallery, a library of books on Tibet and Buddhism, a rooftop bar and an Ayurvedic massage room. The cheapest rooms have shared bathrooms and mattresses that might be too narrow for some couples. The new-wing rooms are much swankier. The only catch is the location, which, though peaceful, makes it tricky for getting a taxi.

TOP END

Soaltee Crowne Plaza (Map pp110–11; ☎ 4273999; www .soaltee.crowneplaza.com; s/d US$180/190, s/d deluxe US$200/210, discounts of 60%; 🖳) Space and tranquillity are precious commodities in Kathmandu but the Soaltee has acres of both; 11 acres, to be precise. Spread around the palatial grounds are some excellent restaurants, a lovely poolside area, a casino and even a bowling alley. The price you pay is the crummy location on the western edge of town, a 15-minute taxi ride from the centre.

Dwarika's Hotel (Map pp110–11; ☎ 4470770; www .dwarikas.com; s/d US$155/165, s/d deluxe US$200/210, discounts of 15%; 🖳) For stylish design and sheer romance, this outstanding hotel is unbeatable. Over 40 years the owners have rescued thousands of wood carvings from around the valley (from buildings facing demolition or collapse) and incorporated them into the hotel design, which consists of clusters of traditional Newari buildings (including a library and pool) separated by brick-paved courtyards. The end result is a beautiful hybrid – a cross between a museum and a boutique hotel, with a lush, pampering ambience. All the rooms are unique and some have lovely open-plan granite bathrooms. Its only disadvantage is its poor location – on a busy street in the east of town – but finding a taxi is never a problem.

Hyatt Regency Kathmandu (☎ 4491234; www .kathmandu.regency.hyatt.com; d from US$210, 60% discounts; 🖳) No expense has been spared on this superb palace-style building, from the dramatic entrance of Newari water tanks to the modern Malla-style architecture. It's worth popping in en route to Bodhnath just to admire the gorgeous stupas in the foyer, which set the stylish tone for the hotel (there's a lamp-lighting ceremony at dusk). As you'd expect, the rooms are furnished tastefully and many have views over nearby Bodhnath stupa. The large swimming pool, tennis courts, excellent fitness centre, good restaurants and popular bar, make this the perfect spot for a splurge, especially when package rates dip as low as US$50. The Hyatt is a couple of km outside Kathmandu, on the road to Bodhnath.

Long-Stay Accommodation
If you are in and around the valley for some time, it's worth looking into something other than a regular hotel, although bear in mind that most hotels will offer highly discounted long-term rates. You should be able to get a three- or four-bedroom local apartment for about US$100 to US200 per month, or a house for about double this. Many longterm renters prefer to live in Patan.

Arcadia Apartments (Map p136; ☎ 4260187; arcadia@mos.com.np; apt per day/month US$18/350) It would be weird to self-cater when surrounded by so many great restaurants but if for some reason you do need a kitchen in the heart of Thamel try the top floor of the Arcadia Building. The apartments have basic cooking facilities, fridge, TV, sofa, separate bedroom and a balcony. There are only six apartments, so reserve ahead of time.

The **Intercultural Training & Research Centre** (Map p136; ☎ 4414490) can put you in touch with a Nepali homestay if you contact them in advance. See p357 for more details.

EATING
Kathmandu has an astounding array of restaurants. Indeed, with the possible exception of the canteen at the UN building,

there are few places where you can choose between Indian, Chinese, Japanese, Mexican, Korean, Middle Eastern, Italian or Irish cuisines, all within a five-minute walk. And there are even some Nepali restaurants… After long months on the road in India or long weeks trekking in Nepal most travellers find Kathmandu a culinary paradise.

Thamel's restaurant scene has been sliding upmarket for a few years now, with a slew of places now costing US$5 per meal – still a great bargain but unthinkable a few years ago. However, if you stay away from beer, you can eat until you burst for less than Rs 200. A bottle of beer will nearly double your bill in a budget restaurant.

Thamel
Thamel restaurants spill into Paknajol, Jyatha and Chhetrapati, just like the hotels. The junction outside Kathmandu Guest House is the epicentre of Thamel dining and you'll find dozens of excellent restaurants within a minute's walk in either direction.

Beyond the restaurants listed here, there are dozens of other budget restaurants, all offering the same standard menu of, well, pretty well anything, and all serving remarkably similar and often very bland food. What marks the difference between these places is the atmosphere, music, service and who happens to be there on the night.

BUDGET
Old Tashi Delek Rest (Map p136; mains Rs 90-140) This place, a long-time favourite, feels like a trekking lodge that's been transplanted from the Everest trek into a Thamel time warp. Prices are cheap, the Tibetan momos (and especially the *richosse* momo soup)

THE AUTHOR'S CHOICES

Nargila Restaurant (Map p136; ☎ 4700712; mains Rs 60-150) Across from the Northfield Café, on the 1st floor, this Israeli budget favourite is one of the very few places to offer good Middle Eastern food and is a quiet place to just take a break from the bustle outside. Try a *shwarma* (grilled meat and salad in a pitta; Rs 145) or hummus served with pitta (Rs 70), washed down by a mint tea (Rs 15). The hot waffle with fruit and yogurt (Rs 80) is just the best in Kathmandu. The staff are endearingly brusque.

Koto Restaurant (Map p136; ☎ 4256449; set meals Rs 150-500; ⊙ 11.30am-3pm, 6-9.30pm) When you need a break from endless 'same same but different' backpacker food, head for this budget branch of the acclaimed Durbar Marg restaurant. The Japanese flavours are subtle and complex and the bamboo décor is bright, elegant and clean. The sukiyaki 'young person' set meal (Rs 260) is a great deal, with all kinds of salad trimmings, miso soup, green tea and unlimited rice.

are authentic and the spinach mushroom enchilada (Rs 100) is surprisingly good for Tibetan-Mexican food (Tib-Mex?). It's down a corridor, slap bang in the centre of the Thamel action.

Yak Café (Map p136; mains 60-120) Another unpretentious and reliable Tibetan-run place at the other end of Thamel. The booths give it a 'Tibetan diner' vibe and the clientele is a mix of trekkers, Sherpa guides and local Tibetans who come to shoot the breeze over a cigarette and a tube of *tongba* (hot millet beer). The menu includes Tibetan dishes, with good *kothey* (fried momos), and South Indian food, at unbeatable prices. It feels just like a trekking lodge, down to that familiar electronic sound of a chicken being strangled every time a dish is ready.

Delima Garden Café (Map p136; mains Rs 90-250) If you can't decide whether you want baked beans or *tom kha gai,* this garden restaurant down an alleyway away from the traffic in Paknajol covers all the bases. The surroundings are nice but the food is a bit hit and miss. There are plenty of breakfast choices.

Helena's (Map p136; ☎ 4266979; mains Rs 150-295; ⏲ 7am-10pm) Helena's is deservedly popular for its set breakfasts (Rs 65), one of the highest rooftops in Thamel, cosy interior and super friendly service, with a wide range of coffee, good cakes, tandoori dishes and steaks. It's warm and cosy in winter. If you are headed off trekking, consider breakfast on the eighth floor a form of high-altitude training.

Chang Cheng Restaurant (Map p136; Centre Point Hotel; veg dishes Rs 80-120, meat Rs 180-300) The real deal for Chinese food, and often full of visiting Chinese business people and Chinese Tibetans who shout, smoke, slurp and burp their way through large portions of wonderfully spicy Sichuanese food.

Dahua Restaurant (Map p136; ☎ 4410247; dishes Rs 60-110) In contrast, this definitely isn't 'real' China – sticky sweet-and-sours and egg foo yong are the rule here – but it's cosy and tasty and the price is right. It's on the eastern edge of Thamel.

Thakali Kitchen (Map p136; ☎ 4701910; veg/non-veg daal bhaat Rs 85/115; ⏲ 10am-10pm) If, after having travelled all this way to Nepal, you actually fancy some Nepali food (!), this upstairs restaurant is a modern place popular with local people working in Thamel. Most opt for the daal bhaat but there's also a range of Newari food such as *aa lang kho,* a dried meat, cheese and radish soup.

Utse Restaurant (Map p136; Tibetan dishes Rs 60-80) In the hotel of the same name, this is one of the longest-running restaurants in Thamel and it turns out excellent Tibetan dishes, such as momos (meat/veg-filled ravioli), *kothey* (fried momos) and *talumein* (egg noodle soup). For a group blowout, *gacok* (also spelt *gyakok*) is a form of hotpot named after the brass tureen that is heated at the table and from which various meats and vegetables are served (Rs 675 for two).

MIDRANGE

Yin Yang Restaurant (Map p136; ☎ 4425510; Thai curries Rs 280) Just south of the intersection, this is one of Thamel's most highly regarded restaurants. It serves authentic Thai food cooked by a Thai chef in either garden or floor seating. It's not cheap but the food is a definite cut above the imitation Thai food found elsewhere. The green curry is authentically spicy – the massaman curry (with onion, peanut and potato) is sweeter. There's a good range of vegetable choices.

Third Eye Restaurant (Map p136; mains Rs 200-230) Next door to Yin Yang, and run by the same people, this is a long-running favourite that retains something of the old Kathmandu atmosphere. There's a sit-down section at the front, and a more informal section with low tables and cushions at the back and a rooftop terrace. Indian food is the speciality and the tandoori dishes are especially good.

Roadhouse Café (Map p136; pizzas Rs 260-350; Arcadia Bldg) The big attraction here is the pizzas from the wood-fired oven (we have been assured the wood is off cuts from a Terai timbermill). The pizzas are pretty darn good, and the décor, especially the courtyard out back, is warm and intimate. The starters, pasta dishes and coffees are all good, as is the service. Top it all off with a scoop of Baskin Robbins ice cream for Rs 70. Credit cards are accepted.

Four Season Restaurant (Map p136; ☎ 4701715; Trilok Plaza; dishes 250-280) A great location and some of the tastiest Thai and Indian food in town, make this a good compromise if you fancy a chicken tikka masala but your date wants a green papaya salad. You can sit overlooking the road, in the warm orange and black bar area or on the rooftop under what looks like an aircraft hanger. One of the chefs is Thai, the other worked at the Rum Doodle for 17 years, so they know their stuff.

K-Too Beer & Steakhouse (Map p136; ☎ 4700043; www.kilroygroup.com; mains Rs 160-450, glass of wine Rs 160-245, plus 13% tax) Run by the same people who run Kilroy's (see p149), the décor and furnishings here are deliberately rough and ready pub-style, and the food and atmosphere are excellent. Dishes range from Irish stew to spinach and potato salad with honey

NEPALI & NEWARI RESTAURANTS

There is a growing number of restaurants around town that specialise in Nepali (mostly Newari) food (see p102 for a rundown of Newari dishes). These run the gamut from unobtrusive little places in Thamel to fancy converted palaces with cultural shows, linen tablecloths and 15-course banquets. Most places offer a set meal, either veg or nonveg, and you dine on cushions at low tables. The 'cultural shows' consist of musicians and dancers performing 'traditional' song and dance routines. The whole thing is pretty touristy, but it's a fun night out nonetheless. At most places it's a good idea to make a reservation during the high season.

Thamel House Restaurant (Map p136; ☎ 4410388; www.thamelhouse.com; dishes Rs 75-200, set meal veg/nonveg Rs 500/600) In Paknajol, this place is set in a traditional old Newari building and has bags of atmosphere. The food is traditional Nepali and Newari. Ask for the à la carte menu and choose individual dishes or go for the blowout set meal. It's also open for lunch.

Bhanchha Ghar (Map p116; ☎ 4225172; Rs 1000 per person, beer Rs 250; ⏰ 11am-10pm) In a traditional three-storey Newari house in Kamaladi, just east of Durbar Marg, next to a Ganesh Temple. There is an upstairs loft bar where you can stretch out on handmade carpets and cushions for a drink, snacks and the obligatory cultural show (try to arrive before 7pm). You can then move downstairs to take advantage of an excellent set menu of traditional Nepali dishes and delicacies. Musicians stroll between the tables playing traditional Nepali folk songs. It's not all that cheap but the food is very good and you can also order a la carte.

Bhojan Griha (Map pp110-11; ☎ 4416423; www.bhojangriha.com; set menu Rs 997, plus 13% tax) In the same vein as Bhanchha Ghar, but perhaps more ambitious, is Bhojan Griha in a recently restored 150-year-old mansion in Dilli Bazar, just east of the city centre. It's worth eating here just to see the imaginative renovation of this beautiful old building, once the residence of the caste of royal priests. Again, dancers and musicians stroll through the various rooms throughout the evening, representing Nepal's major ethnic groups. Most of the seating is traditional (ie, on cushions on the floor), although these are actually legless chairs, which saves your back and knees. In an effort to reduce waste, plastic is not used in the restaurant and mineral water is bought in bulk and sold by the glass. *Went here*

Nepali Chulo (Map p115; ☎ 4220475; www.nepalichulo.com, set menu Rs 960, mains Rs 280, plus 13% tax) Closer to Thamel is this new restaurant in the wing of a 157-year-old Rana palace, the Phora Durbar. Most people choose the fixed menu of 11 dishes but ordering à la carte is possible. Choose between floor or table seating but get here before 7pm to catch the live music and dance. A *chulo* is a Nepali-style stove.

Krishnarpan Restaurant (Map pp110-11; ☎ 4470770; ⏰ dinner only) One of the best places for Nepali food is the Krishnarpan Restaurant at Dwarika's Hotel, east of the centre near the Ring Rd. The atmosphere is superb and the food gets consistent praise from diners. Prices range from US$22 for a six-course meal up to a wallet- (and stomach-) busting US$34, 22-course extravaganza. Bookings are advisable. If you are coming on Friday, arrive in time for the 6pm dance show in the hotel courtyard.

Baithak Restaurant (Map p116; ☎ 4267346; 12-course set menu Rs 945, mains Rs 250; ⏰ 10am-10pm) At Babar Mahal Revisited, southeast of the centre (see p153), this restaurant has a dramatic and regal, almost Victorian, setting, with crystal and linens and where diners are attended by waiters dressed in royal costume and watched over by looming portraits of various disapproving Ranas. The menu features 'Rana cuisine', a courtly cuisine created by Nepali Brahmin chefs and heavily influenced by North Indian Mughal cuisine. The setting is probably the most memorable part of the restaurant. Vegetarians will find plenty to eat here. The attached K2 Bar has a nice terrace for a predinner drink. A *baithak* is a royal suite or state room.

mustard dressing, and the excellent pepper steak (Rs 295) is already a post-trekking classic. There is always some promotion going on here (currently free fried potato skins and an Irish coffee for every main course) and live European football is broadcast on the TV. But really, guys, Barbara Streisand on the stereo – what were you thinking?

Everest Steakhouse (Map p136; steaks Rs 300-450) If K-Too represents the new breed of slickly-run Thamel eateries, then the Everest Steak house is very much old-school. The red curtains haven't changed in 20 years and the waiters can be fascinatingly rude – it's hard to know if they really are taking the piss or not. The menu spreads to 30 types of steak (garlic, pepper, Mexican, even a curry steak…), all imported from Kolkata (Calcutta) and served up rare unless you request well done. It's very popular with European trekking groups but, then, after three weeks' of daal bhaat, anything tastes good.

La Dolce Vita (Map p136; ☎ 4700612; pasta Rs 175-225, pizzas Rs 250) Thamel's best attempt at comfort Italian cuisine offers up such delights as gnocchi, spinach and walnut ravioli, tasty baked potatoes (Rs 55), tiramisu (Rs 125) and wines by the glass (from Rs 175). Choose between the rustic red and white tablecloths and terracotta tiles of the main restaurant, a rooftop garden, the yummy-smelling espresso bar or sunny lounge space; either way the atmosphere and food are excellent. It's right on the corner opposite Kathmandu Guest House.

Nuovo Marco Polo (Map p136; ☎ 4413724; www .kathmanduitalianfood.com; Bhagwan Bahal; mains Rs 150-250) Further out on the fringes of Thamel, this restaurant is also good for authentic Italian food, including Italian *permigiano* cheese and good espresso.

Pilgrims Feed 'N Read (Map p136; ☎ 4700942; mains Rs 110-180, set meal Rs 250) Keep walking past the Self-Help section of Pilgrims Book House and you'll end up in this quiet and classy café, with indoor and garden seating. The focus is on herbal teas (Rs 60 per pot) and vegetarian Indian food (including *dosa*s) and there's no shortage of reading material.

Northfield Café (Map p136; breakfasts Rs 150-190, mains Rs 180-270; ☯ 7am-10.30pm) Next door to Pilgrims, this open-air spot is the place for serious breakfast devotees (huevos rancheros included), with fresh juice and smoothies, and bottomless filter coffee (Rs 50). The

Mexican and Indian tandoori dinner dishes are excellent and the sunny garden is a real plus in winter.

New Orleans Café (Map p136; ☎ 4700736; mains Rs 220-390) Hidden down an alley near the Brezel Bakery, New Orleans boasts an intimate candlelit vibe and a great selection of music, often live. It's a popular spot for a drink (see p151) but the menu also ranges far and wide, from Thai curries to Creole jambalaya (Rs 220).

Krua Thai Restaurant (Map p136; ☎ 4414291; soups Rs 210-270, mains Rs 230-430) North of Sam's Bar, this is another good open-air Thai place. The food is reasonably authentic (ie spicy), with good curries, tom yam soup and papaya salad, although some dishes taste more Chinese than Thai. The Thai chef recently passed away so it remains to be seen whether standards will suffer.

Himalatte Café (Map p136; ☎ 4256738; mains Rs 180-285) A North-American coffeehouse feel here, right down to the comfy sofas and Friday night music jams (courtesy of the owner's band). The impressive array of coffees are some of the best in Thamel (Rs 40-70), as are the cheeseburgers (Rs 195). The menu ranges from Caesar wraps to fruit crêpes and the Tuesday and Thursday set meal specials are good value. We recommend the excellent chicken saltimbocca (Rs 210) – cheese, sage and bacon inside a chicken breast. If you are feeling a little fragile, try the hangover helper – carrot juice with ginger and parsley.

Fire & Ice Restaurant (Map p136; ☎ 4250210; 219 Sanchaya Kosh Bhawan, Tridevi Marg; pizzas Rs 240-350, glass of wine Rs 195; ☯ 11am-10pm) Rumour has it that this was a favourite of Prince Dipendra and his girlfriend, before he massacred his entire family in 2001 (see p38). Regardless, it's an excellent and informal Italian place, serving some of the best pizzas in Kathmandu, imported Italian soft-serve ice cream, seriously good coffee and rousing opera – Italian, of course. It's very popular and you'll need a reservation in the high season.

Dechenling Beer House (Map p136; ☎ 4412158; mains Rs 120-350, fixed meal Rs 390) Quality Tibetan and Indian food is served up in this attractive beer garden and it's one of the few places in town to offer interesting Bhutanese dishes (Rs 220), such as *kewa dhatsi* (potatoes and cheese curry). The *thentuk* (Tibetan noodle soup, Rs 120) is the best in Thamel. If you can't decide, opt for a set meal at Rs 350 to Rs 390.

Via Via Café (Map p136; ☎ 4700184; www.viaviacafé .com; closed Mon; mains Rs 120-240) This century-old red house at the end of Seven Bends is part of a Belgian-run chain of travellers' cafés that is part restaurant, part lounge bar, and part cultural centre. The food is European, with some specifically Belgian touches, and the brunch menu includes French toast, crêpes and Greek omelette with spinach, cheese and black olives (Rs 120). If you like the food, sign up for the weekly cookery course (see p105).

Kilroy's of Kathmandu (Map p136; ☎ 4250441; www .kilroygroup.com; ⏰ 7am-10pm) Named after the self-promoting Irish owner and head chef, this place is a definite cut above the average Thamel restaurant. The menu ranges from Balti chicken (Rs 295) to beef and Guinness hotpot (Rs 355) and interesting hybrids such as seafood *thugpa* (Tibetan noodle soup) with lemongrass (Rs 360), plus great desserts, especially the bread and butter pudding (Rs 185). The menu is posted online. There's always some kind of special going on, from Friday specials to champagne brunches. You can sit inside, or outside in the shady garden, complete with waterfall.

Freak Street (Jochne)

Freak St has a number of restaurants where you can find good food at lower prices than Thamel. Even if you're staying in other areas of the city it's nice to know there are some good places for lunch if you're sightseeing around Durbar Sq.

Diyalo Restaurant (Map p116) At the Annapurna Lodge, this is a cosy, popular little garden restaurant with a large menu, including crêpes, burgers and a few Chinese and Indian dishes, all for less than Rs 90.

Kumari Restaurant (Map p116; mains Rs 70-90, set Nepali meals Rs 60-80) Next to the Century Lodge, this friendly hang-out attracts the densest collection of dreadlocked travellers in Kathmandu and is one of very few places that seems to have hung onto some of the mellowness of times past. All the travellers' favourites are here and the prices are some of the best in town.

Ganesh Restaurant (Map p116; mains Rs 70-90) A slightly gloomy but good vegetarian place, with generous portions of such dishes as lasagne and spinach mushroom burgers.

There are two lovely *chaitya*s in front of the restaurant.

Snowman Restaurant (Map p116; cakes Rs 30-40) A long-running and mellow place, this is one of those rare Kathmandu hang-outs that attracts both locals and backpackers, drawn to some of the best cakes and crème caramel in town. The chocolate cake has been drawing travellers for close to 40 years now (it's not the same cake…). When John Lennon starts singing 'goo goo g'joob' on the stereo it really does feel very 1967…

Festive Fare Restaurant (Map p115) Overlooking Basantapur Sq, this restaurant has unsurpassed views from its top-floor terrace and attracts more of a tour-group crowd. Prices are about double those of the Freak St cheapies.

A cheaper nearby option is **Café de Cosmopolitan** (Map p115; mains Rs 90-150).

Central Kathmandu

The restaurants in the Kantipath and Durbar Marg areas are generally more expensive than around Thamel, although there are a few exceptions. See the last few listings here and the boxed text, p147 for some of Kathmandu's worthwhile splurges.

BUDGET

Dudh Sagar (Map p136; ☎ 4412047; Kantipath; dishes Rs 35-60; ⏰ 8am-8pm) This is the place to reacquaint yourself with South Indian snacks like *dosa*s (crêpes filled with potato curry) and *idly* (pounded rice cakes), topped off with Indian sweets like *barfi* (fudge) and *gulab jamun* (deep-fried milk balls in rose-flavoured syrup). A special *masala dosa* followed by a *dudh malai* (cream cheese ball in chilled pistachio milk) makes a great meal for less than Rs 70.

MIDRANGE & TOP-END

Koto Restaurant (Map p116; ☎ 4226025; Durbar Marg; dishes Rs 250-300, set menu Rs 500) Some say Koto prepares the best Japanese food in town. If not the best, then it's close, with a wide range of dishes from cold soba noodles to sukiyaki and even fresh mackerel, plus several set menus. It's up a dingy little stairwell but the décor is cosy and intimate. There's a less expensive branch in Thamel (see p145).

Seoul Arirang (Map p116; ☎ 4232105; Durbar Marg; mains Rs 200, set menus Rs 350-500) This excellent Korean place has a pleasant rooftop area and serves dishes barbecued at your table, as well as Korean classics such as *bulgogi* (beef and ginger) and *bibimbap* (rice with beef, vegetables and hot sauce; Rs 200). The owner is Korean but the chefs are Nepali. The picture menu guarantees no nasty surprises.

Ghar-e-Kebab (Map p116; dishes Rs 350-500) Outside and run by the Hotel de l'Annapurna, this has some of the best North Indian and tandoori food in the city. Indian miniatures hang on the walls and in the evenings classical Indian music is played and traditional Urdu *ghazals* (love songs) are sung. A complete meal for two, including drinks, costs about Rs 2000, and you get stung for bread and rice at Rs 100 each. Try one of the traditional sherbets for dessert.

Chimney Room (Map p116; ☎ 4248999; mains Rs 600-1100; ☺ dinner only) At the Yak & Yeti Hotel, northwest of the centre, this is one of Kathmandu's most famous restaurants, named after the famous open fireplace. It now serves mostly continental cuisine, with the excellent borscht and chicken à la Kiev two of the last links with its Russian roots.

1905 (Map p136; ☎ 4225272; Kantipath; mains Rs 200-700) You can dine with ambassadors and ministers in Thomas Kilroy's latest venture, set in a lovely old house. The tables on a bridge over a wonderful lily pond adds a definite colonial Burmese feel, so it's fitting that there are several southeast Asian dishes on offer. You'll need some time to wade through the seven different menus (including one just for teas!). Lunches are a great deal, with wraps and specials around Rs 195 (the chef's roots are showing with the cheese and Branston pickle sandwich) and there's a great Sunday brunch. Dinner is a more serious affair so dress up for dishes such as Roquefort, apricots and Asian pear salad Rs 395, or salmon fishcakes in saffron and vermouth sauce (Rs 675).

Elsewhere
BUDGET
Lazimpat Gallery Café (Map p116; ☎ 4428549; Lazimpat) This friendly place occupies a unique niche, somewhere between a greasy spoon and an art café, with a menu boasting both sausage, bacon and beans (Rs 110) and carrot and coriander soup (Rs 60). It's run by a British former VSO worker and so is popular with local volunteers. It's great for cheap, light lunch if you're out in Lazimpat.

MIDRANGE & TOP-END
Mike's Breakfast (Map pp110-11; ☎ 4424303; breakfasts Rs 160-290; ☺ 7am-9pm) As the name suggests, this place specialises in big American-style breakfasts (Mike is a former Peace Corps worker), and it does them well. It's a bit out of the way but it's certainly a laid-back way to start (and occupy most of) the day, in the attractive, leafy garden of an old Rana house. The breakfast menu includes excellent waffles with yogurt, fruit and syrup (Rs 210) and great eggs Florentine (Rs 260); all prices include organic Nepali coffee. Lunch extends to Mexican quesadillas and salad/soup combos. Friday is pizza night and the barbeque fires up Sunday evenings (Rs 250). While you're here take a look at the excellent Indigo Gallery (see p127). The restaurant is in the suburb of Naxal, about a 15-minute walk from the top end of Durbar Marg.

Royal Hana Garden (Map p116; ☎ 4416200; www.royalhana.com; Lazimpat; mains Rs 260-420; ☺ 10.30am-10pm) This place is a bit of a find – there are two outdoor hot-spring baths (admission Rs 280, includes towel and shampoo) where you can luxuriate for as long as you like before heading inside for a very reasonably priced Japanese meal. It's perfect for small groups and it's worth ringing ahead to book a soak. The restaurant is in Lazimpat, just north of the Hotel Ambassador.

Chez Caroline (Map p116; ☎ 4263070; mains Rs 200-550; ☺ 9.30am-10pm) In the Babar Mahal Revisited complex (p153), Caroline's is a swanky (pretentious even?) outdoor restaurant popular with expat foodies. It offers French-influenced main courses such as 'wild mushroom tart with walnut sauce', quiche and crêpes, plus a wide range of patisseries, teas and wines. After a swift couple of glasses of pastis (liquorice-flavoured liqueur), head upstairs for some steamy salsa dancing at Latin Quarter (see p152).

Dwarika's Hotel (p144) has a candlelit Friday night poolside barbecue (Rs 675 plus 13% tax) and dance show that makes for a great splurge. See the boxed text, p147 for details of the hotel's Krishnarpan Restaurant.

Quick Eats
Weizen Bakery (Map p136; mains Rs 150-280) Down from the Yin Yang, this bakery restaurant serves good vegetarian food. It has a pleasant garden and is a nice quiet place for breakfast, with newspapers to read and

music playing in the background. The bakery out front has decent cakes, breads (particularly the pretzels!) and pastries, with bakery goods (but not cakes) discounted by 50% after 8pm.

Pumpernickel Bakery (Map p136) Bleary-eyed tourists crowd in here every morning for fresh croissants, yak-cheese sandwiches, pastries and filter coffee in the pleasant garden area at the back. The restaurant is self service.

Hot Bread (Map p136) The bakery in the supermarket across the road does a roaring trade in sandwiches, bread rolls, pizza slices and pastries. The ham and cheese rolls (Rs 65) make a great lunch on the run. Bakery items are discounted by 50% after 9.30pm.

Brezel Bakery (Map p136) This nearby bakery is also pretty good, especially for breakfast.

BK's Place (Map p136; chips Rs 75-125) Has a steadily growing reputation for good old-fashioned chips (French fries), with a variety of sauces, as well as good momos. It's a tiny place, west of the Rum Doodle.

Sandwich Point (Map p136; rolls Rs 50-70; 24hr) A tiny place back at the main Thamel Chowk, this is a good little spot for a wide variety of rolls; perfect for the late-night munchies.

Dolma Momo Center (Map p136) This is typical of the Tibetan eateries dotted around town – it's just a hole in the wall, and momos and a few stains are the only things on the menu. But the momos are excellent, and at Rs 12 to Rs 16 for a plate and Rs 5 for milk tea, they're top value. Head south from the Hotel Utse.

Bakery Café (Map p136; 4422616; www.nanglos .com; Tridevi Marg; 7am-9.30pm) With branches on the edge of Thamel, on Durbar Marg and in Patan, this buzzy chain offers excellent value coffees and snacks for when you just need to take a break over an Americano and a plate of momos. The management have commendably hired deaf staff, which is perhaps one reason why the music is so bad. See also p193.

Self-Catering

For trekking food such as noodles, nuts, dried fruit and cheese, there are a number of small supermarkets in Thamel, including the Best Shopping Centre (Map p136) on the edge of Thamel at the end of Tridevi Marg.

The Bluebird supermarkets (Map p136) have a wide variety of goods. There's a branch by the main bridge across the Bagmati River to Patan, and another branch in Lazimpat, near the French embassy (both are on Map p116). The Kasthamandap Bazaar Supermarket (Map p116), just off Durbar Marg, also has a good selection.

DRINKING

There are a few bars scattered around Thamel, all within a short walk of each other. Just poke your nose in to see which has the crowd and style that appeals. Most places have a happy hour between 5pm and 8pm, with two-for-one cocktails.

Rum Doodle Restaurant & Bar (Map p136; 4701 208; mains Rs 220-350; 10am-10pm) Named after the world's highest mountain, the 40,000½ft Mt Rum Doodle (see p21), this famous bar is still milking a dusty (1983!) *Time* magazine accolade as 'one of the world's best bars'. It's long been a favourite meeting place for mountaineering expeditions – Edmund Hillary, Reinhold Messner, Ang Rita Sherpa and Rob Hall have left their mark on the walls – and trekking groups have added hundreds of giant yeti trek report footprints. The restaurant serves up steaks, pasta and pizza and there's often live music. You can eat here free for life – the only catch is that you have to conquer Everest first!

Maya Cocktail Bar (Map p136; cocktails Rs 200; 4pm-11pm) is a long-running favourite. The two-for-one cocktails between 4pm and 7pm (with free popcorn) are a guaranteed jumpstart to a good evening.

Pub Maya (Map p136) This place is associated to the Maya, but it's noisier.

Tom & Jerry Pub (Map p136) Close to Nargila Restaurant, this is a long-running, rowdy upstairs place with pool tables (Rs 50 per half hour) and a dance floor. Thursday is ladies' night.

Jatra (Map p136; 4211010; mains Rs 160-220) An intimate and pretty cool venue for a beer or dinner, with indoor and outdoor seating. Friday nights bring live music jams; on Wednesdays ladies get a free cocktail.

J-Bar (Map p136; 4418209; 6pm-midnight Tue-Fri & Sun, 3pm-2am Sat; drinks Rs 250-300, plus 13% tax) At the back of Himalayan Java, the J-Bar kicks in around 10pm when the Thamel bars shut and keeps going to 2am on Fridays and Saturdays. It's more like New York than Nepal, with cream leather interiors and pricey drinks, but it's a place

KATHMANDU

to meet Nepal's beautiful set. After 10pm access is via the side alley.

Sam's Bar (Map p136; ☼ 4-11pm) This is a cosy place with reggae every Saturday.

Full Moon (Map p136; ☼ 6pm-11pm; beer Rs 175) A tiny chill-out bar and den of iniquity, with a mixed Nepali-foreign clientele.

Via Via Café (see p146) This café has a small but sociable bar, with a happy hour from 4pm to 7pm, and Friday and Saturday night club music in the downstairs lounge.

Himalayan Java (Map p136; ☎ 4422519; Tridevi Marg; coffee Rs 45-70, breakfast Rs 120-160) Above the Bakery Café, this modern and buzzing coffeehouse serves good teas, coffees and snacks. There's a sunny balcony, lots of sofas, a nonsmoking section, and big-screen TV for the football, but from certain angles it feels a bit like a hotel foyer. It's popular with cool middle-class Nepalis.

Just Juice 'n' Shakes (Map p136; drinks Rs 25-90) Little more than a hole in the wall, hidden down a side alley, with just four cramped seats, but the juices, espresso and fruit/yogurt smoothies are just great. Try a carrot juice with lemon and ginger.

ENTERTAINMENT

Nepal is an early-to-bed country and even in Kathmandu you'll find few people on the streets after 10pm, especially when the capital's political situation is tense. Most bars close their doors by 11pm, though a few keep serving those inside.

Bands play at various Thamel restaurants on Friday and Saturday nights in the high season, particularly at Himalatte, Jatra and New Orleans – just follow your ears.

Beyond this, you could take in a Bollywood blockbuster or try to earn back your flight money at one of half a dozen casinos. Major sporting events such as Premier League football and Formula 1 grand prixs are televised in all the major bars.

There are also several cultural performances which generally involve local youths wearing a variety of dress over their jeans and performing traditional dances from Nepal's various ethnic groups, accompanied by a live band that includes a tabla, harmonium and singer.

Casinos

Kathmandu's casinos are all attached to upmarket hotels and open 24 hours. Dust off your tuxedo, polish up your best Sean Connery impersonation (*Aah, Mish Moneypenny…*) and make a beeline for the **Casino Royale** (Map p116; ☎ 4271244), set in a former Rana palace at the Yak & Yeti Hotel. Hang around the tables long enough and staff will ply you with free drinks and a dinner buffet (with Russian dancing girls!).

The other casinos, like **Casino Anna** (Map p116; ☎ 4225228) at the Hotel de l'Annapurna, attract a mainly Indian crowd.

At all casinos you can play in either Indian rupees or US dollars, and winnings (in the same currency) can be taken out of the country when you leave. The main games offered are roulette and blackjack, and the main clients are Indians. Nepalis are officially forbidden from entering.

Music & Dance

There are a few performances of Nepali music and dancing in the restaurants of the top-end hotels but little is scheduled.

The **New Himalchuli Cultural Group** (Map pp110-11; ☎ 4415280; himalchuli@enet.com.np) is a dance troupe that performs nightly at a crummy restaurant in Lazimpat. The hour-long show costs Rs 350 and starts at 7pm in summer (October to April) and 6.30pm in winter (May to September). Ring in advance to check that a performance is planned.

Kalamandapa Institute of Classical Nepalese Performing Arts (Map p116; ☎ 4271545; admission with tea Rs 400) Nepali dances (and occasional theatre) are performed here at the Hotel Vajra most Tuesdays at 7pm. Phone ahead to check schedules. There are sometimes Newari music concerts (Rs 500) on Fridays or Sunday evenings.

Gandharba Association (Map p136; ☎ 4700292; http://gandharbas.nyima.org) This is an organisation for the city's musician caste. There are informal music jams between 5pm and 7pm at their offices on the third floor above Equator Expeditions (tourists are welcome) but they play in local restaurants such as the Northfield Café (see p148). Individual musicians offer music lessons for around Rs 100 per hour (see p357) and they also sell their own CDs.

Upstairs Jazz Bar (Map p116; ☎ 4410436) This place in Lazimpat has live jazz in its tiny bar every Wednesday and Saturday that is patronised by an interesting mix of locals and expats.

Latin Quarter (Map p116; 4254260; www.salsanepal
.com; drinks Rs 200-300) This place has hot and
sweaty salsa dance nights on Friday and
Wednesday and you can even arrange salsa
dance tuition here. It's owned by a famous
Nepali singer/actor and is in the Babar
Mahal Revisited complex (see below).

Weekly **sitar concerts** accompany dinner
at Feed 'N' Read Restaurant in Pilgrim's
Book House in Thamel.

Cinemas

As made famous by the title of Pico Iyer's
book *Video Night in Kathmandu* (see p22),
a dwindling number of Thamel restaurants
show Western movies almost as soon as
they hit the cinemas in the West. There's
no charge to watch the films as long as
you order dinner but the food is average
at best and the film sound quality is often
atrocious, since the films are pirate copies
(it's not uncommon to see someone's head
walking past the camera on screen!) You'll
see the movies chalked up on pavement
blackboards.

Kathmandu Guest House Minitheatre (Map
p136; admission Rs 200) The Kathmandu Guest
House shows nightly films in its 25-seater
theatre.

Jai Nepal Cinema (Map p116; ☎ 4442220; www
.jainepal.com; stalls Rs 100-140, balcony Rs 175) On the
south side of the new Royal Palace; shows
some foreign films and is the best in town.

Kumari Cinema (Map p116) This cinema has
the same owners and prices as the Jai Nepal
and shows more foreign films in English.

Elsewhere, Bollywood-style Hindi and
Nepali films are the usual fare. Entry
charges are minimal (Rs 30) and the films
are well worth attending, since understanding the language is only a minor hin-
drance to enjoying these comedy-musical
spectaculars. Indians call them 'masala
movies' as they have a little bit of everything in them.

SHOPPING

Everything that is turned out in the various
centres around the valley can be found in
Kathmandu, although you can often find a
better choice, or more unusual items, in the
centres that produce the items – Jawlakhel
(southern Patan) for Tibetan carpets; Patan
for cast metal statues; Bhaktapur for woodcarvings; and Thimi for masks.

Thamel in particular can be a pretty
stressful place to shop, what with all the
tiger balm sellers, rickshaw drivers and high
speed motorbikers. Dive into a side street
or garden haven when stress levels start to
rise.

Amrita Craft Collection (Map p136; ☎ 4240757;
www.amrita.com.np) This is a good place to start,
with a broad collection of crafts and clothing. Subtract 20% from its fixed prices and
you get a good benchmark for what you
should aim to pay on the street if you don't
mind haggling. The branch across the road
has the larger selection.

Babar Mahal Revisited (Map p116) This unique
complex of old Rana palace outbuildings,
originally built in 1919, has been rede-
veloped to house a warren of chic clothes
shops, designer galleries, handicraft shops
and even a wine shop, as well as a couple
of top-end restaurants and bars. It's aimed
squarely at local expats and wealthy locals
so prices are as high as the quality. It's
southeast of the city near the Singh Durbar
government offices.

The royal palace of the Singh (or Singha)
Durbar, now home to Nepal's government,
was built in 1907. With over 1700 rooms,
it was once the largest private residence in
Asia, until fire destroyed 90% of the complex in 1973.

Aroma Garden (Map p136; ☎ 4420724) As the
name suggests, this is Thamel's sweetest-
smelling shop. It's a good one-stop shop
for incense, essential oils, soaps and almost
anything else that smells great.

There are dozens of shops in Thamel
that sell hand-made paper products from
photo albums to paper lamps. One of the
better shops is **Paper Park** (Map p136; ☎ 4700475;
www.handmadepaperpark.com), next to the Hotel
Marshyangdi.

Bronze Statues

Patan is the place to shop for statues (see
p194). This is one area where research is
vitally important, as quality and prices do
not necessarily correlate. The best shops in
central Kathmandu are on Durbar Marg;
Curio Arts (Map p116; ☎ 4224871; www.devasarts.com)
is a good place to start.

Clothing

Kathmandu is the best place for ready-to-
wear Western clothes. Embroidered T-shirts

are a popular speciality (our favourite has 'Same Same...' on the front and '...But Different' on the back!) and you can custom any design or logo, preferably on your own higher quality t-shirt.

A few tailors in central Thamel and Lazimpat stock Chinese silks and can make pretty much anything that you can explain, including copies of your favourite shirt or dress. There are lots of funky hats, felt bags, jumpers etc, particularly on the twisting road known as Saatghumthi, but *please* think twice before buying those red stripy juggling pants… Always try clothes on before handing over the cash.

Popular and unique items include felt bags (from Rs 250) and impossibly cute baby-sized North Face fleeces (Rs 300) or Tibetan jackets.

Curios
An endless supply of curios, art pieces and plain old junk is churned out for the tourist trade. Most does not come from Tibet but from the local Tamang community and doesn't date back much further than, well, last month, but that doesn't put most people off. Basantapur Sq is the headquarters for this trade, but before you lock wits with these operators, visit the **Amrita Craft Collection** (Map p136; ☎ 4240757).

Gems & Jewellery
Buying gems is always a risky business unless you know what you're doing – see p359 for a warning on gem scams. Be immediately suspicious of anyone who tells you that you will be able to make an enormous profit – if this was possible and legal they would do it themselves.

There are dozens of jewellery shops in Kathmandu – including in Thamel, on New Rd and Durbar Marg. The merchandise is produced both in India and locally. When walking between Thamel and Durbar Sq you'll often come across the tiny silver workshops.

The prices for silver jewellery are very low compared with what you'd pay at home, and many people have jewellery made to order. You buy the stones or draw the design and they'll make it up, usually in just a day or two. The quality is usually excellent, but be sure to agree on a price before giving the go-ahead.

Handicrafts
For general handicrafts such as handmade paper, ceramics and woodwork – much of it made by disadvantaged or minority groups – the best places are the showrooms of the nonprofit development organisations that are based in the Kopundol district of Patan. Two of these shops, **Mahaguthi** (Map pp110-11; ☎ 4438760; ☽ 10am-6.30pm) and **Sana Hastakala** (Map pp110-11; ☎ 4436631), have outlets in Lazimpat. See p194 for details.

Other nearby fair trade shops include **Folk Nepal** (Map p116; ☎ 4426009; ☽ 9am-7pm) and **Third World Craft Nepal** (Map p116; ☎ 2090500; www .thirdworldcraft.com), which although not as interesting are worth a quick look.

Maheela is an NGO that makes clothes, cushions, scarves, bags and Lao-like weavings from *dhaka* cloth, as well as carpets. The organisation is part of the Women's Foundation (see p60) and 25% of profits are donated to women's shelters and to educational, legal assistance and counselling programmes, including for those affected by Nepal's political violence. Their showroom is currently in Patan but plans to move to Thamel in 2006.

Indian Goods
Since the war in Kashmir killed the tourist trade there, many Kashmiris have migrated to Nepal to sell traditional crafts such as carpets, cushions, tapestry, woollen shawls and papier-mâché. These guys are excellent salespeople, so buy with caution.

You'll also find a fair amount of embroidered clothing, cushions and bed linen from Gujarat and Rajasthan. Prices are higher than if you buy in India, but considerably less than if you buy in the West. Tridevi Marg is lined with colourful Indian bedspreads.

Photography
Bandari Photo Shop (Map p136; ☎ 4700604) in central Thamel is a reliable source of film and can print out digital shots, as can **Color Link** (Map p136; ☎ 4251468; JP Rd) further south and **Advanced Photo Finisher** (Map p136) in the north of Thamel.

Hicola Tridevi Marg (Map p136; ☎ 4250163); Lazimpat (Map p116; ☎ 4429284) is fairly reliable and can handle colour prints and E-6 or Ektachrome slides. Mounted slide processing will cost you around Rs 400 for 36 slides;

prints costs Rs 360 for 36 photos. There are branches in Thamel and Lazimpat.

Ganesh Photo Lab (Map p116; ☎ 4216898), in an alley southwest of Durbar Sq, is an unlikely looking but reputedly good place for B&W processing.

New camera equipment can be a good deal in Nepal and the range of cameras and lenses is good. New Rd in central Kathmandu is the best place to look. In Thamel try **Snapper Photo** (Map p136; ☎ 4700494; JP School Rd). Just be sure to ascertain whether what you are buying has an international warranty.

Tea

One reliable place for high-quality tea is **Tea World** (Map p136; ☎ 4252588), down a long corridor beside the Student Guest House in Thamel. The manager offers free tasting and will tell you a lot about the teas on offer. Prices range from Rs 100 to Rs 600 per 100g. See p370 for more on Nepali tea.

Thamel's tea shops carry a wide range of spices and masala mixes.

Thangkas

The main centre for thangkas is just off Durbar Sq, and this is where you'll find the best salespeople (not necessarily the best thangkas). For modern work there are plenty of places in Thamel.

Phapa Chengreshi Thangka Painting School (Map p136) You can see thangkas being painted on the spot at this school in Thamel.

Dharmapala Thangka Center (Map p116; ☎ 4223 715; www.thangka.de) Down an arcade, off Durbar Marg, this is a showroom for a local school of thangka painting. You can see the thangkas being painted at the nearby **workshop** (Map p116).

Tibetan Thangka Gallery (Map p116; ☎ 4428863) Just past the Hotel Ambassador, this is another good little place. Thangkas are painted on the spot (you can watch the artists at work) and many pieces from here end up in the Durbar Sq shops with higher price tags.

Tibetan Antiques

Kathmandu seems to be the global clearing house for a continual stream of antiques from Tibet, including thangkas, carpets, jewellery, storage chests, religious objects, saddles and clothing. Since the Chinese have done their utmost to destroy Tibetan culture over the last 50 years, removing some of

what remains to safety is perhaps more morally acceptable than some other 'collecting' that goes on in Nepal. There are a number of good shops on Durbar Marg, but don't go without a very healthy wallet.

For prayer flags and Tibetan and Bhutanese cloth, the best place is the street in front of the Kathesimbhu Stupa. Choose between cheaper polyester and better quality cotton flags and remember, this is your karma that we are talking about.

Trekking Gear

Thamel has some excellent trekking gear for sale, though don't think that you are getting the genuine article. Most of the 'Columbia' fleeces and 'North Face' jackets are made locally but with imported fleece and Gore-Tex. See p328 for details on hiring and buying trekking gear. For reliable rentals and purchase try **Shona's Alpine Rental** (Map p136; ☎ 4265120).

One useful tip: you can revitalise an old down sleeping bag by having a reliable trekking shop add 500g to 1kg of down, for around US$20 per kilo. Most places do an excellent job.

GETTING THERE & AWAY

See p376 for details of getting to/from Kathmandu both by air and by land from neighbouring countries.

Air

There are three important rules with flights out of Kathmandu: reconfirm, reconfirm and reconfirm! This particularly applies to Royal Nepal Airlines (RNAC); at peak times when flights are heavily booked you should reconfirm when you first arrive in Nepal and reconfirm again towards the end of your stay. Even this may not guarantee you a seat – make sure you get to the airport very early as people at the end of the queue can still be left behind. Thai doesn't require reconfirmation.

For a list of airline offices in Kathmandu see p376.

DOMESTIC AIRLINES

The various domestic airlines have sales offices around the city but locations and phone numbers seem to change with the weather. Anyway, it's far less hassle to buy tickets through a travel agency and you'll probably get a better deal this way. See p376 for an overview of domestic airlines.

RNAC has computerised booking only on five routes: Pokhara, Jomsom, Lukla, Bharatpur and mountain flights. These can be booked at the main **RNAC office** (Map p116; ☎ 4248614; Kantipath; ☼ 9am-1pm & 2-6pm) on the corner with New Rd.

All other RNAC domestic flights are booked in a haphazard manner at a small **domestic office** (Map p116; ☎ 4224497, 4226574; ☼ 10am-1pm, 2-5pm) just around the corner. Here it seems the booking clerk keeps issuing tickets as long as people keep fronting up with money. With no apparent reservation charts to speak of, the potential for overbooking is high. Confirm more than once, and get to the airport early. The other domestic carriers are much better organised.

Bus

LONG DISTANCE BUSES

The **Kathmandu bus station** (Map pp110-11; Ring Rd, Balaju) is north of the city centre. It is officially called the Gongbu Bus Park, but is generally known as the Kathmandu Bus Terminal, or simply 'bus park'. This bus station is basically for all long-distance buses, including to Pokhara and destinations in the Terai. It's a huge and confusing place and there are very few signs in English but most of the ticket sellers are very helpful. There's often more than one reservation counter for each destination. Bookings for long trips should be made a day in advance – Thamel travel agents will do this for a fee.

See the table, left for a list of longdistance destinations served from Kathmandu. Bus No 23 (Rs 7) runs to the bus station from Lekhnath Marg on the northern edge of Thamel.

The exceptions to this are the popular tourist buses to Pokhara (seven hours, Rs 250) that depart daily at around 7am from a far more convenient location at the Thamel end of Kantipath (see Map p136). Buses are comfortable and you get a fixed seat number with your ticket. For more details see p263.

Greenline (Map p136; ☎ 4257544, www.catmando .com/greenline; Tridevi Marg; ☼ 7am-5.30pm) offers air-con deluxe services that are considerably more expensive than the tourist buses (but include lunch). There are daily morning buses to Pokhara (US$12, seven hours) and Chitwan (US$10, six hours), with a lunch break and bus change in Kurintar. The Lumbini service is currently on hold. You should book a day in advance. They also offer 'drive there, fly back' packages to Pokhara (US$59) and Chitwan (US$59 to US$67).

BUSES FROM KATHMANDU BUS STATION

Destination	Km	Duration (hr)	Cost (Rs) night/day	Ticket window
Besisahar	150	6	175 bus, 235 minibus	25 & 27
Bhairawa/Sunauli	282	8-10	280/230 (Rs 305 minibus)	23 & 24
Biratnagar	541	18	525/-	9
Birganj	298	10	250 night bus or minibus	15 & 17
Butwal	237	7-9	261/207, 282 minibus	22, 23, 24
Dhunche	119	8	-/159 minibus	28
Gorkha	141	5	-/120 big bus	25
Hile	635	24	608/-	7
Ilam	697	13	700/-	3
Janakpur	375	12	410/380 minibus	11 & 14 (day bus)
Kakarbhitta	610	18	607/530	2 & 29
Mahendranagar	695	18	667/667	6
Narayangarh	146	5	150	17
Nepalganj	531	12	520/500	19
Pokhara	202	8	200/250 minibus	15, 16 & 25 (minibus)
Tansen (Palpa)	302	10-12	300/235	23 & 24
Trisuli Bazaar	68	4	78	30

* Duration is daytime driving time. Night buses take around 50% longer, with a sleep stop

KATHMANDU

Golden Travels (Map p116; ☎ 4220036; Woodlands Hotel, Durbar Marg) also runs similar services, departing at 7am, to Pokhara (US$12) and Sunauli (Rs 525), changing buses in Kalanki.

THE KATHMANDU VALLEY

Buses for destinations within the Kathmandu Valley, and for those on or accessed from the Arniko Hwy (for Jiri, Barabise, and Kodari on the Tibetan border) operate from the **City (Ratna Park) bus station** (Map p116), also known as the old bus stand, in the centre of the city on the eastern edge of Tundikhel parade ground. The station is a bit of a horror; drenched in diesel fumes, with no English signs and not much English spoken. Keep shouting out your destination and someone will eventually direct you to the right bus.

Services include to Banepa (Rs 20), Dhulikhel (Rs 25), Barabise (Rs 86; last bus 4pm), Kodari (7am, Rs 160), Jiri (departures between 5.30am and 8am; Rs 247, express Rs 290 to Rs 320). Unless otherwise noted buses depart when full.

As with anything in Nepal, however, there are exceptions to the rule. Buses to Bhaktapur (Rs 12, 45 minutes) run from a **stand** (Map p116) on Bagh Bazar.

A single direct minibus to Nagarkot (Rs 150, three hours) leaves from just north of Leknath Marg, north of Thamel, at 1.30pm – see the Greater Thamel map.

Buses to Pharping (Dakshinkali) leave from Shahid Gate (Martyrs' Memorial) at the southern end of the Tundikhel parade ground (Map p116), as well as the Ratna Park station.

Buses to Bungamati, Godavari and Chapagaon in the southern valley leave from Patan – see p195.

Car

Although you cannot rent cars on a drive-yourself basis they can be readily rented with a driver from a number of operators. The rental cost is high, both in terms of the initial hiring charge and fuel. Charges are as high as US$50 per day, although they can be lower, especially if you are not covering a huge distance.

Wayfarers (see p114) can arrange car hire for a one-way drop to Pokhara (Rs 5500) or Chitwan (Rs 4100). Sightseeing around the Kathmandu Valley costs around RS 2500 per day depending on the itinerary.

Taxis

A better option than hiring a car is to hire a taxi for the day. Between several people, longer taxi trips around the valley, or even outside it, are affordable. A half-/full-day sightseeing trip within the valley costs around Rs 800/1500. For longer journeys outside the valley count on about Rs 2500 per day plus fuel, which is generally cheaper than hiring a car through a travel agency.

GETTING AROUND

The best way to see Kathmandu and the valley is to walk or ride a bicycle. Most of the sights in Kathmandu itself can easily be covered on foot, and this is by far the best way to appreciate the city. If and when you run out of steam, there are plenty of reasonably priced taxis available.

To/From the Airport

Kathmandu's international airport is called **Tribhuvan Airport** (Map pp110-11; ☎ 4472256) after the late king; the area's former name Gaucher (literally 'cow pasture') speaks volumes about Kathmandu's rapid urban expansion. See p376 for details of arrival and departure procedures.

Getting into town is quite straightforward. Both the international and domestic terminals offer a prepaid taxi service, currently fixed at Rs 350 to Thamel.

Once outside the international terminal you will be confronted by hotel touts, who are often taxi drivers making commission on taking you to a particular hotel. Many hold up a signboard of the particular hotel they are connected with, and if the one you want is there, you can get a free lift. The drawback with the taxis is that the hotel is then much less likely to offer you a discount, as it will be paying a hefty commission (up to 50% of the room) to the taxi driver. If you book a room in advance, most hotels will pick you up direct for free and there's no commission.

Public buses leave from the main road – about 300m from the terminal – but they're only really practical if you have very little luggage and know exactly how to get to where you want to go.

From Kathmandu to the airport you should be able to get a taxi for Rs 200 during daylight hours, around Rs 250 for a late or early flight.

Cycle-Rickshaw

Cycle-rickshaws cost Rs 30 to Rs 50 for most rides around town – because you have to negotiate all fares they can actually be more expensive than going by taxi. The tourist rate from Thamel to Durbar Sq is Rs 40. You *must* agree on a price before you start.

Bicycle

Once you get away from the crowded streets of Kathmandu, cycling is a pleasure, and if you're in reasonable shape this is the ideal way to explore the valley. See p80 for general information on biking and some route ideas.

Mountain bikes start at around Rs 150 per day for poor-quality Chinese- or Indian-made bicycles, fine for light use around the city. Imported bicycles can be rented for around Rs 400, and this is generally money well spent. Check the brakes before committing and be certain to lock the bike whenever you leave it.

For longer trips around the valley, the major mountain bike companies such as Dawn Til Dusk, Himalayan Mountain Bikes and Massif hire out high-quality bikes with front-suspension for around Rs 600. Bike Nepal and Nepal Mountain Bike Tours are a bit cheaper but the former's bikes are pretty battered. See p83 for company details.

If you want to make an early start, most are happy to give you the bike the evening before. For all bikes, negotiate discounts for rentals of more than a day.

Bus

Buses are very cheap, but often unbelievably crowded and limited in where they can go to in Kathmandu. The smaller minibuses are generally quicker and can be useful to places like Bodhnath and Patan if you can work out the routes.

Motorcycle

There are a number of motorcycle rental operators in Thamel. Officially, you will need an international driving licence, however no-one ever checks. You will have to leave a deposit of either your passport or air ticket. For Rs 350 per day you'll get a 125cc Indian-made Honda road bike, which is generally fine for road trips in the Kathmandu Valley. A 250cc trail bike costs around Rs 600 per day.

Singh Motorbike Centre (Map p136; ☎ 4418594; ☻ 8am-7pm) is a reliable place for in Thamel.

Pheasant Motor Bikes (Map p136) in the courtyard of the Pheasant Lodge has somewhat slippier prices, ranging from Rs 350 for a Yamaha RX 125 to Rs 600 for a Hero Honda or Exciter.

Motorcycles can be great fun outside the town, once you master the traffic. The main problem is getting out of Kathmandu, which can be a stressful, choking and dangerous experience. You will need a pair of goggles and some kind of face mask (available in most pharmacies).

Fuel currently costs Rs 67 (and rising) per litre and you'll only need a couple of litres for a day trip. Beyond the ring road petrol stations are few and far between.

Safa Tempos

These electric and ecofriendly three-wheeled vans serve various routes around town from a confusing collection of stands alongside the main post office on Kantipath (Map p116). Unfortunately few drivers speak English, there are few english signs and the routes can be fiendishly complicated. The tempos are green; petrol driven *tuk-tuk's* are blue. Blue signs marked with the white outline of a tempo indicate a stop.

Taxi

Taxis are quite reasonably priced. The charge for a metered taxi is Rs 8 flagfall and Rs 3 for every 200m; drivers don't usually take too much convincing to use the meter for short trips, although from major tourist centres you may have to negotiate. Shorter rides around town (including to the bus station) rarely come to more than Rs 60. Night-time rates cost 50% more between 8pm and 6am. Most taxis are tiny Suzuki Marutis, which can just about fit two backpackers and their luggage.

Taxis can be booked in advance on ☎ 4420987, at night call ☎ 4224374.

Other approximate taxi fares from Thamel include:

Pashupatinath Rs 90
Bodhnath Rs 130
Patan Rs 110 to 130
Bhaktapur Rs 350
Changu Narayan Rs 600
Nagarkot Rs 700
Dhulikhel Rs 1000

Around the Kathmandu Valley

The fertile, mountain-sheltered Kathmandu Valley is the historic heart of Nepal, where the Himalaya's most sophisticated kingdoms rose and fell and where Nepali art and culture were developed and refined. In many ways the Kathmandu Valley *is* Nepal.

The artistic richness of the valley is reflected in the six Unesco World Heritage sites that lie scattered around the valley like jewelled confetti. They include the ancient Buddhist stupas of Swayambhunath (affectionately known as the 'Monkey Temple') and Bodhnath. The Pashupatinath Temple ranks as Nepal's most important Hindu site and attracts pious pilgrims and dreadlocked sadhus (holy men) from all over the subcontinent. Newari architecture reaches its pinnacle in the breathtaking Durbar squares of Patan and Bhaktapur, the third and most traditional of the valley's three former kingdoms. Just outside Bhaktapur is the Changu Narayan Temple, an open-air museum of stone-carved masterpieces. All these sites are easily visited as day trips from Kathmandu.

The valley has a host of lesser-known, but still wonderful, temples, viewpoints and traditional Newari villages, and half the fun is getting to and from these sights, by foot, mountain bike or motorbike. Many people miss out on these sights in a feverish rush to get to Chitwan, Pokhara or Everest, but the irony is that you'll find far fewer tourists just 10km outside Kathmandu than you will jostling for a view at Everest Base Camp.

With a rapidly expanding population of 1.5 million the valley has certainly changed over the years, but aspects of traditional life endure. Rural life continues to move to the rhythms of the seasons and spectacular festivals, and the timeless demands of the fields, the family and the gods remain the fundamental priorities of most people's lives.

HIGHLIGHTS

- View the stunning Newari architecture of **Patan's Durbar Square** (p186), with its superb art museum
- Explore the fascinating backstreets of **Bhaktapur** (p196), Nepal's most intact medieval town
- Follow Tibetan refugees around the Buddhist stupa of **Swayambhunath** (p162), with its excellent views of Kathmandu
- Get a taste of Tibetan culture at the **Bodhnath Stupa** (p170), the largest in Nepal
- Order room service and savour the Himalayan views direct from your hotel balcony in **Nagarkot** (p223) or **Dhulikhel** (p227)
- Take a bike ride out to the lovely traditional Newari village of **Bungamati** (p220)

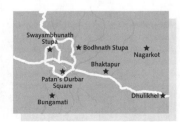

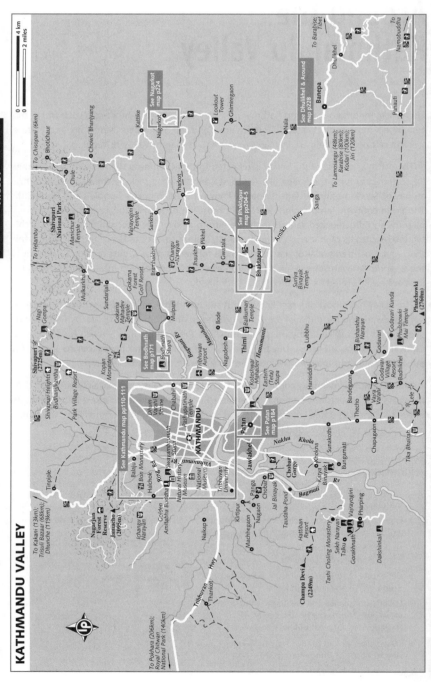

AROUND THE KATHMANDU VALLEY

KATHMANDU VALLEY

History

An important entrepôt on the trade route from India to Tibet, the Kathmandu Valley has long been a cultural and racial melting pot, with migrations from all directions adding to the stew. This fusion has resulted in a unique Newari culture that found its expression in the valley's superb art and architecture. For more information on Newari culture see p44 and p47.

The Newari golden age peaked in the 17th century when the valley consisted of three glorious but rival city-states, all of which grew rich from the transit trade. It was during the reign of the Malla kings (see p30), particularly in the 17th and 18th centuries, that many of the valley's finest temples and palaces were built, as each kingdom strove to outshine the other.

The unification of Nepal in 1768 by Gorkha's King Prithvi Narayan Shah signalled the end of the Kathmandu Valley's fragmentation. Nepali, an Indo-European language spoken by the Khas of western Nepal, replaced Newari as the country's language of administration.

Climate

In summer (May to September) Kathmandu and the valley can get very hot, with temperatures often above 30°C. Even in the winter months (December to February) the bright sunny days often reach 20°C, although with nightfall the mercury may plummet to near freezing.

It never snows in the Kathmandu Valley, but climb higher to the valley edge at Nagarkot and it gets significantly colder, so bring a jumper.

Dangers & Annoyances

The Kathmandu Valley remains largely immune to the political violence wracking the rest of the country, largely due to a strong-army presence. Rural areas to the east and on either side of the road to the Tibetan border are considered Maoist strongholds.

Women in particular should avoid hiking alone in remote corners of the valley. Don't venture out during a *bandh* (strike) and avoid travelling outside the valley after dark. For general security advice see p359.

Getting Around

If you intend to do any biking, hiking or just plain exploring it's worth getting Nepa Maps' 1:50,000 *Around the Kathmandu Valley* (Rs 450) or Himalayan Maphouse's *Biking Around Kathmandu Valley* (Rs 550), both are available in Kathmandu.

BICYCLE & MOTORBIKE

By far the easiest and most economical way of getting around the valley is by bicycle or motorbike. Bicycle speed allows you to appreciate your surroundings and gives you the freedom to wander wherever you like. If you are aiming for somewhere on the rim of the valley, make sure you have a multigeared mountain bike (see p158 for places to hire bikes in Kathmandu). A reasonably fit person can cycle almost anywhere in the valley and return to Kathmandu before dusk.

See the Outdoor Activities chapter for details on the demanding but rewarding routes from Kathmandu to Dhulikhel (p84); Panauti to Patan (p85); and the Scar Route through Shivapuri National Park (p83).

Other excellent DIY day-trip itineraries that combine a great ride with some lesser-visited cultural gems include the following:

- Kirtipur to Chobar to Pharping and then Dakshinkali
- Bungamati to Khokna and onto Chobar
- Chapagaon to the Lele Valley to Badhikhel and to Bishanku Narayan

---

TOP FIVE TEMPLES IN THE KATHMANDU VALLEY

The following five are our favourite temples in the valley:

- Changu Narayan (p165) – A treasure house of sculpture at this Unesco World Heritage site.
- Gokarna Mahadev (p212) – A visual A to Z of Hindu iconography.
- Vajrayogini Temple (p214) – Peaceful and powerful spot visited by troops of playing monkeys.
- Budhanilkantha (p182) – Impressive monolithic stone carving of a sleeping Vishnu.
- Dakshinkali (p219) – Spooky place of blood sacrifices and wrathful goddesses.

- Budhanilkantha to Nagi Gompa to Mulkarkha to Sundarijal to Gokarna Mahadev
- Nagarkot to Vajrayogini Temple to Sankhu and onto Bodhnath
- Bodhnath to Gokarna Mahadev Temple to Sankhu and Vajrayogini Temple.

BUS & TAXI
Buses and minibuses service all of the roads, but although they're cheap, they are uncomfortable and limiting. If you are part of a group or if the budget allows, you could consider hiring a car or taxi (Rs 600 to 800 per half day, or Rs 1000 to 1500 per full day).

FOOT
There are a great many interesting walks around the valley, the best of which link up some of the most interesting sights in the valley and avoid backtracking by bus or bicycle. See below for our favourite walks. Other excellent day hikes include from Nagi Monastery (in Shivapuri National Park) to Kopan Monastery, and from Nagarkot to Sankhu or Changu Narayan. For something more extreme, try the full-day cardio-hikes up to the peaks of Shivapuri, Phulchowki or Nagarjun.

If you don't have the time for an Everest or Annapurna trek but still want to hit some trails for a couple of days, it's possible to link up a series of day hikes around the valley to form a multiday trek of anything from two days to a week, staying in lodges and hotels and taking in a combination of Panauti, Namobuddha, Dhulikhel, Banepa, Nagarkot, Chisopani, Sundarijal, Budhanilkantha and Kakani.

TOP FIVE VALLEY HIKES

Get the blood moving with these excellent half-day hikes.

- Nagarkot to Nala via Ghimiregaon (p224)
- Dhulikhel to Panauti via Namobuddha (p230)
- Gokarna Mahadev to Bodhnath, via Kopan Monastery (p214)
- Kirtipur to the Jal Binayak Temple via Chobar (p216)
- Hattiban to Champa Devi (p219)

ORGANISED TOURS
Wayfarers Travel Service (Map p136; ☎ 4266010; www.wayfarers.com.np; Thamel, Kathmandu) offers one-day guided walks of the settlements of the southern valley rim: Kirtipur, Khokna, Bungamati and Chapagaon. It also offers a three-day guided 'Valley Vistas' hike, which take in Sankhu, Namobuddha, Dhulikhel and Nagarkot. Day hikes cost US$30 per person with a guide, transport, lunch and breakfast, or US$20 if you travel by bus. Three-day hikes cost US$110, including accommodation, lunch, breakfast and a porter guide.

See p82 for information on organised mountain-bike trips around the valley

AROUND KATHMANDU

The sights in this section can all be visited as easy day trips, or even half-day trips, from the capital.

SWAYAMBHUNATH
The great Buddhist temple of **Swayambhunath** (admission Rs 75), on the top of a hill west of Kathmandu, is one of the most popular and instantly recognisable symbols of Nepal. The temple is known affectionately as the 'Monkey Temple', after the large troop of handsome monkeys that guards the hill and amuses visitors and devotees with tricks (including sliding gracefully down the banisters of the main stairway to the temple).

Legends relate that the Kathmandu Valley was once a lake (geologists agree on this point) and that the hill on which Swayambhunath stands was 'self-arisen' *(swayambhu)*, much like a lotus leaf risen from the muddy waters of the lake (see also the boxed text, p217). It is also said that Emperor Ashoka paid a visit to the site over 2000 years ago.

An inscription indicates that King Manadeva ordered work done here in AD 460 and certainly by the 13th century it was an important Buddhist centre. In 1346 Mughal invaders from Bengal broke open the stupa in the search for gold. King Pratap Malla added the stairway in the 17th century.

From its hilltop setting, Swayambhunath offers fine views over Kathmandu and the valley. It's particularly striking in the early evening when the city is illuminated, and the site is also very attractive under the soft glow of moonlight. There are several curio

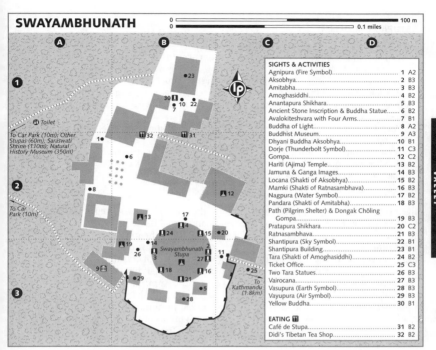

SWAYAMBHUNATH

AROUND THE KATHMANDU VALLEY

shops around the stupa, as well as a couple of reviving cafés.

Sights

EASTERN STAIRWAY
Although you can get closer to the temple by vehicle from the west, the long climb up the eastern stairway is by far the best way of approaching Swayambhunath. Look for the trinity of yellow-and-red stone Buddhas at the base of the hill. Halfway up the steps there is another small collection of stonework, including a scene depicting the birth of the Buddha, with his mother Maya Devi grasping a tree branch and the Buddha taking seven miraculous steps immediately after his birth. You'll see Tibetan astrologers reading fortunes here.

As you climb the final (steepest) stretch, look for the pairs of animals – Garudas, lions, elephants, horses and peacocks – the 'vehicles' of the Dhyani Buddhas. Near the end of the climb is the ticket office (there's another one around the back of the site). When you reach the top, remember to walk around the stupa in a clockwise direction.

GREAT THUNDERBOLT
As well as building the great stairway, Pratap Malla added a pair of *shikharas* (corncoblike Indian-style spires) and the stone snow lions and *dorje*, which visitors see immediately upon reaching the top of the stairs. *Dorje* is the Tibetan word for this thunderbolt symbol; in Sanskrit it is called a *vajra*. In Tantric thought the *dorje* symbolises male force or compassion and the bell symbolises female wisdom. Around the pedestal supporting Swayambhunath's mighty *dorje* are the animals of the Tibetan calendar.

STUPA
Atop the soaring swell of the whitewashed dome, a gold-coloured square block depicts the watchful eyes of the Buddha, which gaze out across the valley in each direction. The question mark–like 'nose' is actually the Nepali number *ek* (one) and a symbol of the unity of all life. Between and above the two eyes is a third eye, which symbolises the Buddha's insight.

Set around the base of the central stupa is a continuous series of prayer wheels, which

STUPA SYMBOLISM

The Buddhist stupas of Swayambhunath and Bodhnath are among the most impressive and most visited monuments in Nepal, as well as the most complex. The earliest stupas were simply domed burial mounds, built to hold relics of the Buddha, but they have evolved over the centuries to become complex structures that represent Buddhist philosophy.

The lowest level of the stupa is the plinth, which may be simply a square platform, but may also be terraced, as at Bodhnath. Atop the plinth is the hemispherical *kumbha* (dome; *kumbha* literally means 'pot'), which is freshly whitewashed each year.

Atop the dome is a *harmika,* a square base usually painted on each side with a pair of eyes. Topping the *harmika* is a tapering section of 13 stages, said to represent the 13 stages of perfection on the way to nirvana. The stupa is topped by a protective umbrella.

The five elements are also represented in the stupa's structure: the base symbolises earth; the dome water; the spire fire; the umbrella air; and the pinnacle ether.

pilgrims, circumambulating the stupa, spin as they pass by. Each prayer wheel carries the sacred mantra *om mani padme hum* (hail to the jewel in the lotus). The prayer flags fluttering from the lines leading to the stupa's spire also carry Tibetan mantras. Also here, at cardinal points, are statues of the Dhyani Buddhas (Vairocana, Ratnasambhava, Amitabha, Amoghasiddhi and Aksobhya) and their shaktis (consorts).

STUPA PLATFORM

The great stupa is only one of many points of interest at Swayambhunath. Two white temples in the Indian *shikhara* style, both dating from 1646, flank the *dorje* at the top of the stairs.

Behind the stupa, adjacent to a poorly lit museum of Buddhist statuary, is a **path** (pilgrim shelter) with an open ground floor and a Kargyud-school gompa above it.

North of the pilgrim shelter is the pagoda-style **Hariti (Ajima) Temple,** with a beautiful image of Hariti, the goddess of smallpox. This Hindu goddess (to the Newars she is known as Ajima), who is also responsible for fertility, illustrates the seamless interweaving of Hindu and Buddhist beliefs in Nepal.

Near the Hariti Temple are pillars on which figues of many gods and goddesses are seated. Look for the figures of Tara making the gesture of charity, with an upturned palm. Actually, there are two Taras, Green Tara and White Tara, who are sometimes believed to be the two wives, Chinese and Nepali, of King Songtsen Gampo, the first royal patron of Buddhism in Tibet. The Taras are two of the female consorts to the Dhyani Buddhas. Nearby bronze images of

the river goddesses **Jamuna** and **Ganga** guard an eternal flame in a cage.

Back at the northeast corner of the complex is a Kargyud school gompa where, with a great deal of crashing, chanting and trumpeting, a service takes place every day at around 4pm. Inside the gompa is an inner pilgrim path that encircles a 6m-high figure of Sakyamuni, the historical Buddha.

Symbols of the five elements – earth, air, water, fire and ether – can be found around the hilltop. Behind the Anantapura *shikhara* are **Vasupura,** the earth symbol, and **Vayupura,** the air symbol. **Nagpura,** the symbol for water, is the muddy pool just north of the stupa, while **Agnipura,** the symbol for fire, is the red-faced god on a marble stone on the northwestern side of the platform. **Shantipura,** the symbol for the sky, is north of the platform, in front of the Shantipura building. Also here are statues of a yellow Buddha and an Avalokiteshvara with four arms.

AROUND THE STUPA

A smaller stupa stands on the hillock just west of the main stupa, with an adjacent gompa, a huge tangle of prayer flags and an important **shrine** to Saraswati, the goddess of learning. At exam time, many scholars come here to improve their chances and schoolchildren fill the place during Basant Panchami, the Festival of Knowledge.

The **Natural History Museum** (admission Rs 30; 🕙 10am-5pm Sun-Fri, closed government holidays), below Swayambhunath by the road that climbs to the west entrance, has a quirky collection of stuffed animals (see p132), including a sarus crane, Himalayan monal pheasant and a pangolin.

There are Tibetan settlements, shrines and monasteries scattered around the base of the Swayambhunath hill. It's worth investing an hour or so to join the elderly Tibetan pilgrims in a clockwise *kora* (pilgrim circuit) of the entire hill, past hundreds of prayer wheels (some 9m tall), chapels, and stone carvings. The route dips to the left just before the Natural History Museum to skirt a pool and later passes a huge golden Amitabha Buddha statue on the west side, before returning via the north side of the hill.

NATIONAL MUSEUM
Around 800m south of Swayambhunath, the **National Museum** (admission foreigner/SAARC/ Nepali Rs 50/10/5; 🕑 10.30am-4.30pm Wed-Sun & 10.30am-2pm Mon Apr-Oct, 10.30am-3pm Wed-Mon Nov-Mar) is a bit hit-and-miss, but has a fine collection of religious art and is worth a visit. A visit can easily be combined with a trip to Swayambhunath.

The history section has a rather eclectic collection that includes some moon rock and whale bones, a number of moth-eaten stuffed animals, some horrific-looking weaponry and a fine portrait gallery. The most interesting exhibit is a leather Tibetan cannon seized in the 1792 Nepal–Tibet War; the most eccentric is an electrical contraption that fires a normal rifle. The dull Numismatic Museum sets the tone for the Postal Museum, where some visitors have apparently passed out from the sheer tedium of it all.

The art gallery, in contrast, displays a superb collection of mainly Hindu statues and carvings (stone, wood, bronze and terracotta), housed in a 19th-century former Rana palace. Some pieces date to the 1st century BC. You can climb to the roof for fine views of Swayambhunath.

Also worth a look is the Gallery of Buddhist art, which offers an excellent and informative overview of Buddhist art and iconography, with a strong emphasis on Tibetan art.

Ticket sales stop an hour before closing time. It costs Rs 50 to bring in a camera. Bags must be deposited at the gate.

Eating & Drinking
If you need a break, you can grab a reviving cup of milk tea at the hole-in-the-wall **Didi's Tibetan Tea Shop**, or stop and get lunch at tourist-oriented **Café De Stupa**.

Getting There & Away
You can approach Swayambhunath by taxi (Rs 80), by bicycle or as part of an easy stroll from Kathmandu. See the map on pp110–11 for an overview of the area.

Taxis can drop you at the bottom of the eastern stairway or at the car park atop the western side. The latter is closer to the stupa but the steep eastern pilgrim stairway offers the more interesting approach.

Safa tempo No 20 (Rs 7) shuttles between Swayambhunath's eastern stairway and Kathmandu's Sundhara district (near the main post office).

WALKING & CYCLING
There are two popular walking or bicycle routes to Swayambhunath – using both offers a pleasant circuit, either in the direction described or in reverse.

Starting at the Chhetrapati Tole junction near Thamel, the road descends to the Vishnumati River (with the Swayambhunath stupa clearly visible in the distance), and passes three interesting temples. The **Indrani Temple**, just beside the river on the Kathmandu side, is chiefly notable for the brightly coloured erotic scenes on its roof struts and its cremation ghats (riverside steps).

Across the river and just upstream is the **Shobabaghwati Temple**. A footpath runs from here up the steep hill to the **Bijeshwari Temple**, from where the road continues to Swayambhunath. This final section passes a couple of teahouses and shops selling rosary beads.

The alternative route starts at Durbar Sq, and follows Maru Tole (Pie Alley) down to the Vishnumati River, where a footbridge crosses to the western side by some stone cremation ghats. From here, the path heads north, then west, through a Tibetan district and past the National Museum.

ICHANGU NARAYAN
At the edge of the valley floor, about 3km northwest of Swayambhunath, the shrine of **Ichangu Narayan** (admission free; 🕑 dawn-dusk) – not to be confused with Changu Narayan east of Kathmandu – is one of the Valley's important Vishnu shrines. This two-storey, 18th-century temple is fronted by two square stone pillars bearing Vishnu's symbols, a *sankha* (conch) and a *chakra* (disc), atop a tortoise. The site was consecrated in 1200

and an earlier temple was built here after a famine in 1512. The walk here is probably of more interest than the temple itself.

The 3km road to Ichangu Narayan begins at Kathmandu's Ring Rd, opposite the statue of Amitabha Buddha, on the western side of the Swayambhunath hill. The track climbs a steep hill to Halchok village (look back for the views) and continues past three Mughal-style Shiva shrines and a bamboo swing (erected anew each year during the Dasain festival) to the temple compound. Going back to Kathmandu by bicycle is one long downhill breeze, but you'll certainly work up a sweat getting to the temple.

PASHUPATINATH

Nepal's most important Hindu **temple** (admission Rs 250, under-10s free) stands on the banks of the holy Bagmati River, on the eastern fringes of Kathmandu, not far from the Tribhuvan Airport. Pashupatinath is also one of the most important Shiva temples on the subcontinent and draws devotees and sadhus (wandering Hindu holy men) from all over India.

Shiva is the destroyer and creator of the Hindu pantheon and is best known in his 'terrible' forms, particularly in Nepal as the cruel and destructive Bhairab, but he also has peaceful incarnations including those of Mahadev and Pashupati, the lord of the beasts. As the shepherd of both animals and humans, Pashupati shows Shiva's most pleasant and creative side.

Pashupati is considered to have a special concern for Nepal and, accordingly, he features in all official messages from the king. Before commencing an important journey, the king will always pay a visit to Pashupatinath to seek the god's blessing. Nepal's Dalit (untouchable) community was only allowed access to the shrine in 2001.

You can visit Pashupatinath as a half-day trip from central Kathmandu or en route to Bodhnath, as the two sites are an interesting short walk apart. Of all the valley's entry fees Pashupatinath offers the least value, as many of the temple buildings are closed to non-Hindus.

Sights
PASHUPATINATH TEMPLE
Non-Hindus are not allowed in the main temple so you'll have to be satisfied with

---

RESPECT FOR THE DEAD

The cremations along the Bagmati often attract a crowd of tourists – cameras and video cameras at the ready – watching like vultures from the opposite bank. Photography is permitted, but please be discreet; many tourists behave with an amazingly insensitive disregard for the funeral parties, some even muscling their way between the mourners to get close-ups of the burning pyre! However extraordinary the sights might seem, this is a religious ceremony, often marking a family tragedy, and the participants should be accorded respect. Behave as you would wish people to behave at a funeral in your home town.

---

glimpses from outside the compound. From the main western entrance you may catch a flash of the mighty golden backside of Nandi, Shiva's bull. The temple dates from the 19th century but the bull is about 300 years old. The black, four-headed image of Pashupati inside the temple is said to be even older; an earlier image was destroyed by Mughal invaders in the 14th century.

For non-Hindus there is more to be seen by heading east of the taxi stand to the riverbanks, where you can look down into the temple from the terraced hillside on the opposite bank.

En route to the riverbanks you'll pass the **Panch Deval** (Five Temples), a former five-shrined complex that now acts as a social welfare centre for a heartbreaking collection of destitute local elderly. A donation box offers a way for visitors to directly contribute. The ticket office is just before the entry to the riverbank.

THE RIVERBANKS OF THE BAGMATI
The Bagmati is a holy river and, like Varanasi on the Ganges, Pashupatinath is a popular place to be cremated. The burning ghats (called Arya Ghats) immediately in front of the temple, north of the footbridges, are for the cremation of royalty, though you'll often see ritual bathing taking place in the river here. Ten members of the royal family were cremated here after the massacre (see the boxed text, p38).

Just north of the main bridge across the Bagmati, but still on the western bank of the river, is the 6th-century **Bachhareshwari Temple**, with Tantric figures, painted skeletons and erotic scenes. It is said that at one time the Maha Shivaratri festival activities included human sacrifices at this temple.

The six square **cremation ghats** just south of the bridges are for the common people and there is almost always a cremation going on here. The log fires are laid, the shrouded body lifted on top and the fire lit with remarkably little ceremony. It's a powerful place to contemplate notions of death and mortality.

Right at the southern end of the western embankment, past the funeral pyres, is a half-buried, but still quite beautiful, 7th-century **standing Buddha image**.

Two footbridges cross the Bagmati River. Facing the temple from across the river are 11 stone *chaityas* (small stupas) each containing a lingam (a phallic symbol of Shiva's creative powers).

From the northern end of the embankment you can see the **cavelike shelters**, once used by hermits and sadhus. These days the yogis (yoga masters), babus and sadhus head for the elaborately frescoed **Ram Temple**, next to the main bridge, especially during the festival of Maha Shivaratri (see p168).

THE TERRACES

Climb up the steps from the eastern riverbank to the terrace, where you can look down into the Pashupatinath Temple from

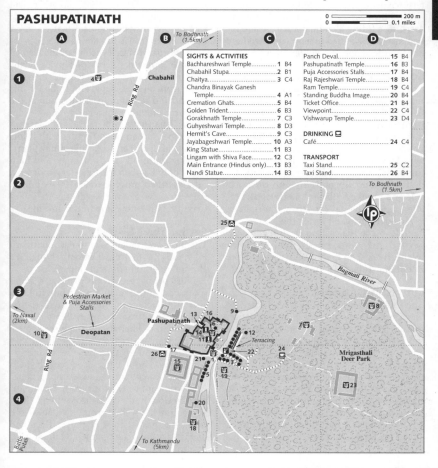

PASHUPATINATH

0   200 m
0   0.1 miles

SIGHTS & ACTIVITIES
Bachhareshwari Temple............**1** B4	
Chabahil Stupa..........................**2** B1	
Chaitya.....................................**3** C4	
Chandra Binayak Ganesh	
Temple...................................**4** A1	
Cremation Ghats.......................**5** B4	
Golden Trident..........................**6** B3	
Gorakhnath Temple...................**7** C3	
Guhyeshwari Temple.................**8** D3	
Hermit's Cave............................**9** C3	
Jayabageshwari Temple...........**10** A3	
King Statue..............................**11** B3	
Lingam with Shiva Face...........**12** C3	
Main Entrance (Hindus only)....**13** B3	
Nandi Statue............................**14** B3	

Panch Deval.............................**15** B4	
Pashupatinath Temple.............**16** B3	
Puja Accessories Stalls.............**17** B4	
Raj Rajeshwari Temple.............**18** B4	
Ram Temple.............................**19** C4	
Standing Buddha Image...........**20** B4	
Ticket Office............................**21** B4	
Viewpoint................................**22** C4	
Vishwarup Temple....................**23** D4	

DRINKING
Café...**24** C4	

TRANSPORT
Taxi Stand................................**25** C2	
Taxi Stand................................**26** B4	

To Bodhnath (1.5km)

To Bodhnath (1.5km)

Chabahil

Ring Rd

Bagmati River

Pedestrian Market & Puja Accessories Stalls

To Naxal (2km)

Deopatan

Ring Rd

Pashupatinath

Terracing

Mrigasthali Deer Park

Battis Putali

To Kathmandu (5km)

several convenient benches. The central two-tiered pagoda dates from 1696. Look for the enormous **golden trident** rising up on the right (northern) side of the temple and the golden figure of the king kneeling in prayer under a protective hood of *nagas* (snake spirits) on the left side. Behind the temple, you can see a brightly coloured illustration of Shiva and his *shakti* (female aspect) looking out over the temple.

At the northern end of this terrace is a **Shiva lingam** on a circular pedestal. A finely featured face of the god has been sculptured on one side of the lingam. It is an indication of the richness of Nepal's artistic heritage that this piece of sculpture, so casually standing on the grassy terrace, is actually a masterpiece dating from the 5th or 6th century! The hillside is now home to the **Mrigasthali deer park**, a fitting blending of nature and religion, as Shiva is said to have frolicked here once in the shape of a golden deer.

GORAKHNATH & VISHWARUP TEMPLES

The steps continue up the hill from the terraces to the Gorakhnath Temple complex at the top of the hill. A red and white *shikhara*, fronted by a towering Shiva trident, is the main structure, but surrounding this is a jungle of temples, sculptures and *chaityas*, with Shiva imagery everywhere. Images of the bull Nandi stand guard, tridents are dotted around, lingams rise up on every side and monkeys play in the treetops, creating a peaceful and evocative atmosphere.

Non-Hindus can't enter the Vishwarup Temple, off to the east, so continue instead beyond the Gorakhnath Temple down to the river. You'll soon get views of the Bodhnath stupa rising up in the distance.

GUHYESHWARI TEMPLE

The Guhyeshwari Temple is dedicated to Shiva's *shakti* in her terrible manifestation as Kali. Entry is banned to non-Hindus, and the high wall around the temple prevents you from seeing anything except the four huge gilded snakes arching up to support the roof finial. Guhyeshwari was built by King Pratap Malla in 1653 and the temple stands in a paved courtyard surrounded by *dharamsalas* (pilgrims' resthouses).

The temple's curious name comes from *guhya* (vagina) and *ishwari* (goddess) – it's the temple of the goddess' vagina! Legend

has it that when Shiva was insulted by his father-in-law, Parvati was so incensed that she burst into flames and it was this act of self-immolation that gave rise to the practice of *sati* (or *suttee*), where a widow is consigned to the same funeral pyre as her deceased husband. The grieving Shiva carried off the corpse of his *shakti* but as he wandered aimlessly, the body disintegrated and this is where her *yoni* (genitals) fell.

Festivals & Events

Pashupatinath is generally busiest (with genuine pilgrims, not tourists) from 6am to 10am and again from 6pm to 7.30pm. The best time to visit the temple is on **Haribodhini Ekadashi** – 11 days after the full and new moon each month. On those days there will be many pilgrims and in the evening the ringing of bells will indicate that the *arati* (light) ceremony is to take place.

In February/March each year, the festival of **Maha Shivaratri** celebrates Shiva's birthday with a great fair at the temple. Pilgrims come from all over Nepal and India for this festival, and if you're in Kathmandu at the time you shouldn't miss it.

The **Bala Chaturdashi** fair takes place in November/December, bringing with it lots of pilgrims, stalls and a fairlike atmosphere. Pilgrims burn oil lamps at night and bath in the holy Bagmati the following morning. Pilgrims then move through the complex, scattering sweets and seeds for their deceased relatives to enjoy in the afterlife.

Getting There & Away

The most convenient way to Pashupatinath is by taxi (Rs 100 from Thamel), though it's also an easy (but stressful) bicycle ride.

Most people are dropped off at a stand southwest of the main temple but you can also approach from the ring road to the west, by the Jayabageshwari Temple (with its painting of Bhairab), through the suburb of Deopatan, where twin lanes are lined with stalls selling marigolds, incense, *rudraksha* beads (made from dried seeds), conch shells and other essential religious paraphernalia.

If you want to walk on from Pashupatinath to Bodhnath, it's a pleasant and short (20 minutes) walk through villages and farmland, past strings of prayer flags and *dhobi* washing, accompanied by the sounds of Hindi music. Take the footbridge across

DIPANKHA JATRA

The Dipankha Jatra is a remarkable day-long 60km pilgrimage that happens once every blue moon. Not literally a blue moon but almost; a planetary combination of a full moon in the month of Ashwin, the first or last day of the month, a Sunday or Monday, a lunar eclipse and other planetary configurations. Unsurprisingly, it doesn't happen very often – twice in the last 50 years, in fact. Over 100,000 people joined the pilgrimage in 2005 to 140 sacred sights in the Kathmandu Valley, including Patan, Bungamati, Ichangu Narayan, Swayambhunath and Pashupatinath.

the river right in front of the Guhyeshwari Temple and head north for five minutes, then turn right at the signposted junction, by a tree temple. At the next junction follow the Buddha's example and take the middle (straight) path. You eventually come out on the main road, right across from the main Bodhnath stupa.

CHABAHIL

The Chabahil Stupa is like a small replica of Bodhnath, about 1.5km west of Bodhnath, in Kathmandu's northeastern suburbs. The original stupa is said to have been built by Ashoka's daughter, Charumati. It certainly predates Bodhnath, and around the main stupa are a number of small *chaityas* from the Licchavi period, dating back to some time between the 5th and 8th centuries. The site includes a 1m-high, 9th-century statue of a bodhisattva, which is claimed to be one of the finest pieces of sculpture in the valley.

Nearby is the small **Chandra Binayak Ganesh Temple** (Map p167), with a double roof in brass. Ganesh's shrew stands on a pillar in front of the shrine, waiting on the tiny image of the god inside.

BODHNATH (BOUDHA)

On the eastern side of Kathmandu, just north of the airport and around 6km from Thamel, is **Bodhnath** (admission foreigner/SAARC Rs 50/20), home to one of the world's largest stupas. The village, also known as Boudha (pronounced *boe*-da), is the religious centre for Nepal's considerable population of Tibetan exiles, and the sidestreets are full

of maroon-robed Tibetan (and foreign) monks, gleaming monastery roofs and shopfronts full of Tibetan texts and yak butter. This is one of the few places in the world where Tibetan culture is accessible, vibrant and unfettered.

Bodhnath has always been linked to Tibetan Buddhism and Lhasa. A major trade route coming from Lhasa went through Sankhu, and Bodhnath therefore lies at the Tibetan traders' entry to Kathmandu. One can easily imagine the traders giving thanks for their successful journey across the Himalaya, or praying for a safe return. People (including mountaineers and Sherpas) still come here to pray before undertaking a journey in the Himalaya.

Many of today's Tibetans are refugees who fled Tibet following the unsuccessful uprising against the Chinese Communists in 1959. They have been both energetic and successful in the intervening years, as the large houses surrounding Bodhnath testify. Apart from the local Tibetans and Nepalis there's a sizeable community of foreign Buddhist students, which contributes to occasional bitchy factional tensions between the different schools (apparently the lessons on nonattachment aren't going so well…).

Late afternoon is a good time to visit Bodhnath, when the group tours depart and the place once again becomes a Tibetan village. Prayer services are held in the surrounding gompas and, as the sun sets, the community turns out to circumambulate the stupa – a ritual that combines religious observance with social event. It's a wonderful feeling to be swept around by the centrifugal force of faith – remember to walk around the stupa in a clockwise direction.

Most people visit for an hour or two before returning to Thamel but the accommodation and facilities in Bodhnath are good and it's not a bad place to be based, especially if you have an interest in Tibetan culture. The atmosphere of cultural exchange and spiritual curiosity is unrivalled.

Information

Internet access is available at **Dharana Internet** (per hr Rs 30; 6am-10pm), on the west side of the stupa, and **Dharma Internet** (per hr Rs 25, 7am-9pm), which has broadband connections, north of the stupa. The ticket office is at the main southern entrance to the stupa.

AROUND THE KATHMANDU VALLEY

VISITING TIBETAN MONASTERIES

The crash of cymbals, thump of Tantric drums, murmuring of Tibetan chants and wafting smells of yak butter and juniper incense combine to make a visit to a gompa (Tibetan monastery) a dramatic and sometimes moving experience. What you'll soon notice beyond this is that monasteries share a remarkable continuity of design, decoration and symbolism.

All gompas are decorated with impressive mural paintings and thangkas (paintings on cotton, framed in brocade and hung). The subjects are usually either meditational deities, revered past lamas or ritual mandalas (diagrams that represent the forces of the universe and aid meditation). As you enter a monastery you will commonly see murals of the four guardian protectors and the Wheel of Life, a highly complex symbolic diagram representing the Buddha's insights into the way humans are chained by desire to the endless cycle of birth, death and rebirth. Rigid rules govern these traditional arts, stressing spirituality, order and symmetry over originality, flair and personal expression.

Symbolism extends throughout the monastery: prayer wheels (sometimes 10m high) are filled with thousands of Buddhist prayers which are 'activated' with each turning of the wheel; prayer flags work on a similar precept and are printed in the five elemental colours. On the monastery roof you'll see the statue of two deer on either side of the Wheel of Law, symbolising the Buddha's first sermon at the deer park of Sarnath.

Past the rows of monks' cushions, the main monastic prayer hall is headed by an altar adorned with seven bowls of water, butter lamps, and offerings of grain and fruit. Here you'll find the main statues, often of the Past, Present and Future Buddhas, along with pictures of the Dalai Lama and other lamas related to the monastery's particular school of Tibetan Buddhism. Fierce protector deities often occupy side chapels and loose-leafed Tibetan manuscripts line the side walls.

Cultural Considerations

Visitors are welcome in most monasteries, and to keep the good faith please bear in mind the following guidelines, particularly if prayers are in progress.

- Remove your shoes and hat before you enter a gompa.
- Ask before taking photos and avoid taking photos during a service.
- Smoking is not permitted anywhere in the main compounds.
- Do not step over or sit on the monks' cushions, even if no-one is sitting on them.
- During ceremonies, enter quietly and stand by the wall near the main entrance; do not walk around in front of the altar, or between the monks, or cross the central area of the temple.
- It is appropriate to make an offering, especially if you do take photographs. A khata (white scarf) is traditional, but these days rupees are also appreciated; monasteries depend for their existence on the donations of the faithful. Pilgrims touch the money to their forehead before donating it.

Sights

THE BODHNATH STUPA

There doesn't seem to be much agreement on how old the Bodhnath site is, but it is likely that the first stupa (chörten in Tibetan) was built some time after AD 600, after the Tibetan king, Songtsen Gampo, was converted to Buddhism by his two wives: the Nepali princess Bhrikuti and Wencheng Konjo from China. The stupa was said to have been built by a prince as penance for unwittingly killing his father. The current stupa structure was probably built after the depredation of the Mughal invaders in the 14th century.

Stupas were originally built to house holy relics. It is not certain if there is anything interred at Bodhnath, but some believe that there is a piece of bone that once belonged to the Buddha.

Around the base of the stupa's circular mound are 108 small images of the Dhyani Buddha Amitabha (108 is an auspicious number in Tibetan culture). A brick wall around the stupa has 147 niches, each with four or five prayer wheels bearing the mantra *om mani padme hum*. Access to the inner stupa is gained through the northern entrance, where there is a small shrine dedicated to Ajima, the goddess of smallpox. It's possible to walk up onto the upper layers of the stupa. Pilgrims find a private space in the inner lower enclosure and perform full-body prostrations. It's a powerful, evocative place that's brought alive by the Tibetan pilgrims who circumambulate the stupa, twirling their prayer wheels, chatting and murmuring prayers.

For more on the symbolic structure of stupas, see the boxed text, p164.

THE GOMPAS

A number of monasteries have been rebuilt since the 1960s but none compares with the great monasteries of Tibet, Ladakh or Bhutan. Most are closed during the middle of the day. See the boxed text, opposite for some guidelines on visiting the gompas.

Tsamchen Gompa is the only gompa that opens directly onto the stupa (on the western side). There are some fine paintings and a magnificent Maitreya (Jampa in Tibetan),

the Future Buddha, covered in beautiful embroideries. Don't miss the massive enclosed prayer wheel on the left of the entrance.

The new **Tamang Gompa** and Guru Lhakhang are currently being built on the north side of the stupa enclosure. A small plaque here honours Ekai Kawaguchi (1866–1945), the first Japanese to make it to Tibet (he passed through Bodhnath in 1899). For an excellent account of his remarkable travels see Scott Berry's book *A Stranger in Tibet*, available in Thamel bookshops.

East of the stupa, the Gelugpa **Samtenling Gompa** is the oldest monastery in Bodhnath.

The Sakyapa school **Tarik Gompa** to the northeast of the stupa does not have the imposing architectural unity of the others – it has obviously been built in stages over a number of years – but there are some high-quality frescoes inside the ground-floor chapel and you can climb upstairs to a splendidly adorned Sakyamuni Buddha. Just east of here is **Tabsang Gompa**, a Kargyud monastery.

North of here, down a side alley, is the large 'white gompa' of **Ka-Nying Sheldrup Ling**

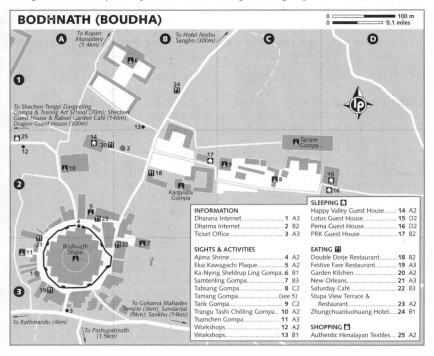

BODHNATH (BOUDHA)

Gompa, one of the largest monasteries in Bodhnath, with nice gardens and a richly decorated interior with some fine paintings and thangkas. The gompa hosts a popular annual seminar on Vajrayana training in November (see p357). You'll hear the tap-tap-tapping of handicraft workshops in the street leading up to the monastery.

Northwest of the stupa, the impressive **Shechen Tengyi Dargyeling Gompa** was established by the famous Nyingmapa lama Dilgo Khyentse Rinpoche to act as an exiled version of Shechen Gompa in eastern Tibet. It has a large and thriving community of over 180 monks and is a popular destination for Tibetan pilgrims. The fine interior decorations are the work of artists from Bhutan. To the right of the main building is the Tsering Art School (see p181).

Festivals & Events
The **Losar** (Tibetan New Year) festival in February or March is celebrated by crowds of pilgrims. Long copper horns are blown, a portrait of the Dalai Lama is paraded around, and masked dances are performed.

Sleeping
There are a number of excellent guesthouses in the tangle of lanes north and east of the stupa, which offer an interesting and infinitely peaceful alternative to basing yourself in Kathmandu. Prices are marginally higher than in Thamel.

Lotus Guest House (☎ 4472320; s/d without bathroom Rs 250/350, with bathroom Rs 290/390, deluxe r Rs 490-750) The next-door Tabsang Gompa runs this very pleasant two-storey option. Rooms are spotlessly clean and spacious, and there is a large garden and sitting area. Upper-floor rooms are best.

Pema Guest House (☎ 4495662; pemaguesthouse@hotmail.com; r with/without bathroom Rs 650/450, deluxe r Rs 850) A multistorey place right across the lane from the Lotus Guest House, with comfortable rooms, clean bathrooms and lots of sun in winter. Ground-floor rooms are darker and slightly cheaper.

Shechen Guest House (☎ 4479009; www.shechenguesthouse.com; s/d/tr Rs 580/800/1210, discounts of 15% May-Aug) There's a nice mix of tourists and dharma students in this well-run guesthouse attached to Shechen Gompa. Rooms are spacious and comfortable and there's a relaxing garden and excellent vegetarian

restaurant. It's an excellent choice if you are interested in Tibetan Buddhism.

Dragon Guest House (☎ 4496117; dragon@ntc.net.np; s/d without bathroom Rs 280/380, d with bathroom Rs 550) This friendly, family-run place is one of Bodhnath's best-kept secrets. The owners (from Mustang) cater to most needs, there's a small garden, a good vegetarian restaurant, a library and a useful little shop. The sunny side rooms on the upper floor are the best. It's in the backstreets northwest of the stupa; the easiest way to find it is to head north out of the main gates of Shechen Guest House.

PRK Guest House (☎ 4465055; www.sakyatharig.org.np; s Rs 700, d Rs 1000-1500) The Pal Rabten Khangsar is a new and surprisingly stylish guesthouse run by next-door Tharig Gompa. Rooms are well tended and decorated with Tibetan rugs and bedspreads, and there's a small library.

Happy Valley Guest House (☎ 4471241; happy@mos.com.np; s US$15-25, d US$20-30, ste US$40-45, discounts of 25%) A modern midrange hotel north of the main stupa, this is another good choice, popular with visiting Western Buddhists and tour groups. It has excellent rooftop views out over the stupa, but only the deluxe rooms have views. There's a good library of books and magazines in the lobby.

Hotel Norbu Sangpo (☎ 4482500; www.norbusangpo.com; s/d US$30/40, discounts of 50%) A highly recommended modern midrange place in the north of the town, with 26 bright, comfortable and spacious rooms and a nice garden. Corner rooms are generally the best. Suites with kitchen (but no appliances) and living room are available from US$250 per month.

Eating
There are a number of restaurants around the stupa itself. The views are often more inspiring than the food, but what views! Buddhist Bodhnath is nirvana for vegetarians.

Double Dorje Restaurant (☎ 4488947; dishes Rs 50-120) A cosy Tibetan-run place that's popular with backpackers and the local dharma crowd, both attracted to the sofa seating and low prices. There's plenty of Western food, plus Tibetan specials, but don't be in a hurry as service can be slow. This is a great place to try out Tibetan butter tea and *tsampa* (Rs 50; on the menu as 'champa') – roasted barley meal that tastes a bit like porridge.

(Continued on page 181)

A roof-top café in the popular Thamel area (p145), Kathmandu

RICHARD I'ANSON

RYAN FOX

Old town (p114), buildings at
night, Kathmandu

Nepali puppets (p371) for sale near Mahendreshwar
temple, Kathmandu

ANDERS BLOMQVIST

ANDREW PEACOCK

Butter lamps at Bodhnath stupa (p170)

Swayambhunath temple (p162)

CAROL POLICH

The unusual octagonal Krishna Temple (p188) in Patan's Durbar Square

Crossing a traditional bridge over Marsyangdi Khola near Bryaga on the Annapurna Circuit Trek (p347)

View of the Annapurnas on the Jomson Trek (p345) near Naudanda

A festival in Gorkha (p239)

GARETH McCORMACK

Bamboo bridge on the Marsayangdi River
on the Annapurna Circuit Trek (p347)

Art at a temple in Sarangkot (p265)

MARK ANDREW KIRBY

Boatman in a canoe on Phewa Tal (p250) in the Pokhara Valley

RICHARD I'ANSON

RICHARD I'ANSON

Rice terraces and the Yamdi River above the village of Suikhet in the Pokhara Valley (p268)

World Peace Pagoda (p255), Pokhara

LINDSAY BROWN

LINDSAY BROWN

Annapurna mountains and Machhapuch-hare from the World Peace Pagoda (p255), Pokhara

ANDERS BLO

Elephant having a bath (p280) in the Rapti River, Royal Chitwan National Park

CHRISTIAN ASLUND

Rhinoceroses in Royal Chitwan National Park (p275)

Thatched-roof house in Terai mustard field, near Royal Bardia National Park (p308)

CAROL POLICH

Porter with a heavy load of chickens on the Annapurna Circuit Trek (p347)

RICHARD I'ANSON

RICHARD I'ANSON

Campsite with views of Annapurna South, Mt Hiunchuli and Machhapuchhare on the Annapurna Circuit Trek (p347)

Trekking store in Thamel (p155), Kathmandu

PAUL DYMOND

Buddhist prayer wheel (p170) in the Everest trekking region, Sagarmatha

RICHARD I'ANSON

Traffic jam on the Annapurna Circuit (p347)

TONY WHEELER

Trekkers heading for the snow, Annapurna Ranges (p269), Annapurna, Gandaki

GRE

(Continued from page 172)

Stupa View Terrace & Restaurant (☎ 4480262; mains Rs 140-250) For good food with a stupendous view this German-run place has a range of vegetarian dishes and good pizza (from a clay oven), plus some unusual dishes such as Middle Eastern *meze*, 'sliced zucchini with mint and olive-oil bread' and special candle-lit meals during the full moon.

Saturday Café (☎ 2073157; mains Rs 100-200) On the east side of the stupa square, come here for good cakes and cookies, organic coffee and frozen sorbet, plus light vegan and organic meals, such as ginger tofu and vegetables, or tomato, lentil and coriander soup. Come early for a seat on the rooftop.

Festive Fare Restaurant (set meals Rs 510, snacks Rs 200) On the southwest side of the stupa, this place serves up set meals to tour groups. The rooftop tables have fabulous views.

Rabsel Garden Café (Rs 85-120; ☺ 11am-8.30pm; Shechen Guest House) For some peace and quiet, head past the row of *chörtens* west of the Shechen Tengyi Dargyeling Gompa to this garden oasis. The vegetarian-only dishes stretch to lasagne, quiche, soup with homemade bread and veggie wraps, and there are good daily specials.

Zhungchuanluohuang Hotel (☎ 4495914; dishes Rs 100) This may be a bit of a mouthful, but it's a damn good-tasting mouthful. It's a bit unnerving to see Chinese characters in the heart of Tibetan Bodhnath but the authentic Sichuanese food is tasty. Try *gongbaojiding* (chicken with chilli and peanuts).

There are plenty of other places to eat, including a branch of **New Orleans** (see p148) and the relaxed **Garden Kitchen** (☎ 4470760).

For those on a shoestring budget, there are plenty of small Tibetan eating houses in the streets behind the stupa that serve up authentic Tibetan *thugpa* (noodle soup) – any place with a curtain across an open door is probably one.

Shopping

There are lots of shops around the stupa selling Tibetan crafts, prayer wheels, prayer flags and Tibetan cowboy hats, most imported from China, but you'll have to negotiate hard to get a decent price.

Authentic Himalayan Textiles (☎ 4490073; ☺ 9am-7pm) 'From exile to textiles' could be the slogan here. It specialises in antique striped Tibetan aprons, known as *pangden,* that have been collected from across the Himalaya (each region has its own characteristic design). Older pieces are used to create patchwork wall hangings, cushions and bags. Any spare threads are rewoven into carpets, even the carpet dust is reused in paper production! Products aren't cheap but you can be sure that only traditional vegetable dyes have been used.

Tsering Art School (☺ 9am-5pm Mon-Fri, 9am-noon Sat; Shechen Tengyi Dargyeling Gompa) The shop at this art school has an on-site tailor and workshop that produces thangkas, incense and clay sculptures. The shop also sells incense, CDs and a few Buddhist books.

Bodhnath has lots of tailors who can whip you up a traditional Tibetan dress or cloak in a couple of days.

Getting There & Away

Buses to Bodhnath depart regularly from Kathmandu's City (Ratna Park) bus station (Rs 7, 30 minutes). The *Safa* tempos that leave from Kantipath in Kathmandu (routes 2 and 28) are slightly quicker. A taxi is by far the easiest option at around Rs 130. The road to Bodhnath is very busy and a bit of a nightmare for bicycles.

There's also an interesting short walk between Bodhnath and Pashupatinath (see p168), or you could combine Bodhnath with a visit to Gokarna Mahadev Temple and Kopan Monastery (see the boxed text, p214).

AROUND BODHNATH
Kopan Monastery

The **Kopan Monastery** (☎ 4481268; www.kopan-monastery.com), a popular centre for courses on Buddhism and other Tibetan-related subjects, stands on a hilltop to the north of Bodhnath. If you've ever thought of learning a little more about Tibetan Buddhism, this could well be the place to do it.

The centre has short courses on Tibetan medicine, thangka painting and other subjects, but the major attraction for Westerners are the 10-day residential courses introducing Buddhist psychology and philosophy. See p357 for more details.

Kopan's founder, Lama Thubten Yeshe, died in 1984, and a young Spanish boy, Osel Torres, was declared his reincarnation. The young reincarnation, who was partly the inspiration for Bernardo Bertolucci's film *Little Buddha,* no longer resides at Kopan.

You can visit Kopan on the pleasant walk between Bodhnath and the Gokarna Mahadev Temple (see the boxed text, p214).

BALAJU

The industrial centre of Balaju is less than 3km north of Thamel, just beyond the Ring Rd, but the capital has virtually swallowed up this nearby suburb. The only reasons to come here are to see the sleeping Vishnu image in Mahendra Park or hike in the nearby Nagarjun Forest Reserve.

The 18th-century gardens at Balaju, now known as **Mahendra Park** (admission Rs 5; 7am-7pm), are somewhat of a disappointment – there's a lot of concrete and litter. Most interesting are the statues in the right-hand corner as you enter the park. The famous Balaju Vishnu image is said to be a copy of the older image at Budhanilkantha.

Apart from the Vishnu image, there are a couple of small temples, an interesting group of *chörtens* (Tibetan Buddhist stupas) and lingams. The 19th-century **Shitala Mai Temple** stands in front of the Vishnu image. The 22 painted waterspouts from which the park takes its local name, Bais Dhara Balaju, are in the centre of the park.

Getting There & Away

Tempos, buses and minibuses (No 23, Rs 5) go to Balaju from Lekhnath Marg, on the northern edge of Thamel. A taxi from Thamel costs around Rs 70.

NAGARJUN FOREST RESERVE

On the hill behind Balaju is the walled **Nagarjun Forest Reserve** (admission per person Rs 10, per car/motorcycle/bicycle Rs 100/30/10; 7am-7pm, 7am-5pm in winter), also known as the Rani Ban (Queen's Forest), which is home to pheasants, deer, monkeys and a couple of military posts. This, along with the former Gokarna Park and Phulchowki, is one of the last significant areas of untouched forest in the valley.

A winding unpaved road and a much more direct footpath lead to the summit (2095m), which is a popular Buddhist pilgrimage site (the reserve is named after the Buddhist saint Nagarjuna). There's a small shrine at the summit to Padmasambhava (Guru Rinpoche in Tibetan) and a viewing tower offers one of the valley's widest mountain panoramas, stretching on a clear day all the way from the Annapurnas to Langtang Lirung, via Machhapuchhare, Manaslu and the Ganesh Himal (a plaque at the bottom of the tower identifies all the peaks). There are also grand views of Kathmandu and its valley laid at your feet to the south.

It's possible to make an enjoyable two-hour cardio-hike up to the summit from near the main gate but there are some security issues to consider (see below).

An excellent sign by the main entry gate specifies an entry fee of Rs 100 if you want to bring an elephant into the park.

Dangers & Annoyances

In October 2005 the reserve was temporarily closed to foreigners after two female foreign hikers were murdered here in separate incidents. Don't hike alone here, be sure to register at the main gate and sign out afterwards.

Getting There & Away

The main entrance to the reserve, Phulbari gate, is about 2km north of Balaju (a 5km bicycle ride from Thamel). It's not a pleasant walk along the busy main road from Balaju so it makes sense to take a taxi to the gate. It's also possible to exit the park at the Mudkhu Bhanjyang gate, 3km further to the northwest, though check this when you register.

BUDHANILKANTHA

Vishnu has many incarnations and in Nepal he often appears as Narayan, the creator of all life, the god who reclines on the cosmic sea. From his navel grew a lotus and from the lotus came Brahma, who in turn created the world. Ultimately everything comes from Vishnu, and at **Budhanilkantha** (admission free; dawn to dusk) the legend is set in stone.

The 5m-long image of Vishnu as Narayan was created in the 7th or 8th century from one monolithic piece of stone and is the most impressive, if not the most important, Vishnu shrine in the country. It was sculpted during the Licchavi period, probably somewhere outside the valley, and laboriously dragged here.

Narayan lies peacefully on a most unusual bed: the coils of the multiheaded snake, Ananta (or Shesha). The snake's 11 hooded heads rise protectively around Narayan's head. Narayan's four hands hold the four symbols of Vishnu: a *chakra* disc (representing the mind), a conch shell (the four elements), a mace (primeval knowledge), and a lotus seed (the moving universe).

During the early Malla period, Vishnuism went into decline as Shiva became the dominant deity. King Jayasthiti Malla is credited with reviving the popularity of Vishnu, and he did this in part by claiming to be an incarnation of the multi-incarnated god. To this day, the kings of Nepal make the same claim and because of this they are forbidden, on pain of death, from seeing the image at Budhanilkantha.

The sleeping Vishnu image, which lies in a small sunken pond enclosure, attracts a constant stream of pilgrims, and prayers take place at 9am every morning (the best time for photos due to the angle of the sun).

Vishnu is supposed to sleep through the four monsoon months, waking at the end of the monsoon. A great festival takes place at Budhanilkantha each November, on the day Vishnu is supposed to awaken from his long annual slumber (for dates see p366).

Non-Hindus cannot enter the enclosure, but there are some unobstructed views from outside the fence surrounding it. There is a Rs 5 parking fee.

Sleeping

Park Village Hotel (☎ 4375280; www.kghhotels.com; r US$60-90, discounts of 50%) If you need to escape Kathmandu, this peaceful midrange retreat just downhill from the Vishnu image may fit the bill. The villa-style accommodation is set in a five-acre garden, with a health club, spa, sauna and pool, and most rooms come with some sort of balcony. The excellent standard rooms are as good as the deluxe, so save yourself US$10 for an Ayurvedic massage or drinks by the pool. The hotel is run by the Kathmandu Guest House (p135) and you'll often get the best discount (and maybe free transport) by booking there.

Shivapuri Heights (☎ 4372518, 9841 371927; www .escape2nepal.com; per person full board US$55) Perched on the hillside above Budhanilkantha, this three-bedroom house floats high above the chaos of Kathmandu. The fully furnished house is equipped with stunning valley views, even from the living room, a CD/DVD player, library, open fireplace and even your own personal chef. As a secret getaway for a romantic couple (you're guaranteed to have the place to yourself) or a relaxing weekend

break from Kathmandu it's hard to beat. The ground-floor room has an ensuite bathroom and the two upper-storey loft rooms share a bathroom, so it's also great for families. Staff will help arrange transport when you make a booking (essential).

Getting There & Away

The No 5 minibuses are the fastest and easiest way to get to Budhanilkantha (Rs 8, route 5), though there are also tempos (from Sundhara) and buses (from the Kathmandu City (Ratna Park) bus station). Pick up a ride from the northern end of Kantipath. The shrine is about 100m east of the terminus. From Thamel a taxi costs around Rs 200 one way.

By bicycle it's a gradual, uphill haul of 15km – hard, sweaty work rewarded with a very pleasant return trip. You could pause at the Dhum Varahi Shrine (see p127).

SHIVAPURI NATIONAL PARK

The northern part of the Kathmandu Valley forms the **Shivapuri National Park** (☎ 4371644; admission foreigner/SAARC/Nepali Rs 250/25/10, car Rs 75, motorbike Rs 15), upgraded to national park status in 2002 to protect the valley's main water source, as well 177 species of birds, orchids, rhesus monkey and even, it is alleged, leopard and bear.

Several good hikes and mountain-bike routes criss-cross the park. The Scar Rd is one of the best biking routes in the valley and follows the old forestry road through the western part of the park – see p83 for details.

The Tibetan nunnery of **Nagi Gompa** is perched near the Tarebhir cliffs, on the lower slopes of the park, 3km from the main gate above Budhanilkantha. Bodhnath's Ka-Nying Sheldrup Ling Gompa holds retreats here for foreign students every November. It's a very bumpy 20-minute 4WD drive or a 1½ hour hike up to the nunnery, which has lovely views and is home to about 100 nuns.

From the gompa it's possible to hike up about 800 vertical metres (three hours) to Shivapuri peak (2725m), via Baghdwar (where the source of the holy Bagmati River pours out of two tiger mouths), then back down via the Pani Muhan water tank (near the park entrance), for a very long day of around seven hours. This is a serious hike that you shouldn't do alone. Take a map, plenty of water and preferably a guide.

An excellent alternative is to walk down-hill from Nagi Gompa to Budhanilkantha, or continue down the ridgeline south to Kopan (three hours) and Bodhnath.

Another good mountain-bike or hiking option from Nagi Gompa is to follow the dirt road east to Mulkarkha and then descend to Sundarijal – a mostly level 11km trip.

PATAN

☎ 01 / pop 190,000

Patan (pa-tan) is separated from Kathmandu by the Bagmati River and is the second-largest town in the valley. It has historically been known by its Sanskrit name

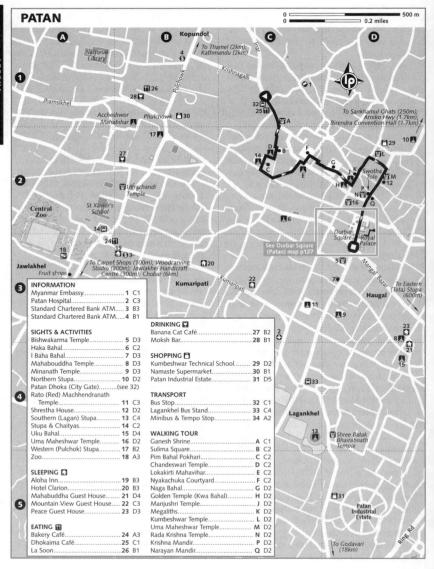

PATAN

0 ————————— 500 m
0 ————————— 0.2 miles

INFORMATION
Myanmar Embassy......................1 C1
Patan Hospital............................2 C3
Standard Chartered Bank ATM....3 B3
Standard Chartered Bank ATM....4 B1

SIGHTS & ACTIVITIES
Bishwakarma Temple..................5 D3
Haka Bahal.................................6 C2
I Baha Bahal...............................7 D3
Mahabouddha Temple................8 D3
Minanath Temple........................9 D3
Northern Stupa..........................10 D2
Patan Dhoka (City Gate)..........(see 32)
Rato (Red) Machhendranath
  Temple..................................11 C3
Shrestha House.........................12 D2
Southern (Lagan) Stupa...........13 C4
Stupa & Chaityas......................14 C2
Uku Bahal.................................15 D4
Uma Maheshwar Temple...........16 D2
Western (Pulchok) Stupa...........17 B2
Zoo..18 A3

SLEEPING
Aloha Inn..................................19 B3
Hotel Clarion.............................20 B3
Mahabuddha Guest House.........21 D4
Mountain View Guest House......22 C3
Peace Guest House....................23 D3

EATING
Bakery Café...............................24 A3
Dhokaima Café..........................25 C1
La Soon.....................................26 B1

DRINKING
Banana Cat Café........................27 B2
Moksh Bar.................................28 B1

SHOPPING
Kumbeshwar Technical School........29 D2
Namaste Supermarket....................30 B1
Patan Industrial Estate...................31 D5

TRANSPORT
Bus Stop....................................32 C1
Lagankhel Bus Stand..................33 C4
Minibus & Tempo Stop...............34 A2

WALKING TOUR
Ganesh Shrine.............................A C1
Sulima Square.............................B C2
Pim Bahal Pokhari.......................C C2
Chandeswari Temple....................D C2
Lokakirti Mahavihar......................E C2
Nyakachuka Courtyard.................F C2
Naga Bahal..................................G D2
Golden Temple (Kwa Bahal).........H D2
Manjushri Temple.........................J D2
Megaliths....................................K D2
Kumbeshwar Temple....................L D2
Uma Maheshwar Temple..............M D2
Rada Krishna Temple....................N D2
Krishna Mandir............................P D2
Narayan Mandir...........................Q D2

Kopundol

To Thamel (2km);
Kathmandu (2km)

Krishnagalli

Jhamsikhel

Accheshwor
Mahabihar
Phulchowk

Central Zoo

St Xavier's
School

Ugrachandi
Temple

National
Library

Puchowk

To Sankhamul Ghats (250m);
Arniko Hwy (1.7km);
Birendra Convention Hall (1.7km)

Swotha
Tole

See Durbar Square
(Patan) map p127

Durbar
Square
Royal
Palace

Mangal Bazar

Jawlakhel

To Carpet Shops (100m); Woodcarving
Studio (200m); Jawlakhel Handicraft
Centre (300m); Chobar (6km)

Fruit shops

Kumaripati

Kumaripati

Haugal

To Eastern
(Teta) Stupa
(600m)

Lagankhel

Shree Batak
Bhairabnath
Temple

Patan
Industrial
Estate

To Godavari
(18km)

Ring Rd

PATAN WALKING TOUR

The Patan Tourist Development Organisation has developed a fascinating walk that winds its way through the complex interlinked courtyards and laneways of the old town. The route gives a great insight into the communal lifestyle and traditional structure of Newari villages, with their many *bahal* (courtyards), *hiti* (water tanks) and *tun* (wells). It's great fun diving through the tunnelled passageways into hidden courtyards.

The walk is marked on Map p184 and outlined briefly here, but is described in more detail in a recommended small booklet entitled *Patan Walkabout* (Rs 100). The booklet is hard to find these days but you might be able to get a photocopied version from the Dhokaima Café (see p193). The walk starts at the Patan Dhoka, ends at Durbar Sq and takes about an hour.

The Route

Walk through Pathan Dhoka to the nearby **Ganesh shrine (A)** and its popular water well, then turn right into **Sulima Sq (B)**, with its central 17th-century Shiva shrine. On the east side of the square is the semi-destroyed house of a famous 16th-century Tantric master; on the south side is a shrine with a fine wooden balustrade.

Continue south to the **Pim Bahal Pokhari (C)** pond and go round it anticlockwise, past the **Chandeswari Temple (D**; 1663) to a large 600-year old whitewashed stupa that was damaged by the Muslim invader Shams-ud-din in the 14th century.

At the road junction take the angled road northeast past some fine wooden windows to an open courtyard. On the south side is the **Lokakirti Mahavihar (E)**, once a monastery and now a school. As you enter the monastery compound you will step over the wooden frame of the chariot used to transport Rato Machhendranath during his festival (see the boxed text, p191). Masked dances are performed at festival time on the *dabali* (platform) in front of the monastery.

Look for the alley leading north off the square, signposted 'Bhaskar Varna Mahabihar', to the **Nyakachuka Courtyard (F)**. There's always something going on in this interesting courtyard. Look for the central stupas and the deities painted over the lintels on the right (east) side of the square. Head to the eastern wall, to the end of a row of four stupas, and go through the covered entrance, across an alley, into another courtyard, the **Naga Bahal (G)**. Walk past the statue of a golden bull to a *hiti* (water tank) and look for the painting of a *naga* (snake) on the wall behind, repainted every five years (most recently 2006) during the Samyak festival.

Go through the eastern passageway to a further courtyard with the red-walled Harayana library in the corner. Follow a diagonal path to a lovely stupa with prayer wheels in its four corners. Behind is an excellent carved wooden monastery shrine room and a sacred well. Pass through the nearby wooden *torana* into the back courtyard of the **Golden Temple (H**; see p190). After visiting the temple, exit east onto the main street, turn left and after 10m, next to a money-changer, you'll see a sign for yet another courtyard, the **Manjushri Temple (J)**. From here continue north past a group of ancient **megaliths (K)**, possibly the oldest objects of worship in the entire Kathmandu Valley, down to the **Kumbeshwar Temple (L**; see p190). From here head east and then south back to Durbar Sq via the **Uma Maheshwar Temple (M**; see p190) and Swotha Tole, with its pagoda-style **Rada Krishna Temple (N)**, Indian-influenced **Krishna Mandir (O)** and Garuda-faced **Narayan Mandir (P)**.

Lalitpur (City of Beauty) and its Newari name, Yala.

Patan's Durbar Sq is full of temples, with a far greater concentration of architecture per square metre than in Kathmandu or Bhaktapur. Moreover, more than 600 stupas and 185 *bahals* are scattered throughout the fascinating backstreets.

Patan makes a great full day trip from Kathmandu. It is possible to stay the night here, although it's so close to Kathmandu that it's not really necessary. The choice of hotels and restaurants is limited, but you'll likely to have the town largely to yourself at the beginning and end of the day.

HISTORY

Patan has a long Buddhist history, and the four corners of the city are marked by stupas said to have been erected by the great

Buddhist emperor Ashoka around 250 BC. Inscriptions refer to the city's 5th-century palaces. The town was ruled by local noblemen until King Shiva Malla of Kathmandu conquered the city in 1597, temporarily unifying the valley. Patan's major building boom took place under the Mallas in the 16th, 17th and 18th centuries.

ORIENTATION

Durbar Sq forms the heart of Patan. From here, four main roads lead to the four Ashoka stupas (see the boxed text, p192). Jawlakhel, to the southwest of the city, has a major Tibetan population and is the centre for carpet weaving in the valley. South of Jawlakhel is the Kathmandu ring road.

Kathmandu buses stop at Patan Dhoka, the original entrance to the city, about a 15-minute walk from Durbar Sq. Taxis might drop you here, but will probably go to the south side of Durbar Sq, known as Mangal Bazar. The Lagankhel bus station, 10 minutes' walk south of Durbar Sq, near the Southern (Lagan) Stupa, has a few bus services to the southern Kathmandu Valley.

INFORMATION

Patan Hospital (p184; ☎ 5521034), in the Lagankhel district, is the best in the Kathmandu Valley (see p113).

There are Standard Chartered Bank ATMs on Kumaripati and Pulhowk Rds.

SIGHTS

Patan's sights are centred around its Durbar Sq but there are several temples located to the south. Don't miss the walking tour of the courtyards and pools to the north (see the boxed text, p185).

Durbar Square (Patan)

As in Kathmandu, the ancient Royal Palace of Patan faces on to **Durbar Square** (Royal Square; Map p187; admission foreigner/SAARC Rs 200/25; ticket office ⏰ 7am-7pm) and this concentrated mass of temples is undoubtedly the most visually stunning display of Newari architecture to be seen in Nepal.

The square rose to its full glory during the Malla period (14th to 18th centuries), and particularly during the reign of King Siddhinarsingh Malla (1619–60). Patan's major commercial district, the Mangal Bazar, runs to the southern edge of the square.

The entry fee is payable at the southern end of Durbar Sq. For repeated visits to Durbar Sq ensure that your visa validity date is written on the back of your ticket.

BHIMSEN TEMPLE

At the northern end of Durbar Sq, the Bhimsen Temple (Map p187) is dedicated to the god of trade and business, which possibly explains its well-kept and prosperous look. Bhimsen, a hero of the Mahabharata, was said to be super strong. Look out for the place settings with bowls, spoons and cups nailed on the roof struts as offerings.

The three-storey temple has had a chequered history. Although it is not known when it was first built, an inscription records that it was rebuilt in 1682 after a fire. Restorations also took place after the great 1934 earthquake, and again in 1967. A lion tops a pillar in front of the temple, while the brick building has an artificial marble façade and a gilded façade on the 1st floor.

MANGA HITI

Immediately across from Bhimsen Temple is the sunken Manga Hiti (Map p187), one of the water conduits with which Patan, and even more so Bhaktapur, are so liberally endowed. This one has a cruciform-shaped pool and three wonderfully carved stone *makara* (mythological crocodiles) head waterspouts. Next to it is the **Mani Mandap**, twin pavilions built in 1700 and used for royal coronations.

VISHWANATH TEMPLE

South of the Bhimsen Temple stands the Vishwanath (Shiva) Temple (Map p187). This elaborately decorated two-roofed temple was built in 1627 and has two large stone elephants guarding the front entrance. The pillars are particularly ornate. Shiva's vehicle, the bull, is on the other side of the temple, while inside is a large lingam. The temple has been restored in recent years.

KRISHNA MANDIR

Continuing into the square, the third temple you reach is the Krishna Mandir (Map p187), which was built by King Siddhinarsingh Malla. Records indicate that the temple was completed with the installation of the image on the 1st floor in 1637. With

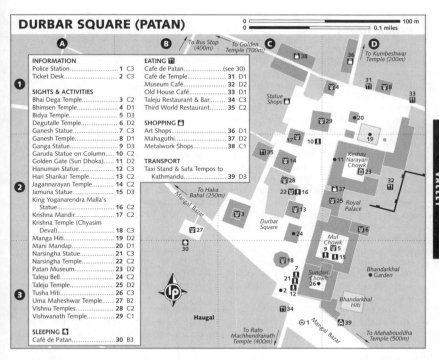

DURBAR SQUARE (PATAN)

0 ———————————— 100 m
0 ———————————— 0.1 miles

INFORMATION
Police Station.......................... 1 C3
Ticket Desk............................... 2 C3

SIGHTS & ACTIVITIES
Bhai Dega Temple.................... 3 C2
Bhimsen Temple....................... 4 D1
Bidya Temple............................ 5 D3
Degutalle Temple..................... 6 D2
Ganesh Statue.......................... 7 C3
Ganesh Temple......................... 8 D1
Ganga Statue............................ 9 D3
Garuda Statue on Column...... 10 C2
Golden Gate (Sun Dhoka)...... 11 D2
Hanuman Temple..................... 12 C3
Hari Shankar Temple................ 13 C2
Jagannarayan Temple.............. 14 C2
Jamuna Statue.......................... 15 D3
King Yoganarendra Malla's
  Statue.................................... 16 C2
Krishna Mandir......................... 17 C2
Krishna Temple (Chyasim
  Deval).................................... 18 C3
Manga Hiti............................... 19 D2
Mani Mandap............................ 20 D1
Narsingha Statue...................... 21 C3
Narsingha Temple..................... 22 C2
Patan Museum.......................... 23 D2
Taleju Bell................................. 24 C2
Taleju Temple........................... 25 D2
Tusha Hiti.................................. 26 C3
Uma Maheshwar Temple......... 27 B2
Vishnu Temples........................ 28 C2
Vishwanath Temple................. 29 C1

SLEEPING
Café de Patan........................... 30 B3

EATING
Cafe de Patan......................(see 30)
Café de Temple........................ 31 D1
Museum Café............................ 32 D2
Old House Café......................... 33 D1
Taleju Restaurant & Bar........... 34 C3
Third World Restaurant............ 35 C2

SHOPPING
Art Shops.................................. 36 D1
Mahaguthi................................ 37 D2
Metalwork Shops...................... 38 C1

TRANSPORT
Taxi Stand & Safa Tempos to
  Kathmandu............................ 39 D3

To Bus Stop (400m)
To Golden Temple (100m)
To Kumbheshwar Temple (200m)
Statue Shops
Keshav Narayan Chowk
Royal Palace
To Haka Bahal (250m)
Durbar Square
Mangal Bazar
Mul Chowk
Bhandarkhal Garden
Sundari Chowk
Bhandarkhal Hiti
Haugal
To Rato Machhendranath Temple (400m)
Mangal Bazar
To Mahabouddha Temple (500m)

its strong Mughal influences, this stone temple is clearly of Indian design, unlike the nearby brick-and-timber, multiroofed Newari temples. The 1st and 2nd floors of this temple are made up of a line of three miniature pavilions, from the top of which rises a *shikhara*-style spire. Musicians can often be heard playing upstairs.

Krishna is an incarnation of Vishnu, so the god's vehicle, the man-bird Garuda, kneels with folded arms on top of a **column** facing the temple. The stone carvings along the beam above the 1st-floor pillars recount events of the Mahabharata, while on the 2nd floor there are scenes from the Ramayana. These fine friezes are accompanied by explanations in Newari of the narrative scenes. Non-Hindus are not allowed inside.

A major festival is held here in August/ September (Bhadra) for Krishna's birthday, Krishnasthami.

JAGANNARAYAN TEMPLE
The two-storey Jagannarayan (or Char Narayan) Temple (Map p187) is dedicated to Narayan, one of Vishnu's incarnations.

Dating from 1565, it is reputed to be the oldest temple in the square, although an alternative date in the late 1600s has also been suggested. The temple stands on a brick plinth with large stone lions, above which are two guardian figures. The roof struts are carved with explicit erotic figures.

KING YOGANARENDRA MALLA'S STATUE
Immediately north of the Hari Shankar Temple is a tall column (Map p187) topped by a figure of King Yoganarendra Malla (1684–1705) and his queens. The golden figure of the kneeling king, atop a lotus bud and protected by the hood of a cobra, has been facing towards his palace since 1700. On the cobra's head is a bird figure; legend has it that as long as the bird remains there the king may still return to his palace. A door and window of the palace are always kept open and a hookah (a water pipe used for smoking) is kept ready for the king should he return. A rider to the legend adds that when the bird flies off, the elephants in front of the Vishwanath Temple will stroll over to the Manga Hiti for a drink!

NEWARI TOWNS

The Newars have over the centuries created an urban culture unequalled in the Himalaya. The cities and towns of the Kathmandu Valley are a compact network of interlocking squares, courtyards, twisting alleyways, ponds and temples, often centred on a main square. Though modern building methods have affected aesthetics and village structure, much of the traditional structure remains. Decorated with carved windows and doorways, statues and shrines, and filled with locals drying grain, fetching water from the local carved well, or resting on a pilgrim's shelter, a Newari town is a remarkable synthesis of art and everyday life.

The family house was the starting point for urban development. Rich Newars build handsomely proportioned brick houses that are up to five storeys high with tiled roofs. Symbolically a Newari house becomes ritually purer as you ascend floors. The *chhayli* (ground floor) is used for commerce or the stabling of animals, or both. The *mattan* (first floor) consists of a bedroom and a room for visitors. Windows are small and latticed for both privacy and security. The *chota* (second floor) is the most active floor in the house and holds the living room, bedrooms and workroom for weaving and the like. It also houses a *dhukuti* (storeroom). Windows on this floor are larger and have outward-opening shutters. The *baiga* (attic floor) has the kitchen and dining room, a *pujakuthi* (shrine room) and a roof terrace.

Newari community life developed when a series of houses was built in a rectangle around a chowk (courtyard or square), often by a single clan or extended family. The chowk, with its water supply and a temple or shrine, became the centre of day-to-day life, as it is today to a large extent. Elaborately decorated *hitis* (water tanks) provide a communal washing area and running water. Shrines, temples and *pathi* (platforms used by the community and travellers) were erected over time by philanthropists.

In larger towns like Patan, monastery complexes were built and run by a unique cooperative religious and social institution known as a *guthi*. Today many of the *bahals* (monastery courtyards) formerly run by the *guthis* have been converted into courtyard communal living spaces (Patan alone has over 260 *bahals*). Here, the markets buzz, children play, women chat and work (weaving, washing, drying grain), old people doze in the sun, men talk over the community's business, and religious ceremonies take place, as they have for centuries.

Behind the statue of the king are three smaller **Vishnu temples**. The small, brick and plaster *shikhara*-style temple was built in 1590 and is dedicated to Narsingha, Vishnu's man-lion incarnation.

HARI SHANKAR TEMPLE

This three-storey temple to Hari Shankar (Map p187), the half-Vishnu, half-Shiva deity, has roof struts carved with scenes of the tortures of the damned – a strange contrast to the erotic scenes on the Jagannarayan. It was built in 1704–05 by the daughter of King Yoganarendra Malla.

TALEJU BELL

Diagonally opposite Taleju Temple, the large bell (Map p187), hanging between two stout pillars, was erected by King Vishnu Malla in 1736. An earlier bell, erected in 1703, was then moved to the Rato Machhendranath Temple. Petitioners could ring the bell to alert the king to their grievances.

Shop stalls occupy the building under the bell platform, and behind it is a lotus-shaped pool with a bridge over it.

KRISHNA TEMPLE

This attractive, octagonal stone temple (Map p187), also known as the Chyasim Deval, completes the 'front line' of temples in the square. The stairway to it, which faces the palace's Sundari Chowk, is guarded by two stone lions. It was built in 1723 and, like the Krishna Mandir, is a stark contrast to the usual Newari pagoda temple designs.

BHAI DEGA TEMPLE

Behind the Krishna Temple stands the squat Bhai Dega, or Biseshvar (Map p187), dedicated to Shiva. It's a singularly unattractive temple, although it is said to contain an impressive lingam. A few steps back from the square is another stone *shikhara*-style **Uma Maheshwar Temple**, clearly owing inspiration to the square's important Krishna Mandir.

ROYAL PALACE
Forming the whole eastern side of the Durbar Sq is the Royal Palace of Patan (Map p187). Parts of the palace were built in the 14th century, but the main construction was during the 17th and 18th centuries by Siddhinarsingh Malla, Srinivasa Malla and Vishnu Malla. The Patan palace predates of Kathmandu and Bhaktapur. It was severely damaged during the conquest of the valley by Prithvi Narayan Shah in 1768 and also by the great earthquake of 1934, but it remains one of the architectural highlights of the valley, with a series of connecting courtyards and three **temples** dedicated to the valley's main deity, the goddess Taleju.

KESHAV NARYAN CHOWK
The northern courtyard of the Royal Palace is entered from the square by the **Golden Gate** (Map p187), or Sun Dhoka. Completed in 1734, this is the newest part of the palace. The courtyard is entered through a magnificent gilded door topped by a golden *torana* showing Shiva, Parvati, Ganesh and Kumar. Directly above it is a golden window, where the king would make public appearances. The bench to the side of the gate is a favourite of Patan's retirees.

PATAN MUSEUM
The section of the palace around Keshav Narayan Chowk (the former residence of the Malla kings) has been superbly renovated and houses one of the subcontinent's finest **museums** (Map p187; ☎ 5521492; www.patan museum.gov.np; admission foreigner/SAARC Rs 250/50; ⌚ 10.30am-5.30pm). There have been some modern elements added to the building as part of the renovations, and the result is a beautiful synthesis of old and new.

The main feature of the museum is an outstanding collection of cast-bronze and gilt-copper work, mostly of Hindu and Buddhist deities. One gallery shows the stages involved in the production of hammered sheet-metal relief designs (known as repoussé) and the 'lost-wax' (*thajya* in Nepali) method of casting. Gallery H at the back of the complex, near the café, houses some fascinating photos of Patan at the turn of the 19th and 20th centuries. The text gives an excellent introduction to Nepal's Buddhist and Hindu iconography, religion and art and is available as an illustrated museum book (Rs 1000).

You need at least an hour, and preferably two, to do this place justice, and it's worth taking a break at the excellent Museum Café (see p193) before diving in for another round. The café is in a rear courtyard, which was used for dance and drama performances during the Malla period. The museum also has a shop (selling good museum posters) and toilets. Photos are allowed.

For a sneak preview of the museum's highlights and the story of its renovation go to www.asianart.com/patan-museum.

MUL CHOWK
This central courtyard (Map p187) is the largest and oldest of the palace's three main chowks (squares). Unfortunately, it's open haphazardly at best, generally when you slip the caretakers some *baksheesh* (a tip). Two stone lions guard the entrance to the courtyard, which was built by Siddhinarsingh Malla, destroyed in a fire in 1662 and rebuilt by Srinivasa Malla in 1665–66. At the centre of the courtyard stands the small, gilded **Bidya Temple**.

The palace's three Taleju temples stand around the courtyard. The doorway to the Shrine of Taleju or Taleju Bhawani, on the southern side of the courtyard, is flanked by the statues of the river goddesses **Ganga**, on a tortoise, and **Jamuna**, on a carved *makura* (mythical crocodile).

The five-storey **Degutalle Temple**, topped by its octagonal triple-roofed tower, is on the northeastern corner of the square. The larger, triple-roofed **Taleju Temple** is directly north, looking out over Durbar Sq. It was built by Siddhinarsingh Malla in 1640, rebuilt after a fire and again after the 1934 earthquake completely destroyed it. The goddess Taleju was the personal deity of the Malla kings from the 14th century, and Tantric rites were performed to her here.

SUNDARI CHOWK
South of Mul Chowk is the smaller Sundari Chowk (Map p187), with its superbly carved sunken water tank known as the Tusha Hiti. Unfortunately the courtyard is currently closed. Behind Sundari Chowk, and also not open to the public, is the Royal Garden and Kamal Pokhari water tank. The area is slated for renovation as a park by Unesco.

Back in main Durbar Sq the blocked-off entrance to Sundari Chowk is guarded by statues of **Hanuman**, **Ganesh** and Vishnu as **Narsingha**, the man-lion. The gilded metal window over the entrance from the square is flanked by windows of carved ivory.

North Of Durbar Square

The following sights are north of Durbar Sq. They can be visited as part of the Patan Walking Tour (see the boxed text, p185).

GOLDEN TEMPLE (KWA BAHAL)

Also known as the Hiranya Varna or Suwarna Mahavihara (Golden Temple), this unique Buddhist **monastery** (Map p184; admission Rs 25; ☉ dawn-dusk) is just north of Durbar Sq. Legends relate that the monastery was founded in the 12th century, although the earliest record of its existence is 1409. The doorway, flanked by gaudy painted guardian lions, gives no hint of the magnificent structure within.

The inner courtyard has a railed walkway around three sides and the entry is flanked by two stone elephants. Shoes and other leather articles must be removed if you leave the walkway and enter the inner courtyard. Look for the sacred tortoises pottering around in the courtyard – they are temple guardians. The main priest of the temple is a young boy under the age of twelve, who serves for 30 days before handing the job over to another boy.

The large rectangular building has three roofs and a copper-gilded façade. Inside the main shrine is a beautiful statue of Sakyamuni (no photos allowed). In the far right of the courtyard is a statue of Vajrasattva wearing an impressive silver-and-gold cape.

In the centre is a small, richly decorated temple with a golden roof that has an extremely ornate *gajur* (bell-shaped top). Inside in the oldest part of the temple is a 'self-arisen' (*swayambhu*) *chaitya*.

The four corners of the courtyard have statues of four Lokeshvaras and four monkeys, which hold out jackfruits as an offering. On the south side is Tara. A stairway leads up to a upper-floor chapel lined with Tibetan-style frescoes. Finally, as you leave the temple, look up to see a Kalachakra mandala carved into the ceiling.

KUMBESHWAR TEMPLE

Directly north of Durbar Sq is **Kumbeshwar Temple** (Map p184), one of the valley's three

---

JANAI PURNIMA AT KUMBESHWAR

Thousands of pilgrims visit the Kumbeshwar Temple during the **Janai Purnima festival** in July or August to worship the silver-and-gold lingam that is set up in the tank. It's a colourful occasion: bathers immerse themselves in the tank while members of the Brahmin and Chhetri castes replace the sacred thread they wear looped over their left shoulder. *Jhankris* (faith healers) beating drums and wearing colourful headdresses and skirts dance around the temple to complete the dramatic scene.

---

five-storey temples. The temple dominates the surrounding streets and is said to date from 1392, making it the oldest temple in Patan. The temple is noted for its graceful proportions and fine woodcarvings and is dedicated to Shiva, as indicated by the large Nandi, or bull, facing the temple.

The temple platform has two ponds whose water is said to come straight from the holy lake at Gosainkund, a long trek north of the valley (see p344 for more information). An annual ritual bath in the Kumbeshwar Temple's tank is claimed to be as meritorious as making the arduous walk to Gosainkund.

On the southeastern edge of the courtyard, behind a black lacquered grill, is an important **Bhairab Temple**, with a life-size wooden image of the god. Next door is the more active single-storey **Baglamukhi (Parvati) Temple**. On the western side of the Kumbeshwar Temple courtyard is the large **Konti Hiti**, a popular gathering place for local women. On the northern side is the Kumbeshwar Technical School (p194).

UMA MAHESHWAR TEMPLE

En route from Kumbeshwar Temple to Durbar Sq, the small and inconspicuous double-roofed **Uma Maheshwar Temple** (Map p184) is set back from the road on its eastern side. Peer inside the temple (a light will help) to see a very beautiful black-stone relief of Shiva and Parvati in the pose known as Uma Maheshwar – the god sitting cross-legged with his *shakti* (consort) leaning against him rather seductively. A similarly named temple near the Golden Temple has a similar statue.

South Of Durbar Square

The following sights are south of Durbar Sq in the backstreets of the bustling Haugal district.

BISHWAKARMA TEMPLE

Walk south from Durbar Sq, past several brassware shops and workshops. There is a small *bahal* almost immediately on your right (west) and then a laneway also leading west. A short distance down this lane is the brick **Bishwakarma Temple** (Map p184), with its entire façade covered in sheets of embossed copper. The temple is dedicated to carpenters and craftspeople and, as if in proof, you can often hear the steady clump and clang of metalworkers' hammers from nearby workshops.

MINANATH TEMPLE

Further south is a two-storey **temple** (Map p184) dedicated to the Buddhist Bodhisattva who is considered to be the little brother of Rato Machhendranath. The Minanath image is towed around town during the Rato Machhendranath festival, but in a much smaller chariot (look out for the epic chariot runners). The quiet temple dates from the Licchavi period (3rd to 9th centuries), but has undergone several recent restorations and has roof struts carved with figures of multi-armed goddesses, all brightly painted. There's a large *hiti* (water tank) in front.

RATO MACHHENDRANATH TEMPLE

South of Durbar Sq, on the western side of the road, is the **Rato (Red) Machhendranath Temple** (Map p184). Rato Machhendranath, the god of rain and plenty, comes in a variety of incarnations. To Buddhists he is the Tantric edition of Avalokiteshvara, while to Hindus he is a version of Shiva.

Standing in a large courtyard, the three-storey temple dates from 1673, although an earlier temple may have existed on the site since 1408. The temple's four carved doorways are each guarded by lion figures and at ground level on the four corners of the temple plinth are reliefs of a curious yeti-like demon known as a *kyah*. A diverse collection of animals (including peacocks, horses, bulls, lions, elephants and a snake) tops the freestanding pillars facing the northern side of the temple. The roof is supported by struts, each showing Avalokiteshvara standing above figures being tortured in hell.

MAHABOUDDHA TEMPLE

Despite its height, the Mahabouddha Temple (Temple of a Thousand Buddhas; Map p184) is totally hidden in a courtyard dwarfed by other buildings. The *shikhara* temple takes

---

RATO MACHHENDRANATH FESTIVAL

The image in the Rato Machhendranath Temple may just look like a crudely carved piece of red-painted wood, but each year during the **Rato Machhendranath Festival** celebrations it's paraded around the town on a temple chariot during the valley's most spectacular festival. Machhendranath is considered to have great powers over rain and, since the monsoon is approaching at this time, this festival is an essential plea for good rain.

As in Kathmandu, the Rato Machhendranath festival consists of a day-by-day chariot procession through the streets of the old town, but here it takes a full month to move the chariot from the Phulchowki area – where the image is installed in the chariot – to Jawlakhel, where the chariot is dismantled.

The main chariot is accompanied for most of its journey by a smaller chariot, which contains the image of Rato Machhendranath's companion, which normally resides in the nearby Minanath Temple.

The highlight of the festival is the Bhoto Jatra, or showing of the sacred vest. Machhendranath was entrusted with the jewelled vest after there was a dispute over its ownership. The vest is displayed three times in order to give the owner the chance to claim it – although this does not actually happen. The king of Nepal attends this ceremony, which is also a national holiday.

From Jawlakhel, Rato Machhendranath does not return to his Patan temple, but rather is conveyed on a *khat* (palanquin) to his second home in the village of Bungamati, 6km to the south, where he spends the next six months of the year. The main chariot is so large and the route is so long that the Nepali army is often called in to help transport it.

its name from the terracotta tiles that cover it, each bearing an image of the Buddha. It's modelled on the Mahabouddha Temple at Bodhgaya in India, where the Buddha gained enlightenment.

The building probably dates from 1585, but suffered severe damage in the 1934 earthquake and was totally rebuilt. Unfortunately, without plans to work from, the builders ended up with a different-looking temple and there were enough bricks left over to construct a *shikhara*-style shrine to Maya Devi, the Buddha's mother, which stands to the southwest!

The Mahabouddha Temple is about 10 minutes' walk southeast of Durbar Sq. A signpost points down a lane full of shops selling Buddhist statuary to the temple. The roof terrace of the shops at the back of the courtyard has a good view of the temple; follow the signs as there's no pressure to shop here.

UKU BAHAL (RUDRA VARNA MAHAVIHAR)

This Buddhist **monastery** (Map p184) near the Mahabouddha Temple is one of the best known in Patan. The main courtyard is absolutely packed with interesting bits and pieces – *dorjes*, bells, peacocks, elephants, Garudas, rampant goats, kneeling devotees and a regal-looking statue of a Rana general. The lions are curious, seated on pillars with one paw raised in salute, look as if they should be guarding a statue of Queen Victoria in her 'not-amused' incarnation rather than a colourful Nepali monastery.

As you enter the main courtyard from the north look for the finely carved wooden struts above, on the northern side of the

courtyard. They are said to be among the oldest of this type in the valley and prior to restoration they were actually behind the monastery, but were moved to this safer location inside the courtyard. The monastery in its present form probably dates from the 19th century, but certain features and the actual site are much older.

Behind the monastery is a small Swayambhunath-style stupa.

West of Durbar Square

HAKA BAHAL

Take the road west from the southern end of Durbar Sq, past Café de Patan, and you soon come to the **Haka Bahal** (Map p184), a rectangular building with an internal courtyard. Traditionally, Patan's Kumari (living goddess) is a daughter of one of the priests of this monastery.

Zoo

Nepal's only **zoo** (Map p184; ☎ 5528323; admission foreigner/SAARC Rs 100/40, children Rs 50/30, camera/video Rs 10/50, paddle boats Rs 40; ⏰ 9am-5pm Tue-Sun) is in the southwestern part of Patan, just north of Jawlakhel. It includes an exotic collection of Nepali wildlife, including rhinos, Bengal tigers, cloud leopards, red pandas, gharial, and something called a spotted lingsang, which we couldn't spot. While in places it's yet another depressing animal prison, steps are being made to improve the animals' environment. Huge hippos and lazy sloth bears open their mouths on cue whenever tourists walk by, ignoring the signs that say 'Don't feed the animals'. Stoners routinely get freaked out by the 60cm-long squirrels.

ASHOKA STUPAS

Legend claims that the four stupas marking the boundaries of Patan were built when the great Buddhist emperor Ashoka visited the valley 2500 years ago. Though there's little chance that Ashoka actually made it to the valley, the stupas do rank as the Kathmandu Valley's oldest Buddhist monuments. Although remains of all four can still be seen today, they probably bear little similarity to the original stupas.

The Northern Stupa is just beyond the Kumbeshwar Temple, on the way to the Sankhamul ghats. It's well preserved and whitewashed. The other three are all grassed over, which lends them a timeless air. The Southern, or Lagankhel, Stupa is just south of the Lagankhel bus stop and is the largest of the four. The smaller Western, or Phulchowk Stupa is beside the main road from Kathmandu that runs through to Jawlakhel. Finally, the small Eastern, or Teta, Stupa is well to the east of centre, across Kathmandu's Ring Rd and just beyond a small river.

Buddhist and Tibetan pilgrims walk around all four stupas in a single day during the auspicious full moon of August.

Keen naturalists, students of the grotesque and young kids will enjoy a visit.

FESTIVALS & EVENTS

Patan's most dramatic festival is the **Rato Machhendranath Festival** (p191) in April or May, followed by the **Janai Purnima Festival** (p190) at Kumbeshwar Temple in August.

SLEEPING

There's a small but decent spread of accommodation for all budgets in Patan, and a few tourists base themselves here.

Budget

Café de Patan (Map p187; ☎ 5537599; pcafé@ntc.net .np; s/d without bathroom Rs 300/400, s/d with bathroom Rs 500/600) The pleasant downstairs café (right), a great location near Durbar Sq and easy transport are the big draws here. The good-value rooms are bright, clean and of a good size, though for any kind of view you'll have to head up to the rooftop. Only two rooms come with private bathrooms.

Mahabuddha Guest House (Map p184; ☎ 5540575; mhg@mos.com.np; s/d Rs 300/400) Near the Mahabuddha Temple, southeast of Durbar Sq, this simple place has an atmospheric location away from the traffic. Rooms come with a bathroom but can be dark so aim for a room higher up, near the pleasant rooftop. Singles are much smaller than doubles. Prices for laundry and breakfast are good value.

Peace Guest House (Map p184; ☎ 5551189; peaceg house@wlink.com.np; s/d without bathroom Rs 200/300, with bathroom Rs 450/550) Another quiet and well-run guesthouse right next to the Mahabuddha Temple, with a range of rooms. The bathrooms are a bit hit-and-miss but the views on the west side are great and a couple of rooms have balconies.

Mountain View Guest House (Map p184; ☎ 55 38168; s/d without bathroom Rs 200/250, with bathroom Rs 300/400) Between Jawlakhel and Durbar Sq, down a sidestreet off the main road, this isn't great, with small rooms, sullen adolescent staff and noise from the neighbouring motorbike repair workshop, but it's cheap. Rooms at the back are best.

Midrange & Top End

All of these places accept credit cards.

Aloha Inn (Map p184; ☎ 5522796; www.alohainn .com; s/d US$30/40, deluxe s/d US$35/45, discounts of 30%; 🌐 🖳) Sadly, there's nothing remotely trop-ical about this old-fashioned but friendly place. It's clean, quiet, a little plain and a little overpriced. Deluxe rooms come with a desk and fridge and are worth the extra US$5. Located in the Jawlakhel area, a bit far to walk from the old city.

Hotel Clarion (Map p184; ☎ 5524512; www.ho telclarion.com; s/d US$50/60, discounts of 40%) More popular with aid consultants than tourists, the Clarion has nine comfortable, well-kept rooms and a pleasant garden but is still close to the noisy road, so ask for a room at the back. The restaurant is good and you can dine with a cocktail in the pleasant garden. It's near the Aloha Inn on the main drag. Credit cards accepted

Summit Hotel (Map p116; ☎ 5521810; www.sum mit-nepal.com; Kopundol; s US$25-100, d US$30-110, discounts of 20-35%; 🌐 🌐 🖳) For those in the know, this stylish Dutch-run resort is a firm favourite and a great alternative to staying in Kathmandu. Carved woods and terracotta tiles frame lovely lush gardens, creating a relaxing, romantic mood. The swimming pool is a plus in summer; open fires keep things cosy in winter. The original garden-view rooms are smaller but all have modern bathrooms and lovely sitting areas and offer the best value. Guests have been known to fight over the coveted corner Himalayan view rooms, with sweeping views across the river to Kathmandu. The budget rooms are worth avoiding.

Hotel Greenwich Village (Map pp110-11; ☎ 5521 780; www.godavariresort.com.np; s/d US$60/70, deluxe r US$80, discounts of 66%; 🌐 🌐) Also topping the Kopundol hill near the Summit Hotel, this is another peaceful but more downmarket (and cheaper) resort. Rooms are a little old-fashioned but then you'll probably spend most of your time at the lovely poolside terrace and café. Foreign exchange and a free airport pickup are useful perks.

Shrestha House (Map p184) is due to open soon as a boutique guesthouse after years of resto-ration under the support of Unesco.

EATING

Most of Patan's restaurants overlook Durbar Sq and are aimed at day-tripping tour groups. Prices are inflated but not out-rageously so, and the views are superb.

Café de Patan (Map p187; ☎ 5537599; dishes Rs 120-250) Just a few steps from the southwest-ern corner of Durbar Sq, this is a small, long-running favourite, with a pleasant open-air courtyard and a rooftop garden (with one table right at the very top of the building!). It turns out a superb lassi, plus pizza and Newari dishes.

Taleju Restaurant & Bar (Map p187; ☎ 5538358; mains Rs 115-165) Head for the 5th-floor terrace of this place at the southern end of the square, as the views from here are outstanding, especially on a clear day when you have the snow-capped Ganesh Himal as a backdrop. The prices are the most reasonable in the square and the food is acceptable, making this the best budget bet with a view. The '100% drinkable' organic Ukrainian wine is hard to turn down.

Museum Café (Map p187; light meals Rs 110-240, coffee Rs 60, plus 13% tax) In the rear courtyard of the Patan Museum, this is a stylish open-air place operated by the Summit Hotel. Prices are a little higher than elsewhere, but the gorgeous garden setting more than compensates. The organic salads are grown on site. You don't need to buy a museum ticket to eat at the café.

Café de Temple (Map p187; ☎ 5527127; mains Rs 170-300, set meal Rs 350-400) On the northern edge of the square, the excellent rooftop views are even more expansive than the menu, which offers both snacks and main meals. Try a cup of Tibetan herbal Yarchagumpa tea (Rs 50).

Prices are a little lower at the similar **Old House Café** (Map p187; ☎ 5555027), set in an old Newari house in the northeastern corner of the square, and **Third World Restaurant** (Map p187; ☎ 5522187), on the quiet western side of the square, with good rooftop views of the Krishna Mandir.

Bakery Café (Map p184; ☎ 5522949; mains Rs 80-160; www.nanglos.com; 💻) Near the zoo roundabout at Jawlakhel, the Bakery is an excellent place to drop in for a reviving café Americano (espresso with hot water), a *badam* (pistachio) milkshake or a light snack. The staff here are all deaf and the service is excellent.

Dhokaima Café (Map p184; ☎ 5522113; mains Rs 100-200; Sunday brunch Rs 300) A pleasant café 'next to the gate' (Patan Dhoka), with a nice garden and bar set under a sprawling walnut tree. It's a good place for a light snack after an exploration of Patan's backstreets, or come for the excellent Sunday brunch (10am to 3pm). The café is part of the Yala Maya Kendra, a Rana-era storehouse that is used for occasional cultural events.

La Soon (Map p184; ☎ 5537166; mains Rs 200-385; 🕙 10.30am-10pm Mon-Sat) Down a side alley (feel the stress melt away as you leave the main street), this relaxing garden restaurant and wine bar is filled at lunchtimes with local NGO staff. The food is international with good pasta, feta wraps and peanut soup.

New York Pizza (☎ 5520294; Kopundol) Boasts the (allegedly) largest commercial pizza in the world at 25 inches. A 12-inch pizza with a couple of toppings costs around Rs 340 and delivery is free anywhere in Patan.

For something special, Friday-night barbeques (Rs 500) at the Summit Hotel (see sleeping) are a treat. The hotel also hosts an organic produce market on Sundays, from 10am to 1.30pm.

DRINKING

Moksh Bar (Map p184; ☎ 5526212; beer Rs 150; 🕙 Tue-Sun) Across from La Soon, Moksh has some of the best live rock, funk and folk music in town (not just the normal Thamel cover bands) on Tuesday, Friday and Saturday.

Banana Cat Café (Map p184; ☎ 5522708; teas Rs 70; snacks Rs 200-300; 🕙 11.30am-6pm Thu-Tue) An artsy Japanese-run teahouse that serves herbal, Ayurvedic and Japanese teas, plus afternoon cream teas and Japanese snacks. The garden space and attached bead shop are a favourite hangout for local expat women.

SHOPPING

Patan has many small handicraft shops and is the best place in the valley for statuary and fair-trade products. The Jawlakhel area in Patan's southwest is great for Tibetan crafts and carpets.

Patan Industrial Estate (Map p184; 🕙 10am-6pm), in the south of Patan, doesn't sound like a very promising place to shop for crafts but it does boast a number of factory-cum-showrooms of carpets, wood- and metalwork. While they are definitely aimed at the group tourist, there is nothing to stop individuals having a wander around. Generally there's no pressure to buy and you can often see craftspeople at work.

Namaste Supermarket (Map p184; 🕙 9am-8pm), in the old Hotel Naryani building, is one of best in the city and an expat favourite.

Fair Trade Shops

Those interested in crafts should definitely visit the string of interesting shops at Kopundol, just south and uphill from the main Patan bridge. A number are run as nonprofit development organisations, so the prices are fair, and the money actually goes to the craftspeople, and some goes into training and product development.

One of the best of these 'crafts with a conscience' is **Mahaguthi** (☎ 5521607; www.mahaguthi .com; ☽ 10am-6.30pm), which was established with the help of Oxfam. It has three shops and sells a wide range of crafts produced by thousands of people across Nepal. It's a one-stop shop for beautiful hand-woven *dhaka* weavings, paper, pottery, block prints, woven bamboo, pashminas, woodcrafts, jewellery, knitwear, embroidery and Mithila paintings (see the boxed text, p315). The main showroom is in Kopundol but there are also branches in Patan's Durbar Sq (Map p187; ☽ 10am-5.30pm Sun-Fri), and in Kathmandu's Lazimpat district (see p154).

Other shops worth looking at nearby include **Dhukuti** (☎ 5535107; ☽ 9am-7pm; www.acp .org.np) for a wide range cloth, batiks, bags and even Christmas decorations, produced by over 1200 low-income women; **Sana Hastakala** (☎ 5522628) for paper and batiks; and **Dhankuta Sisters** (☽ 10am-6pm Sun-Fri) for tablecloths, cushion covers and the like, made of woven *dhaka* cloth from eastern Nepal. The other craft shops in this area are commercially run and mostly stock larger home-design items aimed at local expats.

Near to the Kumbeshwar Temple, the **Kumbeshwar Technical School** (Map p184; ☎ 5537484; http://kumbeshwar.com) provides Patan's lowest castes with skills; they produce locally made carpets, jumpers and woodwork direct to the consumer. The small showroom is on the ground floor of the school, down a short alley to the right of the school entrance.

Metalwork & Woodwork

Patan is the centre for bronze casting and other metalwork. The statues you see on sale in Kathmandu were probably made in Patan and there are a number of excellent metalwork shops just to the north of Durbar Sq. Good-quality gold-plated and painted bronze figures will cost Rs 2000 to 5000 for smaller ones, and up to more than Rs 10,000 for large images.

Woodcarving Studio (☎ 5538827; www.leebirch .com; Jawlakhel; ☽ 10am-5pm Sun-Fri) Artist Lee Birch's studio displays some of the best carvings in the valley, made on site by Newar woodcarvers. Prices are generally high, but so is the quality. It's best to call ahead.

Carpets

Anyone who likes Tibetan carpets should visit Jawlakhel, the former Tibetan refugee camp, where Nepal's enormous carpet industry was born. Tibetan carpet shops line the approach road south of the zoo.

The **Jawlakhel Handicraft Centre** (☎ 5521305; ☽ 9am-5pm Sun-Fri), established in 1960, is a large cooperative workshop where you can watch the carpet-making process, as well as check out the centre's showrooms (with marked prices). It's opposite a Tibetan monastery.

The carpets at the **Kumbeshwar Technical School** (opposite) are fairly priced, and this is possibly the only place where you can buy carpets made from 100% pure Tibetan wool. Carpets cost around US$100 for a 1m by 1.5m size or US$150 for 1.75m by 1.2m. For more on Tibetan carpets see p57.

GETTING THERE & AWAY

You can get to Patan from Kathmandu by bicycle, taxi, bus or tempo. It's an uphill and choking 5km bike ride from Thamel to Patan's Durbar Sq. The trip costs around Rs 130 by taxi.

Safa (electric) tempos (Rs 7, route 14A) leave from Kantipath, near the Kathmandu main post office in Sundhara district, as soon as they are full. Double-check the destination when getting in, as some run to Mangal Bazar/Durbar Sq, others to Lagankhel bus station. When returning, a few tempos branch right to Koteshwar instead of continuing to Kathmandu centre.

Local buses run frequently between Kathmandu's City (Ratna Park) bus station and Patan Dhoka (Rs 7).

Buses and faster minibuses to the southern valley towns leave when full from Patan's chaotic Lagankhel bus stand, including to Godavari, Bungamati and Chapagaon.

An interesting route back to Kathmandu is to continue northeast from the Northern Stupa down to the interesting ghats of Sankhamul, across the footbridge over the Bagmati River and then up to the Arniko Hwy near the big convention centre, from where you can take a taxi or cycle back to Thamel.

BHAKTAPUR

☎ 01 / pop 65,000

Bhaktapur, also known as Bhadgaon (pronounced *bud*-gown and meaning 'City of Rice') in Nepali, or Khwopa (City of Devotees) in Newari, is the third major town of the valley. Traffic free, the traditionally intact town is also in many ways the most timeless. The cobblestone streets link a string of temples, courtyards and monumental squares, and the sidestreets are peppered with shrines, wells and water tanks.

The lack of traffic makes walking through Bhaktapur a pleasure and certainly more enjoyable than walking in Kathmandu. The town's cultural life is also vibrant, with centuries-old traditions of craftsmanship and strong communities of potters, woodcarvers and weavers. Look for rice laid out to dry in the sun, people collecting water or washing under the communal taps, dyed yarns hung out to dry, children's games, fascinating shops and women pounding grain – there's plenty to see.

Perhaps most entrancing of all is Bhaktapur's effortless blending of the modern and medieval, thanks largely to the German-funded Bhaktapur Development Project, which restored buildings, paved dirt streets and established sewerage and wastewater management facilities in the 1970s.

HISTORY

Bhaktapur's historical roots lie in its position on the early trade route to Tibet, though the credit for the formal founding of the city goes to King Ananda Malla in the 12th century. The oldest part of the town is around Tachupal Tole, to the east.

From the 14th to the 16th century, as Bhaktapur became the most powerful of the valley's three Malla kingdoms, the focus of the town shifted west to the Durbar Sq area. Much of the town's great architecture dates from the rule of King Yaksha Malla (1428–82), who built the Pashupatinath and Dattatreya temples, but also from the end of the 17th century, during King Bhupatindra Malla's reign. At its peak the city boasted 172 temples and monasteries, 77 water tanks, 172 pilgrim shelters and 152 wells.

The 15th-century royal palace in Durbar Sq remained the seat of power until the city's defeat by Prithvi Narayan Shah in 1768 relegated the former capital to a market town. The 1934 earthquake caused major damage to the city.

ORIENTATION

Bhaktapur rises up on the northern bank of the Hanumante River. Public buses, minibuses and taxis from Kathmandu stop at Navpokhu Pokhari on the western edge of town. Tour buses unload at the tourist-bus and taxi park on the northern edge of town. Both are a short walk from the city centre.

For the visitor, Bhaktapur is really a town of one curving road – the old trade route to Tibet – that links several squares. From the bus stop at Navpokhu Pokhari you come first to Durbar Sq, then Taumadhi Tole with its famous five-storey Nyatapola Temple, then to Tachupal Tole.

INFORMATION

Visiting foreigners are charged a hefty fee of Rs 750 (US$10). This is collected and checked zealously at over a dozen entrances to the city. If you are staying here for up to a week, you need only pay the entrance fee once, but you must state this at the time of buying the ticket and write your passport number on the back of the ticket.

For longer stays (up to one year), a Bhaktapur Visitor Pass is available within a week of purchasing your entry ticket. Passes are issued by the **Bhaktapur Municipality office** (Map p187; ☎ 6610310; ☙ 6am-7pm) at the ticket booth on the western end of Durbar Sq and require two photos and a photocopy of your visa and passport details. SAARC nationalities pay Rs 50. Children under 10 are free.

There are moneychangers in Taumadhi and Tachupal Tole and a couple of Internet cafés, including **Surfer's Edge** (Map pp204-5; per hr Rs 20; ☙ 9am-10pm) just north of Potters' Sq.

SIGHTS

The following sights will lead you on a walk from west to east through the old town. To dive into the backstreets follow the walking tour (p203), which is marked on the Bhaktapur map (Map pp204–5).

The Western Gates to Taumadhi Tole

The main road heading through Bhaktapur from the west forks at Siddha Pokhari. The northern road leads to Durbar Sq but the main southern road is the more interesting of the two.

To get onto this west–east road from Navpokhu Pokhari turn south from the corner of the *pokhari* (large water tank) and then left on the road, passing a ticket office by the town's Lion Gate. Unless otherwise indicated all of the following sights are on the Bhaktapur map pp204–5.

LION'S GATE TO POTTERS' SQUARE

Heading east from Lion's Gate you pass a small tank on your right and then the much larger **Teka Pokhari** (Map pp204-5). Just 10m before the next major junction, to your left, is the constricted, tunnel-like entrance to the tiny **Ni Bahal** (signposted as 'Jet Barna Maha Bihar'), dedicated to Maitreya Buddha, the Buddha yet to come. The entrance is easy to miss, just before the carved pillars of a pilgrim resthouse.

Cross the junction, where the road runs downhill to the Mangal Tirtha Ghat, and you will see on your left the red-brick **Jaya Varahi Temple**. There are elaborately carved wooden *toranas* over the central door and the window above it. At the eastern end of the temple is the entrance to the upper floor, flanked by stone lions and banners. The two ornate windows, on either side of the upper *torana*, have recently been re-painted their original gold.

A few more steps bring you to a small **Ganesh shrine**, jutting out into the street and covered in bathroom tiles. Continue to **Nasamana Square**, which is somewhat decrepit but has a Garuda statue without a temple. Almost immediately after this is a second square with the **Jyotirlingeshwar**, a *shikhara*-style temple that houses an important lingam. Behind the shrine is an attractive *hiti*, one of Bhaktapur's many sunken water conduits. Continue straight and you will arrive at the turn-off right to Potters' Sq. Walk a little further on and you will come to Taumadhi Tole.

POTTERS' SQUARE

Potters' Sq (Bolachha Tol) can be approached from Durbar Sq, Taumadhi Tole or along the western road into town from Lion's Gate.

On the northern side of the square a small hillock is topped by a **Ganesh shrine** and a shady pipal tree. There are fine views over the river to the hills south of Bhaktapur. The square itself has two small temples:

a solid-brick central **Vishnu Temple** and the double-roofed **Jeth Ganesh Temple**. The latter is an indicator of how long the activity all around the square has been going on – a wealthy potter donated the temple in 1646 and to this day its priest is chosen from the potter caste.

Pottery is very clearly what this square is all about; the southern side of the square is lined with clay stores and potters' wheels, and the square (and other parts of town) is often filled with hundreds of pots drying in the sun. After the harvest in October, which is when most tourists visit, the pots have largely been exchanged for piles of drying rice. An alleyway to the south reveals a traditional mud-and-straw-covered kiln.

Taumadhi Tole

A short walk from Potters' Sq or Durbar Sq reveals the second great square of Bhaktapur, the Taumadhi Tole (Map p198). Here you'll find Nyatapola Temple, the highest temple in the valley and also the Café Nyatapola (p207), where the balconies provide a great view over the square. The latter was renovated for its new purpose in 1977 and it has some finely carved roof struts.

NYATAPOLA TEMPLE

The five-storey, 30m-high Nyatapola Temple (Map p198) is not only the highest temple in Nepal, but also one of the best examples of traditional Newari temple architecture. From the Arniko Hwy or Suriya Binayak Temple (see p209), the temple appears to soar above Bhaktapur's rooftops, with the snow-capped Himalaya as a dramatic backdrop.

The elegant temple was built during the reign of King Bhupatindra Malla in 1702, and its design and construction were so solid that the 1934 earthquake caused only minor damage. The stairway leading up to the temple is flanked by guardian figures at each plinth level. The bottom plinth has the legendary Rajput wrestlers Jayamel and Phattu, said to have the strength of 10 men. On the plinths above are two elephants, then two lions, then two griffins and finally two goddesses – Baghini and Singhini. Each figure is said to be 10 times as strong as the figure on the level below. Presiding over all of them, but hidden away inside, is the mysterious Tantric goddess Siddhi Lakshmi, to whom the temple is dedicated.

AROUND THE KATHMANDU VALLEY

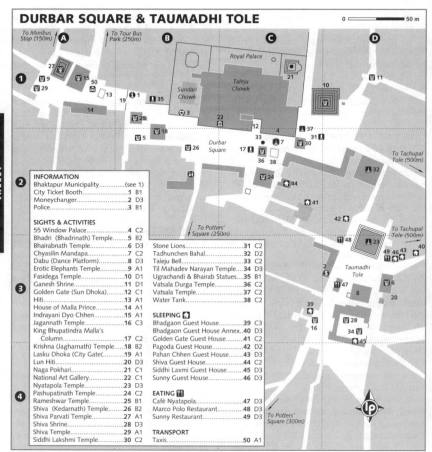

DURBAR SQUARE & TAUMADHI TOLE

0 ————— 50 m

To Minibus Stop (150m)
To Tour Bus Park (250m)
Royal Palace
Sundari Chowk
Taleju Chowk
Durbar Square
Taumadhi Tole
To Tachupal Tole (500m)
To Potters' Square (250m)
To Potters' Square (300m)

INFORMATION
Bhaktapur Municipality...............(see 1)
City Ticket Booth.........................1 B1
Moneychanger.............................2 D3
Police...3 B1

SIGHTS & ACTIVITIES
55 Window Palace.......................4 C2
Bhadri (Bhadrinath) Temple........5 B2
Bhairabnath Temple....................6 D3
Chyasilin Mandapa.....................7 C2
Dabu (Dance Platform).................8 D3
Erotic Elephants Temple...............9 A1
Fasidega Temple........................10 D1
Ganesh Shrine...........................11 D1
Golden Gate (Sun Dhoka)...........12 C1
Hiti..13 A1
House of Malla Prince.................14 A1
Indrayani Dyo Chhen.................15 A1
Jagannath Temple......................16 C3
King Bhupatindra Malla's
  Column..................................17 C2
Krishna (Jagharnath) Temple.......18 B2
Lasku Dhoka (City Gate(............19 A1
Lun Hiti....................................20 D3
Naga Pokhari............................21 C1
National Art Gallery...................22 C1
Nyatapola Temple......................23 D3
Pashupatinath Temple................24 C2
Rameshwar Temple....................25 B1
Shiva (Kedarnath) Temple...........26 B2
Shiva Parvati Temple..................27 A1
Shiva Shrine..............................28 D3
Shiva Temple.............................29 A1
Siddhi Lakshmi Temple...............30 C2

Stone Lions...............................31 C2
Tadhunchen Bahal......................32 D2
Taleju Bell.................................33 C2
Til Mahadev Narayan Temple.......34 D3
Ugrachandi & Bhairab Statues....35 B1
Vatsala Durga Temple.................36 C2
Vatsala Temple..........................37 C2
Water Tank................................38 C2

SLEEPING
Bhadgaon Guest House................39 C3
Bhadgaon Guest House Annex.....40 D3
Golden Gate Guest House............41 C2
Pagoda Guest House...................42 D2
Pahan Chhen Guest House..........43 D3
Shiva Guest House......................44 C2
Siddhi Laxmi Guest House...........45 D3
Sunny Guest House.....................46 D3

EATING
Café Nyatapola.........................47 D3
Marco Polo Restaurant...............48 D3
Sunny Restaurant......................49 D3

TRANSPORT
Taxis..50 A1

Only the temple's priests are allowed to see the image of the goddess, but the temple's 108 carved and painted roof struts depict her in her various forms. Various legends and tales relate to the temple and its enigmatic inhabitant. One is that she maintains a balance with the powers of the terrifying Bhairab, comfortably ensconced in his own temple just across the square.

BHAIRABNATH TEMPLE

The well-restored, triple-roofed Bhairabnath Temple (also known as the Kasi Vishwanath or Akash Bhairab; Map p198) has an unusual rectangular plan and a somewhat chequered history. It was originally built as a one-storey temple in the early

17th century, but was rebuilt with two storeys by King Bhupatindra Malla in 1717. The 1934 earthquake caused great damage to the temple and it was completely rebuilt and a third floor added.

Casually stacked by the north wall of the temple are the enormous wheels and temple chariot runner on which the image of Bhairab (a fearsome form of Shiva) is conveyed around town during the Bisket festival in mid-April – see the boxed text, p203. There are more chariot runners on the north side of the Nyatapola Temple.

Curiously, despite Bhairab's fearsome powers and his massive temple, his bodiless image is only about 15cm high! A small hole in the central door (below a row of carved boar snouts) is used to push offerings into the temple's interior, but the actual entrance to the Bhairabnath Temple is through the small Betal Temple, on the south side of the main temple.

The temple's façade is guarded by two brass lions and includes an image of Bhairab painted on rattan with real dried intestines draped across it! Head here at dusk to catch nightly devotional music.

TIL MAHADEV NARAYAN TEMPLE

It's easy to miss the square's third interesting temple (Map p198), as it is hidden away behind the buildings on the southern side of the square. You can enter the temple's courtyard through a narrow entrance through those buildings, or through an arched entrance facing west, just to the south of the square.

This double-roofed Vishnu temple has a Garuda kneeling on a high pillar in front, flanked by pillars bearing Vishnu's *sankha* and *chakra* symbols. Some of the temple's struts also depict Garudas. A lingam in a yoni (female equivalent of the phallic symbol) stands inside a grilled structure in front and to one side of the temple. A plaque to the lower right of the door depicts the goddess Vajrayogini in characteristic pose with her left leg high in the air.

Despite the temple's neglected setting it is actually an important place of pilgrimage as well as one of the oldest temple sites in the town: an inscription indicates that the site has been in use since 1080. Another inscription states that the image of Til Mahadev installed inside the temple dates from 1170.

Durbar Square

Bhaktapur's Durbar Sq (Map p198) is larger than Kathmandu's, much less crowded with temples than Patan's and less vibrant than either. However it wasn't planned that way: Victorian-era illustrations show the square packed with temples and buildings, but the disastrous earthquake of 1934 destroyed many of them, and today empty plinths mark where temples once stood.

Durbar Sq is the one place where you'll be approached by a string of tiresome guides and thangka painting school touts.

EROTIC ELEPHANTS TEMPLE

Just before you enter the square, coming from the minibus and bus stop, pause for a little bit of Newari humour. On your right, perhaps 70m before the main Durbar Sq entrance gate, is a tiny double-roofed **Shiva Parvati temple** (Map p198) with some erotic carvings on its temple struts. Among the series of copulating animals are elephants in the missionary position with their trunks entwined in pleasure! It's a *hathi* (elephant) Kamasutra.

UGRACHANDI & BHAIRAB STATUES

When you enter Durbar Sq from the west you'll pass by an entry gate (to a school) with two large stone lions built by King Bhupatindra Malla. On the northern wall to the left are statues of the terrible Bhairab (right) and the equally terrible Ugrachandi, or Durga (left), the fearsome manifestation of Shiva's consort Parvati. The statues date from 1701 and it's said that the unfortunate sculptor had his hands cut off afterwards, to prevent him from duplicating his masterpieces.

Ugrachandi has 18 arms holding various Tantric weapons and symbols (symbolising the multiple aspects of her character) and she is in the act of casually killing a demon with a trident (symbolising the victory of wisdom over ignorance). Bhairab has to make do with just 12 arms. Both god and goddess are garlanded with necklaces of human heads. The gates and courtyard that these powerful figures guard are no longer of any particular importance.

CHAR DHAM

A number of less significant temples crowd the western end of Durbar Sq. They include the lopsided **Rameshwar Temple** (Map p198) dedicated to Shiva and the **Bhadri Temple** dedicated to Vishnu as Narayan. In front of them is an impressive, larger **Krishna Temple** and just beyond that is a brick *shikhara*-style **Shiva Temple** erected by King Jitamitra Malla in 1674.

Together the four temples are called the Char Dham, after the four Hindu pilgrimage sites of the same name, to provide a place of worship for those unable to make the pilgrimage to the real sites.

KING BHUPATINDRA MALLA'S COLUMN

King Bhupatindra Malla was the best known of the Malla kings of Bhaktapur and had a great influence on the art and architecture of the town. Like the similar column in Patan's Durbar Sq, this one (built in 1699) was based on the original in Kathmandu but remains the most beautiful of the three. The king sits with folded arms, studying the magnificent golden gate to his palace.

VATSALA DURGA TEMPLE & TALEJU BELL

Beside the king's statue and directly in front of the Royal Palace is the stone Vatsala Durga Temple (Map p198), which was built by King Jagat Prakash Malla in 1672 (some sources say 1727). The *shikhara*-style temple has some similarities to the Krishna Mandir in Patan. In front of the temple is the large **Taleju Bell**, which was erected by King Jaya Ranjit Malla in 1737 to mark morning and evening prayers at the Taleju Temple.

A second, smaller bell stands on the temple's plinth and is popularly known as 'the barking bell'. It was erected by King Bhupatindra Malla in 1721, supposedly to counteract a vision he had in a dream, and to this day dogs are said to bark and whine if the bell is rung.

ROYAL PALACE

Bhaktapur's Royal Palace (Map p198) was founded by Yaksha Malla (r 1428–82) and was added to by successive kings, particularly Bhupatindra Malla. As with the old palaces of Kathmandu and Patan, visitors are restricted to certain areas. The palace suffered great damage in the terrible 1934 earthquake and only half a dozen of the original 99 courtyards survived.

NATIONAL ART GALLERY

The western end of the palace has been made into an **art gallery** (Map p198; admission Rs 20; ☻ 10am-5pm Wed-Mon). The entrance to the gallery is flanked by figures of Hanuman the monkey god and Vishnu as Narsingha, his man-lion incarnation. These guardian figures date from 1698 and Hanuman appears in Tantric form as the four-armed Hanuman-Bhairab. This part of the palace was once known as the Malati Chowk.

The gallery has a fine collection of Hindu and Buddhist paintings, palm-leaf manuscripts, *paubha* (thangka like paintings on cloth) and metal, stone and woodcrafts; it's the best of the town's three museums.

Once paid, your entry ticket is valid for both the Woodcarving and Brass & Bronze Museums in Tachupal Tole (see opposite).

GOLDEN GATE & 55 WINDOW PALACE

Adjacent to the gallery, the magnificent Golden Gate, or Sun Dhoka, is the entrance to the 55 Window Palace (Map p198). The Golden Gate is generally agreed to be the most important piece of art in the whole valley. The gate and palace were built by King Bhupatindra Malla, but were not completed until 1754 during the reign of Jaya Ranjit Malla, the last of the Bhaktapur Malla kings.

A Garuda, the vehicle of Vishnu, tops the *torana* and is shown here disposing of a number of serpents, which are the Garuda's sworn enemies. The four-headed and 10-armed figure of the goddess Taleju Bhawani is featured directly over the door. Taleju Bhawani is the family deity of the Malla dynasty and there are temples to her in the royal palaces in Kathmandu and Patan as well as Bhaktapur.

The Golden Gate opens to the inner courtyards of the palace, but you cannot proceed further than the ornate entrance to colourful Taleju Chowk (1553). Non-Hindus can check out the nearby **Naga Pokhari**, a 17th-century royal water tank encircled by a writhing stone cobra *(naga)*. The *nagas* rise up on scaled pillars and water pours from a goat's head that protrudes from the mouth of a *makara* (crocodile demon). The tank was traditionally used for the daily ritual bath of the goddess Taleju.

At the time of research, the 55 Window Palace was under major renovation, slated to continue until 2007.

CHYASILIN MANDAP

Beside Vatsala Durga Temple is an attractive **water tank** and in front of that is the Chyasilin Mandap (Map p198). This octagonal temple was one of the finest in the square until it was destroyed by the 1934 earthquake. Using some of the temple's original components, it was totally rebuilt in 1990; note the metal construction inside this outwardly authentic building.

PASHUPATINATH TEMPLE

Behind the Vatsala Durga Temple, this temple (Map p198) is dedicated to Shiva as Pashupati and is a replica of the main shrine at Pashupatinath. Originally built by King Yaksha Malla in 1475 (or 1482), it is the oldest temple in the square and is sometimes called the Yaksheswor Mahadev Temple.

AROUND THE KATHMANDU VALLEY

For adults only, the roof struts depict some of the rudest erotic art in the valley. Unexpected humour is provided by one bored-looking woman who multitasks by washing her hair while pleasuring her husband at the same time. Don't even ask what the dwarf with the bowl is doing…

SIDDHI LAKSHMI TEMPLE

By the southeastern corner of the palace stands the stone Siddhi Lakshmi Temple (Map p198), also known as the Lohan Dega, or Stone Temple. The steps up to the temple are flanked by male and female attendants, each leading a rather reluctant child and a rather eager-looking dog. On successive levels the stairs are flanked by horses, rhinos, man-lions and camels.

The 17th-century temple marks the dividing line between the main and secondary parts of Durbar Sq. Behind the temple is another **Vatsala Temple**, while to one side of it are two rather lost-looking curly-haired **stone lions**, standing by themselves out in the middle of the square.

FASIDEGA TEMPLE

The large and ugly Fasidega Temple (Map p198) is dedicated to Shiva and stands in the centre of the second part of Durbar Sq. There are viewpoints all around the valley – the Changu Narayan Temple is one of them – from where you can study Bhaktapur at a distance. The white bulk of the Fasidega is always an easy landmark to pick out. The temple sits on a six-level plinth with elephant guardians at the bottom of the steps, and with lions and cows above them.

TADHUNCHEN BAHAL

The southern and eastern side of the second part of the square is made up of a double-storey *dharamsala* (rest house for pilgrims), now used as a school. As you enter the street leading east from the square, the restored monastery of the Tadhunchen Bahal (Map p198), or Chatur Varna Mahavihara, is on the southern side. It dates from 1491 and is where the cult of the Kumari, Nepal's living goddesses, originally started. Bhaktapur actually has three Kumaris but they lack the political importance of Kathmandu's (see the boxed text, p119).

In the inner courtyard the roof struts on the eastern side have highly unusual carvings showing the tortures of the damned. In one a snake is wrapped around a man, another shows two rams butting an unfortunate's head, while a third strut shows a nasty tooth extraction being performed with a large pair of pliers! You may see copper chasing going on in the courtyard.

Taumadhi Tole to Tachupal Tole

The curving main road through Bhaktapur runs from beside the Bhairabnath Temple in Taumadhi Tole to Tachupal Tole, the old centre of town. The first stretch of the street is a busy shopping thoroughfare selling everything from porters' tumplines (the leather or cloth strips across the forehead or chest used to support a load carried on the back) to Hindi movie DVDs.

At the first bend there are two interesting old buildings on the right-hand (southern) side. The **Sukul Dhoka** (Map pp204–5) is a *math* (Hindu priest's house), with superb woodcarving on its façade. Next door is the **Lun Bahal**, originally a 16th-century Buddhist monastery that was converted into a Hindu shrine with the addition of a stone statue of Bhimsen. If you look into the sanctum, in the inner courtyard, you can see the statue, dating from 1592, complete with a ferocious-looking brass mask.

A little further along, the road joins **Golmadhi Square** (Map pp204–5) with a deep *hiti*, the small, triple-roofed **Golmadhi Ganesh Temple** and adjacent to it a **white chaitya**. Just down on the left is the well-restored façade of the **Jhaurbahi Dipankar Bihar**.

A further 100m brings you to another small open area with a *path* (pilgrim shelter) on your right. Behind it is a tank and, set behind a gateway, is the **Inacho Bahal** (Map pp204–5; see p203). A few more steps bring you to Tachupal Tole.

Tachupal Tole

Tachupal Tole was probably the original central square of Bhaktapur and the seat of Bhaktapur royalty until the late 16th century, so this is most likely the oldest part of the town. South from this square a maze of narrow laneways, passageways and courtyards runs down to riverside ghats.

The tall, square **Dattatreya Temple** (Map p202) was originally built in 1427, but alterations were made in 1458. Like some other important structures in the valley it is said

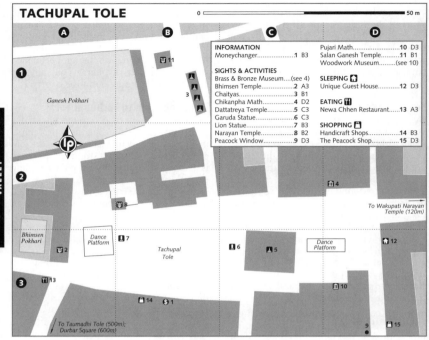

TACHUPAL TOLE

INFORMATION	
Moneychanger.................1 B3	

SIGHTS & ACTIVITIES	
Brass & Bronze Museum....(see 4)	
Bhimsen Temple.................2 A3	
Chaityas............................3 B1	
Chikanpha Math.................4 D2	
Dattatreya Temple..............5 C3	
Garuda Statue....................6 C3	
Lion Statue........................7 B3	
Narayan Temple..................8 B2	
Peacock Window.................9 D3	

Pujari Math........................10 D3	
Salan Ganesh Temple..........11 B1	
Woodwork Museum.........(see 10)	

SLEEPING	
Unique Guest House...........12 D3	

EATING	
Newa Chhen Restaurant......13 A3	

SHOPPING	
Handicraft Shops.................14 B3	
The Peacock Shop...............15 D3	

Ganesh Pokhari

Bhimsen Pokhari

Dance Platform

Tachupal Tole

Dance Platform

To Wakupati Narayan Temple (120m)

To Taumadhi Tole (500m); Durbar Square (600m)

to have been built using the timber from a single tree. The temple is dedicated to Dattatreya, a blending of Brahma, Vishnu and Shiva, although the Garuda-topped pillar and the traditional weapons of Vishnu (conch and a disc) on their pillars indicate the strong influence of Vishnu. The temple is important to Shaivites, Vaishnavites and Buddhists.

The three-storey temple is raised well above the ground on its base, the sides of which are carved with some erotic scenes. The front section, which was a later addition to the temple, stands almost separate and the temple entrance is guarded by the same two Malla wrestlers who watch over the first plinth of the Nyatapola Temple.

At the other end of the square is the two-storey **Bhimsen Temple** (Map p202), variously dated to 1605, 1645, 1655 or 1657! The temple is squat, rectangular and open on the ground floor. It's fronted by a platform with a small double-roofed Vishnu/Narayan Temple and a pillar topped by a brass lion with his right paw raised. Steps lead down behind it to the deeply sunken Bhimsen Pokhari.

There are 10 buildings around the square that were originally used as *maths* (Hindu monasteries). The best known was the **Pujari Math**. It was originally constructed in the 15th century during the reign of King Yaksha Malla, but was rebuilt in 1763. German experts renovated the building in 1979 as a wedding gift for the then King Birendra. Until the 20th century, an annual caravan brought tributes to the monastery from Tibet.

The Pujari Math is principally famed for the superb 15th-century **peacock window**, 30m down a small alley on the right-hand side. It is reputed to be the finest carved window in the valley and is the subject of countless postcards and photographs. The shop opposite allows photos from its upper-floor window.

The building now houses a **Woodcarving Museum** (Map p202; admission Rs 20; 9am-4pm Wed-Mon), which has some fine examples of the woodcarving for which Bhaktapur has long been famous. It costs an extra Rs 20 to take photos; but there's not really enough light to make that worthwhile; bring a torch (flashlight). The ticket also covers entry to the Brass & Bronze Museum and the National Art Gallery (p200).

Across the square from the Pujari Math is the **Brass & Bronze Museum** (Map p202; admission Rs 20; ⏲ 9am-4pm Wed-Mon), with poorly lit examples of metalwork and ceremonial vessels from around the valley.

On the north side of Tachupal Tole is another open area, with the small **Salan Ganesh Temple** (Map p202), dating from 1654. The open temple is ornately decorated, but the image is just a rock with only the vaguest elephant-head shape. To one side of the temple is the Ganesh Pokhari, a large tank.

WALKING TOUR
See Map pp204–5 for the route of this circular walking tour, The letter following the sights corresponds to the map position.

Part I – North of Durbar Square
Starting from the northeastern corner of Durbar Sq, walk to the east of the high Fasidega Temple, continue north past a multicoloured Ganesh shrine to a little alleyway on the right, next to a thangka painting school. Follow the alleyway into a longer tunnel and out onto the main path. Continue past a shrine to a traditional building with **sun and moon plaques (A)** on the west side. Swing north (look for the strange leather face hanging on the north wall) and

then take a right turn, quickly swinging to the left just past a momo restaurant.

Three quarters of the way up the alleyway, look for the **terracotta Ganesh window (B)** on your right. At the junction take a right, past some lovely carved windows, and then swing left. Head north past a Mahakali Temple, a water pool and a city ticket office until you hit the main road on the north edge of the town.

Turn right (east) on the road towards Nagarkot and you soon come to the modern **Mahakali Temple (C)**, where a lovely shrine tops a small hill reached by a steep flight of steps.

Just beyond this temple, turn right back into town, walk uphill and then turn left just before a small pool. Continue walking until you reach the tiny, open, yellow-roofed **Mahalakshmi Temple (D)**. Turn right (south) here and continue down to another large tank, the Naga Pokhari. Here the typically green water contrasts nicely with the dyed yarns hung out to dry alongside the tank. On the western side of the tank, two **temples (E)** flank a central white **shikhara temple (F)**, while a cobra rears up from the centre of the tank.

Pass along the north side of the tank, swing north and then, 10m before a roofed **Ganesh shrine (G)**, pop into a low doorway on the right (marked by three steps) into a tiny

---

BISKET JATRA AT KHALNA TOLE

Bisket Jatra heralds the start of the Nepali New Year and is one of the most exciting annual events in the valley. In preparation, Bhairab's huge triple-roofed chariot is assembled from the parts scattered beside the Bhairabnath Temple and behind the Nyatapola Temple in Taumadhi Tole. The huge and ponderous chariot is hauled by dozens of villagers to Khalna Tole with Betal, Bhairab's sidekick from the tiny temple behind the Bhairabnath Temple, riding out front like a ship's figurehead, while Bhadrakali, his consort, accompanies them in her own chariot.

The creaking and swaying chariots lumber around the town, pausing for a huge tug of war between the eastern and western sides of town. The winning side is charged with looking after the images of the gods during their week-long riverside sojourn in Khalna Tole's octagonal *path* (pilgrim shelter). After the battle the chariots slither down the steep road leading to Khalna Tole, where a huge 25m-high lingam (phallic symbol) is erected in the stone *yoni* (female genital symbol) base.

In the evening of the following day (New Year's day), the pole is pulled down, again in an often-violent tug of war. As the pole crashes to the ground, the new year officially commences. Bhairab and Betal return to Taumadhi Tole, while Bhadrakali goes back to her shrine by the river.

Other events take place around Bhaktapur for a week preceding New Year and then for days after, with locals often dressed in the town's traditional red, white and black striped cloth, known as *haku patasi*. Members of the potters' caste will put up and haul down their own lingam, and processions also carry images of Ganesh, Lakshmi and Mahakali around town.

courtyard with lovely woodcarvings and a central *chaitya*. Continue out the far end, follow the alley past another courtyard and then on the left you'll see the white-pillared entrance of the **Prashan Nashil Maha Bihar (H)**. This Buddhist temple has some nice stone carvings, some prayer flags and occasional devotional music.

Continue east to the road junction, marked by a lotus-roofed shrine, and take

WALK FACTS

Duration Two hours
Start Durbar Sq
Finish Taumadhi Tole

a left to the large pool known as the Kwathandau Pokhari. Head right along the tank to its southeast corner and the **Nava Durga Temple (I)**, a Tantric temple. The golden door is surmounted by a golden window and is guarded by metal lions. It all contrasts nicely with the red-painted brick frontage.

Continue southeast past some wonderfully carved balconies (look up to see garlic and corn drying) to the main east–west road, which runs through Tachupal Tole and Taumadhi Tole. Around this area there are more potters at work. Turn right and immediately on your left is the elaborate entrance to the **Wakupati Narayan Temple (J)**, built in 1667. The ornate, golden temple is double-roofed and is fronted by a line-up of

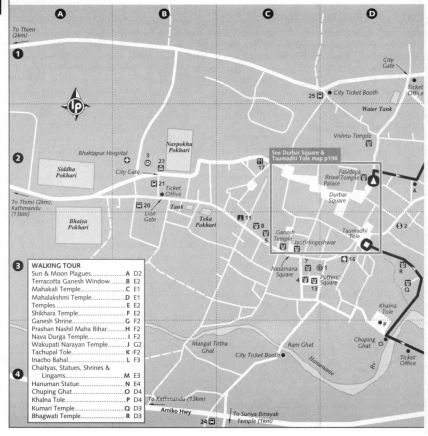

BHAKTAPUR

no less than five Garudas supported on the backs of turtles. You can often find wood-carvers or spinners in this courtyard. Continue from here to **Tachupal Tole** (**K**; p201).

Part II – South of Tachupal Tole
From Tachupal Tole turn left down the side of the Pujari Math; directions to its famous peacock window are well signposted. At a square jog right (by a small deity), left, right at a second small square and left again at the main square. Then immediately on your left is the unassuming gateway to the ornate little **Inacho Bahal (L)** – signposted the 'Sri Indravarta Mahavihar' – with prayer wheels, figures of the Buddha and a lopsided miniature pagoda roof rising up above the courtyard.

From here the road drops down to the Hanumante River, and enters rural surroundings. At the bottom of the hill is a Ram Temple and a curious collection of **chaityas**, **statues**, **shrines** and **lingams (M)**, including a bas-relief of a nude Shiva (obviously pleased to see you) next to what are said to be the largest Shiva lingam in Nepal. Head down to the sacred river confluence for a collection of shrines and statues including one of **Hanuman (N)**, the faithful ally of Rama and Sita. On the nearby building are four paintings, partly obscured by a photogenic tree, including one on the far right showing Hanuman returning to Rama from his Himalayan medicinal herb foray, clutching a whole mountain in his hand.

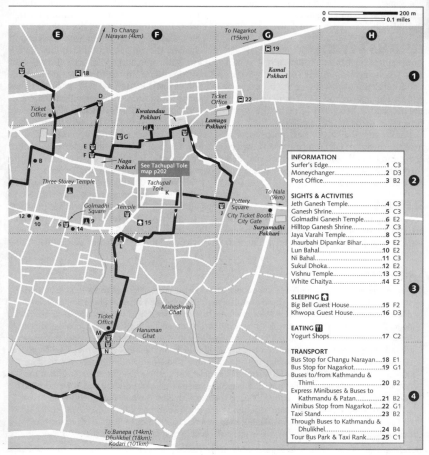

Cross the bridge and then take a hairpin turn back from the road onto a small footpath. This rural stroll ends by another temple complex, where you cross the river by the **Chuping Ghat (0)**, where there are areas for ritual bathing and cremations.

Above the river is **Khalna Tole (P)**, the centre for the spectacular activities during the Bisket Jatra festival (see the boxed text, p203). On the south side of the square look for the huge wooden poles (known as *yosin*) that are erected in the central plinth during the festival. Just south is a pretty temple complex that now serves as Tribhuvan University's Department of Ethnomusicology.

The circular walk ends with a gentle climb back into the town, past the modern **Kumari Temple (Q)** and **Bhagwati Temple (R)**, emerging at a small livestock market on the southern side of Taumadhi Tole.

FESTIVALS & EVENTS

Bhaktapur celebrates **Bisket Jatra** (Nepali new year's day) on April 14th with a stupendous chariot festival (see the boxed text, p203). The nearby town of Thimi celebrates the dramatic **Balkumari Jatra** at the same time (see the boxed text, p209).

Bhaktapur is also the best place to witness the antics of **Gai Jatra** (see p364), where cows and boys dressed as cows are paraded through the streets. It's not the running of the bulls but it is a lot of fun.

SLEEPING

A growing number of visitors to Bhaktapur are staying overnight. There's plenty to see, no screaming motorbikes or air pollution,

and once dusk falls all the Kathmandu daytrippers melt away, not to return until after breakfast the next day.

Most guesthouses have only a handful of (generally small) rooms so you may have to hunt around the first night. In general you are paying more for the location and views than the quality of your room, and your rupees won't go quite as far in Bhaktapur as they do in Kathmandu. Single rooms are in short supply.

Budget

Pagoda Guest House (Map p198; ☎ 6613248; www
.pagodaguesthouse.com.np; r without bathroom US$5-10,
with bathroom US$15-25) This friendly and family-run place is just off the northwestern edge of Taumadhi Tole. There are only six rooms, all different and neat as a button, though perhaps a little bit overpriced these days. The cheaper rooms come with towels and a heater; the pricier upstairs rooms have a clean bathroom and TV. There's also a decent rooftop restaurant but the views are limited.

Shiva Guest House (Map p198; ☎ 6613912; www
.shivaguesthouse.com; s/d/tr without bathroom US$6/8/12,
s/d with bathroom US$15/20, discounts of 20% Dec-Aug)
Bang on Durbar Sq, this well-maintained place has corner rooms with fantastic views over Durbar Sq, but the other rooms are overpriced. There's a cosy restaurant on the ground floor (mains Rs 150 to 300).

Golden Gate Guest House (Map p198; ☎ 6610534;
www.goldengateguesthouse.com; s/d without bathroom Rs
200/300, with bathroom Rs 400/700, deluxe Rs 1300/1500)
A friendly place entered through a passageway from Durbar Sq or from the laneway between Durbar Sq and Taumadhi Tole.

NAGA PANCHAMI

During the festival of Naga Panchami people across Nepal leave offerings to the *naga*s (serpent spirits). Among the offerings is a bowl of rice, offered because of an incident at the Siddha Pokhari pond on the western outskirts of Bhaktapur which, legend has it, was once inhabited by an evil *naga*. A holy man determined to kill the *naga* himself by taking the form of a snake, and told his companion to be ready with a bowl of magic rice. If, after he entered the pond, the water turned white then the *naga* had won and it was all over. If, on the other hand, the water turned red, then he had defeated the *naga* and although he would emerge from the pond in the form of a snake, the magical rice could restore his original form. Sure enough the water turned red, but when the holy man in the form of a hideous serpent emerged from the water, his horrified companion simply turned tail and ran, taking the rice with him. The holy man tried to catch him, but failed, and eventually decided to return to the pond and remain there.

To this day the inhabitants of Bhaktapur keep well clear of the Siddha Pokhari pond, and on the day of Naga Panchami a bowl of rice is put out – just in case the holy man/snake turns up.

Rooms lack much style but are generally clean and some have balconies. The top-floor deluxe rooms are best. There are fine rooftop views and there's also a good restaurant downstairs, featuring a stunning 400-year-old carved window.

Big Bell Guest House (Map pp204-5; ☎ 6611675; r without bathroom Rs 300-400) A modern friendly family-run cheapie, a stone's throw from Tachupal Tole. There are no creaking floorboards here to give it charm but the common bathrooms are clean and the best rooms overlook the small garden restaurant.

Khwopa Guest House (Map pp204-5; ☎ 6614661; khwopa12@hotmail.com; s Rs 350, d Rs 450-500) Low ceilings and a lack of views give this well-run place a hobbit-like vibe, but it's a decent budget choice just off Taumadhi Tole. The upstairs rooms are quieter.

Siddhi Laxmi Guest House (Map p198; ☎ 6612 500; siddhilaxmi.guesthouse@gmail.com; r Rs 250-600, ste Rs 1050; Til Mahadev Naryan Temple Complex) The best thing about this tiny five-roomed guesthouse is the hidden location in one of Bhaktapur's nicest courtyards. The huge top-floor suite is great but it's all downhill as you head downstairs. The mid-floor rooms are good value and one comes with a shared balcony. The ground-floor rooms have thin mattresses and tiny bathrooms.

Midrange

Bhadgaon Guest House (Map p198; ☎ 6610488; www .bhadgaon.com.np; Taumadhi Tole; s/d US$15/20) From the lovely foyer seating to the great rooftop views over Taumadhi Tole and the Langtang Himalaya beyond, this place is a good choice. Rooms are clean and comfortable but vary in size; everyone wants the top-floor double with its private balcony. The rooftop restaurant is popular and reasonably priced. The new nine-roomed annex (☎ 2133124) across the square is just as good, with views on the east side through carved wooden windows, but no restaurant.

Pahan Chhen Guest House (Map p198; ☎ 6612 887; srp@mos.com.np; s Rs 500-700, d Rs 800-1000) On the northeastern corner of Taumadhi Tole, with comfortable cosy rooms with clean bathrooms, although they are a bit small (especially the singles). Black-and-white photos lend a dash of style and the views from the roof are as good as you'll get.

Sunny Guest House (Map p198; ☎ 6616094; sunnyres@hotmail.com; r Rs 700-1200, ste Rs 2000) Next

door to the Pahan Chhen, this is a similar deal, with only six rooms. The front-facing rooms offer some of the best views of Taumadhi Tole, and rooms are quite chic, with nice lighting and carved window lattices but small bathrooms. The suite has a gorgeous carved window seat. There's a relaxing balcony restaurant (below).

Unique Guest House (Map p202; ☎ 6611575; unique@col.com.np; s/d US$10/15) A tiny, vertical place with four rooms on four floors in a low-ceilinged, creaky and slightly claustrophobic old building on Tachupal Tole. It's the only hotel in this part of the town, which helps create a powerful atmosphere once the crowds disappear. It's probably no good if you are much over six feet tall, though.

EATING

Bhaktapur is certainly no competition for Kathmandu when it comes to restaurants, but don't worry, you won't starve. Don't forget to try Bhaktapur's famous speciality: *juju dhau*, 'the king of curds' (yogurt) while you are here. You can find it in tourist restaurants, but there are also several holes-in-the-wall between Durbar Sq and Navpokhu Pokhari (look for the pictures of curd outside), where you can get a small cup for Rs 7 or a giant family-sized bowl for Rs 60.

Café Nyatapola (Map p198; ☎ 6610346; snacks Rs 150, set meals Rs 450-550, pot of tea Rs 55; ☼ 8am-7pm) Right in Taumadhi Tole, this is in a building that was once a traditional pagoda temple – it even has erotic carvings on some of the roof struts. It's a cramped tourist-only zone but the location is irresistible. Prices are comparatively high but part of the profits go to a local hospital.

Marco Polo Restaurant (Map p198; mains Rs 70-120) On the corner of the square and beside the Nyatapola Temple, this is a cheaper bet if you want a substantial meal, and it's open in the evenings when many of the other tourist places are shut. There's a small balcony with limited views over Taumadhi Tole.

Sunny Restaurant (Map p198; mains Rs 140-200) Consists of two places; one atop the guesthouse of the same name and the other next door. Both offer a terrace and great views over the square, though the hotel restaurant is 10% more expensive. Local specials include the Newari set meal and king curd.

The best-value food in town is in the courtyard of the Big Bell Guest House

---

KITE FLYING IN THE KATHMANDU VALLEY

No visitor to the Kathmandu Valley in autumn, around the time of Dasain, can fail to notice the local penchant for kite flying – kids can be seen flying kites on rooftops, on streets, in open spaces and in parks.

To the uninitiated, this looks like, well, kids flying kites, but there is a lot more to it than meets the eye. First and foremost is the fact that kites are flown to fight other kites – downing your opponent is the objective, and this is done by cutting their line.

The way to protect yourself from the ignominy of becoming a dreaded *hi-chait* (kite with a cut line) and to make your own kite as lethal as possible is to armour the line of the kite. In the past, people used to make their own *maajhaa* (line armour) and everyone had their own secret recipe, often involving a combination of crushed light bulbs, boiled slugs and gum. The trick was to make it sharp enough to cut an opponent's line, but not so sharp that it would cut itself when wound on to the *lattai* (wooden reel). These days people use ready-made threads, which cost anything from Rs 40 for 1000m up to Rs 25 per metre for pre-armed line from India.

The other hazard that may catch the unwary is the *mandali*, a stone on a string launched by a pirate on low-fliers – the idea being that they cross your string, bring down your kite and then make off with said kite!

The paper kites themselves look very basic but are surprisingly manoeuvrable, the so-called Lucknow kites being the most sought after. Prices for kites start as low as Rs 5 and go to a modest Rs 50 or so. Popular places to buy kites are Asan Tole and Bhotahiti in Kathmandu's old city.

(p207), near Tachupal Tole, where you can get standards like sweet-and-sour vegetables with rice for Rs 50.

Newa Chhen Restaurant (Map p202; Tachupal Tole; snacks Rs 30-70) Serves up local snacks in a creaky old building but wouldn't be noteworthy if it weren't for the single corner table which has killer views of Tachupal Tole. Grab it early and don't let go.

If you are on a tight budget, there are several basic momo restaurants around town. The food is fairly low grade but the momos are tasty and you can fill up for pennies.

SHOPPING

Bhaktapur is famed for its pottery and woodcarving. Shops and stalls catering to visitors are concentrated around Tachupal Tole.

Woodcarving & Puppets

Bhaktapur is renowned for its woodcarving and you'll see good examples in stalls around Tachupal Tole and the alley beside the Pujari Math, right under the peacock window in fact. Popular pieces include copies of the peacock window or masks depicting the god Bhairab.

Some of the best puppets, which are on sale in their thousands in all the valley towns, come from Bhaktapur and nearby Thimi.

Paper

Hand-made paper, cards, albums and other paper products are available throughout town. One good place to check out is **The Peacock Shop** (Map p202; ☎ 6610820; ☟ 9am-6pm, factory closed Sat), near the Peacock Window down the side of Pujari Math. You can visit the workshop out back and observe the pressing, drying, smoothing, cutting and printing processes involved in making the paper. You can also see the raw *lokta* (daphne bush) plant material from which the paper is made.

GETTING THERE & AWAY
Bicycle

The main Arniko Hwy to Bhaktapur carries a lot of bellowing, belching buses and trucks so it's better to follow the parallel road to Bhaktapur via the northern end of Thimi. See p84 for a description of the route. Avoid peak hours.

Bus, Minibus & Taxi

Minibuses from Kathmandu (Rs 12, 40 minutes) drop off/depart from a stand just southwest of Bhaktapur's Navpokhu Pokhari, a short walk from Durbar Sq. The last minibus back to Kathmandu leaves at about 6.45pm. Express buses are the best bet, as local buses stop in Thimi en route.

Taxis from Kathmandu cost around Rs 350 one way.

Buses for Nagarkot (Rs 15, one hour) leave regularly from the northeastern corner of the city.

Buses to Changu Narayan (Rs 8, 30 minutes) leave every 30 minutes or so from the northern junction with the Changu Narayan road.

For Dhulikhel you'll have to walk 10 minutes down to the Arniko Hwy (via Potters' Sq and Ram Ghat) and catch a (probably packed) through bus from Kathmandu.

AROUND BHAKTAPUR

SURIYA BINAYAK TEMPLE

About 1km south of town, this 17th-century Ganesh Temple is said to be a good place to visit if you're worried about your children being late developers! It's also popular with marriage parties. To get there take the road down past Potters' Sq to Ram Ghat (where there are areas for ritual bathing and cremations), cross the river and continue to the main road. The road continues on the other side and has fine views back over the rice paddies to Bhaktapur. It's about a 45-minute walk from central Bhaktapur.

Where the road turns sharp right, a steep stairway climbs up to the temple on a forested hilltop. As you step inside the temple enclosure, the very realistic-looking rat, on top of a tall pillar, indicates that this temple belongs to Ganesh. The image of the god sits in an enclosure, awash in red paste,

marigolds, rice offerings and melted candles. Statues of kneeling devotees in a range of traditional headdresses face the image and the *shikhara* is flanked by large bells.

There are twice-weekly puja ceremonies on Tuesday and Saturday mornings; get here early and grab a tea-and-omelette breakfast at the pilgrim stalls. If you are feeling energetic, steps lead up the hillside to the right of the temple for the best valley views.

THIMI

Thimi (known historically as Madhyapur) is the fourth-largest town in the valley, outranked only by Kathmandu, Patan and Bhaktapur. It's a typical Newari town and its 'capable people' (the name of the town is derived from this Newari expression) operate thriving cottage industries producing pottery and papier-mâché masks. You'll pass a string of mask shops if you head west from Thimi along the northern road to Bhaktapur. Thimi isn't spectacular but the lack of traffic or tourists make it a pleasant stop-off en route to Bhaktapur.

The town's main road runs north–south between the old and new (Arniko Hwy) Bhaktapur roads, which form the northern and southern boundaries of the town.

Sights

From the southern gate on the main highway there's a short, stiff walk up to the main southern square and the 16th-century **Balkumari Temple**. Balkumari is one of Bhairab's

---

BALKUMARI JATRA

The small town of Thimi welcomes the new year with an exciting festival instituted by King Jagat Jyoti Malla in the early 1600s in which Balkumari, one of Bhairab's consorts, is honoured. All through the first day of the new year devotees crowd around the Balkumari Temple in Thimi and as dusk falls hundreds of *chirags* (ceremonial oil lamps) are lit. Some devotees lie motionless around the temple all night with burning oil lamps balanced on their legs, arms, chests and foreheads.

The next morning men come from the various *toles* or quarters of Thimi and from surrounding villages, each team carrying a *khat* (palanquin) with images of different gods. As the 32 *khats* whirl around the temple, red powder is hurled at them and the ceremony reaches fever pitch as the *khat* bearing Ganesh arrives from the village of Nagadesh. The crowds parade up and down the main street until late in the morning when Ganesh, borne by hundreds of men, makes a break for home, pursued by the other *khats*. Sacrifices are then made to Balkumari.

In the nearby village of Bode another *khat* festival, with just seven *khats* rather than 32, takes place at the Mahalakshmi Temple. Here a volunteer spends the whole day with an iron spike piercing his tongue. Successful completion of this painful rite brings merit to the whole village as well as the devotee.

shaktis and the temple's entrance is plastered in feathers from previous sacrifices. A statue of Balkumari's vehicle, a peacock, stands in front of the temple. Further north, past a Lokeshwar temple (safe behind four sets of locked doors!), a school flanked by painted images and a *shikhara*-style temple, is a 16th-century **Narayan Temple** and a **Bhairab Temple**, with erotic carvings on the struts and a small brass plaque of Bhairab's face, his mouth stuffed with rice offerings. North of here are silversmiths, flour grinders and basket makers, and a stupa complex where men gather to play cards.

At the north end of Thimi is the crossroads with the old road to Bhaktapur; turn left, and head downhill past a small shrine and water tank. Take a detour right off the main road for a couple of minutes to see the village of **Nagadesh** and the impressive Ganesh Dyochen (a *dyochen* is a Tantric temple). Through the gateway and to the right is the triple-roofed **Ganesh Temple**, where the façade is often smeared with sacrificial blood.

Back at the northern crossroads, a 15-minute walk north will bring you to the village of **Bode**. From a crossroads marked by a couple of corner stores take a left for five minutes into the brick alleys of the village. Take a right at the first pool to the Nil Barahi Temple and the interesting belt-driven contraption that's used to roast corn. Head left (west) one block, and then take a right to the 17th-century **Mahalakshmi Temple** with an image of a reclining Vishnu behind it.

Getting There & Away

Any Bhaktapur-bound minibus from Kathmandu will be able to drop you at Thimi, probably at the southern entrance but possibly the northern entrance, and you catch another minibus on to Bhaktapur from either junction. A taxi from Kathmandu to the southern entrance costs around Rs 200.

If you are continuing by bike to Bhaktapur, the northern (old) road offers a far more pleasant ride.

CHANGU NARAYAN TEMPLE

The beautiful and historic temple of **Changu Narayan** (admission Rs 60; ☼ dawn-dusk) stands on a hilltop at the eastern end of the valley,

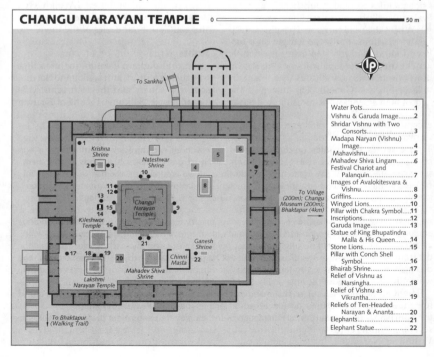

HIKING THE SHORTCUT BETWEEN CHANGU NARAYAN & SANKHU

From Changu Naryan you can avoid having to backtrack by hiking an hour or so north to the main Bodhnath-Sankhu road and then continuing east to Sankhu or west to Bodhnath.

From the northern entrance of the Changu Narayan Temple a short and steep path descends to the Manohara River, which is crossed easily by wading or by a temporary bridge during the dry season (impossible in the monsoon). This brings you out to the Sankhu road at Bramhakhel, which is about 3.5km southeast of Gokarna. Frequent minibuses head east and west from here.

Coming from the other direction, you'll see a small sign for Changu Narayan on a building wall on the south side at the entry to Bramhakhel. It's a five-minute walk across the fields to the river and the temporary bridge. It's quite a steep and difficult scramble up the hill that will take at least 45 minutes (especially if you're carrying a bicycle). There's quite a labyrinth of paths up the hill and it's not a bad idea to have a guide (and bicycle carrier). You will probably find boys offering their carrying services – establish a price in advance. You can recognise the temple by its golden roof atop the final bump of a lengthy spur running down from the eastern edge of the valley.

about 6km north of Bhaktapur and 22km from Kathmandu. It dates from 1702, when it was rebuilt after a fire, however its origins go back to the 4th century and many of the stone sculptures date from the Licchavi period (4th to 9th centuries). The temple is a Unesco World Heritage site.

Despite the temple's beauty, its easy access from Bhaktapur and the proximity of some fine walks nearby, it attracts relatively few visitors.

The one street of Changu Village leads up from the car park past a central *path* (pilgrim shelter), water tank and Ganesh shrine, before ascending past thangka and wooden mask shops to the temple entrance.

The double-roofed temple is dedicated to Vishnu in his incarnation as Narayan and is exceptionally beautiful, with quite amazingly intricate roof struts depicting multi-armed Tantric deities. It is fronted on the west side by a kneeling figure of Garuda said to date from the 5th century. The man-bird mount of Vishnu has a snake around his neck and kneels with hands in the *namaste* position facing the temple. Stone lions guard the wonderfully gilded door, which is flanked by equally detailed gilded windows. Two pillars at the front corners carry a conch and disc, the traditional symbols of Vishnu. Non-Hindus are not allowed inside the temple itself, which is normally shut anyway.

The temple's true gems are the wonderful, much older sculptures dotted around the courtyard. In the southwest corner are several notable images, including one of Vishnu as Narsingha, his man-lion incar-

nation, disembowelling a demon. Another, to the left, shows him as Vikrantha/Vamana, the six-armed dwarf who transformed into a giant capable of crossing the universe in three steps during his defeat of King Bali. He is in a characteristic 'action pose', with his leg raised high. To the side of these images is a small black slab showing a 10-headed and 10-armed Vishnu, with Ananta reclining on a serpent below. The scenes are divided into three sections – the underworld, the world of man and the heavens. The beautifully carved image is around 1500 years old.

In the northwestern corner there is a 7th-century image of Vishnu astride the Garuda, which is illustrated on the Rs 10 banknote. In front of the Garuda figure that faces the front of the temple is the oldest stone inscription in the valley, dating from 464 AD. The inscription is in Sanskrit and tells how the king persuaded his mother not to commit *sati* (ritual suicide) after his father's death.

Also interesting are the statues of King Bhupatindra Malla and his queen, kneeling in a gilded cage in front of the temple. In the centre of the courtyard, triangular bricks are used, while out towards the edge there are older, rounded-corner bricks.

Just outside the temple complex is the Bhimsen Pati, with its stone guardians; the remains of the Balamphu royal residence on the north side; and a small open-air collection of sculptures to the south, behind the Changhu Peaceful Cottage.

Back in Changu is the **Changu Museum** (admission Rs 140; ☻7am-6pm), which gives a funky introduction to traditional valley life, exhibited in a 160-year-old house. Look for the rhino-skin shield, the 2nd-century leather coins, Tantric astrology books and 225-year-old rice! It's worth a visit, though the recent 300% ticket hike is a bit cheeky.

Sleeping & Eating

Changhu Guest House (☎ 6616652; saritabhatta@ hotmail.com; s/d lower fl Rs 300/400, s/d upper fl Rs 350/500) Just before the temple, the four simple but clean rooms here offer a peaceful and offbeat place to spend the night. The upper-floor rooms are worth the extra money as they come with a balcony and views over Bhaktapur. The owners can arrange visits to local Tamang villages and distilleries.

Changu Narayan Hill Resort (☎ 6617691; r Rs 300) 600m east of the village, along the track to Nagarkot, this secluded guesthouse could be really nice, with great views and a homely atmosphere, but the basic concrete rooms and cold-water bathrooms spoil it a little.

The **New Hill Restaurant**, by the car park at the entrance to Changu, and the slightly pricier **Changhu Peaceful Cottage**, near the temple, both offer a decent place for lunch.

Getting There & Away

Regular public buses run the 6km between Changu Narayan and Bhaktapur (Rs 8, 30 minutes), with the last bus around dusk. A taxi from Kathmandu costs around Rs 800 return, or Rs 250 from Bhaktapur.

By bike it's a downhill run to Bhaktapur (30 minutes), but a steep climb on the way there. Perhaps the best option is to take a bus or taxi to Changu Naryan and then walk back via the village of Jhaukhel (1½ hours). A network of walking trails lead back to Bhaktapur; just keep asking the way.

If you're headed to Nagarkot you can take the footpath east to Tharkot and catch a bus for the final uphill stretch – see p224 for details of the hike.

THE NORTHEASTERN VALLEY

This quiet corner of the Kathmandu valley is probably the least visited but it offers visoters a couple of charming temples, a lovely mountain-bike itinerary and access to the start of the Helambu trek (p339).

GOKARNA MAHADEV TEMPLE

Only 2km northeast of Bodhnath, past the ugly suburb of Jorpati, the road to Sundarijal branches north off the Sankhu road and, after 3.5km of twists and turns, takes you to the old Newari village of Gokarna, 10km from Kathmandu. The village is notable for its fine riverside Shiva temple.

Built in 1582, the triple-roofed Mahadev (Great God) or **Gokarneshwar (Lord of Gokarna) Temple** (admission free) stands on the banks of the Bagmati River; its inner sanctum enshrines a particularly revered Shiva lingam. Over the temple entrance is a golden *torana*, with Shiva and Parvati making an appearance in the centre in the Uma Maheshwar position (where Parvati sits on Shiva's thigh and leans against him) and a figure of the Garuda above them.

The temple's great interest is the surprisingly varied collection of sculptures and reliefs all around the site, some dating back more than a thousand years. They even line the pathway down from the road to the temple courtyard.

The sculptures illustrate an A to Z of Hindu mythology, including early Vedic gods such as Aditya (Sun God), Chandra (Moon God), Indra (on an elephant) and Ganga (with four arms and a pot on her head from which pours the Ganges). Shiva

---

NARSINGHA

The image of Vishnu as Narsingha (or Narsimha) is a common one throughout the valley. In his man-lion incarnation the god is traditionally seen with a demon stretched across his legs, in the act of killing the creature by disembowelling it. You can find Narsingha at work at Changu Narayan, in front of the palace in Patan, just inside the Hanuman Dhoka entrance in Kathmandu and at the Gokarna Mahadev Temple.

The demon was supposedly undefeatable as it could not be killed by man or beast, by day or night or by any weapon. Vishnu's appearance as Narsingha neatly overcame the first obstacle, for a man-lion is neither a man nor a beast. He then waited until dusk to attack the demon, for dusk is neither day nor night. And instead of a weapon Narsingha used his own nails to tear the demon apart.

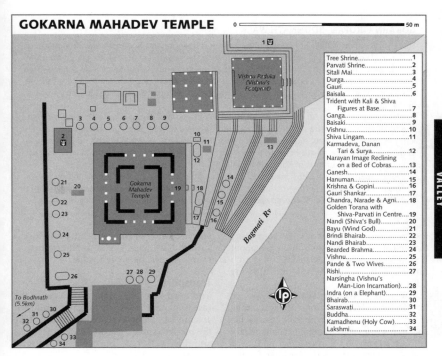

GOKARNA MAHADEV TEMPLE

Tree Shrine	1
Parvati Shrine	2
Sitali Mai	3
Durga	4
Gauri	5
Baisala	6
Trident with Kali & Shiva Figures at Base	7
Ganga	8
Baisaki	9
Vishnu	10
Shiva Lingam	11
Karmadeva, Danan Tari & Surya	12
Narayan Image Reclining on a Bed of Cobras	13
Ganesh	14
Hanuman	15
Krishna & Gopini	16
Gauri Shankar	17
Chandra, Narade & Agni	18
Golden Torana with Shiva-Parvati in Centre	19
Nandi (Shiva's Bull)	20
Bayu (Wind God)	21
Brindi Bhairab	22
Nandi Bhairab	23
Bearded Brahma	24
Vishnu	25
Pande & Two Wives	26
Rishi	27
Narsingha (Vishnu's Man-Lion Incarnation)	28
Indra (on a Elephant)	29
Bhairab	30
Saraswati	31
Buddha	32
Kamadhenu (Holy Cow)	33
Lakshmi	34

appears in several forms, including as Kamadeva, the God of Love, and Vishnu appears as Narsingha, making a particularly thorough job of disembowelling a nasty demon (see the boxed text, opposite). The god Gauri Shankar is interesting since it contains elements of both Shiva and Parvati. The Brahma figure in the southwest corner appears to have only three heads (he should have four) until you peer around the back and discover the hidden head.

The finest of the Gokarna statuary is in the small shrine house, which is in the northwestern corner of the courtyard. This 8th-century sculpture of the beautiful goddess Parvati shows her at her radiant best.

To one side of the main temple, just above the river, is the small, open, single-storey **Vishnu Paduka**. This relatively recent addition shelters a metal plate bearing Vishnu's footprint. Outside, set into the steps above the river, is an image of Naryan reclining on a bed of cobras, just like the images at Budhanilkantha and Balaju. To the north, behind the pavilion, is a remarkable shrine that has been almost entirely taken over by

a tree that must have started as a seed on its roof. There's a spiritual message in there somewhere, we're sure...

Those who have recently lost a father often visit the temple, particularly during Gokarna Aunsi, the Nepali equivalent of Father's Day, which falls in September.

Getting There & Away
You can walk, cycle, take a minibus (easiest from Bodhnath) or hire a taxi to Gokarna. For the latter, expect to pay a Rs 500 return fare from Kathmandu or Rs 150 one way from Bodhnath.

For a great day out on a mountain bike you can combine a visit to the temple with a trip to Sankhu (p214); it's more enjoyable if you avoid the heavy traffic and set off from Jorpati.

GOKARNA FOREST
At Gokarna, 4km east of Bodhnath, the 18-hole **Gokarna Forest Golf Resort** (☎ 4451212; www .gokarna.com) is one of the finest in South Asia. The Gleneagles-designed course has a beautiful setting in a 470-acre former royal hunting

GOKARNA–KOPAN–BODHNATH WALK

There's a pleasant walking or biking route between Gokarna and Bodhnath via the monastery at Kopan. The obvious trail starts from just opposite the Gokarna Mahadev temple, to the right of a roadside statue, and quickly branches left at the Sahayogi Higher Secondary School. After five minutes, branch right onto a dirt road as it follows the side of a pine-clad hill. You can see the yellow walls of Kopan Monastery ahead atop a hill and the Bodhnath stupa down below in the valley.

After another five to 10 minutes, branch left when you meet a junction with a paved road. The track soon becomes a footpath (OK for mountain bikes). After another five minutes, branch left, passing below a new monastery and follow the hillside to a saddle on the ridge. A couple of minutes later take a path heading uphill to the right – this takes you up the side of another monastery to the entrance of Kopan (45 minutes).

From Kopan, just follow the main road south for 40 minutes to Bodhnath, or jump on one of the frequent minibuses. Before you hit the built-up area of Bodhnath you want to branch left into the village, otherwise you'll end up west of Bodhnath, close to the Hyatt Regency Hotel.

reserve – one of the valley's few remaining forested areas. An 18 hole round costs about US$40/50 for weekdays/weekend, plus club hire (US$10), shoes (US$5) and a caddy (US$3).

The resort's **Harmony Spa** (🕑 7am-8pm) at Le Meridian (see sleeping) offers a range of top-end massages, Ayurvedic treatments and wraps from staff trained in Thailand (try an hour's tamarind and oatmeal polish for US$25). US$20 gets you a day pass for the gym, pool, sauna and Jacuzzi; on Saturdays you get a barbeque lunch thrown in for free. Half-day spa packages start at Rs 3000.

In front of the Harmony Spa entrance is a 200-year old pipal tree, where the Buddha (played by Keanu Reeves, of all people) in Bertolucci's film *Little Buddha* was tempted by the demon Mara and called the earth to witness his victory. Not a lot of people know that…

Le Meridian also arranges forest walks (Rs 250 for a guide) within the reserve to the Bandevi (Forest Goddess) Temple and elephant steps, or to the Gokarna Mahadev Temple (one hour; see p212).

Sleeping

Le Meridien (☎ 4451212; www.gokarna.com/html/the _hotel.html, www.lemeridien.com; s/d US$160/180, discounts of 50-60%) Top-of-the-line resort accommodation is provided in this superbly peaceful modern-day palace. Wicker furniture and dark woods add a colonial feel inside, as do the forests of deer and monkeys outside. The old block rooms are housed in a former Rana hunting lodge. It's perfect if

you need some pampering after a trek or a spell in Kathmandu. The clubhouse restaurant is surprisingly good value.

Transport

You need your own transport to get to the resort, or take a taxi from Kathmandu for around Rs 300 one way. Alternatively, take the bus to Sankhu, get off at the hotel gates and then walk 1km (but try not to let anyone see you…).

SANKHU

Sankhu was once an important post on the trading route between Kathmandu and Lhasa (Tibet), and although the town's flower has faded, you can still see many signs of its former prosperity. Although many traditional aspects of Newari life continue here, the most persuasive reason to visit is the beautiful Vajrayogini Temple complex, an easy 45-minute (2km) walk or bicycle ride northeast of town.

As well as visiting the temple, it's worth devoting an hour or so to meandering around Sankhu village. At Dhalna Tole make a left (east) to Salkha Tole, then a diversion north to the Salkha Mahadev Temple, then south back to the bus station.

Vajrayogini Temple

Perched high above the valley, in a grove of huge, ancient trees, this complex of temples is well worth a visit. The main temple was built in 1655 by Pratap Malla of Kathmandu, but it seems likely the site has been used for much longer than that. It's a sublimely peaceful site, the silence broken only by the chatter of wild monkeys drinking from the many water spouts.

At Sankhu, turn left at the bus stop and walk north through the village, past some lovely old Newari architecture (a map at the bus stop highlights the nicest buildings). The road jogs right and left at Dhalna Tole and continues north out of the village, under an ugly concrete archway. There are some fine stone carvings of Vishnu and Ganesh after the arch. The road then forks. The left fork is the traditional approach for pedestrians and descends down to the small river; the right fork is drivable (though rough) to the base of the hill. Park at the teashop.

The climb up the stone steps to the temples is steep and hot. About halfway up there is a shelter and some carvings of a withered-looking Kali and orange Ganesh. A natural stone here represents Bhairab, and sacrifices are made at its foot.

There are two temples in the main courtyard and the one nearest to the entrance is the **Vajrayogini Temple**, a pagoda with a three-tiered roof of sheet copper. There is some beautiful repoussé work on the southern façade, though the actual image of the goddess can only be seen when the priest opens the door for puja (religious ritual).

The two-tiered temple furthest from the entrance enshrines a *chaitya* and commemorates Ugra Tara, a Hindu-ised version of Vajrayogini. The woodcarving around the doors is particularly fine. The rock between the two temples represents the *naga* god, as indicated by the encircling stone snake. In the far left corner of the courtyard as you enter are some caves once used for Tantric practices. Behind the temples and up some stairs are buildings that were once used as pilgrim resthouses and priests' houses.

Getting There & Away

Buses and minibuses to Sankhu leave from Kathmandu's City (Ratna Park) bus station (Rs 15 to Rs 20, one hour) and pass a major checkpoint. The last bus back to Kathmandu leaves Sankhu around 6pm.

It's easy to reach Sankhu by bicycle from Kathmandu (20km). The road is sealed and flat (with a few minor exceptions), and it's an attractive and interesting ride, once you get past Jorpati. Figure on a 1½-hour ride (11.5km) from Bodhnath.

For a loop trip it's possible (in the dry season at least) to cross the Manohara River near Bramhakhel and climb to the fascinating Changu Narayan Temple (see the boxed text, p211). For a longer loop you could cycle or bus to Nagarkot and then cycle or walk down from there (see p224 for details).

SOUTHERN VALLEY

The destinations in this section lie on four radial routes that branch off the southern Kathmandu Ring Rd like spokes from a wheel, making it hard to combine more than a couple of sites in one out-and-back trip. A couple of useful connector routes link some of these radial routes to make a useful loop itinerary.

The Chapagaon and Godavari routes can be combined on a bike, motorbike or foot trip. Kirtipur, Chobar and Bungamati can be combined on another bike or motorbike trip by crossing the Bagmati River at Chobar Gorge. Kirtipur, Chobar, Pharping and Dakshinkali can also be visited in one trip.

Most of these destinations make for excellent day trips on a mountain bike. Many involve steep uphill stretches as you approach the valley walls – which is all the better for the return trip. Of these, the best mountain-bike runs are probably the roads to Bungamati and to the Lele Valley via Chapagaon.

KIRTIPUR

Strung out along a ridge 5km southwest of Kathmandu, the small town of Kirtipur retains an unhurried, timeless air despite its proximity to the capital. Its impressive but little-visited temples point to a golden age that has long passed.

During the 1768/9 conquest of the valley by Prithvi Narayan Shah it was clear that Kirtipur, with its superbly defensible hilltop position, would be the key to defeating the Malla kingdoms, so it was here the Gorkha king struck first and hardest. Kirtipur's resistance was strong, but eventually, after a bitter siege, the town was taken and the inhabitants paid a terrible price for their courageous resistance. The king, incensed by the long struggle his forces had endured, ordered that the nose and lips be cut off every male inhabitant in the town.

AROUND THE KATHMANDU VALLEY

Fortunately for a small minority, he was practical as well as cruel, and those who could play wind instruments were spared.

At one time there were 12 gates into the city; traces of the old city wall can still be seen. As you wander through Kirtipur, you can see dyed yarn hanging from upstairs windows and hear the background clatter of the town's handlooms. Many of the town's 9000 inhabitants are weavers or farmers; the lower-caste people generally live outside the old city wall, lower down the hill. Kirtipur's hilltop position offers fine views over Kathmandu, with the Himalaya rising behind.

The campus of Nepal's Tribhuvan University stands at the base of Kirtipur's hill and has the best library facilities to be found in Nepal.

Sights

Kirtipur stretches across two hills, with a lower saddle between them. The **Chilanchu Vihara** (built 1515) tops the southeastern hill and consists of a central stupa surrounded by four smaller stupas, numerous statues and some dilapidated Buddhist monastery buildings. The entrance to the courtyard is marked by a tree that has completely encased a small shrine.

From the rear of the stupa go right, down to the 16th-century stone *shikhara*-style **Lohan Dehar**. Continue beyond the temple, then take a left to the 12th-century **Bagh Bhairab Temple**, at the bottom of the saddle where the town's two hills meet. The upper wall of this famous triple-roofed temple is decorated with the swords, machetes and shields of the Newari troops defeated by King Prithvi Narayan Shah. The temple sides are decorated with buffalo horns. The temple's principal image is of a terrible Bhairab in his tiger form and is sacred to both Hindus and Buddhists. Look for the temple's *torana* to the left of the entrance door with a green image of Vishnu astride the Garuda and, below him, blue Bhairab between Ganesh and Kumar. To the far right of the courtyard is a fertility shrine under a tin umbrella. Animal sacrifices are

---

KIRTIPUR TO CHOBAR WALK

Instead of simply returning from Kirtipur to Kathmandu the same way, you can continue by foot or bike from Kirtipur to Chobar and the Chobar Gorge. The route is rideable, but is also an interesting walk.

From the Chilanchu Vihara at the southeastern end of Kirtipur, head south downhill past a brick base (built as the foundations of a stupa) to the main road around the base of the village. Take a left and then a right after 100m and then, after another 100m, take the dirt road that branches off to the left.

Head southeast to the hilltop village of **Panga**, which has a number of temples. You'll probably arrive in the northwest corner of the town so head south through the village to a three-storey temple and pool complex and then swing back to the northeast corner of the village where you'll find the road to Chobar, up on the hill.

There are two parallel roads to Chobar village; both join at the **Vishnu Devi Mandir**, marked by a large trident. The temple has a tiny Garuda on a pillar and a small image of a reclining Vishnu surrounded by *naga* serpents. If you get lost at any point just ask for the road to Vishnu Devi Mandir.

Continue past the temple for around 60m, join a cart path to the right (south) and after a couple of minutes branch left up a cobbled path by a red brick house and then left again up a steep footpath past clumps of bamboo. At the next junction take a right up another path up to the first square of the interesting small village of Chobar, right on the top of the hill. Curve to the left around the southern end of the town and you'll arrive at the **Adinath Lokeshwar Temple** (see opposite/). If in doubt, just ask directions.

After you've visited the temple head out the east entrance to the Chobar Le Village Resort and then follow the path down past the monastery, east and then southeast, past a small quarry to the main Pharping road. A path shortcuts down from the other side of the road to the Jal Binayak Temple and the bridge across the Chobar Gorge. It's possible to catch a bus from here back to Kathmandu or south to Pharping.

made early on Tuesday and Saturday mornings. The square and pond in front of the temple once formed part of a royal residence and as a consequence feature some fine woodcarvings.

From the temple exit, take a right, heading west through the village to a Ganesh shrine and then a stone stairway that leads to the triple-roofed **Uma Maheshwar Temple**. The temple is flanked by two stone elephants that wear spiked saddles to keep children from riding them! Unusually, the main image of Shiva and Parvati is a standing one, not in the standard Uma Maheshwar pose. To the left of the central image of the god and his consort is a smaller image in the standard pose. The temple was originally built in 1673 (some sources say 1655) with four roofs until it was badly damaged by the earthquake of 1934. Kirtipur's residents made their last stand here during the 1768 siege. The bell to the right was cast in 1895 by 'Gillett & Johnston Founders, Croydon'.

Getting There & Away
BUS, MINIBUS & TAXI
Numerous buses (No 21) depart from Kathmandu's City (Ratna Park) bus station (Rs 7, 30 minutes) for Kirtipur. Alternatively, it's a short trip by taxi (around Rs 250).

From the east entrance to town you'll notice a modern Thai-designed Buddhist temple to the left of Kirtipur's Naya Bajaar (New Bazaar) at the foot of the Kirtipur hill. From the beginning of Naya Bazaar, climb the stairway straight ahead and at the top take a right and then a left to get to the Chilanchu Vihara.

It takes around one hour to Kirtipur by mountain bike from Kathmandu; the turn-off to the right is 1.3km south of the Kathmandu Ring Rd.

CHOBAR
The picturesque little village of Chobar, 6km from Kathmandu, tops a hill overlooking the Bagmati River where it flows through the Chobar Gorge.

Sights
The town's main attraction is the **Adinath Lokeshwar Temple**, originally built in the 15th century and reconstructed in 1640. The temple is dedicated to red-faced Rato

---

LEGEND OF THE CHOBAR GORGE
Geologists and theologians rarely find much common ground but in Kathmandu they both agree that eons ago the Kathmandu Valley was a lake and the hill of Swayambhunath was an island. Gradually the lake dried up to leave the fertile valley floor we see today.

Local legends relate that the change from lake to valley was a much more dramatic one, for the Buddhist deity Manjushri is said to have taken his mighty sword and with one blow cut open the valley edge to release the pent-up waters. The place where his sword struck rock was Chobar on the southern edge of the valley and the result was the Chobar Gorge.

Countless *nagas*, or snake spirits, were washed out of the valley with the departing waters, but many, including Kartotak, 'king of the snakes', made it to the nearby Taudaha pond, next to the road to Pharping. The pond is a popular breeding area for migratory birds.

Machhendranath and is sacred to both Hindus and Buddhists. Six figures of the Buddha are lined up beneath the temple's golden *torana*, but the most interesting feature is the astounding array of metal pots, pans and water containers that are fixed to boards hanging all around the temple roofs next to photos of the recently deceased. These kitchen utensils are donated to the temple by newlyweds in order to ensure a happy married life.

The small Chobar Gorge is 1km southeast of Chobar village, where the Bagmati River cuts through the edge of the Chobar hill. Down by the river, just south of the gorge and the now defunct cement factory, is the important **Jal Binayak Temple** (1602), one of the valley's most important Ganesh shrines. The temple's Ganesh image is simply a huge rock in a brass case. The temple's roof struts depict eight Bhairabs and the eight Ashta Matrikas (Mother Goddesses) with whom Ganesh often appears.

A neat little suspension bridge spans the river just by the gorge; a plaque states the bridge was made in Aberdeen in 1903. There are fine views of the gorge on one side and the Jal Binayak Temple on the other.

Sleeping & Eating

Chobar Le Village Resort (☎ 4333555; www.nepalvil lageresort.com; r US$30-50; mains Rs 75-140) This gorgeous 200-year old house nestled between the Adinath Temple and a Tibetan gompa has been converted into a tiny two-room guesthouse, garden restaurant and sculpture garden. It's a pleasant place to stop for lunch (the *shish taouk,* or chicken kebabs, are great) but the admittedly charming rooms are overpriced. The resort can help arrange meditation classes at the next-door monastery.

Getting There & Away

Buses to Pharping and Dakshinkali pass by the turn-off to Chobar, from where it's a short but steep walk uphill, and also Chobar Gorge, a couple of kilometres later. The nicest way to get to both sites is on foot from Kirtipur – see the boxed text, p216.

From the Chobar Gorge you can cross the suspension bridge and follow a trail on the left uphill to a small village junction. A left here will take you the Kathmandu Ring Rd, entering Patan at Jawlakhel. A right turn will take you on a convoluted bike path that eventually links up with the Bungamati road.

PHARPING

Pharping is a thriving, traditional Newari town, 19km south of Kathmandu and surprisingly untouched by the swarms of tourists that visit Dakshinkali. The town is famous for its pilgrimage sites, the Hindu origins of which have been largely absorbed by the now predominant Tibetan Buddhist monasteries. The town is popular with both Tibetan and Hindu pilgrims.

The Pilgrimage Route

The best way to visit the sights of Pharping is to join the other pilgrims on a clockwise pilgrim circuit (a *parikrama* in Nepali, or *kora* in Tibetan).

As you enter the town from the main road, take the first right by the football pitch and head uphill, past the large Tibetan-style Dzongsar *chörten* (pop inside to turn its prayer wheels), a couple of restaurants, and the Sakyapa school **Tharig Gompa** with its huge *chörten.* Beyond here, at the bend in the road, is a Tibetan monastery signposted 'Pharping Ganesh and Saraswati Temple'. The chapel to the left is actually a Tibetan-style **Drölma Lhakhang** (Drölma is the Tibetan name for Tara, who is identified here with Saraswati), with images of Ganesh and the 21 manifestations of Tara.

To the right of this chapel is the **Rigzu Phodrang Gompa,** which is identified with the Indian sage Padmasambhava (known to Tibetans as Guru Rinpoche), who is credited with introducing Buddhism to Tibet. He is clearly recognisable by his curly moustache and *katvanga* (staff of skulls).

Ascend the flight of stairs between the two temples, past prayer flags and a rock fissure, where cracks are stuffed with little bags of wishes and human hair. Eventually you'll come to the **Guru Rinpoche Cave** (also known as the Gorakhnath Cave), surrounded by monastery buildings. With its butter lamps and soot-blackened walls it feels like an ancient Tibetan shrine, were it not for the Liza Minnelli–style row of coloured light bulbs. Take off your shoes to enter.

Continue out of the cave enclosure, down a flight of stairs lined with prayer flags to the 17th-century Newari-style **Vajra Yogini Temple**. The Tantric Buddhist goddess Vajrayogini (known to Hindus as Ugra Tara) is featured in the temple's *toranas*. Check out the lovely Rana-style courtyard to the side.

From here, pilgrims continue east up a pathway to the Nyingmapa school **Do Ngak Chöling Gompa**, where the main chapel features a central statue of Sakyamuni flanked by Padmasambhava and Vajrasattva. It's often locked so try to slide in with a band of pilgrims. From the monastery head down to the junction and branch downhill to the main road and the Tashi Delek Happy Restaurant for a post-pilgrimage cup of tea.

Sleeping & Eating

Dakchhinkali Village Inn (☎ 4710053; dik_vinn@ wlink.com.np; s/d US$12/18) On a bluff right by the main gate which marks the start of the descent to Dakshinkali, this spot is quiet and relaxing (except on Saturdays when it's busy with pilgrim traffic), with 10 rustic but cosy rooms. There's also a very pleasant garden restaurant (mains Rs 150-250).

Family Guest House (☎ 4710412; r Rs 500-800) A new, modern place in Pharping town, with clean but somewhat overpriced rooms and a good rooftop restaurant.

The nearby **Snowland Restaurant** is a good little Tibetan restaurant, but all food is made to order so it doesn't pay to be in a hurry. **Tashi Delek Happy Restaurant** is another good place for a cheap Chinese lunch, or try the nearby **Bajrayoginee Restaurant**.

Hattiban Resort (☎ 4710122, city office 4371397; www.intrekasia.com; s/d US$52/62; mains Rs 300) is perched on a ridge high above the Kathmandu Valley. With stunning views, this small resort has 24 good-quality rooms, most with a balcony. The terrace is a superb place to soak up the views. From the resort it's an excellent two-hour hike up to the peak of Champa Devi (2249m), 200 vertical metres above the resort. A very rough, steep and winding 2km track branches off the main road, 2.5km before Pharping. A taxi from Kathmandu costs around Rs 1000, though the price may go up when the driver sees the state of the road.

Getting There & Away
Buses leave throughout the day for Pharping from Kathmandu's City (Ratna Park) bus station (Rs 20, two hours), or catch the less frequent No 22 bus from Kathmandu's Shahid Gate. The last bus back to Kathmandu leaves around 5.30pm.

AROUND PHARPING
Dakshinkali
At the southern edge of the valley, in a dark, somewhat spooky location in the cleft between two hills and at the confluence of two rivers, stands the blood-soaked temple of **Dakshinkali**. The temple is dedicated to the goddess Kali, Shiva's consort in her most bloodthirsty incarnation, and twice a week faithful Nepalis journey here to satisfy her bloodlust.

Sacrifices are always made to goddesses, and the creatures to be sacrificed must be uncastrated male animals. Saturday is the major sacrificial day of the week, when a steady parade of chickens, ducks, goats, sheep, pigs and even the occasional buffalo come here to have their throats cut or their heads lopped off by professional local butchers. Tuesday is also a sacrificial day, but the blood does not flow quite as freely. During the annual celebrations of Dasain in October the temple is literally awash with blood and the image of Kali is bathed in it.

After their rapid dispatch the animals are butchered in the stream beside the temple and their carcasses are either brought home

for a feast or boiled up on the spot for a picnic in the grounds. You'll see families arriving with pots, bags of vegetables and armfuls of firewood for the big day out.

Non-Hindus are not allowed into the actual compound where Kali's image resides (there is often an incredibly long queue for Hindus to get in), but it is OK to take photos from outside. Many tourists behave poorly here, perching vulturelike from every available vantage point in order to get the goriest possible photos. However extraordinary the sights might seem, this is a religious ceremony, and the participants should be treated with respect, not turned into a sideshow.

The path down to the temple is lined with tea stalls, sadhus, souvenir sellers and hawkers selling offerings of marigolds, fruit and coconuts, as well as *khuar,* a sweet treat somewhere between cottage cheese and fudge (Rs 20 per 100g). The snack stalls at the bus park serve up reviving tea and pappadums for Rs 5 each.

Despite the carnival spirit, witnessing the sacrifices is a strange and, for some, confronting experience. The slaughter is surprisingly matter-of-fact (and you won't get to see much of it), but it creates a powerful atmosphere.

A pathway leads off from behind the main temple uphill to the Mata Temple, which offers good views.

GETTING THERE & AWAY
Bus
Buses operate from Kathmandu's Shahid Gate (Martyrs' Memorial) and City (Ratna Park) bus station (Rs 20) daily. There are extra buses on Tuesday and Saturday – the most important days for sacrifice – but they are still very crowded. From Pharping it's an easy 1km downhill walk or ride.

Cycling
It is an enjoyable but exhausting two-hour (20km) bicycle ride from Kathmandu. The views are exhilarating, but it is basically uphill all the way – so mountain bikes are the way to go. Tuesday is probably the better day to pick as the traffic fumes are not too thick. Make sure you get an early start, as the shrine is busiest early in the morning. There's a small charge to park your bike in the car park. Be warned – the climb from Dakshinkali back up to Pharping is a killer.

Walking

If you are travelling by public transport and have walked or got a lift to Dakshinkali, consider the short-cut hiking route back up to Pharping. A path on the southern side of the sacrificial compound brings you to an open picnic area. From the cooking area at the back of this area there's a steep scramble up a goat track that follows a ridge on the northwestern side of the gorge. At the top you come out on a plateau – you'll immediately see the white monastery surrounded by prayer flags on a nearby hill. Make your way through the paddy fields, on the narrow paths between the rice. It takes about 40 minutes to get to Pharping.

Sekh Narayan Temple

The Sekh (or Shesh) Narayan Temple is the centrepiece of an interesting collection of temples, crystal-clear pools and sculpture. The main temple is above the pools, under a multi-hued, overhanging cliff and next to a Tibetan monastery.

The main temple, one of the most important Vishnu temples in the valley, was built in the 17th century, but it is believed that the cave to the right (now dedicated to Padmasambhava, or Guru Rinpoche) has been a place of pilgrimage for much longer. To the right of the temple is a bas-relief of Vishnu Vikrantha, also known as the dwarf Vamana, which probably dates from the Licchavi period (5th or 6th centuries).

Half-submerged in the lowest, semi-circular pond is a 12th- or 13th-century sculpture of Aditya, the sun god, framed by a stone arch and with a lotus flower at each shoulder. If you are lucky you might catch devotional religious music being played in the pavilion by the pools.

Sekh Narayan is less than 1km from Pharping and is easily reached by foot. You can hail a returning bus from here on to Kathmandu.

BUNGAMATI

Bungamati is a classic Newari village dating from the 16th century. It is perched on a spur of land overlooking the Bagmati River, 10km from Kathmandu, and is shaded by large trees and stands of bamboo. Fortunately, the village streets are too small and hazardous for cars. There are quite a few woodcarving shops in the village and a cou-

ple of carpet looms but visitors have yet to arrive en masse, so tread gently.

Sights

Bungamati is the birthplace of Rato Machhendranath, the patron god of the valley, who resides in the large *shikhara*-style **Rato Machhendranath Temple** in the centre of the village square for six months of the year (he spends the rest of his time in Patan). The process of moving him around Patan and backwards and forwards to Bungamati is central to one of the most important annual festivals in the valley – see the boxed text, p191 for details.

To get to the temple from the bus stop at the edge of the town, follow the signs for the **Newari Cultural Museum**, worth a quick visit for its displays of local traditional lifestyle, and take a right at the Ganesh shrine. There's a useful map of the village near the bus stand.

The *chowk* around the temple is one of the most beautiful in the valley – here one can see the still-beating heart of a functioning Newari town. There are many *chaityas* and a huge prayer wheel, clearly pointing to the capacity of Newari religion to weld together elements from different religious traditions.

Head out of the square's northern gate and follow the cobblestone road as it curves to the right, past the Padmapur Mahadev Temple and a Ganesh shrine to the big water tank of the **Dey Pukha** (Central Pond). Continue to the village gates; from here it's right back to the bus stand, or left to the Karya Binayak Temple.

Between Bungamati and Khokna, the **Karya Binayak Temple** is dedicated to Ganesh. It's not particularly interesting and Ganesh is simply represented by a stone, but the view is impressive and the locals often stage a Saturday *bhoj* (feast) and *bhajan* (devotional music) – the Newari version of a barbeque and karaoke. When the path from Bungamati meets a larger track, take a left for the temple.

If you take a right at this crossroads, you'll join a tarmac road and after five minutes you'll arrive at the village of **Khokna**. The town is not as appealing as Bungamati, as it was seriously damaged in the 1934 earthquake, but it has retained many traditional aspects of Newari life, and is famous for its mustard-oil presses. There is no central square, unlike in Bungamati, but there's plenty of action in the main street, including women spinning wool. The impressive main temple is a two-tiered construction dedicated to Shekala Mai, a mother goddess. From the central temple, return back along the tarmac road, turning left at the large pool to rejoin the main Patan–Bungamati road.

Getting There & Away

Buses to Bungamati leave frequently from Patan's Lagankhel station (Rs 8, 30 minutes).

The road to Bungamati provides yet another ideal mountain-biking expedition (16km return from Patan). From Patan, continue over Kathmandu's Ring Rd from the main road through Jawlakhel. After you cross the Nakhu Khola, veer left; the right fork takes you to the Chobar Gorge – see p217. It's a pleasant ride along a gradually climbing ridge to get to Bungamati.

Approximately 6km from the Ring Rd are two restaurants and a viewpoint overlooking Bungamati with its white temple (to the left), the Karya Binayak temple (centre) and Khokna (to the right).

To get to Khokna directly from the main Kathmandu road take the road signposted to the 'Gyanadaya Residential School', 1.5km before the viewpoint.

CHAPAGAON

Chapagaon is a prosperous village with a number of shops, temples and shrines. Near the entrance to the village is a small Ganesh shrine. There are temples dedicated to Narayan and Krishna, the latter with some erotic roof struts, and there's a Bhairab shrine at the top end of the village.

Sights

The forested complex of the **Vajra Varahi Temple** (parking Rs 5), an important Tantric site, lies about 500m east of the main road. As you enter Chapagaon take the road on your left after the Narayan and Krishna temples. Note the disused irrigation system, with stone channels and bridges, behind the village.

The temple was built in 1665 and is popular with wedding parties, pilgrims and picnickers who descend en masse on Saturdays. The two-roofed temple is unusual as it lacks a central pinnacle. Visitors pour milk and offerings over the statue of a bull in front

of the temple, whose main image is often submerged in offerings of flowers, milk, coconuts, radishes, boiled eggs, coloured powder and animal blood. It's an interesting and atmospheric place that has probably been a centre for worship for millennia.

Getting There & Away

Local minibuses leave from Lagankhel in Patan to Chapagaon (Rs 15, one hour). By mountain bike, Chapagaon is 13km and about an hour (yes, that's the same as the bus!) from Kathmandu's Ring Rd.

A useful connector road east of the Vajra Varahi Temple links up to the Godavari road just south of Bandegaon and allows you to combine the Chapagaon and Godavari roads into one route. The dirt road makes for a nice bike trip or you can walk it in an hour and then catch a minibus up to Godavari.

AROUND CHAPAGAON
Lele Valley

The peaceful, beautiful Lele Valley seems a million miles from the bustle of Kathmandu and is in many ways untouched by the 21st (or 20th) century. You won't find many other tourists here.

Apart from touring the lovely scenery, the main thing to head for is the **Tika Bhairab**, a large multicoloured painting at the confluence of two rivers, about 4km south of Chapagaon.

Malla Alpine Resort (☎ 01-4410320; s/d US$61/72, discount 30%), signposted at Kalitar, 3km beyond the Tika Bhairab up a dirt road, is a forgotten place that offers eight bungalows in a wonderfully secluded location, but it's in need of a bit of upkeep these days. Make enquiries and reservations at the Malla Hotel in Kathmandu (p143). You really need your own transport to get here.

GETTING THERE & AWAY

There are a couple of route options to consider if you are making a bike trip to the valley. The main road south of Chapagaon splits and offers two ways of getting to the Lele Valley, or more importantly a loop option for a return trip of around 12km. The only downer is that the main (western) branch sees lots of truck traffic heading to a quarry behind the Tika Bhairab.

A more adventurous mountain-bike option would be to continue from the Tika

Bhairab to the far end of Lele village (4km) and then climb northeast along a dirt track to a forested pass above the lovely upper Lele Valley, then descend the slippery single track to Badhikhel (8km from Lele). Continue north from here and you'll quickly meet the Chapagaon–Godavari track (see p221); a left turn will take you back to Chapagaon for a total 16km loop. A right will take you on to Godavari.

GODAVARI

Godavari is not an especially interesting village but there are a number of places to visit in the area, such as the Godavari Kunda, Phulchowki Mai Temple and enjoyable walks to the giant Shanti Ban Buddha or shrine of Bishankhu Narayan (opposite). It's not a must-see sight but it does make for a nice day trip from the capital on a motorbike or mountain bike.

The 10km sealed road from the Kathmandu Ring Rd south of Patan passes through the village of Godavari to an open space at the foot of the hills. Here a partially sealed road continues south to Phulchowki Mai Temple and on to Phulchowki Mountain; the main road veers left (northeast) 1km past an ashram to the gardens and Godavari Kunda.

The road from Kathmandu passes several large plant nurseries, highlighting the region's botanical importance and commercial viability.

Sights

The verdant **Royal Botanic Gardens** (☎ 5560546; admission foreigner/SAARC/Nepali Rs 100/25/10, children under 10 50% discount; ☷ 10am-5pm, until 4pm mid-Nov to mid-Feb) is a quiet and peaceful spot for a walk or picnic (except on Friday and Saturday when the place is overrun with schoolkids and local couples). The visual highlight is the Coronation Pond with its 7m commemorative pillar. The visitor centre has some good exhibits on Nepal's flora.

A road continues past the turn-off to the botanical gardens and after 100m or so you come to the **Godavari Kunda** – a sacred spring – on your right. The hill behind the spring is covered in colourful prayer flags and there's a Tibetan monastery nearby. Every 12 years (next in late 2015) thousands of pilgrims come here to bathe and gain merit. Clear mountain water collects in a pool in

a closed inner courtyard, flows through carved stone spouts into a larger pool and then drains down to a photogenic line of five stupas that offer a perfect picnic spot.

If you return towards the main crossroads and take the partially sealed road to the south, the **Phulchowki Mai Temple** is 600m up the hill, near an ugly marble quarry. The a three-tiered pagoda is dedicated to a Tantric mother goddess and is flanked by a temple to Ganesh. The two large pools before the temple compound are fed by nine spouts (known as the Naudhara Kunda) that represent the nine streams that flow off Phulchowki.

You can see the **Shanti Ban Buddha**, a huge golden statue of the Buddha, on the hillside behind Godavari as you approach the village. To get a closer look (be warned – it looks better from a distance) and for fine views over the valley, take the signposted road to the right at the end of the village. From the turn-off it's a 15-minute walk past some lovely traditionally thatched houses.

Sleeping & Eating

Godavari Village Resort (☎ 5560675; www.godavari resort.com.np; s/d US$150/165, discounts of 80%; ☲) This comfortable resort consists of a number of attractive Mediterranean-style villas and Newari-style buildings spread over a hillside, with idyllic views over rice paddies and the Himalaya. It's perfect as a quiet base for local hiking or biking (staff recommend the nearby Santanisur Temple), and there's a pool (Rs 250 for nonguests), sauna, clay tennis courts and even bowling (all at extra cost), plus five shuttle buses a day to Kathmandu's New Rd. Bike hire is available (Rs 600 per day) and the weekend barbecues (Rs 599) are popular with out-of-towners. Request a balcony or mountain-view room when booking. The resort is signposted off the road, 3km before Godavari.

Hotel View Bhrikuti (☎ 5560542; www.hotelview bhrikuti.com.np; US$60/70, discounts of 40%) A brand spanking new option, all modern and marbly, with a chintzy bar and bright and clean rooms, some with balcony. It's comfortable but a bit soulless, 1.5km south of the centre.

There are some cheap restaurants in front of the Godavari Kunda that are popular with local students and make for an excellent lunch break.

Getting There & Away

Local minibuses (No 5) and buses (No 14) run between Lagankhel in Patan and Godavari (Rs 12, one hour). It would be quite feasible to get here on a mountain bike and return to Kathmandu via Chapagaon.

AROUND GODAVARI
Bishankhu Narayan

If you're looking for an excuse to get off the beaten track, the **shrine of Bishankhu Narayan** may do nicely. There's not much to see, despite the fact that it is one of the most important Vishnu shrines in the Kathmandu Valley, though the site has a timeless, almost animistic feel. A steep stairway leads up to the chain mail–covered shrine and then down into a narrow fissure in the rock, where pilgrims test their sin levels (and need for an immediate crash diet) by trying to squeeze through the tiny gap.

There are two main ways to get to the shrine. By vehicle, the unsealed 2.5km road to Bishankhu Narayan takes off to the east from the village of Bandegaon, then veers southeast and crosses a small stream. After 1km you come to Godamchowr village. The road forks left at the village football ground; from here it's a steep uphill climb (if in doubt keep taking the steepest path) for around 1.5km to reach the shrine.

The best way to the shrine on foot is from Godavari village. You'll have to ask the way, as there are several trails that wind around the contoured terraces of the valley to the shrine.

On the way back, the Bishanku Naryan Village Restaurant offers snacks and drinks, 700m from the shrine.

Phulchowki Mountain

This 2760m-high mountain is the highest point around the valley and there are magnificent views from the summit. It's also home to over 570 species of flowering plants and one third of all the bird species in Nepal, as well as one of the last surviving 'cloud forests' in central Nepal. Government officials have been saying that it is to be declared a conservation area for years now. The mountain is famous for its springtime (March and April) flowers, in particular its magnificent red and white rhododendrons.

The unsealed road is very rough in places and you really need a 4WD or a trail motorbike (take care on the slippery gravel sections). You may need to register with the local army base if someone stops you.

You would need to be very keen to undertake the climb on a mountain bike, though it could certainly be done. On foot it would be a strenuous full day hike; start early in the morning, bring plenty of water and follow the footpaths from Phulchowki Mai Temple, not the main road which snakes around the mountain. Locals warn of robberies in the area so do not hike this remote route alone.

THE VALLEY FRINGE

Beyond Bhaktapur the Kathmandu Valley walls start to rise, revealing views beyond the valley bowl. Dhulikhel and the destinations around it actually lie beyond the valley, but are easily visited from Kathmandu and from other destinations in the valley. You could combine them all for an excellent four-day itinerary on mountain bike, motorbike or on foot. See p83 for ideas on a bike ride through the eastern valley.

NAGARKOT

☎ 01 / **elevation 2175m**

There are various places around the edge of the Kathmandu Valley that offer great mountain views, but the resort village of Nagarkot, 32km from Kathmandu, is generally held to be the best. Dedicated mountain watchers make their way up to the village, stay overnight in one of Nagarkot's lodges, then rise at dawn to see the sun appear over the Himalaya.

Between October and March a trip to Nagarkot will nearly always be rewarded with a view, but you will be very lucky to catch more than a glimpse through the monsoon clouds between June and September. During the summer, sweaty valley residents escape the heat for the resort's cool mountain air; in winter they rush up if there's even a chance of being able to throw a tiny snowball. It can get very cold at Nagarkot in autumn and winter, so if you're staying overnight come prepared with warm clothing.

The original army camp at Nagarkot never developed into a traditional village, so while the views can be stunning, the unplanned scatter of lodges is messy. Relations with the local army base were severely strained during a religious festival in December 2005 when a deranged soldier massacred 12 locals during a drunken rampage.

Nagarkot is very much a one-night stand, and few visitors stay longer. The best way to leave Nagarkot is on foot, on downhill hikes west to Sundarijal, Sankhu, or Changu

Narayan, north to Chisopani or south to Banepa.

Orientation & Information

Nagarkot's accommodation is spread out along the dirt track that heads north from the bus stop at the town's only intersection. The main group of guesthouses crowd around a hill topped by a Mahakali shrine, a 15-minute walk from the bus stop.

Tibet Net Cafe (per hr Rs 150), across from the Hotel Dragon Resort, offers expensive Internet access and can burn photos onto a CD.

Sights

The only thing to do is to soak up the outrageous views, from Dhaulagiri in the west to Mt Everest (little more than a dot on the horizon) and Kanchenjunga in the east, via Ganesh Himal (7406m), Langtang Lirung (7246m), Shisha Pangma (8012m), Dorje Lakpa (6975m) and Gauri Shankar (7146m).

An hour's uphill walk (4km) just south from the village will give an even better 360-degree view from a **lookout tower** on a ridge, passing a former Rana palace (now part of the army camp) en route. The main hotel area has a small hilltop Mahakali Temple.

Activities
HIKING

There are a number of hiking routes to and from Nagarkot. If you only want to walk one way it's a good idea to take the bus to Nagarkot and walk back down. The following walks are all written heading downhill from Nagarkot.

Nepa Maps' 1:25,000 *Nagarkot – Short Trekking on the Kathmandu Valley Rim* is useful, though its 1:50,000 *Around the Kathmandu Valley* is probably good enough.

To Changu Narayan (1½ hours from Tharkot)

From Nagarkot it is very easy to see the long spur that extends into the Kathmandu Valley. At the very end of the spur the ridgeline gives one final hiccup and then drops down to the valley floor. The beautiful temple of Changu Narayan is on the top of this final bump on the ridgeline.

The walking trail from Nagarkot parallels the road to Bhaktapur along a ridge, branching off at the sharp hairpin bend at

---

NAGARKOT

0 ————— 300 m
0 ————— 0.2 miles

INFORMATION
Tibet Net Café.........................(see 15)

SIGHTS & ACTIVITIES
Mahakali Shrine.........................1 B3

SLEEPING
Club Himalaya Resort................2 B5
Galaxy View Tower.....................3 B4
Hotel at the End of the
  Universe.................................4 B3
Hotel Chautari...........................5 B3
Hotel Country Villa....................6 B3
Hotel Dragon Resort..................7 B3
Hotel Green Valley.....................8 B3
Hotel Snowman.........................9 B4
Hotel Sunshine........................10 B3
Hotel View Point......................11 B3
Nirvana Village Resort.............12 B3
Peaceful Cottage......................13 B3
The Fort Resort........................14 B3
Tibet Home..............................15 B3

EATING
Berg House Café......................16 A4
Sherpa Alpine Cottage.............17 B4
Teahouse Inn...........................18 A4

TRANSPORT
Bus Stop..................................19 A4

To Nagarkot Farmhouse Resort (1.5km); Kattike (2.5km); Bhotichaur (8km); Sankhu (8km)

To Changu Narayan

To Bhaktapur (15km)

Army Camp

Army Checkpost

To Lookout Tower (3km)

Tharkot (marked on some maps as Deural-ibhanjhang). Catching a bus to here from Nagarkot saves you the tedious first half of the walk.

From the bend, take the dirt road heading west and take the left branch (the right drops towards Sankhu). The track climbs uphill through a pine forest for about 20 minutes until it reaches the top of the ridge and then it simply follows the ridgeline, undulating gently down to Changu Narayan. The trail passes several Chhetri villages, with wonderful views over the valley to the Himalaya. See p210 for details of the temple and hikes on from here to Bhaktapur or the road to Bodhnath.

To Sankhu (2½ hours)

From Nagarkot a dirt road leads all the way to Sankhu, offering an easy and interesting way to return to Kathmandu on foot or bike.

From Nagarkot take the northwest road down to the Nagarkot Farmhouse Resort and follow the switchbacks down to the village of **Kattike**, which has a teahouse and shop. Take a left at the junction at the edge of town. You can continue all the way down this track, or for a more interesting walk take a minor road that turns off sharply to the right 15 minutes down this track. Follow this footpath for 20 minutes as it shrinks to a trail and then take a sharp left downhill past several houses to join the main track. From here it's an hour's slog to Sankhu and the town's east gate.

To Banepa (3½ hours)

The town of Banepa is outside the valley and is the major junction town on the way to Dhulikhel on the Arniko Hwy (the road to the Tibetan border). From Nagarkot, head south for an hour to the lookout tower, at the walk's highest point. From here, follow the dirt road west and then south. The dirt road follows the western ridge downhill all the way to Nala.

A more adventurous backcountry hiking route peels off to the left by the telecom tower and descends steeply. When you hit a dirt track head left and keep asking directions to the village of **Ghimiregaon**. Following a precise trail is difficult, but stick to the left side of the valley – all trails lead to **Nala**, 1¾ hours and 600m below the lookout tower. At Nala, visit the four-roofed Newari-style

Bhagwati Temple in the centre of town and then walk or catch a bus for the remaining 3km to Banepa.

From Banepa, you can take a bus back to Kathmandu or on to Dhulikhel or Panauti.

To Sundarijal (1–2 days)

It takes two easy days or one very long one to reach Sundarijal from Nagarkot on a trail that follows the valley rim. From Sundarijal you can take the road to Gokarna, Bodhnath and Kathmandu or you can continue for another day along the rim to Shivapuri and Budhanilkantha. Some trekking agencies operate treks on this valley-rim walk, but it is also possible to find accommodation in village inns. There are many confusing trail junctions, so ask for directions frequently.

The trail follows the same route as to Sankhu as far as Kattike (about one hour) and then turns right (north) to Jorsim Pauwa. Walk further down through Bagdhara, with its village inns, to Chowki Bhanjyang (about one hour). From Chowki Bhanjyang, another hour's walk will take you through Nagle to **Bhotichaur**, a good place to stop overnight in a village inn.

The walk continues by returning towards Chowki Bhanjyang for a short distance and taking the fork by a *chautara* (porters' resting place) uphill, then continues more steeply uphill to cross a ridge line before dropping down on the middle of three trails to Chule (or Jhule). From here the trail enters the Shivapuri National Park (see p183) and contours around the edge of the valley, before dropping down to Mulkarkha (about 10km from Chule). Here the trail drops past small waterfalls and a reservoir and along the water pipeline to Sundarijal. The last part of this trail to Sundarijal is the first part of the popular Helambu trek (p339).

Another variant on this hike is to continue northwest from Bhotichaur to **Chisopani**, where there are several trekking lodges (Chisopani is an overnight stop on the Helambu trek), and then the next day to hike southwest back over the ridge through Shivapuri National Park to Sundarijal.

Sleeping

Nagarkot has a fair selection of guesthouses and hotels, most of them far from pretty. Most are relatively expensive for the facilities you get, but the views are priceless.

AROUND THE KATHMANDU VALLEY

BUDGET

Hotel Snowman (☎ 6680146; r Rs 300-400) This is the first place you come to heading north from the intersection. The fairly uninspiring location leads to decent prices and the rooms vary from damp, dark doubles to nice rooms with good views. Published rates of up to US$40 are pure fiction.

Galaxy View Tower (☎ 6680122; r US$5-15) Just where the road splits, this has a wide range of good-value rooms spread across the hillside. Rooms are more comfortable than stylish but most have at least partial views. The best-value rooms are in the middle bracket. There's a cosy restaurant.

Hotel at the End of the Universe (☎ 6680011; www.endoftheuniverse.com.np; chalets Rs 200-700, cottage Rs 1000, ste Rs 2000-3000) A switched-on budget hotel close to the Mahakali shrine, this is a character-filled place, with a wide range of rooms types from basic bamboo cabins to gingerbread-style cottages and luxury suites; the latter are perfect for small groups or families.

Peaceful Cottage (☎ 6680077; peacefulcottage@ hotmail.com; partitioned r without bathroom US$8-10, s/d with bathroom US$12/16, deluxe US$16/24) Further down the road, the rooms here are comfortable enough, except for the overpriced cheapies which are little more than cells divided by plywood. The real draw is the terrace restaurant and the friendly management. Climb to the top of the octagonal tower for the best views in town.

Hotel Dragon Resort (☎ 6680179; r Rs 800, deluxe Rs 1200, ste Rs 1500, discounts of 50%) Has some rooms below its restaurant. The cheaper ones are clean, bright and good value with discounts, though they don't have views. Deluxe rooms come with a sunny terrace.

Hotel Green Valley (☎ 6680078; r Rs 250-500, deluxe Rs 800-1000) At the end of the dirt road, perched on the edge of a steep slope and a fair old walk from the bus station, the building here is a concrete lump, but the rooms are decent and modern, there's a good-value restaurant and the terrace has a fabulous view. New deluxe rooms are in the Newari-style upper floor.

There are lots of other choices, including the orange-and-yellow **Tibet Home** (☎ 6680015; r Rs 400-500), a cosy modern place across from the Hotel Dragon Resort, and the **Nirvana Village Resort** (☎ 6680126; r Rs 300), a cheaper, ramshackle place at the end of the line.

MIDRANGE & TOP-END

The Fort Resort (☎ 6680149; www.mountain-retreats .com; s/d US$65/80, discounts of 30%) Next to the Hotel View Point, this is a stylish place built in a Newari style on the site of the original *kot* (fort). The secluded and peaceful cottages offer the best value, with private balcony, high ceilings and large bathrooms. There's a good restaurant and the four gardeners ensure the lovely garden terrace is always at its peak. A spa is planned, as are new tower rooms, with excellent corner suites.

Hotel View Point (☎ 6680123; www.hotelviewpoint .com; s/d US$24/35, deluxe US$55/65, discounts of 40%) The highest hotel in Nagarkot, this is something of a blot on the skyline. The rooms are on the small side, but the views are superb and there are lots of lovely terraces to relax on. The pine walls give the rooms the feel of a sauna, which is the closest thing you'll get to heating during the winter.

Hotel Country Villa (☎ 6680128; www.hotelcoun tryvilla.com; s US$10-20, d US$15-25) Down from the Peaceful Cottage, this is another good choice, with a great restaurant, terrace and bar. Rooms vary but most have a private balcony. Half-board rates start around US$30/50.

Nagarkot Farmhouse Resort (☎ 6228087; nfh@mos .com.np; s/d without bathroom US$25/40, with bathroom US$32/50, deluxe US$42/60, discounts of 20%, rates include 3 meals) Well away from the sprawl of Nagarkot, and with the feel of a rural retreat, this highly recommended Newari-inspired complex has just 15 rooms. It's run by Kathmandu's Hotel Vajra (p144) and is a great place to get away from it all or use as a hiking base. The resort is about 1.5km past the Hotel Country Villa down the dirt track to Sankhu.

Club Himalaya Resort (☎ 6680080; www.nepalsho tel.com; s/d US$60/75, discounts of 15%; ⍰) A large construction like this really does nothing for the rural ambience but it is a quality place. Each room is named after a Himalayan peak and has a private balcony with awesome views, and there are more views from the rooftop terrace. Ask for an upper-floor room. The stylish atrium-type foyer has a restaurant, library and indoor plunge pool. It's at the south end of the ridge, near the bus stop. A free hotel shuttle bus leaves the Ambassador Hotel in Kathmandu daily at 3pm, returning the next morning at 11am.

The **Teahouse Inn** annex (☎ 6680045; per person half board US$14) has cheaper and smaller rooms (without views).

Other midrange options include the rambling old **Hotel Chautari** (☎ 6680075; keyman@wlink .com.np; s/d US$45/60, discount 50%), which has the musty air of a British boarding school but offers great mountain views, or the modern **Hotel Sunshine** (☎ 6680105; r US$10-30), where room rates correspond directly with how many window views you get.

Eating

There's limited choice in the food department and most people eat at their lodge.

Teahouse Inn (mains Rs 150-225, set meal Rs 350) A modern place attached to the Club Himalaya Resort, with a nice terrace and aimed at day-trippers. It's above the main intersection (look for the blue roof). The manager recommends the chicken momos.

Hotel Dragon Resort (mains Rs 300-350) The restaurant here has the most interesting menu in town and a modern open kitchen, a legacy of the times when Kilroy's of Kathmandu ran the show. The largely Continental menu ranges from fish and chips to apple crumble but it remains to be seen whether they can actually deliver the goods.

Sherpa Cottage (mains Rs 150-235) A Sherpa couple from Lukla run this relaxing little spot and the menu is trekking-inspired, with dishes like Swiss rosti (a potato dish) and Tibetan *phing* noodles dishes, plus good breakfasts.

Berg House Café (breakfasts Rs 50-90) Right by the bus stop, this is a cosy little place serving Western food and is handy if you are waiting for a bus. Any place that has 'hot chocolate cake' listed on the breakfast menu is good with us.

Getting There & Away

Direct buses from Kathmandu are elusive beasts. One tourist minibus runs daily from Kathmandu at 1.30pm from a stand on Lekhnath Marg, west of the Hotel Malla (Rs 150, two hours). Return buses depart from the Galaxy View Tower at 10am.

Buses from Kathmandu may not run out of season, in which case you'll probably have to get a bus to Bhaktapur and change, which is a pain, since you get dropped off at the west end of town and have to pick up the next bus in the east. Extremely crowded buses return from Nagarkot to Bhaktapur every half hour or so (Rs 15, 1½ hours).

A one-way taxi to Nagarkot costs around Rs 1400 from Kathmandu, or Rs 700 from Bhaktapur.

Walking to, or preferably from, Nagarkot is an interesting alternative. For route ideas see p224.

BANEPA
pop 16,000

Just outside the valley, the small town of Banepa is a busy crossroads, 29km from Kathmandu. It was an important stop on the trade route to Tibet and once even boasted diplomatic relations with China's Ming dynasty. Dhulikhel is 5km to the east, the temple town of Panauti is about 7km south and Nala is 3km to the northwest.

The pleasant squares and laneways in the older northwest section of Banepa are worth exploring. Right beside the turn-off to Chandeshwari is a pretty tank with bas-reliefs of gods at one end.

Only 1km or so northeast of Banepa is the **Chandeshwari Temple**. Legend has it that the people of this valley were once terrorised by a demon known as Chand. When Parvati, in her demon-slaying mode, got rid of the nuisance she took the name Chandeshwari, 'Slayer of Chand', and this temple was built in her honour.

The temple is entered through a doorway topped by a brilliantly coloured relief of Parvati disposing of the demon. The triple-roofed temple has roof struts showing the eight Ashta Matrikas and eight Bhairabs, but the temple's most notable feature is a huge and colourful fresco on the west wall of Bhairab at his destructive worst. The temple had been almost totally deconstructed in 2006 as part of its major renovation.

The ghats below the temple, beside the stream, are an auspicious place to die and people come here when their end is nigh.

Getting There & Away

Regular buses leave from Kathmandu's City (Ratna Park) bus station (Rs 20, two hours) and continue on to Dhulikhel and beyond. Buses to Panauti turn off the Arniko Hwy at the main Banepa junction.

DHULIKHEL
☎ 011 / pop 9,800 / elevation 1550m

Only 3km southeast of Banepa (32km from Kathmandu) is the interesting small town of

AROUND THE KATHMANDU VALLEY

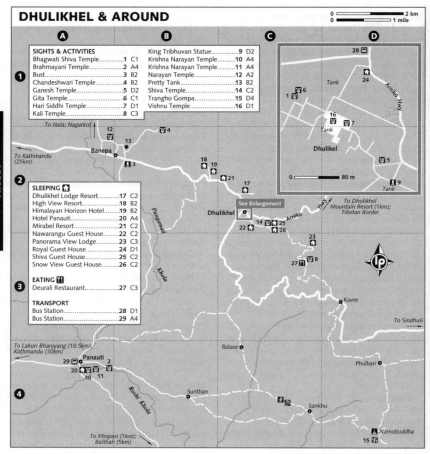

DHULIKHEL & AROUND

Dhulikhel. It's popular as a Himalayan view-point, in part because the road to Dhulikhel is an easier route than the steep and winding road to Nagarkot, but also because Dhulikhel is a real Newari town, not just a tourist resort. It's also a good centre for short day treks – many visitors come here to stretch their legs before setting off on longer treks.

The peaks on view stretch from Langtang Lirung (7246m) in the east, through Dorje Lakpa (6966m) to the huge bulk of Gauri Shankar (7145m) and nearby Melungtse (7181m) and as far as Numbur (5945m) in the east.

A new highway from Dhulikhel to Sind-huli is being finalised with Japanese as-sistance and will considerably shorten the travelling time between Kathmandu and the towns of the eastern Terai. What an increase in heavy vehicle traffic will do for the peaceful ambience of Dhulikhel – and the narrow and already inadequately engin-eered Arniko Hwy back to Kathmandu – is not yet clear. Construction was seriously delayed in 2002; every time the government workers laid some tarmac, Maoist rebels would creep up in the middle of the night and blow it up!

Sights

The old part of the town, west of the bus stop, is an interesting area to wander around. The town's main square has a tank, the small triple-roofed **Hari Siddhi Temple** and a **Vishnu**

Temple fronted by two worshipful Garudas in quite different styles. One is a kneeling stone Garuda topping a low pillar, while the second Garuda is in bright metal, more like the bird-faced Garudas of Indonesia than the conventional Nepali Garudas.

Walking in the other direction you pass the Nawarangu Guest House and after 1.5km you reach the junction where the road turns right (west) towards the Kali Temple. Continue straight on from the junction and dip down to a picturesque little **Shiva Temple** at the bottom of a gorge. Water flows through the site, where the main sanctum features a four-faced lingam topped with a metal dome with four *nagas* arching down from the pinnacle. This temple has everything – Nandi, kneeling devotees, Ganesh, Hanuman, Saraswati, Shiva and Parvati, lingams, tridents and more.

Dhulikhel's final temple attraction is the **Kali Temple** high up the hill towards Namobuddha. Climb up the hill for the excellent mountain views, not for the shrine, which is occupied by the army. To get there, take the right branch of the junction mentioned earlier and follow the footpath shortcuts, not the winding 2km-long mud road. It's a 20- to 30-minute uphill walk. The peaceful Deurali Restaurant is just below the temple.

Sleeping
BUDGET
Nawarangu Guest House (☎ 661226; s/d without bathroom Rs 125/250, with bathroom Rs 200/350) If you ever wondered what Dhulikhel was like c 1974, check out this classic budget backpacker hangout that's been going for almost 40 years now. The pie oven is long gone and part of the old building collapsed during a recent monsoon, but there are still cheap (basic) rooms, a cosy restaurant decorated with local paintings (for sale) and good honey pancakes (Rs 50). The owner, Purna, remains a gracious host, despite some hard times, and can take you to a great lookout point just two minutes' walk from the hotel. The hotel is southeast of the main *chowk*, towards the Shiva Temple.

Snow View Guest House (☎ 661229; d with/without bathroom Rs 500/300) Another couple of minutes' walk towards the Shiva Temple, this is a friendly place set in a pleasant garden with bright clean rooms, a rooftop sitting area and mountain views. Rooms are comfortable and good value; the more expensive doubles are carpeted.

Shiva Guest House (☎ 9841-254988; d without bathroom Rs 200-300, with bathroom Rs 500-700) A tiny family-run farmhouse with only five clean, fresh rooms and great views from the top-floor rooms and rooftop. Food comes fresh from the organic garden and you can pick mandarins right off the trees in October. It's very secluded and there's no road here; follow the signposted path one minute on foot from the Shiva Temple (a 15-minute-walk from the main road).

Royal Guest House (☎ 664010; s/d without bathroom Rs 200/300, with bathroom Rs 400/500) Another good budget place, back on the main junction. Rooms are good value (though the singles are small) and the common bathrooms are clean, plus there's a cosy lodge-style restaurant (mains Rs 110 to Rs 160) with BBC World on the TV.

Panorama View Lodge (☎ 663086; r lower/upper fl Rs 300/600) For those who really want to get away from it all, follow the dirt track that leads to the Kali Temple for 1.5km to this peaceful place (a 45-minute hike from the main road). The views are huge and the rooms are clean and quiet. In fact, you'll most likely be the only guest.

MIDRANGE & TOP END
Dhulikhel Lodge Resort (☎ 661114; www.dhulikhel lodgeresort.com; s/d US$70/80, discounts of 55%) Just off the main road, near the Dhulikhel bus stop, this large, modern but tastefully built place has comfortable rooms and superb views (try to get a room on the top floor). There's also a block of newer rooms, but some don't have the views. The great circular fireplace in the bar provides an après-ski atmosphere. The reception offers information on walks around Dhulikhel and can provide a birding checklist.

Mirabel Resort (☎ 661972; www.ournepal.com/mi rabel; s/d US$90/100, discounts of up to 70%) A rather out-of-place Mediterranean-style resort, but it is very well done and offers the top accommodation in Dhulikhel. The rooms have great views, a balcony, fridge and TV and the rooftop terrace is as good as it gets. It was offering amazing discounts during our last visit.

Himalayan Horizon Hotel (☎ 661296; www.hima layanhorizon.com; s/d US$62/66, discounts of 20%) Also known as the Hotel Sun-n-Snow, this hotel is a bit of a monster, but it does feature traditional woodcarving, has a pleasant restaurant and garden terrace area, and all the rooms face straight out on to the Himalayan peaks. The spacious split-level rooms come with private balcony views and are a good bet, although not if the other resorts are offering bigger discounts.

High View Resort (☎ 661966; www.highviewresort .com; s/d US$30/40, deluxe US$60/65, discounts of 35-50%) An excellent place, 700m further down the same side road as the Himalayan Horizon and then a stiff five-minute climb up some steps. Huge deluxe rooms come with a private balcony and the views are excellent, even from the shower! The cheaper rooms by the restaurant are smaller but still pleasant.

Dhulikhel Mountain Resort (☎ 661466; www.cat mando.com/dhulikhel-mt-resort; s/d US$76/78, discounts of 20%) If you have transport, head 4km downhill from Dhulikhel towards the Tibetan border to this lovely resort. Accommodation is in luxurious thatched cottages surrounded by gorgeous gardens and staff can lead guests on walks to the local villages of Baralgaon, Tin-

pipal and Manegaon. Ring them in advance and they'll pick you up in Dhulikhel.

Eating

The hotels offer the best places to eat. For a cheap lunch the Royal Guest House is a good bet. If you're headed to the Kali Temple you could grab breakfast or a snack at the nearby **Deurali Restaurant**.

Getting There & Away

Frequent buses to Dhulikhel leave from Kathmandu's City (Ratna Park) bus station (Rs 25, two hours). The buses skirt Bhaktapur and then climb out of the valley over the Sanga Pass, passing a major military checkpoint en route. The last bus goes back to Kathmandu at around 6pm.

A taxi from Kathmandu costs about Rs 900, or about Rs 650 from Bhaktapur.

The walk to Dhulikhel from Nagarkot is an interesting alternative. After watching the sunrise at Nagarkot you can walk down through Nala to Banepa, from where you can take a bus the last 4km to Dhulikhel (see p224 for details).

DHULIKHEL TO NAMOBUDDHA HIKE

The hike or mountain-bike trip from Dhulikhel to Namobuddha is a fine leg-stretcher. It takes about three hours each way, so it makes a good day walk. The walk can be made either as a return-trip loop from Dhulikhel or a one-way hike to the interesting village of Panauti, from where you can stay the night or return by bus to Dhulikhel via Banepa. Most of the hike follows a dirt road and route finding is easy.

From Dhulikhel the trail first climbs up to the Kali Temple lookout (p228) then drops down (take the left path after the Deurali Restaurant) for half an hour to the village of **Kavre**, by the new road to Sindhuli. Cross the road, take the road by some battered old prayer flags and pretty much follow this for the next hour until you round a ridge to the village of **Phulbari**, where you can get a cold drink or cup of tea. Soon you crest a hill and in the distance you'll see a Tibetan monastery atop a hill, with Namobuddha just below it. Just before Namobuddha the main track branches left; take the right branch to the stupa. There are several teahouses by the stupa where you can get a basic lunch.

There is very little known about the stupa at **Namobuddha**, but it is an important destination for Tibetan pilgrims. A legend relates that the Buddha came across a tigress close to death from starvation and unable to feed her cubs. The sorrowful Buddha allowed the hungry tigress to consume him. A marble tablet depicting the event in **Trangho Gompa** on the hill above the stupa marks the holy site where this event is supposed to have taken place. It's worth hiking the steep 10 minutes up to the huge monastery; take the path uphill to the left of the stupa.

From Namobuddha the trail to **Sankhu** descends to a track from the right side of the stupa, through forest to the temple and mini-ghats of Sankhu. About an hour from Namobuddha the path splits right uphill to Batase and Dhulikhel, or left along the road past terraced fields to **Sunthan** and **Panauti**, about two hours from Namobuddha. The tarmac picks up about 1.5km from Panauti. As you approach Panauti, cross the stream over a suspension bridge to the ghats and then follow the road as it curves round to the Indreshwar Mahadev Temple (see opposite).

PANAUTI

In a valley about 7km south of Banepa (36km from Kathmandu), the small town of Panauti sits at the junction of the Roshi Khola and Pungamati Khola. Like Allahabad in India, a third 'invisible' river, the Padmabati, is said to join the other two at the confluence (see the boxed text, right). A popular tradition asserts that the entire town is built on a single piece of solid stone, making it immune to earthquakes.

Panauti once stood at the junction of important trading routes and had a royal palace in its main square. Today it's just a quiet backwater, but is all the more interesting for that. The village has retained and restored (with French help) much of its traditional architecture and has a number of interesting temples, one of which may be the oldest in Nepal.

Sights

INDRESHWAR MAHADEV TEMPLE

The three-storey Indreshwar Mahadev Temple in the village centre is a Shiva temple, built in 1294 and rebuilt in the 15th century. In 1988 an earthquake caused serious damage. In its original form it may well have been the oldest temple in Nepal – Kathmandu's Kasthamandap may predate it, but Kasthamandap was originally built as a *dharamsala,* not as a temple.

The temple is certainly a fine one and the roof struts depicting the various incarnations of Shiva and some discreetly amorous couples are masterpieces of Newari woodcarving.

To the south of the main temple is the rectangular Unamanta Bhairab Temple, with three faces peering out of the upstairs windows, rather like the Shiva-Parvati Temple in Kathmandu's Durbar Sq. A small, double-roofed Shiva temple stands by the northwestern corner, while a Vishnu shrine with an interior 2m-high image of the god faces the temple from the west.

OTHER TEMPLES

On the east side of the village, at the junction of the Roshi Khola and Pungamati Khola, is the interesting **Krishna Narayan Temple** complex, with some woodcarvings of similar age to the Indreshwar Mahadev Temple (look for Krishna playing his flute on the roof struts). The riverbank stone sculptures are also of interest, but unfortu-

TRICKERY & REPENTANCE AT PANAUTI

Legends relate that Ahilya, the beautiful wife of a Vedic sage, was seduced by the god Indra, who tricked her by assuming the shape of her husband. When the sage returned and discovered what had happened he took a bizarre revenge upon Indra by causing Indra's body to become covered in *yonis,* female sexual organs! Naturally, Indra was somewhat put out by this and for many years he and his wife Indrayani repented at the auspicious *sangam* (river confluence) at Panauti. Eventually, Parvati, Shiva's consort, took pity upon Indrayani and turned her into the invisible river, which joins the two visible ones in Panauti. More years passed and eventually Shiva decided to release Indra from his strange predicament. Shiva appeared in Panauti as a great lingam and when Indra bathed in the river his *yonis* disappeared. The Shiva lingam is the one that stands in the temple.

nately the late 1980s were cruel to Panauti: as well as an earthquake there were severe floods, which swept away the cremation ghats at the river junction.

Across the Pungamati Khola is the 17th-century **Brahmayani Temple**; a suspension bridge crosses the river at this point. Brahmayani is the chief goddess of the village and her image is drawn around the town each year in the town's chariot festival.

As you enter Panauti through the northwestern gate, near the bus station, look for a pilgrim resthouse 70m down on the left, next to the old runners of a temple chariot. By a lovely *hiti,* turn right to get to a collection of interesting buildings, including the wonderfully restored municipality office, a pilgrim resthouse and a temple with some lovely golden window frames. There are lots of other temples and shrines hidden in the backstreets around here.

Festivals & Events

Panauti celebrates a **chariot festival** at the end of the monsoon each year around September, when images of the gods from the town's various temples are drawn around the streets in temple carts. The festival starts from the town's old Durbar Sq.

Every 12 years (next in 2010), the **Magh Sankranti festival** (in mid-January, or the Nepali lunar month of Magh) is celebrated with a great *mela* (religious fair) in Panauti that attracts large crowds of pilgrims, worshippers and sadhus.

Sleeping & Eating

Hotel Panauti (☎ 011-661055; panauti@wlink.com .np; r with/without bathroom Rs 500/300) You aren't spoilt for choice in Panauti but luckily this is a good place, about a five-minute walk south from the main western gate by the bus stand. Rooms are simple but bright, clean and comfortable (though the hot water is only solar heated) and there's a decent rooftop terrace and restaurant.

Getting There & Away

Buses run frequently between Panauti and Kathmandu's City (Ratna Park) bus station (Rs 19, two hours) via Banepa; the last bus leaves Panauti around 6pm. For Dhulikhel you'll have to change in Banepa.

See p230 for information on walking to Panauti from Dhulikhel.

If you are travelling by mountain or motorbike you could return to Kathmandu along the remote little-used dirt road via Lakuri Bhanjyang. See p85 for a description of the 30km route, a two-hour ride by motorbike.

AROUND PANAUTI

The terraced fields, villages and lush hills southeast of Panauti offer great scope for hiking and village exploration. It's a far less visited area than Dhulikhel.

The only place to stay is the good **Balthali Resort** (☎ 01-4108210; www.balthalivillageresort .com; s/d US$35/45, half board US$47/69, discounts of 25%), perched on top of a hill above the village of the same name, with sweeping Himalayan views. The rooms lack much architectural charm, but are decent and clean. Staff there can lead you on hikes to Tamang villages like Dada Gaun, across the Roshi Khola to the Namobuddha stupa or deep into the Mahabharat range to the south.

To get to Balthali take a bus (Rs 5) or walk from Panauti to Kholpasi, past the sericulture (silk) cooperative, and then continue on foot over the Saladu Khosi for an hour or so to Balthali village.

BEYOND THE VALLEY

While the following destinations are well beyond the confines of the Kathmandu Valley, they can be visited as part of an overland vehicle tour from Kathmandu in a relatively short period.

ARNIKO HIGHWAY TO TIBET

The Arniko Hwy provides Nepal's overland link with Tibet and China. Past Barabise the road is particularly vulnerable to landslides and during the monsoon sections are likely to be closed temporarily between May and August. Even when the highway is passable it's of limited use in breaking India's commercial stranglehold on Nepal, as it's still cheaper to ship Chinese goods via Kolkata (Calcutta) than to truck them through Tibet.

After Dhulikhel the road descends into the beautiful **Panchkhal Valley**. A turnoff at Lamidanda, around 12km from Dhulikhel, leads for 9km on a tarmac road to Palanchowk, where there is a famously beautiful black stone image of the goddess Bhagwati (a form of Durga, itself a terrifying form of Parvati). About five minutes' drive beyond the town of Panchkhal a dirt road takes off to the left, giving road access to the Helambu region.

About 8km later you arrive at **Dolalghat**, a thriving town at the confluence of the Indrawati and Sun Kosi Rivers and the departure point for many rafting trips. The turn-off to Jiri is another 14km away, on the right. **Lamosangu** is a few kilometres after the Jiri turn-off, on the Arniko Hwy. North of Lamosangu is a hydroelectric plant with a tedious military checkpoint.

For a more detailed description of this route see p86.

Barabise

Barabise is the region's main bazaar town and transport centre. There's little reason to stay here, but you might find yourself caught here at the end of the day, particularly if the night-time curfew continues to shut down transport options early.

Bhotekhosi Guest House (s/d Rs 125/150), by the bridge in the centre of town, is the best of a bad bunch. Other options include the very basic **Milan Guest House** (tr Rs 150), by the noisy southern bus stand for buses to Kathmandu, or the fairly miserable **Hotel Chan-**

deshwori (d Rs 250) in the north of town, with a patchy restaurant.

Buses run frequently from different ends of town to Kodari (Rs 55, three hours) and Kathmandu (Rs 86, last bus 4pm). A single express bus to Kathmandu leaves at 7am (Rs 110, 3½ hours).

Borderlands Resort

Tucked away in a bend of the Bhote Kosi River, 97km from Kathmandu, the superb **Borderlands Resort** (www.borderlandresorts.com; tw per person US$40) is a quiet and isolated riverside retreat. It consists of a central bar and dining area, and a number of luxury thatch-roofed safari tents dotted around a lush tropical garden. Activities offered include rafting, canyoning and trekking, but it's also a great place to just hang out for a day or two.

Accommodation includes meals and transport from Kathmandu. Packages that include activities offer the best value; drop in to the resort's **Kathmandu office** (Map p136; ☎ 01-4425836; next to the Northfield Café) for more details. As an idea of prices, two days of canyoning/rafting costs US$110/70, including transport and accommodation.

Last Resort

Another 4km towards Tibet, **Last Resort** (www.tlrnepal.com; US$25-35 full board per person) sits in a beautiful spot on a ridge above the Bhote Kosi river, 12km from the Tibet border. Access is by suspension bridge across the river, and it's here that Nepal's only bungee jump is set up (see p77).

Accommodation at the resort is in comfortable standard (four-person) or deluxe (two-person) safari tents, with the focus being the soaring stone-and-slate dining hall and Instant Karma bar. There are gas-heated showers, a plunge pool and a sauna (Rs 300 per person), with massage and yoga to come. The cost of accommodation includes meals and transport to and from Kathmandu. Bring mosquito repellent and a torch (flashlight).

The resort also offers canyoning, rafting on the Bhote Kosi (US$40, if already staying at the resort), trekking, mountain biking and rock climbing, plus kayak clinics at its less glamorous Riverside Resort (US$40 per day per person). See p78 for details.

Like Borderlands, the Last Resort does a range of packages that combine any or all of the above activities, so it's not a bad idea to

---

OFF THE BEATEN TREK

Both Borderlands and Last Resort offer trekking trips up to the Tibetan border. A four- or five-day trek takes in the ruins of Duganagadi Fort, built in 1854 to defend Nepal during the Nepal-Tibet war, the Tibetan monastery at Bagam, the nunnery at Gumba and the villages of Yemershing, Tasitham and Listikot.

A six- to seven-day option heads to Bhairab Kunda, a holy lake at 4080m with great views of the Langtang range. Thousands of pilgrims trek up to the lake during the full moon of August.

Prices hover around US$40 per person per day for the fully supported camping trek and you are almost guaranteed to have these places to yourself.

---

call into its **Kathmandu office** (Map p136; ☎ 01-4439525; near Kathmandu Guest House) for more information and to book.

Tatopani

The next point of interest is the **hot springs** (admission Rs 2) of Tatopani, 3.5km south of the Tibetan border at Kodari. Five minutes' walk north of the central bazaar, look for a turnstile and sign on the right-hand side. The springs come out as a set of showers (great after a hard bicycle ride from Dhulikhel).

There is a small gompa on the southern edge of town and a large *mani lhakhang* (shrine with a prayer wheel) in the centre.

Family Guest House (☎ 091-633011; d Rs 250; daal bhaat Rs 60) is probably the best accommodation in town, with a decent restaurant and basic but clean rooms.

Other local lodges such as the Tibetan Lodge & Restaurant and Sonam Lodge are more basic.

Kodari

Nepal's border town with Tibet (China), Kodari is little more than a collection of shabby wooden shanties and a snaking line of squealing Tata trucks, ferrying Chinese goods down into the subcontinent.

It is possible to walk past the Nepali checkpoint and stop in the middle of the **Friendship Bridge** to pose for photos on the red line drawn across the road. From here on is Tibet, which right here looks just like

Nepal. The Chinese border post is 8km up-hill at Khasa (Zhangmu). A Chinese visa and Tibetan travel permit is needed to progress further than this.

INFORMATION

The **immigration office** (8.30am-4pm) gives arrivals a Nepali visa for US$30 and also accepts Nepali rupees or Chinese yuan, but you must supply one photo.

You can change cash and travellers cheques at the **Nepal Bangladesh Bank** (10.15am-3.30pm Sun-Fri), 20m from immigration, for a Rs 100 commission or 1% of the transaction.

SLEEPING & EATING

There is a string of five or so similar guest-houses right by the border, the best of which is the **Kailash Tashi Delek Guest House** (d Rs 250; mains Rs 100-180), which has a nice river view restaurant. They are mostly used as lunch stops by groups headed to or from Tibet.

GETTING THERE & AWAY

There is one express bus a day at 2pm to Kathmandu (Rs 160, 4½ hours). Otherwise take a local bus to Barabise (Rs 55, three hours), and then another on to Kathmandu (Rs 86, last bus around 4pm). Buses are packed and most people ride on the roof.

After 2pm your only option to get to Kathmandu the same day is to take a taxi for around Rs 2000 (Rs 500 a seat). Taxis generally won't leave for Kathmandu after 5pm due to security concerns between Barabise and Panchkhal.

THE ROAD TO LANGTANG

A tarmac road heads northwest out of Kathmandu for 23km to Kakani, perched on the edge of the Kathmandu Valley with spectacular views of the Ganesh Himal, and continues to Trisuli Bazaar. Beyond here the road to Dhunche deteriorates to very rough gravel, and is travelled only by mountain bikers and trekkers headed for the Langtang region (see p341).

Just before Malekhu, on the Kathmandu–Pokhara (Prithvi) Hwy, there's a bridge over the Trisuli and the turn-off for the new road to Trisuli Bazaar. It makes an interesting circular bicycle ride a possibility, taking in Kakani, Trisuli Bazaar, Dhading and Male-khu. See Map pp238–9 for this route.

Kakani

Standing at 2073m on a ridge northwest of Kathmandu, Kakani is nowhere near as popular as Nagarkot, but it does offer mag-nificent views of the Ganesh Himal and the central and western Himalaya. The 24km road to Kakani also offers a great bike ride from the capital.

Apart from staring open-mouthed at the view (one could argue this is enough), there's not much to do. The century-old summer villa used by the British embassy, large police training college and army posts crowd out the views somewhat.

The peaceful Thai Memorial Park com-memorates the 113 victims of a 1992 Thai Airlines crash. The Shiva shrine across the road offers wider Himalayan views. The government is constructing an Interna-tional Mountaineer Memorial Park below the hillside.

The fairly basic Kakani Guest House and Waiba Guest House were both closed in 2005 but are expected to reopen soon. The former Tara Gaon Hotel is currently oc-cupied by the army.

GETTING THERE & AWAY

Kakani is an hour by car or motorcycle from Kathmandu, and is a long, though rewarding, bicycle trip. There are a number of restaurants along the route. The road is sealed almost all the way and it is a fairly gentle climb – downhill all the way home! See p83 for details of the route to Kakani and on through Shivapuri National Park.

Kakani is 3.5km off the main Dhunche road; turn right at the crest of the hill, be-fore the Kaulithana police checkpoint.

For Kakani, catch a Trisuli Bazaar or Dhunche bus from counter 30 of the Kath-mandu bus station, get off at Kaulithana (Rs 25) and walk the 3km uphill to Kakani.

Nuwakot

The small village of Nuwakot, a few kilo-metres southeast of Trisuli Bazaar, has the remains of a 16th-century **fortress** built by Prithvi Narayan Shah when he was plan-ning his campaign to take the Kathmandu Valley in 1744, he later died in the fortress. The impressive main seven-storey Newari-style tower is the forerunner of Kathman-du's Basantapur Tower. The fort is an interesting spot and can be reached by a

TAMANG HERITAGE TRAIL

As part of its Tourism for Rural Poverty Alleviation Programme (TRPAP), the Nepal Tourism Board has helped establish a new village tourism project in the Tibetan-influenced Rasuwa district bordering Langtang (see map pp342–3). The aim of the Initiative is to bring tourism money to communities off the main tourist routes. Profits from homestay accommodation, food sales, handicrafts and Tamang cultural performances are split between the individuals concerned and village social funds. It's a sometimes uneasy mix of community-based tourism and free-market economics but it's a worthy program that deserves support and provides an excellent add-on or alternative to the more commercialised Langtang area.

The highlights of the region include Gatlang, the largest Tamang village in the area, the Tatopani community-run hot springs at Tatopani, the lake of Parvati Kunda near Gutlang, Tibetan monasteries around Goljung, and Himalayan views from Nagthali Danda. The star of the show is the village of Briddim (2229m), where you can stay at one of 24 homes that take in tourists on a rota system (there are only 43 houses in the village!). It's also possible to trek along the old Tibetan trade route via Timure to Rasuwagadhi Fort on the border with Tibet's Kyirong Valley, though for this you need a travel agency to help arrange a border permit (US$10) from the Department of Immigration in Kathmandu (p112).

A five- or six-day loop of the region is the best option, starting in Syabrubesi and taking in Syabrubesi, Gatlang, Tatopani, Thuman, Timure, Briddim and Syabrubesi, each of which are around four hours' hike apart. If nothing else, spend a night in Briddim to get a taste of the region.

Accommodation is available in a community lodge in Gatlang, the homestay programme in Briddim, or in private houses or lodges in Goljung, Tatopani, Timure and Thuman. Costs are around RS 150 per person per night, plus Rs 100 per meal. In general, the village homestays offer a more intimate experience than the large-scale lodges of Langtang.

You should be able to find a licensed guide in Syabrubesi for around RS 650 per day, which includes food and accommodation. There are plans to open an information office and small museum in Dhunche.

If you want to get off the beaten track and experience the Tibetan-influenced Tamang culture, then give it a try. For more details you can download brochures and maps at the website www.welcomenepal.com/trpap or contact the Nepal Tourism Board's **Sustainable Tourism Unit** (☎ 01-4256909; info_trpap@ntb.org.np) in Kathmandu.

steep 1½ hours uphill climb from Bidur, or a 30-minute detour by car.

There are a couple of basic restaurants and lodges in Trisuli Bazaar if you get stuck here. Buses leave from the Kathmandu main bus station on the ring road every 15 minutes between 6.30am and about 2.30pm (Rs 53, four hours).

Dhunche & Syabrubesi

By the time you reach Dhunche, 119km from Kathmandu, you will have been inspected by countless redundant police and army checkpoints, plus paid Rs 1000 to enter the Langtang National Park. Irritation evaporates quickly, however, because there are spectacular views of the Langtang Valley, and although the modern section of Dhunche is pretty tacky, it's definitely a Tamang town, and the old section is virtually unchanged. Many people start trekking

from Dhunche, although there is a bus to Syabrubesi as well (see p341).

SLEEPING & EATING

There are a number of decent trekking-style hotel restaurants, including the **Langtang View** (r with/without bathroom Rs 300/200), Dhunche Guest House, Tibetan View Guest House, Annapurna Guest House and others.

Syabrubesi has the Buddha Hotel, Lhasa Hotel and half a dozen other smaller lodges.

GETTING THERE & AWAY

The road to Dhunche is bad, but it deteriorates further if you continue 15km to Syabrubesi. The views on both stretches are spectacular.

Minibuses leave Kathmandu at 6.30am, 7.30am and 8.30am for Dhunche (Rs 159, eight hours) and Syabrubesi (Rs 202, nine hours), returning at 6.30am and 7.30am.

Kathmandu to Pokhara

Most travellers rush the journey between Kathmandu and Pokhara, missing some of Nepal's hidden gems. The hills that flank the 206km Prithvi Hwy contain some of the most important religious sites in Nepal, but most visitors whistle through on tourist buses and see little of what the area has to offer. We strongly recommend taking at least two days for the journey between Kathmandu and Pokhara to see more of this interesting and unspoiled region.

Heading west from Kathmandu, the first of several possible places to break the journey is the Manakamana Mandir near Mugling, one of the oldest temples in central Nepal and an important destination for Hindu pilgrimages. Further west, Gorkha is the former capital of the Shah dynasty, while the nearby hill town of Bandipur is a living museum of Newari architecture and culture.

As well as these historic points of interest, the highway is lined with modern townships that have sprung up around important road junctions and river crossings. Most are fairly unappealing but there's always the chance you could end up staying overnight while changing buses. Dotted between these settlements are numerous roadhouses where buses stop for snacks and toilet breaks. Where you end up will depend on the bus company but the food is normally hygienic and cheap.

Even if you don't stop between Kathmandu and Pokhara, the scenery along the road is dramatic. The highway follows a series of deep river valleys, passing ancient stone villages, cascading rice terraces, rocky gorges and roaring rapids crossed by precarious suspension bridges. On clear days, most of the way to Pokhara there are views of Machhapuchhare and the Annapurna massif.

HIGHLIGHTS

- Experience the exhilarating valley views from the **Manakamana Cable Car** (opposite)
- Hike to Gorkha's magnificent hilltop **Gorkha Durbar** (p239), a triumph of Newari architecture
- Enjoy a lunchtime swim at the luxurious **River Side Springs Resort** (p238) in Kurintar
- Step back in time at **Bandipur** (p242), a perfectly preserved Newari village on an ancient trade route
- Walk to untouched Magar villages and mountain shrines in the **Bandipur hills** (p244)

DANGERS & ANNOYANCES

Most places along the Prithvi Hwy are currently under government control, but this could change at any time. Gorkha and Bandipur have been targeted by Maoists in the past and there are army checkpoints all along Prithvi Hwy. As elsewhere, you should check the security situation before you travel. Note that many towns impose curfews during flare-ups of violence.

GETTING THERE & AWAY

Assuming things are peaceful, several dozen public and tourist buses run daily between Kathmandu and Pokhara, linking most of the important towns en route. There are several army checkpoints along the way and the journey takes at least seven hours. Foreigners are usually waved straight through, but locals must disembark and show their bags to the authorities.

Note that bus fares are often hiked up for foreigners. Buy at the ticket office to reduce the chances of getting stung. Another hassle for travellers is theft during meals stops – keep an eye on your gear, and don't leave valuables on the bus.

For details of the mountain bike ride between Kathmandu and Pokhara see p88.

KATHMANDU TO MUGLING

People living in Kathmandu often complain about being trapped in the Kathmandu Valley. There are only really two roads out of Kathmandu, one leading northeast to Lhasa in Tibet and one running west along the gorge of the Trisuli River to Pokhara. Named in honour of Prithvi Narayan Shah, the Prithvi Hwy is the busiest road in Nepal and it passes through a string of small villages on its way to Mugling, the turn-off for Narayangarh and the Terai.

At **Naubise**, 29km from Kathmandu, the Tribhuvan Hwy branches south and makes a dramatic passage across the hills of the Mahabharat Range to the Terai (see p304 for details). It's a thrilling journey but it takes an age and most people skip it in favour of the faster route via Mugling and Narayangarh. For details of mountain biking along this route see p86.

From Naubise, the Prithvi Hwy follows the valley of the Mahesh Khola to meet the mighty Trisuli River, which twists and contorts along a narrow gorge. The next big

settlement is **Malekhu**, famous for its smoked river fish; if your bus stops here, hawkers will line up at the windows selling rolls of smoked fish from long wooden rakes.

About 3km before Malekhu, a side road leads north to **Dhading**, a tiny cluster of stone houses on a terraced ridge overlooking the Ganesh Himalaya. The **Shreeban Rock Climbing Nature Camp** (☎ 01-4258427; www.shreeban.com.np; in Kathmandu; B&B per person per day US$25, rates for activities vary; ☘ closed winter) offers rock climbing, hang-gliding, mountain biking and trekking in the hills around Dhading – arrange visits in advance in Kathmandu. Accommodation is in an old village house, on a stepped ridge with vertigo-inducing views.

Back on the highway, the next village after Malekhu is **Benighat**, where the roaring Buri Gandaki River merges with the Trisuli. The increased bore of the river creates some impressive rapids and many whitewater rafting companies put in at Charaudi, about 20km downriver. **Himalayan Encounters** (☎ 01-4700426; rafting&trekking@himenco.wlink.com .np; in Kathmandu) runs an attractive, low-key rafting centre, the Trisuli Center, in the small village of Bandare. See p95 for more on rafting on the Trisuli.

About halfway between Benighat and Mugling, the tiny village of **Hugdi** is a possible starting point for treks to the Chitwan Hills – see p288 for details. The Manakamana Cable Car, the longest in Asia, begins its dramatic journey up the hillside at **Cheres**, about 6km before Mugling.

MANAKAMANA

From the tiny hamlet of Cheres, an Austrian-engineered cable car sweeps up an almost impossibly steep hillside to the ancient **Manakamana Mandir**, one of the most important temples in Nepal. Hindus believe that the goddess Bhagwati, an incarnation of Parvati, has the power to grant wishes, and newlyweds flock here to pray for male children. Pilgrims seal the deal by sacrificing a goat or pigeon in a gory pavilion behind the temple. There's even a dedicated carriage on the cable car for sacrificial goats (humans can book the return journey – goats get a one-way ticket).

Built in the tiered pagoda style of the Kathmandu Valley, the temple dates back to the 17th century and the atmosphere is electric, particularly on feast days, when

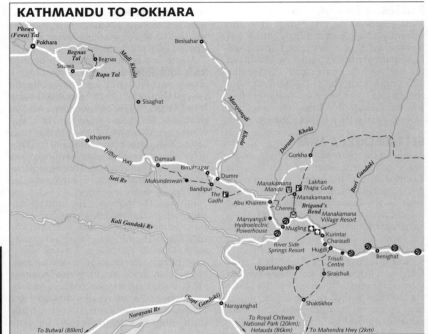

KATHMANDU TO POKHARA

Manakamana almost vanishes under a sea of pilgrims, pigeons and sacrificial goats. For views of the Himalaya, continue uphill for about 3km past the small Shiva mandir to **Lakhan Thapa Gufa**, a sacred cave offering uninterrupted views of the mountains. Trekkers can continue west along the ridge, reaching Gorkha in about four hours.

Until 1998, the only way to get here was the arduous 18km trek from Abu Khaireni, 8km west of Mugling on the way to Pokhara. Visitor numbers have soared since the construction of the cable car, but foreigners are still a novelty and most things here exist for the benefit of pilgrims rather than tourists.

Sleeping & Eating
There are dozens of simple pilgrim lodges in the village surrounding the temple. Probably the best is **Sunrise Home** (☎ 064-460055; d/t with bathroom Rs 300/400); rooms are spotless and spacious and the restaurant downstairs serves delicious veg and nonveg curries.

There are a couple of upmarket options down in the valley at **Kurintar**, about 3km east of the cable car station.

River Side Springs Resort (☎ 056-540129; nang int@ccsl.com.np; s/d from US$50/60, discounts of 25%; ❄ ☲) This surprisingly sophisticated hotel and restaurant has a prime location on the banks of the Trisuli. Accommodation is in classy cabins and an airy central lodge and there's a glorious ring-shaped swimming pool with a semisubmerged bar (open to nonguests for a Rs 250 fee). Many of the upmarket tourist buses stop here for lunch.

Manakamana Village Resort (☎ 056-540150; om@hons.com.np; r with bathroom Rs 900, r with air-con Rs 1200; ❄) Across the road, this simpler tin-roofed resort offers simple but clean rooms in cottages dotted around a small, flower-filled garden.

Getting There & Away
The awesome **Manakamana Cable Car** (foreigner/Nepali US$12/Rs 320, luggage Rs 8; ☽ 9am–noon & 1.30–5pm) rises nearly 1000m as it covers the 2.8km from the Prithvi Hwy to the Manakamana ridge. The views are breathtaking but Maoists have targeted the cable car in the past so check that everything is calm before you visit.

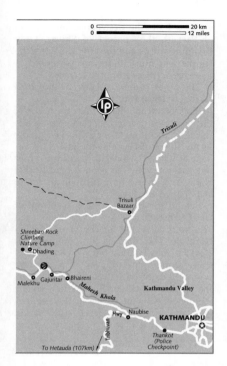

All buses that run between Kathmandu and Pokhara or Narayangarh pass the turn-off to the cable car (look for the red brick archway). If you want to walk to Manakamana, the trail starts at the village of Abu Khaireni, about 8km west of Mugling.

MUGLING
☎ 056

Mugling marks the junction between the Prithvi Hwy and the main road to the plains. From here, it's 110km to Kathmandu, 96km to Pokhara, and 34km to Narayangarh. The town isn't particularly interesting or attractive, but many buses travelling between Kathmandu and Pokhara stop here for meals and you may end up staying if you change buses on your way to the Terai.

Mugling is also a possible start and end point for rafting trips, including the leisurely drift down the Narayani River to Royal Chitwan National Park. Most people arrange rafting trips in Kathmandu or Pokhara – see p89 for more information.

Many of Mugling's hotels are fronts for prostitution, but **Machhapuchhare Hotel &**

Lodge (☎ 540029; r with bathroom Rs 250) accommodates the occasional stranded backpacker. For food, there are dozens of 'hotel and lodging' places along the main road.

ABU KHAIRENI

At this small junction town, a rutted road branches north to Gorkha; buses and minibuses around the junction offer transfers to Gorkha for Rs 40. Abu Khaireni is also the starting point for the four- to five-hour climb to the **Manakamana Mandir**.

To reach the temple, turn off the highway onto the road to Gorkha and turn right by the Manakamana Hotel; the trail crosses the river on a small suspension bridge and climbs steadily through terraced fields and small villages to reach the ridge.

GORKHA
☎ 064

About 24km north of Abu Khaireni, Gorkha was the birthplace of Prithvi Narayan Shah, conqueror of the Kathmandu Valley and founder of modern Nepal. It's a major pilgrimage destination, particularly for Newars, who regard the Shah kings (including the current one) as living incarnations of Vishnu. The main attraction here is the Gorkha Durbar, the former palace of the Shahs, which lords over Gorkha from a precarious ridge above the town.

In the current political climate, being linked to the Shahs is a mixed blessing. The town is a major target for Maoist attacks and there are numerous military checkpoints along the road from Abu Khaireni. During times of political tension, Gorkha is often placed under curfew – check with your hotel before going out at night.

Sights
GORKHA DURBAR

Regarded by many as the crowning glory of Newari architecture, **Gorkha Durbar** (admission free; ⏱ 6am-6pm) is a fort, a palace and a temple all in one. This magnificent architectural confection is perched high above Gorkha on a knife-edge ridge, with superb views over the Trisuli Valley and the soaring peaks of the Annapurna and Ganesh Himalaya.

As the birthplace of Prithvi Narayan Shah, the Durbar has huge significance for Nepalis. The great Shah was born here in around 1723, when Gorkha was a minor feudal kingdom, in thrall to the larger city-states in the Kathmandu Valley. Upon gaining the throne, Prithvi Narayan forced the Kathmandu Valley into submission, forging a kingdom that extended far into India and Tibet. In 1769 the capital was shifted from Gorkha to Kathmandu and Gorkha was relegated to the status of a national monument.

To reach the durbar, you must climb an exhausting stairway of 1500 stone steps, snaking up the hillside above the Gorkha bus stand. Most pilgrims enter through the **western gate**, emerging on an open terrace in front of the exquisite **Kalika Mandir**. Built in the reign of King Ram Shah (1606–36), but extensively remodelled over the years, the temple is a psychedelic fantasy of carved peacocks, demons and serpents. The wood-carving around the doors and windows is particularly striking – note the ornate peacock windows and the erotic scenes on the root struts.

Gory sacrifices of goats, chickens, doves and buffaloes are carried out in the courtyard in front of the temple to honour the goddess Kali (the destructive incarnation of Parvati, the consort of Shiva). Only Brahmin priests and the king can enter the temple, but non-Hindus are permitted to observe sacrifices from the terrace.

The other major structure in the compound is **Dhuni Pati**, the former palace of Prithvi Narayan Shah. Like the temple, the palace is covered in elaborate wood-carvings, including a magnificent window in the shape of Garuda (the man-bird vehicle of Vishnu). Non-Hindus cannot enter but you can view the room where Prithvi Narayan Shah was born through an ornate star-shaped window.

Behind the palace is the mausoleum of **Guru Gorkhanath**, a reclusive saint who acted as a spiritual guide for the young Prithvi Narayan. This part of the compound is closed to non-Hindus, but you can descend some stone steps to peek into the **cave** where the saint once lived. If you leave via the northern gate, you'll come to a vividly painted carving of **Hanuman**, the monkey god, and a series of carved stone steles. A path leads east from here past a large

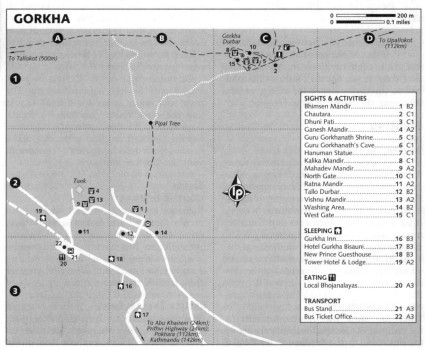

BLOOD SACRIFICE

Although revered as the consort of Shiva, Kali is also an incarnation of the Tantric goddess Shakti, a pre-Hindu deity linked to the worship of female mystical power. The followers of Shakti were notoriously bloodthirsty and human sacrifices to Shakti continued long after Tantric worship was absorbed into mainstream Hinduism. These days, buffaloes, goats, chickens and doves are the preferred victims; hundreds meet their maker each *astami* (the eighth day of the waning moon in the lunar calendar) at the Kalika Mandir in Gorkha. It's a grimly fascinating spectacle but be warned – the air is heavy with tension and the paving stones are slick with sacrificial blood. During Dasain in October, more than 1000 goats and buffalo are slaughtered at the Kalika Mandir to honour the victory of Durga (another incarnation of Shakti) over the buffalo demon Mahisasura.

---

chautara (stone resting platform) to an exposed rocky bluff with awesome views of the mountains and a set of carved stone footprints, attributed variously to Sita, Rama, Gorkhanath and Guru Padmasambhava.

The durbar is an important religious site, and visitors must follow strict rules. Shoes should be removed and photography and leather (including belts) are banned inside the Gorkha Durbar complex. This is strictly enforced by soldiers so use the lockers at the shoe stand near the western gate (bring your own padlock) or leave your camera at the guard house.

To get to Gorkha Durbar, go north from the bus station and follow the main cobbled street through the bazaar. The steps to the durbar start just before the post office – if you reach the public **washing area**, you've gone too far. The final ascent to the durbar is steep and strenuous but there are several stalls selling bottled water. Look out for the huge tin steamers used to strip the feathers off sacrificial chickens to prepare them for the cookpot.

OTHER MONUMENTS

There are more historic monuments in the old part of Gorkha. Immediately above the bus stand is the fortified **Ratna Mandir**,

the official Gorkha residence of King Gyanendra. If you follow the road uphill, you'll reach a small compound with three small temples – the two-tiered temple is dedicated to **Vishnu**, the squat white temple with the Nandi statue is dedicated to **Mahadev** (Shiva) and the small white *shikhara* (temple tower) by the tank is sacred to **Ganesh**.

A little further along, the road opens onto a large square with a small wooden temple dedicated to **Bhimsen**, the Newari god of commerce. A monumental gateway leads off the square to **Tallo Durbar**, a huge Newari-style palace, built in 1835 for an errant Rana; it's currently occupied by soldiers but you can peek through the gate.

There are two ruined **forts** on the ridge above Gorkha Durbar, but both are occupied by the Nepali army.

Sleeping & Eating

Gorkha has a decent range of places to stay. The best restaurants are at the hotels, but there are numerous cheap **bhojanalayas** (snack restaurants) near the bus stand.

New Prince Guesthouse (☎ 420030; d/q with bathroom Rs 150/250) Downhill from the bus stand above an arcade of shops, New Prince is basic but good for the price. Some rooms need a lick of paint so see a few before deciding.

Tower Hotel & Lodge (☎ 420335; r without bathroom Rs 150) On the other side of the bus stand, this humble place is run by the friendly shopkeepers downstairs. It's handy for the buses and rooms are basic but clean.

Gurkha Inn (☎ 420206; s/d US$25/35) Styled like a Spanish hacienda, and set in a lovely stepped garden facing the valley, this comfortable place has a cosy patio restaurant and bright, airy rooms.

Hotel Gorkha Bisauni (☎ 420107; ghbisauni@wlink .com.np; s/d without bathroom US$12/18, s/d with bathroom US$21/32, discounts of up to 60%) With the current discounts, the posh-looking Gorkha Bisauni is a bona fide bargain. It's set in landscaped grounds about 200m downhill from Gurkha Inn and rooms have carpets, TV and private or shared bathrooms with hot showers. The restaurant serves a reassuringly familiar, globe-trotting traveller menu.

Getting There & Away

The bus stand is right in the middle of town and the ticket office is on the road to Tower Hotel & Lodge. There are three daily buses to Pokhara (Rs 110, five hours) and 10 daily buses to Kathmandu (Rs 105 to 120, five hours), or you can ride a local bus or minibus to Abu Khaireni (Rs 40, 30 minutes) and change there. A single bus leaves Gorkha at 7am for Bhairawa (Rs 210, five hours) and several morning buses run to Narayangarh (Rs 90, three hours).

DUMRE

About 17km west of Abu Khaireni, Dumre is a dusty (or muddy) roadside bazaar with little to recommend it. Plenty of travellers pass through town on the way to Bandipur or Besisahar (the starting point for the Annapurna Circuit Trek) but few people stop overnight. If you do find yourself stuck here, **Mustang Lodge** (☎ 065-580106; r without bathroom Rs 150) is friendlier than most and the owners speak English.

Any bus travelling between Kathmandu and Pokhara can drop you on the highway in Dumre. Local buses and jeeps run regularly to Besisahar; the official fare for the bumpy three-hour journey is Rs 65 but don't be surprised if the starting price is five or six times this. Jeeps to Bandipur (Rs 20 per person, one hour) loiter around on the highway about 200m west of the Besisahar junction. If you're in a hurry, you can charter the whole jeep for Rs 300.

BANDIPUR

☎ 065

Bandipur (pronounced 'ban-DI-pur') is a national treasure. Draped like a silk scarf along a high ridge above Dumre, the town is a living museum of Newari culture. People here seem to live centuries apart from the rest of the country and more than 70% of the buildings are traditional Newari houses, with carved wooden windows and overhanging slate roofs. It's hard to believe that somewhere so delightful has managed to escape the ravages of tourist development.

The Bandipur Social Development Committee has shown remarkable maturity in opening Bandipur up to tourism. There are just a few places to stay and eat and money from tourism ventures is ploughed back into restoring temples and houses. Bandipur remains very much a living community – as you wander around the narrow streets, you'll see farmers tending market gardens, women carrying baskets of freshly cut fodder, children stacking cobs of corn on wooden stakes, and goats, buffaloes and chickens wandering around as if they owned the place.

Bandipur was originally part of the Magar kingdom of Tanahun, ruled from nearby Palpa (Tansen), but Newari traders flooded in after the conquest of the valley by Prithvi Narayan Shah. The town became a major stop on the trade route between India and Tibet and traders invested their profits in temples, slab-paved roads and towering brick shop-houses. Then, 50 years ago, it all fell apart. The new Pokhara–Kathmandu highway passed far below town and traders picked up sticks and relocated to Narayangarh. Even today, many buildings are empty, though some have found a new life as restaurants and guesthouses.

As you may have gleaned from the communist graffiti, locals have some sympathy with the Maoist cause, but there have been no real problems here since the police post was abandoned in 2002. For more information on Bandipur, visit the website www.bandipure.com.

Sights

With its medieval ambiance and glorious 18th-century architecture, all of Bandipur is a sight. You could spend days wandering around the town and surrounding Magar villages. The residents are singularly hospitable and for now at least, Bandipur has escaped the 'one bonbon, one pen, one rupee' phenomenon that plagues towns in more established tourist areas.

As well as the following sights and monuments, there are some interesting walks in the hills, including the trek to **Siddha Gufa**, the largest cave in Nepal – see the boxed text p244 for details.

TUNDIKHEL

This ancient parade ground is perched on a flat-topped ridge near the village hospital. Back when Bandipur was a stop on the trade route between India and Tibet, this was the setting for trade fairs and archery contests. The views of the Himalaya from here are breathtaking – come here at dusk when the setting sun picks the peaks out in shades of pink and gold. At the start of the Tundikhel are five enormous fig trees. In

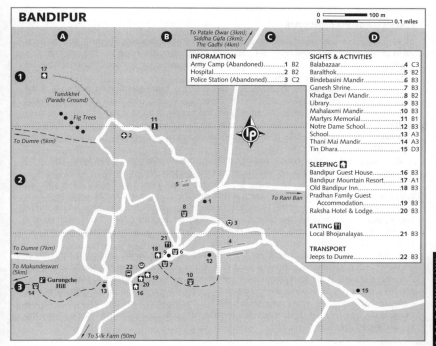

BANDIPUR

INFORMATION	
Army Camp (Abandoned)..........1	B2
Hospital.................................2	B2
Police Station (Abandoned)........3	C2

SIGHTS & ACTIVITIES	
Balabazaar.............................4	C3
Baralthok..............................5	B2
Bindebasini Mandir...................6	B3
Ganesh Shrine........................7	B3
Khadga Devi Mandir..................8	B2
Library................................9	B3
Mahalaxmi Mandir...................10	B3
Martyrs Memorial....................11	B1
Notre Dame School..................12	B3
School...............................13	A3
Thani Mai Mandir....................14	A3
Tin Dhara............................15	D3

SLEEPING	
Bandipur Guest House..............16	B3
Bandipur Mountain Resort........17	A1
Old Bandipur Inn.....................18	B3
Pradhan Family Guest Accommodation..................19	B3
Raksha Hotel & Lodge..............20	B3

EATING	
Local Bhojanalayas..................21	B3

TRANSPORT	
Jeeps to Dumre.......................22	B3

Nepali mythology, the different types of fig tree are symbols for different Hindu gods, and Vishnu, Brahma and Hanuman are all represented here.

If you follow the path north from the Tundikhel past the hospital, you'll reach the **Martyrs Memorial**, a stone pillar commemorating the local men who died fighting the Ranas in the political turmoil that followed Indian Independence. Further along the same track is the abandoned Magar settlement of **Baralthok**, with some stately brick shop-houses. The trail to Siddha Gufa turns off to the left near the abandoned army camp; if you take the right fork after 50m you'll come to **Rani Ban**, a peaceful area of public woodland.

TEMPLES
The most interesting temple in town is the large, two-tiered **Bindebasini Mandir** at the northeast end of the main bazaar. Dedicated to Durga, the temple is covered in ancient carvings and an elderly priest opens the doors each evening so locals can pay homage to the idol inside. Facing the tem-

ple across the square is the town **library**, a striking 18th-century building with carved windows and beams. Nearby, a set of stone steps runs east to the small **Mahalaxmi Mandir**, another centuries-old Newari-style temple.

Behind the Bindebasini Mandir, a wide flight of stone steps leads up the hillside to the unusual **Khadga Devi Mandir**. The squat, barnlike building houses the sacred sword of Mukunda Sen, the 16th-century king of Palpa (Tansen). According to legend, the sword was a gift from Shiva, but the king gave away all his material possessions to become a wandering ascetic and his sword somehow ended up in Bandipur. With hindsight, it seems likely that the mendicant king swapped his sword for food while wandering in the hills, but the blade is still revered as a symbol of *shakti* (female mystical power). Once a year during Dasain, the sword is marched to the main bazaar and anointed with the blood of a sacrificial sheep.

OTHER SIGHTS
If you take the path leading east from the Bindebasini Mandir, you'll pass the famous

WALKS AROUND BANDIPUR

It's easy to pass several peaceful days exploring the hills around Bandipur. There are gobsmacking views of the Annapurna Himalaya from dozens of points along the ridge and the countryside is a gorgeous patchwork of terraced rice and mustard fields and small orchards. Most guesthouses can arrange walking guides for around Rs 300.

One of the easiest walks is the 30-minute ascent to the **Thani Mai temple**, just west of the village at the top of Gurungche Hill. The trail starts near the big pink school at the southwest end of the bazaar (near Bandipur Guest House). The temple is set in a peaceful copse of trees on top of the hill and there are epic views over the mountains and Bandipur village. Don't be surprised if local children make flying gestures as you pass – paragliders have launched from here in the past.

With more time on your hands, you can walk down to the famous **Siddha Gufa**, said to be the largest cave in Nepal. The entrance is narrow but it opens up into a vast vaulted chamber, full of stalactites, stalagmites and bats. The cave has never been fully explored but you can scramble some 200m with a decent torch or lantern. The 1½-hour trek to the cave starts near the abandoned army camp at the north end of the village, but it helps to have a local guide. Some people continue down the hillside to Bimalnagar on the Prithvi Hwy. You can combine a visit to Siddha Gufa with a trip to **Patale Dwar** (literally 'Gateway to the Underworld'), another cavern full of eye-catching geological formations.

An hour's hike northeast of Bandipur is the hill known as the **Gadhi**, topped by the ruins of an ancient *kot* (fort). The view from here takes in an incredible sweep of Himalayan peaks; you can trace the path of the Marsyangdi River north between the Annapurna and Manaslu massifs and most of the way to Manang. Another interesting walk is the two-hour trek to **Mukundeswari**, a Magar shrine atop the distinctive twin-peaked hill northwest of Bandipur. Locals believe that this was the forest retreat of Mukunda Sen and the hilltop is adorned with tridents, knives and swords left by devotees.

Notre Dame School, established by Catholic nuns from Japan in 1985. As well as providing an international education to children from rural families, the nuns set up numerous pioneering social projects in the area, which may explain the high levels of education and politeness in Bandipur! The school was closed after pressure from Maoists in 2001, but it reopened in 2003.

Just east of the school is **Balabazaar**, a striking arcade of old shop-houses formerly occupied by Newari cloth merchants. Turn right where the road forks and you'll reach the public washing area known as **Tin Dhara**, where clean, cool spring water emerges from beneath the Rani Ban forest. The name means 'three spouts', but in fact there are five spouts, carved in the shape of mythical beasts. There are several small temples dotted around the spring where you can sit and watch the comings and goings of village life.

Another interesting detour is the **Bandipur silk farm**, an easy 30-minute walk south of the village. The staff don't speak much English but they'll happily show you around.

Sleeping & Eating

There are several simple food and lodging places along the main bazaar but many are actually hostels for the Notre Dame School.

Bandipur Guest House (☎ 520103; r without bathroom Rs 200) Housed in a majestic, crumbling shop-house at the start of the bazaar, this charming place offers simple wooden rooms with tiny balconies overlooking the village. The building is a real museum piece and good meals (of the daal bhaat variety) are available in the dining room. Similar rooms to the Bandipur Guest House are available for similar prices at Raksha Hotel & Lodge and Pradhan Family Guest Accommodation further along.

Old Bandipur Inn (☎ 520110; r per person per night with meals US$20) Run by the highly professional team behind Himalayan Encounters (see p90), this beautifully restored Newari mansion is full of Buddhist art and the elegant wooden rooms look right out over the mountains. Rates include Nepali meals and guides for local walks and you can include Bandipur as part of longer rafting and trekking tours.

Bandipur Mountain Resort (☎ 520125, 01-220162; www.islandjungleresort.com/bandipur, in Kathmandu; r per person with meals US$30; 🏊) This midrange resort offers spacious rooms, set amongst the pines at the west end of Tundikhel. It's a little faded, and the pool is frequently empty, but it's not bad for the price. Advance reservations are essential.

Getting There & Away
The 7km link road to Bandipur branches off the Prithvi Hwy about 2km west of Dumre; jeeps to Bandipur hang around on the highway in Dumre and charge Rs 20 per person or Rs 300 for the whole jeep.

It's also possible to walk to Bandipur from Dumre along the old traders' path. The trail starts on the highway about 500m west of the last house in Dumre, and climbs steeply through small villages, terraced fields and patches of forest, emerging at the southwest end of the Tundikhel. Allow three hours on the way up or 1½ hours on the way down.

DUMRE TO POKHARA
Heading west from Dumre, the highway follows the winding gorge of the Madi Khola to the district headquarters of **Damauli**, the largest town between Kathmandu and Pokhara with little to recommend it. Beyond Damauli, the Prithvi Hwy enters the broad floodplain of the Seti River, a surreal landscape of truncated gorges and hanging valleys. From here, the magnificent pyramid of Mt Machhapuchhare looms over the highway like a beacon – if you're travelling on the roof of a public bus, the sense that the mountain is calling you is quite profound.

The next town of any size is **Khaireni**, about 24km west of Damauli, but again, there are no real sights to speak of. This final stretch of road is hot and dusty and there are several army checkpoints that slow traffic to a crawl. Most people can't wait to get to Pokhara for a hot shower or a cold drink.

KATHMANDU TO POKHARA

Pokhara

Imagine a perfect triangular mountain, capped by snow and buffeted by the icy winds of the Himalaya. Imagine a millpond calm lake, perfectly reflecting the snowy peaks. Now imagine a village on the lakeshore, thronged by travellers and reverberating to the sound of 'om mani padme hum' from a hundred shops selling prayer flags, carpets, masks, singing bowls and CDs of Buddhist mantras. That's Pokhara.

Nepal's second city, at least in tourist terms, Pokhara is the end point for the famous Annapurna Circuit trek and the starting point for a dozen more treks through the mountains of the Annapurna Range, including the perennially popular Jomsom Trek and the equally dramatic (but less busy) trek to the Annapurna Sanctuary. It's unashamedly touristy, in the Thamel mould, but the setting is spectacular – the perfect pyramid of Mt Machhapuchhare looms high above Pokhara, reflected in the placid waters of Phewa Tal.

For many travellers, Pokhara represents a last chance to stock up on creature comforts before hitting the mountain trails. For others, it's a place to enjoy a steak dinner and cold beer after weeks of daal bhaat in the hills. Even if you aren't a dedicated trekker, there's plenty here to keep you busy. Pokhara has numerous museums and there are some fascinating caves, waterfalls and Tibetan villages in the surrounding hills.

For the adventurous, travel agents in Pokhara offer a slew of adventure activities, from trekking and microlight flights to river rafting and jungle safaris. Paragliding from Sarangkot viewpoint has to be one of the most thrilling experiences in the subcontinent. Alternatively, bring a good book and spend your days reading in a café overlooking languorous Phewa Tal.

POKHARA

HIGHLIGHTS

- Go boating on serene **Phewa Tal** (p250)
- Follow the exploits of great mountaineers at the **International Mountain Museum** (p252)
- Enjoy steak dinners and beery evenings in the **restaurants** (p261) of Lakeside
- Stroll through the forest to Pokhara's tranquil **World Peace Pagoda** (p255)
- Revel in the sunset views of the Annapurna range from lofty **Sarangkot** (p265)
- Escape the crowds at **Begnas Tal** (p267), the second largest lake in the Pokhara Valley

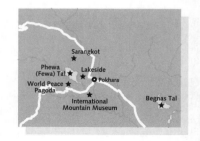

■ AREA CODE: ☎ 061　　　■ POPULATION: 171,000　　　■ ELEVATION: 884 M

POKHARA IN...

Two Days
Two days will give you a decent taste of Pokhara. Start with a browse through the souvenir shops of **Lakeside** (p263) then rent a boat for a leisurely row around **Phewa Tal** (p253). Lunch on the strip then head inland for a wander round old Pokhara. On day two, wriggle through the **Bat Cave** (p267) and drop in on one of Pokhara's interesting museums.

Four Days
With four days, visit the huge **International Mountain Museum** (p252) and walk north around the lake. Take a trip to one of the **Tibetan settlements** (p253) north and south of Pokhara and trek up to the sublime **World Peace Pagoda** (p255). On day four, hike or take a taxi to **Sarangkot** (p265) for epic views of the Annapurna massif.

One Week
With a week in Pokhara, you'll have time to try some of the adventure activities – **paragliding** (p254) from Sarangkot is strongly recommended. Consider the walk to **Poon Hill** (p268) or hire a bike or motorcycle to explore **Begnas Tal** (p267) and the villages on the northern lakeshore.

HISTORY

Before the construction of the Prithvi Hwy, getting to Pokhara involved a 10-day pony trek, with numerous deadly river crossings along the way. When the Swiss explorer Toni Hagen visited in 1952, he found ambling buffalo carts and streets lined with brick Newari houses. Hints of this time can still be seen in old Pokhara, just north of the Mahendra Pul bazaar.

Aside from the odd explorer, the first Westerners to reach Pokhara were hippies in the 1970s. With its lakeshore setting, laid-back pace and plentiful supply of marijuana, Pokhara made a perfect endpoint for the south Asian overland trail. From these barefoot beginnings, it developed rapidly. By the 1980s, it had transformed into a modern mountain resort, with hundreds of hotels, shops, bars and restaurants.

Today, Pokhara is basically Thamel by the water, but you only have to wander north around the lakeshore to find the peaceful idyll that first attracted people here in the 1970s.

CLIMATE

Pokhara sits about 400m lower than Kathmandu so the autumn and winter temperatures are generally much more comfortable. Even in the height of winter you can get away with a T-shirt during the day time and you'll only need a sweater or jacket for evenings and early morning starts. From June

to September the skies open and the views vanish behind blankets of grey cloud; bring a brolly and be prepared to wade when the streets are flooded.

ORIENTATION

Famed as the city by the lake, Pokhara sprawls along the eastern shore of gorgeous Phewa Tal (Fewa Tal). Most travellers stay on the lake shore in Lakeside, a seemingly endless string of budget hotels, restaurants, bars, Internet cafés and souvenir shops, extending right around the lake from Basundhara Park to the northern shore.

More budget accommodation is available near the Phewa dam in Damside, which also has the tourist office, the Annapurna Conservation Area Project (ACAP) office and the immigration office.

Inland from Lakeside, you'll find the airport and the bus stand for tourist buses to Kathmandu (also known as the Mustang bus stand). The main public bus stand is at the north end of the Pokhara airstrip, while local buses to Baglung (for treks to the Annapurna Range) leave from the highway north of town.

The main shopping area for locals is Mahendra Pul, running north from the public bus stand. Just north of here is Pokhara's old town, bound by the Baglung Hwy and the Seti River gorge.

For convenience, we've divided the lakeshore into several sections. Starting from the

POKHARA

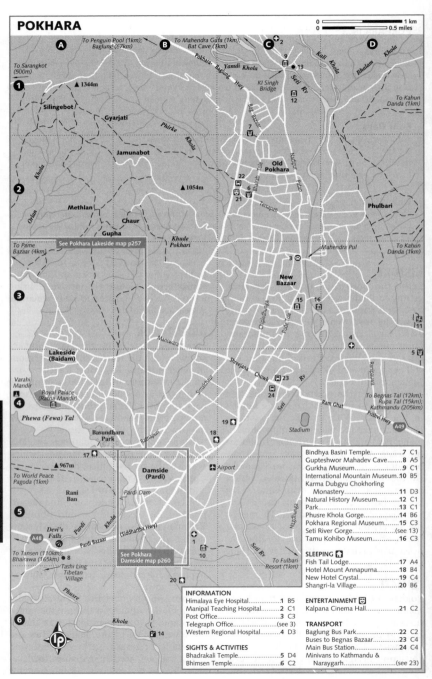

POKHARA

Bindhya Basini Temple	7	C1
Gupteshwor Mahadev Cave	8	A5
Gurkha Museum	9	C1
International Mountain Museum	10	B5
Karma Dubgyu Chokhorling Monastery	11	D3
Natural History Museum	12	C1
Park	13	C1
Phusre Khola Gorge	14	B6
Pokhara Regional Museum	15	C3
Seti River Gorge	(see 13)	
Tamu Kohibo Museum	16	C3

SLEEPING 🏠

Fish Tail Lodge	17	A4
Hotel Mount Annapurna	18	B4
New Hotel Crystal	19	C4
Shangri-la Village	20	B6

ENTERTAINMENT 🎭

Kalpana Cinema Hall	21	C2

TRANSPORT

Baglung Bus Park	22	C2
Buses to Begnas Bazaar	23	C4
Main Bus Station	24	C4
Minivans to Kathmandu & Naraygarh	(see 23)	

INFORMATION

Himalaya Eye Hospital	1	B5
Manipal Teaching Hospital	2	C1
Post Office	3	C3
Telegraph Office	(see 3)	
Western Regional Hospital	4	D3

SIGHTS & ACTIVITIES

Bhadrakali Temple	5	D4
Bhimsen Temple	6	C2

Seti River dam, you'll pass through Damside, then Lakeside East (from Basundhara Park to the Royal Palace), then Central Lakeside (from the palace to the junction known as Camping Chowk), then Lakeside North (from Camping Chowk to the northern shore). All these places have Nepali names, but most people use 'Lakeside' for the whole strip.

INFORMATION
Bookshops
There are dozens of bookshops along the strip at Lakeside. All sell maps, guidebooks, postcards and reams of glossy coffee-table books. **Mandala Book Shop** (Map p257; ☎ 523203; ⌚ 10am-9pm) opposite the Hotel Snowland probably has the best stock.

Emergency
The direct phone number for the police is ☎ 100. For medical emergencies, contact the hospitals directly (see Medical Services, below).

Internet Access
All the Internet cafés in Pokhara charge the same rate – Rs 2 per minute with a minimum Rs 20 charge.
E-Mail One (Map p257; ⌚ 8am-11pm)
MS Communications (Map p257; ⌚ 7am-11pm)

Internet Resources
For online information on Pokhara, visit www.pokharacity.com.

Immigration Office
The **immigration office** (Map p260; ☎ 521160; ⌚ 10am-5pm Sun-Thu, 10am-3pm Fri) shares a building with the tourist office and Annapurna Conservation Area Project in Damside. Visa extensions cost US$30 for 30 days – bring your passport and two photos, plus the visa fee in Nepali rupees. For more on visa extensions see p375.

Laundry
Hotels can arrange same day laundry services if you drop your clothes off first thing in the morning, or there are plenty of small laundry shops along the strip in Lakeside.

Medical Services
There are several pharmacies in Lakeside selling everyday medicines. For anything

serious, there are two modern hospitals on the east bank of the Seti River.
Western Regional Hospital (Map p248; ☎ 520066)
Manipal Teaching Hospital (Map p248; ☎ 526416)

Money
There are several foreign exchange offices in Lakeside that change cash and travellers cheques in major currencies. All are open daily but rates are usually better at the **Standard Chartered Bank** (Map p257; ⌚ 9.45am-4.15pm Sun-Thu & 9.45am-1.15pm Fri), near Camping Chowk. The bank has two ATMs, one here and one next to the Hotel Snowland.

Post
The main **post office** (Map p248; ⌚ 10am-5pm Sun-Thu & 10am-3pm Fri) is a hike from Lakeside at Mahendra Pul. If you want to send anything valuable, **UPS** (Map p257; ☎ 536585) in Lakeside is costly but reliable.

Telephone
There's no real need to go to the **telegraph office** (Map p248; ⌚ 24 hr) in Mahendra Pul – Internet cafés in Lakeside offer phone calls to Europe and most other places for around Rs 50 per minute. Call back costs Rs 5.

Tourist Information
Nepal Tourism runs a helpful **tourist office** (Map p260; ☎ 535292; ⌚ 9am-1pm & 2-5pm Sun-Fri) in Damside, sharing a building with the Annapurna Conservation Area Project and the immigration office.

Travel Agencies
Most of the travel agents in Lakeside can book tours, flights and bus tickets, but be

POKHARA

TREKKING PERMITS

If you plan to trek anywhere inside the Annapurna Conservation Area, you'll need a permit from the **Annapurna Conservation Area Project** (ACAP; Map p260; ☎ 540376; ⌚ 9am-5pm Sun-Fri, 9am-4pm in winter) in Damside. The entry fee to the conservation area is Rs 2000/200 (foreigner/SAARC) and permits are issued on the spot (bring two passport-sized photos). There are ACAP checkpoints throughout the reserve and if you get caught without a permit, the fee rises to Rs 4000/400 (foreigner/SAARC).

BEATING THE BOTTLE

Abandoned plastic drinking water bottles are one of the plagues of the Himalaya. Some trekking routes are vanishing under a tide of plastic rubbish that will take thousands of years to decay. You can do your bit to keep the Himalaya beautiful by purifying your own water – there are springs and wells in most villages and water can easily be purified using water purification tablets or a water filter. Some lodges in the Annapurna Conservation Area now offer refills of purified water for a nominal charge – part of a joint initiative by the Annapurna Conservation Area Project and the New Zealand government. Start off on the right foot by visiting the **Kathmandu Environmental Education Project** (KEEP; Map p257; ☎ 531823), based in the Amrit Guest House in Lakeside. KEEP provides all sorts of information on environmental pollution in the hills and offers a canteen refilling service for Rs 10.

---

wary of anyone offering direct bus trips to towns in India; without exception, you must change buses at the border. The following travel agents are reputable.

Blue Sky Travel (Map p257; ☎ 521435; www.blue-sky-tours.com)

Wayfarers (Map p257; ☎ 532274; www.wayfarers.com.np) See p114 for details.

DANGERS & ANNOYANCES

There was a time when the worst thing that could happen in Pokhara was paying too much for a Kashmiri carpet. Sadly, the downturn in tourism has led to an upsurge in crime. A number of travellers have been mugged on the walk to the World Peace Pagoda and on the trek from Phewa Tal to Sarangkot and it pays to check the current situation before you set off (see p19). You should be safe if you travel in a group and walk in daylight hours.

Like many traveller towns, Pokhara is mobbed by touts, and the problem has become worse as visitor numbers have fallen. It's almost impossible to get a taxi from the tourist bus stand to Lakeside without a tout coming along to steer you towards a commission paying hotel where you'll pay twice the going rate. The best way to escape their clutches is to claim you have an advance booking somewhere else.

Swimmers should watch out for syringes and other sharp pieces of junk on the edges of Phewa Tal and steer clear of the dangerous dam. If you hire a motorcycle, be aware of the standard Asian obstacles – potholes, speeding trucks, rogue cows and suicidal chickens.

The insurgency is not currently affecting travel around Pokhara or inside the Annapurna Conservation Area, but road transport to Kathmandu and the Terai may be affected by any sudden upsurges in violence. As always, check the situation locally before you travel.

SIGHTS
Phewa Tal

Spreading majestically westwards from Pokhara, Phewa Tal is the second-largest lake in Nepal. On calm days, the mountains of the Annapurna Range are perfectly reflected in the mirrored surface of the *tal*. Away from the shore, the water is clean and deep and the dense forest along the south side of the lake provides shelter for brilliant white egrets.

The best way to appreciate Phewa Tal is by rowboat – see p253. Many people walk or cycle around the lakeshore – the trek up to the World Peace Pagoda (see the boxed text p255 for details) affords breathtaking views over the *tal* and the mountains beyond.

Mountains

Most people come to Nepal for the Himalaya and Pokhara is one of the best places to get an up close view of the peaks. From west to east, the peaks are Hiunchuli (6441m), Annapurna I (8091m), Machhapuchhare (6997m), Annapurna III (7555m), Annapurna IV (7525m) and Annapurna II (7937m). The dramatic Annapurna Massif looms over the city and the lake. There are few places in town where you can't see one or other of the snow-capped peaks jutting up into the clear blue sky.

The skyline is dominated by Mt Machhapuchhare ('Fish Tail' in Nepali) – at 6997m, it's actually one of the smaller peaks of the Annapurna Range, but it looks taller as it's closer to Pokhara. If you walk for a few days along the Jomsom Trek you'll see the second summit that gives the mountain its name, hidden away behind the main peak.

POKHARA

If you get the chance, visit Sarangkot (p265) to see all the Annapurnas lined up against the horizon. Another good place to see the mountain vista is the World Peace Pagoda – you'll see all the peaks twice, reflected in the surface of the lake.

Old Pokhara

For a taste of what Pokhara was like before the rafting agencies and German bakeries set up shop, head to the old town (Map p248), north of Mahendra Pul. The best way to explore is on foot or by bike.

From the Nepal Telecoms building at Mahendra Pul, head north along Tersapati, passing a number of small **religious shops** selling Hindu and Buddhist paraphernalia. At the intersection with Nala Mukh, check out the **Newari houses** with decorative brick-work and carved wooden windows.

Continue north on Bhairab Tole to reach the small two-tiered **Bhimsen Temple**, a two hundred-year-old shrine to the Newari god of trade and commerce, decorated with erotic carvings. The surrounding square is full of shops selling baskets and ceramics.

About 200m further north is a small hill, topped by the ancient **Bindhya Basini Temple**. Founded in the 17th century, the temple is sacred to Durga, the warlike incarnation of Parvati, worshipped here in the form of a *saligram* (ammonite fossil).

Varahi Mandir

Pokhara's most famous Hindu temple, the two-tiered pagoda-style **Varahi Mandir** (Map p257) stands on a small island near the Ratna Mandir (Royal Palace). Founded in the 18th century, the temple is dedicated to Vishnu in his boar incarnation, but it's been extensively renovated over the years. Rowboats to the temple (Rs 20) leave from near the city bus stand in Lakeside.

Karma Dubgyu Chokhorling Monastery

Overlooking Pokhara on the east side of the Seti River, this huge **gompa** (Map p248; ☙ daylight hr) is worth visiting just for the views. The main prayer hall has a gilded statue of Sakyamuni (the historical Buddha) and there are more Buddhist statues in the monastery gardens. To get here, take the road leading east across the river from Mahendra Pul.

In the same area is the hilltop **Bhadrakali Temple**, a two-tiered Newari-style mandir (Hindu temple) dedicated to the eight-armed Bhadrakali, one of several violent incarnations of Parvati. To get here, walk east from the Karma Dubgyu gompa and go right at the next two junctions.

Museums

GURKHA MUSEUM

Housed in a new building just north of Mahendra Pul and near to the KI Singh Bridge, this **museum** (Map p257; ☎ 541966; entry foreigner/SAARC/Nepali Rs 50/20/10; ☙ 8am-4.30pm Thu-Tue) focuses on the history and achievements of the famous Gurkha regiment – see the boxed text, below for more information on the Gurkhas.

POKHARA

SIMPLY THE BEST

It might seem like an odd leftover from the days of empire, but the British army maintains a recruiting centre on the outskirts of Pokhara. Every year, hundreds of young men from across Nepal come to Pokhara to put themselves through the rigorous selection process to become a Gurkha soldier.

Prospective recruits must perform a series of backbreaking physical tasks, including a 5km uphill run carrying 25kg of rocks in a traditional *doko* basket. Only the most physically fit and mentally dedicated individuals make it through – it is not unheard of for recruits to keep on running with broken bones in their determination to get selected.

The primary motivation for most recruits is money. The average daily wage in Nepal is less than one British pound, but Gurkha soldiers earn upwards of £1000 per month, with a commission lasting up to 16 years and a British Army pension for life, plus the option of becoming a British citizen on retirement.

Identified by their curved *khukuri* knives, Gurkhas are still considered one of the toughest fighting forces in the world. British Gurkhas have carried out peacekeeping missions in Afghanistan, Bosnia and Sierra Leone and Gurkha soldiers also form elite units of the Indian Army, the Singapore Police Force, and the personal bodyguard of the sultan of Brunei.

INTERNATIONAL MOUNTAIN MUSEUM

The newest cultural offering in Pokhara, this vast **museum** (Map p248; ☎ 525742; www.mountainmuseum.org/; foreigner/SAARC/Nepali Rs 300/100/50; ⏱ 9am-5pm) is devoted to the mountains of Nepal and the mountaineers who climbed them. Inside you can see original gear from many of the first Himalayan ascents, as well as displays on the history, culture, geology and flora and fauna of the Himalaya. The museum is south of the airstrip near the Himalaya Eye Hospital – a taxi from Lakeside will cost around Rs 400 return.

NATURAL HISTORY MUSEUM

At the north end of town, in the Prithvi Narayan University campus, this **museum** (Map p248; ☎ 521102; admission free, donations appreciated; ⏱ 9am-12.45pm & 1.30-5pm Sun-Thu 9am-12.45pm Fri) is devoted to the natural history of the Pokhara region. Local wildlife is represented by preserved specimens and some kooky-looking concrete models.

POKHARA REGIONAL MUSEUM

North of the bus station on the road to Mahendra Pul, this interesting little **museum** (Map p248; ☎ 520413; foreigner/SAARC/Nepali Rs 10/5/2; ⏱ 10am-5pm, until 3pm Mon, closed Tue) is devoted to the history and culture of the Pokhara valley, including the mystical shamanic beliefs followed by the original inhabitants of the Pokhara Valley. There's an additional fee for cameras and video cameras. In winter, the museum closes an hour earlier, except on Fridays.

TAMU KOHIBO MUSEUM

Over on the east bank of the Seti River, this small but intriguing **museum** (Map p248; admission Rs 20; ⏱ 10am-5pm Mon-Sat) is dedicated to the culture and customs of the Gurung (Tamu) people, the indigenous inhabitants of the Pokhara Valley, who follow a mix of animist, Shamanistic and Bonist beliefs, brought here from Tibet in the days before Buddhism. See p45 for more information on the Gurung people. To get here, cross the river via the small bridge just south of Mahendra Pul and head for the cluster of white towers on the side of the gorge.

Seti River Gorge

The roaring Seti River passes right through Pokhara, but you won't see it unless you go looking. The river has carved a deep, narrow gorge through the middle of town, turning the water milky white in the process. At points, the gorge is less than a metre across and the river gushes by more than 50m below street level.

The best place to catch a glimpse of the Seti River is the **park** (Map p248; ⏱ 7am-6pm, entry Rs 10) near the KI Singh Bridge, just north of old Pokhara on the road to Batulechaur. If you peer down through the darkness, you can just see the water churning through the gorge. Nearby is a small Buddhist gompa with friendly novice monks.

In the same area, you can get a dramatic view of the much larger **Phusre Khola Gorge** from the Phewa Power House – the track to the power station leaves the Butwal Hwy just south of Pardi Birauta Chowk, near the small road bridge. Locals come here in the afternoons to watch planes performing giddying turns as they come in to land at Pokhara's tiny airport.

Devi's Falls

Also known as Patale Chhango, this **waterfall** (Map p248; admission Rs 20/10 foreign/Nepali; ⏱ 6am-6pm) marks the point where the Pardi Khola stream vanishes underground. When the stream is at full bore, the sound of the water plunging over the falls is deafening, but the concrete walkways don't add much to the atmosphere.

According to locals, the name is a corruption of David's Falls, a reference to a Swiss visitor who tumbled into the sinkhole and drowned, taking his girlfriend with him! The falls are about 2km southwest of the airport on the road to Butwal, just before the Tashi Ling Tibetan Village.

Gupteshwor Mahadev Cave

Across the road from Devi's Falls, this **Hindu cave** (Map p248; admission Rs 20, Rs 70 to falls viewpoint; ⏱ 6am-6pm) contains a huge stalagmite worshiped as a Shiva lingam. The standard ticket only covers the temple, but you can pay extra to clamber through a low tunnel behind the shrine, emerging in a damp cavern behind the thundering waters of Devi's Falls. If you look at the ceiling of the cave, you can see branches and other detritus, forced into cracks by the force of the waters when the cave floods every monsoon.

Tibetan Settlements

Most of the Tibetan refugees who hawk souvenirs in Lakeside live in the Tibetan refugee settlements north and south of Pokhara. Both settlements make interesting detours from Pokhara by bike, bus or on foot.

The largest settlement is **Tashi Palkhel** (Map p266), a few kilometres north of Pokhara on the road to Baglung. The colourful **Jangchub Choeling Gompa** in the middle of the village is home to around 100 monks and masked dances are held here in January/February as part of the annual Losar (Tibetan New Year) celebrations. To reach the gompa you have to run the gauntlet past an arcade of persistent handicraft vendors. Nearby is a *chörten* piled with carved mani stones bearing Buddhist mantras and a carpet weaving centre, where you can see all stages of the process and buy the finished article.

Heading southwest from Pokhara on the road to Butwal, you'll come to the smaller **Tashi Ling Tibetan Village** (Map p248). There are several shops selling momos and Tibetan carpets and handicrafts, plus the small **Shree Gaden Dargay Ling Gompa**.

ACTIVITIES
Boating

If the commercialism of Lakeside gets too much, just head out onto the calm waters of Phewa Tal. Colourful wooden *doongas* (rowboats) are available for rent at several boat stations, including near the city bus stand and next to the Fewa Hotel. Rates start at Rs 200 per hour with a boatman, or RS 140/500 per hour/day if you row yourself. You can also rent plastic pedalos (Rs 250 per hour) and miniature sailboats (Rs 200 per hour). If you are boating alone near Damside, keep well away from the dam wall.

Cycling

Pokhara is fairly flat and the traffic is quite light once you get away from the main highway – perfect for cycling. Indian mountain bikes are available from dozens of places on the strip in Lakeside for Rs 20/100 per hour/day. For a description of the day-long or overnight bike ride out to Sarangkot and Naudanda see p88. Contact any of the Lakeside travel agents for details of mountain biking trips in the hills around Pokhara.

Golf

Golfers can hire everything they need at **Himalayan Golf** (Map p266; ☎ 577204; green fees 9/18 holes US$30/45), about 7km east of Pokhara. There's also a nine-hole golf course at the luxurious Fulbari Resort – see p261.

Horse Riding

Travel agents in Pokhara offer pony treks to various viewpoints around town, including Sarangkot, Kahun Danda and the World Peace Pagoda. Half-day trips (US$10) stick to the lakeshore; you'll need a full day (US$19) to reach the viewpoints.

Kayaking & Rafting

Another popular way to explore Phewa Tal is by kayak. **Ganesh Kayak Shop** (Map p257; ☎ 522657; ☺ 8am-9pm) near Moondance Restaurant rents out decent plastic kayaks for Rs 150/650 per hour/day and offers longer kayaking safaris around Nepal.

Pokhara is a good place to organise rafting trips, particularly trips down the Kali Gandaki and Seti Rivers, but also kayak clinics on the Seti River and the scenic drift down the Narayani River to Royal Chitwan National Park. See p92 for more information. Reliable rafting operators include:

Himalayan Encounters (Map p257; ☎ 520873; rafting&trekking@himenco.wlink.com.np)

Swissa/Raging River Runners (Map p257; ☎ 526839; www.swissatravel.com)

Ultimate Descents/Adventure Centre Asia (Map p257; ☎ 523240; www.upnepal.com)

Massage

Trekkers with aching muscles can get traditional Ayurvedic massage at several places in Lakeside. Next to the Koto restaurant, **Natural Health Center** (Map p257; ☎ 538624) offers Shiatsu and reflexology as well as the usual herbal rubs (from Rs 700 per hour).

Meditation & Yoga

Pokhara is a great spot to contemplate the nature of the universe and several centres around the lake offer meditation and yoga training.

Ganden Yiga Chopen Meditation Centre (Pokhara Buddhist Meditation Centre; Map p257; ☎ 522923; pokharacentre@yahoo.com) This place holds three-day meditation and yoga courses (Rs 3000) as well as daily sessions at 10am (Rs 200) and 5pm (Rs 150). It's down a lane in Lakeside North near the Hungry Feel Restaurant.

POKHARA

Nepali Yoga Center (Map p257; ☎ 532407; www .nepaliyoga.com) Near the Hotel Octagon, this place holds daily Hatha yoga classes (Rs 300, 1½ hours) at 7.30am and 4.30pm and various longer courses can be arranged.
Sadhana Yoga (Map p266; ☎ 542601; www.sadhana -yoga.org.np) This friendly and secluded retreat is hidden away on a ridge overlooking Phewa Tal, about 2.5km northwest of Lakeside. The energetic Asanga offers one- to six-day courses in Hatha yoga for Rs 1600 per day, including tuition, steam and mud baths, accommodation and meals. Call for directions.

Microlight Flights
Based near the Hotel Snowland, **Avia Club Nepal** (Map p257; ☎ 540338; www.avianepal.21bc .net) offers exhilarating microlight flights around the Pokhara Valley. In 15 minutes (US$65), you can buzz around the World Peace Pagoda and lakeshore, but you'll need 30 minutes (US$112) or one hour (US$198) to get up above Sarangkot for the full Himalayan panorama.

Paragliding
Paragliding from the top of Sarangkot must be one of the most exciting experiences in the Himalaya. **Sunrise Paragliding** (Map p257; ☎ 521 174; www.nepal-paragliding.com) offers 30-minute flights exploring the thermals above Sarangkot (US$75) and one-hour cross-country jumps across the valley north towards Annapurna (US$120). **Blue Sky Paragliding** (☎ 534737; www .paragliding-nepal.ch) is the other big operator. See p79 for more details.

If conventional paragliding fails to thrill, there's always parahawking. Invented by British falconer Scott Mason, parahawking is an unlikely combination of falconry and paragliding where eagles and pariah kites are trained to lead gliders to the best thermal currents (see p79 for more details). If you want to literally soar with the eagles, you'll need to train up as a solo paraglider first – paragliding centres in Lakeside can start you on your way. Less brave souls can see the avian guides at their roost at Maya Devi Village on the northern shore of Phewa Tal (see right).

Swimming
The cool waters of Phewa Tal are perfect for a dip but there's a fair bit of pollution around at Lakeside so walk around to the northern shore or hire a boatman to take you out onto the lake. Watch out for cur-

rents wherever you swim and don't get too close to the dam in Damside.

The only public pool in the area is the open-air **Penguin Pool** (Map p266; ☎ 527470, 522275; admission Rs 100; ☉ 10am-12.30pm & 1.30-6.30pm, closed Nov to Jan), a few kilometres north of Pokhara along the road to Baglung.

Several upmarket hotels let nonguests swim in their pool for a fee. In Lakeside, **Hotel Barahi** (see p258) charges Rs 200; **Shangri-la Village** (see p261) charges Rs 565 including a buffet lunch (weekends only).

Walking
Even if you don't have the energy or perhaps the inclination to attempt the mighty Annapurna Circuit, there are plenty of short walks in the hills around Pokhara. If you just want to stretch your legs and escape the crowds, just stroll along the north shore of Phewa Tal. A dirt road leads west along the shoreline to the village of Pame Bazar, where you can pick up a bus back to Pokhara.

Another possible hike is the three-hour trip to the viewpoint at **Kahun Danda** (1560m) on the east side of the Seti River. There's a modern viewing tower on the crest of the hill, built over the ruins of an 18th century *kot* (hill-fort). The easiest trail to follow begins near the Manipal Teaching Hospital in Phulbari – ask for directions at the base of the hill. You can also get up here by pony (see p253).

One of the most popular walks around Pokhara is the trip to the World Peace Pagoda (see opposite). For longer walks in the Pokhara area see p268.

TOURS
Travel agents in Pokhara can arrange local tours and activities, but it's just as easy to rent a bike or motorcycle and do things under your own steam – see p253 and p250 for some suggestions.

FESTIVALS & EVENTS
Every August, Pokhara's Newari community celebrates **Bagh Jatra**, which recalls the slaying of a deadly marauding tiger. Gurungs celebrate **Tamu Dhee** (Trahonte) at around the same time, beating drums to drive away evil spirits. August is also time for **Gai Jatra**, when cows are decorated with paint and garlands, and villagers perform

WALKING TO THE WORLD PEACE PAGODA

Balanced on a narrow ridge high above Phewa Tal, the brilliant-white World Peace Pagoda was constructed by Buddhist monks from the Japanese Nipponzan Myohoji organisation to promote world peace. There are three paths up to the pagoda and several small cafés for snacks and drinks once you arrive, but be warned that there have been muggings on the trails in the past. Check the latest situation before you head off. Lone women are particularly at risk because of the perception, justified or otherwise, that they are an easy target.

The Direct Route (One hour)

The most obvious route up to the pagoda begins on the south bank of Phewa Tal, behind the Fewa Resort. Boatmen charge around Rs 200 to the trailhead from Lakeside and the path leads straight up the hillside on cut stone steps. Ignore the right-hand fork by the small temple and continue uphill through woodland to reach the ridge just west of the pagoda. You can either continue on to Pokhara via the scenic route (described below) or go back the way you came.

The Scenic Route (Two hours)

A more interesting route to the pagoda begins near the footbridge over the Pardi Khola, just south of the Phewa dam. After crossing the bridge, the trail skirts the edge of padi fields before turning uphill into the forest near a small brick temple. From here, the trail climbs for about 2km through gorgeous open *sal* forest and follows the ridge west. When you reach a clearing with several ruined stone houses, turn left and climb straight uphill to reach the flat, open area in front of the pagoda. An alternative start point for this route is Devi's Falls – a small but obvious trail crosses the padi fields behind the falls and runs up to meet the main path at the bottom of the forest.

The Easy Route (20 minutes)

For views without the fuss, take a local bus from the public bus stand to Kalimati on the road to Butwal for Rs 5. Several small trails lead up from the road to the school in Kalimati village and on to the entrance to the pagoda.

---

dances to bring peace to the souls of the departed. See p363 for more.

Tibetan Buddhists hold celebrations and masked dances at *gompas* (monasteries) around Pokhara to celebrate **Losar** (Tibetan New Year) in January/February and **Buddha Jayanti** (Buddha's birthday) in April/May. Every April in Basundhara Park, the popular **Annapurna Festival** features dance, music and stalls serving regional foods.

SLEEPING

Most people stay near the lake in Lakeside, a nonstop strip of hotels, budget guesthouses, travel agents, traveller restaurants and souvenir shops. People looking for peace and quiet tend to head to the north end of the strip or skip Lakeside altogether in favour of Damside.

Most hotels in Pokhara have a garden and almost all offer rooms with ceiling fans and hot showers, either in private or shared bathrooms. However, showers tend to be solar-powered, which means no hot water in the morning. Midrange places and better budget hotels provide cable TV, phones and air-con. At the top end, expect the full range of international luxury facilities.

Hotels at the budget end of the spectrum tend not to bother with tax, but midrange and top end hotels add 13% to the bill for VAT and service. Many places list prices in US dollars, but you can always pay in rupees.

Lakeside

As the main traveller centre in Pokhara, Lakeside is packed with hotels – the following hotels are the current pick of the bunch but new places open up all the time so talk to other travellers for recommendations. Take care of your valuables and shut your windows before going out – there have been thefts in the past.

Several of the larger lodges will let you camp in the gardens for a fee, or you can

POKHARA

DISCOUNTS

Rates at Pokhara hotels were always negotiable and with the decline in tourist numbers, this is truer than ever. Most places offer discounts of between 20% and 40% on the published rates, which can bring many midrange hotels down into the budget category. If hotels normally discount their rates, we have mentioned this in the reviews. It may still be worth asking for discount at other hotels, but rates at the cheaper places are often as low as they can go. Most guests at Pokhara's top end hotels arrive on package tours, so there is less incentive for these hotels to offer discount rates. Hotels in this price range normally quote their full rack rates, but discounts may be available if you ask at reception when you check in and discounts are sometimes available during the monsoon.

set up your tent for free in the basic **camping ground**, next to the lake at Camping Chowk. However, there are no facilities, and the nearest toilets are to be found at neighbouring restaurants.

LAKESIDE EAST

Lakeside East is separated from Central Lakeside by the Royal Palace, but it doesn't take long to walk between the two.

Budget

Orient Youth Hostel (Map p257; ☎ 522619; hotel orient@hotmail.com; r with bathroom Rs 250-450, discounts of 20%) On the same alley as Base Camp Resort, this small hotel offers incredibly neat, clean rooms with carpets and colourful bed linen. It's more of a hotel than a hostel, but the rates are a bargain.

New Nanohana Lodge (Map p257; ☎ 522478; nanohana_lodge@hotmail.com; d with bathroom US$4-12, discounts of 20%) Nearby, this banana-yellow hotel is popular with Korean and Japanese travellers and it's excellent value. Each level has a terrace with table and chairs and some rooms have cracking Annapurna views. Before you get too excited about the giant hemp tree in the garden, it's a male.

Blue Planet Lodge (Map p257; ☎ 537472; www .blueplanetlodge.com; r with bathroom Rs 500) No relation to Lonely Planet, this cosy lodge is run by a friendly Belgian-Nepali couple. Rooms

are tidy, comfortable and colourful and a portion of the room rent goes to help disadvantaged children.

Gauri Shankar Guest House (Map p257; ☎ 520 422; dm Rs 100, r with/without bathroom Rs 300/200) Calm, quiet and reasonably priced, Gauri Shankar has small rooms set in a secluded garden of pebbles and bushes. It's simple but friendly and there's a dorm.

Hotel Nirvana (Map p257; ☎ 523332; nirvana@cnet .wlink.com.np; r with bathroom Rs 400-1000, discounts of 30%; 🕸) Almost invisible behind a giant bougainvillea hedge, Hotel Nirvana has high standards. There's a prim garden and the spacious rooms have colourful ethnic bedspreads and curtains.

New Tourist Guest House (Map p257; ☎ 521479; ntgh2002@yahoo.com; s/d Rs 100/120, d with bathroom Rs 150-500) The best of several cinderblock hotels on an alley near the Hindu shrine at Lakeside East. All rooms are no frills but the newer building has nicer rooms than the old building at the back.

Midrange

Almost all the midrange places are in Central Lakeside or Lakeside East. With the slump in tourism, hefty discounts are almost guaranteed. Rooms at all the following hotels come with bathrooms, TVs and phones, unless otherwise indicated.

Hotel Trek-o-Tel (Map p257; ☎ 528996; trekotel@ acehotels.wlink.com.np; s/d US$35/40, discounts of 20%; 🕸) Subtlety is the watchword at this smart modern hotel located in Lakeside East. Everything is tasteful and understated and rooms are housed in octagonal stone blocks in a pretty garden. Many guests are workers for international NGOs – a good marker of quality.

Base Camp Resort (Map p257; ☎ 521226, 522949; basecamppkr@wlink.com.np; s/d US$51/55, discounts of 30%; 🕸) Good service raises this midrange hotel above the crowd. Rooms are contained in tasteful two-storey villas in a garden of palms and bougainvilleas. In-room facilities include cable TV and minibars.

Hotel View Point (Map p257; ☎ 532648; www .hviewpoint.com; r US$25-30, discounts of 30%; 🕸) Another mini-skyscraper, Hotel View Point has excellent mountain views, particularly from the 5th floor terrace. Doubles are roomy and well-appointed and the more expensive rooms have air-con. It's down the alley beside the Laxman Restaurant.

POHKARA LAKESIDE

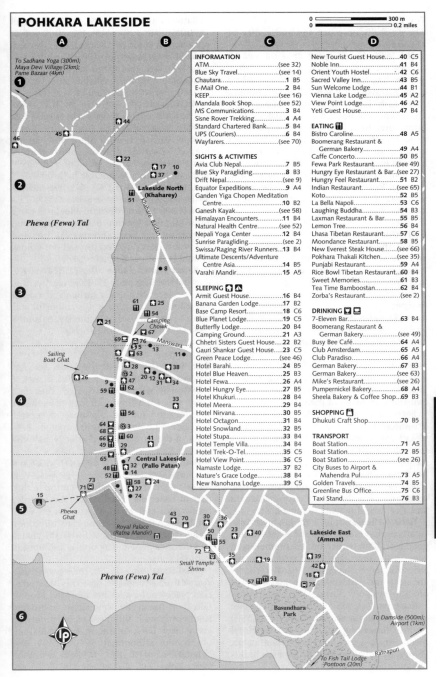

0 ————————— 300 m
0 ————————— 0.2 miles

To Sadhana Yoga (300m);
Maya Devi Village (2km);
Pame Bazaar (4km)

Lakeside North
(Khaharey)

Phewa (Fewa) Tal

Khahare Baidan

Camping
Chowk

Manswara

Sailing
Boat Ghat

Central Lakeside
(Pallo Patan)

Phewa
Ghat

Royal Palace
(Ratna Mandir)

Small Temple
Shrine

Phewa (Fewa) Tal

Lakeside East
(Ammat)

Basundhara
Park

To Damside (500m);
Airport (1km)

To Fish Tail
Pontoon (20m)

Ratnapuri

POKHARA

INFORMATION
ATM..................................(see 32)
Blue Sky Travel...................(see 14)
Chautara..................................1 B5
E-Mail One..............................2 B4
KEEP...................................(see 16)
Mandala Book Shop.............(see 52)
MS Communications................3 B4
Sisne Rover Trekking................4 A4
Standard Chartered Bank.........5 B4
UPS (Couriers).........................6 B4
Wayfarers............................(see 70)

SIGHTS & ACTIVITIES
Avia Club Nepal........................7 B5
Blue Sky Paragliding.................8 B3
Drift Nepal............................(see 9)
Equator Expeditions.................9 A4
Ganden Yiga Chopen Meditation
   Centre..............................10 B2
Ganesh Kayak......................(see 58)
Himalayan Encounters............11 B4
Natural Health Centre...........(see 52)
Nepali Yoga Center 12 B4
Sunrise Paragliding................(see 2)
Swissa/Raging River Runners...13 B4
Ultimate Descents/Adventure
   Centre Asia........................14 B5
Varahi Mandir.......................15 A5

SLEEPING
Armit Guest House..................16 B4
Banana Garden Lodge.............17 B2
Base Camp Resort...................18 C6
Blue Planet Lodge...................19 C5
Butterfly Lodge.......................20 B4
Camping Ground.....................21 A3
Chhetri Sisters Guest House.....22 B2
Gauri Shankar Guest House.....23 C5
Green Peace Lodge................(see 46)
Hotel Barahi...........................24 B5
Hotel Blue Heaven...................25 B3
Hotel Fewa..............................26 A4
Hotel Hungry Eye....................27 B4
Hotel Khukuri.........................28 B4
Hotel Meera............................29 B4
Hotel Nirvana.........................30 B5
Hotel Octagon........................31 B4
Hotel Snowland......................32 B5
Hotel Stupa............................33 B4
Hotel Temple Villa..................34 B4
Hotel Trek-O-Tel.....................35 C5
Hotel View Point.....................36 C5
Namaste Lodge.......................37 B2
Nature's Grace Lodge..............38 B4
New Nanohana Lodge.............39 C5

New Tourist Guest House........40 C5
Noble Inn...............................41 B4
Orient Youth Hostel................42 C6
Sacred Valley Inn....................43 B5
Sun Welcome Lodge................44 B1
Vienna Lake Lodge..................45 A2
View Point Lodge....................46 A2
Yeti Guest House.....................47 B4

EATING
Bistro Caroline........................48 A5
Boomerang Restaurant &
   German Bakery....................49 A4
Caffe Concerto........................50 B5
Fewa Park Restaurant............(see 49)
Hungry Eye Restaurant & Bar..(see 27)
Hungry Feel Restaurant...........51 B2
Indian Restaurant..................(see 65)
Koto.......................................52 B5
La Bella Napoli.......................53 C6
Laughing Buddha....................54 B3
Laxman Restaurant & Bar........55 B5
Lemon Tree............................56 B4
Lhasa Tibetan Restaurant........57 C6
Moondance Restaurant...........58 B5
New Everest Steak House.......(see 66)
Pokhara Thakali Kitchen........(see 35)
Punjabi Restaurant..................59 A4
Rice Bowl Tibetan Restaurant..60 B4
Sweet Memories.....................61 B3
Tea Time Bamboostan.............62 B4
Zorba's Restaurant................(see 2)

DRINKING
7-Eleven Bar...........................63 B4
Boomerang Restaurant &
   German Bakery..................(see 49)
Busy Bee Café.........................64 A4
Club Amsterdam......................65 A5
Club Paradiso..........................66 A4
German Bakers........................67 B3
German Bakery......................(see 63)
Mike's Restaurant..................(see 66)
Pumpernickel Bakery...............68 A4
Sheela Bakery & Coffee Shop...69 B3

SHOPPING
Dhukuti Craft Shop.................70 B5

TRANSPORT
Boat Station............................71 A5
Boat Station............................72 B5
Boat Station..........................(see 26)
City Buses to Airport &
   Mahendra Pul......................73 A5
Golden Travels........................74 B5
Greenline Bus Office................75 C6
Taxi Stand..............................76 B3

Top End

There's really only one top-end choice in Lakeside.

Fish Tail Lodge (Map p257; ☎ 526428; www.fish tail-lodge.com.np; s/d US$95/105, deluxe US$110/120, monsoon discounts of 25%; ✸ ◻ ✿) Reached by a rope-drawn pontoon from Basundhara Park, Fish Tail is charmingly understated and rooms are housed in low slate-roofed bungalows in a lush tropical garden. Its probably the most sensitively designed building in Pokhara and facilities include an outdoor pool and an excellent restaurant and bar (open to nonguests for lunch and dinner). Rooms 16, 17 and 18 have excellent lake and mountain views but you'll need to book well in advance.

CENTRAL LAKESIDE

This is the heart of the action at Lakeside and you're never more than 20 metres from a budget hotel, traveller restaurant, travel agent or Tibetan souvenir shop.

Budget

Sacred Valley Inn (Map p257; ☎ 531792; svalley@cnet .wlink.com.np; r with bathroom US$8-12, upstairs US$15-20, discounts of 20%) Set in a tidy garden across from the Royal Palace, Sacred Valley is a long-established traveller favourite. All the rooms are well maintained and those upstairs have gleaming marble floors and windows on two sides, allowing in plenty of light.

Hotel Snowland (Map p257; ☎ 520384; snow land@cnet.wlink.com.np; rear wing s/d US$15/20, deluxe US$35/45, super deluxe US$55/65, discounts of 30%) Close to the Royal Palace and the city bus stand, the inviting Snowland is a midrange hotel with budget prices. You don't get much of a garden, but you do get huge, clean rooms with red-hot power showers and a calm and relaxing atmosphere.

Yeti Guest House (Map p257; ☎ 520394; r with/without bathroom from Rs 300/250) Some places have a good feel about them from the moment you walk in the door. Yeti is set back from the strip in a large, shady patio garden, rooms are neat and bathrooms are massive. It's often full so book ahead.

Noble Inn (Map p257; ☎ 524926; www.nobleinn .com; r with/without bathroom from Rs 400/250, ste US$15) About 50m along the alley beside Hotel Meera, this big, airy place is excellent value. Plenty of cool air moves through the building and the garden is a delight.

Butterfly Lodge (Map p257; ☎ 522892; pahari _govinda@hotmail.coml; dm Rs 150, r with/without bathroom from Rs 500/200) Spread over several Newari-style buildings down the alley beside 7-Eleven, this lodge feels a bit like a miniature mountain village. Some of the money goes to supporting local children.

Hotel Temple Villa (Map p257; ☎ 521203; temple villa_hotel@hotmail.com; d with/without bathroom from US$10/6, discounts of 30%) A few doors down, Temple Villa feels a bit like a posh family home. The garden is full of exotic butterflies and the bedrooms are spacious and nicely furnished, with large marble bathrooms.

Hotel Octagon (Map p257; ☎ 526978; hotelocta gon@hotmail.com; r with/without bathroom US$10/5, discounts of 20%) Down the same alley, you can't miss this odd-looking octagonal building. Rooms are spotless, showers are hot and the building is carpeted throughout (shoes should be left outside).

Nature's Grace Lodge (Map p257; ☎ 527220; d with/without bathroom Rs 250/150) Nearby, this simple place has a shady garden and a small guest lounge at the back. It's colourful and clean inside and some of the larger rooms have small divan seating areas.

Midrange

Hotel Fewa (Map p257; ☎ 520151; mike@fewa.mos .com.np; s/d US$15/30, s/d cottage US$20/35, discounts of 30%) Run by Mike Frame of Mike's Breakfast fame, this appealing midrange place has a fine location on the lakeshore in central Lakeside. The best rooms are in stone cottages in the garden, styled after Nepali village houses.

Hotel Barahi (Map p257; ☎ 523017; www.barahi .com; s/dUS$32/41, s/d deluxe US$65/81, discounts of 35%; ✸ ✿) A surprisingly refined option in this part of Lakeside, Hotel Barahi has a large, lovely pool and smart air-con rooms with small balconies. The stone-clad buildings make it look a bit like a Swiss ski chalet and there's a pool and a popular and upbeat cultural show.

Hotel Stupa (Map p257; ☎ 522608; hstupa@yahoo .com; s/d US$25/40, discounts of 40%) This big stone-clad place on the alley beside Hotel Mountain Top has a pleasing air of grandeur. Rooms are swish and there are balconies on every level. Look for the miniature statues of the stupa at Bodhnath

Hotel Khukuri (Map p257; ☎ 532549; www.samrat travel.com/hotel; r US$10, r with air-con US$30, discounts of 30%; ❄) Down the alley near 7-Eleven, this smart-looking place attracts lots of Indian tourists on package tours. Rooms are bright and spacious and there's the inevitable rooftop terrace.

Hotel Blue Heaven (Map p257; ☎ 532647; s/d from US$15/22; discounts of 30%; ❄) Just north of Camping Chowk, Blue Heaven is a monumental blue building that gets the best of the views by being taller than all its neighbours. It's not the most sensitive development, but it's a favourite of Indian travellers and rooms are very snug.

Hotel Hungry Eye (Map p257; ☎ 520908; bikram yoshiya@hotmail.com; r US$15, r with air-con US$30, discounts of 30%; ❄) This hotel was one of the first hotels at Lakeside and it's maturing nicely rather than growing old. Rooms are above the Hungry Eye Restaurant and have all the expected midrange mod cons, including spotless tiled bathrooms.

Hotel Meera (Map p257; ☎ 521031; meera@cnet .wlink.com.np; s with/without bathroom US$30/7, d with/without bathroom US$40/10, discounts of 40%; ❄) A huge place covered in New England–style shingles, Hotel Meera attracts an older crowd looking for peace and quiet. There's a good restaurant in a secluded courtyard and rooms have decent midrange facilities.

LAKESIDE NORTH
Things become simpler, quieter, cheaper as you head northwest from Camping Chowk. Call ahead before traipsing out here with all your baggage.

Budget
Banana Garden Lodge (Map p257; ☎ 542401; s/d Rs 80/100) The best and brightest of the budget guesthouses, Banana Garden benefits from genial owners and a lovingly maintained garden. There are two shared solar-heated showers and the owners provide home-style Nepali meals.

Namaste Lodge (Map p257; r without bathroom Rs 100) Next door, Namaste offers simple rooms with two or three beds and ceiling fans, facing the lake. Rooms are smarter upstairs than down.

View Point Lodge (Map p257; ☎ 526218; r with/without bathroom Rs 150/120) Perched above the lakeshore on a small bluff, this charming guesthouse is one of the last old-fashioned traveller hang-outs. Guests tend to be bookish types in search of peace and quiet and

you can swim in the cooling waters of the tal right in front of the lodge. Rooms are basic but clean and some have gorgeous lake views; there's also a brilliant restaurant.

Green Peace Lodge (Map p257; ☎ 532780; r without bathroom Rs 150, d with bathroom from Rs 300) Very similar, Green Peace has two buildings, a rustic lodge overlooking the lake and a larger guesthouse set amongst the padi fields 100m west on the road to Pame Bazar.

Chhetri Sisters Guest House (Map p257; ☎ 524066; trek@3sistersadventure.com; dm Rs 200, r with bathroom Rs 400-700) Much smarter than the surrounding hotels, this tidy brick guesthouse is owned the same people as Chhetri Sisters Trekking. Rooms are tasteful, the location is peaceful and there's a small atrium garden.

Vienna Lake Lodge (Map p257; ☎ 528228; r with bathroom Rs 150, with views Rs 250-350) Up a small track at the north end of the lakeshore development, this spic and span guesthouse has small, bright rooms and balconies full of pot plants looking out over the lake.

Sun Welcome Lodge (Map p257; ☎ 531732; r without bathroom Rs 100) The most inviting of several cheap places on a track leading inland by the Panorama Restaurant. Don't expect the Ritz as rooms contain just a bed and a fan.

DAMSIDE
The area around the Phewa dam is officially known as Pardi, but most people call it Damside. This was one of the first areas to be developed for tourists but with visitor numbers falling, it feels pretty quiet these days. It takes longer than you might think to walk to Lakeside – it's worth investing in a rental bike or motorcycle.

Budget
Rooms at all the following hotels have private bathrooms unless otherwise stated.

Hotel Pokhara Prince (Map p260; ☎ 532632; roshan_tamang@yahoo.com; r Rs 500, discounts of 20%) Near the start of the trail to the World Peace Pagoda, this modern, crazy-paved place has marble floors throughout and small balconies with mountain views. It's not bad value and the bathrooms have tubs and reliably hot showers.

Hotel Twin Peaks Map p260; (☎ 522867; www .pokharainfo.com; s/d from US$8/12, discounts of 30%) Supported by the Pahar Trust, a charity run by ex-Gurkha soldiers, Hotel Twin Peaks feels a bit like a family home. It's spread

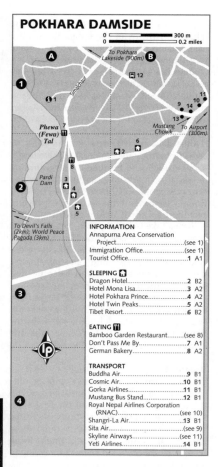

POKHARA DAMSIDE

0 _____ 300 m
0 _____ 0.2 miles

INFORMATION
Annapurna Area Conservation
    Project...................................(see 1)
Immigration Office....................(see 1)
Tourist Office..............................**1** A1

SLEEPING 🏠
Dragon Hotel...............................**2** B2
Hotel Mona Lisa..........................**3** A2
Hotel Pokhara Prince..................**4** A2
Hotel Twin Peaks........................**5** A2
Tibet Resort................................**6** B2

EATING 🍴
Bamboo Garden Restaurant.........(see 8)
Don't Pass Me By.........................**7** A1
German Bakery.............................**8** A2

TRANSPORT
Buddha Air....................................**9** B1
Cosmic Air...................................**10** B1
Gorka Airlines.............................**11** B1
Mustang Bus Stand......................**12** B1
Royal Nepal Airlines Corporation
    (RNAC)...................................(see 10)
Shangri-La Air.............................**13** B1
Sita Air..(see 9)
Skyline Airways...........................(see 11)
Yeti Airlines................................**14** B1

over two buildings linked by a walkway and
some rooms have mountain views.

Hotel Mona Lisa (Map p260; ☎ 520863/523680;
s with/without bathroom US$20/6, d with/without bathroom US$25/10, discounts of) The best and brightest of several similar places in this area, Mona Lisa tempts Japanese visitors with brightly coloured rooms and lounges with low *kokatsu* tables and cushions.

Midrange
There are just a few midrange choices near
the dam.

Dragon Hotel (Map p260; ☎ 520391; dragon@mos
.com.np; s/d with private bathroom Rs 600/700, with bathtub Rs 700/800, discounts of 20%; 🖳) A huge building reached through a private court-

yard, Dragon Hotel is a Pokhara survivor. A timely renovation has raised standards to their old levels and the foyer is full of Tibetan knick-knacks.

Tibet Resort (Map p260; ☎ 520853; tibetres@cnet
.wlink.com.np; s/d with bathroom US$23/34, discounts of 40%; 🖳) Set back from the road in a huge garden full of marigolds, Tibet Resort has mountain views and an air of peace and seclusion. Rooms are homely and there's a restaurant upstairs.

Elsewhere
You don't have to stay by the lake. There are several hotels inland by the airport and a selection of big luxury places outside the centre by the Seti River or high in the hills above town.

WESTERN SHORE
If you want to escape the tourist bustle of Lakeside, there are two peaceful getaways on the southern shore of the lake.

Fewa Resort (Map p266; ☎ 520885; s/d with bathroom US$15/25, discounts of 20%) Right on the lakeshore on the south bank of Phewa Tal, this is the place to come for blissful peace and quiet. Rooms are simple but inviting and each has a massive sun deck facing the lake. Call ahead for transfers from Lakeside.

Raniban Retreat (Map p266; ☎ 531713, 522219; www.raniban.co.uk/ranibanretreat.html; s/d with bathroom US$45/50) Along the ridge from the World Peace Pagoda, this secluded hilltop guesthouse is made up of several attractive stone cottages with awe-inspiring views over the lake and mountains. It's a genuine retreat and all sorts of activities can be arranged by the friendly staff. Call ahead for directions.

AIRPORT AREA
There are a few midrange and top end places near the airport.

Hotel Mount Annapurna (Map p248; ☎ 520037; lodrik@mos.com.np; s/d with bathroom from US$20/30, discounts of 30%; 🖳) Tibetan-owned and decked out with Tibetan knick-knacks, this '60s-style place is faded but friendly and it's very convenient for the airport. Rooms are plain but well-appointed and there's a large walled garden.

New Hotel Crystal (Map p248; ☎ 520035; s/d from US$62/72, discounts of 40%; 🖳) Almost opposite the airport, this sprawling place was once the poshest hotel in town, but it's show-

POKHARA

ing its age these days. Nevertheless, rooms are bright and well-appointed and there's a gloriously chintzy bar, backed by a mural of Bhairab's teeth.

Shangri-la Village (Map p248; ☎ 522122; www .hotelshangrila.com; r with bathroom US$180; 🔀 🖳 🔊) Close to the Seti River, about 1km southeast of the airport, the Shangri-la is a peaceful haven with a wonderful secluded swimming pool. The tasteful rooms are contained in several imaginatively-designed stone buildings and there are glorious mountain views from the gardens. Other luxury facilities include a fine-dining restaurant, sauna and health spa. Ask about discounts during the monsoon.

OUTSKIRTS

If money is no object, there are several luxury resorts hidden away in the hills around Pokhara. Discounts may be available during the monsoon.

Fulbari Resort (Map p266; ☎ 523451; www.fulbari .com; s/d from US$140/150; 🔀 🖳 🔊) South of Pokhara on the east bank of the Seti River, the Fulbari is a vast, five-star resort hotel. It's far enough from town for uninterrupted mountain views and inside you'll find every conceivable luxury, including a huge pool, health spa and golf club.

Tiger Mountain Pokhara Lodge (Map p266; ☎ 01-4361500 in Kathmandu; www.tigermountain.com; cottages per person US$100; 🔀 🖳 🔊) Set on a lofty ridge, Tiger Mountain is about 10km east of town. It's owned by the same team as Tiger Tops at Chitwan and the owners have made a real effort to make the place blend into the surroundings. Rooms are contained in stylish stone bungalows and there's a wonderful mountain-view swimming pool. Rates include meals and transfers to/from Pokhara.

EATING

Pokhara has dozens of restaurants and cafés serving up Western, Nepali and Indian food to hungry travellers and trekkers. Almost every restaurant has the same menu – expect daal bhaat (Nepali plate meals with lentils and rice), momos (Tibetan dumplings), macaroni, pizza and spaghetti, tandoori chicken, chicken in a basket, nachos and burritos, steaks, fish (from the lake) and chips and *rosti* (Swiss potato pancakes).

As well as the following restaurants, there are dozens of ultracheap local canteens offer-

ing momos, chow mein (fried noodles), daal bhaat and fresh fruit juices. Most are fine but do insist on purified water for juices.

Unless otherwise stated, the following restaurants are open from 8am to 10pm.

Lakeside

Lakeside has the best of the traveller restaurants and bars.

LAKESIDE EAST

Caffe Concerto (Map p257; pizzas Rs 120-180) Potted marigolds and jazz on the stereo add to the bistro atmosphere at this cosy Italian place. The thin-crust pizzas are the best in town, wine is available by the glass and the *gelato* (Italian ice cream) is delicious.

Lhasa Tibetan Restaurant (Map p257; meals from Rs 100-250) Piped temple music adds atmosphere at this big Tibetan place near the Royal Palace. The menu runs through familiar momos and *thugpa* (noodle soup) territory and you can warm up after dinner with a tankard of *tongba* (warm millet beer).

Laxman Restaurant & Bar (Map p257; dishes from Rs 90) With video movies, a good selection of north Indian curries and not one but two open fires, Laxman is a great choice for lunch or dinner.

La Bella Napoli (Map p257; pizzas & pasta from Rs 120) Another stalwart on the strip, this traveller restaurant tries its hand at everything. The pizzas and pasta are tasty and good value.

Fish Tail Lodge (Map p257; ☎ 526428; buffet breakfast Rs 525, buffet lunch or dinner Rs 700; 🕑 6am-10pm) The restaurant at the Fish Tail Lodge offers a feast of an evening buffet in exclusive surroundings, over on the south bank of the lake. On clear days, it's worth coming here for a drink in the garden.

CENTRAL LAKESIDE

Moondance Restaurant (Map p257; dishes Rs 80-350) Good service, good food and a roaring open fire all contribute to the popularity of this upmarket-looking place near the palace. The menu features salads, pizzas, steaks and decent Indian curries. There are pool tables upstairs but watch the spiral staircase after a few beers.

New Everest Steak House (Map p257; steaks Rs 175-350) Carnivores flock to this old-fashioned steak house for two-inch thick hunks of freshly grilled beef. Steaks come with a carnival of sauces, but purists go for the

POKHARA

'half steak' – just grilled meat, veg and fries. Steaks come quite rare – ask for 'well done' unless you like it bloody.

Koto (Map p257; mains Rs 100-300 ⏲ 11.30am-3pm & 6-9pm) The Pokhara branch of this popular Kathmandu chain (see p145), never seems that busy but the Japanese food is faultless. The teriyaki beef is highly recommended.

Bistro Caroline (Map p257; mains Rs 90-250) Run by the same people as Chez Caroline in Kathmandu (see p150), this swanky place targets older travellers. It's more a place for a quiet romantic dinner than a noisy evening in the company of strangers but the European, Indian and Nepali food is excellent and there's a good wine list.

Pokhara Thakali Kitchen (Map p257; mains Rs 60-300; ⏲ 11am-9pm) Attached to the Trek-O-Tel, this upmarket Nepali restaurant specialises in the traditional cuisine of the Mustang valley and the menu includes regional delicacies such as dried meat rolled in buckwheat.

Hungry Eye Restaurant & Bar (Map p257; mains Rs 75-350) Close to the Royal Palace, the restaurant at the Hungry Eye Hotel is a long-standing survivor. It looks a bit dated but the food is good and there's a popular cultural show from 6.30pm daily.

Punjabi Restaurant (Map p257; curries Rs 40-200) An authentic, Punjabi-run place churning out tasty vegetarian curries and tandoori breads. The front dining room has quite a lot of character and the vegetarian curries with paneer (Indian cheese) are excellent.

Indian Restaurant (Map p257) A little further along the strip, this place serves similarly good food but it has less atmosphere.

Boomerang Restaurant & German Bakery (Map p257; main dishes Rs 80-350) Probably the best of the 'garden and dinner show' places in central Lakeside, Boomerang has a large, shady garden and cultural shows nightly from 7pm. The roadside bakery is also popular – see the entry for Drinking.

Fewa Park Restaurant Located next door to the Boomerang, Fewa Park Restaurant is almost identical.

Tea Time Bamboostan (Map p257; mains Rs 100-300) This place probably wins the prize for the most imaginative name in Pokhara. It's small and cosy and evenings feature DVD movies and cold bottles of Tuborg and Everest beer. The food isn't bad either.

Rice Bowl Tibetan Restaurant (Map p257; mains Rs 80-200) This inexpensive and laid-back place

opens till late, serving decent Tibetan staples like momos and *thugpa*.

Lemon Tree (Map p257; meals Rs 100-300) Quite smart and sophisticated, Lemon Tree has a broader menu than most and excellent service. It's one of the few restaurants in central Lakeside to serve fresh lake fish.

LAKESIDE NORTH

Things get decidedly quieter as you go north of Camping Chowk, but **Sweet Memories** and **Laughing Buddha** offer the usual traveller standards.

Hungry Feel Restaurant (Map p257; meals Rs 50-150; ⏲ 8am-9pm) North of Lakeside on the road to Pame Bazaar, this welcoming Nepali-style restaurant sits right on the water. Views are the main attraction but the chef cooks up a mean curried lake fish.

Damside

Most people staying in Damside eat in their hotel, but there's a branch of the **German Bakery** chain for breakfast buns and a few traveller restaurants on the road to Birauta Chowk.

Bamboo Garden Restaurant (Map p260; mains Rs 90-200) Above the German Bakery, this laid-back place serves all the usual traveller favourites and the terrace catches evening breezes.

Don't Pass Me By (Map p260; mains Rs 100-250) A cosy little restaurant on the edge of the lake, where you can sit outside and enjoy pretty good travellers' fare at reasonable prices.

DRINKING
Bars

Pokhara nightlife generally winds down around 10pm, but if you've just come back from the hills and you want to party late, a handful of bars flaunt the rules and rock till around midnight. Local bands move from bar to bar on a nightly rotation, playing covers of Western rock hits.

Club Amsterdam (Map p257; ⏲ 11am-midnight) An old favourite on the strip, Club Amsterdam is lively and loud. Head out to the firepit in the garden if you want a quiet conversation.

Club Paradiso (Map p257; ⏲ noon-11.30pm) Loud and brash may be just what you are looking for after weeks in the hills. Club Paradiso has a pool table and deafening pop and it pulls in as many local teenagers as foreigners.

Busy Bee Café (Map p257; ⏲ 10am-11.30pm) Down an alley opposite the Maya Restaurant, Busy Bee is a relatively new arrival on the Pokhara scene. Live bands play on a cramped stage inside, but most drinkers hang out by the fire in the cosy courtyard.

7-Eleven Bar (Map p257; ☻ 6pm-11pm) Just before Camping Chowk, this is a dark bar with loud Hindi pop. It's popular with Indian visitors, less so with Westerners.

Cafés

There are plenty of cafés along the strip in Lakeside where you can sit back with a book and snacks, pastries and a reasonable interpretation of a proper cup of coffee. The following cafés open at around 7am.

Pumpernickel Bakery (Map p257; cakes & sandwiches Rs 20-100) Down an alley off the main drag, this down to earth place has a quiet garden where you can read and munch on sticky cakes with convincing coffee.

Boomerang Restaurant & German Bakery (Map p257; breakfast from Rs 50) The bakery in front of the Boomerang Restaurant serves up fresh baked cakes and buns and decent coffee. There are two other German Bakery branches in Lakeside and one in Damside.

Mike's Restaurant (Map p257; sandwiches Rs 100 to Rs 140) Another enterprise by Mike of Mike's Breakfast in Kathmandu, this lakeside café at Hotel Fewa serves good tea and coffee and gourmet sandwiches.

Sheela Bakery & Coffee Shop (Map p257; sandwiches & cakes from Rs 40) Right by Camping Chowk, this popular little bakery tempts early risers with cakes and freshly-baked baguettes.

If you run out of steam on the walk to Pame Bazaar, **Maya Devi Village** (p266) serves daal bhaat and cold drinks and you can see the parahawks at their roost.

ENTERTAINMENT

Dozens of restaurants and bars offer cheap beers and pirate DVDs of the latest Hollywood blockbusters. Just walk along the strip at Lakeside to see which venues are pulling in a crowd.

Another option is to take in a Nepali cultural show in Lakeside. Several restaurants along the strip have nightly song and dance shows that are enthusiastic, if not entirely authentic. There's no additional charge and most shows start at 6.30pm or 7pm – try **Fewa Park Restaurant**, **Boomerang Restaurant** or **Hungry Eye Restaurant** (see p261).

In Central Lakeside, **Hotel Barahi** (p258) has an upmarket evening buffet dinner and cultural show from 6.30pm (US$10). If you reserve a table early, you can use the pool for free during the day.

Next to the Baglung bus park, the **Kalpana Cinema Hall** (Map p248; ☎ 520157) screens Nepali films and Bollywood imports, plus the occasional Western blockbuster.

SHOPPING

If you've been to Thamel in Kathmandu, you know what to expect. Dozens of traveller boutiques in Lakeside sell pirate CDs, Buddhist masks, prayer flags, counterfeit trekking gear, Kashmiri carpets, Indian wall hangings, Nepali *khukuri* knives and antiques of dubious antiquity. Pokhara is also a good place to pick up *saligrams* – fossilised sea creatures from the Kali Gandaki valley – but these are often overpriced.

Close to the Royal Palace in Lakeside East, **Dhukuti** (Map p257; www.acp.org.np; ☻ 9am-7pm, from 10am Sat/Sun) sells an interesting selection of arts and crafts produced by village cooperatives around Nepal, and prices are fixed.

As well as the shops in Lakeside, legions of Tibetan refugee women wander from restaurant to restaurant offering Tibetan knick-knacks for sale. For a better selection of Tibetan arts and crafts, including handmade carpets, head to the Tashi Palkhel and Tashi Ling Tibetan communities north and south of Pokhara – see p253.

GETTING THERE & AWAY

Pokhara has good bus and air links to other parts of the country, but overland routes are often affected by the security situation in the country. Check locally before making any long journeys by bus.

Air

Royal Nepal Airlines Corporation (RNAC; ☎ 521021) and several private airlines offer regular daily shuttle flights between Kathmandu and Pokhara (US$65 to US$76, 20 minutes). There are great Himalayan views if you sit on the right-hand side of the plane heading into Pokhara (or the left, on the way to Kathmandu).

RNAC and **Gorkha Airlines** (☎ 525971) also offer flights to Jomsom (from US$54, 20 minutes), on the Annapurna Circuit trail. RNAC also has a flight to Manang (US$54,

POKHARA

25 minutes). The only flights to the Terai are the four weekly RNAC shuttle flights to Bharatpur (US$44, 20 minutes).

All the airlines have offices opposite the airport near Mustang Chowk but it's usually easier to get one of the travel agents in Lakeside to do the running around for a ticket. The domestic departure tax from Pokhara is Rs 170.

Bus

There are three bus stations in Pokhara. The dusty and chaotic main public bus stand at the northeast end of the Pokhara airstrip has buses to Kathmandu and towns in the Terai. The main ticket office is at the back and the office for night buses is at the top of the steps near the main highway.

Tourist buses to Kathmandu and Royal Chitwan National Park leave from the Mustang bus stand at Mustang Chowk, while buses to the trailheads for the Annapurna Conservation Area leave from the **Baglung bus park** (Map p248), about 2km north of the centre on the main highway.

Day buses run from around 5am to noon, while night buses leave between 4pm and 6pm. However, night services only run during lulls in violence between Maoist rebels and the government.

TO/FROM KATHMANDU

The bus trip between Kathmandu and Pokhara takes six to eight hours, depending on the condition of the road and the number of army checkpoints along the way. All buses make a stop at a roadside restaurant along the way.

Tourist buses are the most hassle-free option – in Pokhara buses leave from the Mustang bus stand near Lakeside. It costs Rs 250 to Rs 300, depending on which travel agent you book with, buses leave at 7am from either end. Taxis meet the tourist buses on arrival but watch out for touts.

Greenline (Map p257; ☎ 531472; www.catmando .com/greenline) has a daily air-con bus to Thamel (US$12, with breakfast) at 7.30am from its depot in Lakeside South. **Golden Travels** (Map p257; ☎ 523096) has a similar service to Durbar Marg in central Kathmandu, leaving from the Mustang bus stand at 7.30am (US$10/12 with/without lunch).

Public buses to Kathmandu (day/night Rs 190/210) leave from the main public bus station. Faster minibuses run to Kathmandu (Kalanki) for Rs 325. In Pokhara, you can pick up minibuses on the highway in front of the public bus stand.

Stops along the road to Kathmandu include Dumre (Rs 75, two hours), Abu Khaireni (Rs 90, three hours) and Mugling/ Manakamana (Rs 95, four hours). There are also four daily direct buses to Gorkha (Rs 110, five hours). See p236 for more information on sights and stopovers along the way.

TO/FROM ROYAL CHITWAN NATIONAL PARK

With the slump in tourism to the Terai, the best way to get to Chitwan is by tourist bus. Buses leave the Mustang bus park daily at 7.30am for Chitrasali (Rs 300 to Rs 350, seven hours) on the outskirts of the park, where jeeps wait to transfer travellers to Sauraha – see p275 for details. Any travel agent in Lakeside can book tickets.

Greenline (left) has a daily deluxe air-con bus to Chitrasali (US$10) at 7.30am from its depot in Lakeside South.

Public buses to Sauraha Chowk/Tadi Bazaar (Rs 90, five hours), on the Mahendra Hwy 5km north of Sauraha, leave from the public bus stand but it's a long, slow rickshaw ride from the junction to Sauraha village.

TO/FROM THE INDIAN BORDER

The closest border crossing to Pokhara is Sunauli, just south of the town of Bhairawa, but you can also cross at Mahendranagar, Nepalganj, Birganj and Kakarbhitta. See the individual towns in the Terai chapter for more details on transport to India.

Travel agents may try to tempt you with the offer of tourist buses to the border and direct buses to towns in India. Don't be fooled – there are no tourist buses to Sunauli and no through-buses to India; without exception, you must change at the border.

From the main public bus stand, there are nearly 20 day and night buses daily for Bhairawa (Rs 230/270/305 day/night/minibus; eight hours), where you can pick up a local bus to the border post at Sunauli.

There are also day/night buses to Birganj (Rs 225/270, nine hours) and Nepalganj (Rs 400/520, 12 hours), Mahendranagar (Rs 728, 16 hours) and Kakarbhitta (Rs 530, 13 hours).

TO/FROM THE TERAI

As well as the buses to the Indian border, there are regular day/night services to Narayangarh (Rs 120/140, four hours), where you can changes to buses east and west along the Mahendra Hwy. A few buses leave early in the morning for Biratnagar (Rs 480, 12 hours) and Janakpur (Rs 325, 10 hours). All buses leave from the main bus stand.

Most buses go via Mugling, but there are also buses along the dramatic Siddhartha Hwy to Butwal (Rs 160, six hours) and Tansen (Rs 130, four hours).

TO/FROM TREKKING ROUTES

Buses to the trailheads for most treks in the Annapurna Conservation Area (such as the Jomsom Trek) leave from the Baglung bus park at Bhairab Tole. One important exception is the Annapurna Circuit trek, which normally starts at Besisahar. See p333 and p268 for more information on these trekking routes.

The following stops are all on the bus route from Pokhara to Beni:

Stop	Fare (Rs)	Duration (Hrs)	Trek
Hyangja	15	1	Ghachok Trek
Phedi	30	1½	Ghorapani (Poon Hill) to Ghandruk Trek
Naya Pul	55	2	Ghorapani (Poon Hill) to Ghandruk Trek, Annapurna Sanctuary Trek, Jomsom Trek
Baglung	80	3	Jomsom Trek
Beni	130	4	Jomsom Trek

Buses leave about every half hour from 5.30am to 3.30pm. Cranky old Toyota taxis leave from the same bus stand – the fare is Rs 600 to Phedi and Naya Pul, Rs 1250 to Baglung and Rs 2000 to Beni.

For Besisahar (Rs 120, five hours), there are two early morning and two lunchtime buses from the main public bus stand, or you can take a bus bound for Kathmandu and change at Dumre.

GETTING AROUND
Bicycle

There are lots of bicycle rental places at Lakeside – see p253 for hire prices.

Boat

Boatmen at Lakeside offer shuttle services around the lake. Expect to pay Rs 250 from Lakeside to the Fewa Resort (for the trail to the World Peace Pagoda) and Rs 350 between Lakeside and Khapeudi (for the alternative trail to Sarangkot).

Bus

Small local buses shuttle between Lakeside, the airport, the public bus stand and Mahendra Pul but routes are erratic and there isn't much space for baggage. Fares start at Rs 9.

Local buses to Pame Bazaar (Rs 5) and other places on the north shore of Phewa Tal leave Camping Chowk every hour or so until mid-afternoon.

Motorcycle

Several places in Lakeside rent out motorcycle and scooters for around Rs 400 per day. Check the bikes out first to make sure they start up easily and brake smoothly.

Taxi

Taxis meet tourist buses at the Mustang Chowk bus stand, but you can expect a hotel tout to come along for the ride. The fare to Lakeside is Rs 80 whether you take the tout's advice or not, so insist on being taken where you want to go. Heading out from Lakeside, you'll pay Rs 100 to the public bus stand, the Baglung bus stand or the airport.

AROUND POKHARA

Trekking in the Annapurna Conservation Area is easily the biggest attraction around Pokhara (see p323 for details) but you don't have to be a seasoned trekker to appreciate the glory of the peaks. There are several dramatic viewpoints on the rim of the Pokhara Valley that can be reached by taxi, mountain bike or rented motorcycle from Pokhara, and gorgeous Begnas Tal and Rupa Tal offer similar lake and mountain vistas to Phewa Tal, but without the crowds.

SARANGKOT

The view of the Annapurna Himalaya from **Sarangkot** (foreigner/Nepali Rs 25/10) is almost a religious experience. From here, you can see a panoramic sweep of Himalayan peaks, from Dhaulagiri (8167m) in the west to the

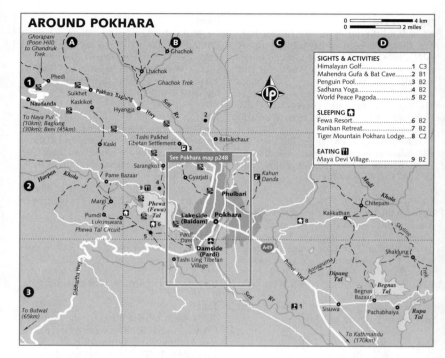

AROUND POKHARA

0		4 km
0		2 miles

SIGHTS & ACTIVITIES
Himalayan Golf..............................1 C3
Mahendra Gufa & Bat Cave........2 B1
Penguin Pool.................................3 B2
Sadhana Yoga................................4 B2
World Peace Pagoda....................5 B2

SLEEPING 🛏
Fewa Resort...................................6 B2
Raniban Retreat............................7 B2
Tiger Mountain Pokhara Lodge...8 C2

EATING 🍴
Maya Devi Village.........................9 B2

perfect pyramid that is Machhapuchhare (6997m) and the rounded peak of Annapurna II (7937m) in the east. Most people come here at dawn or dusk, when the sun picks out the peaks in brilliant colours.

The main village is just below the ridge, but a set of steps leads uphill to a dramatic viewpoint in the ruins of an ancient *kot* (hill fort). It is currently occupied by the army, but photography is fine, as long as you don't take pictures of the soldiers.

There's another ruined fort at **Kaskikot** (1788m), a one-hour walk west of Sarangkot along the ridge road, with similarly jaw-dropping views.

Sleeping & Eating

There are loads of places to stay and eat in Sarangkot. The cheapest options are along the concrete steps to the fort.

Lake View Lodge (r with/without bathroom Rs 250/150) The best of the cheapies, Lake View is honest about its assets – some rooms do indeed have lake views.

There are a few upmarket choices just downhill from the village.

Hotel Annapurna & Sherpa (☎ 9851088746; r from Rs 350) This inviting hotel is set in a neat garden and the cosy rooms have hot showers.

Mountain View Lodge (☎ 9846028278; r with/without bathroom Rs 250/250) Nearby, the Mountain View doesn't actually have mountain views, but it's comfortable, quiet and welcoming.

Getting There & Away

Taxi drivers in Lakeside offer dawn rides up to the ridge to catch the morning sunrise for around Rs 500, but you must walk the final 1km along a pitted motorcycle track. The taxi fare is the same whether the driver waits to drive you back or you walk down.

By motorcycle or mountain bike, follow the road that branches off the Baglung Hwy near the Bindhya Basini Temple. When the road levels out below the ridge, look for the Sarangkot turning on the right, opposite a large group of tin-roofed school buildings. For details of the ride out to Sarangkot and on to Naudanda see p88.

A more challenging option is the three- to four-hour walk from Pokhara. The most popular path begins on the highway opposite the Baglung bus park. The obvious trail runs west across the fields and up the side of Gyarjati Hill, meeting the dirt road at Silangabot, about 1km east of the Sarangkot turning.

There's also a scenic route from Phewa Tal but the trail is hard to follow and there have been muggings along this path. The trail begins near the village of Khapeudi on the road to Pame Bazaar (look for the signpost about 50m after the Green Peace Lodge), meeting the road just west of the turn-off to Sarangkot. It's usually easier to follow this trail on the way down.

MAHENDRA GUFA & BAT CAVE

The limestone bedrock of the Pokhara Valley is perforated by caves and underground streams, several of which can easily be visited from Pokhara on foot, by bike or by taxi. A return taxi to the following sites will cost Rs 500, including waiting time. A return taxi ride to these sites will cost Rs 500 including waiting time. Alternatively, the caves can be reached on foot or by bicycle from Lakeside.

The first large cave to be discovered near Pokhara, **Mahendra Gufa** (Map p266; foreigner/Nepali Rs 10/5; ◷ 7am-6pm) is popular with Indian and Nepali tourists, but the main tunnel is lit by electric bulbs and it doesn't have much atmosphere. Several stalactites are revered as Shiva lingams. The cave is about 6km north of Lakeside in the suburb of Batulechaur.

You won't find Michael Keaton, Val Kilmer or Christian Bale lurking in the dark and spooky **Bat Cave** (Map p266; Chameri Gufa; foreigner/Nepali Rs 10/5; ◷ 6am-6pm). What you will find is thousands of live horseshoe bats, clinging to the ceiling of a damp and slippery chamber and occasionally chirruping into the darkness – claustrophobics beware. A slippery path leads down into the darkness to a low vault where thousands of horseshoe bats cling to the ceiling – claustrophobics beware! Daredevils can continue to the back of the vault and wriggle out through a tiny chute to the surface. Torches can be hired for Rs 15, and guides (no fixed rate) can show you the narrow exit tunnel. Ask about tours to other newly-discovered caves. The cave is a 10-minute walk south from Mahendra Gufa.

BEGNAS TAL & RUPA TAL

About 10km southeast of Pokhara, a road leaves the Prithvi Hwy for Begnas Tal and Rupa Tal, two gloriously serene lakes that see few foreign visitors, despite their proximity to Pokhara. The hiking trail between the lakes forms the final leg of the popular Annapurna Skyline Trek.

Local buses run from the highway opposite the main Pokhara bus stand to Begnas Bazaar on the shore of picturesque Begnas Tal. It's a peaceful spot and the mountains of the Annapurna Range are brilliantly reflected in the rippling waters. If you feel energetic, you can rent boats for leisurely paddles on the lake for Rs 200/150 per hour (foreign/Nepali).

Rupa Tal is via a 3km hike along the trail that winds uphill from the bus stand in Begnas Bazar. It's much more isolated than Begnas Tal but the surrounding countryside is delightful and you can stay at several laid-back teahouses on the ridge overlooking the lake.

Sleeping & Eating

There are guesthouses in Begnas Tal and along the ridge above Rupa Tal.

Hotel Day Break & Restaurant (☎ 560011; s/d with bathroom Rs 150/200) At the start of the walking trail in Begnas Bazaar, this friendly, family-run place has bright rooms with Formica floors, hot showers and mountain views from the roof.

Annapurna Lake View (r Rs 200) Reached via the path across the Begnas Tal dam, this rustic ridge-top guesthouse has two rudimentary rooms and a café looking out over the lake.

Rupa View Point (d Rs 200) A lovely family-run place above the village of Pachabhaiya, overlooking Rupa Tal. There are just two rooms and evening meals are prepared by the farmer's wife. To get here, follow the signposted path off the main trail, then take the steps on the left, then the path on the right.

Getting There & Away

Buses to Begnas Tal (Rs 20, 20 minutes) stop on the highway opposite the main public bus stand in Pokhara. By bike or motorcycle, take the Prithvi Hwy towards Mugling and turn left at the obvious junction in Tal Chowk.

POKHARA

SHORT TREKS AROUND POKHARA

Without the Himalaya, there would be no Pokhara, at least in tourist terms. You'll need at least a week to reach the snowline on the Jomsom or Annapurna Sanctuary Treks (see p323 for details), but there are some fascinating short treks in the lower foothills that afford epic views of the Annapurna Himalaya.

Most villages in the area have basic teahouses where you can find a meal (almost invariably chow mein or daal bhaat) and a bed for the night, and the only specialist gear required is a sleeping bag and a warm jacket for the evenings. Nevertheless, the usual precautions for safe and responsible trekking apply (see p330 and p330).

Most of the trails are easy to follow, but there have been robberies along a few of the routes, so it makes sense to travel in a group. You should also equip yourself with a suitable map, particularly if you fancy branching off the established tourist route. Lonely Planet's *Trekking in the Nepal Himalaya* has more detail on trekking options around Pokhara.

The Phewa Tal Circuit (One Day)

If you get an early start, it's possible to walk right around the shore of Phewa Tal, beginning on the path to the Peace Pagoda. Starting from the Peace Pagoda, continue along the ridge to the village of Lukunswara and take the right fork where the path divides. Once you reach Pumdi, ask around for the path down to Margi on the edge of the lake. From Margi, you can either cut across the marshes over a series of log bridges or continue around the edge of the valley to the suspension bridge at Pame Bazaar, where a dirt road continues along the northern shore to Pokhara. If you run out of energy, local buses pass by every hour or so.

Ghachok Trek (Two Days)

This interesting two-day trek goes north from Pokhara to the traditional Gurung villages around Ghachok. It starts from Hyangja, near the Tashi Palkhel Tibetan settlement, and crosses the Mardi Khola to Lhachok before ascending to the stonewalled village of Ghachok, where you can stop overnight before turning south and returning to Pokhara via Batulechaur. With more time, you can extend this walk to visit some even more remote villages in the valley leading north from Ghachok.

Ghorapani (Poon Hill) to Ghandruk Loop (Six Days)

In an area packed with mountain viewpoints, Poon Hill (3210m) stands out. A steep 1.5km walk above Ghorapani, this exposed bluff looks out over an incredible vista of snowy peaks, including Annapurna South (7273m) and Machhapuchhare (6997m). Some people include Poon Hill as a detour on the Annapurna Circuit or Jomsom Treks, but it's also a popular trekking destination in its own right.

Most people include Poon Hill as part of the popular six-day Ghorapani to Ghandruk Loop, which also includes a stop at the Gurung village of Ghandruk. However, there have been robberies on this trail, particularly between Ghorapani and Ghandruk, so travel in a group.

The trail starts at Naya Pul, on the road from Pokhara to Baglung, and follows the Jomsom trail for the first two days, with overnight stops in Tikedhunga and Ghorapani. On day three, most people leave before dawn for the hike to Poon Hill and relax in Ghorapani for the rest of the day.

Day four involves a gentle descent to Tadapani, and day five continues downhill to Ghandruk, a scenic village of stone and slate houses with a colourful Buddhist monastery. The final day is an easy descent back to Naya Pul, where you can pick up buses back to Pokhara. Alternatively, head east across the valley to Landruk and stop overnight at Tolka, before continuing to Phedi on the Baglung hwy.

Tatopani (Hot Spring) Loop (Four Days)

A variation on the same theme, this four-day trek follows the Jomsom trail for three days to the geothermal springs at Tatopani, before turning south along the gorge of the Kali Gandaki River. The most popular route begins at Naya Pul and runs north through Tikedhunga and Ghorapani to Tatopani before turning south to Beni (see p345 for details of the route as far as Ghorapani). An alternative five-day route follows the Annapurna Sanctuary Trek to Landruk before branching west to meet the main trail at Ghorapani.

From Ghorapani, the route follows the Jomsom trail to Tatopani ('hot springs' in Nepali), an attractive village on the Kali Gandaki River. The eponymous hot springs (Rs 10 entry per person) are down on the river bank and you'll need a swimming costume if you want to experience the soothing effect of warm water on tired muscles. The return leg is a long day following the Kali Gandaki down to Beni, where you can pick up a bus back to Pokhara.

ANNAPURNA SKYLINE TREK (ROYAL TREK)

Following a low ridge east of Pokhara, with spine-tingling views of the Annapurna peaks, the four-day Annapurna Skyline Trek (or Royal Trek) was famously walked by Britain's Prince Charles in 1980. It's an ideal walk for families with children as the path is wide and easy to follow and the highest point is less than 2000m. However, because it lies off the main tourist circuit, there is no teahouse accommodation en route, except at Begnas Tal. Most people bring a stove and camp at basic campsites along the route.

The trail starts near the army camp on the Prithvi Hwy, just east of the Bijayapur Khola, and cross a flat area of rice fields before climbing the ridge to the village of Kalikathan (1370m), which has two basic campsites with fine views. On the second day, the trail follows the forested ridge through Thulokot to Mati Thana, where you can take a teashop lunch, before climbing to Naudanda, Lipini and finally Shaklung (1730m) with another simple camping ground.

On day three, the trail descends to the valley floor, then rises to the attractive Gurung village of Chisopani (1629m) – the campsite is a short walk beyond the village near a ridge-top temple and the views are sublime. The final day involves a leisurely stroll along the ridge that separates Rupa Tal and Begnas Tal, emerging on the valley floor at Begnas Bazaar (see p267), where buses leave regularly for Pokhara.

The Terai & Mahabharat Range

Hanging out in the plains might not be the first thing that comes to mind when visiting the world's most mountainous nation, but the Terai is a fascinating and varied place and most people see only a tiny fraction of it as they rush between the Indian border and the hills. There are plains and jungles, forts and temples, ancient monuments and national parks, wilderness and bustling bazaars, plus the lush green landscape of the Chure and Mahabharat hills. If you thought the Terai was all pancake flat, prepare to be pleasantly surprised.

The vast majority of travellers follow a well-established route through the Terai, from Kathmandu or Pokhara to Royal Chitwan National Park and on to the Indian border crossing at Sunauli. However, more and more people are escaping this touristy circuit and discovering the cities of the Terai – places like Janakpur and Tansen – and the historical birthplace of the Buddha at Lumbini. If you're heading to India, don't restrict yourself to Sunauli – there are four other border crossings between India and Nepal, providing easy access to Delhi, Agra, Varanasi, Lucknow and Darjeeling.

Tourism to the Terai dropped off markedly in the early years of the Maoist uprising, but visitor numbers seem to be slowly creeping upwards. However, the situation remains volatile and the long-term future of tourism in the Terai depends on the government and Maoists finding a political solution to their grievances. At the time of writing, the most obvious signs of the insurgency were the army roadblocks along major highways, but it's essential to check the latest security situation before you visit (see p19).

HIGHLIGHTS

- Spot rhinos from the back of another jungle giant – the Indian elephant – in **Royal Chitwan National Park** (p281)
- Visit **Sauraha** (p280) to scrub a jumbo at elephant bathtime
- Hike to **Chepang villages** (p288) on the new trekking route to the Chitwan Hills
- Tour terrific temples and hike to the fabulous Ranighat Durbar from the hill town of **Tansen** (p298)
- See the jungle without the crowds at **Royal Bardia National Park** (p308) in the western Terai
- Support women artisans at the **Janakpur Women's Development Centre** (p312) in Janakpur
- When the hills are peaceful, stay in a traditional Tibetan lodge in lofty **Hile** (p320)

History

Travelling through the Terai today, it's hard to believe that this was once one of the most important places in the subcontinent. In 563 BC, the queen of the tiny kingdom of Kapilavastu gave birth to a son named Siddhartha Gautama and 35 years later, under a Bodhi tree at Bodhgaya in India, Buddhism was born. The Indian Buddhist emperor Ashoka made a famous pilgrimage here in 249 BC, leaving a commemorative pillar at the site of the Buddha's birth in Lumbini.

Nepal also played a pivotal role in the development of Hinduism. Sita, the wife of Rama and heroine of the Ramayana, was the daughter of the historical king Janak, who ruled large parts of the plains from his capital at Janakpur. Janak founded the Mithila kingdom, which flourished until the third century AD, when its lands were seized by the Gutpas from Patna in northern India.

The depopulation of the Terai began in earnest in the 14th century, when the Mughals swept across the plains of northern India. Hundreds of thousands of Hindu and Buddhist refugees fled up into the hills, many settling in the Kathmandu valley, which later rose to prominence as the capital of the Shah dynasty. Aided by legions of fearsome Gurkha warriors, the Shahs reclaimed the plains, expanding the borders of Nepal to twice their modern size.

Although the British never conquered Nepal, they had regular skirmishes with the Shahs. A treaty was signed in 1816 that trimmed the kingdom to roughly its current borders. Nepal later regained some additional land (including the city of Nepalganj) as a reward for assisting the British in the 1857 Indian Uprising.

The Terai was covered by swathes of jungle well into the 1950s. The indigenous people of the plains, the Tharu, lived an almost stone-age existence until 1954, when DDT was used to drive malaria from the plains and thousands of land-hungry farmers flocked into the Terai from India and the Nepali hills.

Today, the Tharu are one of the most disadvantaged groups in Nepal, and huge areas of the forest have been sacrificed for farmland and industrial development. Nevertheless, some large patches of wilderness remain, preserved in a series of excellent national parks, and the massive industrial and agricultural development in the plains is slowly raising the quality of life for the nation, at least in economic terms.

Climate

The Terai has a similar climate to the northern plains of India – hot as a furnace from May to October and drenched by monsoon rains from June to September. Try to visit in winter (November to February) when skies are clear and temperatures are moderate. The annual monsoon rains can severely affect transport in the region – dirt roads turn to mud, dry stream beds become raging torrents and roads and bridges are routinely washed away. Allow extra time for any long-distance journeys and be prepared to fly if necessary to get around these obstacles.

Dangers & Annoyances

There is a lot of misinformation about the safety of travel in the Terai. Tourist offices often insist that everything is safe while embassies claim that it's dangerous to even leave the Kathmandu Valley. In reality, the safety of travel depends on the current status of negotiations between the Maoists and the Nepali government. During ceasefires, everything operates as normal, but violence can flare up quickly so it's important to check the security situation before you visit. There are few areas where travel is particularly risky – the far west of Nepal is the heartland of the Maoist insurgency and attacks on government installations are common, particularly north of the Mahendra Hwy. The hills in the far east of Nepal are another potential flashpoint, particularly close to the border with Sikkim. Things are generally peaceful in the central Terai but there have been attacks in the villages around Royal Chitwan National Park (including Sauraha), and more recently, near Lumbini. For more on security issues see p19).

The most obvious sign of the insurgency for travellers is the network of army checkpoints on all major roads. Foreigners are usually waved straight through, but locals must disembark for questioning and bag checks, which can add hours to journey times. At times of conflict, night-time curfews are imposed across the Terai.

An equally pressing problem for tourists is the risky nature of road transport in the Terai, see p272 for more information. Another potential problem for travellers is the annual monsoon. Rivers already swelled by meltwater from the mountains are inundated by rainwater and floods are inevitable.

Getting There & Away

The Terai is easily accessible from Kathmandu and Pokhara in Nepal and from West Bengal, Bihar and Uttar Pradesh in India. The Indian rail network passes close to several of the most important border crossings and there are frequent bus and air connections from the Terai to towns and villages across Nepal.

AIR

Royal Nepal Airlines Corporation (RNAC; www .royalnepal.com) and many private airlines offer flights around the Terai. Currently, you can fly from Kathmandu or Pokhara to Nepalganj, Biratnagar, Bharatpur, Bhairawa, Janakpur, Simara (for Birganj) and Bhadrapur (for Kakarbhitta) – see these individual towns for details. Prices for flights around the Terai are also listed on the Nepal Air Fares map, p383.

LAND

All of Nepal's land border crossings are in the Terai. Heading from east to west, you can cross between India and Nepal at the following points:

Border crossing (Nepal to India)		Page
Mahendranagar to Banbassa	for Delhi & hill towns in Uttaranchal	p311
Nepalganj to Jamunaha	for Lucknow	p307
Belahiya to Sunauli	for Varanasi, Agra & Delhi	p290
Birganj to Raxaul Bazar	for Patna & Kolkata	p302
Kakarbhitta to Panitanki	for Darjeeling, Sikkim & Kolkata	p322

The Sunauli crossing is by far the most popular route between the two countries, but immigration staff are used to seeing foreign tourists at all the crossings and Nepali visas are available on arrival. You need one passport photo and US dollars cash for the visa fee (currently US$30 for a single entry visa and US$80 for multiple entry).

Details of border opening times and onwards travel into India are included in the

'Crossing the Border' boxed texts under Sunauli, Nepalganj, Birganj, Mahendranagar and Kakarbhitta. For more on crossing between Nepal and India, see p380.

Getting Around

Buses and minibuses are the main form of transport around the Terai with the Maoist ceasefire, night services have resumed between Kathmandu and Pokhara and the main border crossings. However, road safety can be an issue, particularly for night travel – see below for more information.

BICYCLE

On the face of it, the Terai is perfectly suited for cycling – the terrain is pool-table flat, there are villages every few miles and traffic is relatively sparse. However, the condition of the roads leaves a lot to be desired – a sturdy mountain bike is strongly recommended. If you run out of steam along the way, you can usually put your bike on the roof of the bus. See p86 for details of biking routes from Kathmandu to Hetauda and Hetauda to Mugling (p87), as well as general biking information.

BUS

Buses are the main form of transport around the Terai, but road safety is a big concern. Hundreds of Nepalis are killed every year in bus crashes and many expats and NGO workers prefer to fly rather than gamble on the buses. Night buses are by far the worst offenders. To maximise safety, travel in daylight hours and avoid the front seats.

Roof riding is prohibited in the Kathmandu Valley but there is no such proscription in the Terai. Riding on the luggage rack with the wind in your hair can be an exhilarating experience, but you also need to consider deadly hairpin turns and hanging power cables – all in all, it's best to stick to short local bus routes.

Buses in the Terai are divided into 'day' and 'night' services – day buses generally leave between 5am and noon, while more expensive night buses typically depart between 4pm and 6pm. There are separate ticket desks for day and night buses at many bus stations – you'll have to ask around to find the right desk. See p385 for more details on bus travel.

CAR

To avoid the hassle of local bus services, you can hire a car and driver in Kathmandu. Most travel agencies can make arrangements and the going rate for a Toyota Corolla and driver is around Rs 4000 per day, including petrol. On top of this, you must also pay for road tolls and meals and accommodation for the driver.

TRAIN

A single narrow-gauge train line runs between Janakpur and the Indian border. Foreign tourists can't cross into India via this route but the train makes for a great excursion from Janakpur – see p312 for details.

CENTRAL TERAI

Bound by the winding Tribhuvan Hwy from Kathmandu to Hetauda and the dramatic Siddhartha Hwy from Pokhara to Butwal, the central Terai is far and away the most visited part of the plains. The road from Mugling to Narayangarh is the principal route south from the Kathmandu valley and the border crossing at Sunauli is the most popular land route between India and Nepal. On the way, you can detour to Royal Chitwan National Park, the largest and most famous wilderness in Nepal, and the birthplace of the Buddha at Lumbini is just a short bus ride from Sunauli.

NARAYANGARH & BHARATPUR

☎ 056

Narayangarh (also spelt Narayangadh and Narayanghat) sits at the junction of the Mugling Hwy and the Mahendra Hwy, which runs the length of Nepal, from Mahendranagar to Kakarbhitta. It's the first major town you come to once you leave the hills and it's an important transport hub, though most people only come here to change buses on the way to Royal Chitwan National Park.

If you do find yourself stopping over, there are several small **mandirs** (temples) along the Narayani River that offer pleasing views of the forested west shore. A more rewarding detour is the 20-minute bus trip to the pilgrimage centre of **Devghat** (p274).

There are no foreign exchange facilities but you can check your email at **Pulchowk Cyber Cafe** (☎ 523953; per hr Rs 25; ⊗ 7.30am-8.30pm).

Sleeping

There are several hotels at Pulchowk, the junction of the Mahendra Hwy and the road to Mugling, and more near the Pokhara bus stand.

Royal Rest House (☎ 522898; Pulchowk; s/d with bathroom from Rs 600/750, with air-con from Rs 1000/1200; ⊠) Right on the highway at Pulchowk, the Royal has a tandoori restaurant downstairs and good rooms with hot showers upstairs. It's quite popular and it may be full if you arrive late in the day.

Regal Rest House (☎ 520755; Pulchowk; s/d without bathroom Rs 100/150, s/d with bathroom & hot water Rs

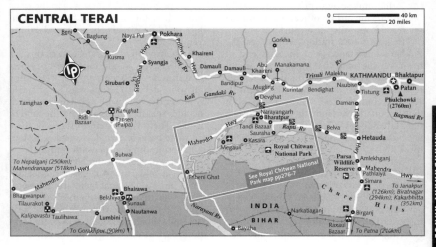

CENTRAL TERAI

0   40 km
0   20 miles

200/250) One block west, Regal is very similar. Rooms at the back are preferable to the noisy rooms at the front. The clean rooms have tiled floors and showers are hot.

Hotel Satanchuli (☎ 521151; Pokhara Bus Stand; r without bathroom from Rs 300, d with bathroom & TV Rs 500) This is the smartest option at the Pokhara bus stand. It's very clean and you can jump straight out of bed and onto the bus.

There are a couple of upmarket choices in Bharatpur, which are handy for the airport.

Island Jungle Resort Bharatpur Heights (☎ 01-4220162 in Kathmandu; www.islandjungleresort.com; r with bathroom & TV US$15; 🏊) Run by the same people as the Island Jungle Resort at Chitwan, this upmarket place has plush rooms with TVs and hot showers, a good restaurant and a swimming pool.

Eating

All the hotels have restaurants and there's a good upmarket choice at Pulchowk.

Kitchen Café (☎ 520453; mains RS 60-200; ✾ 8am-8.30pm) Just before the bridge over the Narayani, this baroque colonial garden restaurant serves the best food in town. The spicy Chinese dishes are particularly recommended and the beers are cold.

Getting There & Away

Bharatpur (2km south of Narayangarh) is the closest airport to Royal Chitwan National Park. There are regular flights to/from Pokhara (US$44, 20 minutes) and Kathmandu (US$54, 30 minutes) with **RNAC** (☎ 530470) and several private airlines. In Bharatpur, the airline offices are all on the main road opposite the airport.

The main bus station, known as the Pokhara bus stand, is at the east end of town, on the road to Mugling. Buses run regularly to Pokhara (day/night Rs 120/140, four hours) and Kathmandu (day/night Rs 150/160, four hours). Minivans to both destinations leave from the road between the Mahendra Hwy and the bus station. A few buses also run north to Gorkha (Rs 90, three hours).

There are also regular buses to Butwal (Rs 80, two hours), Sunauli/Bhairawa (Rs 150, three hours), Birganj (Rs 140, three hours), Janakpur (Rs 150, six hours), Nepalganj (Rs 380; eight hours), Biratnagar (day/night Rs 380/400, nine hours), Kakarbhitta (day/night Rs 405/475, 12 hours) and Mahendranagar (Rs 565, 12 hours). Buses also pull into the new bus station in Bharatpur and Pulchowk on the Mahendra Hwy.

For Chitwan, you could take a local bus to Sauraha Chowk/Tandi Bazaar (Rs 10, 20 minutes) and then a rickshaw to Sauraha, but it's usually better to take a taxi all the way from Pulchowk (Rs 600).

Around Narayangarh

DEVGHAT

Hidden away in the forest about 6km northeast of Narayangarh, Devghat (Deoghat) marks the confluence of the Kali Gandaki and Trisuli Rivers, two important tributaries of the River Ganges. Hindus regard the point where the rivers meet as especially sacred and many elderly high-caste Nepalis come here to live out their final years and eventually die in the sight of god on the banks of the holy river. Far from being gloomy, it's an uplifting place and the calm, contemplative atmosphere is wonderfully soothing after the hectic pace of the plains.

The sacred confluence was first mentioned in the *Skanda Purana,* written in around the 5th century BC by Indian devotees of Shiva. The best way to see Devghat is to wander around and discover – the modern village is reached by a suspension bridge over the rushing waters of the Trisuli and the streets are lined with ashrams (spiritual training centres) and temples. From about 10am each morning, large crowds of Nepali pilgrims make their way to the exact point where the rivers meet for ritual bathing, wedding rituals, picnics and Hindu cremations.

Western visitors are rare, and as this is a holy place, you should take care to respect local attitudes. Residents are very welcoming but some devout Hindus may be offended by physical contact with non-Hindus, which includes shaking hands and sharing food or drinks. There is nowhere to stay, but there are some basic *bhojanalayas* (snack restaurants) around the suspension bridge.

On the first day of the Nepali month of Magh (in mid-January), thousands of pilgrims flock to Devghat from around Nepal and India to immerse themselves in the river to celebrate the Hindu festival of **Magh Sankranti**, which marks the end of the dark months of winter – see p363.

Getting There & Away

Local buses to Devghat (Rs 7, 20 minutes) leave from near Hotel Satanchuli at the Pokhara bus stand in Narayangarh. If you feel energetic, you can walk back along the eastern bank of the river through the forest.

ROYAL CHITWAN NATIONAL PARK

☎ 056

Royal Chitwan National Park has long been regarded as Nepal's third biggest attraction after trekking and the Kathmandu Valley. This huge and beautiful nature reserve protects 932 sq km of sal forest, water marshes and rippling grassland. The park is one of the last refuges of the endangered one-horned Indian rhino and there are sizeable populations of tigers, leopards and rare Gangetic dolphins.

Before the Maoist insurgency, Chitwan was visited by an impressive 92% of all visitors to Nepal, but tourist numbers have plummeted since 2001. The upmarket lodges inside the park still attract decent numbers of visitors, but several budget resorts in Sauraha have closed and others have dropped their rates significantly.

On one level, the wildlife has probably benefited from the reduced visitor numbers – it's a lot easier to hunt when you don't have an elephant-load of tourists shouting and scaring off your prey. However, poaching has increased significantly since the Nepali army stopped patrolling the park, and the rhino population has been hit particularly badly.

Many people visit Chitwan on package tours arranged through travel agents in Kathmandu, Pokhara or overseas. This is by far the easiest approach if you plan to stay at one of the upmarket lodges inside the park.

If you can't afford one of the expensive lodges deep inside the park, the nearby town of Sauraha is an excellent alternative. A small but lively tourist centre has grown up along the river bank about 6km south of Sauraha Chowk (Tandi Bazaar) on the Mahendra Hwy, with hotels, restaurants, bars, moneychangers, travel agents, Internet cafés and dozens of shops selling the full range of Nepali souvenirs, from pirate CDs to tiger pugmark ashtrays.

Careless development has undermined some of the safari atmosphere at Sauraha, but the setting is impressive – perched beside a wide, slow-flowing river with a wall of dense jungle looming tantalisingly on the far bank. An incredible range of jungle activities can be arranged and the surrounding countryside is a peaceful patchwork of rice fields and Tharu villages. In fact, there's probably more to do here than at the big, expensive lodges inside the park.

When planning a visit to Chitwan, try to give yourself enough time for several safaris. The wildlife is unpredictable and you can't rely on sightings every time. Two whole days in the park is really the minimum for wildlife spotting. Be aware that the popular four-day, three-night packages to Chitwan include a day of travel at either end.

MAKING THE FOREST PAY

During the 1980s and 1990s, Chitwan experienced a wave of poaching and illegal forest clearing, linked to the desperate economic situation in the villages around the park. Army patrols were able to drive off the poachers, but fuel wood gathering proved an ongoing thorn in the side of park wardens, until the creation of the community forests at Baghmara and Kumrose.

Backed by the World Bank and the King Mahendra Trust for Nature Conservation, these two areas bordering the national park were replanted with fast growing trees to provide villagers with an alternative source of fire wood and fodder. Ownership and responsibility for the forests was then handed over to local committees, with representatives from every family in the area.

Unlike many of the Nepal government's social policies, the community forests have proved a major success. Forest clearance inside the park has fallen dramatically and the community forests have provided new economic avenues for local people in terms of nature management and eco-tourism.

Between them, the two community forests now cover 2500 hectares, providing fuel, fodder and tourism opportunities for more than 2000 local people. Canoe and elephant safaris in Kumrose Community Forest can be arranged in Sauraha and most of Chitwan's signature species have been spotted in the reserves.

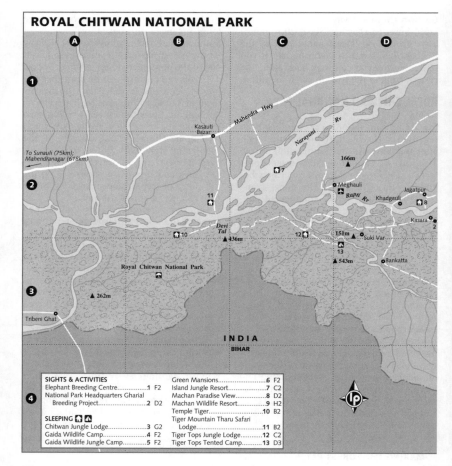

ROYAL CHITWAN NATIONAL PARK

SIGHTS & ACTIVITIES
Elephant Breeding Centre.................1 F2
National Park Headquarters Gharial
  Breeding Project..........................2 D2

SLEEPING
Chitwan Jungle Lodge....................3 G2
Gaida Wildlife Camp.......................4 F2
Gaida Wildlife Jungle Camp...........5 F2

Green Mansions............................6 F2
Island Jungle Resort......................7 C2
Machan Paradise View...................8 D2
Machan Wildlife Resort..................9 H2
Temple Tiger..............................10 B2
Tiger Mountain Tharu Safari
  Lodge...................................11 B2
Tiger Tops Jungle Lodge..............12 C2
Tiger Tops Tented Camp.............13 D3

History

Royal Chitwan National Park was created in 1973, but the area has been protected since at least the 19th century as a hunting reserve for Nepali and foreign aristocrats. King George V and his son, the young Edward VIII, managed to slaughter a staggering 39 tigers and 18 rhinos during just one blood-soaked safari to Chitwan in 1911.

Despite all the toffs firing buckshot into the jungle, Chitwan's status as a hunting reserve probably protected more animals than it killed. The biggest threat to wildlife in lowland Nepal has always been habitat loss, and the forest and malarial swamps were preserved to provide cover for game, keeping human encroachment to a minimum.

Until the late 1950s, the only inhabitants of the Chitwan Valley were small communities of Tharu villagers, who were blessed with a natural resistance to malaria. After a massive malaria eradication programme in 1954, land-hungry peasants from the hills swarmed into the region and huge tracts of the forest were cleared to make space for farmland.

As their habitat disappeared, so did the tigers and rhinos. By the mid 1960s, there were fewer than 100 rhinos and 20 tigers. News of the dramatic decline reached the ears of King Mahendra and the area was declared a royal reserve, becoming a national park in 1973. Some 22,000 peasants were removed from within the park boundaries, but it was only when army patrols were introduced to

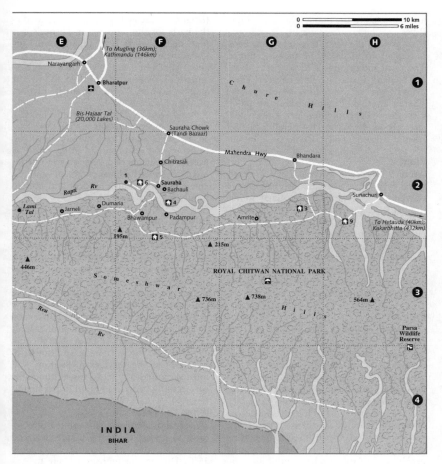

stop poaching that animal numbers really started to rebound. Chitwan was added to the Unesco World Heritage list in 1984.

At the time of the 2000 census, wildlife populations were looking quite respectable, with 544 rhinos and an estimated 80 tigers, plus 50 other species of mammals and 450 species of birds. Sadly, a lot of that ground has been lost since the start of the Maoist rebellion. Poachers have reduced rhino and tiger numbers by a quarter, selling the animals parts on to middlemen in China and Tibet. One single consignment seized near the Nepal–Tibet border in 2003 contained the pelts of 32 tigers and 579 leopards.

The situation hasn't been helped by the falling visitor numbers, which have put a massive dent in the livelihoods of Tharu villagers around the park fringes. To make things worse, many resorts were damaged by monsoon floods in 2002, particularly around Sauraha. A swift resolution to Nepal's civil war is essential if Chitwan's endangered animals are to have any chance of survival.

Geography

Royal Chitwan National Park covers an impressive 932 sq km. A further 499 sq km is set aside as the Parsa Wildlife Reserve and new conservation areas have been created in the community forests at Baghmara and Kumrose – see the boxed text p275. Because of the topography, most tourist activities are restricted to the floodplain of the Rapti River.

As well as the river, there are numerous *tal* (small lakes) dotted around the forest. The most interesting of these, particularly for viewing birds, are **Devi Tal** near Tiger Tops Jungle Lodge and **Lami Tal** near Kasara. There's another group of lakes and pools just outside the park boundary, known collectively as **Bis Hajaar Tal** (literally '20,000 lakes').

Plants

Around 70% of the national park is covered in sal forest, but there are also large areas of *phanta* (grassland), particularly along the banks of the Rapti and Narayani Rivers. Growing up to 8m in height, the local elephant grass provides excellent cover for rhinos and tigers. In the forest, you'll find *shisham,* kapok, *palash,* pipal and strangler fig and scarlet-flowered *kusum* trees, as well as the ubiquitous *sal,* the principal hardwood species in the Terai.

Animals

Chitwan boasts more than 50 different species of mammals, including monkeys, tigers, leopards, sloth bears, wild boar, hyenas, deer, elephants, and rhinos. Bird-watchers can tick off 450 different species of birds and butterfly-spotters have identified at least 67 species of butterfly, some as large as your hand.

The *gaida* (one-horned Indian rhinoceros) is the most famous animal at Chitwan and you stand a good chance of seeing one on an elephant safari, despite the recent upsurge in poaching. Chitwan also has significant populations of tigers, crocodiles and Gangetic dolphins – see the boxed text opposite for more on Chitwan's signature species.

As well as these high-profile animals, you may spot muntjacs (barking deer), chitals (spotted deer), *laghunas* (hog deer) and *jarayos* (sambar) and massive gaurs (Indian wild oxen) skulking in the bushes. Other predators in the park include hyenas and sloth bears, but like the tigers, these animals are threatened by the illegal trade in animal parts for Chinese medicine.

The most commonly seen monkey at Chitwan is the stocky rhesus macaque (the same monkey seen hanging around in Nepali temples) but you also stand a good chance of spotting the larger and more elegant *bandar*

(langur). These agile grey apes were used as the basis for the monkeys in Disney's cartoon of the *Jungle Book* (apart from King Louie, who was plainly an orang-utan and about 3000km from his native home in Sumatra!). Spotted deer often follow the langurs around, taking advantage of their profligate feeding habits.

Birds seen in Chitwan include bulbuls, mynahs, egrets, parakeets, jungle fowl, peacocks, kingfishers, orioles and various species of drongos. Birders should bring a pair of decent binoculars and keep an eye out for rarer species such as scarlet crested sunbirds, emerald doves, jungle owlets and crested hornbills.

Information

Sauraha's **park office and visitor centre** (☎ 521 932; admission per day foreigner/SAARC/Nepali Rs 500/200/20; ❤ 7am-6.30pm) handles admission fees to the park. If you're staying at a lodge inside the park this is usually bundled into the overall charge, but if you stay in Sauraha you have to pay the fee separately.

There's no bank in Sauraha, but several private moneychangers accept pounds, dollars and euros in cash and travellers cheques at reasonable rates. There are a number of STD/ISD phone services in Sauraha and most also offer Internet access, although the connection is very slow (Rs 120 per hour).

When to Visit

The ideal time to visit Chitwan is from October to February, when skies are clear and the average daily temperature is a balmy 25°C. During the monsoon (May to August), many lodges close and tracks through the park become impassable. Whenever you come, remember to pack insect repellent – mosquitoes are an inescapable fact of life in the jungle and malaria is present in some areas of the park.

Dangers & Annoyances

Maoist rebels are active in the area around Chitwan and the army post and telephone exchange at Sauraha have been attacked on several occasions. In June 2005, a public bus was destroyed by a landmine near Narayangarh, killing 38 people. Travel is generally safe during ceasefires, but things can change rapidly so it's essential to check the security situation before you visit.

THE TERAI &
MAHABHARAT RANGE

SIGNATURE SPECIES

Chitwan has some high profile species that everyone wants to see, including the following:

The One Horned Indian Rhino (gaida)

Chitwan is one of the last refuges of the rare one-horned Indian rhinoceros. Only about 2000 survive worldwide, most of them in Chitwan and nearby Kaziranga National Park in India. Until recently, Chitwan was actually exporting rhinos to other Terai parks, including Royal Bardia and Sukla Phanta in western Nepal. Sadly, poaching has increased significantly since the start of the Maoist insurgency. In 2000, there were 500 rhinos in the park, but only 372 animals were found in the 2005 census and more kills were reported throughout 2005. Nevertheless, rhinos are still one of the most commonly seen animals on elephant safaris in the park.

Indian Elephants (hathi)

The Indian elephant is the largest animal in the subcontinent, reaching five tonnes in weight. There are no longer any wild elephants at Chitwan, but the park has a highly successful breeding programme and dozens of domesticated elephants ferry visitors around the park on wildlife-spotting safaris. This is definitely the most interesting way to explore the park and you can even help wash the elephants at the daily elephant bathtime at Sauraha (see p280).

The Royal Bengal Tiger (bagh)

This lean, mean, killing machine is the top predator in the jungles of Nepal and the cunning, intelligence and savage power of the royal Bengal tiger make it one of the most feared animals in the subcontinent. Both locals and foreigners have been attacked by tigers at Chitwan – something to think about before joining a guided walk. There are currently around 60 tigers in Chitwan – sightings are rare as tigers lay low during daylight hours, but keep your eyes peeled.

Marsh Muggers

The most common large reptile in Chitwan, the marsh mugger, is a distant relative of the Australian saltwater crocodile. This small, stocky croc grows to 4m and feeds on anything it can catch, including humans. In case you were wondering, the word 'mugger' originally comes from India – the British borrowed the term after observing marsh muggers dragging unsuspecting villagers to a sudden watery grave!

Gharials

Another distant relative of the Australian saltie, the gharial is a bizarre looking beast, with a slender, elongated snout crammed with ill-fitting teeth. In fact, the gharial is perfectly evolved for its diet of river fish – 110 million-year-old fossils have been found with exactly the same body plan. Gharials are endangered, but there are breeding programmes at Chitwan and other national parks and young gharials have been released into many rivers in the Terai.

Gangetic Dolphins (susu)

Perhaps the rarest of all animals at Chitwan, the Gangetic or freshwater dolphin is occasionally seen in the Narayani and Rapti Rivers. This freshwater relative of the oceanic dolphins is almost completely blind and it hunts using sonar in the murky waters of Nepal's rivers. There are estimated to be only a hundred surviving dolphins in Nepal, with fewer than 20 in the waterways of Chitwan.

Another small but significant risk comes from the wildlife in the park. Tigers, leopards and rhinos are all quite capable of killing human beings, and there have been serious attacks on tourists taking guided walks through the park. Most people have a good experience on jungle walks, but you should be aware that there's a small but significant risk – being chased by a rhino seems a lot less funny when you consider

THE TERAI &
MAHABHARAT RANGE

the phrase 'trampled to death'. See the boxed text p282 for a first-person account of a tiger attack at the reserve!

Bugs are another unwelcome aspect of life in the jungle. Mosquitos are present in large numbers year round and during the monsoon, the forest comes alive with *jukha* (leeches). See p395 for tips on how to deal with these pests. There is also a small risk of contracting typhus fever from a tick bite – always inspect exposed skin after walking.

Sights
NATIONAL PARK HEADQUARTERS
The main **National Park Headquarters** (☎ 521932; ☉ 7am-6.30pm) is inside the park at Kasara, about 13km west of Sauraha on the south bank of the Rapti River. Most people visit as part of an organised jungle safari and there's a small visitor centre with displays on wildlife and a gharial breeding project where you can see these kooky-looking reptiles up close.

There's also a smaller **National Park Visitors Centre** (☉ 7am-6.30pm) in Sauraha, with displays on wildlife and an office where you can book rides on park elephants. Every lunchtime, dozens of elephants come to the river for their daily bath and the main elephant breeding centre is a short cycle ride west of the centre.

ELEPHANT BREEDING CENTRE
About 3km west of Sauraha on the far side of the small Bhude Rapti River, this interesting **breeding centre** (☎ 580154; foreigner/SAARC/Nepali Rs 50/25/10; ☉ 6am-6pm) supplies most of the el-

---

ELEPHANT BATHTIME
There are few experiences that create such a feeling of childlike wonder as helping to bath an elephant. Every day from 11am to noon, the elephants in Sauraha march down to the river near the Riverside Hotel for their morning scrub and everyone turns out to watch the spectacle. If you bring your swimming costume, you can join in the fun. There's no better way of cooling off on a hot day than sitting on the back of a submerged elephant and shouting *chhop!* – if you get the accent right you'll be rewarded with a refreshing trunk-full of cold water! Lodges with their own elephants offer similar elephant bathtimes at similar times.

---

ephants for elephant safaris at Chitwan. The elephants spend much of the day grazing in the jungle so come before 10.30am or after 3.30pm if you want to see the indescribably cute baby elephants. Look out for mahouts preparing *kuchiis* – elephant sweets made from molasses and rice wrapped in grass. The breeding centre is an easy walk or cycle along the road past Lun Tara – a canoe ferry carries visitors across the Bhude Rapti River for a nominal charge.

ELEPHANT POLO
About 25km southwest of Narayangarh, the Tharu village of Meghauli is a sleepy place, full of thatched huts and wandering chickens, and there is no tourist development, though plans are afoot to develop the town for cultural tours. However, the town wakes up every December for the annual **Elephant Polo Championships**, a jumbo-sized sporting spectacular held on the Meghauli airstrip. The event attracts teams from around the world, including several countries that don't have native elephants. Few travellers visit at other times, but you can get here by bike from Sauraha or by local bus from Narayangarh.

BIRD EDUCATION SOCIETY
Run by local volunteers, this friendly **bird-watching centre** (☎ 580113; www.besnepal.org; ☉ 7am-5.50pm) should be the first port of call for birders, twitchers and other avian enthusiasts. The centre has a library of bird books and a binocular rental service (Rs 10/80 per hour/day) and they also have guided bird-watching excursions every Saturday from 7am to 11am. There's no charge but donations help fund the activities.

THARU CULTURAL SHOW
Most of the big park lodges put on shows of traditional Tharu songs and dances for guests, including the popular stick dance, where a great circle of men whack their sticks together in time – it's the Nepali equivalent of Morris dancing! It's very much a tourist experience, but the shows are fun and they provide employment for local people. In Sauraha, there's a nightly performance at the **Tharu Culture Program**, near the Rainforest Guest House. The show starts at 7.30pm each evening and tickets cost Rs 60.

PACHYDERM POLO   *Bradley Mayhew*

One of Nepal's more unusual spectator sports is the annual World Elephant Polo Championships, held every November at Tiger Tops in Meghauli. Eight international teams compete during the week-long tournament, though local heroes the 'Tiger Tops Tuskers' are always firm favourites. Each game consists of two 10-minute *chukka*s of playing time, with a 10-minute interval. Players are tied onto the elephants by rope but if they happen to fall off their elephant, play is stopped while they remount. Scotland are the current reigning world champions, which is a bit odd.

Each team consists of elephants with a range of speeds – the best player tends to go on the fastest, smallest elephant. Each elephant has a *mahout* (driver), as well as a player with a 2m mallet. As the website says 'it's slower than horse polo but faster than you might think'!

Elephants seem to love the game, so much so that the initial use of soccer balls had to be abandoned after the animals realised how much fun it was to stamp on and explode the balls. One of the first rules made it a foul for any elephant to lie down in front of the goal mouth, since scoring then becomes almost impossible.

It may come as no surprise to hear that the sport was allegedly invented during a heavy bout of drinking… For more details see the website www.elephantpolo.com.

THARU VILLAGES

Sauraha is surrounded by small Tharu villages that provide a glimpse of life on the Terai plains. You can explore many of the villages by bike or on foot, but resist the urge to hand out sweets, pens and money. If you want to help local people, shop in the village shops or eat in village *bhojanalayas*. Farming is the main industry and many people still decorate their houses with Mithila paintings and adobe bas-reliefs of animals. The nearest Tharu village is **Bachauli**, east of Sauraha towards Gaida Wildlife Camp.

Activities

There are loads of ways to keep busy at Chitwan. The following sections cover the most popular options, but special trips can be arranged for bird-watchers and other special interest groups.

ELEPHANT RIDES

Lumbering through the jungle on the back of a five tonne jumbo is by far the best way to see wildlife in the park. Elephant-back safaris offer a fantastic vantage point high above the tall grasses of the *phanta* and the wildlife is much more tolerant of elephants than of noisy jeeps or walkers.

Riding an elephant is thrilling rather than comfortable. Elephants move with a heavy, rolling gait and three or four passengers are crammed into each wooden *howdah* (riding platform). Each elephant is controlled by a *pahit* (mahout), who works with the same elephant throughout its life.

There are both private and government-owned elephants in the park but there isn't much difference in price and all safaris run in the early morning or late afternoon.

Government-Owned Elephants

The national park has its own herd of domesticated elephants, and jungle safaris (foreigner/SAARC/Nepali Rs 1000/400/200) leave the visitor centre at Sauraha daily at 8am and 4pm. There are no advance bookings so you should come to the national park visitor centre at 6am or 1pm to buy a ticket. Safaris last 1½ hours and run through the dense *phanta* along the Rapti River, a favourite feeding ground for deer and rhinos.

Privately Owned Elephants

Most of the lodges inside the park have their own elephants and elephant safaris are included in most package tours. In Sauraha, you can arrange inexpensive elephant safaris through **Unique** (☎ 580080) and **United** (☎ 580219). Both run morning and afternoon safaris in the Kumrose Community Forest, a buffer zone on the east edge of the park with decent wildlife populations. Safaris last 2½ hours and the cost is Rs 550, plus the park fees.

JUNGLE WALKS

Visitors are allowed to enter the park on foot with a mandatory guide and this can be a fantastic way to get close to the wildlife. However, several people have been attacked by rhinos and tigers over the years – see the

CHASED BY A TIGER *Joop van Pijkeren, Netherlands*

We were some of the first tourists to enter the park early in the morning and it was still misty. We hadn't been walking long when our guide suddenly gave us a signal. We froze and saw a small yellowish animal running away a few metres in front of us. We initially thought it was a leopard, but suddenly a huge tiger leapt out in front of us and brought down one of our guides with its claws. We were terrified!

The tiger disappeared into the bush then wheeled around for a second attack – we could see its enormous head coming through the bush and hear it roaring. Our guides beat the tiger back with walking sticks while we stood terrified behind them. Then one of our guides hit the tiger hard on the nose and it vanished as quickly as it had appeared. We were all alive, we had survived a tiger attack in Nepal and we had a second chance at life.

We decided to continue the walk – after all, what were the chances of getting attacked by a tiger twice in one day? Minutes later we saw the footprints of an adult tiger and cub – obviously the tigress had a baby and was protecting it.

boxed text above for a first-person account of a tiger attack in Chitwan. Generally, the bigger the group, the safer the walk, but the experience of your guide counts for a lot. Levels of experience vary and some of the guides have a worryingly devil-may-care attitude to creeping up on rhinos.

Walks can be arranged through any of the lodges or travel agents in Sauraha. The going rate is Rs 400 for a half-day and Rs 600 to Rs 800 for a full day and you'll also have to pay the daily park fees.

You can also arrange overnight trips to the Kumrose Community Forest for Rs 500 per person. Walkers spend the night on top of the wildlife viewing tower, enveloped by the noises of the jungle. Supper, breakfast and a sleeping bag are included in the price.

CANOEING

An altogether more relaxing way to explore the park is on a canoeing trip on the Rapti or Narayani River. You have a good chance of spotting water birds and crocodiles and if you get really lucky, you might even catch a glimpse of a rare Gangetic dolphin. Canoe trips from Sauraha cost Rs 850 per person, which includes a one-hour trip down river, followed by a two-hour guided walk back to Sauraha, with a stop at the elephant breeding centre.

4WD SAFARIS

It may not have quite the same romance as riding through the jungle on the back of an elephant, but jeep safaris are another popular way to explore the national park. Animals are less phased by the rumble of

jeep engines than you might suspect and you'll have the opportunity to get much deeper into the jungle.

The route for safaris depends on the current security situation and the state of the roads after the monsoon – popular destinations include Bis Hajaar Tal, Lami Tal and the gharial crocodile–breeding centre near Kasara. Half-day safaris start at Rs 800 per person. You'll pay Rs 8000 per jeep for a full-day safari, so try to get a group together to reduce the cost.

CYCLING

You can't cycle inside the park itself, but the surrounding countryside is ideal for bicycle touring. You can visit dozens of small Tharu farming communities where you're guaranteed to be mobbed by enthusiastic children. Another possible destination is Bis Hajaar Tal, a collection of bird-filled lakes and ponds about 1½ hours northwest of Sauraha, accessible via the Mahendra Hwy.

Mountain bikes made in India can be rented from various shops in Sauraha for around Rs 70 per half day and Rs 140 per full day.

For information on a mountain bike trip that passes Chitwan see p87.

SWIMMING

There are some excellent swimming holes and rivers to splash around in at Chitwan, but you need to be a little careful as marsh muggers are not averse to the odd human meal. The golden rule is only swim where there are large numbers of people. The northern bank of the Rapti River is a popular spot for a dip, but watch out for the current and avoid the south bank. Seek local advice before swimming elsewhere in the park.

If you've brought your swimming costume, don't miss the chance to help out at elephant bathtime – see p280.

Sleeping

You can stay either inside the park, or at Sauraha, the small traveller centre on the north shore of the Rapti River. Wherever you stay, be aware that visitor numbers are greatly reduced at Chitwan. You may prefer the company of an organised tour to being the only guest at a lodge outside the park.

One important consideration at Chitwan is when to shower – almost all of the lodges

use environmentally friendly solar showers, but these only provide hot water at the end of the day, not in the morning. Another consideration is mosquitos – most places have nets but bring repellent or you *will* get bitten.

INSIDE THE NATIONAL PARK

By far the most atmospheric way to visit Chitwan is to stay at one of the upmarket resorts inside the park. The resorts are expensive, but it's hard to put a price on the experience of staying deep in the forest, surrounded by the sounds of the jungle. Most of the lodges offer a choice of Tharu-style jungle cottages or comfortable safari tents, all with private bathrooms and hot showers. The lodges all have bars and restaurants but

there are few other mod cons, reflecting the 'getting back to nature' ethos.

Most people visit the lodges on package tours arranged from Kathmandu or Pokhara. The standard package last three days and two nights and the rates include all meals and activities once you arrive, including elephant rides, jungle walks, canoe trips and cultural shows. Drinks are not included and you may also have to pay the park entry fees (see p278). Transport to the resorts is also extra, and it can be expensive as most transfers involve a rented car and driver. You can make arrangements directly through the resorts or go through a travel agent in Kathmandu or Pokhara.

The following rates are based on two people sharing – if you come alone, you'll pay a 50% surcharge. All the lodges inside the park charge 13% government tax. Most of the park resorts have lowered their rates because of falling visitor numbers, and this is reflected in the prices quoted here. It may be worth inquiring about additional discounts, but as most visitors arrive on prepaid package tours, there is no real incentive for the lodges to cut prices for walk-in guests.

Easily the most famous accommodation at Chitwan, the three **Tiger Tops lodges** (☎ 01-4361500 in Kathmandu; www.tigermountain.com) are run by Tiger Mountain, which also manages the Tiger Mountain Lodge in Pokhara and the Karnali Jungle Lodge and Tented Camp at Bardia. The company has a deserved reputation for high standards and the facilities, guides and overall ethos are superb. Rates at all the lodges include meals and activities, but not park fees. The Jungle Lodge and Tented Camp close from May to September, when the jungle roads become impassable. Children aged three to 10 pay half the adult rates.

Tiger Tops Jungle Lodge (packages per person per night US$350; discounts available May-Sep) The original tree-top guesthouse that forged the Tiger Tops brand. The famous stilt houses are still some of the most characterful accommodation anywhere in Nepal and everything is constructed from local materials. The lodge sits beside the small Reu Khola at the western end of the park and the spacious rooms have solar-powered lights and fans and solar-heated water. There are always elephants wandering about the place, adding to the jungle atmosphere.

Tiger Tops Tented Camp (packages per person per night US$200; discounts available May-Sep) 3km east of the Jungle Lodge in the serene Surung Valley, this feels much more like a traditional jungle safari and it's easy to imagine what life must have been like for the *pukkah sahibs* (colonial gentlemen) who came here to hunt in the early 20th century. The comfortable safari tents have twin beds, modern bathrooms and small balconies and there's a delightful raised bar and restaurant.

Tiger Mountain Tharu Safari Lodge (packages per person per night US$200; discounts available May-Sep; 🔊) This is the newest addition to the Tiger Tops family. Located outside the park boundary on the north bank of the Narayani River, it doesn't have quite the same jungle feel as the other Tiger Tops lodges but rooms are contained in attractive Tharu-style long houses, decorated with Mithila paintings, and there's a stylish restaurant and pool.

Temple Tiger (☎ 01-4221637 in Kathmandu; www.catmando.com/temple-tiger; packages per person per night US$250) On the south bank of the Narayani River in the west of the park, Temple Tiger offers raised wooden cabins with thatched roofs and private bathrooms, each with a private viewing platform looking over the *phanta*. Rates are high but the camp is surrounded by dense jungle – it's the real safari deal. Children under 12 are charged 50%. Park fees are extra.

Island Jungle Resort (☎ 01-4220162 in Kathmandu; www.islandjungleresort.com; 3-day/2-night package per person US$230; discount of 20% Jun-Sep) This place has a superb location on a large island in the middle of the Narayani River at the western end of the park. The cottages at the main resort are simple but tasteful and decorated with animal paintings. There's a lovely riverside breakfast terrace, plus the obligatory Tharu-style restaurant and bar. Children aged three to 10 are charged 50%. Rates include park fees.

Gaida Wildlife Camp (☎ 01-4215409/4215431 in Kathmandu; www.visitnepal.com/gaida; safari tents/bungalows per person US$100/110, not incl park fees; 🌙 Oct-May) Gaida is the closest lodge to Sauraha and it's the only park accommodation on the north bank of the Rapti River. Visitors have a choice of appealing timber bungalows at the main lodge or safari tents at the Gaida Wildlife Jungle Camp, across the river at the base of the Someshwar hills. Wildlife is not particularly prolific at the main camp, but there are loads of animals around the jungle camp. You can stay in both as part of the same package. There's an extra camping fee of US$7 per person per night for the jungle camp.

Chitwan Jungle Lodge (☎ 01-4442240 in Kathmandu; www.chitwanjunglelodge.com; 3-day/2-night package US$220, additional nights US$100) Set on the south bank of the Rapti River in the eastern part of Chitwan, this sensitively-themed resort makes extensive use of thatch and natural materials. There's a very inviting open-air bar and restaurant and the spacious rooms are lined with reed matting. Rates include park fees and children pay half rates. The resort is closed from June to August.

Machan Wildlife Resort (☎ 01-4225001; www.nepalinformation.com/machan; package rates per person 1-/2-nights US$110/220, additional nights US$90, discounts of 30% May-Sep; 🐾) At the eastern end of the park, this attractive place is the closest resort to the Parsa Wildlife Reserve. Wildlife is plentiful around the resort and guests stay in well-designed, timber-frame bungalows with bathrooms, set among the trees. The striking Mithila paintings on the walls were created by women from the villages around Janakpur. Facilities here include a delightful natural swimming pool, a bar and restaurant and a video library of wildlife films.

For more creature comforts, **Machan Paradise View** is a large, modern hotel-style resort set in large grounds near the park headquarters at Kasara, charging the same rates. Park fees are extra.

SAURAHA

Most independent travellers to Chitwan stay in the village of Sauraha, on the northern fringes of the park. There are dozens of lodges and resorts here, from upmarket package tour places to simple cottage resorts run by local villagers. However, visitor numbers are significantly down from the levels seen before the start of the insurgency. It may be some time before the tourism revival seen in Kathmandu and Pokhara spills over to Chitwan.

Most of the resorts and hotels are strung out along the National Park boundary or the road to Chitrasali, but there are also some laid-back options on the road to the Elephant Breeding Centre. Most resort names are made up of some combination of the words jungle, safari, wildlife, river,

---

DISCOUNTS

At the time of writing, most of the lodges at Sauraha were offering significant discounts on their printed rates – as much as 50% in some cases. If lodges offer discounts, we have mentioned this in the reviews. Places that don't offer discounts have usually dropped their prices as low as they can go, but it may still be worth asking when you check in. In these difficult times, competition is doubly fierce and most of the lodges send jeeps to the bus stand at Chitrasali to jostle for customers. The villagers of Sauraha are some of the friendliest people in Nepal so try not to let this colour your view of the place.

---

park, resort, lodge and camp – read the signs carefully to make sure you are going to the right place.

Budget

All the budget options are very similar so choosing between them is often just a spot decision. Most lodges consist of simple mud-and-thatch cottages with small verandas, set around a central restaurant in a small tropical garden. You'll normally have a choice of shared or private bathrooms and most places have solar powered showers which only run hot after a few hours of morning sunshine. Call ahead to make sure the following places are open for business before turning up at the door.

Jungle Adventure World (☎ 580064; jaw_resort@ hotmail.com; cottages Rs 500, discounts of 20%) Handy for the park entrance and the riverside restaurants, this place has recently been taken over by Buddhist owners, which explains all the prayer flags and Tibetan wall hangings. The bungalows are very inviting and each has a solar shower.

River View Jungle Camp (☎ 580096; adhikari46@ hotmail.com; cottages from Rs 400) A decent place, with several different styles of cottages and a long garden with viewing towers looking over the river. The mood is calm and the rooms are tidy.

Travellers Jungle Camp (☎ 580013; tiger@gnet .com.np; s/d with bathroom Rs 200/400, r with tub Rs 500) Across the road, Travellers Jungle Camp has its own elephant stand and cottages are decorated with bird murals. Rooms are spic and span, as are the grounds, and these are the cheapest bathtubs in town.

Hotel Wildlife Camp (☎ 580322; www.hotelwild lifecamp.com; cottages with bathroom Rs 300, r in villa Rs 500-1000; discounts of 20%) Rates are refreshingly low at this big package place on the road north from the bazaar. The hotel is set in a neatly manicured garden full of royal palms and you have a choice of tidy modern cottages or two-storey villas with balconies. It's often full so call ahead.

Annapurna View Lodge (☎ 580072; 2-bed cottages Rs 100, s/d with bathroom from Rs 150/200) Opposite the army post, this is one of the better budget places and the pleasant garden is divided into small squares by miniature hedges. Rooms are in long blocks and all have fans, mozzie nets and bathrooms.

Crocodile Safari Camp (☎ 580053; cottages with bathroom Rs 150-200) Back from the river near the park entrance, this is another option for travellers who are watching the pennies. It's fairly rustic but the owners are friendly and the cottages are clean.

Lun Tara (☎ 580145; www.luntara-nepal.com; r without bathroom Rs 300, with bathroom US$10-20) If you're a getting-back-to-nature kind of person, look no further than Lun Tara, about 3km west of Sauraha near the Elephant Breeding Centre. Everything here has been designed with upmost consideration for the environment. The Tharu-style cottages have lots of home comforts, the restaurant serves tasty Thai, Italian and Nepali meals and various wellness activities are available on site. The connection to Chitrasali and Sauraha is by horse and cart.

Chitwan Safari Camp & Lodge (☎ 580078; cottages Rs 300) Set among mustard fields at the back of the village, this place benefits from a quiet location and friendly local owners. It's a short walk from both the bazaar and the park entrance.

Family Guest House (☎ 580081; old&wild@hotmail .com; r without bathroom Rs 250) Close to the main bazaar, this small village-style resort has clean, economically priced rooms in an intimate garden.

Chitwan Resort Camp (☎ 580082; ☎ 01-4227711 in Kathmandu; r with bathroom Rs 400, discounts of 20%) The best of several very similar places on the road leading north from the bazaar, Chitwan Resort Camp has attractive cottages with latticed verandas, set in a maze of tiny topiary.

Hotel Jungle Lodge (☎ 580006; ☎ 01-4443599 in Kathmandu; www.hjlchitwan.com; r with bathroom from Rs 500, discounts of 20%) A long-established place in a shady garden on the northwest edge of Sauraha. Rooms are in raised huts with bathrooms, wooden floors and verandas. It's all quite tasteful and there's a big central restaurant.

Rainforest Guest House (☎ 580007; sharad2029@ yahoo.com; cottages without bathroom Rs 100, r with bathroom Rs 200-300) At the northern end of town, this place has a wide choice of rooms, from basic thatched cottages to hotel rooms with bathrooms in a modern concrete block.

Jungle Sunset Camp (☎ 580112; jungle_sunset@ hotmail.com; cottages with shared bathroom Rs 150, r with private bathroom Rs 200-300) A cheap and cheerful option right on the river bank, with a modern hotel block at the back and simple cottages at the front. It's just off the road to the Elephant Breeding Centre.

Jungle Wildlife Camp (☎ 580093; junglewcamp@ yahoo.com; r with bathroom Rs 250) Next door, this place has two green hotel blocks in a modest garden and a sundeck right by the water. Rooms are simple but clean with mosquito nets, fans and large bathrooms with solar showers.

Jungle Tourist Camp (☎ 580030; www.adventure chitwan.com.np; cottages Rs 300, discounts of 20%) Out on the edge of the village, this isn't a bad choice. Clean rooms with bed nets and lino floors are set in a small garden.

Midrange

Most of the midrange lodges are set up for visitors on package tours, but all give out rooms to independent travellers if there are vacancies. With the current discounts, some of these places are excellent value – you can get a top notch room with private bathroom and balcony for as little as US$10/15 per single/double.

Many hotels offer their own packages, with accommodation, meals and various jungle activities. The standard package lasts three days and two nights – you'll have to make your own way to Sauraha, but lodges will pick you up from Chitrasali. Alternatively, you can book an all inclusive package with transfers by bus, plane or car through any travel agency in Pokhara or Kathmandu.

Rhino Residency Resort (☎ 580095; ☎ 01-4420431 in Kathmandu; www.rhino-residency.com; 3-day/2-night package US$200, s/d room only US$50/60, discounts of 50%; 🌐 🛢) Right by the entrance to the national park, this elegant resort has rooms in slate-roofed bungalows with flagstone patios. The styling falls somewhere between English Regency and Malay Colonial and there's a pool, bar and restaurant. Discounts extend to the tour packages.

Royal Park Hotel (☎ 580061; www.royalparkhotel .com.np; 1-day/2-night packages US$80, r only per night US$20) Set in grounds you could get lost in, this appealing upmarket hotel has an open-air bar, a restaurant full of old photos and rooms in elegant, widely spaced cottages or two-storey villas in the garden. Rates include breakfast and there's a tiny pool, though it's not always full. Rooms are the best in town for wheelchair users.

Hotel River Side (☎ 5800098; hriverside@hotmail .com; downstairs r with bathroom Rs 500, 1st-/2nd-fl r US$15/25, discounts of 30%) This big, modern block by the river is much more attractive once you get round the back. There's a riverside restaurant, a garden full of hammocks and a good selection of well-maintained rooms with carpets, reed furniture and powerful fans.

Rhino Lodge Hotel (☎ 580065; rhinolodge@wlink .com.np; downstairs/1st-fl r with bathroom US$10/15, discounts of 30%) A large modern two-storey place set in a large, well-kept garden that runs most of the way to the river. Rooms on the second floor have garden and river views. It's popular with package groups so book in advance.

Jungle Safari Lodge (☎ 580046, in Kathmandu ☎ 01-4416300; www.nepal-safari.com; r from US$20, with air-con & TV US$40, discounts of 50%; 🌐) Set back from the road in a huge garden, this is more like a hotel than a jungle resort. Rooms are cavernous and extremely comfortable and some have bathtubs. The cottages here are currently not in use.

Chitwan Paradise Hotel (☎ 580048, in Kathmandu ☎ 01-4444544; paradise@mos.com.np; 3-day/2-night package US$60, cottages only Rs 800, discounts of 20%) Down the road to the Elephant Breeding Centre, this calm and modern place has a lovingly manicured lawn that could have been trimmed with nail scissors. Rooms are in tidy, modern bungalows and a portion of the profits goes to rural communities.

Chitwan Tiger Camp (☎ 580060; www.chitwanti gercamp.com; standard/deluxe r with bathroom Rs 400/800, discounts of 20%; 🌐) A timely refurbishment is raising standards at Tiger Camp, but

the riverside restaurant is still the main attraction. Rooms are housed in an odd assortment of buildings: deluxe rooms are upstairs, standard rooms are downstairs.

Jungle Safari Park (☎ 580128; in Kathmandu ☎ 01-4263054, www.islandjungleresort.com; r with bathroom Rs 500-1000, discounts of 30%) The location by the army camp may put some people off, but the brick cottages here are modern and well looked after and the lodge arranges its own elephant safaris. Ask about package rates including activities.

Green Mansions (☎ 580088, in Kathmandu ☎ 01-4221854; green@mansions.wlink.com.np; 3-day/2-night packages US$190, additional nights US$80, discounts of 20%) An upmarket option near the Elephant Breeding Centre, Green Mansions is pleasantly low-key and the smart tiled cottages are tastefully styled with plenty of local trim.

Eating

Most lodges have restaurants and there are several independent places in the main bazaar at Sauraha. All serve jungle-themed cocktails and a familiar menu of travellers fare – Nepali, Indian, Italian, Mexican, you know the drill. One unusual European dish to join the throng is *patatje oorlog* – an unlikely-sounding combination of chips, mayonnaise, ketchup, onions, and peanut-sauce, invented in Holland.

Al Fresco (mains Rs 50-200; ☷ 6am-10pm) Probably the best of the terrace restaurants, with two levels, street-side views and all your traveller favourites.

KC's Restaurant (mains Rs 70-300; ☷ 6am-10pm) The most upmarket choice at Sauraha, KC's is set in a Spanish-style hacienda with an open terrace and a fire pit at the back. The chefs here cook up a feast and the menu runs from Nepali and Indian curries to pizzas and pasta.

There's another cluster of laid-back traveller restaurants on the sandy banks of the river that get quite busy around elephant bath-time and sunset. Probably the most popular is **River Sunset Restaurant** (meals Rs 40-200; ☷ 6am-10pm), attached to Chitwan Tiger Camp.

For real bargain basement meals, there are a few rustic *bhojanalayas* in the bazaar.

Shopping

Souvenir shops in Sauraha sell the usual range of Tibetan, Kashmiri and Nepali arts and crafts. Local specialities include tiger pugmark ashtrays and wood carvings of elephants and rhinos, including dubious mating scenes. For something a bit more upmarket, head to **Happy House** (☎ 580026; ✆ 7am-9pm) near the Al Fresco Restaurant (there's a branch near the Bird Education Society). This small, family-run business produces its own honey (in various delectable varieties) and sells gorgeous Mithila paintings produced by women's craft co-operatives near Janakpur.

Getting There & Away

AIR

When there is sufficient tourist demand, Yeti has daily scheduled flights from Kathmandu to the tiny runway at Meghauli for US$82, but you'll need to make advance arrangements with your lodge for a pick-up as there is nothing in Meghauli. If you're bound for Sauraha, it's better to fly into Bharatpur near Narayangarh and take a taxi. RNAC and several private airlines offer daily flights to Bharatpur from Kathmandu (US$54 to US$70, 30 minutes) and Pokhara (US$44, 20 minutes). A taxi from the airport to Sauraha will cost around Rs 600. Travel agents and hotels can make bookings.

BUS

By far the easiest way to reach Chitwan is by tourist bus from Kathmandu or Pokhara. In either direction, the journey takes six to seven hours and the fare is Rs 300 to Rs 350, depending on which travel agent you book with. Buses leave from the Mustang bus stand in Pokhara and the Thamel end of Kantipath in Kathmandu at 7am. The final stop is Chitrasali, about 5km from Sauraha – jeeps and hotel touts wait at the bus park to transfer new arrivals to Sauraha for Rs 50. There's no obligation to commit to staying at any particular resort, regardless of what the touts say. In the opposite direction, buses leave Chitrasali at 9.30am. Any hotel or travel agent can make bookings.

A more comfortable option is the daily air-con bus operated by **Greenline** (☎ 560126), which runs to Kathmandu or Pokhara for US$10 including brunch. From Kathmandu or Pokhara it leaves at 7.30am; from Chitrasali, it leaves at 8am.

You can pick up public buses to Kathmandu and Pokhara and destinations in the Terai at Sauraha Chowk (also known as Tandi Bazaar), on the Mahendra Hwy about 6km north of Sauraha. However, it's usually easier to take a local bus to Narayangarh (Rs 10, 20 minutes) and change there – see p274 for more information.

CAR

Travel agents and upmarket lodges can arrange transfers to Chitwan by private car. The going rate for a car and driver is around US$60 and the journey from Pokhara or Kathmandu takes about five hours. Cars usually drop guests off at the turn-offs to

---

WALKS IN THE CHITWAN HILLS

After the success of the Sirubari village tourism project near Daman, the Nepal Tourism Board has created a new network of trekking routes in the hills north of Chitwan. Several Chepang, Magar and Gurung villages have been developed as destinations for cultural tourism, with accommodation in village homestays, cultural activities and treks to mountain viewpoints. So far, the development has been very low-key, and the walks offer a much more authentic experience of Nepali life than the established trekking routes around Everest and Annapurna.

The main trailheads for walkers are **Shaktikhor**, accessible by local bus from Narayangarh, and **Hugdi**, near Kurintar on the Prithvi Hwy. From either starting point you can follow a long loop around the top of the ridge, visiting the Rana-era fort at **Uppardangadhi** and the dramatic Himalayan viewpoint at **Siraichuli** (1945m). On the way you'll pass through a string of traditional villages; locals are very friendly, if a little bemused by the sight of foreigners.

Because of the poor transport links, most people stay at least one night, but two days will give you more time to explore this interesting area. Simple homestay accommodation is available in **Hattibang**, on the trail up from Hugdi, and in Shaktikhor, where you can also hire guides. Alternatively, you can make all the arrangements through a travel agency in Kathmandu, Pokhara or Sauraha. As elsewhere, the safety of walking in this area depends on the status of the Maoist insurgency. See www.welcomenepal.com/trpap/areas_chitwan.html for more information.

the resorts and you must complete the journey by lodge 4WD or elephant!

RAFT

A rather more interesting way to arrive at Chitwan is by river raft. Most of the big Kathmandu rafting operators offer trips down the Trisuli and Narayani Rivers, culminating at the national park, usually as park of a package tour. Don't expect wild white water – the rafting experience is more of a leisurely drift – but there are some fine views and the sandy beaches along the riverside offer great camping spots.

Mugling is the main embarkation point on the Prithvi Hwy, about halfway between Kathmandu and Pokhara. It takes two or three days to raft down to Chitwan. Most people combine rafting with a safari package in the national park – expect to pay around US$80 per person for the rafting section of the trip. Most rafting companies (see p90) can make arrangements – however, trips only run if there is enough demand.

Getting Around

BICYCLE & MOTORCYCLE

Several shops in Sauraha rent out bicycles that are perfectly good for exploring the surrounding villages; the going rate is Rs 140 per day.

A few places rent out decrepit motorbikes for Rs 150 per hour or Rs 500 per day, but make sure the bikes start up properly before heading off into the Styx.

JEEP

Shared jeeps to Chitrasali cost Rs 50 but they only leave to coincide with the departure of the tourist buses. A reserve jeep will cost Rs 200 to Chitrasali, Rs 400 to Sauraha Chowk/Tandi Bazaar and Rs 600 to the airport at Bharatpur.

RICKSHAW

A rickshaw from Sauraha Chowk/Tandi Bazaar to Sauraha will cost around Rs 70, but allow 40 minutes for the journey.

SUNAULI & BHAIRAWA

☎ 071

About 165km southwest of Narayangarh, Sunauli (pronounced 'so-nor-li') is the most popular border crossing between India and

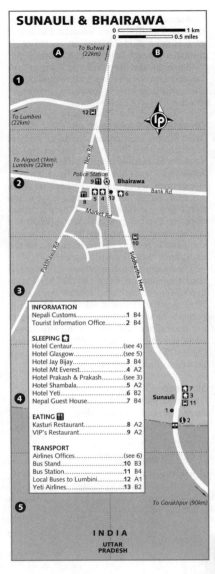

SUNAULI & BHAIRAWA

INFORMATION	
Nepali Customs................................1	B4
Tourist Information Office.........2	B4

SLEEPING 🏠	
Hotel Centaur...............................(see 4)	
Hotel Glasgow..............................(see 5)	
Hotel Jay Bijay.............................3	B4
Hotel Mt Everest...........................4	A2
Hotel Prakash & Prakash............(see 3)	
Hotel Shambala............................5	A2
Hotel Yeti.......................................6	B2
Nepal Guest House.......................7	B4

EATING 🍽	
Kasturi Restaurant........................8	A2
VIP's Restaurant...........................9	A2

TRANSPORT	
Airlines Offices............................(see 6)	
Bus Stand.....................................10	B3
Bus Station..................................11	B4
Local Buses to Lumbini..............12	A1
Yeti Airlines................................13	B2

Nepal. There's not much here – just a strip of hotels along the dusty highway – and most travellers just whistle through on their way south to Delhi and Varanasi or north to Kathmandu and Pokhara. If you do choose to stop over, there are more places to stay in Bhairawa, a more substantial town 4km north of the border.

Bhairawa is also the starting point for trips to Lumbini, the historical birthplace of Gautama Buddha and an increasingly popular place to break the journey between India and Nepal. If you want to visit Lumbini, you can skip both Sunauli and Bhairawa and stay in one of the friendly guesthouses at Lumbini Bazaar.

Orientation & Information

Most people use Sunauli for both sides of the border, but the Nepali border post is actually at Belahiya, about 4km south of Bhairawa. Buses run directly from the border to most major towns in Nepal so there's no need to go into Bhairawa unless you don't like the look of the hotels in Belahiya. To further confuse things, Bhairawa is also known as Siddharthanagar but you can usually get away with Bhairawa for the town and Sunauli for the border.

The Government of Nepal runs a small **tourist information office** (☎ 520304; 🕑 10am-5pm Sun-Fri) on the Nepal side of the border. Bhairawa has several banks but it's usually easier to change money at the border. There are several net cafés around the junction of Bank Rd and New Rd in Bhairawa, charging Rs 25 per hour. Net cafés in Sunauli are slower and much more expensive.

Sleeping

There are plenty of hotels at Belahiya, but the border post is noisy, dusty and plagued by mosquitoes – bring coils or a mozzie net or end up as supper. All in all, Bhairawa is a much more wholesome place to stay.

SUNAULI/BELAHIYA

All the hotels are strung out along the road to Bhairawa.

Hotel Jay Bijay (☎ 523029; r with/without bathroom Rs 250/150) A quite bright, friendly place, with dated but cheerful décor. Rooms are simple but reasonably clean.

Nepal Guest House (☎ 520876; 4-bed dm Rs 50, r with bathroom & cold/hot shower Rs 150/240) Travellers on a tight budget need look no further. Rooms here are pretty basic, but good for the money, and there's also a pretty decent restaurant.

Hotel Prakash & Prakash (☎ 526994; www.hotelprakash.com; s/d with bathroom Rs 800/1000, with air-con Rs 1200/1500; ❄) Unexpectedly posh for this locale, this business-class hotel is further up the road towards the border. It's popular with Indian travellers and the guest rooms are spacious and reasonably quiet.

BHAIRAWA

Most of the hotels in Bhairawa are strung out along Bank Rd, which runs west off the Siddhartha Hwy.

Hotel Centaur (☎ 527266; Bank Rd; r with bathroom Rs 200) A typical no-frills, budget place. Rooms are reasonably large and clean but showers are cold.

Hotel Glasgow (☎ 523737; mermaid@mos.com.np; Bank Rd; s/d with TV & bathroom Rs 500/700, with air-con Rs 1000/1200, discounts of 20%; ❄) The best place in

CROSSING THE BORDER

Border Hours

The Nepali side of the border is open 24 hours, but the Indian border post is only staffed from 6am to 10pm. After 7pm and before 7am, you may need to go searching for the immigration officials on either side.

Foreign Exchange

Several moneychangers on the Nepali side of the border exchange Nepali and Indian rupees, and cash and travellers cheques in US dollars, UK pounds and euros. Shops and hotels on both sides of the border accept Indian and Nepali rupees at a fixed rate of 1.6 Nepali rupees to one Indian rupee.

Onward to India

All travellers bound for India must change buses at the border. From the bus station on the Indian side of the border, there are direct morning buses to Delhi (INRs 405, 24 hours) and Varanasi (INRs 150, 10 hours). There are also buses to Gorakhpur (INRs 50, three hours) where you can connect with the Indian broad-gauge railway.

town. Hotel Glasgow has attentive staff, an excellent restaurant, huge rooms and properly hot showers. Rooms are pretty much perfect and you have the option of air-con.

Hotel Shambala (☎ 520167; Bank Rd; r with bathroom from Rs 400, with TV & air-con from Rs 800; ✷) A solid, midrange choice on the main street. There's a restaurant and rooms have fans, phones and hot showers.

Hotel Mt Everest (☎ 520410; hotelmteverest@yahoo .com) Rates and facilities are similar at this affiliated hotel down from the Shambala.

Hotel Yeti (☎ 520551; hotelyeti@wlink.com.np; cnr Bank Rd & Siddhartha Hwy; s/d US$30/35, s/d with air-con US$35/45, discounts of 25%; ✷) This is the preferred choice of upmarket tour groups and it's very modern and comfortable. All rooms have TVs, phones and reliably hot showers.

Eating

All the hotels have restaurants serving the usual range of Nepali, Indian and continental dishes. In Sunauli there are a few small restaurants near the bus station.

Kasturi Restaurant (snack meals from Rs 50; ✸ 7am-8pm) One of several upmarket *misthan bandhars* (Indian snack restaurants) along Paklihawa Rd, this place serves excellent vegetarian curries and *dosas* (lentil-flour pancakes), as well as Indian sweets.

VIPs Restaurant (Bank Rd; mains Rs 50-120; ✸ 8am-9pm) If you must have meat, try this small Indian, Nepali and Chinese place around the corner on Bank Rd.

Getting There & Away
AIR
Yeti Airlines (☎ 527527) and other private airlines offer flights between Kathmandu and Bhairawa (US$90, 40 minutes, daily). Bhairawa airport is about 1km west of town, easily accessible by rickshaw. Most **airline offices** are around the junction of Bank Rd and the Siddhartha Hwy.

BUS
Buses for Kathmandu and Pokhara leave regularly from both Belahiya and Bhairawa. For other destinations, you're best off going to Bhairawa. Be suspicious of travel agents in India or Nepal who claim to offer 'through tickets' between the two countries. Everyone has to change buses at the border. For more on this see p381.

There are regular day and night buses to Pokhara (day/night Rs 230/270, eight hours) and Kathmandu (day/night Rs 230/280, eight hours) via Narayangarh (Rs 150, three hours). Minivans to Pokhara/Kathmandu cost Rs 305/300.

A slightly more comfortable option is the daily **Golden Travels** (☎ 520194) air-con bus to Kathmandu (Rs 525); it leaves Kathmandu at 7.30am and Sunauli at 7am.

From the **bus stand** in Bhairawa, buses leave every 15 minutes to Butwal (Rs 28, 30 minutes) where you can change for destinations in the western Terai. Heading east, there's a 6.10am bus to Janakpur (Rs 320, eight hours), a 5am bus to Biratnagar (Rs 470, 10 hours) and a 4.15am service to Kakarbhitta (Rs 520, 12 hours).

Local buses for Lumbini (Rs 25, 1½ hours) and Taulihawa (Rs 50, three hours) leave from the junction of the Siddhartha Hwy and the road to Lumbini, about 1km north of Bank Rd.

Getting Around
Regular jeeps and local buses shuttle between the border and Bhairawa for Rs 7. A rickshaw will cost Rs 20.

LUMBINI
☎ 071
As the historical birthplace of Gautama Siddhartha Buddha, Lumbini is one of the most important religious sites in the world. The man who would later achieve enlightenment under a Bodhi tree, inspiring a global philosophy of peace and reflection, was born under a sal tree in Lumbini in the month of May in 563 BC.

Despite being an important destination for pilgrimages, Lumbini is nothing like Haridwar, Mecca or Lourdes. Pilgrims here come in a slow, respectful trickle and many stay on to meditate in the monasteries surrounding the sacred site. That said, Lumbini has undergone a major renaissance over the last few years, and new monasteries are springing up here faster than you can say 'om mani padme hum'.

The centre of Lumbini is the Maya Devi Temple, which marks the exact spot where Queen Maya Devi of Kapilavastu gave birth to Gautama Siddhartha. Surrounding the temple is a sacred garden containing the pillar of Ashoka as well as the ruined

THE TERAI & MAHABHARAT RANGE

CHINESE TEAM TO SHOOT THE BUDDHA! *Bradley Mayhew*

Scan the Nepali newspapers and you'll come across some great news stories. Our favourite headline was the eyecatching 'Chinese team to Shoot the Buddha!', actually a Chinese documentary film crew that had arrived in Lumbini.

---

foundations of dozens of ancient stupas and monasteries. Extending for miles around the sacred garden is a huge park known as the Lumbini Development Zone, designed by Japanese architect Kenzo Tange in 1978. It's a work in progress but the grounds are already full of landscaped lakes and Buddhist monasteries, constructed by Buddhist communities from around the world.

You can easily spend one or two days exploring the site so it's well worth an overnight stay. There are hotels all around the perimeter of the Development Zone and plenty of small guest houses in the peaceful village of Lumbini Bazaar, directly opposite the main entrance to the site.

History

After years of work at Lumbini, archaeologists are now fairly certain that Gautama Siddhartha, the historical Buddha, was indeed born here in 563 BC. A huge complex of monasteries and stupas was erected on the site by his followers and the Indian emperor Ashoka made a pilgrimage here in 249 BC, erecting one of his famous pillars.

Shortly after this, some unknown cataclysm affected Lumbini. When the Chinese pilgrim, Fa Hsien (Fa Xian), visited in AD 403, he found the monasteries abandoned and the city of Kapilavastu in ruins. Two hundred years later, Hsuan Tang (Xuan Zang), another Chinese pilgrim, described 1000 derelict monasteries and Ashoka's pillar, shattered by lightning and lying on the ground. However, the site was not entirely forgotten. The Nepali king, Ripu Malla, made a pilgrimage here in 1312, possibly leaving the nativity statue that is still worshipped in the Maya Devi Temple.

Mughal invaders arrived in the region at the end of the 14th century and destroyed the remaining 'pagan' monuments at both Kapilavastu and Lumbini. The whole region then returned to wilderness and the sites were lost to humanity, until the governor of Palpa, Khadga Shumsher Rana, began the excavation of Ashoka's pillar in late 1896.

Lumbini is now creating a new archaeology for itself in the Lumbini Development Zone – if explorers rediscover the site in a thousand years, they'll find the ruins of dozens of vast 21st century monasteries, reflecting Buddhist cultures from across the globe.

Dangers & Annoyances

Travel around Lumbini is generally safe, but Maoists have carried out several attacks in the area during the latest upsurge in violence, including at Taulihawa. As elsewhere, check the security situation before wandering off into the countryside.

Sights

MAYA DEVI TEMPLE

The revered **Maya Devi Temple** (foreigner/SAARC/Nepali Rs 50/10/free; 6am-5.30pm) sits on the exact site of the birth of the Buddha, according to Buddhist scholars. Excavations carried out in 1992 have revealed a succession of ruins on the site dating back at least 2200 years, including a commemorative stone on a brick plinth, matching the description of a stone laid down by Emperor Ashoka in the third century BC. There are plans to raise a grand monument on the site, but for now, the ruins are protected by a plain brick pavilion.

If you remove your shoes, you can walk around the ruins on a raised boardwalk. The focal point for pilgrims is a famous sandstone carving of the birth of the Buddha, reputedly left here by the Malla king, Ripu Malla, in the 14th century, when Maya Devi was worshipped as an incarnation of the Hindu mother goddess. The carving has been worn almost flat by centuries of veneration, but you can just discern the shape of Maya Devi grasping a sal branch and giving birth to the Buddha, with Indra and Brahma looking on. There's a modern reproduction in the Bihari monastery near the temple.

The pond beside the temple is believed to be where Maya Devi bathed before giving birth to the Buddha and dotted around the grounds are the ruined foundations of a number of brick stupas and monasteries, dating from the 2nd century BC to the 9th century AD.

Opposite the temple are two small Buddhist monasteries: the **Dharma Swami Maharaj Buddha Vihar** (☎ 580132) was constructed by pilgrims from Mustang in Nepal, while the **Nepal Buddha Vihara** (☎ 580172) was constructed by monks from Bihar in India. You can pick up incense and other bits of Buddhist paraphernalia at the religious **market** on the pathway to the temple.

ASHOKAN PILLAR

The Indian emperor Ashoka visited Lumbini in around 249 BC, leaving behind an inscribed sandstone pillar to commemorate the occasion. After being lost for centu-

ries, Ashoka's pillar was rediscovered by the governor of Palpa, Khadga Shumsher Rana, in 1896. The 6m high pink sandstone pillar has now been returned to its original site in front of the Maya Devi temple – the pillar isn't much to look at, but it is highly revered by Nepali Buddhists. King Mahendra of Nepal tried to match the feat with his own **column** in the 1980s, but it languishes, largely forgotten, at the south end of the park.

BUDDHIST MONASTERIES

Since the Lumbini Development Zone was founded in 1978, Buddhist nations from around the world have constructed extravagant monasteries around the birthplace of

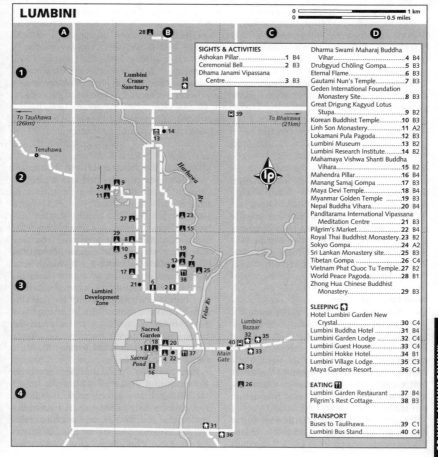

LUMBINI

SIGHTS & ACTIVITIES	
Ashokan Pillar	1 B4
Ceremonial Bell	2 B3
Dhama Janami Vipassana Centre	3 B3
Dharma Swami Maharaj Buddha Vihar	4 B4
Drubgyud Chöling Gompa	5 B3
Eternal Flame	6 B3
Gautami Nun's Temple	7 B3
Geden International Foundation Monastery Site	8 B3
Great Drigung Kagyud Lotus Stupa	9 B2
Korean Buddhist Temple	10 B3
Linh Son Monastery	11 A2
Lokamani Pula Pagoda	12 B3
Lumbini Museum	13 B2
Lumbini Research Institute	14 B2
Mahamaya Vishwa Shanti Buddha Vihara	15 B2
Mahendra Pillar	16 B4
Manang Samaj Gompa	17 B3
Maya Devi Temple	18 B4
Myanmar Golden Temple	19 B3
Nepal Buddha Vihara	20 B4
Panditarama International Vipassana Meditation Centre	21 B3
Pilgrim's Market	22 B4
Royal Thai Buddhist Monastery	23 B2
Sokyo Gompa	24 A2
Sri Lankan Monastery site	25 B3
Tibetan Gompa	26 C4
Vietnam Phat Quoc Tu Temple	27 B2
World Peace Pagoda	28 B1
Zhong Hua Chinese Buddhist Monastery	29 B3

SLEEPING	
Hotel Lumbini Garden New Crystal	30 C4
Lumbini Buddha Hotel	31 B4
Lumbini Garden Lodge	32 C4
Lumbini Guest House	33 C4
Lumbini Hokke Hotel	34 B1
Lumbini Village Lodge	35 C3
Maya Gardens Resort	36 C4

EATING	
Lumbini Garden Restaurant	37 B4
Pilgrim's Rest Cottage	38 B3

TRANSPORT	
Buses to Taulihawa	39 C1
Lumbini Bus Stand	40 C4

THE TERAI & MAHABHARAT RANGE

THE BIRTH OF THE BUDDHA

The historical Buddha, Siddhartha Gautama, was the son of Suddhodana, ruler of Kapilavastu, and Maya Devi, a princess from the neighbouring kingdom of Devdaha. According to legend, the pregnant Maya Devi was travelling between the two states when she came upon a pond of extraordinary beauty, surrounded by flowering sal trees. After bathing in the cool water, she suddenly went into labour, and just had time to walk 25 steps and grab the branch of a tree for support before the baby was born. The year was 563 AD and the location has been positively identified as Lumbini.

After the birth, a seer predicted that the boy would become a great teacher or a great king. Eager to ensure the later, King Suddhodana shielded him from all knowledge of the world outside the palace. At the age of 29, Siddhartha left the city for the first time and came face to face with an old man, a sick man, a hermit and a corpse. Shocked by this sudden exposure to human suffering, the prince abandoned his luxurious life to become a mendicant holy man, fasting and meditating on the nature of existence. After some severe austerities, the former prince realised that life as a starving pauper was no more conducive to wisdom than life as a pampered prince. Thus was born the middle way.

Finally, after 49 days meditating under a Bodhi tree on the site of modern-day Bodhgaya in India, Siddhartha attained enlightenment – a fundamental grasp of the nature of human existence. He travelled to Sarnath, near Varanasi, to preach his first sermon, and Buddhism was born. Renamed Buddha ('the enlightened one'), Siddhartha spent the next 46 years teaching the 'middle way' – a path of moderation and self-knowledge through which human beings could escape the cycle of birth and rebirth and achieve Nirvana, a state of eternal bliss.

The Buddha finally died at the age of 80 at Kushinagar, near Gorakhpur in India. Despite the Buddha's rejection of divinity and materialism, all the sites associated with his life have become centres for pilgrimage and the Buddha is worshipped as a deity across the Buddhist world. The ruins of Kapilavastu were unearthed close to Lumbini at Tilaurakot (see p297), and devotees still cross continents to visit Bodhgaya, Sarnath and Kushinagar in India. More recently, the site of Devdaha, the home of Maya Devi, was identified on the outskirts of the Nepali town of Butwal.

the Buddha. Each reflects the unique interpretation of Buddhism of its home nation and together the monasteries create a fascinating map of world Buddhist philosophy.

The site is *extremely* spread out, so hire a bicycle in Lumbini Bazar or rent one of the waiting rickshaws at the entrance to the archaeological zone. Unless otherwise stated, all the monasteries are open daily during daylight hours.

West Monastic zone

The West Monastic Zone is set aside for monasteries from the Mahayana school. Starting at the **Eternal Flame** (just north of the Maya Devi Temple), follow the dirt road along the west bank of the pond to the **Panditarama International Vipassana Meditation Centre** (☎ 580118; www.panditarama-lumbini.info), where serious practitioners of meditation can study for a nominal donation.

Heading north, a track turns west to the **Drubgyud Chöling Gompa** (☎ 580241), a classic Tibetan-style gompa built in 2001 by Bud-

dhists from Singapore and Nepal. The mural work inside is quite refined and a gigantic stupa is under construction next door. A small track veers south to the tasteful **Manang Samaj Gompa** (☎ 580135), a giant *chörten* (Tibetan reliquary stupa) constructed by Buddhists from Manang in northern Nepal.

Further west is the elegant **Zhong Hua Chinese Buddhist Monastery** (☎ 580264), one of the most impressive structures at Lumbini. Reached through a gateway flanked by Confucian deities, this elegant pagoda-style monastery looks like something from the Forbidden City. Not to be outdone, the government of South Korea is building a huge new **Korean Buddhist Temple** (☎ 580123) on the other side of the road.

Just north of the Chinese temple is the charming **Vietnam Phat Quoc Tu Temple** (☎ 580178), due to be completed in 2006. The pagoda-style monastery is beautifully landscaped and the dragon tiled roof is delightful. Nearby is a new complex of stupas and monastery buildings being constructed by the Austrian **Geden International Foundation**. New monasteries are also planned by the governments of Mongolia and Bhutan.

Further north is a second group of Mahayana monasteries, set around an L-shaped pond. The truly extravagant **Great Drigung Kagyud Lotus Stupa** (☎ 580275; 🕑 8am-noon & 1-5pm) was constructed by the German Tara Foundation and the domed ceiling of the main prayer room is covered in some inspired Buddhist murals.

Behind the German monastery is the **Sokyo Gompa** (☎ 580111), a traditional Tibetan-style gompa built by the Japanese Sokyo Foundation. The new **Linh Son Monastery** (☎ 580198) is being constructed by French Buddhists next door.

East Monastic Zone

The East Monastic Zone is set aside for monasteries from the Theravada school. The area is less developed than the western zone and the track is bumpier, but many of the monasteries have peaceful woodland settings.

Close to the north end of the pond, the **Royal Thai Buddhist Monastery** (☎ 580222) is an imposing *wat* (Thai-style monastery) built from gleaming white marble. Next door is the rather plain and austere **Mahamaya Vishwa Shanti Buddha Vihara** (☎ 580144), constructed as a joint venture between Japanese Buddhists and the Indian Mahabodhi Society.

A short cycle ride south is the **Myanmar Golden Temple** (☎ 580179), one of the oldest structures in the compound. There are three prayer halls here – the most impressive is topped by a corncob-shaped *shikhara* (tower), styled after the temples of Bagan. Nearby is the **Lokamani Pula Pagoda**, a huge gilded stupa in the southern Burmese style, inspired by the Shwedagon Paya in Yangon.

Behind the stupa is the modest **Gautami Nun's Temple** (☎ 580177), the only monastery in the compound built for female devotees. Across the road is the small **Dhama Janami Vipassana Centre** (☎ 580282), where followers of the Theravada school can practice meditation.

Further south, a track leads down to the site earmarked for the new **Sri Lankan Monastery** (☎ 580193). A short walk south from here takes you back to the Eternal Flame, passing a huge **ceremonial bell**, inscribed with Tibetan characters.

LUMBINI MUSEUM

Tucked away at the back of the compound, near the bridge at the north end of the pond, this **museum** (☎ 580318; foreigner/SAARC/Nepali Rs 50/10/10; 🕑 10am-3pm Wed-Mon) is devoted to the life of the Buddha, with artefacts and photos from Buddhist sites around the world, from Kathmandu to Candy.

Across the road is the **Lumbini Research Institute** (☎ 580175; liri@mos.com.np), but this is only open to serious scholars of Buddhist history.

WORLD PEACE PAGODA & LUMBINI CRANE SANCTUARY

Outside the main compound, but easily accessible by bike, the gleaming white **World Peace Pagoda** (🕑 daylight hr) was constructed by Japanese Buddhists at a cost of US$1 million. Near the base of the stupa is the grave of a Japanese monk, murdered by anti-Buddhist extremists during the construction of the monument.

The surrounding wetlands are protected as part of the **Lumbini Crane Sanctuary** and you stand a good chance of seeing rare sarus cranes stalking through the water meadows. There's no formal entrance to the park and no entrance fee – just stroll into the damp meadows behind the pagoda.

Tours

Recently, a number of traditional villages around Lumbini have been developed for grassroots tourism as part of the **Tourism for Rural Poverty Alleviation Programme** (TRPAP; ☎ 01-4269768; www.welcomenepal.com/trpap). The project is just getting off the ground but several of the lodges and hotels around the Development Zone now run village tours with a focus on traditional lifestyles and livelihoods.

Lumbini Village Lodge arranges interesting tours that really get under the surface of life in the Terai. Guides are available for Rs 500 per day, or you can get a map (Rs 20) and make your own way by bike.

Festivals & Events

The most important Buddhist celebration at Lumbini is the annual **Buddha Jayanti** festival in April or May, when busloads of Buddhists from India and Nepal come here to celebrate the birth of the Buddha. Pilgrims also come here to worship each

purnima (the night of the full moon) and **astami** (the eighth night after the full moon).

Many Hindus regard the Buddha as an incarnation of Vishnu and thousands of Hindu pilgrims come here on the full moon of the Nepali month of Baisakh (April–May) to worship Maya Devi as **Rupa Devi**, the mother goddess of Lumbini.

Sleeping

It is possible to day trip to Lumbini from Bhairawa, but there are plenty of places to stay around the compound.

BUDGET

Most of the budget options are in Lumbini Bazaar, the small village opposite the entrance to the Lumbini Development Zone. All are simple but very clean, and all serve homestyle Nepali meals.

Lumbini Village Lodge (☎ 580432; lumbinivillage lodge@yahoo.com; r without bathroom per person Rs 100, s/d with bathroom Rs 250/350) This charming lodge has a central courtyard shaded by a mango tree and big, clean rooms with fans and window nets. Internet access is available for Rs 80 per hour, you can rent bikes for Rs 100 per day, and the owners run tours of surrounding villages.

Lumbini Garden Lodge (☎ 580146; r with/without bathroom Rs 300/200) A few doors down, this is a tidy, family-run place with small, clean rooms. Some get more sunlight than others so see a few before deciding.

Lumbini Guest House (☎ 580142; s/d/tr Rs 250/300/400) On the other side of the main bazaar, this place is a bit more upmarket but still good value. Some rooms have squat toilets and some have western-style toilets so you have the choice.

MIDRANGE & TOP END

Most of the upmarket hotels are on the main road around the outside of the Development Zone. Unless otherwise stated, rooms at all the following hotels have bathrooms, TVs and air-con.

Lumbini Buddha Hotel (☎ 580114; lama_raa chit@hotmail.com; s/d US$15/20; ☒) In a small area of woodland at the south end of the Development Zone, this calm, institutional place has rooms in safari-style buildings linked by raised walkways.

Maya Gardens Resort (☎ 580220; bmaya@kghouse .com.np; s/d from US$60/70; ☒) Set in large grounds about 500m southeast of the site, this up-market resort offers very comfortable rooms in calm surroundings. There's a good restaurant. Ask about discounts.

Hotel Lumbini Garden New Crystal (☎ 580145; lumcrystal@ntc.net.np; s/d from US$90/99, ☒) Partner hotel to the New Crystal in Pokhara, this huge, swish place is almost opposite the gate to the Development Zone. It's aimed at well-heeled pilgrims and all sorts of religious paraphernalia is available in the foyer.

Lumbini Hokke Hotel (☎ 580236; subhokke_btw@ wlink.com.np; s/d US$90/120; Apr-Aug; ☒) Built with real style, the Hokke targets wealthy Japanese pilgrims who come to pray at the nearby World Peace Pagoda. It looks a bit like a traditional Japanese village and rooms come Western-style or Japanese-style, with tatami floors, paper partitions and Japanese furniture. The restaurant serves top-notch Japanese set meals.

Eating

Most people eat at their hotels, but there are a few restaurants in the development zone serving snack meals and cold drinks.

By the main car park, **Lumbini Garden Restaurant** (☻ 6am-6pm) is a modern red-brick place serving the usual mix of cold Cokes and veg thalis (plate meals).

Pilgrim's Rest Cottage (☻ 6am-6pm), near the Burmese stupa, serves good value Nepali set meals to hungry pilgrims and school groups.

Getting There & Away

Local buses run regularly between Lumbini and the local bus stand in Bhairawa (Rs 25, 1½ hours). The road to Lumbini is lined with traditional farms and tall mango trees – a perfect setting for a bit of roof riding.

To reach Taulihawa from Lumbini, take a local bus to the junction with the Bhairawa road (Rs 5) and change to a bus bound for Taulihawa (Rs 25, 1½ hours).

If you need to be in Bhairawa in a hurry, taxis in Lumbini Bazaar charge Rs 500 to the main Bhairawa bus stand and Rs 600 to the border at Belahiya.

Getting Around

The best way to get around the compound is by bicycle – Lumbini Village Lodge in Lumbini Bazaar charges Rs 100 per day for fairly reliable Chinese Hero bikes.

If you can't get a bike, a rickshaw can be a good alternative. Loads of rickshaw-wallahs loiter near the entrance to the development zone, charging Rs 50 to Rs 150 per hour, depending on your bargaining skills.

TAULIHAWA & TILAURAKOT

About 27km east of Lumbini, Taulihawa is another sleepy Terai town, but nearby Tilaurakot has been identified as the historical site of **Kapilavastu**, where Gautama Siddhartha spent the first 29 years of his life. For years, archaeologists waged an ongoing battle with a rival site at Piprahwa in India, but the discovery of artefacts dating back to the time of the Buddha at Tilaurakot have pretty much sealed the deal.

The site sits in a peaceful meadow, about 3km from Taulihawa, on the banks of the Banganga River, and you can still see the foundations of a large residential compound and the remains of the city moat and walls. However, the ruins have degraded over the centuries and it takes a certain amount of imagination to visualise the city of extravagant luxury that drove the Buddha to question the nature of existence.

Entry to the site is free and the surrounding farm land looks much the same today as it did in the time of Siddhartha Gautama. It isn't hard to imagine Siddhartha walking out through the imposing city gateway for the first time and seeing an old man, a sick man, a hermit and a corpse.

About 400m from the ruins, a small **museum** (☎ 076-560128; entry Rs 15; ⏲ 10am-5pm Wed-Mon) displays some of the artefacts found at the site, including a large collection of coins and pottery.

Taulihawa was the victim of a major Maoist assault in 2006. Check locally to make sure travel is safe before visiting from Lumbini.

Sleeping & Eating

There are plenty of basic food stalls in Taulihawa and there are reasonably clean, inexpensive rooms at **Lumbini Hotel** (s/d without bathroom Rs 80/100), on the road to Tilaurakot. There are no facilities at Tilaurakot so bring water and food from Taulihawa.

Getting There & Away

Lumbini lies a few km off the road from Bhairawa to Taulihawa. To reach Taulihawa from Lumbini, catch a local bus to the junction (Rs 5, 10 minutes) and change to a bus bound for Taulihawa (Rs 25, 1½ hours).

Tilaurakot is 3km north of Taulihawa. At the end of the bitumen the museum is on the left and the ruins are 400m away down a dirt track on the right. A rickshaw from Taulihawa will cost Rs 30.

THE SIDDHARTHA HWY

Most travellers heading north from Sunauli to Pokhara follow the Mahendra Hwy to Narayangarh then the Prithvi Hwy from Mugling to Pokhara, but a more interesting route is the dramatic Siddhartha Hwy, which winds through a series of landslide-scarred valleys between Butwal and Pokhara. Public buses run fairly regularly on this route, but the road is often blocked by landslides and floods during the monsoon. There are several temples at either end of the highway where drivers toss coins from their windows to pray for a safe journey.

Butwal

☎ 071

Butwal is fairly typical Terai town – hot, flat, dusty and crowded – but it sits at a very important junction. From here, the Mahendra Hwy runs east to Kakarbhitta and west to Mahendranagar and the Siddhartha Hwy runs north to Pokhara and south to Bhairawa/Sunauli. Even if you don't stop here, it's quite likely that you'll pass through town on your way across the plains.

There isn't a great deal to see, but the **old town** on the west bank of the Tinau River is worth exploring. A small pedestrian suspension bridge leads across the river from just west of Traffic Chowk. If you follow the Siddhartha Hwy north into the spooky looking Tinau Gorge, you'll come to a series of dramatic **waterfalls**, reached by another mini-suspension bridge.

Archaeologists have recently identified a village just east of Butwal as the site of the kingdom of **Devdaha**, home to the mother of Siddhartha Gautama Buddha. So far, only limited excavations have been carried out, but there's a small memorial park on the site, signposted off the Mahendra Hwy towards Narayangarh.

INFORMATION

Numerous Internet centres on the main road near Traffic Chowk offer slow Internet access for Rs 30 per hour. The Nabil Bank on Traffic Chowk has an ATM that takes international cards.

SLEEPING & EATING
There are plenty of hotels north of Traffic Chowk on the main road in the centre of town.

Hotel New Gandaki (☎ 540928; d without bathroom Rs 250) On the alley behind Traffic Chowk, this is a reliable cheapie – rooms are old but OK for the money.

Hotel Siddhartha (☎ 540380; s/d with bathroom Rs 500/700, s/d with air-con Rs 1000/1200; ✷) One of the better choices in town, the Siddhartha is bright and friendly and rooms have big TVs and hot showers – ask for one at the back away from the traffic noise. There's also a good restaurant.

Hotel Royal (☎ 542730; s/d with bathroom Rs 400/500) Across Traffic Chowk from the Siddhartha, Hotel Royal has compact but reasonably cosy rooms and an above-average restaurant.

There are lots of cheap and cheerful restaurants along the main road in Butwal, plus a few interesting options in the old town.

Kasturi Misthan Bhandar (meals from Rs 40; ⏱ 7am-8pm) This simple *misthan bhandar* (sweet shop and snack house) serves a wide range of sticky Indian sweets and healthy south Indian vegetarian meals.

Nanglo West (☎ 546184; Samaya Devi Tole; mains Rs 50-250; ⏱ 9am-8pm) Hidden away in the old

---

MISTHAN BHANDARS

An unlikely blend of sweet shop and vegetarian restaurant, *misthan bhandars* offer the full range of Indian sweetmeats, from *gulab jamun* (dough balls in sweet syrup) to *barfi* (milk and nut fudge) and *halwa* (soft fruit slices). Alongside these sweet treats, you'll find the spicy vegetarian flavours of South Indian cuisine – *dosas* (lentil flour pancakes), *idly* (steamed rice cakes) and *vadai* (gram flour donuts), all served with coconut chutney and *sambar* (a spicy dipping sauce with cinnamon and tamarind). If you travel for any length of time in the Terai, you'll find yourself visiting *misthan bhandars* quite regularly for a break from the daal bhaat, chow mein and chilli chicken.

---

town on the west bank of the river, this sophisticated Nepali restaurant is run by the same people as Nanglo West in Tansen. The menu features some interesting regional specialities.

GETTING THERE & AWAY
All long-distance buses leave from the main bus park, just south of Traffic Chowk. There are buses every half hour or so to Kathmandu (day/night/minibus Rs 207/261/282, seven hours) and Pokhara (day/night/minibus Rs 160/210/240; five hours) via Mugling and the Prithvi Hwy. There are also several daily buses on the scenic route to Pokhara via Tansen (Rs 50, two hours).

Along the Mahendra Hwy, there are regular buses to Narayangarh (Rs 80, two hours), Nepalganj (Rs 215-247, four hours) and Mahendranagar (Rs 467, nine hours). Kia minibuses zip along the hwy to Narayangarh for Rs 130.

Local buses leave for Sunauli/Bhairawa (Rs 28, 30 minutes) every 10 minutes.

Tansen (Palpa)
☎ 075
The former capital of the Magar kingdom of Tanahun, Tansen (Palpa) is a romantic medieval hill town, perched high above the Kali Gandaki River on the road between Butwal and Pokhara. The narrow, winding streets are full of Newari shop-houses and temples and most of the centre is too steep for cars, which all adds to Tansen's charm. Few tourists make it out this way, but it's easy to fill several days exploring the town and there are some excellent walks in the hills. Sadly, Tansen has been targeted by Maoists on several occasions, including a major assault on the Tansen Durbar compound in 2006. Check locally to make sure travel is safe before venturing here from Kathmandu or Pokhara.

Until the rise of the Shahs, Tanahun was one of the most powerful kingdoms in Nepal. Troops from Palpa even came close to conquering Kathmandu in the 16th century under the leadership of King Mukunda Sen. The power of the Magars waned in the 18th century and Tansen was reinvented as a Newari trading post on the trade route between India and Tibet. Metalworking and weaving *dhaka*, the fabric used for traditional Nepali jackets and

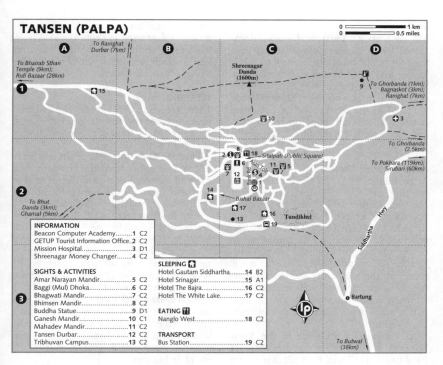

TANSEN (PALPA)

INFORMATION	
Beacon Computer Academy..........1	C2
GETUP Tourist Information Office.2	C2
Mission Hospital.........................3	D1
Shreenagar Money Changer........4	C2

SIGHTS & ACTIVITIES	
Amar Narayan Mandir.................5	C2
Baggi (Mul) Dhoka.....................6	C2
Bhagwati Mandir........................7	C2
Bhimsen Mandir.........................8	C2
Buddha Statue............................9	D1
Ganesh Mandir..........................10	C1
Mahadev Mandir.......................11	C2
Tansen Durbar...........................12	C2
Tribhuvan Campus.....................13	C2

SLEEPING	
Hotel Gautam Siddhartha.........14	B2
Hotel Srinagar..........................15	A1
Hotel The Bajra.........................16	C2
Hotel The White Lake..............17	C2

EATING	
Nanglo West.............................18	C2

TRANSPORT	
Bus Station...............................19	C2

topis (cloth hats), are still important local industries.

The tourist office can recommend some excellent walks to viewpoints and villages around Tansen and there are great views over the bowl-shaped Madi Valley from several points around town. A sheet of mist normally hangs over the valley till mid-morning, earning it the nickname 'White Lake'. For sweeping Himalaya views, head up to Shreenagar Danda, the forested peak above Tansen – see the boxed text p301.

ORIENTATION

Tansen is veritable maze of narrow alleys, but getting lost is part of the pleasure. The main road snakes around the western edge of town, but most places of interest are tucked away on the cobbled streets of the old town. The most important landmark is the octagonal pavilion in the middle of Sitalpati, the main market square. The main shopping street is Bank Street (Makhan Tole), running south from Sitalpati; the bus stand is about 500m south of the centre on the main road.

INFORMATION

Enterprising locals have set up an excellent tourist information service, **Getup** (Group for Environmental & Tourism Upgrading Palpa; ☎ 521341; getup@hons.com.np; ☼ 10am-1pm & 2-5pm Sun-Fri), about 30m west of Sitalpati. Staff can arrange guided trips to metalworking centres and fabric workshops and the office also sells excellent trekking maps (Rs 10) for short treks around Tansen, including the classic loop to Ranighat – see p301 and the boxed text, p301 for more information.

For foreign exchange, the best option is **Shreenagar Money Changer** (☼ 7.30am-6pm) on Bank Rd, just east of Sitalpati. There are several Internet cafés on Bank Rd but power cuts are common – the best connection is at **Beacon Computer Academy** (☎ 520239; per hr Rs 35; ☼ 7am-8pm).

For more information on Tansen, visit www.tansenpalpa.net.

SIGHTS

For a little visited hill town, Tansen is packed with interesting sights.

Sitalpati

The main market square in Tansen is dominated by a curious octagonal pavilion, used for public functions in the days when Tansen was ruled by the governors of the Shah regime. At the northwest corner of the square, the small, two-tiered **Bhimsen Mandir** is sacred to the Newari god of trade and commerce. Several shops on the square, and along nearby Bank Street, sell *dhaka* fabric and local metalware.

Amar Narayan Mandir

At the bottom of Asan Tole (the steep road running east from Sitalpati), the Amar Narayan Mandir is a classic three-tiered, pagoda-style temple. The mandir was built in 1807 by Amar Singh Thapa, the first governor of Tansen, and it's considered to be one of the most beautiful temples outside the Kathmandu Valley. Note the erotic scenes on the roof struts and the alternating skulls and animal heads on the lintel. Devotees come here every evening to light butter lamps in honour of the patron deity, Lord Vishnu.

At the start of the steps to the Amar Narayan Mandir is the smaller **Mahadev Mandir**, sacred to Shiva. It's built in the same tiered Newari style and inside, a pot of water drips continually onto a stone lingam. Local women fill their brass *gaagri* (water ewers) at the waterspout behind the temple.

Leather items and shoes should be removed before entering either temple.

Tansen Durbar

Probably the most striking building in Tansen, this bureaucratic-looking palace was built for the provincial governor in 1927. A fan of pomp and circumstance, the governor used to ride out to greet his subjects on an elephant through the huge gateway on the south side of Sitalpati (known locally as **Baggi Dhoka** or Mul Dhoka). The Durbar is now the administrative centre for the local government but it's heavily fortified and foreigners are only allowed to peek in through the gate.

Bhagwati Mandir

This large modern-looking temple is hidden in a courtyard on the west side of the Durbar, but it sits on the site of several older shrines. As the only shrine dedicated to Durga, the patron saint of the Newars, it's probably the most popular temple in town. The idols from the temple are paraded through town on chariots each August as part of the Bhadra Krishna Nawami festival.

SLEEPING

There are some cheap 'hotel and lodging' places around the bus station, but they're all pretty awful – most of the decent choices are uphill in the old town.

Hotel The Bajra (☎ 520443; s/d with bathroom Rs 150/250) Just uphill from the bus park, this cheerful cheapie has a good Nepali restaurant and basic rooms with cold showers (hot water is available by the bucket).

Hotel The White Lake (☎ 520291; s/d without bathroom Rs 200/300, s/d with bathroom Rs 400/600, deluxe s/d Rs 900/1200) The deluxe rooms here are very comfortable, but the cheaper rooms are overpriced. However, the welcome is friendly, the restaurant serves decent grub and the terrace at the back has excellent valley views.

Hotel Gautam Siddhartha (☎ 520280; d/tr without bathroom Rs 150/250) Nearby, on the small square known as Bishal Bazaar, this small local hotel is a good find. The owners run a Nepali restaurant downstairs and rooms are plain but clean.

Hotel Srinagar (☎ 520045; www.hotelsrinagar.com; s/d with bathroom & TV US$24/32; discounts of 30%) The most luxurious option, about 2km away on the ridge above town, a 20-minute walk west of the summit. Although rather isolated, rooms are sumptuous, the views are sensational and there's a good restaurant.

EATING

All the hotels have restaurants, but it would be a shame to leave Tansen without sampling the Nepali delights at **Nanglo West** (☎ 520184; Nepali mains Rs 50-250; ⏰ 10.30am-8.30pm), on the north side of Sitalpati. As well as familiar staples like daal bhaat, you can sample the local *choyla* (dried buffalo or duck meat with chilli and ginger), served with *chura* (flattened rice) and spiced potatoes in curd. The restaurant is styled like a Nepali house and diners sit on low cushions (shoes should be removed at the door).

GETTING THERE & AWAY

The **bus station** is at the southern entrance to Tansen and the ticket office is at the east end of the stand. Buses to Pokhara (Rs 130,

---

WALKS AROUND TANSEN

Tansen is set in the middle of fantastic walking country and the tourist office **GETUP** (p299) can recommend some excellent walks in the surrounding hills.

One of the nicest short walks is the one-hour stroll up **Shreenagar Danda**, the 1600m-high hill directly north of town. The trail starts near the small **Ganesh mandir (temple)** above Tansen and climbs steeply through open woodland to the crest of the hill. When you reach the ridge, turn right; a 20-minute stroll will take you to a modern **Buddha statue** and a viewpoint with fabulous views over the gorge of the Kali Gandaki River and the Himalaya.

Another short and easy walk is the two-hour stroll to the **Bhairab Sthan Temple**, 9km west of Tansen. The courtyard in front of the temple contains a gigantic brass trident and inside is a silver mask of Bhairab, allegedly plundered from Kathmandu by Mukunda Sen. The walk follows the road from Tansen to Tamghas.

If you fancy something more challenging, the three-hour walk to the village of **Ghansal** passes several hilltop viewpoints, emerging on the highway about 3km south of Tansen. The walk is mainly downhill and there are spectacular valley views from Bhut Dada, about halfway along the route. GETUP sells a map (Rs 10) with a detailed description of the trail.

Other possible destinations for walks include **Ghorbanda**, a traditional potters village northeast of Tansen on the way to Pokhara and **Bagnaskot**, on the ridge east of Gorkhekot, which has a small Devi temple and a wonderfully exposed hilltop viewpoint. You can also follow the old **trade route** from Tansen to Butwal – GETUP has a map (Rs 10) with a detailed description of the trail. All three walks can be completed in a day if you get an early start.

---

four hours) leave at 5.30am, 6.15am and 9.30am, or there are regular services down to Butwal (Rs 50, two hours) from 6.30am to 5pm. Local buses for Ridi Bazaar (Rs 50, two hours) leave fairly regularly during the same hours – get an early morning start if you want to get back the same day.

Around Tansen

As well as the popular walks around Tansen (see the boxed text above), there are a few interesting villages that you can reach on foot or by bus.

RANIGHAT

The most famous sight near Tansen is probably the **Ranighat Durbar** on the east bank of the Kali Gandaki. Fancifully referred to as Nepal's Taj Mahal, this crumbling baroque palace was built in 1896 by Khadga Shamsher Rana, an ambitious politician who was exiled from Kathmandu for plotting against the prime minister. Khadga made another abortive attempt to seize power in 1921 and was exiled again, this time to India. After his departure, the Durbar was stripped of most of its valuable fittings, but the building still stands, slowly fading on the banks of the Kali Gandaki.

You can walk to the Durbar in around four hours along an easy-to-follow trail, beginning in Gorkhekot at the east end of Shreenagar Danda. The route down to the river is mainly downhill, but the return leg follows a steeply ascending trail on the next ridge, emerging near Hotel Srinagar. GETUP sells an excellent route guide and map (Rs 10). Rafting trips on the Kali Gandaki sometimes make it as far as the palace – see p97.

RIDI BAZAAR

About 28km northwest of Tansen by road (or 13km on foot), the Newari village of Ridi Bazaar sits at the confluence of the Kali Gandaki and Ridi Khola. As a sacred confluence, Ridi is a popular destination for pilgrimages, and the site is further sanctified by the presence of *saligrams* – the spiral fossils of ancient sea creatures, distantly related to the modern nautilus – revered as symbols of Vishnu.

Pilgrims believe that if they fast and worship for three days and take a ritual bath in the Kali Gandaki, all their sins will be forgiven. The most important feast day is **Magh Sankranti** (see p363), the first day of the Nepali month of Magh (mid-January), when hundreds of devotees bathe in the icy waters of the Kali Gandaki to mark the passing of winter. Worshippers also gather every *ekadashi* (the 11th day after the full moon).

The principal religious monument in Ridi is the **Rishikesh Mandir**, founded by Mukunda Sen in the 16th century. According to legend, the Vishnu idol inside was discovered fully-formed in the river and has miraculously aged from boy to man. The temple is on the south bank of the Ridi Khola, near the bus stand.

To reach Ridi on foot, take the trail leading northwest from the Tansen–Tamghas road near Hotel Srinagar. Buses to Ridi (Rs 50, two hours) leave from the public bus stand in Tansen.

SIRUBARI

About 80km northwest of Tansen, the remote Gurung village of Sirubari has been developed as a destination for cultural tourism by the Nepal Tourism Board. Far from a tacky tourist experience, this is more like a rural homestay – accommodation and meals are provided by local farmers and the only way in is on foot, via a four-hour trek from Syangja on the Siddhartha Hwy. The village is full of traditional stone buildings, including a charming gompa (Buddhist monastery), and there's a rugged viewpoint nearby at **Thumro** (2300m) overlooking the full sweep of Himalayan peaks. The villagers are mainly Buddhist and most families have at least one member in the Gurkha Regiments.

The trail to the village begins at the small village of Arjunchaupari near Syangja, on the road between Pokhara and Tansen. However, few people in Sirubari speak English and you may have problems if you drop in unannounced. The easiest way to visit is to make advance arrangements with a travel agent in Kathmandu or Pokhara – they'll arrange your accommodation and a guide and put you on the right bus to the trailhead.

BIRGANJ
☎ 051

Unlovely would be a good way to describe Birganj. As the main transit point for freight between India and Nepal, the town is mobbed by trucks, deafened by car horns, jostled by rickshaws and choked by traffic fumes. Most of Nepal's exports leave the country via the hectic border crossing at Raxaul Bazaar, but travellers tend to skip this crossing entirely in favour of the much saner border crossings at Sunauli and Kakarbhitta.

If you can get over the heat and noise, there are some interesting buildings dotted around town. The fanciful **clock tower** in the centre of town is covered in Buddhist and Hindu iconography and just west is the popular **Gahawa Maysan Mandir**, sacred to Durga. On the other side of Main Rd is the **Ghariarwa Pokhari**, a sacred pond used by locals as an impromptu swimming pool. Nearby is **Bal Mandir**, a meeting hall styled after the Buddhist stupa at Bodhnath, and

---

CROSSING THE BORDER

Border Hours

The Nepali side of the border is open 24 hours but the Indian side is usually only staffed from 4am to 10pm, though you may be able to find someone to stamp you through outside these times. Nepali visas are available on arrival from the Nepal immigration office but payment must be in US dollars.

Foreign Exchange

There are no facilities at the border but there are banks and moneychangers in Birganj.

Onwards to India

The border is 5km south of Birganj and it's about 500m from the Nepali border post to the bus station in Raxaul Bazaar. Most people take a rickshaw straight through from Birganj (Rs 40). From Raxaul, there are regular buses to Patna (INRs 90, five hours) or you can take the daily Mithila Express train to Kolkata's Howrah train station – it leaves Raxaul at 10.20am, arriving into Howrah at 5am the next morning. Seats cost INRs 276/748/1165 in sleeper class/air-con 3-tier/air-con 2-tier.

further south is a colourful **Shiv Temple** with a giant statue of Lord Shiva.

ORIENTATION & INFORMATION

Birganj follows a simple grid system. Main Rd runs through the middle of town to the Indian border and most of the hotels are on the streets running west. The bus stand is at the end of Ghantaghar Rd (New Rd), which runs east from the clocktower at the north end of town.

There's a government-approved **money-changer** (7am-7pm) opposite Hotel Makalu on the corner of Campus Rd and Main Rd. You can change US dollars, euros, UK pounds and Indian and Nepali rupees, but only in cash. For travellers cheques, try the **Nepal Bangladesh Bank**, further along Campus Rd.

Fast Internet access is available from **Shree Shyam Cyber Cafe** (529947; per hr Rs 20; 6.30am-8.30pm), around the corner from Hotel Kailas.

SLEEPING

There are a number of noisy budget places near the main bus stand, and a handful of more upmarket choices in the centre.

Hotel Welcome Nepal (524057; Ghantaghar Rd; s/d without bathroom Rs 125/150, d with bathroom Rs 300-250) The most salubrious choice in this area, Hotel Welcome Nepal gets slightly less traffic noise than the places right next to the bus stand.

There are more hotels further west along Ghantaghar Rd and Main Rd.

Hotel Kailas (522384; Adarshnagar; s without bathroom Rs 100, s/d with bathroom from Rs 280/430, r with air-con Rs 990;) Bellboys in bow ties and chintzy '60s décor add charm at this big budget hotel one block west of Main Rd. Rooms are moderately tasteful and the attached Dewan-E-Khas restaurant serves tasty Indian and Chinese food.

Hotel Diyalo (522370; vishuwa@nepalexpo.com; Adarshnagar; r with bathroom Rs 400, with air-con Rs 600-1000;) Almost next door to Hotel Kailas, this big institutional place has large, un-cluttered rooms and a cosy little restaurant. The styling is a bit dated but rooms are comfortable.

Hotel Makalu (523054; hmakalu@atcmail.com.np; cnr Campus & Main Rds; r with bathroom Rs 800, with air-con from Rs 1200;) This recommended business-class hotel is very calm and relaxed – just

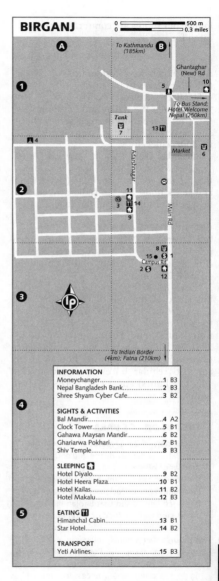

BIRGANJ

0   500 m
0   0.3 miles

To Kathmandu (185km)

Ghantaghar (New) Rd

To Bus Stand; Hotel Welcome Nepal (250km)

Tank

Market

Adarshnagar

Main Rd

Campus Rd

To Indian Border (4km); Patna (210km)

INFORMATION	
Moneychanger	1 B3
Nepal Bangladesh Bank	2 B3
Shree Shyam Cyber Cafe	3 B2

SIGHTS & ACTIVITIES	
Bal Mandir	4 A2
Clock Tower	5 B1
Gahawa Maysan Mandir	6 B2
Ghariarwa Pokhari	7 B1
Shiv Temple	8 B3

SLEEPING	
Hotel Diyalo	9 B2
Hotel Heera Plaza	10 B1
Hotel Kailas	11 B1
Hotel Makalu	12 B3

EATING	
Himanchal Cabin	13 B1
Star Hotel	14 B2

TRANSPORT	
Yeti Airlines	15 B3

what you need in hectic Birganj. Rooms have TVs, carpets and 24-hour hot showers and there's a very good restaurant.

Hotel Heera Plaza (523988; giris@atcnet.com .np; Ghantaghar Rd; s/d with bathroom & TV Rs 700/800, with air-con Rs 1200/1400;) Midway between the clock tower and the bus station, this gigantic place feels a bit like a 1970s airport lounge but rooms are comfortable and well cared for.

EATING

All the hotels have restaurants, or try the following places in the town centre.

Star Hotel (Adarshnagar; meals Rs 40-100; 🕑 9am-9pm) Between the Kailas and Diyalo hotels, this simple tandoori canteen serves cheap and tasty *thalis* (Indian plate meals) and tandoori chicken.

Himanchal Cabin (Main Rd; mains under Rs 60; 🕑 7.30am-8.30pm) Close to the clock tower, this reliable *misthan bhandar* (sweet shop and snack house) serves Indian sweets and tasty south Indian vegetarian snacks.

GETTING THERE & AWAY

Yeti Airlines (☎ 525389; Campus Rd) and other private carriers fly daily between Simara (the airport for Birganj) and Kathmandu (US$64; 20 minutes).

Buses leave from the large and hectic bus stand at the end of Ghantaghar Rd. There are plenty of day and night buses to Kathmandu (day/night Rs 225/280, nine hours), and Pokhara (day/night Rs 225/270; nine hours), via Narayangarh (day/night Rs 140/150, three hours). There are also regular buses to Janakpur (Rs 140, five hours) and Hetauda (Rs 65, two hours).

THE BUDDHA OF BARA

At the start of 2005, nobody had heard of Ram Bahadur Banjan. By the end of the year, thousands of Nepali Buddhists were hailing the 16-year-old Tamang boy as the second incarnation of the Buddha. Followers of the teenaged lama claim that Banjan has been meditating without food or water in the forest east of Birganj for at least six months. Although that sounds unlikely, the Nepali government asked the Royal Nepal Academy of Science and Technology to investigate the claim, and if necessary, declare a miracle. Before any conclusions could be reached, Banjan mysteriously disappeared, most likely spirited away by his followers to a location more conducive to inner reflection. However, this is unlikely to be the end of the story – check the Nepali news media for the latest developments.

GETTING AROUND

Rickshaws charge Rs 40 to go from town to the Nepali border post and on to Raxaul Bazaar. Alternatively, you can take a tempo or tonga (horse cart) from the bus station to the Nepali border post for Rs 8 and then walk to the Indian side.

THE TRIBHUVAN HWY

From Birganj, the easiest and fastest route to Kathmandu or Pokhara is along the Mahendra Hwy to Narayangarh and then north to Mugling, but when were the best travel experiences ever easy? It's much more fun to take the winding and dramatic Tribhuvan Hwy, which leaves the Mahendra Highway at Hetauda, just east of Chitwan. The road is sometimes blocked by floodwaters and landslides after the monsoon, but the scenery is breathtaking and you can stop on way at Daman for some of the best Himalayan views in Nepal. For details of the mountain bike ride along this route see p86.

Hetauda

☎ 057

The bustling town of Hetauda marks the junction between the flat Mahendra Hwy and the steep, spectacular Tribhuvan Hwy. From here, a Heath-Robinson cableway carries cement and gravel uphill from the Terai to satisfy Kathmandu's insatiable appetite for construction. There isn't any great reason to stop here except to change buses, but the locals are friendly and the town is known for its brassware, particularly the brass *gaagri* pots that locals use to store water.

There are no foreign exchange facilities but several Internet cafés on the main road offer Internet access for Rs 30 per hour.

SLEEPING & EATING

There are several cheap lodges by the bus stand, but quieter rooms are available around Mahendra Chowk on the main road.

Neelam Lodge (☎ 520900; Main Rd; s/d without bathroom Rs 90/140, s/d with bathroom Rs 170/250) On the main road, about 200m north of Mahendra Chowk, this simple lodge is a favourite stop for traders from the hills. There are no frills but the rooms are clean and the welcome warm.

Hotel Seema (☎ 520124; seema@mos.com.np; Main Rd; s/d with bathroom & TV Rs 600/800, s/d with air-con Rs 1500/2000; 🖵) This big, modern business-class hotel is a short walk south of Mahendra Chowk. The restaurant cooks up excellent Indian and Chinese food and the rooms have a touch of class, with carpets, TVs and hot showers.

Motel Avocado & Orchid Resort (☎ 520429; www.orchidresort.com; Tribhuvan Hwy; Nissan hut s/d Rs 350/500, hotel s/d from Rs 500/800, deluxe s/d from Rs 1200/1600, discounts of 20%; 🏊) Further north, where the Tribhuvan Hwy leaves Hetauda, this quirky resort is set in a peaceful garden of rhododendron and avocado trees. Accommodation is in Nissen huts or in two plush hotel blocks at the back of the garden and the cheerful restaurant has a notebook where cyclists and motorcyclists have recorded their travels through Nepal.

GETTING THERE & AROUND
The main bus stand is just west of Mahendra Chowk. There are regular morning and afternoon buses to Pokhara (Rs 250/270, six hours), and Kathmandu (day/night Rs 200/210, six hours) via Narayangarh (Rs 75/90, one hour). You can also pick up services to destinations east and west along the Mahendra Hwy. Local buses and minibuses run regularly to Birganj (Rs 65, two hours).

Buses along the Tribhuvan Hwy leave from a smaller bus stand, just north of Motel Avocado. There are buses every hour or so to Kathmandu (Rs 200, eight hours) via Daman (Rs 90, four hours) until around 2pm. Rickshaws and auto-rickshaws can ferry you from town to the bus stand for Rs 30.

Daman
☎ 057

Perched 2322m above sea level, with clear views to the north, east and west, Daman boasts what is arguably *the* most spectacular outlook on the Himalaya in the whole of Nepal. There are unimpeded views of the entire range from Dhaulagiri to Mt Everest from the concrete **viewing tower** (admission foreigner/Nepali Rs 20/10) inside the Daman Mountain Resort. Alternatively, head to the helipad at the Everest Panorama Resort.

There are several interesting detours from Daman. About 1km south of the village, towards Hetauda, a trail leads west through the forest to the tiny **Shree Rikheshwar Mahadev Mandir,** sacred to Shiva. On the way, you can drop into a gorgeous little **gompa** (Buddhist monastery) in a glade

---

WALKS AROUND DAMAN
Beyond Daman, the Tribhuvan Hwy plunges into the heavily cultivated Palung Valley, an idyllic patchwork of mustard, rice and millet fields, small orchards, trickling streams and peaceful villages of brick and stone houses. Few people pass through the area, let alone take time to explore it, but this is probably the closest place to Kathmandu where you can experience Nepal as it was before the Internet cafés and banana pancakes.

The valley is a fascinating base for walks and mountain biking trips. Most towns in the area have basic lodges and *bhojanalayas* (snack restaurants). Just equip yourself with a decent topographical map and go explore. Probably the best starting point for walks is **Shikharkot**, about 40km south of Naubise. There are several rustic lodges on the main road and buses between Kathmandu and Daman pass through several times a day.

Sadly there have been clashes between government forces and Maoist rebels in this area. Make sure that things are calm before setting off into the hills.

---

of trees draped with thousands of prayer flags. From the highway, it's 1km to the gompa and 1.5km to the temple.

SLEEPING & EATING
There are just a few places to stay, but all budgets are catered for.

In the middle of the village are three simple guest houses – **Everest Hotel & Lodge, Hotel Daman & Lodge** and **Gauri Shankar Hotel & Lodge** – owned by local families and sharing a single phone number (☎ 057-540387). All offer Nepali meals and simple rooms in rustic village houses – don't be surprised if you end up sleeping near a pile of onions! Single/double rooms cost Rs 100/200, and daal bhaat is Rs 50.

Daman Mountain Resort (☎ 01-4438023 in Kathmandu; safari-style tents Rs 400, r with/without bathroom Rs 800/700) This ageing resort at the start of the village is a more comfortable option. It's not the Savoy, but rooms are clean and cosy and the viewing tower has the best views in Daman. The tents are probably best avoided in winter.

Everest Panorama Resort (☎ 057-540382, ☎ 01-4415372-3 in Kathmandu; s/d US$70/80, discounts of 20%)

Easily the most charming place to stay in Daman, this upmarket mountain resort offers tasteful cottages with sun decks scattered across a sunny hillside facing the Himalaya. All the rooms have heaters, TVs, hot showers and mountain views and you can arrange guided walks, mountain biking and pony treks. Reception is a 200m walk from the highway along a winding boardwalk.

GETTING THERE & AWAY

Buses leave Daman every hour or so from 7am to 2pm to Kathmandu (Rs 175, four hours) and Hetauda (Rs 90, four hours). Alternatively, this is one of the most spectacular (and gruelling) mountain-bike routes in Nepal (see p86 for details).

WESTERN TERAI

The Mahendra Hwy runs west from Butwal to meet the Indian border at Mahendranagar, passing through one of the least developed parts of Nepal. Few travellers pass through the area and fewer still stop to investigate its little-visited national parks. Unfortunately, western Nepal is also the heartland of the Maoist insurgency. Bridges, telephone exchanges, government offices and army bases have been attacked on numerous occasions and it's important to check the security situation before planning any trips through this area.

NEPALGANJ
☎ 081

Few travellers use the border crossing at Nepalganj (Nepalgunj), even though the Indian city of Lucknow is just four hours away by bus. Nepalganj is a fairly typical Nepali border town – mobbed by traders and full of cheap hotels and contraband goods – but the border crossing is hassle free and there are good bus and air connections on to other parts of Nepal.

If you find yourself spending time in Nepalganj, take a stroll through the old bazaar. Shop windows are crammed with smuggled goods and there are half a dozen small temples strung out along the main road through the bazaar. Probably the most interesting is the garish **Bageshwari Mandir**, devoted to Kali. Nearby is a large pond with a pavilion containing a gaudy **statue** of Mahadev (Shiva).

As the main administrative centre for the region, Nepalganj is a popular target for rebel attacks. The centre of town is heavily fortified and it's wise to check the security situation before attempting to cross the border here.

Orientation & Information

Nepalganj is 16km south of the Mahendra Hwy and 6km north of the Indian border. It's about 1km from the Nepali border post at Jamunaha to the Indian border post at Rupaidha Bazaar – walkable, but easier by rickshaw.

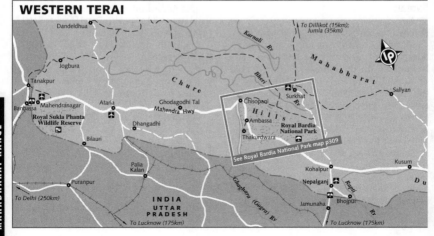

WESTERN TERAI

Most of the hotels in Nepalganj are strung out along Surkhet Rd near the Birendra Chowk roundabout. The bus stand is 1km northeast of Birendra Chowk and the airport is 6km northwest.

A couple of places on Surkhet Rd offer slow Internet access for Rs 40 per hour.

Sleeping & Eating

Most hotels are on the main road north of Birendra Chowk.

Manakamana Guest House (☎ 520664; Surkhet Rd; d with bathroom Rs 150) Budget travellers will find rudimentary rooms with fans and cold showers at this basic lodge on the main road.

Hamro Guest House (☎ 520818; Surkhet Rd; d without bathroom Rs 100-200, with bathroom Rs 300-500) Many Indian tourists choose this cheap and informal place, set around a courtyard just north of Birendra Chowk.

Hotel Pahuna Ghar (☎ 522358; Surkhet Rd; d with bathroom/hot water Rs 250/400) North of the centre towards the bus stand, this reliable mid-range place offers a choice of budget rooms with cold showers or deluxe rooms with marble floors, TVs and hot showers.

Hotel Sneha (☎ 520119; hotel@sneha.wlink .np; Surkhet Rd; s/d with air-con US$30/36, discounts of 25%; 🖳) This big old-fashioned conference hotel is set in sprawling grounds on the way to the border. The huge rooms are set around a courtyard full of royal palms. Unfortunately, the hotel is often booked out for government meetings.

> ### CROSSING THE BORDER
>
> **Border Hours**
> Both sides of the border are open from 4.30am to 9pm, but you may be able to cross later if you can find the immigration officials.
>
> **Foreign Exchange**
> There are several moneychangers on the Nepali side of the border, but they only exchange Indian and Nepali rupees. The Nabil Bank in Nepalganj may be able to exchange other currencies.
>
> **Onward to India**
> For Rs 50 you can take a rickshaw from the Nepalganj bus stand to the border at Jamunaha and on to the bus stand in Rupaidha Bazar. From here, buses and share taxis run regularly to Lucknow (INRs 160, seven hours). The nearest point on the Indian rail network is Nanpara, 17km from the border.

All the hotels have restaurants, but there are several upmarket eateries on the main road.

Kitchen Hut (☎ 524349; mains Rs 50-200; 🕙 10am-9.30pm) This bright and bustling place has the best food and atmosphere in town. The menu runs the gamut from *dosas* to momos.

Getting There & Away

AIR

Nepalganj is the main air hub for western Nepal. **RNAC** (☎ 520767) has four weekly flights to Kathmandu (US$103 to US$122, two hours) and numerous flights to small airstrips in the interior, including Jumla (US$61 to US$69, 45 minutes) and Dolpa (US$81 to US$91, 45 minutes). Most of the private airlines also fly to Kathmandu for around US$109.

If the airline offices are closed, try **Neha Tours & Travels** (☎ 523525) or **Sneha Tours & Travels** (☎ 522507) on the main road.

BUS

The well-organised **bus stand** is about 1km northeast of Birendra Chowk. Buses to Kathmandu (day/night Rs 450/540, 12

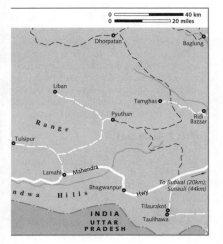

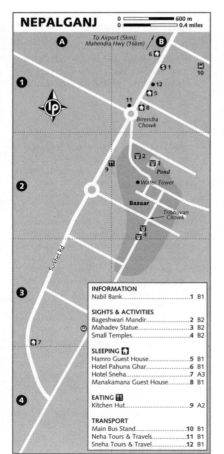

NEPALGANJ

0 ————— 600 m
0 ————— 0.4 miles

To Airport (5km);
Mahendra Hwy (16km)

Birendra
Chowk

Pond

Water Tower

Bazaar

Tribhuvan
Chowk

Surkhet Rd

INFORMATION
Nabil Bank.....................................1 B1

SIGHTS & ACTIVITIES
Bageshwari Mandir.........................2 B2
Mahadev Statue..............................3 B2
Small Temples................................4 B2

SLEEPING
Hamro Guest House.........................5 B1
Hotel Pahuna Ghar..........................6 B1
Hotel Sneha...................................7 A3
Manakamana Guest House...............8 B1

EATING
Kitchen Hut...................................9 A2

TRANSPORT
Main Bus Stand............................10 B1
Neha Tours & Travels.....................11 B1
Sneha Tours & Travel.....................12 B1

hours) and Pokhara (day/night Rs 400/520, 12 hours) leave early in the morning or early in the afternoon; all buses run via Narayangarh (day/night Rs 380/400, eight hours). Buses for Mahendranagar (Rs 300, six hours) leave hourly from 5.30am until 2pm in the afternoon.

Local buses to Thakurdwara (for Royal Bardia National Park) leave at 11.20am and 1.30pm (Rs 126, three hours).

Getting Around

Shared *tempos* (three-wheelers) and tongas run between the bus stand and the border for Rs 15. A cycle-rickshaw costs Rs 50 to the airport and Rs 40 all the way to Rupaidha Bazaar in India.

ROYAL BARDIA NATIONAL PARK

☎ 084

About halfway between Butwal and Mahendranagar, **Royal Bardia National Park** (☎ 429719; admission per day foreigner/SAARC/Nepali Rs 500/200/20) is the largest untouched wilderness in the Terai. The park protects 968 sq km of sal forest and whispering grassland, bordering the Geruwa and Karnali Rivers. The atmosphere is wonderfully tranquil and with the current slump in tourism, you may well have the whole place to yourself.

There are estimated to be around 22 royal Bengal tigers and 100 one-horned rhinos at Bardia but these animals are elusive and sightings are rare. Other mammals in the park include grey langurs, rhesus macaques, leopards, civets, hyenas, sloth bears and barking, spotted, sambar and hog deer. Bardia also has more than 250 species of birds, including the endangered Bengal florican and sarus crane. Gharial and marsh mugger crocodiles and Gangetic dolphins are occasionally spotted on rafting and canoe trips along the Geruwa River.

Be warned that Maoist rebels are active on the fringes of the national park. Visitor numbers have plummeted since the start of the insurgency and most people visit on organised tours, which only run when the army and rebels are observing a ceasefire.

Orientation & Information

Park fees should be paid at the **park headquarters** (☎ 429719; 6am-5pm Sun-Fri) is about 13km south of the Mahendra Hwy in the village of Thakurdwara. The bumpy access road leaves the highway at Ambassa, about 500m before the Amreni army checkpost.

Most of the safari lodges are close to Thakurdwara, but because of the poor condition of the roads, visitors usually arrange to be transferred to the lodges by 4WD. Note that much of the park is inaccessible from May to September because of flooding.

Sights & Activities

Most people visit Bardia on an **elephant safari** and this is by far the most exciting way to explore the park. Rides on the park elephants (foreigner/SAARC/Nepali Rs 1000/400/200) should be booked in advance at the park headquarters. Jeep safaris can be arranged directly through the lodges for around Rs 4000 per jeep.

THE TERAI &
MAHABHARAT RANGE

Guided walks will get you even closer to the wildlife, but this can be a risky activity with angry rhinos around. Any of the lodges can arrange a guide, but rates will depend on the number of people in the group. **Boat trips** along the Geruwa River cost Rs 500/200/50 by canoe and Rs 1000/4000/100 by inflatable raft.

The park headquarters has a small **information centre** (admission free; 🕙 10am-4pm Sun-Fri) and a breeding centre for marsh mugger and gharial crocodiles. Also located here is the intriguing **Tharu Museum** (admission foreigner/Nepali Rs 50/5; 🕙 10am-4pm Sun-Fri), which explores the customs and rituals of the Tharu people.

The Karnali river is also famous for *mahaseer*, the giant South Asian river carp, which can reach 80 kilos in weight. Anglers can obtain fishing permits (foreigner/SAARC/Nepali Rs 500/100/20) at the park headquarters. However, be aware that the World Wildlife Foundation is campaigning for the *mahaseer* to be added to the world list of endangered species because of overfishing and pollution.

Sleeping & Eating

With the collapse of tourism in the Terai, most people visit Bardia on organised package tours. Independent travellers should call ahead to make sure resorts are open for business. Most places are currently offering discounts of up to 40%, though this usually doesn't apply to package rates.

Bardia Jungle Cottages (☎ 429714; in Kathmandu 01-4428552; shakti@travels.wlink.com.np; cottages with/without bathroom from Rs 300/250) Right opposite the park entrance, this friendly, low-key resort has a large, shady garden, a restaurant and comfortable thatched cottages with ceiling fans. In these more quiet times, you'll appreciate being so close to the park headquarters.

Forest Hideaway Cottages (☎ 429716; ☎ 01-4225973 in Kathmandu; www.foresthideaway.com; 4/5 day packages incl meals & activities US$155/206) About 1km north of the park headquarters, this cosy Tharu-style resort is one of the best choices at Bardia. The grass-roofed cottages have solar power and rates include meals, activities, park fees, transfers from Ambassa and an onward bus ticket to your chosen

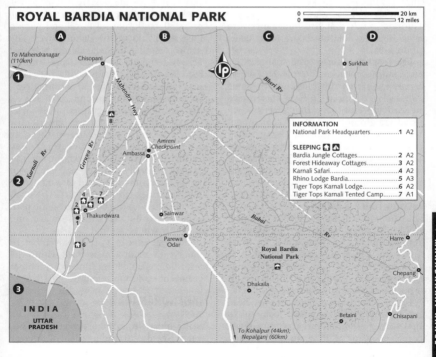

ROYAL BARDIA NATIONAL PARK

0 _____ 20 km
0 _____ 12 miles

To Mahendranagar (110km)

Chisopani

Surkhat

Mahendra Hwy

Bheri Rv

Karnali Rv

Geruwa Rv

Amreni Checkpoint

Ambassa

INFORMATION
National Park Headquarters...............1 A2

SLEEPING 🏠 🏕
Bardia Jungle Cottages.....................2 A2
Forest Hideaway Cottages.................3 A2
Karnali Safari....................................4 A2
Rhino Lodge Bardia..........................5 A3
Tiger Tops Karnali Lodge..................6 A2
Tiger Tops Karnali Tented Camp........7 A1

Thakurdwara

Sainwar

Babai

Parewa Odar

Royal Bardia National Park

Harre

Chepang

Dhakaila

Betani

Chisapani

INDIA

UTTAR PRADESH

To Kohalpur (44km); Nepalganj (60km)

THARU HOMES

The indigenous Tharu people of the western Terai are masters of improvisation. Villagers make almost everything they need
using the natural materials around them.
Even houses are built up from woven twigs
and grass coated in thick layers of river
mud. As well as being extremely environmentally friendly, the mud acts as a natural
heat shield, keeping the homes surprisingly
cool, even in summer. The same technique
is used to produce most of the furniture inside, from cupboards and bedsteads to the
water cooler and wood-fired kitchen range.
However, fresh layers of mud must be applied throughout the year to fill in cracks
and replace material washed away by the
monsoon rains.

---

destination in Nepal. Package rates are discounted by 15% from May to September.

Rhino Lodge Bardia (☎ 429720, ☎ 01-4701200
in Kathmandu; rhinolodge@nepal-safari.com; cottages with
bathroom Rs 150-500) About 4km from the park
entrance, this place looks much nicer now
that the garden has grown in. Accommodation is in tidy thatched bungalows with
small verandas and meals are often taken
on the lawn.

Tiger Tops Karnali Lodge (☎ 01-4361500 in Kathmandu; www.tigermountain.com; GPO Box 242, Kathmandu; package rates per night US$200) Run by the same
team as Tiger Tops in Chitwan, this recommended top-end lodge only opens when
a package group is in town. Accommodation is in stylish Tharu-style cottages near
Thakurdwara or safari tents deep inside the
park overlooking the Karnali River. Package
rates include meals and all activities (park
fees and local transfers are extra).

Getting There & Away

The slump in tourism has meant that most
people visit Royal Bardia on a package tour
from Kathmandu. If you intend to make
your own way to the park, call ahead to
make sure the resorts are open and arrange
a pick up from Thakurdwara. The nearest
airport is at Nepalganj (see p307).

To reach Bardia by public transport, head
to Nepalganj and change to a local bus to
Thakurdwara (Rs 126, three hours) – buses
leave Nepalganj at 11.20am and 1.30pm

and Thakurdwara at 7am and 9am. Change
at Ambassa for buses to Mahendranagar
(Rs 100, 21/2 hours).

JUMLA

Hidden away in the foothills of the Sisne
Himalaya, the tiny village of Jumla (2370m)
is the trailhead for treks to the remote Karnali region in the far northwest of Nepal.
From the airstrip in Jumla, it takes three to
four days to reach **Rara National Park** (admission
foreigner/SAARC/Nepali Rs 1000/100/free) with its famous sky-blue lake. Sadly, the hills around
Jumla are controlled by Maoist rebels and
travel in this area cannot currently be recommended. Should the security situation improve, Kathmandu trekking agencies should
be able to arrange guides and porters.

The only realistic way to reach Jumla is
by air. RNAC flies twice weekly between
Jumla and Nepalganj (US$61 to US$69, 45
minutes).

ROYAL SUKLA PHANTA WILDLIFE RESERVE

Tucked against the Indian border, **Royal
Sukla Phanta Wildlife Reserve** (☎ 099-521309;
admission per day foreigner/SAARC/Nepali Rs 500/200/20)
covers 305 sq km of sal forest and *phanta*
along the banks of the Bahini River. The
terrain is similar to Royal Bardia National
Park and the reserve has tigers, rhinos,
crocodiles, wild elephants and Nepal's largest population of *barasingha* (swamp deer),
currently numbering around 2000, as well
as large numbers of migratory birds.

Visiting Sukla Phanta was always difficult, and since the closure of the only
park lodge, camping is the only way to stay
overnight. The few visitors who make it to
the park generally come on day trips from
Mahendranagar with a hired car and driver.
Elephant rides (foreigner/SAARC/Nepali
Rs 1000/500/200) can be booked at the park
headquarters, but call ahead to make sure
somebody will be around.

The best time to visit is November to
January; the main vehicle track within the
park is impassable from June to September
because of monsoon flooding.

MAHENDRANAGAR

☎ 099

As the most westerly border crossing between Nepal and India, Mahendranagar

offers an interesting back route to Delhi and the hill towns of Uttaranchal. This is one of the more relaxing border crossings and the town itself is surprisingly pleasant. Unfortunately for travellers, the Maoist insurgency affects travel throughout this region. Most people head straight for the border, but the little-visited Sukla Phanta Wildlife Reserve is a short drive east of the airport.

Dangers & Annoyances

Mahendranagar is the gateway to western Nepal, but travel in the region is fraught with difficulties. Maoist rebels have staged numerous attacks on bridges and civic institutions in recent years and vehicles on the Mahendra Hwy are subject to regular army searches, adding hours to journey times. Everything returns to normal during ceasefires, so check the security situation before you visit.

The annual monsoon brings a whole new set of challenges, from flooded roads to collapsed bridges. Even during the dry winter season, the road from Nepalganj to Mahendranagar is a notorious accident black spot. Be prepared for long delays, particularly during the monsoon.

Road travel at night is risky anywhere in Nepal and particularly hairy in a region where buses have been targeted by roadside bombs. Be aware that travel by road may sometimes be impossible because of structural damage to bridges following Maoist attacks.

Orientation & Information

Mahendranagar is just south of the Mahendra Hwy, about 5km east of the Indian border. From the Nepali border post at Gaddachauki, it's about 1km to the Indian border post at Banbassa – a rickshaw is probably the way to go.

It's laid out on a simple grid system. The main road runs east to west and the roads leading south are labelled 'Line 1' to 'Line 5'. The bus stand is right on the Mahendra Hwy so there's no need to come into the centre unless you plan to stay the night.

The Government of Nepal runs a small **tourist information centre** (☎ 523773; ☿ 7am-6.30pm) on the Nepal side of the border. If you need a Hotmail fix, several computer centres on Line 5 offer fast net access for Rs 40 per hour.

Sleeping & Eating

There are lots of cheap hotels near the bus stand, plus more upmarket options on the roads leading south from the main street.

Royal Guest House (☎ 523799; d without bathroom Rs 160) This basic place is the best of the grungy hotels directly opposite the bus stand.

Hotel New Anand (☎ 521693; Line 3; s/d with bathroom from Rs 300/500) Above a small shopping arcade, this good value cheapie offers simple rooms with a geyser, a TV and a comfy chair to watch it from.

Hotel Sweet Dream (☎ 522313; Mahendra Hwy; d with bathroom Rs 350-450, with air-con Rs 1000; ❄) On the highway about 100m east of the bus station, this friendly midrange place has

---

CROSSING THE BORDER

Border Hours

The Nepali side of the border is open to tourists 24 hours, but before 7am and after 5.30pm you may need to go searching for the Nepali officials. The Indian side of the border is only open to vehicles 5am-6am, noon-2pm and 5-6pm.

Foreign Exchange

There's a small bank counter near the Nepali customs post but it only exchanges Indian and Nepali rupees.

Onward to India

From the Indian border post, it's an INRs 10 rickshaw ride to the bus station in Banbassa, where you can pick up long-distance buses to Delhi (INRs 156, 10 hours). Local buses and shared jeeps serve Almora, Nainital and other towns in Uttaranchal. There's also a slow metre-gauge train to Bareilly, where you can pick up trains to other destinations in India.

comfortable rooms with carpets and a decent restaurant. The colour scheme is a bit
overpowering but the welcome is warm.

Most people eat at their hotels, or there
are several simple Nepali *bhojanalayas* on
Line 4.

Getting There & Away
The airport is 3.5km from the centre but
flights to Nepalganj and Kathmandu have
been suspended indefinitely.

The bus station is about 1km from the
centre on the Mahendra Hwy. Long-haul
buses leave for Kathmandu (Rs 735, 16
hours) at 5am, 8.30am and 2.15pm. There's
also a single Pokhara service at 10.30am (Rs
728, 16 hours). Local buses run regularly to
Nepalganj (Rs 300, six hours), passing the
turn off to Royal Bardia National Park.

Getting Around
Buses, tempos and tongas run regularly between the bus station and the border for Rs
10 to Rs 15. Taxis can be hired for trips to
Royal Sukla Phanta Wildlife Reserve for Rs
4000 per day.

EASTERN TERAI

Bound by the Indian states of Sikkim and
West Bengal, the eastern Terai is broadly a
mirror image of the west. The rolling hills of
the Mahabharat Range are squeezed between
the dry eastern plains and the Himalaya,
and the Mahendra Hwy cuts east to meet
the Indian border at Kakarbhitta, providing
easy access to Sikkim and Darjeeling.

The eastern portion of the Terai sees
more visitors than the west, but it's still
a peaceful and untouched region, at least
as far as tourism goes. Probably the most
famous spot is Janakpur, with its ancient
Sita temple and rich tradition of Mithila
painting. Politically, things aren't quite so
peaceful. Maoist rebels operate in the hills
and travel north of the Mahendra Hwy is
often impossible due to skirmishes between
rebels and government soldiers. Check the
security situation before embarking east.
This includes the border crossing to India
at Kakarbhitta.

JANAKPUR
☎ 041
Janakpur has been a centre for Hindu pilgrimages since at least the 4th century BC,
when the story of Sita, wife of Rama and
daughter of King Janak of Mithila, was written down in the Ramayana. Even today,
the town feels closer to the Hindu towns of
India than the tribal townships of Nepal –
there's nowhere better to get a real feel for
life in the plains.

On one level, Janakpur is a tourist town,
but almost all the tourists are pilgrims from
India. The streets are dotted with pilgrims'
hostels and the huge Janaki temple attracts
pilgrims from across the subcontinent. The
best time to visit is during the Hindu festival

EASTERN TERAI

of Sita Bibaha Panchami (see p366), when vignettes from the Ramayana are acted out in the streets, bringing the ancient myth vividly to life.

The other lure in Janakpur is Mithila culture. Janakpur was once the capital of the ancient kingdom of Mithila, a territory now divided between Nepal and India, and more than two million people in the area still speak Maithili as their native tongue. The people of Mithila are famous for their wildly colourful paintings. Mithila art is primitive, in the Fine Art sense, and it offers a fascinating window onto rural life in the Terai – see the boxed text p315.

Janakpur is actually the third city on this site. The city mythologised in the Ramayana existed around 700 BC, but it was later abandoned and sank back into the forest. Simaraungarh grew up in its place, but this city was also destroyed, this time by Muslim invaders in the 14th century. Modern Janakpur is a busy, bustling bazaar town, with winding narrow streets, more rickshaws and bicycles than cars and a real sense of energy and purpose. Many people visit on the way to/from Kakarbhitta and you can make a fascinating detour south to the Indian border (though not across it) on the old metre-gauge train to Jaynagar.

Orientation

About 20km south of the Mahendra Hwy, Janakpur is a maze of narrow, winding streets – the telecom tower and water tower

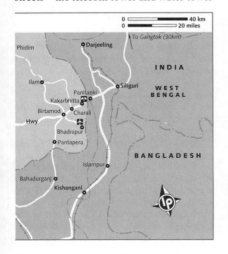

are useful landmarks. The official centre of town is the Janaki Temple in the middle of the bazaar, but most of the hotels are further east on the road running up to Bhanu Chowk and the train station.

If you come in on the highway, you'll arrive at Ramanand Chowk, topped by a giant metal sculpture of crossed elephant tusks. The town centre is east of the junction while the bus stand is due south at Zero Mile Chowk.

Information

There's a small and informal **tourist office** (☎ 520755; ☼ 10am-4pm Sun-Thu, 10am-3pm Fri) upstairs in an arcade near the station on Bhanu Chowk. It closes an hour earlier from November to January.

There's nowhere to change money but **Royal Cyber & Communications** (☎ 525441; Station Rd; per hr Rs 30; ☼ 6.30am-10pm) is a reliable net-café.

Sights
JANAKI MANDIR

Janakpur's most important temple is dedicated to Sita, the wife of Rama and heroine of the Ramayana. According to the ancient text, Sita was kidnapped by Ravana, the demon-king of Lanka and her husband sped south to save her, aided by the loyal monkey god, Hanuman. Although Rama and Sita were historical figures, Hindus regard Rama as an incarnation of Vishnu and Sita as an incarnation of Lakshmi.

Built in extravagant baroque Mughal style, the **Janaki Mandir** is believed to stand on the exact spot where King Janak found the infant Sita lying in the furrow of a ploughed field. In fact, the temple only dates to 1912, but it feels much older with its arches, domes, turrets and screens. It looks a little like a glorious wedding cake, designed for a maharajah.

A steady stream of pilgrims files in through the gatehouse to pay homage to the Sita statue in the **inner sanctum** (☼ 5-7am & 6-8pm). It's a much calmer process than the bloodthirsty goings-on at Nepal's Shaivite temples and many people come here to sit in the cool cloisters and contemplate the lessons of the Ramayana. The temple is particularly popular with women, who wear their best and most colourful saris for the occasion.

Vendors sell coloured powders and religious objects on the square in front of the temple and the surrounding street market

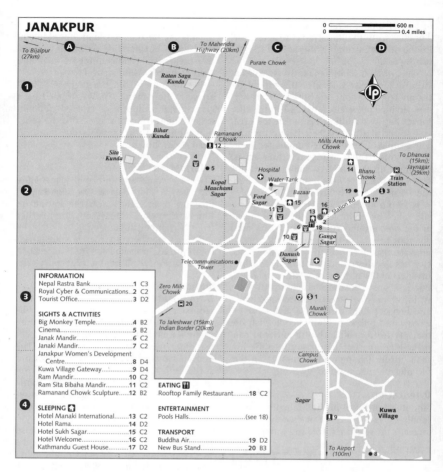

JANAKPUR

INFORMATION
Nepal Rastra Bank.....................1 C3
Royal Cyber & Communications..2 C2
Tourist Office............................3 D2

SIGHTS & ACTIVITIES
Big Monkey Temple..................4 B2
Cinema....................................5 B2
Janak Mandir...........................6 C2
Janaki Mandir...........................7 C2
Janakpur Women's Development
    Centre.................................8 D4
Kuwa Village Gateway..............9 D4
Ram Mandir............................10 C2
Ram Sita Bibaha Mandir..........11 C2
Ramanand Chowk Sculpture.....12 B2

SLEEPING
Hotel Manaki International.......13 C2
Hotel Rama............................14 D2
Hotel Sukh Sagar....................15 C2
Hotel Welcome.......................16 C2
Kathmandu Guest House..........17 D2

EATING
Rooftop Family Restaurant........18 C2

ENTERTAINMENT
Pools Halls................................(see 18)

TRANSPORT
Buddha Air.............................19 D2
New Bus Stand.......................20 B3

has the usual lively hubbub of a plains town bazaar. Look for unusual Indian imports such as *pani phul* (fresh water chestnuts).

RAM SITA BIBAHA MANDIR

Almost next door to the Janaki Temple, this rather bizarre **temple** (admission Rs 2, camera fee Rs 5, video Rs 21; ⏰ 5am-9pm) marks the spot where Rama and Sita were married. The temple is topped by a modernist interpretation of a tiered pagoda roof and the walls are glass so you can peer in at the kitsch life-sized models of Sita and Rama.

RAM MANDIR & DANUSH SAGAR

Hidden away in a stone courtyard southeast of the Janaki Mandir, the **Ram Mandir** is a much older structure, built in the classic tiered pagoda style of the hills. The main temple is sacred to Rama but there are several smaller shrines to Shiva, Hanuman and Durga dotted around the compound. It's busiest in the early evening, when the courtyard is filled with incense smoke and music.

Opposite the entrance are a series of ghats (steps for ritual bathing) leading down into the **Danush Sagar**, the largest ceremonial tank at Janakpur. There are small shrines all around the perimeter and vendors in front sell flower garlands, tikka powder, sacred threads and other ritual objects for pujas (prayers). Nearby is the small **Janak Mandir**, sacred to the father of Sita.

OTHER TEMPLES & PONDS

There are numerous other temples and ponds scattered around the outskirts of town, accessible on foot or by rickshaw.

Over on the other side of town, Hanuman is worshipped in the form of a live rhesus macaque at the **Big Monkey Temple**. The previous monkey grew to 60kg before finally succumbing to morbid obesity and its replacement seems well on the way to following it. It's easy to miss the temple – the gateway is almost opposite the **cinema**, about 100m south of Ramanand Chowk.

If you head west from Ramanand Chowk, you'll reach two more ceremonial tanks – **Bihar Kunda** and **Ratan Saga Kunda**.

TRADITIONAL VILLAGES

The sugar cane fields and Mithila villages around Janakpur form a lush and magical mosaic. Many of the villages are built in the traditional Mithila style, with adobe walls decorated with colourful paintings of people and animals. Probably the easiest village to reach from Janakpur, is **Kuwa**, about 1km south of Murali Chowk. People are very friendly, as long as you aren't too intrusive with your camera, and you can drop in on the Janakpur Women's Development Centre – see the boxed text below. If you feel like roaming further a field, **Dhanusa**, 15km northeast of Janakpur, marks the spot where Rama allegedly drew Shiva's magic bow.

Festivals & Events

By far the most interesting time to visit Janakpur is during **Bibaha Panchami** (Vivaha Panchami) on the fifth day of the waxing moon in November/December. Tens of thousands of pilgrims descend on the town to celebrate the re-enactment of Sita's marriage to Rama and there are processions and performances of scenes from the Ramayana in the streets. **Rama Navami** (March/April), celebrating Rama's birthday, is also accompanied by a huge procession.

On the day before Holi in March, **Parikrama** involves a ritual walk around the town's ring road, attracting thousands of pilgrims. **Holi** itself can get very boisterous but be warned: foreigners are not exempt from a ritual splattering with coloured powder and water. If you visit during **Tihar** (Deepawali) in October/November, you'll see Mithila women repainting the murals on their houses.

Sleeping & Eating

All the following hotels have attached restaurants. Because of all the standing water in the holy ponds, mosquitos come out with all guns blazing. Slap on the DEET or light a coil if you want a decent night's sleep.

Kathmandu Guest House (☎ 521753; Bhanu Chowk; s/d without bathroom Rs 100/200, s/d with bathroom Rs 150/250) A reliable cheapie. Rooms have fans, mosquito nets and clean bathrooms with squat toilets.

MITHILA ART

As the former capital of the kingdom of Mithila, it's appropriate that Janakpur is striving to preserve the ancient art of Mithila painting. More commonly associated with Bihar in India, Mithila painting is part decoration, part social commentary, recording the lives of rural women in a society where reading and writing are reserved for high-caste men. Scenes in Mithila paintings record the female experience of life in the Terai – work, childbirth, marriage and the social network among village women.

Traditionally, Mithila paintings were used for decoration – you can still see houses across the Terai with abstract patterns or complex scenes of village life painted in white and ochre on the mud walls. More recently, Mithila painting has taken off as a collectable art form, creating a whole new industry for women in impoverished rural communities.

One of the best known social projects is the **Janakpur Women's Development Centre** (☎ 521080; www.catgen.com/jwdc; 🕑 10am-5pm Sun-Fri, 10am-4pm Dec-Jan), just outside Janakpur in the village of Kuwa. Around 50 Mithila women are employed at the centre, producing paper paintings, papier-mâché boxes and mirrors, screen-printed fabrics and hand-thrown ceramics. The work is delightful and the money raised goes directly towards improving the lives of rural women. You can meet the artisans and buy directly from the centre – a rickshaw from Janakpur to the centre will cost Rs 30.

Hotel Sukh Sagar (☎ 520488; d without bathroom Rs 200, s/d with bathroom from Rs 250/275) In the bazaar opposite the Janaki Temple, this simple pilgrim's hostel has reasonably clean rooms and hot water by the bucket. There's an inexpensive veg curry house downstairs.

Hotel Rama (☎ 520059; Mills Area Chowk; d with bathroom Rs 300-400, d with air-con Rs 800; ❄) A hike from the centre but excellent value for money, Hotel Rama is about 500m north of Bhanu Chowk. It's popular with NGOs, which is always a good sign, and the rooms are large, clean and painted in soothing shades of lilac.

Hotel Welcome (☎ 520646; Station Rd; s/d with bathroom Rs 300/450, s/d with air-con Rs 1000/1600; ❄) Slightly run down, but still reasonably good value. The location is convenient and some rooms have cheerful Mithila-inspired paintings on the walls. Rooms with air-con cost just Rs 500 if you don't use the air-conditioner.

Hotel Manaki International (☎ 521540; hotel manaki@hotmail.com; Shiv Chowk; s/d with bathroom Rs 1000/1200, s/d with air-con Rs 2000/2500; ❄) The only really upmarket choice in Janakpur, the Manaki International has cavernous deluxe rooms with all mod cons and more modest standard rooms with hot showers but no air-con.

Rooftop Family Restaurant (Station Rd; mains Rs 50-200; ⏱ 9am-10pm) Facing the small Janak Mandir, this upmarket place claims to be 'the only choice of smart people' in Janakpur and we're inclined to agree. The Chinese and Indian food is excellent.

If you're looking for nightlife, there are several **pool halls** near the Rooftop Family Restaurant.

Getting There & Away

Buddha Air (☎ 041-525022) and other private airlines have daily flights between Janakpur and Kathmandu (US$76, 25 minutes). Airline offices are around Bhanu Chowk and the airport is a Rs 70 rickshaw ride south of the centre.

Buses leave from the dusty main bus station southwest of Zero Mile Chowk, a Rs 30 rickshaw ride from central Janakpur. There are day and night buses east to Kakarbhitta (day/night Rs 270/300, five hours) and north to Kathmandu (day/night Rs 350/370, 10 hours) via Narayangarh (day/night Rs 150/170, six hours). A single bus leaves daily for Pokhara (Rs 325, 10 hours) and there are several morning buses for Biratnagar (Rs 160, four hours), Local buses run hourly to Birganj (Rs 140, five hours) until about 3pm.

The station at the north end of Station Rd is the starting point for train rides to local villages – see below for details.

KOSHI TAPPU WILDLIFE RESERVE
☎ 025

This **Wildlife Reserve** (☎ 530897; admission per day foreigner/SAARC/Nepali Rs 500/200/20) was founded in 1976 to protect a small triangle of *phanta* (grassland) and *tappu* (small islands) in the floodplain of the Sapt Kosi River, the last habitat of the endangered *arna* (wild water

---

RIDING THE RAILS

From the train station in Janakpur, a slow metre-gauge train runs east across the Indian border to the dusty plains town of Jaynagar. Only Indians and Nepalis can actually cross the border, but the train ride provides a delicious taste of the subcontinent.

This must be one of the last trains in Asia where people routinely ride on the roof. Passengers are crammed into very square inch of the carriages and bicycles and boxes hang from every window so there's often nowhere else to go. It's a breezy ride up top, but the train passes through some wonderfully unspoiled countryside, stopping at a series of small Terai villages. Along the way you'll see farmers ploughing with bullock carts, children chasing beside the train with paper kites and families winnowing rice in the courtyards of tiny thatched homes.

Foreigners can travel as far as Khajuri (2nd-/1st-class Rs 16/32, three hours), about 21km southeast of Janakpur. Trains leave Janakpur at 6.45am, 11.30am and 3.20pm, returning from Khajuri at around 8.40am, 12.40pm and 4.30pm. If you fancy getting down and stretching your legs, the train stops in the villages of Parbaha (2nd/1st class Rs 7/12, 8km, 30 minutes) and Baidehi (2nd/1st class Rs 10/18, 12km, one hour). To return to Janakpur, you can take the next train or hop on a local bus.

buffalo). At the south end of the reserve, the Kosi Barrage funnels the floodwaters of the Sapt Kosi into a single channel to minimise flood damage in Bihar.

It's a wonderfully serene spot and most travellers who visit are bird-watchers in search of rare species such as the Bengal florican and sarus crane. At least 439 species of birds have been recorded here and migratory species from Siberia and Tibet take up residence from November to February. *Arna* tend to hang out on the tappu and you may also spot deer, wild boars, pythons and crocodiles. There are thought to be a handful of Gangetic dolphins in the Sapt Kosi but they are very rarely seen.

Most visitors come on organised tours from Kathmandu or Pokhara, which include bird-watching walks, elephant rides, boat trips, accommodation and meals at the tented camps inside the park and transfers from Biratnagar airport. There are few facilities for independent travellers.

Information

The **reserve headquarters** (☎ 530897; ⏰ 10am-5pm) at Kusaha has an interesting information centre and museum, with elephant, deer and guar skulls and a desiccated gharial. This is where visitors pay the daily park entry fees.

Sights & Activities

As with other national parks in the Terai, the most popular way to explore is by elephant. Elephant safaris can be arranged at the park headquarters for Rs 1000/400/200 (foreigner/SAARC/Nepali). All the lodges can arrange tours of the *tappu* (river islands) by canoe or *dunga* (wooden boat) – the going rate for a boat and driver is about Rs 1500, covering up to five passengers.

Every lodge has a resident ornithologist who leads bird-spotting walks around the park, usually included in the package rates. If you come here independently, ask about hiring a guide at the park headquarters.

Sleeping

There are several lodges, but call ahead to make sure they're open before turning up at the front door. As well as the package rates, you'll have to pay the park entry fee, the park camping fee (Rs 300 per person) and 13% tax.

Koshi Camp (☎ 01-4429609 in Kathmandu; www .kosicamp.com; 3-day/2-night package per person US$189) A popular choice for birders, Koshi Camp is located on the western edge of the park, near several water holes. It's refreshingly small and low-key and accommodation is in comfortable safari tents.

Aqua Birds Unlimited Camp (☎ 01-4413470 in Kathmandu; aquabirds@ccsl.com.np; 3-day/2-night package US$175) Again, the focus here is on our feathered friends. The resident bird-watching guides are very experienced and accommodation is big safari tents with solar-powered hot showers. Ask the camp about the migratory birds festival that they put on most years in February, depending on tourist demand and the security situation. **Koshi Tappu Wildlife Camp** (☎ 01-4226130 in Kathmandu; www.koshitappu.com; explore@mos.com.np; package per person US$125) This peaceful jungle camp sits out on the northeastern edge of the reserve. Guests stay in simple safari tents and there's no electricity, but the jungle atmosphere is very appealing. A small water course flows through the grounds so you can watch birds from the comfort of the bar.

Getting There & Away

Almost everyone comes here on a package tour with a pre-arranged pick up from Biratnagar airport. If you want to visit under your own steam, the park headquarters is about 3km south of the Mahendra Hwy, signposted 16km northeast of the Kosi Barrage.

ITAHARI

Itahari is an undistinguished town at the junction of the Mahendra Hwy and the roads to Biratnagar and Hile. All long-distance buses along the Mahendra Hwy pull into the well-organised bus stand and there are fast and frequent local services to Biratnagar and places along the road to Hile.

If you get stuck overnight, the **Jaynepal Hotel** (☎ 580113; s/d without bathroom Rs 200/250, r with bathroom Rs 350-450) is right by the roundabout at the turn off to Dharan Bazaar. A rickshaw from the bus stand will cost Rs 30.

BIRATNAGAR

☎ 021

Biratnagar is the second-largest city in Nepal, but it still feels like a small provincial town. There's lots of heavy industry on the road leading south to Biratnagar from the

Mahendra Hwy but the centre of town is surprisingly calm and manageable. Most of the goods produced here go straight across the border to India – the nearest border crossing open to travellers is Kakarbhitta.

Biratnagar doesn't have any must-see sights, but the town is a major air hub for flights to the eastern hills and there are daily air connections to Kathmandu. Jute used to be grown around here in large quantities, but the Tharu and Danuwar villagers who produced the fibres have lost out to mechanised industry. If you find yourself killing time here, drop into the gaily-painted **Hanuman Mandir** and **Kali Mandir** near the public market.

Information & Orientation

Biratnagar is about 22km south of the Mahendra Hwy. The official centre of town is Traffic Chowk and the municipal market is just north on Main Rd. Most of the hotels are further west on Malaya Rd, which runs south to the border. The bus stand is a Rs 30 rickshaw ride southwest of the centre and the airport is a Rs 60 ride northwest.

For foreign exchange, try **Lumbini Bank Ltd** (Himalaya Rd; ☼ 10am-2.30pm Sun-Thu, till 12.30pm Fri). Several Internet cafés at Traffic Chowk offer fast connections for Rs 25 per hour.

Sleeping & Eating

Most people stay near the noisy bus stand, but Traffic Chowk is a more upbeat and welcoming area.

Dhankuta Lodge (☎ 522925; s/d with bathroom from Rs 160/200) Don't expect frills at this rudimentary place opposite the bus station. Rooms are dingy but tolerable; try to get one at the back, away from the traffic noise.

Hotel Geetanjali (☎ 527335; Malaya Rd; s/d with bathroom Rs 350/450) Not far from the bus stand, above some cane furniture shops, this place has big, clean rooms with concrete floors and a reasonably priced restaurant.

Hotel Namaskar (☎ 521199; hotelnamaskar@wlink .com.np; Main Rd; s/d with bathroom Rs 600/800, s/d with air-con Rs 1000/1200; ✖) The smartest option at Traffic Chowk, Namaskar is set in a quiet courtyard. It's run by devotees of Sai Baba and rooms are large and inviting. The restaurant here is one of the best in town.

Hotel Swagatam (☎ 524450; swagat@bcn.com.np; s/ d with TV & bathroom Rs 550/700, r with air-con Rs 1200-1500; ✖) About 500m south of the bus station, this bright pink hotel is covered in bougainvilleas. The bar and restaurant has a nice ambience and the rooms are chintzy but comfortable. Air-con rooms have tubs and carpets.

Getting There & Away

RNAC (☎ 524661) and several private airlines offer flights between Biratnagar and Kath-

BIRATNAGAR

0 ———— 200 m
0 ———— 0.1 miles

To Airport (2.5km); Itahari (22km)

Ⓐ   Ⓑ

❶

4 🏨
Market
3 🏨
Police
Ⓟ @1 Traffic Chowk
Mahendra Chowk
Himalaya Road
💲 2

🏨 7

Malaya Rd

❷

Post Office
✉

❸

6 🏨

9 🚌 🏨 5

● 10

🏨 8

❹

To Indian Border (6km)

THE TERAI & MAHABHARAT RANGE

mandu (US$81 to US$96, one hour). RNAC also flies three times a week to Taplejung (US$64 to US$85, 30 minutes). Travel agents around Traffic Chowk can make bookings. A rickshaw to the airport will cost around Rs 60.

The **bus stand** is a Rs 10 rickshaw ride southwest from Traffic Chowk. There are regular day and night buses to Kathmandu (day/night Rs 475/495, 12 hours) via Narayangarh (day/night Rs 380/400, nine hours), and several buses leave every morning for Birganj (Rs 252, seven hours) and Janakpur (Rs 160, four hours). There are also regular services along the Mahendra Hwy to Kakarbhitta (Rs 120, 3½ hours).

Local buses run regularly to Dharan Bazaar (Rs 40, one hour) throughout the day. There are also early morning buses to Dhankuta (Rs 140, three hours) and Hile (Rs 170, 3½ hours).

DHARAN BAZAR TO HILE

About 17km north of Itahari, Dharan Bazaar marks the start of yet another dramatic route into the hills. From here, a decent tarmac road runs north into the foothills of the Himalaya, providing access to a series of attractive hill towns and trekking trailheads. Sadly, this is another area with Maoist problems and you should check the security situation carefully before venturing north of Dharan Bazaar.

Dharan Bazaar
☎ 025
Just off the Mahendra Hwy, at the foot of the Chure hills, Dharan feels like a hill town that has been transported to the plains. You'll see lots of tribal women wearing their wealth in the form of heavy gold jewellery and the overall mood is prosperous and upbeat – you'd never realise that an earthquake almost destroyed the place in 1988. Dharan is famous for its metalworkers, who produce high quality cauldrons and *gaagri* (brass water jugs) for villages in the hills.

Dharan is also one of the *shakti peeths,* marking the spot where part of the body of Shiva's first wife, Sati, fell after she was consumed by flames. There are several important Shaivite temples northeast of the centre in the village of Bijayapur. Set among dense bamboo thickets down the path beside the four-tiered concrete tower, **Budha Subba Mandir**

contains a curious collection of mud-covered rocks, said to represent the reclining body of Mahadev (Shiva). The smaller **Dantakali** and **Pindeshwar** temples are both on the road leading south from the small roundabout with the concrete football. To reach Bijayapur, take the steps leading uphill near the Panas Hotel, or charter an auto-rickshaw.

Several net cafés around Bhanu Chowk (the square with the bus stand and clocktower) offer fast net access for Rs 30 per hour. The Nabil Bank has an ATM that accepts foreign cards.

SLEEPING & EATING
Accommodation in Dharan is very limited – there are a few cheap hotels near the bus stand and one decent midrange choice about three blocks north.

Hotel Naya Yug (☎ 524797; r with/without bathroom Rs 250/200) Don't be put off by the red lights in the windows – this is actually a fairly respectable cheapie. There's a small restaurant and rooms are simple but perfectly adequate.

Hotel Panas (☎ 523204; Chata Chowk; s/d Rs 400/500) Three blocks north of Bhanu Chowk, near the steps to Bijayapur, this decent midrange place has comfy rooms with TVs, fans, hot showers and thick blankets.

For meals, there are lots of cheap daal bhaat and chow mein places around the bus stand.

House of Sweets & Snacks (snack meals under Rs 50; ☯ 7.30am-8pm) For cheap and tasty *dosas* and other South Indian favourites, try this popular *misthan bhandar* on the road north from Bhanu Chowk.

GETTING THERE & AROUND
Buses leave regularly from Bhanu Chowk for Kathmandu (day/night Rs 475/527, 15 hours) and Biratnagar (Rs 40, one hour). Heading north, local buses run regularly from 4am to 4pm to Bhedatar (Rs 50, one hour), Dhankuta (Rs 95, two hours) and Hile (Rs 118, 2½ hours). Early morning buses continue from Hile to Basantpur and Therathum, but check the security situation before venturing out this far. See p99 for details of treks from Basantapur to The Hide Out and rafting on the Tamur River.

Expect to pay around Rs 300 for an autorickshaw from the bus stand to Bijayapur and back.

Bhedetar

Bhedetar isn't much more than a cluster of wooden shacks and army buildings on the road to Dhankuta, but the location – perched at 1420m with soaring views over Everest and Makalu – is dramatic. There are giddying views over the Terai and mountains from the 20m-high **viewing tower** (foreigner/SAARC/Nepali Rs 50/10/5; ☼ daylight hr) on the bluff behind the army post; these days, the entry fee is rarely collected.

There's nowhere to stay, but several tinroofed *bhojanalayas* serve simple, filling meals, *tongba* (millet beer) and local 'wine' (ie spirits). If you come here by car or motorcycle, watch out for drunk drivers.

Dhankuta
☎ 026

About 50km above Dharan, Dhankuta is a dusty bazaar town, sprawled along an east-facing ridge. It's an important stop for traders from the hills, particularly on Thursdays for the weekly *haat bazaar* (village market), but it dozes quietly the rest of the time. There's a small **museum** (entry Rs 10; ☼ 10am-5pm Sun-Fri) with displays on tribal culture at the top of the bazaar, but you'll need local help to find it.

Maoists are active in this area, but if the security situation improves, it may be possible to walk in the surrounding hills. There's a viewpoint with modest mountain views just south of the centre; take the right fork above the bus station and follow the obvious trail that branches left up the hillside.

Most travellers who visit are bound for loftier locations such as Hile or the remote trekking routes around Kanchenjunga.

Maoists have staged several raids on the police post at Dhankuta in recent years – check that things are safe before you leave Dharan.

SLEEPING & EATING

If you do chose to stop here, there are several decent 'hotel and lodging' places on the main street.

Hotel Parchaya (☎ 520593; s/d Rs 100/175) Along the ridge at the north end of town, this friendly wooden guesthouse has simple, village-style rooms and a nice restaurant where you can hang out in the evenings. To get here, follow the main road through the village and branch right by the police post.

GETTING THERE & AWAY

Plenty of buses travel between Dhankuta and Dharan Bazaar (Rs 95, two hours). Morning buses from Dharan Bazaar continue uphill to Hile (Rs 25, 30 minutes) and on to Basantpur and Therathum.

Hile
☎ 026

The hill town of Hile (pronounced 'high-lay') is the starting point for treks to the Arun Valley (possible for individuals) and to Kanchenjunga and Makalu (only for groups). However, the security situation is not good. The hills around Hile are currently off limits to all but the most intrepid trekking parties, which is a real shame, as Hile is one of the most attractive villages in the eastern highlands.

If you do make it up here, the village is home to a sizeable population of Tibetans, who worship at the colourful **Urgay Namedo Chöling Gompa** in the middle of the village. There's a second Buddhist monastery further along the ridge, near the Don Bosco school. Fans of a nice, hot cuppa can visit the **Guranse Tea Estate** (☎ 01-4478301 in Kathmandu; www.guransetea.com.np) on the road to Dhankuta.

Several high points offer dramatic views over the Makalu section of the Himalaya. For the best views, walk uphill along the main road to the army encampment and climb the grassy ridge beyond.

SLEEPING & EATING

There are several charming Tibetan-run lodges along the main road through the village where you can find a clean bed and a plate of spicy buff chow mein. Most of the lodges also offer *tongba*, the traditional hot millet beer of the Himalaya.

Hotel Himali & Lodge (☎ 540140; d/q without bathroom Rs 120/400) A stone-finished place with bright blue windows, friendly Tibetan owners and a dark but cosy Tibetan-style bar at the back.

Gumba Hotel & Lodge (☎ 540173; s/d/q without bathroom Rs 60/100/200) Next to the Buddhist monastery, Gumba is very similar – dark but cosy, with oodles of character.

GETTING THERE & AWAY

Regular buses run downhill to Dhankuta (Rs 25, 30 minutes) and Dharan Bazaar (Rs 118, 2½ hours) from the dirt bus stand in the middle of the village. Assuming the road is safe, buses run north to Basantpur and Therathum, where you can start treks north into the Himalaya.

BIRTAMOD TO ILAM

The road to the tiny hill station of Ilam (pronounced 'ee-lam') starts just east of Birtamod on the Mahendra Hwy. As the centre of Nepal's small tea industry, Ilam has a lot in common with nearby Darjeeling, but the area is a hotbed of Maoist activity and road to Ilam is often blocked due to clashes between security forces and rebels.

If the security situation does improve, Ilam may resurface as a destination for tea tours, hill walks and treks in the foothills of Mt Kanchenjunga (8598m), the world's third highest peak. The main trailhead for mountain treks is Taplejung, accessible by plane from Biratnagar and bus from Birtamod.

Birtamod
☎ 023
The nondescript highway town of Birtamod is the starting point for buses and jeeps bound for Ilam. With the current security station in the hills, few tourists are heading to Ilam, which means that even fewer are stopping in Birtamod. Check the security situation locally before you head into the hills.

If you need to stop over, **Paradise Restaurant & Lodge** (☎ 542942; s/d without bathroom Rs 100/200, s/d with bathroom Rs 250/350) is a clean, reasonably priced lodge; it's 200m east of the main roundabout, opposite the departure point for Ilam jeeps.

Birtamod sits right on the Mahendra Hwy so any bus heading to Kakarbhitta can drop you off. Buses to Ilam (Rs 130, four hours) leave from the highway, just east of the main roundabout. Jeeps do the same journey in three hours (Rs 140).

Ilam
☎ 027
Ilam is the centre of Nepal's small tea industry and the quality of Ilam tea is recognised around the world. Sadly, this attractive hill town is frequently off limits due to the actions of Maoist rebels. Tea plantation tours and hill walks are the main attractions here but trips to Ilam are probably best avoided until the security situation improves.

If you are able to visit, the best place to stay is **Green View Guest House** (☎ 520103; r with/without bathroom from Rs 350/200). Rooms are large, clean and modern and most do indeed have a green view – of tea plantations.

The road to Ilam branches off the Mahendra Hwy at Charali but buses and jeeps to Ilam originate in Birtamod – see left. If the security situation allows, you can follow the same road north to Taplejung, the starting point for group treks to the base of Kanchenjunga.

KAKARBHITTA
☎ 023
Kakarbhitta (Kakarvitta) is the easternmost crossing between India and Nepal and it's just a few hours drive from Siliguri and Darjeeling in West Bengal and Gangtok in Sikkim. This is one of the easiest border crossings and the bazaar by the bus stand is packed with vendors selling Indian spices, Nepali *khukuris* (Gurkha knives), Chinese radios and other black market goods. The surrounding countryside is full of tea plantations, a taste of things to come on the Darjeeling side of the border, but there's isn't any great reason to linger here.

Information & Orientation
The Nepali border post at Kakarbhitta and the Indian border post at Panitanki are just a few hundred metres apart, so you can cross the border easily on foot. In Kakarbhitta, the bus stand is about 100m west of the border on the north side of the hwy. Most of the hotels are in the surrounding streets.

The Government of Nepal runs a small **tourist information centre** (☎ 562252; ⏱ 7am-6pm) on the Nepal side of the border. You can check your email at **Net Point Cyber Zone** (☎ 562040; per hr Rs 30; ⏱ 8am-8pm) opposite Hotel Mechi.

Sleeping & Eating
Kakarbhitta is tiny and most of the hotels are crammed together in the narrow alleys leading west from the back of the bus stand.

Hotel Deurali (☎ 562115; s without bathroom Rs 50, d with bathroom Rs 250) On an alley west of the bus park, this old-style cheapie is pretty basic but you can't argue with the price. Showers are cold and there's a simple *bhojanalaya* downstairs.

CROSSING THE BORDER

Border Hours

Both sides of the border are staffed between 6pm and before 7pm. You may still be able to cross outside these times but you'll need to go searching for the immigration officials.

Foreign Exchange

Nepal Bank Ltd operates a foreign exchange desk (🕑 7am-5pm) close to the border. You can change cash and travellers cheques in US dollars, UK pounds and Euros, as well as Indian and Nepali rupees.

Onwards to India

It's about 100m from the Kakarbhitta bus stand to the border, and another 100m to the Indian border post at Panitanki. Rickshaws charge Rs 30 from Kakarbhitta all the way through to the bus stand at Panitanki, which has regular services to Siliguri (Rs 15, one hour), where you can pick up buses to Darjeeling (Rs 60, two hours). Jeeps to the same destinations, and Gangtok (Rs 140, 4½ hours) in Sikkim, line up just beyond the Indian visa post. Siliguri lies on the main train line from Kolkata to northeast India.

Hotel Sirijunga (☎ 562122; s/d with bathroom Rs 200/400, s/d with TV Rs 300/500) Full points for character at this unusual temple-topped hotel west of the bus stand. Rooms have a dash of colour and there's a restaurant and bar full of fairy lights.

Hotel Mechi (☎ 562040; s/d with bathroom Rs 500/700, s/d with air-con Rs 800/1400; ❄) On the same road as the Kanchan, Hotel Mechi has hot showers and a recommended restaurant (the same food is available from room service). The usual border price-hike rules don't seem to apply here – the large, comfortable rooms here are excellent value.

Hotel Rajat (☎ 562033; rajeshm_s@yahoo.com; s/d with bathroom Rs 200/300, deluxe s/d with TV Rs 600/800, d with air-con Rs 1000; ❄) The welcome is friendly here and there's a bistro-like restaurant with gingham tablecloths downstairs. Rooms are simple but inviting and the owner is a great source of advice for onward travel.

For meals, all the lodges have restaurants serving Indian, Nepali and Chinese fare.

Getting There & Away

AIR

The nearest airport is at Bhadrapur, 10km south of Birtamod, which in turn is 13km west of Kakarbhitta. **Yeti Airlines** (☎ 522232) and other private carriers have daily flights to Kathmandu (US$113, 50 minutes) – any of the travel agents around the bus park can issue tickets. A taxi from Kakarbhitta bus stand to the airport costs Rs 600 or you can take a local bus to Birtamod, then a second bus to Bhadrapur, then a rickshaw to the airport.

BUS

Travel agents in Kathmandu and Pokhara offer 'through-tickets' to Darjeeling, but you must change buses at Kakarbhitta, then again at Siliguri – it's just as easy to do the trip in stages. The bus stand in Kakarbhitta is the usual, chaotic affair. Be extra wary of your luggage if travelling after dark.

There are several daily services to Kathmandu (day/night Rs 530/607, 17 hours) and Pokhara (day/night Rs 520/622, 17 hours), all travelling via Narayangarh (day/night Rs 405/475, 12 hours). Consider the poor safety record of night buses in Nepal before committing to 17 hours on unlit roads.

Within the eastern part of the Terai, there are four or more daily buses to Janakpur (day/night Rs 270/300, five hours), Biratnagar (Rs 120, 3½ hours) and Birganj (Rs 275, eight hours). If for some reason you wanted to cross Nepal in one go, a single bus leaves daily at 12.40pm for Mahendranagar (Rs 1128, 20 hours) and other towns in the western Terai.

Trekking

The heartland of Nepal is far from any roads, and the only way to get there is by walking through endless ranges of hills. It's a rewarding experience to join local people and walk to remote villages and the foot of the Himalayan peaks.

Trekking in Nepal means a walking trip following trails, many of which have been used for centuries. It is not mountaineering, although some of the popular trekking trails are used by mountaineering expeditions on their approach marches. Their length varies – there are popular treks that only take a day and others that last a week or a month.

Nepal offers some of the most spectacular and beautiful scenery in the world. It has a near monopoly on the world's highest peaks – eight of the 10 highest are found here. Mountain flights may give you superb views, but there is absolutely nothing like waking up on a crystal-clear Himalayan day and seeing an 8000m peak towering over you.

Trekking in Nepal is not like hiking through an uninhabited national park. Local people are constantly passing by on the trails, usually carrying extraordinarily heavy loads of un-expected items. Along many routes there are regularly spaced villages in which to pause and find shelter. In the villages you can meet people from diverse ethnic groups. The warm, outgoing nature, general friendliness and good humour of Nepalis is often noted by trekkers. Religious festivals can make trekking even more enjoyable and interesting.

This chapter outlines the basic requirements for safe trekking on the mountain trails and gives an overview of the major trekking routes where you can stay in local lodges each night. For treks to more remote regions, you will require more detailed advice, maps and route descriptions; check out Lonely Planet's *Trekking in the Nepal Himalaya*. This chapter covers multiday hikes: for our top 10 day hikes, see p77.

HIGHLIGHTS

- Make the approach to **Everest Base Camp** (p334), following in the footsteps of famous mountaineers
- Awake to the uncanny stillness of the **Annapurna Sanctuary** (p352) as dawn reveals the awesome sight of the surrounding peaks soaring overhead
- Visit remote mountain villages, meet the local people and experience Tibetan Buddhist culture in **Namche Bazaar** (p337)
- Witness the raw beauty of the glaciers; hear the crash of avalanches and the roar of raging rivers around **Manang Village** (p351), with a new and more spectacular view day after day

TREKKING

BEFORE YOU GO

PLANNING

Nepal offers plenty of opportunity for treks lasting a day or less, though most are considerably longer. From Pokhara (p268) or around the Kathmandu Valley (p162) you can do a variety of two-, three- or four-day walks, but Nepal's most popular treks take at least a week. For the very popular Everest Base Camp and Annapurna Circuit treks you have to allow three weeks each. Don't take on one of these treks too lightly; the end of the first week is not the time to discover that you're not keen on walking.

When to Trek

The best time to trek is the dry season from October to May; the worst time is the monsoon period from June to September. This generalisation does not allow for the peculiarities of individual treks. Some people even claim that the undeniable difficulties of trekking during the monsoon are outweighed by the virtual absence of Western trekkers.

The first two months of the dry season, October and November, offer the best weather for trekking. The air, freshly washed by the monsoon rains, is crystal clear, the mountain scenery is superb and the weather is still comfortably warm.

December, January and February are still good months for trekking, but the cold can be bitter and dangerous at high altitudes. Getting up to the Everest Base Camp can be a real endurance test and Thorung La on the Annapurna Circuit is often blocked by snow.

In March and April the weather has been dry for a long time and dust is starting to hang in the air, affecting visibility. The poorer quality of the Himalayan views is compensated for by the superb wildflowers, such as the wonderful rhododendrons.

By May it starts to get very hot, dusty and humid, and the monsoon is definitely just around the corner. From June to September the trails can be dangerously slippery due to the monsoon rains, and raging rivers often wash away bridges and stretches of trail. Nepal's famous *jukha* (leeches) are an unpleasant feature of the wet season but, with care, trekking can still be possible and there are certainly fewer trekkers on the trail.

What Kind of Trek?

There are many different styles of trekking to suit your budget, fitness level and available time. You can carry your own pack and tent and rely totally on your own navigation, language skills and prior research. Others find it makes sense to hire a local porter to carry your heavy luggage so that you can walk with only a small pack. A guide will also enhance the trekking experience. Most independent trekkers plan to sleep and eat in lodges every night and forego the complications of camping. To save time, many people organise a trek through a trekking agency, either in Kathmandu or in their home country. Such organised treks can be simple lodge-to-lodge affairs or magnificent expeditions with the full regalia of porters, guides, portable kitchens, dining tents and even toilet tents.

Trekking is physically demanding. Some preparation is recommended, even for shorter treks. You will need endurance and

---

TREKKING SAFELY IN MAOIST COUNTRY

At the time of writing, the Maoist uprising in rural Nepal had significantly affected most trekking routes, though the Maoists have made it clear that they are not targeting foreign tourists. While no tourists have been harmed by Maoist groups, trekkers have been asked for 'donations', ranging from Rs 1000 to US$100, when passing through areas under Maoist control. There have been several ugly confrontations when trekkers initially refused to pay up. Check the current situation before heading out on the trail, as with all treks, and cooperate fully with demands of both government officials and Maoists when required.

Even in the relatively unaffected regions of Annapurna and Everest, telephone booths and ACAP posts have been destroyed and some police checkposts are no longer manned.

Before undertaking any trek you should register with your embassy and follow its travel advice. For up-to-date information visit www.trekinfo.com, which has links to various travel advice and news sites. See also the boxed text, p19.

MOUNTAINEERING IN NEPAL *Bradley Mayhew*

Mountaineering became a fashionable pursuit in Europe during the second half of the 19th century. Having knocked off the great Alpine peaks, Europeans found the much greater heights of the Himalaya an obvious new challenge. An Englishman named WW Graham made a mountaineering visit to Nepal in 1883 and reached the top of a 6000m peak. He was followed by another Englishman, Tom Longstaff, who climbed Trisuli (7215m) in 1907. For the next 20 years this remained the highest summit reached in the world. An Italian attempt on K2, in Pakistan, two years later became the first of the huge Himalayan expeditions involving hundreds of porters.

The West's newfound affluence after its recovery from WWII, together with more modern equipment, vastly improved oxygen apparatus, new mountaineering skills and the reopening of Nepal, led to a golden age of Himalayan mountaineering. The prewar failures were abruptly reversed in the 1950s, beginning with Maurice Herzog's valiant French expedition on Annapurna in 1950. His team's horrific storm-plagued struggle turned an already extremely difficult climb into an epic of human endurance, but for the first time mountaineers had reached the top of an 8000m peak. After descending the mountain they had a month-long struggle through the monsoon with the expedition doctor having to perform amputations of frostbitten fingers and toes.

The success of the 1953 British expedition to Everest began a trend towards larger and larger expeditions. The few climbers who did reach the summit from these expeditions required a huge pyramid of supporters below them. The effect on the environment was devastating, as forests fell to provide firewood for the expeditions and vast amounts of mountaineering equipment and garbage were left behind. The Everest Base Camp has been aptly titled the 'world's highest garbage dump'.

---

stamina to tackle the steep ascents and descents that are so much a part of trekking in the highest mountain range in the world.

On the trail you will begin to realise just how far you are from medical help and the simple comforts that you usually take for granted. For most people, this is part of the appeal of trekking, but for some it is a shock to realise just how responsible they are for their own wellbeing. A simple stumble can have catastrophic results. Even a twisted ankle or sore knee can become a serious inconvenience if you are several days away from help and your companions need to keep moving.

Independent Trekking

Independent trekking does not mean solo trekking. It simply means that you are not part of an organised tour. The trekking trails described here have accommodation along their entire length so there's no need to pack a tent, stove or mat.

For experienced hikers, guides and porters are not necessary on the Annapurna or the Everest treks. A good guide or porter will enhance your experience, but a bad one will just make life more complicated (see right).

There are many factors that influence how much you spend on an independent trek. In most places, dorm accommodation costs around Rs 50 to 100, a simple meal of rice and daal around Rs 50 to 75. As you get further from the road on the Annapurna Circuit and in the Everest region, prices can be more than twice as high. After a long day hiking, most people will weaken when confronted by a cold beer, an apple pie or a hot shower, and these will dramatically add to your costs. Budget for US$10 to US$20 per day in the Annapurna and Everest regions, which will also cover the occasional luxury.

In almost all lodges prices are fixed and are more than reasonable. Remember this – and the real value of the rupee – before you start to get carried away with bargaining.

Guides & Porters

If you can't (or don't want to) carry a large pack, if you have children or elderly people in your party, or if you plan to walk in regions where you have to carry in food and tents, you should consider hiring a porter to carry your heavy baggage.

If you make arrangements with one of the small trekking agencies in Kathmandu, expect to pay Rs 200 to 300 per day for a guide, and Rs 300 to 750 for a porter. The reason a guide is cheaper is that you will be

TREKKING

buying the guide's food – so remember to factor that in.

FINDING GUIDES & PORTERS

To hire a guide, look on bulletin boards, hire someone through a guesthouse or agency, visit a trekking company or check with the office of the Kathmandu Environmental Education Project (KEEP; see p331). **Chhetri Sisters Guesthouse** (☎ 061-524066; trek@3sistersadventure.com) at Lakeside North, Pokhara, organises women porters and guides for women trekkers (see p259).

It's fairly easy to find guides and porters, but it is hard to be certain of their honesty and ability. Unless you have first-hand recommendations, you're best to hire someone through a guesthouse or agency. A porter or guide found at a street corner can easily disappear along the trail with all your gear even if they are carrying a slew of letters from past clients certifying their honesty.

There is a distinct difference between a guide and a porter. A guide should speak English, know the terrain and the trails, and supervise porters, but probably won't carry a load or do menial tasks such as cooking or putting up tents. Porters are generally only hired for load-carrying, although an increasing number speak some English and know the trails well enough to act as guides.

If during a trek you decide you need help, either because of illness, problems with altitude, blisters or weariness, it will generally be possible to find a porter. Most lodges can arrange a porter, particularly in large villages or near a hill-country airstrip where there are often porters who have just finished working for a trekking party and are looking for another load to carry.

OBLIGATIONS TO GUIDES & PORTERS

An important thing to consider when you decide to trek with a guide or porter is that you are placing yourself in the role of an employer. This means that you may have to deal with personnel problems, including medical care, insurance, strikes, requests for time off and salary increases, and all the other aspects of being a boss. Be as thorough as you can when hiring people and make it clear from the beginning what the requirements and limitations are. After that, prepare yourself for some haggling – it's part of the process.

When hiring a porter you are responsible (morally if not legally) for the welfare of those you employ. Many porters die or are injured each year (see the boxed text, opposite) and it's important that you don't contribute to the problem.

These are the main points to bear in mind when hiring a porter.

- Ensure that adequate clothing is provided for any staff you hire. This needs to be suitable for the altitudes you intend to trek to, and should protect against bad weather. Equipment should include adequate footwear, headwear, gloves, windproof jacket and trousers, sunglasses, and blanket, sleeping mat and tent if you are trekking to remote areas or high altitude.
- Ensure that whatever provision you have made for yourself for emergency medical treatment is available to porters working for you.
- Ensure that porters who fall ill are not simply paid out and left to fend for themselves (it happens!).
- Ensure that porters who do fall ill, and are taken down and out in order to access medical treatment, are accompanied by someone who speaks the porter's language and also understands the medical problem.

Whether you're making the arrangements yourself or dealing with an agency, make sure you clearly establish where you will go, how long you will take, how much you are going to pay and what you will supply along the way. With a guide, agree on a fixed daily rate for food rather than pay as you go. Arrangements where you pay for the guide or porter's accommodation and food can end up being surprisingly expensive. The amount of food a hungry Nepali guide can go through, when you're footing the bill, can be stunning. You need to increase the allowance at higher elevations where food is more expensive.

When you do provide equipment for porters, be sure to make it clear whether it is a loan or a gift. In reality it can be very hard to get back equipment that you have loaned unless you are very determined and thick-skinned. If you're hiring your own porters, contact KEEP (see p331) for information about the porter clothing bank, a scheme that allows you to rent protective gear for your porter.

TREKKING WITH A PORTER

Porters are the backbone of the trekking industry in Nepal, and yet every year there are incidents (all of them preventable) involving porters suffering from acute mountain sickness (AMS), snow blindness and frostbite. Some of these illnesses have resulted in fatalities. It seems porters are well down the pecking order with some trekking companies that simply don't look after the porters they hire. This certainly does not apply to all companies, but there are plenty, especially at the budget end of the scale, who are more worried about their own profit than the welfare of those they rely on to generate that profit.

Porters often come from the lowland valleys, are poor and poorly educated, and are often ignorant of the potential dangers of the areas they are being employed to work in. Stories abound of porters being left to fend for themselves, wearing thin cotton clothes and sandals when traversing high mountain passes in blizzard conditions. At the end of each winter a number of porters' bodies are discovered in the snowmelt – they become tired, ill or affected by altitude, and simply sit down in the snow, get hypothermia and die. If you are hiring a porter independently, you have certain obligations to meet. If you are trekking with an organised group using porters, be sure to ask the company how they ensure the wellbeing of porters hired by them.

In order to prevent the abuse of porters, the **International Porter Protection Group** (IPPG; www.ippg.net) was established in 1997. The aim of both the IPPG and its sister organisation **Porters Progress** (www.portersprogress.org) is to improve health and safety for porters at work, to reduce the incidence of avoidable illness, injury and death, and to educate trekkers and trekking and travel companies about porter welfare. Both organisations operate a clothing bank for porters, with branches in Lukla and Thamel. IPPG has an office in the **International Mountain Explorers Connection** (IMEC; Map p136; ☎ 2081407; www.mountainexplorers.org) in Thamel. Porters Progress has an office further north in Thamel (Map p136).

Organised Trekking

Organised treks can vary greatly in standards and costs. Treks arranged with international travel companies tend to be more expensive than trips arranged within Nepal.

INTERNATIONAL TREKKING AGENCIES

After reading the glossy brochure of an adventure-travel company, you pay for the trek and everything is organised before you leave home. The cost will probably include flights to and from Nepal, accommodation in Kathmandu before and after the trek, tours and other activities as well as the trek itself. A fully organised trek provides virtually everything: tents, sleeping bags, food, porters as well as an experienced English-speaking *sirdar* (trail boss), Sherpa guides and usually a Western trek leader. All you need worry about is a daypack and camera.

Companies organising trekking trips in Nepal include some well-known names such as **Mountain Travel-Sobek** (www.mtsobek.com), **Wilderness Travel** (www.wildernesstravel.com) or **Above the Clouds** (www.aboveclouds.com) in the USA, **World Expeditions** (www.worldexpeditions.com.au) or **Peregrine Adventures** (www.peregrineadventures)

.com) in Australia, and **Explore Worldwide** (www.explorewporldwide.com) in the UK. Although the trek leaders may be experienced Western walkers from the international company, the on-the-ground organisation in Nepal will most probably be carried out by a reputable local trekking company.

LOCAL TREKKING AGENCIES

It's quite possible (and it can save a lot of money) to arrange a fully organised trip when you get to Nepal, but if you have a large group it's best to make the arrangements well in advance. Many trekking companies in Nepal can put together a fully equipped trek if you give them a few days notice. With the best of these companies a trek may cost upwards of US$60 or US$70 per person per day and you'll trek in real comfort with tables, chairs, and dining tents, toilet tents and other luxuries.

There are more than 300 trekking agencies in Nepal, ranging from those connected to international travel companies, down to small agencies that specialise in handling independent trekkers. These small agencies will often be able to fix you up with individual porters or guides. A group trek organised through one of these agencies might cost US$30 to US$50 per person per day. Group treks staying at village inns along the route can be cheaper still (around US$25 a day including a guide and food).

Some trekking agencies that have been recommended include:

Adventure Nepal Trekking (☎ 01-4412508; fax 4222026; Tridevi Marg, Thamel, PO Box 915, Kathmandu)

Ama Dablam Trekking (☎ 01-4415372/3; fax 4416029; himalaya.sales@amadablam.wlink.com.np; Lazimpat, PO Box 3035, Kathmandu)

Annapurna Mountaineering & Trekking (☎ 01-4222999; fax 4226153; amtk@ccsl.com.np; Durbar Marg, PO Box 795, Kathmandu)

Asian Trekking (☎ 01-4424249; fax 4411878; Tridevi Marg, Thamel, PO Box 3022, Kathmandu)

Bhrikuti Himalayan Treks (☎ 01-417459; fax 4413612; asianbht@ccsl.com.np; Nag Pokhari, Naxal, PO Box 2267, Kathmandu)

Chhetri Sisters (☎ 061-524066; trek@3sistersadventure.com; Lakeside North, Pokhara)

Crystal Mountain Treks (☎ 01-4416813; fax 4412647; dinesh@crystal.wlink.com.np; Nag Pokhari, Naxal, Kathmandu)

Himalayan Hill Treks & River Tours (☎ 01-4520609; info@hilltreks.com; Patan)

Inner Nepal Treks (☎ 01-4226130; fax 4224237; explore@mos.com.np; Kamaladi, Kathmandu)

Journeys Mountaineering & Trekking (☎ 01-4415092; fax 4419808; journeys@mos.com.np; Baluwatar, Kathmandu)

Lama Excursions (☎ 01-4220186; fax 4227202; trek@lamex.wlink.com.np; Chanddol, Maharajganj, Kathmandu)

Malla Treks (☎ 01-4410089; fax 4423143; info@mallatreks.com; Lekhnath Marg, Kathmandu)

Mountain Travel Nepal (☎ 01-4414508; info@tigermountain.com; Lazimpat, Kathmandu)

Sherpa Society (☎ 01-4470361; fax 4470153; passang@mos.com.np; Chabahil, Chuchepati, Kathmandu)

Sherpa Trekking Service (☎ 01-4220243; fax 4227243; sts@wlink.com.np; Kamaladi, Kathmandu)

Sisne Rover Trekking (☎ 061-520893; fax 523262; sisne@mos.com.np; Lakeside, Pokhara)

Thamserku Trekking (☎ 01-4354491; fax 4354329; info@trekkinginnepal.com; Basundhara, Ring Rd, Kathmandu)

Treks & Expedition Services (☎ 01-4418347; fax 4410488; Kamal Pokhari, Kathmandu)

Venture Treks & Expeditions (☎ 01-4221585; fax 4220178; temtig@mos.com.np; Kantipath, Kathmandu)

Yeti Mountaineering & Trekking (☎ 01-4425896; fax 4410899; ymtrek@ccsl.com.np.wlink.com.np; Ramshah Path, Kathmandu)

Books & Maps

The best series of maps of Nepal is the 1:50,000 series produced by Erwin Schneider for Research Scheme Nepal Himalaya and originally printed in Vienna. Most sheets are now published by Nelles Verlag in Munich. They cover the Kathmandu Valley and the Everest region from Jiri to the Hongu Valley. The 1:100,000 Schneider maps of Annapurna and Langtang are available from many map shops overseas and at bookshops in Kathmandu.

National Geographic produces trekking maps to the Khumbu, Everest Base Camp, Annapurna and Langtang areas, as part of its Trails Illustrated series (Rs 950 to 1050). They are generally good for the most popular treks.

The Finnish government has assisted Nepal's survey department with the production of a series of 1:50,000 and 1:25,000 maps covering most of Nepal, but they don't show all the trekking trails. They are available in some bookshops and from the Maps of Nepal outlet in Baluwatar, Kathmandu, on the road towards Bhaktapur, for Rs 80 per sheet.

There are numerous 'trekking' maps produced locally by Himalayan Map House, Nepa Maps and Shangri-La Maps. They cost from Rs 400 and are readily found in map and bookshops in Thamel. These maps are adequate for trekking the popular trails and are relatively inexpensive. Be aware that there is a great deal of repackaging going on. Don't buy two maps with different covers and names assuming you are getting significantly different maps. Check them first.

All of these maps are available at bookshops in Kathmandu, and some speciality map shops overseas stock a selection. Most are available online from **Stanfords** (www.stanfords.co.uk), **Omni Resources** (www.omnimap.com) or **Melbourne Map Centre** (www.melbmap.com.au).

What to Bring
EQUIPMENT

It's always best to have your own equipment since you will be familiar with it and know for certain that it works. If there is some equipment that you do not have, you can always buy or rent it from one of Nepal's many trekking shops. Much of the equipment available is of adequate quality (but check items carefully) and the rental charges are generally not excessive, but large deposits are often required (usually equal to a generous valuation of the equipment itself). Never leave your passport as a deposit.

Hire rates in Kathmandu vary depending on quality. You can hire a sleeping bag (two to four season) for Rs 25 to 55, a down jacket for Rs 20 to 40 and a tent for Rs 120 to 150.

Thamel is the centre for equipment shopping in Nepal, though Pokhara and Namche Bazaar also have trekking-equipment outlets. It is no longer easy to pick up the leftover gear from trekking expeditions, but there is a great deal of new equipment you can purchase including last-minute sundries such as iodine, sun block and LED head lamps.

Some trekking gear, including sleeping bags, down jackets, duffel bags, backpacks, camera cases, ponchos and wind jackets, is manufactured in Kathmandu and sold in Thamel at very reasonable prices. Much of this locally produced gear is decorated with well-known brand names, but don't be deceived into thinking you're getting top-quality merchandise at a bargain price. Even so, most items are well made and will stand up to the rigours of at least one major trek.

Kathmandu does have a *pukka* (real) North Face showroom on Tridevi Marg but the selection is small and prices are similar to those in the US.

Approximate retail prices for new Nepali-made gear complete with fake brand names are as follows:

Item	Cost (Rs)
sleeping bag (2-4 season)	4000-6000
down jacket	3000
rain/wind jacket	450-1500
pile jacket	300-1000
day-pack	350-1300
expedition pack	1500-3000
duffel bag	300-450
quality socks	160-850

CLOTHING & FOOTWEAR

The clothing you require depends on where and when you trek. If you're going to the Everest Base Camp in the middle of winter you must be prepared for very cold weather and take down gear, mittens and the like. If you're doing a short, low-altitude trek early or late in the season the weather is often

likely to be fine enough for T-shirts and a pile jacket to pull on in the evenings.

Apart from ensuring you have adequate clothing to keep warm, it's important that your feet are comfortable and will stay dry if it rains or snows. Uncomfortable shoes and blistered feet are the worst possible trekking discomforts. Make sure your shoes fit well and are comfortable for long periods. Running shoes are adequate for low-altitude (below 3000m), warm-weather treks where you won't encounter snow, though they lack ankle support. Otherwise the minimum standard of footwear is lightweight trekking boots. Trekking boots can be bought in Kathmandu for Rs 2000 to 3000, but these are generally seconds and are not recommended. The best idea is to bring your own worn-in boots.

OTHER GEAR

In winter or at high altitudes a top-quality four-season sleeping bag will be necessary. If you are going on an organised trek check what equipment is supplied by the company you sign up with. If you need to hire one, it could be grubby; check for fleas or worse.

Rain is rare during most of the trekking season, though weather patterns in the Bay of Bengal can cause massive rainstorms during autumn, and there are sure to be a few rainy days during spring. You should be prepared for rain by carrying waterproof gear, or at least a portable umbrella. The rainy season just before and after the monsoon months also brings leeches with it, and it's good to have some salt or matches to deal with them. Take a torch (flashlight) for those inevitable calls of nature on moonless nights.

MONEY

Except in Solu Khumbu and on the Annapurna treks, changing foreign money is likely to be very difficult if not impossible. Bring enough money for the whole trek and don't count on being able to change Rs 1000 notes except in Namche Bazaar and Jomsom.

DOCUMENTS & FEES
Trekking Permits

Permits are not required for trekking in the Everest, Annapurna and Langtang regions described in this book.

National Park & Conservation Fees

If you trek in the Annapurna, Manaslu, Kanchenjunga or Makalu regions, you will enter a conservation area and must pay a conservation fee; if your trek enters a national park, you must pay a national park fee.

You should buy an entrance ticket for all national parks and conservation areas in advance at the **national parks office** (8am-2pm Sun-Fri) just next to the **Annapurna Conservation Area Project office** (ACAP; Map p136) in the Sanchaya Kosh Bhawan Shopping Centre at the entrance to Thamel in Kathmandu. You can pay the national park fee when you arrive at the park entrance station, but *you must pay the conservation fee in advance.* Currently, the (once-only) fee is Rs 1000 (US$15) for national parks, Rs 2000 (US$30) for Annapurna and Rs 1000 for Makalu-Barun and Kanchenjunga conservation areas.

Conservation fees for the Annapurna area are also payable in Pokhara at the **ACAP office** (061-532275), Pardi Damside inside the Nepal Tourism Board's (NTB) Tourist Service Centre building. Bring Rs 2000 and one photograph. Fortunately the permit is issued on the spot and you should accomplish the task quickly unless there is a long queue. If you arrive at an ACAP checkpoint without a permit you will be charged Rs 4000!

RESPONSIBLE TREKKING

Nepal faces several environmental problems as a result of, or at least compounded by, tourists' actions and expectations. These include the depletion of its forests for firewood; the build-up of nonbiodegradable waste, especially plastic bottles; and the pollution of its waterways. You can help by choosing an environmentally and socially responsible trekking company and heeding some of the following advice.

Trekking Gently in the Himalaya, a booklet by Wendy Brewer Lama, is an excellent resource which has essential tips for trekkers. It's available at the KEEP offices (opposite) in Thamel and Pokhara.

Firewood & Forest Depletion

Minimise the use of firewood by staying in lodges that use kerosene or fuel-efficient wood stoves and solar-heated hot water. Avoid using large open fires for warmth – wear additional clothing instead. Keep showers to a minimum, and spurn showers

altogether if wood is burnt to produce the hot water.

Consolidate cooking time (and wood consumption) by ordering the same items at the same time as other trekkers. Daal bhaat (rice and lentils) is usually readily available for large numbers of people, does not require special lengthy cooking time and is nutritious and inexpensive. Remember that local meals are usually prepared between 10am and 11am, so eating then will usually not require lighting an additional fire. Treat your drinking water with iodine rather than boiling it.

Those travelling with organised groups should ensure kerosene is used for cooking.

Garbage & Waste

You can do several things to reduce the amount of rubbish and pollution in the hills. Purifying your own water instead of buying mineral water in nonbiodegradable plastic bottles is the most important of these.

Independent trekkers should always carry their garbage out or dispose of it properly. You can burn it, but you should remember that the fireplace in a Nepali home is a sacred institution and throwing rubbish into it would be a great insult. Take out all your batteries, as they will eventually leak toxins.

Toilet paper is a particularly unpleasant sight along trails; if you must use it, carry it in a plastic bag until you can burn it. Better yet, carry a small plastic trowel to bury your faeces (well away from any streams) and a small plastic water container so that, like the vast majority of people in the world, you can clean yourself with water instead of toilet paper.

Those travelling with organised groups should ensure that toilet tents are properly organised and that rubbish is carried out. Check on the company's policies before you sign up.

Water

Do your bit to minimise pollution and don't soap up your clothes in the streams. Instead use a bowl or bucket and discard the dirty water away from water courses.

On the Annapurna Circuit, the Annapurna Conservation Area Project (with New Zealand government assistance) has introduced the Safe Water Drinking Scheme – a chain of 16 outlets selling purified water to trekkers.

Its aim is to minimise the demand for plastic mineral-water bottles. An estimated one million plastic bottles are brought into the Annapurna Conservation Area each year, creating a serious litter problem. The outlets are found in Tal, Bargarcchap, Chame, Pisang, Hongde, Manang, Letdar, Thorung Phedi, Muktinath, Kagbeni, Jomsom, Marpha, Tukuche, Khobang, Lete and Ghasa.

USEFUL ORGANISATIONS

Several organisations are attempting to deal with the environmental problems created by trekking. One organisation, the Annapurna Conservation Area Project (ACAP), has done a great deal to encourage sustainable development in the Annapurna region. ACAP has offices in Thamel (Sanchaya Kosh Bhawan Building), Patan and Pokhara.

These organisations in Kathmandu offer free, up-to-date information on trekking conditions, health risks and minimising your environmental impact.

Kathmandu Environmental Education Project (KEEP; Map p136; ☎ 4412944; www.keepnepal.org; ☯ 10am-5pm Sun-Fri), in Thamel, has a library, some useful notebooks with up-to-date information from other trekkers, an excellent notice board and embassy registration forms for most countries. It also sells iodine, biodegradable soap and other environmentally friendly equipment.

The **International Mountain Explorers Connection** (IMEC; Map p136; ☎ 2081407; info@mountainexplorers.org; www.hec.org; ☯ 10am-5pm Sun-Fri) also provides information on trekking. Members can store luggage here and use the mail and email service.

Himalayan Rescue Association (HRA; Map p136; ☎ 4445505, 4440292; ☯ noon-1pm, 2-5pm Sun-Fri; www.himalayanrescue.org; Thamel) has information about AMS and useful notebooks with up-to-date information from other trekkers, plus trail conditions, weather updates and embassy registration forms. It runs health posts at Pheriche, Machermo and Manang. Free lectures on altitude sickness are held at the Thamel office at 3pm Monday to Friday. Both KEEP and the HRA offices are excellent places to visit and advertise for trekking companions

The slide shows held in the Kathmandu Guest House (p135) by Chris Beall, a British freelance photographer, writer and trek leader, are another good source of up-to-date information in Kathmandu for independent trekking. The shows cost Rs 300 (including tea/coffee and biscuits) and you get plenty of time to ask questions at the end. You'll see posters up at the Kathmandu Guest House.

HEALTH

Acute mountain sickness (AMS) or altitude sickness is the major concern on all high-altitude treks, but for the majority of trekkers health problems are likely to be minor, such as stomach upsets and blisters. Commonsense precautions are all that's required to avoid illness.

Basic rules for healthy trekking include taking care that water is always safe to drink. The best method is to treat water with iodine, as this is safe and does not require the use of firewood or kerosene to boil water. Diarrhoea is one of the comparatively minor problems that can ruin a trek so watch what you eat and ensure your medical kit has a medication such as Lomotil or Imodium (for emergencies only) and an antibiotic like Norfloxacin. The food on an organised trek is unlikely to cause problems, but village-inn trekkers are at risk.

At high altitudes the burning power of the sun is strong, so make sure you have a pair of good sunglasses, a hat and a maximum protection sunscreen. If there is any likelihood that you'll be walking over snow, sunglasses are insufficient; you need mountaineering glasses with sidepieces. Ensure that your porters also have adequate eyewear.

Many people suffer from knee and ankle strains, particularly if they are carrying their own pack. If you have a predisposition to these injuries, carry elastic supports or bandages. Lightweight, collapsible trekking poles are invaluable in this regard, providing extra support and stability, especially on those knee-pounding descents. They can also come in handy when the village dogs get a bit too close. You should also carry plasters (Band-Aids) in case of blisters.

Make sure you are in good health before departing, as there is very little medical attention along the trails and rescue helicopters are not only very expensive but *must* be cleared for payment in advance. Your embassy can do this if you have registered with it. See p335 for more information on possible medical assistance along the way.

In general, Himalayan hospitals can offer only very limited facilities and expertise. The **Himalayan Rescue Dog Squad** (☎ 061-523267; www.hrdsnrescue.org.np; Riverside Hospital & Disaster Relief Unit, Shyauli Bazaar, Lamjung) operates the largest rescue organisation in Nepal.

Be ever-alert for the symptoms of AMS. See p388 for more detailed information on staying healthy while trekking.

TREKKING SAFELY

Usually, the further you get from heavily populated centres the less likely it is that your personal safety will be threatened. Assaults in remote places are not unheard of, however. Indeed, some places have earned quite a reputation for violent assaults, almost without exception involving a solo trekker or small party of two or three. On the trails that run from Ghorapani to Tikhedhunga and Ghorapani to Ghandruk it is important to stay in a group and remain alert, particularly towards the end of a long tiring day. Several basic rules should be followed: don't trek alone, don't make ostentatious displays of valuable possessions and don't leave lodge doors unlocked or valuables unattended.

See also p359.

Choosing Companions

You should never trek alone. It's useful to have someone to watch your pack – when you have to run off the trail into the bushes, or even when you are in a lodge and go out to the toilet. It's also important to have someone around in case of injury or illness. Women should choose trekking companions carefully and treat with caution any offer of a massage in a remote hotel.

If you do not already have a travelling companion, then you should find either a guide or another trekker in Kathmandu or Pokhara to trek with. If you're looking for a Western companion, check hotel bulletin boards or just chat with someone who sits next to you in a restaurant and perhaps your schedules and ambitions will coincide. Two websites that you can visit to find trekking companions and guides are www.trekinfo.com and www.yetizone.com. Unless you have a friend to trek with, or are prepared to take a chance on finding a companion in Nepal, booking a group trek may be the safest option.

Trail Conditions

Walking at high altitudes on rough trails can be dangerous. Watch your footing on narrow, slippery trails, and never underestimate the changeability of the weather – at any time of the year. If you are crossing high passes where snow is a possibility, never walk with less than three people. Carry a supply of emergency rations, have a map and compass (and know how to use them), and have sufficient clothing and equipment to deal with cold, wet, blizzard conditions.

You will be sharing the trail with man and beasts, usually carrying large burdens – not for fun but to scrape a living, so show respect. If a mule or yak train approaches, move to the high side of the trail. If you move to the outside you are at risk of being knocked over the edge. Buffalo will happily trample all over you, especially when they are moving downhill – give them a wide berth.

Register with Your Embassy

All embassies and consulates strongly recommend that their citizens register with them before they hit the trail. See the boxed text, p359.

Rescue Insurance

Check that your travel-insurance policy does not exclude mountaineering or alpinism. Although you will not be engaging in these activities on the trekking trail, you may have trouble convincing the insurance company of this fact. Check what insurance is available through your trekking company, if using one. Rescue insurance will need to cover an emergency helicopter evacuation or a charter flight from a remote airstrip. You can purchase rescue insurance from most alpine clubs in Western countries. In Nepal, **Neco Insurance** (☎ 01-4427354; info@necoins.com.np; PO Box 12271, Kathmandu) offers trekking policies. Personal accident, medical and evacuation insurance for trekkers is US$6.88 per day for the first 15 days of trekking and US$4.40 per day thereafter.

Altitude

Walking the trails of Nepal often entails a great deal of altitude gain and loss; even the base of the great mountains of the Himalaya can be very high. Most treks that go through populated areas stick to between 1000m and 3000m, although the Everest

Base Camp trek and the Annapurna Circuit trek both reach over 5000m. On high treks like these ensure adequate acclimatisation, and the maxim of 'walking high, sleeping low' is good advice; your night halt should be at a lower level than the highest point reached in the day.

TREKS

ROUTES & CONDITIONS

Most trekkers want to get away from roads as quickly as possible, and it is still possible to leave them quickly behind. Nepali trails are often steep and taxing. The old adage that 'the shortest path between two points is a straight line' appears to have been firmly drummed into Nepalis, irrespective of any mountains that may get in the way! In compensation, the trails are often very well maintained. Busy trails up steep slopes are often endless stone staircases.

A typical day's walk lasts from between five to seven hours and involves a number of ascents and descents. It's rare to spend much time at the same level. On an organised camping trek the day is run to a remarkably tight schedule. A typical pattern would be: up at 6am, start walking at 7am, stop for lunch at 10am, start after lunch at noon, stop walking at 3pm. Nepalis rise early, eat very little for breakfast, eat a large lunch in the late morning and a second meal before dark, then retire early – you will be best off to try and follow a similar schedule.

A little rudimentary knowledge of the Nepali language will help to make your trek easier and more interesting, although finding your way is rarely difficult on the major trekking routes and English is fairly widely spoken. See p398 for some useful Nepali words and phrases.

Sleeping

Organised treks camp each night and all you have to do is eat and crawl into your tent. Even erecting the tent is handled by the trekking crew, who put it up for you at the site selected by your *sirdar* or group leader.

Independent trekkers stay in the small lodges, guesthouses or village inns that have flourished along the popular trails. These lodges range from simple extensions of a traditional family home (which can sometimes be a plywood firetrap of questionable construction) to quite luxurious places with private rooms, extensive menus and even attached toilets and showers. It's possible to make quite long treks relying entirely on local accommodation and food. Nevertheless, it's still a good idea to carry a sleeping bag as lodges sometimes run out of bedding at peak season.

Eating

On an organised trek your only concern with food is sitting down to eat it. The porters carry virtually all of the ingredients with them, and there will be a cook with well-drilled assistants who can turn out meals of stunning complexity.

Independent trekkers will find numerous places to eat along the most popular trails, although it's wise to carry some emergency food supplies such as cheese, dried fruit or chocolate. On the Everest and Annapurna treks it's unlikely that you will walk more than an hour or two without coming across some sort of establishment that can offer tea, soft drinks, beer, and often a full meal. KEEP and other environmentally concerned organisations point out that the local diet of daal bhaat is nutritious, easily prepared, available everywhere, and requires a minimum of fuel for preparation. You lessen your impact on the environment and usually eat better if you adapt to the local diet.

RESTING – A NEPALI INSTITUTION! *Joe Bindloss*

With the tortuous nature of the Nepali landscape, getting around on foot can be heavy going. To ease the burden on travellers, villagers across Nepal have created thousands of *chautaras* – stone platforms shaded by pipal or banyan trees – where walkers can rest their feet and set down their loads. Many *chautaras* stand on the site of ancient pre-Hindu shrines, and the platforms are still a focal point for village life – a place to meet and chat, or trade and carry out religious rituals. Even today, constructing a *chautara* is seen as a sure-fire way to improve karma (the Buddhist and Hindu law of cause and effect) for future existences.

> **EVEREST NUTS** *Bradley Mayhew*
>
> The world's highest peak has attracted many commendable achievements: the first ascent without oxygen (1978), first summit with an artificial leg (1998), the first ski descent (2000), the first blind ascent (2001), youngest ascent (aged 16), oldest ascent (64) and fastest ascent (eight hours). Sherpa Babu Chiru spent a particularly amazing 21 hours on top of Everest without oxygen in 1999.
>
> But there have also been some admirably silly achievements.
>
> Perhaps most ambitious was the Briton Maurice Wilson, who planned to crash his Gipsy Moth plane halfway up the mountain and then climb from there to the top, not letting his almost total lack of mountaineering, or flying, experience get in the way of an obviously silly plan. (He eventually froze to death at Camp III dressed in a light sweater.)
>
> Maybe it's something in the national psyche (this is after all the nation that gave us Monty Python), for it was also a team of Brits who trekked all the way to Everest Base Camp to play the 'world's highest game of rugby' at 5140m. They lost.
>
> My personal Everest heroes are the British (!) pair who carried an ironing board up Everest to 5440m to do some extreme ironing ('part domestic chore, part extreme sport'). For anyone contemplating a repeat expedition, the duo have revealed that expedition preparation can be limited to three important factors: 'a few beers, a drunken bet and a stolen ironing board'.

The standard of cuisine on the Jomsom Trek is so westernised that it has been dubbed 'the apple pie trail' because that dish features on so many village-inn menus. It's surprising how many places even have cold beer available as well; before you complain about the price, contemplate the fact that somebody had to carry that bottle of beer all the way there and will probably have to carry the empty bottle back again!

CHOOSING A TREK

It is possible to do short treks in Nepal that do not reach demanding altitudes or need sophisticated equipment, years of experience or athletic stamina. A certain level of mental and physical fitness and sensible planning and preparation will ensure that yours is an enjoyable experience. For a selection of short treks see p268 and p162.

One statistic that is difficult to determine is distance. It is easy to judge distances from a map, but a printed map is in two dimensions. With the many gains and losses of altitude – and all the turns and twists of the trail – a map measurement of the routes becomes virtually meaningless. Someday someone will take the time to push a bicycle-wheel odometer over every trail in Nepal to get accurate distance measurements. Until then, we'll just have to be satisfied with the estimate that most of the days listed here are 10 to 20km of trekking,

The six popular longer treks described in this chapter are: the Everest Base Camp,

Helambu, Langtang, Jomsom, Annapurna Circuit and Annapurna Sanctuary treks.

EVEREST BASE CAMP TREK
Duration 21 or 15 days
Max elevation 5545m
Best season October to December
Start Jiri or Lukla
Finish Lukla

This trek takes about three weeks unless you fly in as well as out of Lukla. It reaches a significant height of 5545m at Kala Pattar, a small peak offering fine views of Mt Everest. Although the final part of the trek is through essentially uninhabited areas, small lodges operate during the trekking season so it's quite suitable for independent trekkers.

Everybody has heard of Mt Everest and that's the reason why the Everest Base Camp trek is so popular. The trek has a number of stunning attractions; not least of these is being able to say you've visited the highest mountain in the world. In addition there's the spectacular scenery and the outgoing Sherpa people of the Solu Khumbu region where Mt Everest and its attendant lesser peaks are.

The 15-day trek from Lukla to Kala Pattar has become the most popular trek because it avoids Maoist country. If you fly to Lukla, be sure to schedule acclimatisation days at Namche and Pheriche to avoid altitude sickness.

The trek from Jiri to Lukla is not only a hard slog, but is also pretty sparse in the breathtaking-views department. The trek doesn't follow valleys, as the Annapurna treks do. Instead the trail from Jiri cuts across the valleys, so for day after day it's a tiring process of dropping down one side of a steep valley and climbing up again on the other. By the time you reach the base camp your ascents will total almost 9000m – the full height of Everest from sea level. Most trekkers now avoid the Jiri portion of the trek because the Maoists usually demand Rs 5000 per person on the first or second day of the trek, please check the situation on the ground before committing to this portion of the trek.

The trek starts in Nepali-speaking Hindu lowlands and ends in the Tibetan-Buddhist highlands where the Sherpas are renowned for their enterprise, hard work, civic responsibility and devotion to the practice of Buddhism. In their often inhospitable land, the potato, a relatively recent introduction, is the main crop, but these days trekking and mountaineering are the backbone of the Sherpa economy. More than half the population in the region is now involved with tourism, and Namche Bazaar looks more like an alpine resort than a Sherpa village.

Flights In & Out

Most Everest trekkers opt to fly one way to avoid having to repeat the difficult initial Jiri to Lukla leg. This introduces its own problems, as flights to Lukla are notorious for cancellations, waiting lists and short-tempered trekkers, although things have improved in recent years. If you have the time, walk in from Jiri and fly out from Lukla. For a shorter trip you can fly in to Lukla, trek to Everest and then fly out, again from Lukla, taking around 15 days to trek to Kala Pattar and back. From Lukla you can just visit Thami, Namche Bazaar and Tengboche, which will take about a week.

Emergency Facilities

There are small hospitals in Jiri, Phaphlu and Khunde (just north of Namche Bazaar); the Himalayan Rescue Association (HRA) has a medical facility in Pheriche.

Access: Kathmandu to Jiri

The road to Jiri follows the Kodari road to Lamosangu, 78km from Kathmandu, and turns off there to Jiri, a further 110km. An 'express' (10-hour) bus to Jiri leaves from the Kathmandu bus station at 6am (Rs 320) and 7am (Rs 290), and there are normal buses (Rs 247) between 5.30am and 8am. Keep a close eye on your luggage.

The Trek

DAY 1: JIRI TO SHIVALAYA

The walk starts with a climb to the ridge top at 2370m then drops down to Shivalaya (1750m).

DAY 2: SHIVALAYA TO BHANDAR

From Shivalaya you climb to Sangbadanda (2150m), Kosaribas (2500m), then to Deorali, a pass at 2705m. There are hotels on the pass, or you can descend to Bhandar (2150m). This Sherpa settlement has a *gompa* (Buddhist monastery) and a number of hotels. It's possible to take a short detour between Sangbadanda and Bhandar to visit Thodung (3090m), where there's a cheese factory, established in the 1950s with Swiss aid.

DAY 3: BHANDAR TO SETE

The trail drops down to the Likhu Khola, crosses the river at 1490m, and tracks along it to Kenja (1570m). Now the long ascent to the Lamjura Bhanjyang (pass) begins. The first part of the climb is quite steep, then it traverses to Sete (2575m), an abandoned gompa. From here on the villages are almost all inhabited by Sherpas and have both Nepali and Sherpa names (the Sherpa village names are given in brackets).

DAY 4: SETE TO JUNBESI

It's a long but gradual climb to the Lamjura Bhanjyang (3530m). You're rewarded with frost and often snow along the trail in winter or with lovely flowering rhododendrons in the spring. Goyom (3300m), on your way to the pass, is a good lunch stop. The pass is the highest point between Jiri and Namche Bazaar and from the top you descend to Tragdobuk (2860m), then to the pretty Sherpa village of Junbesi (Jun; 2675m). Junbesi has a monastery and some good hotels. It is a good place for a rest day with some interesting walks in the vicinity.

DAY 5: JUNBESI TO NUNTALA

The trail climbs to Khurtang, on a ridge at 2980m (where for the first time you can

EVEREST BASE CAMP TREK

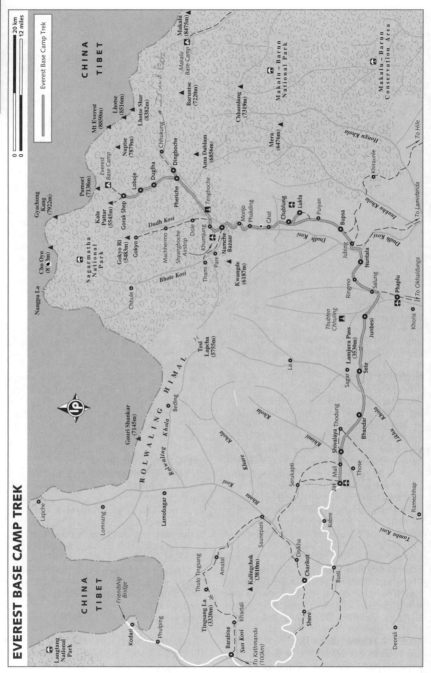

0   20 km
0   12 miles

━━━ Everest Base Camp Trek

see Everest), then on to Salung (2980m). A lower trail from Junbesi leads to the hospital and airstrip at Phaphlu and the district headquarters and bazaar at Salleri. From Salung the trail descends to the Ringmo Khola (2570m). Then it's up to Ringmo where apples and other fruit are grown.

A short climb from Ringmo takes you to the 3071m Trakshindo La, then the trail drops down past the gompa of the same name, and on to Nuntala (Manidingma; 2250m), where there are numerous hotels offering a variety of standards.

DAY 6: NUNTALA TO BUPSA
The trail descends to the Dudh Kosi (1480m) and crosses it to follow the eastern bank. The trail climbs to Jubing (Dorakbuk; 1680m) and continues over a ridge to Khari Khola (Khati Thenga; 2070m). You should arrive in Khari Khola early enough to push on up the steep hill to Bupsa (Bumshing; 2300m). There are several hotels on the top of the ridge and a few less sumptuous hotels at Kharte, 20 minutes' walk beyond Bupsa up the trail to the north.

DAY 7: BUPSA TO CHABLUNG
From Bupsa the trail climbs gradually, offering views of the Dudh Kosi 1000m below at the bottom of the steep-sided valley, until it reaches a ridge at 2840m overlooking Puiyan (Chitok). The trail is very narrow in places as it makes its way down to Puiyan (2730m), in a side canyon of the Dudh Kosi valley. Climb to a ridge at 2750m then drop down to Surkhe (Buwa; 2290m). Just beyond Surkhe is the turn-off to Lukla with its airstrip.

The trail continues to climb through Mushe (Nangbug) and then Chaunrikharka (Dungde; 2630m) to Chablung (Lomdza). If you are flying in to Lukla, trek downhill past Chablung to Phakding for the night.

DAY 8: CHABLUNG TO NAMCHE BAZAAR
From Chablung the trail contours along the side of the Dudh Kosi valley before descending to Ghat (Lhawa; 2530m). The trail climbs again to Phakding, a collection of about 25 lodges at 2800m.

The trail crosses the river on a long, swaying bridge, and then leads you along the river to Benkar (2700m). A short distance beyond Benkar the trail crosses the Dudh Kosi to its east bank on a suspension bridge and climbs to Chomoa.

It's a short climb up to Monjo (2800m), where there are some good places to stay. Show your entrance ticket at the Sagarmatha National Park entrance station, then descend to cross the Dudh Kosi. On the other side it's a short distance to Jorsale (Thumbug; 2810m), then the trail crosses back to the east side of the river before climbing to the high suspension bridge over the Dudh Kosi.

It's a steady climb from here to Namche Bazaar (Nauche; 3480m). As this is the first climb to an altitude where AMS may be a problem, take it easy and avoid rushing. There is another national park entrance station just below Namche where permits are again checked and fees collected.

DAY 9: ACCLIMATISATION DAY IN NAMCHE BAZAAR
Namche Bazaar is the main centre in the Solu Khumbu region and has shops, restaurants, a bakery, hotels with hot showers, a pool hall, a police checkpoint, a moneychanger, a bank and even an Internet service. Pay a visit to the Sagarmatha Pollution Control Committee office to find out about conservation efforts being made in the region, and also visit the national park visitor centre on the ridge above town (well worth a visit).

Namche Bazaar and the surrounding villages have an ample supply of hydroelectricity, used for lighting and cooking as well as powering the video parlours. There is a colourful market each Saturday.

There is plenty to do around Namche Bazaar and you should spend a day here acclimatising. Remember that the victims of AMS are often the fittest and healthiest people who foolishly overextend themselves. It's helpful to do a strenuous day walk to a higher altitude as part of your acclimatisation, coming back down to Namche to sleep. For this purpose the long day walk to Thami (to the west) is worthwhile.

DAY 10: NAMCHE BAZAAR TO TENGBOCHE
The slightly longer route from Namche Bazaar to Tengboche via Khumjung and Khunde is more interesting than the direct one. The route starts by climbing up to the Shyangboche airstrip. Above the airstrip is the Everest View Hotel, a Japanese scheme

to build a deluxe hotel with great views of the highest mountains on earth. The hotel has had a chequered history, but is once again open, with rooms at US$135, plus an extra charge for oxygen if needed!

From the hotel or the airstrip you continue to Khumjung (3790m) and then rejoin the direct trail to Tengboche. The trail descends to the Dudh Kosi (3250m) where there are several small lodges and a series of picturesque water-driven prayer wheels. A steep ascent brings you to Tengboche (3870m). The famous gompa, with its background of Ama Dablam, Everest and other peaks, was burnt down in 1989. It has been rebuilt as a large, impressive structure. There's a camping area and a number of places to stay. During the November to December full moon the colourful Mani Rimdu festival is held here with masked dances in the monastery courtyard, and accommodation becomes extremely difficult to find.

DAY 11: TENGBOCHE TO PHERICHE
Beyond Tengboche the altitude really starts to tell. The trail drops down to Devuche, crosses the Imja Khola and climbs past superb *mani* stones (carved with the Tibetan Buddhist chant *om mani padme hum*) to Pangboche (3860m). The gompa here is worth visiting and the village is a good place for a lunch stop.

The trail then climbs to Pheriche (4240m), where there is an HRA trekkers' aid post and possible medical assistance. Pheriche has a number of hotels and restaurants that may feature exotic dishes left over from international mountaineering expeditions.

DAY 12: ACCLIMATISATION DAY IN PHERICHE
Another acclimatisation day should be spent at Pheriche. As at Namche, a solid day walk to a higher altitude is better than just resting; Dingboche and Chhukung (4730m) are possible destinations. Either walk offers good views.

DAY 13: PHERICHE TO DUGLHA
The trail climbs to Phalang Karpo (4340m) then Duglha (4620m). It's possible to continue on to Lobuje, but the HRA doctors at Pheriche urge everyone to stay a night at Duglha to aid acclimatisation.

DAY 14: DUGLHA TO LOBUJE
From Duglha the trail goes directly up the terminal moraine (debris) of the Khumbu Glacier for about one hour then left into the memorial area (in memory of those who have died making the ascent) Chukpilhara, before reaching the summer village of Lobuje (4930m). The altitude, the cold and the crowding in the lodges can combine to ensure less than restful nights.

DAY 15: LOBUJE TO GORAK SHEP
The trail continues to climb to Gorak Shep (5160m). The return trip from Lobuje to Gorak Shep takes a couple of hours, leaving enough time to continue to Kala Pattar – or you can opt to overnight in Gorak Shep and reach Kala Pattar the next morning. At 5545m this small peak offers the best view you'll get of Everest without climbing it.

Although there is accommodation at Gorak Shep it's cold and the altitude makes life uncomfortable. It's a better plan to return to Lobuje for the night. The altitude hits nearly everybody; getting back down to Lobuje or even better, to Pheriche, makes a real difference.

DAY 16: GORAK SHEP TO LOBUJE
If you want to get to the base camp then it's about six hours round trip from Gorak Shep. There's no view from base camp; if you only have the energy for one side trip, then make it Kala Pattar. The trek back down to Lobuje is easy, but it seems endless because of the many uphill climbs.

DAY 17: LOBUJE TO DINGBOCHE
Staying the night at Dingboche instead of at Pheriche makes an interesting accommodation alternative. It's a 'summer village' at 4410m with numerous large lodges.

DAYS 18 TO 20: DINGBOCHE TO LUKLA
The next three days retrace your steps down to Lukla via Tengboche and Namche Bazaar. There is extreme pressure for a seat on flights out of Lukla, so be sure to have an advance booking, and be there the evening before your flight to reconfirm (the airline offices are generally open from 5pm to 6pm, but sometimes it's 6pm to 7pm). Then be prepared for a torrid time at the airstrip as frustrated trekkers vie for the limited seats. This is especially so when flights have been

cancelled for a few consecutive days due to poor visibility, and there is a huge back-log of passengers all wanting to get back to Kathmandu.

DAY 21: BACK TO KATHMANDU
If the gods are with you, your flight will come in and your reservation won't have been can-celled. Then, after it took you so many days to get here by road and foot, your aircraft only takes 35 minutes to fly you back.

Alternative Routes & Side Trips
An interesting side trip is the nine-day round trip from Namche Bazaar to Gokyo and back. This trek ends at Gokyo Ri, a hill with fine, but different, views of Everest. You can even combine both Gokyo and base camp by crossing the 5420m Cho La, but you need to take this route seriously - it's best to bring your ice axe and crampons and know how to use them.

A shorter side trip from Namche Bazaar is to Thami, the gateway to Tesi Lapcha and the Rolwaling Himal. You can do a round trip to Thami in one very long day, but it's better to stay overnight to catch the morning views.

HELAMBU TREK
Duration 8 days
Max elevation 3640m
Best season October to April
Start/Finish Sundarijal

The Helambu region offers a one-week trek that can start and finish in the Kathmandu Valley. There is not a lot of high moun-tain scenery but it is culturally interesting. There is plenty of accommodation along the route, but you must still carry a sleep-ing bag.

Although it's not as well known and popular as the Everest Base Camp trek or the Annapurna Circuit, this trek offers a number of distinct advantages. The trek is easily accessible from Kathmandu. Indeed, you could leave your hotel in Kathmandu and set foot on the Helambu trail within an hour. The Helambu trek only takes a week so it is ideal for people who do not have the time for one of the longer treks. And since it stays at relatively low altitudes it also does not require sophisticated cold-weather equipment and clothing.

The Helambu trek starts from Sundarijal at the eastern end of the Kathmandu Valley and doesn't climb above 3500m. The trek makes a loop through the Sherpa-popu-lated Helambu region to the northeast of Kathmandu and only the first day's walk is repeated on the return trip. The Sherpa people of the Helambu region are friendly and hospitable, just like their kinfolk of the Solu Khumbu region.

Wherever you trek in the region, you will enter the Langtang National Park. The army is particularly conscientious about collecting the Rs 1000 park entrance fee. On this trek there are park checkposts at Magen Goth, Khutumsang and Sermathang that won't let you pass without a park permit (see p330).

Emergency Facilities
There is a national park radio at Magen Goth. Telephones are available at Tarke Gyang.

Access: Kathmandu to Sundarijal
Occasional buses leave from Kathmandu City bus station (near Bagh Bazaar) to Sun-darijal (Rs 20), 15km from Kathmandu, or get a bus to Jorpati, just beyond Bodhnath, and catch a Sundarijal bus at the road junc-tion. A taxi will cost Rs 650. At Sundarijal you enter the Shivapuri National Park (ad-mission Rs 250; see p183).

The Trek
DAY 1: SUNDARIJAL TO CHISOPANI
From Sundarijal the trail starts off up con-crete steps beside the pipeline that brings drinking water down to the valley. Even-tually the trail leaves the pipeline from near the dam and reaches Mulkharka, sprawling up the ridge around 1895m, 600m above Sundarijal. There are superb views back over the valley and some teashops on the pass for rest and refreshment.

The trail continues to climb, but less steeply, to Chisopani (2300m). Chisopani is rather like a grubby little truck stop without the trucks but the mountain views in the morning can be very fine. Take care of your possessions here; it's still rather close to the Kathmandu Valley. There are a number of lodges at Chisopani.

DAY 2: CHISOPANI TO GUL BHANJYANG
The trail heads down to Pati Bhanjyang (1770m), which has a police checkpoint

and a number of lodges. The trail rises and falls through Chipling (2170m). From here the trail climbs again to reach a 2470m pass before descending a forested ridge to Thodang Betini (2250m). Continuing along the forested ridge, the trail descends to a large *chörten* overlooking the Tamang village of Gul Bhanjyang (2140m). This is a classic hill village with a pleasant main street, several shops and a number of places to stay.

DAY 3: GUL BHANJYANG TO THAREPATI
The trail climbs the ridge from Gul Bhanjyang to another pass at 2620m, then it's downhill to Khutumsang (2470m), in a saddle atop the ridge. The national park office is at the far side of the village. Show your park entry permit or pay Rs 1000 if you started at Sundarijal; you will have to show your permit yet again if you are headed in the opposite direction.

The trail follows a ridgeline with views of the Langtang and Gosainkund peaks through sparsely populated forests to Magen Goth (with an army checkpoint) before finally reaching Tharepati (3640m). The trail to Gosainkund and the Langtang trek branches off northwest from here. Tharepati has several lodges including the very nicely situated Himaliya Lodge on the Khutumsang side.

DAY 4: THAREPATI TO MALEMCHIGAON
From the pass the trail turns east and descends rapidly down a ravine to the large Sherpa village of Malemchigaon (2530m). There are a number of lodges in the village, and a very brightly painted gompa.

DAY 5: MALEMCHIGAON TO TARKE GYANG
From Malemchigaon the trail continues to drop, crossing the Malemchi Khola by a bridge at 1920m and then making the long climb up the other side of the valley to Tarke Gyang (2590m). This is the largest village in Helambu, and the prosperous Sherpas who live here specialise, among other things, in turning out 'instant antiques' for gullible trekkers. There are a number of lodges including the pleasant Mount View Hotel on the Malemchigaon side of the village. Tarke Gyang is a good place for a rest day or you can take a side trip up to the peak (3771m) overlooking the village. This is the end of the route down from the Ganja La.

From Tarke Gyang there is a very pleasant alternative return route via Sermathang (below).

DAY 6: TARKE GYANG TO KIUL
The circuit route back to Sundarijal leaves Tarke Gyang past the guesthouse and *mani* wall (walk to the left), then drops off the west side of the ridge in a rhododendron forest, along a broad, well-travelled path. Passing through the Sherpa villages of Kakani (2070m) and Thimbu (1580m), the trail enters the hot, rice-growing country of the Malemchi and Indrawati valleys.

The steep descent continues down to Kiul (1280m), strung out on terraces above the Malemchi Khola. The trail is now in semitropical banana-and-monkey country at an elevation below that of Kathmandu.

DAY 7: KIUL TO PATI BHANJYANG
There is construction work in this portion of the valley to build a tunnel that will take water from here to the Kathmandu Valley. The trekking route is likely to be confused and dusty while construction is under way.

The trail descends along a river, crossing it on the second suspension bridge at 1190m then joins a wide trail at Mahenkal and follows it to Talamarang (940m). The trail follows Talamarang Khola for some distance, then (it's hard to find at times) climbs steeply to Batache and then Thakani, on the ridge top, at 1890m. From here the trail follows the ridge to Pati Bhanjyang (1770m), where the Helambu circuit is completed.

DAY 8: BACK TO SUNDARIJAL
The final day largely retraces the route of the first day's walk.

Alternative Route from Tarke Gyang to Malemchi Pul Bazaar
An alternative route can be followed from Tarke Gyang through Sermathang and then along a ridge through Dubhachaur to join the road at Malemchi Pul Bazaar, south of Talamarang. This route is very pleasant as far as Malemchi and attracts relatively few trekkers. There are numerous lodges at Sermathang and Malemchi but the choice is limited elsewhere.

From Malemchi the final stretch back to Kathmandu is along a dusty roadway that brings you out on the Kathmandu to Kodari road at Panchkhal, from where you will have to take a bus 55km back to Kathmandu via Dhulikhel and Banepa. You can usually get a ride on a bus or truck down the road from Malemchi and this route does avoid having to duplicate the final stretch from Pati Bhanjyang through Sundarijal.

(Another Helambu alternative is to start and finish from Malemchi Pul Bazaar, completing the shorter loop, which goes through Talamarang, Kiul, Tarke Gyang and Sermathang.)

DAY 1: TARKE GYANG TO SERMATHANG

The easy trail descends gently through a beautiful forest to Sermathang (2620m), the centre of an important apple-growing area. Sermathang is more spread out than the closely spaced houses of Tarke Gyang; there are fine views of the valley of the Malemchi Khola to the south. If you do the trek in the reverse direction this is where you must pay the Rs 1000 entry fee to the Langtang National Park. There are lodges at Sermathang.

DAY 2: SERMATHANG TO MALEMCHI PUL BAZAAR

From Sermathang the trail continues to descend to Dubhachaur (1610m) then steeply down to Malemchi Pul Bazaar at 880m where it meets the road. The village has a collection of lodges and inns. Buses run frequently along the road (known as the Helambu Hwy) from Malemchi Pul Bazaar via Bahunepati and Sipa Ghat to Banepa (via Panchkhal) where you change to a bus or taxi to Kathmandu.

LANGTANG TREK

Duration 7-8 days
Max elevation 3870m
Best season October to May
Start/Finish Syabrubesi

This trek has fine views, interesting villages, and although there are some relatively uninhabited stretches, accommodation is available.

The Langtang trek offers many of the benefits of the Helambu trek, and gives you the opportunity to get right in among the Himalayan peaks and to walk through remote, sparsely populated areas. If you want real adventure then the Langtang

and Helambu treks can be linked by high-altitude passes, via the Gosainkund Lakes or the Ganja La at 5106m (see p344).

The Langtang trek can take up to two weeks (although a three-day approach to the heart of the Langtang Valley is suggested here) and leads to the foot of glaciers high in the Langtang Valley. The trail passes through Tibetan and Tamang villages and offers fine views of the Ganesh Himal across to the northwest. Although the trek passes through lightly populated and undeveloped areas, it is still possible to stay at lodges at various points along the route. Ascending from just 541m at Trisuli Bazaar to 3870m at Kyanjin Gompa, the trail passes through an ever-changing climate and offers trekkers an exceptional diversity of scenery and culture.

The treks all enter the Langtang National Park and the army collects a Rs 1000 park entrance fee. Checkposts are at Dhunche and at Ghora Tabela. Video cameras are only allowed into the national park after paying a whopping US$1000 fee.

Emergency Facilities

There are national park radios at Ghora Tabela and Langtang, and there are telephones at Dhunche and Thulo Syabru. The Yeti Guest House in Kyanjin Gompa has a satellite phone that can be used to summon a helicopter in an emergency.

Access: Kathmandu to Syabrubesi

It's 72km from Kathmandu to Trisuli Bazaar, which takes about four hours by car or six by bus. The road is paved but very winding, with fine mountain views. From Trisuli, the 50km unpaved road leading to Dhunche is steep, winding and rather hairy, passing through Betrawati and Thare. There are buses at 7.30am and 8.30am from Kathmandu to Dhunche (Rs 159, eight hours). Dhunche is a pretty village at 1950m and here you must pay the entrance fee to Langtang National Park, though it's better to buy the permit in Kathmandu before starting your trek. For more details on the road to Dhunche, see p235.

There is a direct bus from Kathmandu to Syabrubesi, about 15km past Dhunche (a one-hour drive). The road descends from Dhunche, gently at first, then in a series of steep loops to a bridge across the Bhote

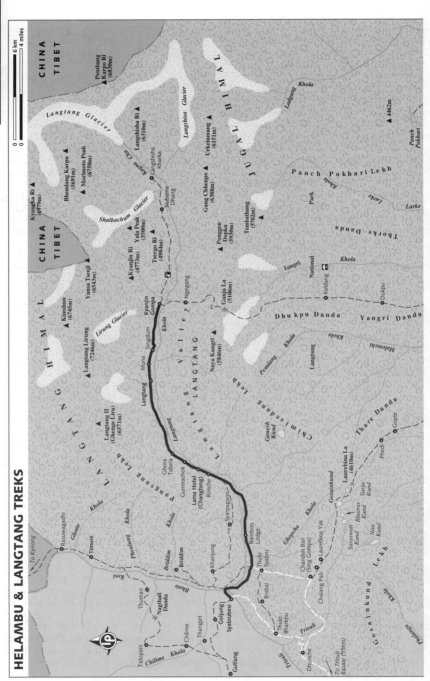

HELAMBU & LANGTANG TREKS

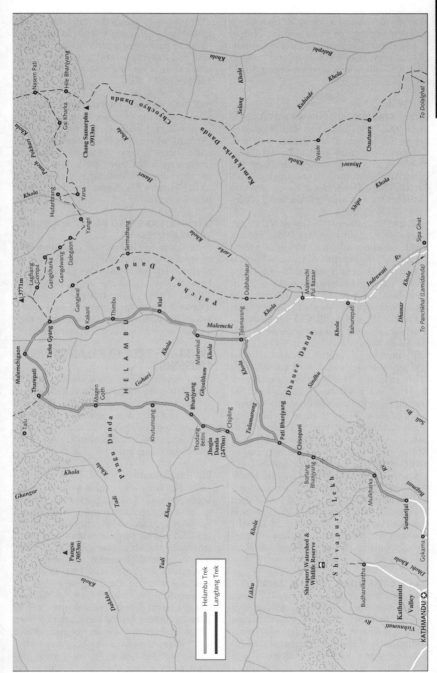

Helambu Trek
Langtang Trek

Kosi. Syabrubesi is a string of shops and lodges along the road just past the bridge. A bus departs Syabrubesi for Kathmandu (Rs 202, nine hours) at 6.30am and 7.30am. You can book a seat in advance at a roadside ticket office.

The Trek

DAY 1: SYABRUBESI TO LAMA HOTEL

Start the trek from the camping area below Syabrubesi (New Syabrubesi) and trek northward past some old government buildings to a suspension bridge over the Bhote Kosi, just north of the junction with Trisuli Khola. Turn right at the eastern end of the bridge and walk into the small settlement of Old Syabru.

The trek becomes a pleasant walk through trees where langur monkeys frolic, passing a side stream and small waterfall before reaching three *bhattis* (village inns) beside a stream at Doman (1680m). The trail then makes a steep climb over a rocky ridge to Landslide Lodge at 1810m, where the route from Thulo Syabru joins from above. Over the rest of the day's walk and the following morning, you will pass few settlements, but the forest abounds with birds.

It's then a long climb in forests to another trail junction with a sign pointing to Syabru (Thulo Syabru). This is a new national park trail that local people rarely use. Beyond the trail junction the trail climbs gently to Bamboo Lodge, a cluster of three hotels (none made of bamboo) at 1960m. Beyond Bamboo Lodge the trail crosses the Dangdung Khola, then climbs to a steel suspension bridge over the Langtang Khola at 2000m.

On the north bank of the Langtang Khola the route climbs alongside a series of waterfalls formed by a jumble of house-sized boulders. Climb steeply to a landslide and the Langtang View & Lodge at Rimche (2400m), and then ascend further to Changtang, popularly known as Lama Hotel, at 2470m.

DAY 2: LAMA HOTEL TO LANGTANG

The trail continues to follow the Langtang Khola, climbing steeply, at times very steeply, to Ghora Tabela (2970m), where there are fine views of Langtang Lirung. Although there is no permanent settlement here, there is a lodge; your national park entry permit will be checked again here.

From Ghora Tabela the trail climbs more gradually to Langtang village (3430m). The national park headquarters is here. Langtang and the villages around are in Tibetan style, with stone walls around the fields, and herds of yaks.

DAY 3: LANGTANG TO KYANJIN GOMPA

It only takes the morning (passing through small villages) to climb to Kyanjin Gompa (3870m), where there is a monastery, lodges and a cheese factory. There are a number of interesting walks from the gompa. If you are intending to continue over the Ganja La to Helambu you should spend some time here acclimatising.

DAYS 4-8: LANGTANG VALLEY & RETURN TO SYABRUBESI

From Kyanjin Gompa you can climb to a viewpoint at 4300m on the glacial moraine to the north for superb views of Langtang Lirung. Day walks can also be made to Yala or further up the valley to Langshisha Kharka for more spectacular views. You can return the same way or take one of the high routes connecting to the Helambu trek.

LANGTANG TREK TO HELAMBU TREK CROSSINGS

If the weather permits, you could tackle the high route via the sacred and picturesque Gosainkund Lakes to join the Helambu Trek. And if you are a very experienced trekker, and adequately equipped with a good map, tent, stove and food, you could tackle the Ganja La.

Via Gosainkund

The trek via Gosainkund is a way of crossing between the Langtang and the Helambu treks. Adequate preparation is necessary, but there are lodges along the route, so finding food and accommodation is not a problem in the trekking season. This route does become impassable during winter.

It takes four days to walk from Dhunche, near the start of the Langtang Trek, to Tharepati in the Helambu region. The trek can also be made from Helambu or it can be done by turning off the Langtang trek from Thulo Syabru, and it is an excellent choice as a return route from the Langtang trek.

Gosainkund is the site for a great pilgrimage in August each year – this is the height of the monsoon, not a pleasant time for trekking. The large rock in the centre of the lake is said to be the remains of a Shiva shrine and it is also claimed that a channel carries water from the lake directly to the tank at the Kumbeshwar Temple in Patan, 60km to the south.

Day 1: Dhunche to Chandan Bari The first day takes you from Dhunche at 1950m to Chandan Bari (Sing Gompa) at 3330m. The route from Thulo Syabru to the gompa can be confusing so take care.

Day 2: Chandan Bari to Laurebina Yak The walk climbs steeply with fine mountain views then heads for Laurebina Yak, which has lodges.

Day 3: Laurebina Yak to Gosainkund Lakes The trail drops to Saraswati Kund at 4100m, the first of the Gosainkund Lakes. The second lake is Bhairav Kund and the third is Gosainkund itself at an altitude of 4380m. There are several lodges, a shrine and numerous paths and small stone shelters for pilgrims on the northwestern side of the lake.

Day 4: Gosainkund Lakes to Gopte The trail climbs from the Gosainkund Lakes to the four lakes near the Laurebina La at 4610m. It then drops down again to Gopte at 3440m where there are seasonal village inns. It was in the Gopte area that an Australian trekker became lost in 1991 and was found alive after 43 days. Nearby is the place where a Thai International Airbus crashed into a mountain in 1992.

Day 5: Gopte to Tharepati The final day's walk descends to a stream and then climbs to Tharepati at 3690m, where this trail meets up with the Helambu trek.

Back to Kathmandu From Tharepati you're on the Helambu Trek and can either take the direct route south to Pati Bhanjyang and Kathmandu or east to Tarke Gyang and then complete the circuit back to Kathmandu.

Across the Ganja La

Walking from the Kyanjin Gompa at the end of the Langtang route south to Tarke Gyang in Helambu involves crossing the 5106m Ganja La. The pass is usually blocked by snow from December to March and at any time a bad weather change can make crossing the pass decidedly dangerous. The walk takes five days; between Kyanjin and Tarke Gyang there is no permanent settlement. The final climb to the pass on both sides is

> **WARNING**
>
> The Ganja La is one of the more difficult passes in Nepal and should not be attempted without a knowledgeable guide, adequate acclimatisation, good equipment and some mountaineering experience.

steep and exposed. During most of the year there is no water for two days south of the pass. You must come adequately equipped for all these complications.

JOMSOM TREK

Duration 9 days
Max elevation 3800m
Best season October to May
Start Naya Pul
Finish Muktinath and back to Jomsom

This trek from Pokhara up the Kali Gandaki valley is among the most popular in Nepal, with superb scenery, interesting people and the best trailside accommodation in the country. It takes a week to reach Muktinath, the end point of the trek. Walking back takes another week or you can fly from Jomsom.

Access: Pokhara to Naya Pul

Like many other treks in Nepal this one is getting shorter as roads gradually extend into the mountains. Eventually it may be possible to drive all the way to Jomsom, and then the trek will no longer exist. A road has already been pushed through the hills from Pokhara to Baglung to the west. Buses leave for Baglung from the bus stop in Bag Bazaar at the northern end of Pokhara. Take the bus up the ridge to Naudanda and then down into the Modi Khola valley and get off at Naya Pul (New Bridge) a few kilometres pass Lumle; the fare is Rs 55, or Rs 600 for a taxi.

ALTERNATIVE ACCESS POINTS

It's still possible to walk all the way from Pokhara to Birethanti. You can reach Naudanda by walking through Sarangkot (p265) and along the ridge to Naudanda. There are fine views of the whole Annapurna Range, Pokhara and Phewa Tal from this large village. Naudanda has a choice of hotels. From Naudanda, follow the road for a bit, then turn off past Khare to Chandrakot and drop to Birethanti.

You can also avoid the long climb over the Ghorapani hill by taking the bus on to Beni further northwest of Pokhara. From here it's a two-day walk up the Kali Gandaki valley to Tatopani.

If you want to trek the route just one way, it can save a lot of time and hassle and make the duration of your trek more predictable to

TREKKING

fly to Jomsom first. In this way, you avoid the predicament of being stuck in Jomsom during flight cancellations. However, you will need to spend some days acclimatising to account for the sudden gain in altitude if you're continuing to Muktinath.

The Trek

DAY 1: NAYA PUL TO TIKEDUNGHA

From Naya Pul it's a short walk up Modi Khola to the large village of Birethanti (1000m), where you can really see how civilised this trek is. Birethanti has a bakery, bank and even sidewalk cafés! A trail north to Ghandruk turns off here. Birethanti has excellent hotels but it's best to continue further in order to shorten the next day's long climb. Sticking to the northern side of the Bhurungdi Khola, the trail climbs to Hille and nearby Tikhedhunga (1525m). Both Tikhedhunga and Hille have places to stay.

DAY 2: TIKEDUNGHA TO GHORAPANI

From Tikedhunga the trail drops down and crosses the Bhurungdi Khola, then climbs very steeply up a stone staircase to Ulleri, a large Magar village at 1960m. It continues to ascend, but more gently, through fine forests of oak and rhododendron to Banthanti (2250m) and then Nangathanti (2460m). Another hour's walk brings you to Ghorapani at 2750m.

Only a short walk beyond Ghorapani is Deorali pass and village (*deorali* means 'pass'), with spectacular views, and this is where most people stay. An hour's climb from here will take you to Poon (or Pun) Hill at 3210m, one of the best Himalayan viewpoints in Nepal. There are hotels at Ghorapani and at Deorali. *Ghora* means 'horse' and *pani* 'water' and indeed, long caravans of pack horses were once a regular sight here. The pack horses now go to Jomsom from Beni along the Kali Gandaki valley.

A trail also runs from Ghorapani/Deorali to Ghandruk. This part of the trek is plagued by leeches during the monsoon and there may be snow on the trail in the winter.

DAY 3: GHORAPANI TO TATOPANI

The trail descends steeply to Chitre (2420m), where there are more lodges. From here the hills are extensively terraced as the trail drops down through Sikha, a large village with

shops and hotels at 1980m, and then descends gently to Ghara (1780m). A further steep descent of 380m takes you to Ghar Khola village where the trail crosses the Ghar Khola on a suspension bridge and then climbs up above the Kali Gandaki before crossing that too. There's also an ACAP checkpost here.

Turning north the trail soon reaches Tatopani (1190m). It's a busy population centre, although a monsoon flood in the late 1980s washed away a number of lodges and bathing pools, and the remainder of the village sits precariously on a shelf above the river. Tatopani offers some of the best food along the whole trail, and you can get a cold beer to go with it. *Tato* means 'hot'; the name is for the hot springs by the river. Tatopani is a popular destination for a shorter trek out of Pokhara. At the south end of the village is the trail to the hot springs and a police checkpost where they enter your details into a register.

DAY 4: TATOPANI TO GHASA

The trail now follows the Kali Gandaki valley to Jomsom. The river cuts a channel between the peaks of Annapurna I and Dhaulagiri, thus qualifying the Kali Gandaki for the title of the world's deepest valley. The two 8000m-plus mountaintops are only 38km apart and the river flows between them at a height of less than 2200m.

The Kali Gandaki valley is home to the Thakalis, an ethnic group noted for their trading and business expertise, particularly in running hotels and lodges, not only here in their homeland but also in Pokhara and elsewhere in Nepal.

From Tatopani the route climbs across several landslides and ascends gradually to Dana at 1400m. This is where the difficult track branches off to Maurice Herzog's base camp, used for his historic ascent of Annapurna in 1950.

The trail continues to climb to the waterfall of Rupse Chhahara (1560m) and at one stage takes a precarious route through a steep, narrow section of the gorge. A suspension bridge crosses the river at 1620m and the trail crosses back again at 1880m, then through Ghasa, the first Thakali village (2120m).

DAY 5: GHASA TO LARJUNG

A steep climb through forest takes you to the Lete Khola, then to the village of Lete

(2430m), with a superb view of the eastern flank of Dhaulagiri, and finally to Kalopani (2530m). Kalopani has great mountain views and some comfortable lodges to view them from.

From Kalopani the trail crosses to the east side of the Kali Gandaki, before crossing back again at Larjung. This village at 2570m has interesting alleyways and tunnels between the houses, an attempt to avoid the fierce winds that often whistle up the Kali Gandaki valley.

DAY 6: LARJUNG TO MARPHA
Khobang (2580m) is a village with a gompa above it, and the mountain views on this stretch are the best to be seen.

Tukuche (2590m) is one of the most important Thakali villages, once a meeting place for traders from Tibet. Despite the growth of tourism in this area, Tukuche is still a quieter, smaller place than it was during this era of trade.

From here the landscape changes as you enter the drier and more desertlike country north of the Himalayan watershed. It also gets windier; gentle breezes from the north shift to a gale from the south as the morning wears on. Marpha (2680m) virtually huddles behind a ridge to keep out of the wind. The village also has some of the most luxurious accommodation to be found along the trail, which makes it a good alternative to staying in Jomsom. A government project between Tukuche and Marpha produces fruit and vegetables for the whole region.

DAY 7: MARPHA TO KAGBENI
The trail continues along the valley side, rising gradually before crossing over a low ridge to Jomsom. At 2713m, Jomsom is the major centre in the region and it has facilities such as a hospital, an ACAP visitor centre and a police checkpost (where you must register and get your ACAP permit stamped). This is the last of the Thakali villages; those further north are inhabited by people of Tibetan descent.

Jomsom has regular flights to Pokhara for US$54.

It's worth following the trail along the river all the way to the medieval-looking village of Kagbeni (2810m). This Tibetan-influenced settlement has a number of good lodges, and is as close as you can get to Lo Manthang, the capital of the legendary kingdom of Mustang further to the north, without paying a US$700 permit fee.

There is a recently built bridge and trail up the west bank of the Kali Gandaki, which provides an alternative to the original trail up the east bank.

DAY 8: KAGBENI TO MUKTINATH
From Kagbeni the path climbs steeply to rejoin the direct trail leading to Khingar (3200m). The trail climbs through a desert landscape then past meadows and streams to the village of Jharkot (3500m). A further climb brings you to Ranipauwa, the accommodation area of Muktinath (3710m).

Muktinath is a pilgrimage centre for Buddhists and Hindus. You'll see Tibetan traders as well as sadhus (holy men) from as far away as the south of India. The shrines, in a grove of trees, include a Buddhist gompa and the Vishnu temple of Jiwala Mayi. An old temple nearby shelters a spring and natural gas jets that provide Muktinath's famous eternal flame. It's the earth-water-fire combination that accounts for Muktinath's great religious significance.

BACK TO POKHARA OR JOMSOM
From Muktinath you can retrace your steps to Pokhara, or simply trek back to Jomsom and hope to catch a flight from there. It is possible to continue beyond Muktinath and cross the Thorung La to walk the rest of the Annapurna Circuit but this long walk is better made in the opposite direction – it's a long, hard climb of 1600m ascent from Muktinath to the pass.

ANNAPURNA CIRCUIT TREK
Duration 16-18 days
Max elevation 5416m
Best season October to November
Start Besisahar
Finish Naya Pul or Beni

It takes nearly three weeks to walk the entire Annapurna Circuit; for scenery and cultural diversity this is the best trek in Nepal. It crosses to the north of the main Himalayan range and crosses a 5416m pass. The last week of the trek is the Jomsom trek in reverse, following the dramatic Kali Gandaki valley.

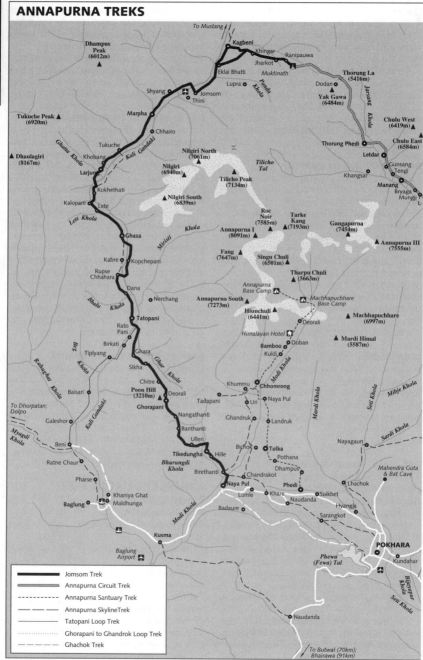

ANNAPURNA TREKS

▬▬▬▬	Jomsom Trek
▬▬▬▬	Annapurna Circuit Trek
- - - -	Annapurna Santuary Trek
— · — ·	Annapurna SkylineTrek
————	Tatopani Loop Trek
··········	Ghorapani to Ghandrok Loop Trek
— — —	Ghachok Trek

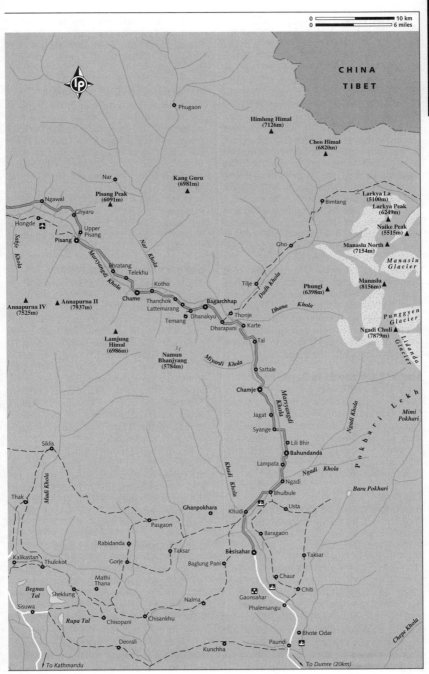

TREKKING

Since it opened to foreign trekkers in 1977, the trek around Annapurna has become the most popular in Nepal. It passes through country inhabited by a wide diversity of peoples, it offers spectacular mountain scenery and it goes to the north of the main Himalayan range to the dry Tibet-like trans-Himalaya. It also has the advantage of having accommodation available each night.

The circuit is usually walked counter clockwise due to the steepness of the track to the Thorung La. For many people, this is too much to manage in one day. The Thorung La at 5416m is often closed due to snow from mid-December to mid-March, and bad weather can move in at any time. The trail to Thorung La can be hard to find when covered in snow. Trekkers should be prepared to turn back due to the weather and altitude. Porters must be adequately equipped for severe cold and snow.

After you cross the Thorung La from Manang to Muktinath, the final seven days of the circuit trek are the same as the Jomsom Trek from Pokhara, but in reverse. Completing the Annapurna Circuit in 16 days allows for only one rest and acclimatisation day at Manang. It's best to slot a few additional days into the schedule.

Access: Kathmandu to Besisahar

It's a long and somewhat tedious 137km from Kathmandu to the turn-off at Dumre. From Dumre, at 440m, buses and 4WDs run regularly to Besisahar (820m). From Pokhara there are two buses (Rs 120, five hours) in the early morning and two at lunchtime. Buses also run frequently from Kathmandu (bus/minibus Rs 175/235, six hours).

The Trek

DAY 1: BESISAHAR TO BAHUNDANDA
Start the trek by taking a taxi or bus from Besisahar along the rough road to Khudi (830m). This is the first Gurung village you reach (many of Nepal's Gurkha soldiers are Gurungs). The Khudi trail offers fine views of Himalchuli (to the northeast) and Ngadi Chuli (aka Manaslu II, and before that, Peak 29) as it climbs to Bhulbule (840m). You enter the Annapurna Conservation Area here and should register at the ACAP checkpoint if it is open. If you did not get your permit in advance, you will have to pay double here.

The trail continues onto Ngadi before reaching Lampata (1135m) and then Bahundanda (1310m). Bahundanda has a few shops, several hotels and a public call office (telephone).

DAY 2: BAHUNDANDA TO CHAMJE
From Bahundanda the trail drops steeply to Lili Bhir and then follows an exposed trail; occasionally the steep drop beside the track is hidden by thick vegetation. Ghermu Phant has a high waterfall and in Syange (1080m) the trail crosses to the west bank of the Marsyangdi Khola on a suspension bridge. The trail then follows the river to the stone village of Jagat, perched strategically in a steep-sided valley and looking for all the world like the toll station for the Tibetan salt trade that it was. The trail descends before climbing through forest to Chamje (1400m).

DAY 3: CHAMJE TO BAGARCHHAP
The rocky trail crosses the Marsyangdi Khola again, then follows the valley steadily uphill to Tal (1700m). Here the valley has been filled by ancient landslides and the river meanders through the fertile flat land before disappearing under some huge boulders. Tal is the first village in the Manang district. The trail crosses the valley floor then climbs a stone stairway before dropping down to another crossing of the Marsyangdi (1850m). The trail continues to Dharapani (1920m), which is marked by a stone-entrance *chörten* typical of the Tibetan-influenced villages from here northward.

Bagarchhap (2160m) has flat-roofed stone houses of typical Tibetan design although the village is still in the transition zone before the dry highlands. A landslide roared through the centre of this village in late 1995 and managed to wipe out much of the village, including two lodges.

DAY 4: BAGARCHHAP TO CHAME
The trail, often rough and rocky, climbs over a ridge through Temang and then continues through forest of pine and fir to Kotho (2640m). Chame (2710m) is the headquarters of the Manang district and its buildings include many hotels, a health post and a bank. At the entrance to the village you pass a large *mani* wall with many prayer wheels. Walk to the left of the wall as the Buddhists do. There are fine views of Annapurna II

as you approach Chame, and two small hot springs are across the river. The route crosses the Marsyangdi Khola here.

DAY 5: CHAME TO PISANG

The trail runs through deep forest in a steep and narrow valley, and recrosses to the south bank of the Marsyangdi Khola at 3080m. Views include the first sight of the soaring Paungda Danda rock face, an awesome testament to the power of glacial erosion. The trail continues to climb to Pisang, which sprawls between 3240m and 3340m and has many lodges.

DAY 6: PISANG TO MANANG

The walk is now through the drier upper part of the Manang district, cut off from the full effect of the monsoon by the Annapurna Range. The people of the upper part of the Manang district herd yaks and raise crops for part of the year, but they also continue to enjoy special trading rights gained way back in 1784. Today they exploit these rights with shopping trips to Bangkok and Hong Kong where they buy electronic goods and other modern equipment to resell in Nepal.

From Pisang there are two trails, north and south of the Marsyangdi Khola, which meet up again at Mungji. The southern route via Hongde at 3420m, with its airstrip at 3325m, involves less climbing than the northern route via Ghyaru, though there are better views on the trail that follows the northern bank of the river.

The trail continues from Mungji (3480m) past the picturesque but partially hidden village of Bryaga (3500m) to nearby Manang (3570m) where there are a number of lodges and an HRA post.

DAY 7: ACCLIMATISATION DAY IN MANANG

It's important to spend a day acclimatising in Manang before pushing on to the Thorung La. There are some fine day walks and magnificent views around the village, and it's best to gain altitude during the day, returning to Manang to sleep. The view of Gangapurna glacier is terrific and can even be enjoyed with a warm Khukri rum from a bar. Manang is a trading centre and the villagers have cottoned on to what trekkers want. You can buy film, batteries, sun-screen, Snickers and just about anything else a trekker could break, lose or crave. The Manangis' legendary trading skills are seen at their keenest here – buy with caution.

DAY 8: MANANG TO LETDAR

From Manang it's an ascent of nearly 2000m to the Thorung La. The trail climbs steadily through Tengi, leaving the Marsyangdi Valley and continuing along the Jarsang Khola valley. The vegetation becomes steadily sparser as you reach Letdar (4250m). The night in Letdar is important for acclimatisation.

DAY 9: LETDAR TO THORUNG PHEDI

Cross the river at 4310m and then climb up to Thorung Phedi (4420m). There are two hotels here – at the height of the season as many as 200 trekkers a day may cross over the Thorung La and beds can be in short supply. Some trekkers find themselves suffering from AMS at Phedi. If you find yourself in a similar condition you must retreat downhill; even the descent to Letdar can make a difference. Be sure to boil or treat water here; the sanitation in Letdar and Thorung Phedi is poor, and giardiasis is rampant. There is a satellite phone here that you can use for US$5 per minute in an emergency.

DAY 10: THORUNG PHEDI TO MUKTINATH

Phedi means 'foot of the hill' and that's where it is, at the foot of the 5416m Thorung La. The trail climbs steeply but is regularly used and easy to follow. The altitude and snow can be problems; when the pass is snow-covered it is often impossible to cross. It takes about four to six hours to climb up to the pass, marked by *chörtens* and prayer flags. The effort is worthwhile as the view from the top – from the Annapurnas, along the Great Barrier to the barren Kali Gandaki valley – is magnificent. From the pass you have a tough 1600m descent to Muktinath (3710m).

Many start out for the pass at 3am. This is not necessary and is potentially dangerous due to the risk of frostbite if you are hanging around waiting in the cold snow for too long. A better starting time is 5am to 6am.

BACK TO POKHARA

The remaining six to seven days of the trek simply follow the Jomsom Trek route but in the opposite direction.

ANNAPURNA SANCTUARY TREK

Duration 10-14 days
Max elevation 4095m
Best season October to November
Start/Finish Phedi

This trek goes into the centre of the Annapurna Range, a magnificent amphitheatre on a staggering scale. Glaciers and soaring peaks and an eerie atmosphere create an unparalleled mountain experience.

At one time this trek was a real expedition into a wilderness area, but now there is a string of lodges that operate during the trekking season. The return trip can take as little as 10 or 11 days but it's best appreciated in 14 days. The walk to the base camp can be tacked on as a side trip from the Jomsom or Annapurna Circuit treks.

There are several possible routes to the sanctuary, all meeting at Chhomrong. The diversion from the Jomsom and Annapurna Circuit Treks is made from near Ghorapani to Ghandruk.

Access: Pokhara to Phedi

You can take a bus (Rs 30, 1½ hours) or taxi from Pokhara a short distance along the Baglung Hwy to Phedi, a cluster of shacks. The start of the trail is outside the Dhampus Mailee Hotel.

The Trek
DAY 1: PHEDI TO TOLKA

From Phedi the trail climbs steeply to Dhampus (1750m), which stretches for several kilometres along the ridge from 1580m to 1700m and has a number of widely spaced hotels. Theft is a real problem in Dhampus, so take care.

The trail climbs to Pothana (1990m) and descends steeply through a forest towards Bichok. It finally emerges in the Modi Khola valley and continues to drop to Tolka (1810m).

DAY 2: TOLKA TO CHHOMRONG

From Tolka the trail descends a long stone staircase, and then follows a ridge to the Gurung village of Landruk (1620m). Ten minutes from here the path splits – north takes you to Chhomrong and the sanctuary, or you can head downhill towards Ghandruk.

The sanctuary trail turns up the Modi Khola valley to Naya Pul (1340m). It then continues from Naya Pul up to Jhinu Danda (1750m) and up again to Taglung (2190m), where it joins the Ghandruk to Chhomrong trail.

Chhomrong, at 2210m, is the last permanent settlement in the valley. This large and sprawling Gurung village has a good choice of hotels, and an ACAP office. Ask about trail conditions in the sanctuary when you register there.

DAY 3: CHHOMRONG TO BAMBOO

The trail drops down to the Chhomrong Khola, and then climbs to Sinuwa and on to Kuldi (2470m) where there is an abandoned ACAP checkpoint. The trek now enters the upper Modi Khola valley, where ACAP controls the location and number of lodges and limits their size. If the lodges are full, you may have to sleep in the dining room, or perhaps the lodge owner can erect a tent for

DANGERS ON THE SANCTUARY TRAIL

There is significant danger of avalanches along the route to the Annapurna Sanctuary between Doban and Machhapuchhare Base Camp. Trekkers have died and trekking parties have been stranded in the sanctuary for days, the trail blocked by tonnes of ice and snow. Always check with the ACAP office in Chhomrong for a report on current trail conditions, and do not proceed into the sanctuary if there has been recent heavy rain or snow.

There is also a theft racket throughout the Annapurna region, particularly in Dhampus and Tikhedhunga, but it can happen anywhere. Thieves often cut the tents of trekkers and remove valuable items during the night. Trekking groups have taken to pitching their tents in a circle like an old-time wagon train and posting a guard with a lighted lantern throughout the night. If you stay in a hotel, be sure that you know who is sharing the room with you, and lock the door whenever you go out – even for a moment (and that includes going to the toilet). The thieves watch everyone in order to decide who has something worth taking or is likely to be careless. If necessary they will wait patiently all night to make their move.

YETI! *Bradley Mayhew*

Along with the equally slippery notion of Shangri-la, the yeti is one of Nepal's most famous cultural exports, occupying a hotly debated biological niche somewhere between zoology and folk religion.

Before you throw your arms up in the air and storm out of the room, bear in mind that the pro yeti camp has some serious proponents. In 1938 mountaineer Bill Tilman tracked yeti footprints for over a mile. Eric Shipton photographed a yeti print on the Menling/Menlungtse Glacier in 1951. Edmund Hilary led an expedition in 1960 to track the yeti, as did Chris Bonnington in 1986 and even travel writer Bruce Chatwin. Reinhold Messner claimed to have seen a yeti in Tibet in 1986 and wrote a book about the subject (*My Quest for the Yeti*).

There are dozens of cases of local sightings. Villages in the Rongbuk region of Tibet apparently discovered a drowned yeti corpse in 1958. In 1998 the official police report on the murder of a Sherpa woman near Dole on the Gokyo trek in Nepal cited 'yeti attack' as the cause of death! Japan's most celebrated yeti-hunter is Yoshiteru Takahashi, who in 2003 claimed to have found a yeti cave on the slopes of Dhaulagiri (his camera froze before he could take a photo…).

The Rolwaling region seems to be the heartland of yeti sightings, followed closely by the Khumbu. Trekkers on the Everest Base Camp trek can still see the yeti scalp at Khumjung Monastery (actually made from the skin of serow, a type of goat/antelope), though the yeti hand of Pangboche, said to have been that of a mummified lama, has mysteriously disappeared. The region's 'yeti pelts' actually belong to the Himalayan blue bear.

The word 'yeti' comes from the Tibetan *yeh-teh*, or 'man of the rocky/snowy places'; the alternative Tibetan names are the *migyu* and *mehton kangmi*, or 'abominable snowman'. First-hand accounts of the yeti describe it having reddish fur, a conical head, a high-pitched cry and strange body odour that smells like garlic (sounds like my friend Andre…), but a sign at Khumjung Monastery outlines the different types of yeti in more subtle and, more importantly, cultural terms. The ape like *dre-ma* and *tel-ma* are messengers of calamity, it says, while the *chu-ti* moves on all fours and preys on goats, sheep and yaks. Worst of all is the *mi-te*, a man-eater, six to eight feet tall, with 'a very bad temperament'. Consider yourself warned.

---

you. In winter, it is common to find snow from this point on. Continue on to Bamboo (2310m), which is a collection of three hotels. This stretch of trail has leeches early and late in the trekking season.

DAY 4: BAMBOO TO HIMALAYAN HOTEL

The trail climbs to Bamboo, then through rhododendron forests to Doban (2540m) and on to Himalayan Hotel at 2840m. This stretch of the trail passes several avalanche chutes. If you arrive early, it's possible to continue on to Deorali to make the following day easier.

DAY 5: HIMALAYAN HOTEL TO MACHHAPUCHHARE BASE CAMP

From Himalayan Hotel it's on to Hinko (3100m). There is accommodation in Deorali (3170m), on the ridge above Hinko. This is the stretch of trail that seems to be most subject to avalanches.

At Machhapuchhare Base Camp (which isn't really a base camp since climbing the mountain is not permitted), at 3700m, there is seasonal accommodation available. These hotels may not be open, depending on whether the innkeeper and the supplies have been able to reach the hotel through the avalanche area.

Be alert to signs of altitude sickness before heading off to Annapurna Base Camp.

DAY 6: MACHHAPUCHHARE BASE CAMP TO ANNAPURNA BASE CAMP

The climb to the Annapurna Base Camp at 4130m takes about two hours, and is best done early in the day before clouds roll in and make visibility a problem. If there is snow, the trail may be difficult to follow. There are four lodges here, which can get ridiculously crowded at the height of the season. Dawn is best observed from the glacial moraine a short stroll from your cosy lodge.

BACK TO POKHARA

On the return trip you can retrace your steps back to Phedi, or divert from Chhomrong to Ghandruk and on to Ghorapani to visit Poon Hill and follow the Annapurna Circuit or the Jomsom Trek route back to Pokhara.

The Ghorapani to Ghandruk walk is a popular way of linking the Annapurna Sanctuary Trek with treks up the Kali Gandaki valley. It's also used for shorter loop walks out of Pokhara (see p268 for more information).

OTHER TREKS

The treks described earlier in this chapter are used by the vast majority of trekkers. Yet there are alternatives that will take you to areas still relatively unvisited: the Kanchenjunga Base Camps, Makalu Base Camp, Mustang, Dolpo, and Rara Lake treks are some of these. There are no lodges on these treks, so you will need to make arrangements through a trekking company and pay a trekking permit fee. At the time of writing, all of these treks, except the Mustang trek, passed through 'Maoist country'; check with your embassy for the latest travel advice.

For information on the popular Annapurna Skyline Trek see p269. See Lonely Planet's *Trekking in the Nepal Himalaya* for the complete story on trekking here. It has comprehensive advice on equipment selection, an excellent health and safety sec-

tion, and comprehensive route descriptions not only of the popular treks covered more briefly in this book, but also of a number of interesting but less heavily used routes.

If you're going right off the beaten track to explore remote areas like Makalu and Kanchenjunga in the east or Jumla and Dolpo in the west, you must be very self-sufficient. In these relatively untouched areas there is probably very little surplus food for sale and the practice of catering to Western trekkers has not yet developed.

Treks in more remote areas are camping treks that must be arranged by a trekking company; the company will arrange the permit.

Area	Fee ($US)
Everest, Annapurna & Langtang	no permit required
Kanchenjunga & Lower Dolpo	$10 per week for first four weeks, $20 per week after that
Upper Mustang & Upper Dolpo	$700 for 10 days, then $70 per day
Manaslu	$75 per week low season, $90 high season
Humla	$90 for seven days, then $15 per day

Directory

CONTENTS

ACCOMMODATION

Accommodation options in this book are arranged according to budget and then subdivided by location. Budget travellers can expect to shell out from US$5 to US$15 for a double room, which will normally have a private bathroom. Midrange rooms range from US$15 to US$50, with top-end groupings heading up from there. Most hotels have a wide range of rooms under one roof, including larger (often top-floor) deluxe rooms which are good for families and small groups.

In Kathmandu and Pokhara there is a wide variety of accommodation from rock-bottom flea pits to five-star international hotels that cost US$150 a night. The intense competition between the many cheaper places keeps prices down and standards up – Kathmandu has many fine places with pleasant gardens and rooms for less than US$10 a night including private bathroom and hot water. Some of Nepal's best deals are now to be found in its stylish midrange and top-end accommodation, discounted by up to 60% in places thanks to the downturn in tourism in Nepal.

The main towns of the Terai have hotels of a reasonable standard, where rooms with fans and mosquito nets cost around Rs 400, down to grimy, basic places catering to local demand from around Rs 50. Some of the cheap places have tattered mosquito nets, if any at all. The cheaper places only have solar-heated hot-water showers, which won't be hot in the mornings or on cloudy days.

Elsewhere in the country the choice of hotels can be very limited, but you will find places to stay along most of the major trekking trails, making Nepal one of the few places in the world where you can trek for three weeks without needing a tent. On lesser-trekked trails places may be Spartan – the accommodation may be dorm-style or simply an open room in which to unroll your sleeping bag – but the Annapurna and Everest treks have excellent lodges and guesthouses every couple of hours.

The recent drop-off in visitor numbers to Nepal means that many places outside of the main tourist centres are deserted. Managers and even chefs may be absent from off-the-beaten-track resorts so phone ahead to these places. Hotels with only one or two guests may be reluctant to turn on

---

BOOK ACCOMMODATION ONLINE

For more accommodation reviews and recommendations by Lonely Planet authors, check out the online booking service at www.lonelyplanet.com. You'll find the true, insider lowdown on the best places to stay. Reviews are thorough and independent. Best of all, you can book online.

DIRECTORY

A NOTE ON HOTEL PRICES

Nepal's hotel prices have always been seasonal and, shall we say, flexible, with peak season running from October to November and February to April. The current drop in tourism has had a deepening effect on hotel discounting rates, so much so that currently there's hardly a hotel in Kathmandu or Pokhara that charges full tariff.

The exact room rate you will be quoted depends partly on the season and partly on general tourist numbers. At the time of research the slump in tourism meant that many midrange hotels were offering discounts of up to 60% even in the high season, particularly in Kathmandu and Pokhara where competition is fiercest. In this guide we have generally given the high-season room rates shown on hotel tariff cards, followed, as a guide, by the maximum discount we were offered during high-season research. You may find even lower rates during the monsoon (June to September). If, however, tourist numbers pick up during the lifetime of this book, you may find that smaller discounts are offered. In reality prices are highly negotiable all the time.

At most hotels the printed tariffs are pure fiction, published partly in the hope that you might be silly enough to pay them, and partly to fulfil government star rating requirements; 20% to 50% discounts are par for the course anywhere these days. If business is slow you can often negotiate a deluxe room for a standard room rate. Some midrange hotels offer discounts for booking online (and a free airport transfer) but you'll get at least this much on the spot, if not more.

You can also negotiate cheaper rates for longer stays. In the cool of autumn and spring you get a further discount on air-conditioned rooms simply by agreeing to turn off the air-con.

---

the hotel heating or hot water. On the plus side (for travellers at least) there are plenty of discounts available, you'll have an excellent choice of rooms and you'll often have smaller towns completely to yourself.

All midrange and top-end hotels charge a value added tax (VAT) of 13% and often quote their prices in US dollars (though you can pay in rupees). Budget places quote prices in rupees and generally forget about the tax.

BUSINESS HOURS

Most government offices in Kathmandu are open from 10am to 5pm Sunday to Friday during summer and 10am to 4pm during the winter (roughly mid-November to mid-February). Offices close at 3pm on Friday and are generally closed for an hour at lunchtime. Saturday is the weekly holiday and almost all offices and banks will be closed. Museums are generally closed on Tuesdays. See p366 for a list of public holidays.

CHILDREN

Few people travel with children in Nepal, yet with a bit of planning it is remarkably hassle-free. Check out Lonely Planet's *Travel With Children* for handy hints and advice about the pros and cons of travelling with children.

In the main tourist centres (Kathmandu and Pokhara), most hotels have triple rooms, and quite often a suite with four beds, which are ideal for families with young children. Finding a room with a bathtub can be a problem at the bottom end of the market. Many Kathmandu hotels have a garden or roof garden, which can be good play areas for kids. Check thoroughly, however, as some are definitely not safe for young children.

Walking the crowded and narrow streets of Kathmandu and other towns can be a hassle with young kids unless you can get them up off the ground – a backpack is ideal, but a pusher or stroller would be more trouble than it's worth unless you bring one with oversize wheels.

Eating out at restaurants with kids can be difficult. While the food is excellent, the service is usually quite slow. By the time the food arrives your kids will be bored stiff and ready to leave. It's less hassle if you eat breakfast at your hotel, have lunch at a place with a garden (there are plenty of these) where the children can let off steam, and in the evening go to the restaurant armed with colouring books, stories and other distractions to keep them busy.

Disposable nappies are available in Kathmandu and Pokhara, but for a price – better to bring them with you if possible. Cloth nappies can be a headache, but remember that disposable nappies are almost indestructible, and waste disposal in Nepal is already a major problem.

CLIMATE CHARTS

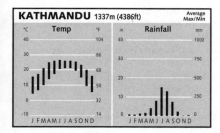

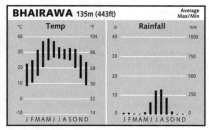

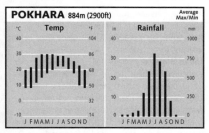

COURSES
Language
Nepali is not a difficult language to learn, and you will see notices around Kathmandu advertising language courses. Most schools offer courses or individual tuition. Expect to pay about US$50 for a two-week course or around US$3 per hour for private tuition.

Places to try in Kathmandu:

Intercultural Training & Research Centre (ITC; Map p136; ☎ 01-4414490; itc@mos.com.np; Kathmandu) Just off Tridevi Marg, this well-respected language centre works with many NGOs, including the UK's Voluntary Service Overseas (VSO). It offers crash courses (three hours), 60-hour beginner courses and six-week intermediate courses. Tuition is one-on-one and costs around Rs 300 per hour.

Kathmandu Institute of Nepali Language (Map p136; ☎ 01-4220295; www.ktmnepalilanguage.com, namrata@mos.com.np; Jyatha, Kathmandu) Offers a week's course of six hours for Rs 1200.

Thamel Nepali Language Institute (Map p136; ☎ 01-4700949; views@wlink.com.np; Thamel; 10am-6.30pm Mon-Fri) Opposite Pilgrims Book House, on the upper floor, this tiny place offers an intensive course of 20 hours or a more relaxed six-hours-a-week course, for roughly Rs 250 per hour for one-on-one tuition, plus around Rs 800 for learning materials. For real linguistic immersion you can stay with a local family.

There are often flyers around Bodhnath advertising Tibetan-language tuition and apartments to rent, as well as opportunities to volunteer-teach Tibetan refugees. The **Centre for Buddhist Studies** (www.cbs.edu .np) based at the Rangjung Yeshe Institute (see p359) is part of Kathmandu University and offers a two-month Tibetan-language course (US$1900) June and July, with accommodation provided with local Tibetan families, it also offers longer university-accredited courses.

Music & the Arts
Gandharba Association (see p152; http://gandharbas .nyima.org; Thamel, Kathmandu) Offers lessons in the *sarangi* (four-stringed instument played with a bow) and they can probably find teachers for other instruments such as the *madal* (drum), *basuri* (flute) and *arbaj* (four-string guitar). Expect to pay around Rs 150 per hour's tuition.

Trekkers Holiday Inn (☎ 01-4480334; www.4free.ch /nepal; Chuchepati) Based at the Hotel Samsara, midway between Kathmandu and Bodhnath, this Swiss-run centre offers cookery courses (see p105) and evening lectures on social welfare and Ayurvedic medicine, as well as a Nepali-language course three days a week (Rs 3500 for 15 hours). You can get a programme of talks and courses from the website. The hotel is hard to find; get yourself to Chuchepati Chowk, by the bust of Pasang Lhamo, head north, take the lane on the left and follow it as it curves.

Yoga, Buddhist Meditation & Massage
Nepal is a popular place for people to take up spiritual pursuits, particularly around the Kathmandu Valley, although Pokhara is becoming increasingly popular.

Check the notice boards in Thamel for up-to-date information about yoga and Buddhism courses, and shop around before you commit yourself.

PRACTICALITIES

■ Nepal's main English-language daily paper, the **Rising Nepal** (www.gorkhapatra.org.np), is basically a government mouthpiece. For a more balanced view of local issues there's the daily **Kathmandu Post** (www.kantipuronline.com) and **Himalayan Times** (www.thehimalayantimes.com) or the weekly **Nepali Times** (www.nepalitimes.com).

■ **ECS** (www.ecs.com.np; Rs 75) is a glossy expat-orientated monthly magazine with interesting articles on travel and culture. **Spotlight** (www.nepalnews.com.np/spotlight.htm) is another local weekly current affairs magazine that is worth a look.

■ The *International Herald Tribune* and *Le Monde* are widely available in Kathmandu, as are *Time* and *Newsweek* (Rs 100).

■ The glossy **Travellers Nepal** (www.tn.com.np) and **Nepal Traveller** (www.nepal-traveller.com) are free monthly tourist magazines with info on sights, festivals and trekking, directories of airlines offices, embassies and so on.

■ In the Kathmandu Valley, tune into Kantipur FM (96.1FM), Hits FM (92.1FM) or HBC FM (104FM), or listen to the BBC World Service on 103FM.

■ Nepal TV has an English news bulletin at 10pm. Most midrange and top-end hotels offer satellite channels, such as BBC World.

■ Electricity, when available, is 220V/50 cycles; 120V appliances from the USA will need a transformer. Sockets usually take three-round-pin plugs, sometimes the small variety, sometimes the large. Some sockets take plugs with two round pins. Local electrical shops sell cheap adapters.

■ Outside Kathmandu blackouts ('load-shedding') are a fact of life. Power surges are also likely so bring a voltage guard with spike suppressor (automatic cut-off switch) for your laptop.

Ananda Yoga Center (☎ 01-4311048; ananda@yoga .wlink.com.np; PO Box 1774, Kathmandu Valley) On the edge of the valley at Satungal, overlooking Matatirtha Village, 8km west of Kathmandu, this is a nonprofit yoga retreat offering courses in reiki, hatha yoga and teacher training.

Ganden Yiga Chopen Meditation Centre (Pokhara Buddhist Meditation Centre; Map p257; ☎ 01-522923; pokharacentre@yahoo.com) Three-day meditation and yoga courses (Rs 3000) as well as daily sessions at 10am (Rs 200) and 5pm (Rs 150).

Healing Hands Centre (www.ancientmassage.com; Maharajganj, Kathmandu) Various monthly courses in Thai massage. The five-day course (20 hours, US$175) teaches you how to give a full body massage; there are also 10-day courses and one-month professional courses for US$800. Accommodation is available at the centre in the northeastern Kathmandu suburbs.

Himalayan Buddhist Meditation Centre (HBMC; Map p136; ☎ 01-4414843; www.fpmt.org) This friendly place offers talks and meditation courses (three to five days, US$50 to US$85). There are also guided meditations Tuesday to Friday and Sunday at 8am, 3pm and 8pm and day-long dharma teachings on Saturday.

Kathmandu Center of Healing (☎ 9851-070786; www.kathmanduhealing.com; Galfutar, Kathmandu)

This place offers one-, two- and five-week professional courses in Thai massage. Other activities include yoga, dance, a monthly four-day reiki course and various 'healing seminars'. Contact Rabin.

Kopan Monastery (☎ 01-4481268; www.kopan-mon astery.com) This monastery, north of Bodhnath, offers reasonably priced and popular seven-day (US$75) or 10-day (US$100) courses on Tibetan Buddhism, generally given by foreign teachers. There's also a popular annual one-month course (US$365) held in November, followed by an optional seven-day retreat. See p181 for more details.

Nepal Vipassana Centre Kathmandu (Map p136; ☎ 01-4250581; nvc@htp.com.np; Jyoti Bhawan Bldg, Kantipath, Kathmandu; ☼ 10am-5pm Sun-Fri); Budhanil-kantha (☎ 01-4371655) Ten-day retreats are held twice a month (starting on the 1st and 14th of the month) at this centre northeast of Kathmandu, just north of Budhanilkantha, and there are also occasional shorter courses. These are serious meditation courses that involve rising at 4am every morning, not talking or making eye contact with anyone over the entire 10 days, and not eating after midday. The fee is donation only.

Nepali Yoga Center (Map p257; ☎ 061-532407; www .nepaliyoga.com) Daily hatha yoga classes (1½ hours, Rs 300) at 7.30am and 4.30pm, plus various longer courses can be arranged.

Osho Tapoban (☎ 01-4353762; www.tapoban.com;
6km northwest of Kathmandu) Commune near the
Nagarjun Forest Reserve based on the teachings of Osho.
Offers daily meditations, Saturday meditation courses and
three-day courses every full moon. Accommodation is
available and there's a decent vegetarian restaurant.

Patanjali Yoga Center (Map pp110-11; ☎ 01-
4278437; www.saptayoga.com) A recommended place for
yoga, west of Kathmandu's city centre. Five- and 10-day
courses involve attending the centre for three hours per
day and include lunch. In theory there are drop-in classes
daily at 7am and 4pm but it's best to call in advance.

Rangjung Yeshe Institute (☎ 01-4490498; www
.shedra.org) At Bodhnath's Ka-Nying Sheldrup Ling
Gompa. The institute offers a fairly advanced 10-day
course ('Vajrayana empowerment') on Tibetan Buddhist
teachings, practice and meditation, led by the monastery's
abbot Chokyi Nyima Rinpoche. The course is held in mid-
November, and costs US$100. Daily meditation at 8am is
open to all.

Sadhana Yoga (www.sadhana-yoga.org.np; Pokhara)
One to 21 days are offered here at the cost of Rs 1600 per
day, which includes accommodation, meals and steam and
mud baths. See p254 for details.

Self-Awakening Centre (Map p116; ☎ 01-4256618;
Babar Mahal Revisited; ☾ closed Sat) Commercial classes
in t'ai chi, yoga, transcendental meditation and anything
else you can dream up. Yoga classes cost Rs 200 per hour;
t'ai chi is Rs 2800 per month.

CUSTOMS

All baggage is X-rayed on arrival and departure. In addition to the import and export of drugs, customs is concerned with
the illegal export of antiques (see right).
You may not import Nepali rupees, and
only nationals of Nepal and India may import Indian currency. There are no other
restrictions on bringing in either cash or
travellers cheques, but the amount taken
out at departure should not exceed the
amount brought in. Officially you should
declare cash or travellers cheques in excess
of US$2000, or the equivalent, but no-one
seems to bother with this.

According to the customs sign in the
Kathmandu airport arrivals hall, visitors are
permitted to import the following articles
for their personal use (and we quote):

Cigarettes, 200 sticks; cigars, 50 sticks;
alcoholic liquor, one bottle not exceed-
ing 1.15 litre; one binocular; one movie
camera films 12 rolls; one tape recorder
with 15 tape reels or cassettes; one per-
ambulator; one bicycle; one tricycle; one
stick; and one set of fountain pens.

Antiques

Customs' main concern is preventing the
export of antique works of art, with good
reason, as Nepal has been a particular victim of international art theft over the last 20
years (see the boxed text, p54).

It is very unlikely that souvenirs sold to
travellers will be antique (despite the claims
of the vendors), but if there is any doubt,
they should be cleared and a certificate obtained from the **Department of Archaeology**
(Map p116; ☎ 01-4250686; Ramshah Path, Kathmandu)
in the National Archives building. If you
visit between 10am and 1pm you should be
able to pick up a certificate by 5pm the same
day. These controls also apply to the export
of precious and semiprecious stones.

DANGERS & ANNOYANCES

Despite the continual stream of bad news
headlines that flows out of Kathmandu, the
most touristed areas of Nepal remain remarkably safe. See the box, p19, for an overview of dangers posed by the current struggle
between the government and the Maoists.

You can minimise the chances of bump-
ing into trouble by heeding the following
general advice:

■ Register with your embassy in Kathmandu (see below).

REGISTERING WITH YOUR EMBASSY

Officials of all embassies in Nepal stress the
benefits of registering with them, telling
them where you are trekking, and report-
ing in again when you return. The offices of
the Kathmandu Environmental Education
Project (KEEP; see p114) and the Himalayan
Rescue Association (see p331) stock registration forms from most embassies, so it's
simple to provide the information.

You can also register online with the **US
Embassy** (https://travelregistration.state.gov),
Australian Embassy and **New Zealand Embassy** (www.nzembassy.com; click on 'India'), and
by sending an email to the **British Embassy**
(ukconsular@mos.com.np). Include the contact
details of your next of kin, and your travel
dates, itinerary, passport number and insurance details.

GOVERNMENT TRAVEL ADVICE

The following governments publish useful travel advisories, highlighting entry requirements, medical facilities, areas with health and safety risks, civil unrest or other dangers, and are generally bang up to date.

Australian Department of Foreign Affairs and Trade (☎ 1300 139 281; www.smarttraveller.gov.au)
Canadian Consular Affairs (☎ 1-800-267 6788; www.voyage.gc.ca)
New Zealand Ministry of Foreign Affairs and Trade (☎ 04-439 8000; www.mft.govt.nz/travel/index .html)
UK Foreign and Commonwealth Office (☎ 0845-8502829; www.fco.gov.uk/travel)
US Department of State (☎ 1-888-407-4747, 1-202-501-4444; http://travel.state.gov/travel)

- Seek out local advice on safe/unsafe areas, but be sceptical of official tourist information and trekking touts.
- Keep an eye on the local press to find out about impending strikes, demonstrations and curfews – see the websites p22.
- Don't ever break curfews – instructions have been given to shoot those who are found breaking curfew.
- Don't travel during *bandh*s (strikes) or blockades. Get very nervous if you notice that you are the only car on the streets of Kathmandu!
- Be flexible with your travel arrangements in case your transport is affected by a *bandh* or security situation.
- Avoid marches, demonstrations or disturbances, as they can quickly turn violent.
- Don't trek alone, even on a day hike. Lone women should avoid travelling alone with a male guide.
- Be familiar with the symptoms of altitude sickness when trekking and observe sensible acclimatisation.
- Consider flying to destinations outside Kathmandu to avoid travelling through areas where there have been disturbances.
- Avoid travelling by night buses and keep bus travel in general to a minimum.
- Be prepared to pay the Maoists a 'tax' if approached while trekking and budget the cash for that eventuality. Trekkers have on occasion been beaten up for not paying this tax. It's just not worth arguing with these guys.
- Keep photocopies of your passport, visa, flight ticket and travellers cheques separate from the originals.

Scams

Be wary of deals offered by gem dealers (especially in Thamel, Kathmandu) that involve you buying stones to sell for a 'vast profit' at home. The dealers' stories vary, but are usually along the lines of the dealer not being able to export the stones without paying heavy taxes, so you take them and meet another dealer when you get home, who will sell them to a local contact and you both share the profit. Travellers falling for this ruse is not as unusual as you might expect.

Other scams include young kids asking for milk; you buy the milk at a designated store at an inflated price, the kid then returns the milk and pockets some of the mark-up (you can prevent this by opening the milk).

Be wary of kids who seem to know the capital of any country you can think of; a request for money will arrive at some point. Then there are the 'holy men' who will do their best to plant a *tika* (a red paste denoting blessing) on your forehead, only to then demand significant payment.

Credit card scam is not unusual; travellers have bought some souvenirs only to find thousand of dollars worth of Internet porn subscriptions chalked up on their bill.

Strikes & Demonstrations

Nepal's political process involves frequent demonstrations and strikes – some called by politicians, some by student groups and some by Maoists, and some by all three! Most common are street processions and rallies in the centre of Kathmandu. It's best to avoid large groups of slogan-chanting youths, in case you end up on the downstream side of a police *lathi* charge (a team of police wielding bamboo staves) or worse.

The US Embassy website gives details of upcoming demonstrations and strikes; go to http://nepal.usembassy.gov and click on 'Demonstration Alert'.

A normal procession or demonstration is a *julus*. If things escalate there may be a *chakka jam* (jam the wheels), when all vehicles stay off the street, or a *bandh,* when all shops, schools and offices are closed as well. When roads are closed the government generally runs buses with armed policemen from the airport to major hotels, returning to the airport from Tridevi Marg at the east end of Thamel.

Theft

While petty theft is not on the scale that exists in many countries, reports of theft from hotel rooms in tourist areas (including along trekking routes) are commonplace, and theft with violence is not unheard of. Never store valuables or money in your hotel room.

One of the most common forms of theft is the rifling of backpacks on the roofs of buses. Try to make your pack as theft-proof as possible – small padlocks and cover bags are a good deterrent.

There's little chance of ever retrieving your gear if it is stolen, and even getting a police report for an insurance claim can be difficult. Try the tourist police, or if there aren't any, the local police station. If you're not getting anywhere, go to **Interpol** (☎ 01-4412602) at the Police Headquarters in Naxal, Kathmandu. The documentation requires a passport photo and photocopies of your passport and visa; the process takes two days.

Traffic, Pollution & Hassle

Traffic on Kathmandu's streets is a rumpus of pollution-belching vehicles with two, three and four wheels. The combination of ancient vehicles, low-quality fuel and lack of emission controls makes the streets of Kathmandu particularly dirty, noisy and unpleasant. Traffic rules exist, but are rarely enforced; be especially careful when crossing streets or riding a bicycle – traffic is supposed to travel on the left side of the road, but many drivers simply choose the most convenient side, which can make walking in Kathmandu a deeply stressful experience. Remember that pedestrians account for over 40% of all traffic fatalities in Nepal.

Consider bringing a face mask to filter out dust and emission particles, especially if you plan to ride a bicycle or motorcycle in Kathmandu.

A minor hassle in Thamel comes from the barrage of irritating flute sellers, tiger-balm hawkers, chess-set sellers, musical-instrument vendors, travel-agency touts, hashish suppliers, freelance trekking guides and rickshaw drivers. In Kathmandu's and Patan's Durbar Squares you'll also come across a string of would-be guides whose trade has been hit badly by the downturn in tourism. There's less hassle in Bhaktapur, though there are some persistent thangka (Tibetan paintings on cotton) touts.

Trekking & Hiking

Fired up by the gung-ho stories of adventurous travellers, it is also easy to forget that mountainous terrain carries an inherent risk. There are posters plastered around Kathmandu with the faces of missing trekkers and travellers. Several solo trekkers go missing every year from the Everest region and one foreign trekker was murdered in Langtang in 2002. In October 2005 two women hikers disappeared (in two separate cases) while hiking in the Nagarjun Forest Reserve, just 5km from Kathmandu. Several tourists have been robbed along the trails to the World Peace Pagoda and Sarangkot, outside Pokhara.

In rural areas of Nepal rescue services are limited and medical facilities are primitive or nonexistent. Moreover, the Maoist insurgency has destroyed many rural phone lines and forced the closure of some park offices and police posts, which have traditionally provided security, information and emergency services for trekkers.

Only a tiny minority of trekkers end up in trouble, but accidents can often be avoided or the risks minimised if people have a realistic understanding of trekking requirements. At a minimum you should never trek alone. See p332 for more advice.

DISABLED TRAVELLERS

Wheelchair facilities, ramps and lifts (and even pavements!) are virtually nonexistent throughout Nepal and getting around the packed, twisting streets of traditional towns can be a real challenge. It is common for hotels to be multilevel, with most rooms on the upper floors, and many places – even midrange establishments – do not have lifts. Bathrooms equipped with grips and railings are not found anywhere, except perhaps in some of the top-end hotels.

There is no reason why a visit and even a trek could not be custom-tailored through a reliable agent for those with reasonable mobility. As an inspiration, consider Eric Weihenmayer who became the first blind climber to summit Everest in 2001 (and wrote a book called *Touch the Top of the World*), or Thomas Whittaker who summited in 1998 with an artificial leg, at the age of 50.

Accessible Journeys (www.disabilitytravel.com) is a US company that has experience in arranging private tours for disabled travellers. **Navyo Nepal** (☎ 01-4280056; www.navyonepal.com) in Nepal has some experience in running cultural tours and treks for people with disabilities. A useful general website is **Access-Able Travel Source** (www.access-able.com).

DISCOUNT CARDS

There aren't any noticeable discounts for holders of a student or seniors card. Those under 30 can get discounts on flights to India without a student card.

EMBASSIES & CONSULATES
Nepali Embassies & Consulates

For embassies and consulates not listed below check out the websites of Nepal's **Ministry of Foreign Affairs** (www.mofa.gov.np) or **Department of Immigration** (www.immi.gov.np/location.php).

Australia Consulate General (☎ 08-9386 2102; gregcam@iinet.net.au; Suite 2, 16 Robinson St, Nedlands, WA 6009); Honorary Consulate-General (☎ 02-9223 6161, fax 9223 6144; Level 13, Pitt St, Sydney, NSW 2000); Honorary Consulate-General (☎ 3220 2007; konbridge@selcon.com.au; Level 7, 344 Queen St, Brisbane, Queensland 4000)

Bangladesh (☎ 02-9892490; rnedhaka@bdmail.net; United Nations Rd, Rd 2, Baridhara, Dhaka)

Canada (☎ 416-865 0200; fax 416-865 0904; Royal Bank Plaza, South Tower, 32nd fl, PO Box 33, Toronto, Ontario M5J 2J9)

China (☎ 010-6532 1795; beijing@nepalembassy.org.cn; No 1, Xi Liu Jie, Sanlitun Lu, Beijing 100600) See also Tibet.

France (☎ 01 46 22 48 67; www.nepalembassy.org; 45 bis rue des Acacias, 75017 Paris) Consulate-General in Toulouse and Rouen.

Germany Embassy (☎ 030-3435 9920; www.nepalembassy-germany.com; Guerickestrasse 27, 10587 Berlin-Charlottenburg); Honorary Consulate (☎ 0221-2 33 83 81; www.konsulatnepal.de, Cologne)

India Embassy (☎ 011-23327361; ramjanki@del.2.vsnl.net.in; 1 Barakhamba Rd, New Delhi 110001); Consulate-General (☎ 033-24561224; rncg@cal.vsnl.net.in; 1 National Library Ave, Alipore, Kolkata/Calcutta 700027)

Japan (☎ 03-3705 5558; nepembjp@big.or.jp; 14-19 Todoroki 7-chome, Setagaya-ku, Tokyo 158-0082)

Myanmar (Burma; ☎ 01-545 880; rnembygn@datseco.com.mm; 16 Natmauk Yeiktha/Park Ave, PO Box 84, Yangon/Rangoon)

Netherlands (☎ 020-6241 530; www.nepal.nl; Keizersgracht 463, 1017 DK, Amsterdam)

Thailand (☎ 0-2391 7240; nepembkk@asiaaccess.net.th; 189 Soi 71, Sukhumvit Rd, Prakanong, Bangkok 10110)

Tibet (☎ 0891-681 5744; rncglx@public.ls.xz.cn; Norbulingka Rd 13, Lhasa, Tibet Autonomous Region)

UK (☎ 020-7229 1594; www.nepembassy.org.uk; 12A Kensington Palace Gardens, London W8 4QU)

USA Embassy (☎ 202-667 4550; www.nepalembassyusa.org; 2131 Leroy Pl NW, Washington, DC 20008); Consulate-General (☎ 270-370 3988; fax 953 2038; 820 2nd Ave, 17th fl, New York, NY 10017) Honorary consulates in San Francisco, Chicago, Boston, Marina Del Rey and Sun Valley, Idaho.

Embassies & Consulates in Nepal

Travellers continuing beyond Nepal may need visas for Bangladesh, China, India, Myanmar (Burma) or Thailand. The only visas dished out in Kathmandu for Tibet (actually a Chinese visa and a travel permit for Tibet) are for organised groups; individuals wishing to travel to China or Tibet may find it easier to get a visa before arriving in Nepal (Delhi is a good place to get one). See p381 for advice about travelling independently in Tibet.

Foreign embassies and consulates located in Kathmandu include:

Australia (Map pp110-11; ☎ 01-4371678; www.embassy.gov.au/np; Bansbari) Beyond the Ring Rd in Maharajganj.

Bangladesh (Map pp110-11; ☎ 01-4372843; fax 4373265; Maharajganj; 🕑 9am-1.15pm & 2-5pm Mon-Fri) Visa application mornings only; tourist visas are not issued here, but are available on arrival in Dhaka.

Canada (Map pp110-11; ☎ 01-4415193; www.cconepal.org.np; Lazimpat)

China (Map pp110-11; ☎ 01-4411740; www.chinaembassy.org.np; Baluwatar; 🕑 9am-noon & 3-5pm Mon-Fri) Visa applications are accepted Monday, Wednesday and Friday 9.30am to 11.30am; passports are generally returned the next working day between 4pm and 4.30pm, though same-day express services are possible. If applying yourself you will need to have proof (such as an air ticket to Beijing or Shanghai) that you are not travelling via Tibet.

France (Map p116; ☎ 01-4412332, 4411740; www.ambafrance-np.org; Lazimpat; 🕑 9am-12.30pm Mon, Tue, Thu, Fri)

Germany (Map pp110-11; ☎ 01-4412786, 4416832; www.kathmandu.diplo.de; Gyaneshwar)

India (Map p116; ☎ 01-4410900; fax 4413132; www
.south-asia.com/Embassy-India; Lainchhaur; ⏱ 9.30am-
noon & 1.30-5pm Mon-Fri) Visa applications 9.30am to
noon, collect visas 4pm to 5pm. Allow up to two weeks
for processing tourist visas, which cost from Rs 2100 to Rs
3200 depending on nationality, plus a Rs 300 telex fee (Rs
1000 telex fee for US citizens) and are valid for six months.
Queues start forming outside the embassy gates around
4am, as only the first 60 or so people get in before the
gates slam shut. Agencies will do the queuing for you for a
service fee of around Rs 1000 to Rs 2000 and will save you
several days of grief. Transit visas (Rs 350; valid for 15 days
from date of issue) are issued the same day, start from that
date and are nonextendable. Two photos and a photocopy
of your passport are required.
Japan (Map pp110-11; ☎ 01-4426680; comjpn@mos
.com.np; Pani Pokhari)
Myanmar (Burma; Map p184; ☎ 01-5524788; fax
5523402; Chakupath, nr Patan Dhoka (City Gate), Patan;
⏱ 9.30am-1pm & 2-4.30pm Mon-Fri) Visa applications
mornings only. Fourteen-day visas are available, four photos are required, 24-hour turnaround; the cost is US$20.
Netherlands (Map p184; ☎ 01-5523444; consulate@
snv.org.np; Bakhundol, Patan; ⏱ 10am-noon Mon &
Wed-Fri, 10am-11am Tue)
New Zealand (Map pp110-11; ☎ 01-4412436; fax
4414750; Dilli Bazaar) Honorary consulate only.
Pakistan (Map pp110-11; ☎ 01-4374011; fax 4374012;
Narayan Gopal Chowk, Ring Rd, Maharajganj; ⏱ 9am-
5pm Mon-Fri)
Thailand (Map pp110-11; ☎ 01-4371410; fax 4371408;
Bansbari; ⏱ 8.30am-12.30pm & 1.30-4.30pm Mon-Fri)
Visa applications accepted 9.30am to 12.30pm, two photos
required, 24-hour turnaround; the cost is about US$10,
though paying the visa fees into a local bank is a pain;
most nationalities don't need a visa for stays of less than
30 days.
UK (Map p116; ☎ 01-4410583; www.britishembassy.gov
.uk/nepal; Lainchhaur; ⏱ 8.30am-noon & 2-4pm Mon-
Thu, 8.30-11.30am Fri)

USA Embassy (Map pp110-11; ☎ 01-4411179; http://nepal
.usembassy.gov; Pani Pokhari; US citizen services ⏱ 1-4pm
Mon, Wed & Fri, 8am-4.30pm Tue, Thu); Consular Section
(Map p116; ☎ 4445577; Yak & Yeti Hotel, Kathmandu)

FESTIVALS & EVENTS
Nepal's colourful holidays and festivals occur
virtually year-round and a visit to Nepal is
almost certain to coincide with at least one,
particularly in the Kathmandu Valley. Certain times of year, most notably towards the
end of the monsoon in August and September, are packed with festivals. They go a long
way towards compensating for the less-than-
ideal weather at this time of year.

Nepal's most spectacular festivities are its
chariot processions, similar to epic processions held in India. These tottering 20m-tall
chariots of the gods are often chronically
and comically unstable (imagine hauling
a 60ft-tall jelly through the streets of Kathmandu) and moving them requires hundreds
of enthusiastic devotees. See the following
Chaitra Dasain, Bisket Jatra, Indra Jatra and
Rato Machhendranath festivals.

Holidays and festivals aren't declared
more than a year in advance, so accurate pre-
diction is difficult. The following calendar
lists Nepal's major festivals in the months
they occur with the Nepali lunar months
listed in brackets. Tibetan festivals are organised by the Tibetan lunar calendar and may
fall in different months in different years.

January–February (Magh)
Magh Sankranti The end of the coldest winter months is
marked by ritual bathing during the Nepali month of Magh.
The festival is dated by the movement north of the winter sun
and is one of the few festivals not timed by the lunar calendar.
Soon after, on the new-moon day, the Tribeni Mela (a *mela*

NEPALI CALENDARS
Nepali holidays and festivals are principally dated by the lunar calendar, falling on days relating
to new or full moons. The lunar calendar is divided into bright and dark fortnights. The bright
fortnight is the two weeks of the waxing moon, as it grows to become *purnima* (the full moon).
The dark fortnight is the two weeks of the waning moon, as the full moon shrinks to become
aunsi (the new moon).

The Nepali New Year starts on 14 April with the month of Baisakh, and is 57 years ahead of
the Gregorian calendar used in the West. Thus the year 2007 in the West is 2064 in Nepal. The
Newars, on the other hand, start their New Year from the day after Deepawali (the third day
of Tihar), which falls on the night of the new moon in late October or early November. Their
calendar is 880 years behind the Gregorian calendar, so 2007 in the West is 1127 to the Newars
of the Kathmandu Valley.

is a fair) is held at various places including Devghat (p274) in the Terai, where over 100,000 people bathe in the nearby Narayani River. Celebrations are also held at Ridi Bazaar, at the confluence of the Kali Gandaki and Ridi Khola (see p301).

Basant Panchami The start of spring is celebrated by honouring Saraswati; since she is the goddess of learning this festival has special importance for students. The shrine to Saraswati just below the platform at the top of Swayambhunath is the most popular locale for the festivities, although Kathmandu is also popular. This is also a particularly auspicious time for weddings.

Losar Tibetan New Year commences with the new moon in February and falls in either Magh or Falgun. It is welcomed with particular fervour at the great stupa of Bodhnath (Boudha), as well as at Swayambhunath and in the Tibetan community at Jawlakhel, near Patan. The Sherpa people of the Solu Khumbu region also celebrate at this time.

February–March (Falgun)

Maha Shivaratri Shiva's birthday falls on the new-moon day of the Nepali month of Falgun. Festivities take place at all Shiva temples, but most particularly at Pashupatinath, and hundreds of sadhus flock here from all over Nepal and India. The king of Nepal makes an appearance late in the day. The crowds bathing in the Bagmati's holy waters at this time are a colourful and wonderful sight.

Holi This exciting festival (also known as Fagu) is closely related to the water festivals of Thailand and Myanmar and takes place on the full-moon day in the month of Falgun. By this time, late in the dry season, it is beginning to get hot and the water which is sprayed around during the festival is a reminder of the cooling monsoon days to come. Holi is also known as the Festival of Colours and coloured powder (particularly red) and water are also dispensed. Foreigners get special attention, so if you venture out on Holi leave your camera behind (or keep it well protected) and wear old clothes that can get colour-stained.

March–April (Chaitra)

Chaitra Dasain Also known as Small Dasain, this festival takes place exactly six months prior to the more important Dasain celebration. Both Dasains are dedicated to Durga and once again goats and buffaloes are sacrificed early in the morning in Kot Sq in central Kathmandu. The Chaitra Dasain sacrifices also signal the start of the month-long Seto (White) Machhendranath chariot festival in Kathmandu (see p125).

Balkumari Jatra The small town of Thimi celebrates this exciting festival at this time (see p209). The New Year is also an important time in the valley for ritual bathing, and crowds of hill people visit the Buddhist stupas of Swayambhunath and Bodhnath.

April–May (Baisakh)

Bisket Jatra Nepali New Year starts in mid-April, at the beginning of the month of Baisakh; the Bisket chariot festival in Bhaktapur is the most spectacular welcome for the New Year, and one of the most exciting annual events in the valley (see p203).

Rato Machhendranath This festival in Patan, whose highlight is the showing of the sacred vest of the god Machhendranath, involves a month-long procession of a temple chariot (see p191).

May–June (Jeth)

Buddha Jayanti (the Buddha's Birthday) A great fair is held at Lumbini, the birthplace of the Buddha, and there are celebrations in Swayambhunath, Bodhnath and Patan. The Swayambhunath stupa's collection of rare thangkas is displayed on the southern wall of the courtyard on this single day each year. There are also colourful monk dances.

July–August (Saaun)

Naga Panchami On the fifth day after the new moon in the month of Saaun, *nagas* (serpent deities) are honoured all over the country. *Nagas* are considered to have magical powers over the monsoon rains. Protective pictures of the *nagas* are hung over doorways of houses and food is put out for snakes, including a bowl of rice. See p206 for more information.

Janai Purnima Around the full moon in the month of Saaun, all high-caste men (Chhetri and Brahmin) must change the *janai* (sacred thread), which they wear looped over their left shoulder. Janai Purnima also brings crowds of pilgrims to sacred Gosainkund Lake, across the mountains to the north of Kathmandu, where they garland a statue of Shiva and throw coins at a sacred lingam. A direct channel is said to lead from the lake to the pond in the Kumbeshwar Temple in Patan and a silver lingam is installed in the pond for the occasion (see p190).

Ghanta Karna This festival is named after 'bell ears', a horrible demon who wore bell earrings to drown out the name of Vishnu, his sworn enemy. This festival, on the 14th day of the dark fortnight of Saaun, celebrates his destruction when a god, disguised as a frog, lured him into a deep well where the people stoned and clubbed him to death. Ghanta Karna is burnt in effigy on this night throughout Newari villages and evil is cleansed from the land for another year.

August–September (Bhadra)

Gai Jatra This 'Cow Festival' takes place immediately after Janai Purnima on the day after the Saaun full moon, and is dedicated to those who died during the preceding year. Newars believe that, after death, cows will guide them to Yama, the god of the underworld, and finding your way on this important journey will be much easier if by chance you should be holding onto a cow's tail at the moment of death. On this day cows are led through the streets of the valley's towns and small boys dress up as cows. The festival is celebrated with maximum energy on the streets of Bhaktapur.

DASAIN FESTIVAL

The pleasant post-monsoon period, when the sky is clearest, the air is cleanest and the rice is ready for harvesting, is also the time for Nepal's biggest annual festival. Dasain lasts for 15 days, finishing on the full-moon day of late September or early October. Although much of Dasain is a quiet family affair, there are colourful events for visitors to see both in Kathmandu and in the country. Dasain is also known as Durga Puja, as the festival celebrates the victory of the goddess Durga over the forces of evil personified in the buffalo demon Mahisasura. Since Durga is bloodthirsty, the festival is marked by wholesale blood-letting and features the biggest animal sacrifice of the year.

Before Dasain commences, Nepalis spring-clean their houses. In the country, swings and primitive hand-powered Ferris wheels are erected at the entrance to villages or in the main squares. On the first day of the festival, a sacred jar of water is prepared in each house and barley seeds are planted in carefully prepared soil; getting the seeds to sprout a few centimetres during Dasain ensures a good harvest.

Fulpati (or Phulpati) is the first really important day of Dasain and is called the 'Seventh Day' although it may not actually fall on the seventh day. Fulpati means 'Sacred Flowers', and a jar containing flowers is carried from Gorkha to Kathmandu and presented to the king at the Tundikhel parade ground. The flowers symbolise Taleju, the goddess of the royal family, whose most important image is in the Gorkha Palace. From the parade ground, the flowers are transported on a palanquin to Hanuman Dhoka (the old Royal Palace) in Durbar Sq, where they are inspected again by the king and his entourage.

Maha Astami or the 'Great Eighth Day' and **Kala Ratri**, the 'Black Night', follow Fulpati, and this is the start of the sacrifices and offerings to Durga. The hundreds of goats you may see contentedly grazing in the Tundikhel parkland prior to Maha Astami are living on borrowed time. At midnight, in a temple courtyard near Durbar Sq, eight buffaloes and 108 goats are beheaded, each with a single stroke of the sword or knife.

The next day is **Navami** and the Kot Sq near Durbar Sq, the scene of the great massacre of noblemen that led to the Rana period of Nepali history (see p33), is the scene for another great massacre. Visitors can witness the bloodshed, but you'll need to arrive early to secure a place. Sacrifices continue through the day and blood is sprinkled on the wheels of cars and other vehicles to ensure a safe year on the road. At the airport, each Royal Nepal Airlines Corporation aircraft will have a goat sacrificed to it! The average Nepali does not eat much meat, but on this day almost everybody in the country will find that goat is on the menu for dinner.

The 10th day of the festival, **Vijaya Dashami**, is again a family affair as cards and greetings are exchanged, family visits are made and parents place a *tika* on their children's foreheads.

In the evening, the conclusion of Dasain is marked by processions and masked dances in the towns of the Kathmandu Valley. The **Kharga Jatra**, or sword procession, features priests dressed up as the various gods and carrying wooden swords, symbolic of the weapon with which Durga slew the buffalo demon. This day also celebrates the victory of Lord Rama over the evil, 10-headed, demon-king Ravana in the Ramayana. The barley sprouts that were planted on the first day are picked and worn as small bouquets in the hair.

Kartika Purnima, the full-moon day marking the end of the festival, is celebrated with gambling in many households, and you will see even small children avidly putting a few coins down on various local games of chance.

Krishna Jayanti (Krishna's Birthday) The seventh day after the full moon in the month of Bhadra is celebrated as Krishna's birthday, sometimes also known as Krishnasthami. An all-night vigil is kept at the Krishna Mandir in Patan on the night before his birthday. Oil lamps light the temple and singing continues through the night.

Teej The Festival of Women lasts three days, from the second to the fifth day after the Bhadra new moon, and is based in Pashupatinath (see p53).

Indra Jatra This colourful and exciting festival manages to combine homage to Indra with an important annual appearance by Kumari (the living goddess), the paying of respects to Bhairab and commemoration of the conquest of the valley by Prithvi Narayan Shah. The festival also marks the end of the monsoon. It was during the Indra Jatra festival back in 1768 that Prithvi Narayan Shah conquered the valley and unified Nepal, so this important event is also commemorated in this most spectacular of Kathmandu occasions (see p134).

September–October (Ashoj/Ashwin)

Pachali Bhairab Jatra The fearsome form of Bhairab, as Pachali Bhairab, is honoured on the fourth day of the bright fortnight in September or early October. Bhairab's blood-thirsty nature means that there are numerous sacrifices.

Dasain Nepal's biggest annual festival. Dasain lasts for 15 days, finishing on the full-moon day of late September or early October. For more about the festival see p365; for information on disruptions to services during the festival see opposite.

October–November (Kartik)

Tihar With its colourful Festival of Lights, Tihar (also called Diwali or Deepawali after the third day of celebrations) is the most important Hindu festival in India, and in Nepal it ranks second only to Dasain. The five days of festival activities take place in late October or early November. The festival honours certain animals, starting with offerings of rice to the crows which are sent by Yama, the god of death, as his 'messengers of death'. On the second day, dogs are honoured with *tikas* and garlands of flowers; in the afterworld it is dogs who guide departed souls across the river of the dead. On the third day cows have their horns painted silver and gold. On the fourth day bullocks are honoured.

Deepawali The third day of the Tihar Festival is the most important day of the festival when Lakshmi, the goddess of wealth, comes to visit every home that has been suitably lit for her presence. No-one likes to turn down a visit from the goddess of wealth and so homes throughout the country are brightly lit with candles and lamps. The effect is highlighted because Deepawali falls on the new-moon day.

Newari New Year The fourth day of Tihar is also the start of the New Year for the Newari people of the Kathmandu Valley.

Bhai Tika On the fifth day of Tihar, brothers and sisters are supposed to meet and place *tikas* on each others' foreheads. Sisters offer small gifts of fruit and sweets to their brothers while the brothers give their sisters money in return. The markets and bazaars are busy supplying the appropriate gifts.

Haribodhini Ekadashi An *ekadashi* falls twice in every lunar month, on the 11th day after each new and full moon, and is regarded as an auspicious day. The Haribodhini Ekadashi, falling in late October or early November (on the 11th day after the new moon) is the most important. On this day Vishnu awakens from his four-month monsoonal slumber. The best place to see the festivities is at the temple of the sleeping Vishnu in Budhanilkantha (p182). Vishnu devotees make a circuit of important Vishnu temples from Ichangu Narayan to Changu Narayan, Bishankhu Narayan and Sekh Narayan, all in the Kathmandu Valley.

Mahalakshmi Puja Lakshmi is the goddess of wealth, and to farmers wealth is rice. Therefore this harvest festi-

val, immediately following Haribodhini Ekadashi, honours the goddess with sacrifices and colourful dances.

Mani Rimdu The Sherpa festival of Mani Rimdu takes place at the monastery of Tengboche in the Solu Khumbu region, on the Everest Base Camp trek. This popular three-day festival features masked dances and dramas, which celebrate the victory of Buddhism over the existing Tibetan Bön religion. The dates for the festivals are worked out according to the Tibetan lunar calendar and occur in October or November. See www.tengboche.org for details and dates. Another Mani Rimdu festival takes place six months later in the lunar month of Jeth (May–June) at Thami Gompa, a day's walk west of Namche Bazaar.

November–December (Mangsir)

Bala Chaturdashi Like *ekadashi*, there are two *chaturdashi*s each month; Bala Chaturdashi falls on the new-moon day in late November or early December. Pilgrims flock to Pashupatinath, burning oil lamps at night, scattering grain for the dead and bathing in the holy Bagmati River – see p193.

Sita Bibaha Panchami On the fifth day of the bright fortnight in late November or early December, pilgrims from all over Nepal and India flock to Janakpur (the birthplace of Sita) to celebrate the marriage of Sita to Rama. The wedding is re-enacted with a procession carrying Rama's image to Sita's temple by elephant (see p315).

GAY & LESBIAN TRAVELLERS

There's little of an open gay scene in Nepal. Homosexuality is not explicitly criminalised but 'any kind of unnatural sex' can bring a year's prison term. Gay Nepalis are frequently subject to police harassment and blackmail. Gay couples holding hands in public will experience no difficulties, as this is socially acceptable, but public displays of intimacy by anyone are frowned upon.

The **Blue Diamond Society** (☎ 01-4427608; www.bds.org.np) is the first gay organisation in Kathmandu. It provides education, support and advice to Nepal's gay and *methi* (transgender) community, and runs the country's only AIDS/HIV prevention programme, partially thanks to a US$40,000 grant donated by Sir Elton John.

Aashnepal Travel & Tours (☎ 01-4228768; www.aashanepal.com.np) is a gay-friendly tour company in Kathmandu.

HOLIDAYS
Public Holidays

Many holidays and festivals affect the working hours of government offices and banks, which close for the following public holi-

DASAIN STOPPAGES

Dasain (15 days in September or October) is the most important of all Nepali celebrations. Tens of thousands of Nepalis hit the road to return home to celebrate with their families. This means that while villages are full of life if you are trekking, buses and planes are fully booked and overflowing, porters may be hard to find (or more expensive than usual) and cars are hard to hire. Many hotels and restaurants in regional towns close down completely, and doing business in Kathmandu (outside Thamel) becomes almost impossible.

The most important days, when everything comes to a total halt, are the ninth day (when thousands of animals are sacrificed), and the 10th day (when blessings are received from elder relatives and superiors). Banks and government offices are generally closed from the eighth day of the festival to the 12th day.

days and some or all of the days of the festivals below (note this list is not exhaustive). The exact festival dates change annually.

Prithvi Narayan Shah's Birthday 10 January
Basant Panchami January/February
Democracy Day 18 February
Maha Shivaratri February/March
Bisket Jatra (Nepali New Year) 14 April
King's Birthday 7 July
Janai Purnima July/August
Teej August/September
Indra Jatra September
Dasain September/October
Tihar October/November
Constitution Day 9 November

INSURANCE

A travel insurance policy to cover theft, loss and medical problems is an excellent idea in Nepal. There is a wide variety of policies available, so check the small print carefully. Some policies exclude 'dangerous activities', which may include riding a motorbike and trekking (and definitely bungee jumping and rafting). Choose a policy that covers medical and emergency repatriation, including helicopter evacuation for trekkers and general medical evacuation to Bangkok or Delhi, which alone can cost a cool US$40,000.

You may prefer a policy that pays doctors or hospitals directly rather than you having to pay on the spot and claim later. If you have to claim later make sure you keep all documentation. Some policies ask you to call back (reverse charges) to a centre in your home country where an immediate assessment of your problem is made.

Bear in mind that many insurance policies do not cover 'acts of terrorism' (ie Maoists), civil war or regions that your country's government advises against travel to, so double-check how your insurance company defines these notions and Nepal's political situation.

Worldwide cover to travellers from over 44 countries is available online at www.lonelyplanet.com/travel_services.

INTERNET ACCESS

Email and Internet services are offered in dozens of places in Kathmandu and Pokhara and are generally cheap at around Rs 30 per hour. Internet access is also available in most other towns – you can even send email from Namche Bazaar on the Everest trek – but connections are usually slow and relatively expensive, as connection may involve a long-distance call to Kathmandu.

LEGAL MATTERS

Hashish has been illegal since 1973, but it's still readily available in Nepal. Thamel is full of shifty, whispering dealers. Possession of a small amount involves little risk, although potential smokers should keep the less-than-salubrious condition of Nepali jails firmly in mind. Don't try taking any out of the country either – travellers have been arrested at the airport on departure.

If you get caught smuggling something serious – drugs or gold – chances are you'll end up in jail, without trial, and will remain there until someone pays for you to get out. Jail conditions in Nepal are reportedly horrific. Bribery may be an option to avoid jail in the first place but unless you can do it in a way which is deniable, you may just end up in deeper strife.

A handful of foreigners currently languish in jails in Kathmandu, mostly for drug offences. If you want to pay a humanitarian visit you can contact your embassy for a list of names and their locations. Take along items of practical use, such as reading matter, blankets and fresh fruit.

Killing a cow is illegal in Nepal and carries a punishment of two years in prison.

MAPS

The best maps in Nepal are those produced by **Karto-Atelier** (www.karto-atelier.com), under the name Gecko Maps. These locally made maps are a result of German-Nepali collaboration and are outstanding. Currently available are maps to Nepal, Kathmandu, Chitwan and Island Peak, for Rs 800 each.

There are many locally produced and cheaper maps available in Nepal which for most trekkers prove quite adequate. The main series is produced by **Himalayan Maphouse** (www.himalayanmaphouse.com) and these include the brand Nepa Maps. They are decent quality and reasonably priced at Rs 200 to Rs 400 each but they definitely aren't reliable enough to use for off-route trekking. These and other maps are sold at a string of glossy map shops throughout Thamel and elsewhere in Kathmandu.

For details of trekking maps and online map shops see p328.

MONEY

The Nepali rupee (Rs) is divided into 100 paisa (p). There are coins for denominations of one, two, five and 10 rupees, and bank notes in denominations of one, two, five, 10, 20, 25, 50, 100, 500 and 1000 rupees. This is a great contrast to a time not long ago, when outside the Kathmandu Valley, it was rare to see any paper money. Mountaineering books from the 1950s often comment on the porters whose sole duty was to carry the expedition's money – in cold, hard cash.

Away from major centres, changing a Rs 1000 note can be very difficult, so it is always a good idea to keep a stash of small-denomination notes. Even in Kathmandu, many small businesses – especially rickshaw and taxi drivers – simply don't have sufficient spare money to allow them the luxury of carrying a wad of change.

ATMs

Standard Chartered Bank has ATMs in Kathmandu and Pokhara; you can get cash advances on both Visa and MasterCard 24 hours a day, though travellers have reported that these machines don't take cards that run on the Cirrus system. Other banks, such as the Himalaya Bank, also have ATMs but some only accept local cards. Using an ATM attached to a bank during business hours will minimise the hassle in the rare event that the machine eats your card.

Cash

Major international currencies, including the US dollar, euro and pounds sterling, are readily accepted. In Nepal the Indian rupee is also like a hard currency – the Nepali rupee is pegged to the Indian rupee at the rate of INRs 100 = Rs 160. Be aware that INRs 500 and INRs 1000 notes are not accepted anywhere in Nepal, apparently due to forgeries.

Changing Money

Official exchange rates are set by the government's Nepal Rastra Bank and listed in the daily newspapers. Rates at the private banks vary, but are generally not far from the official rate.

There are exchange counters at the international terminal at Kathmandu's Tribhuvan Airport and banks and/or moneychangers at the various border crossings. Pokhara and the major border towns also have official moneychanging facilities, but changing travellers cheques can be difficult elsewhere in the country, even in some quite large towns. If you are trekking, take enough small-denomination cash rupees to last the whole trek.

The best private banks are Himalaya Bank Nepal Bank Ltd and Standard Chartered Bank. Some hotels and resorts are licensed to change money but their rates are lower.

When you change money officially, you are required to show your passport, and you are issued with a foreign exchange encashment receipt showing your identity and the amount of hard currency you have changed. Hang onto the receipts as you need them to change excess rupees back into hard currency at banks. You can change rupees back into hard currency at most moneychangers without a receipt.

If you leave Nepal via Kathmandu's Tribhuvan Airport, the downstairs exchange counter will re-exchange the amount shown on 'unused' exchange certificates. Official re-exchange is not possible at any bank branches at the border crossings.

Many upmarket hotels and businesses are obliged by the government to demand payment in hard currency; they will also accept rupees, but only if you can show a foreign exchange encashment receipt that covers the amount you owe them. In practice this regulation seems to be widely disregarded. Airlines are also required to charge tourists in hard currency, either in cash US dollars, travellers cheques or credit cards, and this rule is generally followed.

Credit Cards

Major credit cards are widely accepted at midrange and better hotels, restaurants and fancy shops in the Kathmandu Valley and Pokhara only.

Branches of Standard Chartered Bank and some other banks such as Nabil Bank and Himalaya Bank give cash advances against Visa and MasterCard in Nepali rupees only (no commission), and will also sell you foreign currency travellers cheques against the cards with a 2% commission.

The American Express (Amex) agent is Yeti Travels (p113) in Kathmandu. It advances travellers cheques to cardholders for a standard 1% commission.

International Transfers

In general it's easiest to send money through a private company such as **Western Union** (www.westernunion.com) or **Moneygram** (www.visitnepal.com/moneygram), which can arrange transfers within minutes. Western Union's agents in Nepal include Yeti Travels, Sita World Travel (see p113) and Nabil Bank. Moneygram uses Easylink, with offices in Thamel, Bodhnath, Butwal and Pokhara. To pick up funds at a Western Union branch you'll need your passport and ten-digit transfer code.

Note that money can often only be received in Nepali rupees, not US dollars.

Moneychangers

In addition to the banks there are licensed moneychangers in Kathmandu, Pokhara, Birganj, Kakarbhitta and Sunauli/Bhairawa. The rates are often marginally lower than the banks, but there are no commissions, they have much longer opening hours (typ-

ically from 9am to 7pm daily) and they are also much quicker, the whole process often taking no more than a few minutes.

Most licensed moneychangers will provide an exchange receipt; if they don't you may be able to negotiate better rates than those posted on their boards.

Tipping

Tipping is accepted (and appreciated) in tourist restaurants. Your loose change (or 5%) is fine in cheaper places; around 10% is fine in more expensive restaurants. Round up the fare for taxi drivers.

PHOTOGRAPHY & VIDEO

Bringing a video camera to Nepal poses no real problem, and there are no video fees to worry about. The exception to this is in Upper Mustang and Langtang border regions where an astonishing US$1000 fee is levied.

Airport Security

All luggage (including carry-on cabin baggage) is X-rayed at Kathmandu's Tribhuvan Airport on the way in and the way out of the country; signs on the X-ray equipment state that the machines are not film-safe for undeveloped film. Have exposed film inspected manually when leaving the country.

Film & Equipment

There are numerous camera and film shops in Kathmandu and Pokhara and good-quality film is readily available. Do check, however, that the packaging has not been tampered with, and that the expiry date has not been exceeded. Out in the smaller cities and towns there is little choice and even greater chance of coming across expired film.

In Kathmandu there are numerous places offering a same-day service for print film (see p154). Typically, 100 ASA 36-exposure colour print film costs about Rs 150. Developing is typically around Rs 400 for 36 prints.

Slide film costs Rs 350 to 400 for Sensia (100 ASA) and a bit less for Elitechrome (Rs 280). Slide processing costs around Rs 360 for 36 mounted shots.

Almost all flavours of memory stick, flash card etc and batteries are available in Kathmandu.

A panoramic camera can be very useful if you're trekking; it's the only way to do service to those jaw-dropping views.

Photographing People

Most Nepalis are content to have their photograph taken, but always ask permission first. Sherpa people are an exception and can be very camera-shy. Bear in mind that if someone poses for you (especially sadhus – holy men), they will probably insist on being given *baksheesh* (a donation).

For more advice and general rules for photographing people and events in Nepal, please see p63.

Restrictions

It is not uncommon for temple guardians to disallow photos of their temple, and these wishes should be respected. Don't photograph army camps, checkpoints or bridges.

Technical Tips

Nepal is an exceptionally scenic country so bring plenty of film. To photograph Nepal's diverse attractions you need a variety of lenses, from a wide-angle lens if you're shooting in compact temple compounds to a long telephoto lens if you're after perfect mountain shots or close-ups of wildlife. A polarising filter is useful to increase contrast and bring out the blue of the sky.

Remember to allow for the intensity of mountain light when setting exposures at high altitude. At the other extreme it's surprising how often you find the light in Nepal is insufficient. Early in the morning, in the dense jungle of Royal Chitwan National Park or in gloomy temples and narrow streets, you may find yourself wishing you had high-speed film. A flash is often necessary for shots inside temples or to 'fill in' shots of sculptures and reliefs.

Rechargeable batteries can be juiced up at most trekking lodges for a fee of Rs 100 to 300 per hour. To charge up batteries or an iPod on a trek, consider a solar charger like the iSun or Solio (www.solio.com).

POST

The postal service to and from Nepal is, at best, erratic but can occasionally be amazingly efficient. Most articles do arrive at their destination…eventually.

Rates

Airmail rates for a 20g letter/postcard are Rs 2/1 within Nepal, Rs 18/15 to India/surrounding countries, Rs 35/25 to Europe/UK and Rs 40/30 to the USA/Australia. An aerogramme costs Rs 32 to the US and Australia and Rs 28 to Europe.

Registered mail costs Rs 85 for international destinations.

Courier

For a 500g package of documents **FedEx** (www.fedex.com/np/) and **DHL** (www.dhl.com) charge around US$40 and US$50 respectively to the US and UK; slightly less to Australia. FedEx offers a 25% discount if you drop documents directly to their office. Packages other than documents cost up to 50% more for the same weight.

Parcel Post

Having stocked up on souvenirs and gifts in Nepal, many people take the opportunity of sending them home from Kathmandu. Parcel post is not cheap or quick, but the service is reliable. Sea mail is much cheaper than airmail, but it is also much slower (packages take about 3½ months) and less reliable. As an idea, a 2kg package to the UK/US/India costs Rs 1600/2000/600 at airmail rate, 25% less at 'book post' rate.

The contents of a parcel must be inspected by officials *before* it is wrapped. There are packers at the Kathmandu foreign post office who will package it for a small fee. The maximum weight for sea mail is 20kg; for airmail it's 10kg, or 5kg for book post.

Some specialised shipping companies (see p113) offer air freight, which is considerably cheaper than airmail and not much more expensive than sea mail. It still goes by air; the catch is that it has to be picked up at an international airport and you'll have to deal with customs paperwork and fees there.

If an object is shipped out to you in Nepal, you may find that customs charges for clearance and collection at your end add up to more than the initial cost of sending it. Often it's worth paying extra to take it with you on the plane in the first place.

SHOPPING

Nepal is a shopper's paradise, whether you are looking for a cheap souvenir or a real work of art. Although you can find almost anything in the tourist areas of Kathmandu, there are specialities in different parts of the Kathmandu Valley. Wherever you shop remember to bargain.

Prices are low for foreign products in Kathmandu and Pokhara but you'll soon realise that you get what you pay for. Thamel's shops in particular are full of poor-quality Indian-printed books, Pakistani pirated CDs and locally-made clothes that don't quite fit properly.

Remember that antiques (over 100 years old) cannot be taken out of the country, and baggage is inspected by Nepali customs with greater thoroughness on departure than on arrival (see p359). It helps to get a receipt and a description of any major purchase from the shop where you bought it.

Unless you are sure about the reliability of the shop, do not ask the shop where you made the purchase to send it for you. See opposite for details on posting goods home.

Bargaining

Bargaining is regarded as an integral part of most commercial transactions in Nepal, especially when dealing with souvenir shops, hotels and guides. Ideally, it should be an enjoyable social exchange, rather than a conflict of egos. Remember to keep things light; Nepalis do not ever appreciate aggressive behaviour. A good deal is reached when both parties are happy. Try to remember that Rs 10 might make quite a difference to the seller, but in hard currency it amounts to very little (less than US$0.15).

Clothing & Embroidery

Tibetan and Nepali clothes have always been a popular buy, but Western fashions made strictly for the tourist market have also become a big industry.

Embroidery is popular and there are lots of little tailor shops around Kathmandu where the sewing machines whir away late into the night adding logos and Tibetan symbols to jackets, hats and T-shirts. Mountaineers like to return from Nepal with jackets carrying the message that this was the Country X, Year Y expedition to Peak Z. You can also buy badges for your backpack saying that you walked to Everest Base Camp or completed the Annapurna Circuit.

A Nepali *topi* (cap) is part of Nepali formal wear for a man and they are tradition-

ally made in Bhaktapur. There's a group of cap specialists between Indra Chowk and Asan Tole in the old part of Kathmandu. Caps typically cost from Rs 50 to 300.

Jewellery

Kathmandu's many small jewellery manufacturers turn out a wide variety of designs with an equally wide range of standards. You can buy jewellery ready-made, ask them to create a design for you or bring in something you would like copied. There are several good shops around greater Thamel, particularly down towards Chhetrapati. See p360 if you are approached to buy gems.

These outlets mainly cater to Western tastes but there are also shops for the local market as Nepali women, like Indian women, traditionally wear their wealth in jewellery. For a few rupees you can buy an armful of glass bangles or colourful beads by the handful.

Masks & Puppets

Papier-mâché masks and colourful puppets are sold at shops in Kathmandu, Patan and Bhaktapur. Thimi is the manufacturing centre for masks, which are used in the traditional masked dances in September – it's interesting to see masks being made there. Ganesh, Bhairab and the Kumari are the most popular subjects for masks and they make good wall decorations.

Puppets make good gifts for children and are made in Bhaktapur as well as other centres. They're often of multiarmed deities clutching little wooden weapons in each hand. The puppet heads may be made of easily broken clay or more durable papiermâché. Smaller puppets cost from around Rs 100 to 400 but you can also pay from Rs 500 to 1000 for a larger figure. As usual, quality does vary and the more puppets you inspect the more you will begin to appreciate the differences.

Metalwork

Patan is the valley centre for bronze casting and the best variety of metalwork is found in the shops around Patan's Durbar Sq (see p194 for more details).

Other Souvenirs

A *khukuri* (traditional knife of the Gurkhas) can cost from Rs 300 to 2000. Most are made in eastern Nepal and come with a scabbard and a blade sharpener (chakmak). Notice the notch (kaudi) in the blade which allows blood to run off before hitting the hilt. You may well have troubles explaining the knife to customs officials in your country (always carry it in your check-in, rather than carry-on, baggage).

Bhaktapur is the centre for woodcarving, and you can find good objects in and around Tachupal Tole.

Cassettes and CDs of Nepali, Indian and general Himalayan music are a fine souvenir of a visit to Nepal, though much of it is of the woolly New Age variety. There are lots of music shops in Kathmandu selling local music as well as pirated Western tapes and CDs (Rs 150 to 250). The best-quality recordings are from Russia, though most come from Pakistan or Singapore. It's a good idea to test them out in the shop as there are a few rogues about. MP3 recordings are also available.

Tibetan crafts include a variety of religious items such as the dorje (thunderbolt symbol), prayer flags and the popular prayer wheels. Tibetans are keen traders, and prices at Bodhnath and Swayambhunath are often high. New Age Tibetophiles love Tibetan 'singing bowls', whose alloy of seven metals creates a ringing sound when you rotate a dowel around the rim, creating a sound said to be conducive to meditative thought.

Dhoop (incense) is a popular buy, as are spices, ranging from single spices like jeera (cumin), besar (turmeric) and methi (fenugreek) to various kinds of masala mixes.

Paper Products

Locally produced paper from the lokta (daphne plant) is used to make picture frames, photo albums, cards and lanterns. The lokta bark is boiled and beaten with wooden mallets and the pulp is spread over a frame to dry. The finished product (often mistakenly called rice paper) folds without creasing and is used on all official Nepali documents.

There's a good selection in the shops of Thamel and Bhaktapur, where you can see the manufacturing process.

Pashmina

One of the most popular souvenirs is a shawl or scarf made from fine pashmina

(the under hair of a mountain goat). The cost of a pashmina depends on the percentage of pashmina in the mix and from which part of the goat's body that pashmina originated, starting from the cheapest back wool and rising through the belly and chest to neck hair, which is about five times more expensive than back hair.

There are literally dozens of shops in Thamel selling pashmina items. The cheapest shawls are a 70/30% cotton/pashmina blend, and these cost around Rs 1500 for a 78cm by 2m shawl. Silk-pashmina blends cost around Rs 2500, while a pure pashmina shawl ranges from around Rs 3500 to US$275 for a pashmina ring shawl (named because they are fine enough to be pulled through a finger ring).

Shahtoosh is a form of pashmina that comes from (and results in the death of) the endangered Tibetan antelope. It is illegal in Nepal. See the boxed text, p61, for more information.

Tea

Tea is grown in the east of Nepal, close to the border with India near Darjeeling where the finest Indian tea is grown. The Ilam, Ontu, Kanyan and Mai Valley teas are the best Nepali brands, but they are not cheap. Expect to pay anything from Rs 600 (in Ilam) to Rs 3000 (in Thamel) per kilogram for good Ilam tea, which is not much cheaper than Darjeeling tea. The excellently named 'super fine tipi golden flower orange pekoe' tea is about as good as it gets. Connoisseurs choose the first (March) or second (May) flush, rather than the substandard monsoon flush. Lemon tea flavoured with lemongrass is another favourite (Rs 150 per 100g).

Thangkas

Thangkas are Tibetan Buddhist paintings that depict fierce protector deities, aspects of the Buddha, various Bodhisattvas, historical figures, a mandala (geometric design) or the wheel of life.

Although there are some genuine antique thangkas to be found, it's highly unlikely that anything offered to the average visitor will date from much beyond last week. Judicious use of a smoky fire can add the odd century in no time at all. Thangkas do vary considerably in quality but buy one because you like it, not as a valuable investment.

Thangkas are available in Kathmandu's Thamel, Durbar Marg and Durbar Sq areas, as well as the Tibetan shops around Bodhnath. Like many other crafts, the more you see the more you will appreciate the difference between those of average and those of superior quality. Traditionally thangkas are framed in silk brocade.

Tibetan Carpets

Carpet weaving is a major trade in Nepal. The skill was brought by Tibetan refugees who have transplanted the craft with great success into their new home. Some of their output is now exported to Tibet, where the skills have largely been lost. A genuine Tibetan carpet purchased in Tibet is probably indeed made by Tibetans, but in Nepal the Tamang people also make carpets.

Jawlakhel, on the southern outskirts of Patan, is the carpet-weaving centre in the valley. The traditional size for a Tibetan carpet is 1.8m by 90cm. Small square carpets are often used to make seat cushions.

Carpet quality depends on knots per inch, and the price is worked out per square metre. A 60-knot carpet costs around Rs 1700 per sq metre, while a 100-knot carpet is Rs 4800 per sq metre.

SOLO TRAVELLERS

Kathmandu, Pokhara and trekking lodges everywhere are supersociable places and it's not hard for solo travellers to hook up with other travellers.

Most hotels have different rates for single and double occupancy but the 'single room' may be much smaller than the double. The best deal is to get a double room for a single price.

Organised treks may charge a single supplement if you don't want to share a tent or room, though most other organised adventure activities don't have any such penalties.

TAX

There is a 13% value added tax (VAT) on most purchases. It is possible to get this VAT refunded but it's an ordeal and is probably only relevant if you've bought something like electrical equipment. You need to have spent more than Rs 15,000 in stores that display refund stickers, have bought products less than 60 days before departure, have

been in the country less than 183 days, and depart Kathmandu by air. Each individual receipt must be for more than Rs 1500.

You must complete an application form at the store where you make the purchase and get two copies of the form stamped by customs officers before you check in for your flight. Take two copies of the form, along with photocopies of the photo and visa pages of your passport, to the Rastriya Barijya Bank desk after immigration. You should then get the 13% tax refunded, minus Rs 500 commission. Then you'll have to change those rupees into dollars, losing another commission.

TELEPHONE

The phone system works well, and making local, STD and international calls is easy. Reverse-charge (collect) calls can only be made to the UK, USA, Canada and Japan.

The cheapest and most convenient way to make calls is through one of the hundreds of private call centres that have sprung up across the country. Look for signs advertising STD/ISD services. It's only worth using the government telegraph offices if you need to make a call in the middle of the night when other places are closed. Many hotels offer international direct-dial facilities but always check their charges before making a call.

Private call centres charge around Rs 40 per minute to most countries.

Internet phone calls are cheaper, costing Rs 10 to 20 per minute (calls to mobile phones are often more expensive), but these are available only in Kathmandu and Pokhara. There is some delay (echo) in the line when making Internet calls, but it is generally fine for most purposes.

Local phone calls cost Rs 5 for two minutes, or Rs 5 per minute if calling a local mobile phone.

Mobile Phones

The mobile network in Nepal is spotty and not very reliable. The Nepali government cuts mobile service during times of political tension (activists coordinate demonstrations through text messaging). Even when the network is up, connections are often awful.

Nepal Telecom (www.ntc.net.np) uses the GSM system and has roaming agreements with some companies, such as Vodafone and BT Cellnet. Getting a prepaid SIM card in Nepal is possible but is a laborious process.

DIRECTORY

TIME

Nepal is five hours and 45 minutes ahead of GMT; this curious time differential is intended to make it very clear that Nepal is a separate place to India, where the time is five hours and 30 minutes ahead of GMT! There is no daylight-saving time in Nepal. See the World Time Zones map on p418.

When it's noon in Nepal it's 1.15am in New York, 6.15am in London, 1.15pm in Bangkok, 2.15pm in Tibet, 4.15pm in Sydney and 10.15pm the previous day in Los Angeles, not allowing for daylight saving or other local variations.

TOILETS

Throughout the country, the 'squat toilet' is the norm, except in hotels and guesthouses geared towards tourists. Next to the toilet (*charpi* in Nepali) is a bucket and/or tap, which has a two-fold function: flushing the toilet and cleaning the nether regions (with the left hand only) while still squatting over the toilet. More rustic toilets in rural areas may simply consist of a few planks precariously positioned over a pit in the ground.

TOURIST INFORMATION

The **Nepal Tourism Board** (☎ 01-4256909, 24hr tourism hotline ☎ 4225709; www.welcomenepal.com) operates an office in Kathmandu's Tribhuvan Airport and a more substantial office at the Tourist Service Centre in central Kathmandu (see p114), both of which have brochures and maps.

The other tourist offices in Pokhara, Bhairawa, Birganj, Janakpur and Kakarbhitta are virtually useless unless you have a specific inquiry.

VISAS

All foreigners, except Indians, must have a visa. Nepali embassies and consulates overseas issue visas with no fuss. You can also get one on the spot when you arrive in Nepal, either at Kathmandu's Tribhuvan Airport or at road borders: Nepalganj, Birganj/Raxaul Bazaar, Sunauli, Kakarbhitta, Mahendranagar, Dhangadhi and even the funky Kodari checkpoint on the road to Tibet.

A Nepali visa is valid for entry for three to six months from the date of issue. Children under 10 require a visa but are not charged a visa fee. Your passport must have at least six months validity. Indian nationals do not require a visa. Citizen of South Asian countries and China need visas but these are free.

You can download a visa application form from the websites of the Nepali embassy in Washington, DC (www.nepalembassyusa .org) or London (www.nepembassy.org.uk).

To obtain a visa on arrival by air in Nepal you must fill in an application form and provide a passport photograph. Visa application forms are available on a table in the arrivals hall, though some airlines (like Thai) provide this form on the flight. To get a jump on the immigration queue, you can download the visa-on-arrival form from www.treks.com.np/visa. A single-entry visa valid for 60 days costs US$30. At Kathmandu's Tribhuvan Airport the fee is payable in any major currency but at land borders officials will probably require payment in cash US dollars; bring small bills. Only single-entry visas are routinely available on arrival, though you may be able to score a multiple-entry visa if you ask.

If you have already visited Nepal during the same calendar year the visa fee is the same but you'll only get a 30-day visa. Much of the time you spend in the visa-on-arrival queue is waiting while officers scour your passport for previous entry stamps. It's worth knowing that if you stayed longer than 15 days in Nepal and are planning a second visit within the same calendar year, your second 30-day visa should be free.

At Nepali embassies abroad it's possible to get a multiple-entry visa (US$80 or equivalent), which gives you multiple trips into Nepal for a year, with each stay valid for 60 days, up to a total of 150 days in any calendar year. Multiple-entry visas are useful if you are planning a side trip to Tibet, Bhutan or India. You can change your single-entry visa to a multiple-entry visa at Kathmandu's Central Immigration Office for US$50.

If you are just planning a lightning visit to Kathmandu it's possible to get a free non-extendable three-day transit visa at Kathmandu airport, as long as you have an air ticket out of the country within three days.

If you stay in Nepal for longer than the duration of your initial 60-day visa, you will require a visa extension (see opposite). Transit visas are nonextendable.

Don't overstay a visa. You can pay a fine of US$2 per day at the airport if you have overstayed less than 30 days (plus in theory US$3 per day between 30 and 90 days and US$5 per day for over 90 days). If you've overstayed more than a week get it all sorted out at Kathmandu's Central Immigration Office *before* you get to the airport, as a delay could cause you to miss your flight.

It's a good idea to keep a number of passport photos with your passport so they are immediately handy for trekking permits, visa applications and other official documents.

Visa Extensions

Visa extensions are available from immigration offices in Kathmandu and Pokhara only and cost US$30 (payable in rupees) for a 30-day extension. You get a 30-day extension whether you are staying for an extra day or an extra 30 days. A multiple-entry visa extension costs US$80.

Every visa extension requires your passport, money, photos and an application form. Collect all these before you join the queue. Plenty of places in Kathmandu and Pokhara will make passport photos for you and there are several pricier instant-photo shops near the immigration offices.

Visa extensions are available the same day, sometimes within the hour. For a fee, trekking and travel agencies can assist with the visa extension process and can usually save you the time and tedium of queuing.

You can extend your visa up to a total stay of 120 days without undue formality. You should be able to get a further 30 days extension but you may need to show a flight ticket proving that you are leaving the country during that time period, since you are only allowed to stay in Nepal for a total of 150 days in a calendar year on a tourist visa.

You can get up-to-date visa information at the website of the **Department of Immigration** (www.immi.gov.np). See the Kathmandu (p112) and Pokhara (p249) sections for more details

WOMEN TRAVELLERS

Generally speaking, Nepal is a safe country for women travellers. However, women should still be cautious. Nepali men may have peculiar ideas about the morality of Western women, given Nepali men's exposure to Western films portraying 'immodest' clothing and holiday flings with locals. Dress modestly, which means wearing clothes that cover the shoulders and thighs – take your cue from the local people if you need to gauge what's acceptable. Several women have written to say that a long skirt is very useful for impromptu toilet trips, especially when trekking.

Sexual harassment is low-key but does exist. Trekking guides have been known to take advantage of their position of trust and responsibility and some lone women trekkers who hire a guide have had to put up with repeated sexual pestering – see p361 for more on this. The best advice is never to travel off the beaten track, nor to hike or trek alone with a local guide. The Chhetri Sisters trekking agency in Pokhara is run by women and specialises in providing women staff for treks (see p325 for contact details).

The best chance of making contact with local women is to go trekking, as it is really only here that Nepali women have a role that brings them into contact with foreign tourists – as often as not, the man of the house is a trekking guide or porter, or is away working elsewhere, which leaves women running the lodges and the many teahouses along the routes.

WORK

For Western visitors, finding work in Nepal is very difficult, though not impossible. The easiest work to find is teaching English, as there are many private schools and a great demand for English-language lessons. However, at less than US$100 a month the pay is very low. Other faint possibilities include work with airline offices, travel and trekking agencies, consultants or aid groups.

Officially you need a work (nontourist) visa if you intend to find employment (even unpaid) in Nepal and you should arrange this before you arrive in the country. Changing from a tourist visa once you are in the country is rarely permissible. The work permit has to be applied for by your employer and you are required to leave the country while the paperwork is negotiated. The process can take months and many people don't bother.

For information on volunteer opportunities in Nepal see p64.

Transport

CONTENTS

THINGS CHANGE

The information in this chapter is particularly vulnerable to change: prices for international travel are volatile, routes change, special deals come and go, and rules and visa requirements are amended. You should check carefully to make sure you understand how a fare (and ticket you may buy) works and be aware of the security requirements for international travel.

The upshot of this is that you should get opinions, quotes and advice from as many airlines and travel agencies as possible before you part with your hard-earned cash. The details given in this chapter should be regarded as pointers and are not a substitute for your own careful, up-to-date research.

GETTING THERE & AWAY

ENTERING THE COUNTRY

Nepal is a traveller-friendly country and arrival is straightforward. All entry points to Nepal offer visas on arrival and money exchange.

Flights, tours and railway tickets can be booked online at www.lonelyplanet.com /travel_services.

AIR

In the last couple of years international air connections to Nepal have withered, so don't expect a great deal of choice of routes or heavily discounted fares.

Airports & Airlines
AIRPORTS

Kathmandu is the site of Nepal's only international airport, **Tribhuvan Airport** (☎ 4472 256). The international terminal is a modern building but security measures are a little bit lax.

Bhairahawa airport is being upgraded to become Lumbini International Airport in 2008.

Arrival & Departure

When you arrive, just before immigration, there is a bank that's open for flight arrivals and has decent exchange rates. Next door is the visa counter where you pay for your visa if you haven't got one already (see p374). There is a hotel reservation counter as soon as you get out of customs at the airport.

When departing for an international flight check in at least two hours early, preferably three in the high season, as the check-in desks can be a bit of a scrum. You need to show your ticket as you enter the departure hall, where all baggage is X-rayed and tagged. The X-ray machines that screen cargo baggage are not film safe, so insist that the security officers physically inspect your film.

You pay your departure tax at the airport branch of Nabil Bank. It is possible to re-exchange Nepali rupees into US dollars at the Nabil Bank, if you have your unused foreign-exchange encashment receipts; commission is Rs 50, or 2%. Also here is a sporadically open post office and telephone office.

After immigration there's a VAT refund booth (see p373) and a café, where you can blow your last rupees. Next comes another X-ray and a manual inspection of luggage, before everyone crams into a hall far too small for the purpose.

AIRLINES

The airline offices listed in this section are all in Kathmandu (☎ 01).

DEPARTURE TAX

When leaving Kathmandu by air, an international departure tax of Rs 1695 is payable in Nepali rupees at the Nabil Bank in the departures terminal. The tax is Rs 1356 if you are flying to South Asian Area Regional Cooperation (SAARC) countries (ie India, Pakistan, Bhutan or Bangladesh). This includes a 'Tourism Service Fee' of Rs 565. There's no departure tax if you leave Nepal overland.

When you buy an air ticket in Kathmandu you will probably be quoted a fare without tax, insurance surcharge and, recently, a fuel surcharge, which can add on US$30 to an international ticket. International fares quoted in this section include these taxes.

The notoriously unreliable **Royal Nepal Airlines Corporation** (RNAC; code RA; Map p116; ☎ 4220 757, 4248614; www.royalnepal-airlines.com; Kantipath) has a limited number of international services, currently to Hong Kong, Delhi, Bangkok, Shanghai, Kuala Lumpur, Singapore, Dubai, Bangalore and Mumbai (Bombay), but nothing to Europe. A chronic lack of aircraft means that even these skeleton services are frequently subject to delays and cancellations. It is worth flying with any airline other than RNAC if at all possible, and in fact only a limited number of travel agencies abroad will book RNAC flights. When King Gyanendra embarked on a tour of Africa in 2005, half of Royal Nepal's international flights were cancelled at short notice!

Air Nepal International (code SZ; Map p116; ☎ 2050 678; www.airnepalinternational.com; Kamaladi) is a new (2005) private airline with one lonely jet that flies to Bangkok, Dubai, Doha and Kuala Lumpur, with plans to extend operations to Bangalore, Mumbai, Kolkata (Calcutta) and New Delhi.

Cosmic Air (code F5; Map p115; ☎ 4215771, 4468321; www.cosmicair.com) is a domestic airline that has international services to Delhi, Dhaka, Kolkata and Varanasi, with plans to extend services to Rangoon, Colombo, Bangalore and Mumbai. Flights were suspended briefly in 2005.

The following airlines currently fly into Kathmandu.

Air China (code CA; Map p116; ☎ 4440650; www.airchina.com) Hub Beijing.

Air Sahara (code S2; Map p115; ☎ 4262121; www.airsahara.net) Hub New Delhi.

Biman Bangladesh Airlines (code BG; Map p116; ☎ 4434740; www.bimanair.com; Lazimpat) Hub Dhaka.

Druk Air (code KB; Map p116; ☎ 4239988, fax 4239658; www.drukair.com.bt) Hub Paro airport.

Gulf Air (code GF; Map p116; ☎ 4435322; www.gulfairco.com) Hubs Dubai and Bahrain and Dammam; be warned – this office gets incredibly busy.

Indian Airlines (code IC; Map p116; ☎ 4410906; www.indian-airlines.in) Hub New Delhi.

Jet Airways (code 9W; Map p115; ☎ 4222121; www.jetairways.com) Hub New Delhi.

Pakistan International Airways (PIA; code PK; Map p116; ☎ 4439234; www.piac.com.pk) Hub Karachi.

Qatar Airways (code QR; Map p115; ☎ 2556579, 4256579; www.qatarairways.com) Hub Doha.

Thai Airways International (code TG; Map p115; ☎ 4223565, 4224917; www.thaiair.com) Hub Bangkok. Other airlines that don't fly directly to Nepal but which offer popular routes to the region, and have offices in Kathmandu, include **British Airways** (☎ 4226611), **Cathay Pacific** (☎ 4246155) and **Austrian Airlines** (☎ 4223331). Most airline offices are closed Saturdays, though a few (including THAI) open between 10am and 2pm.

Tickets

There are limited flights into Kathmandu these days, and bargain fares are few and far between. You may find that the cheapest flights from Europe or the US east coast fly into New Delhi, to connect with final short flight to Kathmandu.

Likewise, though you may find Kathmandu as part of a round-the-world ticket, you'll most likely find it cheaper to go overland from Delhi or Kolkata (Calcutta).

From the west coast of North America or from Australasia, Bangkok is the usual

WHERE TO SIT

If you want to see the mountains as you fly into Kathmandu you must sit on the correct side of the aircraft. Flying in from the east – Bangkok, Kolkata (Calcutta), Hong Kong, or Yangon (Rangoon) – you want the right side (seat J on Thai Airways). Flying in from the west – New Delhi, Varanasi or the Gulf – you want the left side (A on Thai). Leaving Kathmandu, you want to sit on the opposite sides.

TRANSPORT

transfer point, although there are also flights to Kathmandu from Hong Kong. Thai Airways and RNAC share the popular Bangkok–Kathmandu route.

Many fares from Australia or the western USA allow stopovers in Bangkok or the hub airport of the main airline (eg Hong Kong for Cathay Pacific). This effectively allows you a multicountry trip to southeast Asia at no additional cost.

Asia

Flights from Kathmandu to Asian destinations include Bangkok (US$240), Dhaka (US$90), Karachi (US$195), Hong Kong (US$353), Lhasa (US$295), Kuala Lumpur (US$260),Dubai (US$253), Osaka (US$618) and Shanghai (US$368).

There are also some interesting through fares; one to consider is with Biman Bangladesh Airlines, whose Kathmandu–Dhaka–Yangon–Bangkok ticket sells for US$380 one way and allows a stop in Yangon and (mandatory) Dhaka. Biman should put you up in a hotel for one night in Dhaka – all other costs are left to you. The Dhaka–Yangon–Bangkok leg runs just once a week.

Thai Airways' Kathmandu to Bangkok flight (US$240) is the most popular connection into and out of Nepal and can get booked up for weeks at a time, particularly mid-December to January. Make your booking as far in advance as possible. Bangkok–Kathmandu tickets are generally cheaper bought in Bangkok.

Air Nepal International is currently offering flights to Bangkok for US$200 each way, twice a week. Royal Nepal costs US$238 and gets you into Bangkok early enough to make a same day connection (whereas the afternoon Thai Airways flight necessitates an overnight stay).

Biman Bangladesh and Cosmic Air operate flights to Dhaka. PIA flies to Karachi three times a week.

Air China has three weekly flights to Lhasa and on to Chengdu (US$320). Foreigners are not allowed to buy a Lhasa ticket without a tour package (see p381) but can buy tickets to Chengdu and on to other Chinese cities like Beijing (US$382) and Shanghai (US$360). The Lhasa flights have traditionally stopped over the winter (November to March) but one flight a week is scheduled for winter 2006/7.

Australia & New Zealand

Fares from Australia depend on the season and typically cost around A$1500 return. Bangkok is the most popular transit point because it links with the reliable Thai Airways flight, although you can also fly via Hong Kong or Kuala Lumpur.

From Kathmandu to east coast Australia, the cheapest one-way ticket at time of research cost US$480 with Cathay Pacific. Thai Airways and Singapore Airlines are more expensive.

Return flight to Kathmandu from Auckland New Zealand start from around NZ$1980.

Agencies in Australia include **Flight Centre** (☎ 133 133; www.flightcentre.com.au), **STA Travel** (☎ 1300 733 035; www.statravel.com.au) and **Trailfinders** (☎ 1300 780 212; www.trailfinders.com.au).

Agencies in New Zealand include **Flight Centre** (☎ 0800 243 544; www.flightcentre.co.nz) and **STA Travel** (☎ 0508 782 872; www.statravel.co.nz).

Online agencies include www.travel.com.au and www.zuji.com.au.

Continental Europe

Austrian Airlines offers the only direct flight between Europe (Vienna) and Nepal, but you may find a cheaper fare with Gulf Air or Qatar Airways. Return airfares in high season start around €1000. One-way air fares from Kathmandu to most European destinations cost around US$560.

STA Travel (www.statravel.com) has branches in major cities across Germany and the rest of Europe.

OTU Voyages (☎ 0820 817 817; www.otu.fr), **Voyageurs du Monde** (☎ 01 42 86 16 00; www.vdm.com) and **Nouvelles Frontières** (☎ 0825 000 747; www.nouvelles-frontieres.fr) all have branches across France.

In Italy try **CTS Viaggi** (☎ 06-462 0431; www.cts.it). In Spain try **Barcelo Viajes** (☎ 902-116226; www.barceloviajes.com). **Just Travel** (☎ 089-7473330; www.justtravel.de) is an English-speaking agency in Munich.

Online European agencies include www.anyway.fr, www.odysia.fr, www.airfair.nl, www.travelchannel.de and the various country sites of www.lastminute.com and www.expedia.com.

India

The main routes between India and Nepal are operated by RNAC, Indian Airlines, Jet

Airways, Cosmic Air and Air Sahara. The first three give a 25% discount to anyone under 30 on flights between Kathmandu and India; no student card is needed.

Fierce competition on the Kathmandu–Delhi route means that at time of research normal fares of US$160 had dropped as low as US$80 with Druk Air (three weekly), or US$100 with Air Sahara.

Other cities in India with direct connections to Kathmandu are Kolkata (US$120), Bangalore (US$233) and Mumbai (US$228 with RNAC). Cosmic Air flies thrice-weekly to Varanasi (US$135).

RNAC has offices in Bangalore (☎ 80-5597878), Delhi (☎ 11-23321572) and Mumbai (☎ 22-22836197), among others.

UK & Ireland
London to Kathmandu costs from £550 to around £650 return in the high season, generally with Gulf Air (via Abu Dhabi) or Qatar Airways (via Doha). Austrian Airways often has cheapish fares via Vienna and New Delhi. The cheapest option is generally to fly to New Delhi and travel overland (train and bus) from there.

From Kathmandu a one-way fare to London costs around US$600 with Gulf Air or Qatar Airways. Try **STA Travel** (☎ 0870-1600 599; www.statravel.co.uk), **Trailfinders** (☎ 0845-058 5858; www.trailfinders.com) or **North-South Travel** (☎ 01245-608291; www.northsouthtravel.co.uk).

Online travel agencies include www.lastminute.com, www.cheaptickets.co.uk and www.expedia.co.uk.

USA & Canada
Intense competition between Asian airlines on the US west coast and Vancouver has resulted in ticket discounting to Bangkok, on top of which you can add on a few hundred dollars to Kathmandu.

Fares to Kathmandu will often be about the same from the east coast (via Europe) or west coast (via Asia) – it's about as far away as you can get in either direction! Multiple connections can make for some mammoth trips, especially as most connections to Kathmandu involve a layover.

From New York the cheapest connection is with Aeroflot to New Delhi via Moscow and then RNAC to Kathmandu.

From the west coast the cheapest flights go to Bangkok via Tokyo (Northwest), Seoul (Asiana), Taipei (China Airlines or Eva Air) or Singapore, overnighting in Bangkok, at your expense, to catch a flight the next day with Thai Airways.

The cheapest return fares start around US$1400. At time of research Cathay Pacific was offering good deals, with the advantage of quality connecting airlines (Thai Airways) and no stopover on the way out.

From Kathmandu, a one-way ticket with Cathay Pacific cost US$511/560 to Los Angeles/New York, or US$584 to Vancouver. Thai Airways and Northwest offer pricier alternatives.

Note that if you have more than three connecting flights you may have problems fitting all these flight details onto your baggage labels and may have to re-check your luggage en route – a real pain.

The *New York Times*, the *Chicago Tribune*, the *LA Times* and the *San Francisco Examiner* all produce weekly travel sections in which you'll find any number of travel-agency ads.

Agencies include **STA Travel** (☎ 800-781 4040; www.statravel.com; 24 hrs), a student specialist with offices throughout the US, and **Travel CUTS** (☎ 1-866-416-2887; www.travelcuts.com), Canada's national student travel agency, with offices in major cities

Specialist Nepal operators like **Third Eye Travel** (☎ 1-800-456-393; www.thirdeyetravel.com) know the best offers and connections and often offer the best deals. Specialist Asia agencies such as **Angel Travel** (☎ 1-800-922 1092; www.angeltravel.com) and **USA Asia** (☎ 1-800-8722742; http://usaasiatravel.com) also book flights to Nepal.

Online booking agencies include **Cheap Tickets** (www.cheaptickets.com), **Orbitz** (www.orbitz .com), **Expedia** (www.expedia.com, www.expedia.ca) and **Travelocity** (www.travelocity.com, www.travelocity.ca).

LAND
Political and weather conditions permitting, there are six main entry points into Nepal by land: five from India, one from Tibet. There are no international bus or train services; everyone changes buses at the borders.

Bring Your Own Vehicle
A steady trickle of people drive their own vehicles overland from Europe, for which an international carnet is required. If you

want to abandon your transport in Nepal, you must either pay a prohibitive import duty or surrender it to customs. It is not possible to import cars more than five years old. Make sure you bring an international driving permit.

India

All of the land borders between India and Nepal are in the Terai. The most popular crossing point is Sunauli, near Bhairawa, which provides easy access to Delhi and Varanasi in India.

Border crossing (Nepal to India)	Page
Belahiya to Sunauli, for Varanasi, Agra and Delhi	p289
Mahendranagar to Banbassa, for Delhi and hill towns in Uttaranchal	p310
Kakarbhitta to Panitanki, for Darjeeling, Sikkim and Kolkata	p321
Birganj to Raxaul Bazar, for Patna and Kolkata	p302
Nepalganj to Jamunaha, for Lucknow	p306

SUNAULI/BHAIRAWA

The crossing at Sunauli is by far the most popular route between India and Nepal and it's also the easiest route from Delhi or Varanasi (see p290 for more information). There are direct buses from Delhi to Sunauli (Rs 405, 24 hours) but many people prefer to do as much of the journey as possible by train – several trains run daily from Delhi to Gorakhpur (22 hours), where you can pick up a bus to Sunauli (Rs 50, three hours). Varanasi also has direct buses to Sunauli (Rs 150, 10 hours).

Once you cross the border, day and night buses run regularly to Kathmandu (day/night Rs 230/280, eight hours) and Pokhara (Rs 230/270, eight hours). A more comfortable option to Kathmandu is the air-con service operated by Golden Travels (see p291), changing buses in Kalanki.

MAHENDRANAGAR

The crossing at Mahendranagar is also used by travellers coming from Delhi, see p311 for more information. There are daily buses from Delhi's Anand Vihar bus stand to Banbassa, the nearest Indian village to the border (INRs 156, 10 hours). Banbassa is also connected by bus with most towns in Uttaranchal, as well as Agra and Dharamsala. Slow and inconvenient trains run

as far as Barielly, about three hours from the border by bus.

From Mahendranagar, there are slow direct bus services to Kathmandu (Rs 735, 16 hours) but it's better to do the trip in daylight and break the journey at Royal Bardia National Park, Nepalganj, Butwal or Narayangarh. Note that this route is often blocked during the monsoon. Maoists are active throughout western Nepal – check the security situation before you travel.

KAKARBHITTA

At the eastern end of Nepal, Kakarbhitta is the closest border crossing to Darjeeling and Sikkim, and trains from Kolkata to northeast India stop close to the border at Siliguri, see p322 for more information. Travel agencies in Kathmandu and Darjeeling offer 'through buses' across the border, but these involve a change in Siliguri and Kakarbhitta, It's just as easy to do the journey in stages, which will also allow you to refresh your batteries with an overnight stop along the way.

From Darjeeling, take a morning bus/jeep to Siliguri (INRs 60/70, two hours) then a bus (INRs 15, one hour) to Panitanki on the Indian side of the border. If cross-border traffic is busy, jeeps sometimes go straight to the border from Darjeeling. Jeeps also run to the border from Kalimpong (Rs 90, three hours) and from Gangtok (Rs 140, 4½ hours), in Sikkim. Coming from Kolkata, you can take an overnight train to Siliguri, then a bus to the border.

From Kakarbhitta, there are day/night buses to Kathmandu (Rs 530/607, 17 hours) but it's more interesting to break the journey at Janakpur, the centre of Mithila culture in Nepal. However, there is Maoist activity in eastern Nepal so you should check things are calm before you travel.

BIRGANJ/RAXAUL BAZAAR

The border crossing from Birganj to Raxaul Bazar is handy for Patna (in India's Bihar province) and you can also get here easily by train from Kolkata. Buses run from the bus station in Patna straight to Raxaul Bazaar (INRs 90, five hours). From Kolkata, you can take the daily Mithila Express – it leaves Kolkata's Howrah station at 4pm, arriving into Raxaul at 9.10am the next morning (INRs 276/748/1165 in sleeper class/air-con 3-tier/air-con 2-tier).

From Birganj, there are regular day/night buses to Kathmandu (Rs 225/280, eight hours) and Pokhara (Rs 225/270, seven hours). All buses pass through Narayangarh, where you can change for Royal Chitwan National Park.

NEPALGANJ
Few people use the crossing at Nepalganj in western Nepal, see p307 for more information. The nearest town in India is Lucknow, where you can pick up slow buses to the border at Jamunaha (INRs 160, seven hours). You might also consider taking a train to Nanpara, 17km from the border.

Over the border in Nepalganj, there are regular day/night buses to Kathmandu (Rs 450/540, 12 hours) and Pokhara (Rs 400/520, 12 hours), passing close to Royal Chitwan National Park. As always, you should check the security situation before crossing at Nepalganj.

Tibet
The bad news is that, officially, only organised 'groups' are allowed into Tibet. The good news is that travel agencies in Kathmandu assemble overland groups to get you into Tibet. Depending on the ever-changing regulations you should then be able to continue on in China (but currently not Tibet) as an independent traveller.

This is not an easy trip by any means. Altitude sickness is a real danger as the maximum altitude along the road is 5140m and budget overland tours do not allow sufficient time to safely acclimatise. The road is often temporarily closed by landslides during the monsoon months (May to August). Political protests, sensitive political dates and political meetings inside Tibet or China are often followed or preceded by additional restrictions on visitors to the region (particularly from mid-September to mid-October).

The bottom line is that if you intend to enter or leave Nepal via Tibet you should come prepared with alternative plans in case travel along this route proves impossible.

In general, travellers face far fewer restrictions entering Tibet through China, so if you are flexible with your plans it makes

---

TICKET PACKAGES TO & FROM INDIA

Some private Indian companies make bus and train bookings all the way through to Kathmandu and Pokhara, including basic accommodation at Sunauli, but many travellers have complained about these services. The package usually involves coordination between at least three different companies, so the potential for an honest cock-up is at least as high as the potential for a deliberate rip-off. In general, if you organise things yourself as you go, it will be cheaper, and you will have more flexibility, including a choice of bus and accommodation within Nepal.

Note that everyone has to change buses at the border whether they book a through ticket or not and, despite claims to the contrary, there are no 'tourist' buses on either side of the border.

Leaving Nepal, the most reliable Nepali company handling through tickets is **Wayfarers** (Map p136; ☎ 4266010; www.wayfarers.com.np) in Thamel, Kathmandu. It requires a minimum of a week to arrange tickets.

Buses through to Varanasi cost around Rs 900 and involve an overnight in Sunauli and then a 10-hour bus ride from the border to Varanasi. Bus-and-train packages to Agra cost Rs 2300/3425 for three-tier/two-tier air-con, or Rs 1275 in a 2nd-class sleeper. Bus and train to Delhi costs Rs 2700/3875 for three-tier/two-tier air-con, or Rs 1475 in a 2nd-class sleeper. For train connections you spend a night in Sunauli, take a morning bus to Gorakhpur (three hours) and then a lunchtime train to Agra (18 hours) or Delhi (22 hours).

These prices are significantly more expensive than buying the tickets as you go, but they do give you confirmed bookings and peace of mind.

It is worth considering making advance bookings on the Indian railways if you are in a hurry or are fussy over which class you want. Some trains, and especially sleeping compartments, can be heavily booked (this is apparently the case for Gorakhpur to Delhi trains). Make sure you get a receipt clearly specifying what you think you have paid for, and hang on to it. For schedules check out www.indianrail.gov.in. For information on booking tickets online see www.irctc.co.in and www.seat61.com/India.htm.

a lot more sense to visit Nepal after a trip through Tibet, not after.

Bear in mind that travel restrictions in Tibet are always in flux and may even be scrapped altogether in the near future.

See p233 for information on getting from the Nepali border town of Kodari to the capital, Kathmandu.

Organised trekking groups only are also allowed to trek from Simikot in far western Nepal to Purang in far western Tibet, and then on to Mt Kailash. For details see Lonely Planet's *Trekking in the Himalaya*.

TRAVEL RESTRICTIONS
At the time of research you can't cross the Chinese border into Tibet without a Tibet Tourism Permit, which can only be arranged through a travel agency when you book a package tour to Lhasa. If you turn up at the border at Kodari with just a Chinese visa you'll be turned away. Air China won't sell you an air ticket to Lhasa without a Tibet Tourism Bureau (TTB) permit.

At the time of research, when people booked this tour they were put on a group visa and any existing Chinese visas in their passports were cancelled. Splitting from this group visa in Lhasa is almost impossible but it is apparently allowed if you fly out of Tibet to Chengdu, making onward independent travel through China possible.

TOUR OPTIONS
A variety of options are currently available in Kathmandu. The quickest way to get into Tibet is to buy a fly-in package to Lhasa from Kathmandu. Depending on the political climate in Tibet, agencies can sometimes offer a one-way flight (US$285) with a visa and permits (US$68) and airport transfers (US$110). At times of political sensitivity you may have to book a pricier tour and a return flight, though you might be able to cancel the return leg in Lhasa.

Several agencies offer fixed-departure (generally Saturdays), overland trips to Lhasa, via Nyalam, Lhatse, Shigatse and Gyantse. The cheapest is a seven-day, one-way, overland trip, currently around US$400 plus US$68 in permit and visa fees, which covers transport by Land Cruiser, accommodation and sightseeing. Dormitory accommodation is provided for the first three nights, then on a twin-sharing basis in en suite rooms.

Packages that include Mt Everest Base Camp (from the Tibetan side) are pricier at US$550 and harder to find. Some agencies also run return trips to Mt Kailash from Kathmandu (from US$1600). Rates are slightly higher in the peak season months of July, August and September and start to dry up by December.

The agency will need one week to get your visa and permits. You will probably get between 12 and 15 days on your group visa so can stay in Lhasa for up to a week after the tour.

Before handing over the cash, ascertain whether you are required to share a room, and how many people will travel in each Land Cruiser (often five, plus a driver and sometimes a guide, which is a real squeeze). Note that agencies may pool customers if numbers are low. Travellers have complained that their promised Land Cruiser turned out to be a dilapidated bus (travel to the Tibet border is always in a minibus), or that the agreed bus wasn't available and that they had to pay an extra US$50 or more per person for a Land Cruiser.

The following agencies in Kathmandu (☎ 01) operate trips to Tibet. Most agencies advertising in Thamel are agents only; they don't actually run the trips.

Ecotrek (Map p136; ☎ 4424112; www.ecotrek.com.np, www.kailashtour.com; Thamel)

Explore Nepal Richa Tours & Travel (Map p136; ☎ 4423064; www.explorenepalricha.com; 2nd fl, Namche Bazaar Bldg, Tri Devi Marg, Thamel)

Green Hill Tours (Map p136; ☎ 4700968; ghill@wlink .com.np; www.greenhilltours.com.np; Thamel)

Royal Mount Trekking (Map p115; ☎ 4241452; www .royal-mt-trekking.com, www.royaltibet.com; Durbar Marg)

Tashi Delek Nepal Treks & Expeditions (Map p136; ☎ 4410746; tashidele@wlink.com.np; Thamel)

Other travel companies in Thamel offering customised tours to Tibet include **Adventure Silk Road** (www.silkroadgroup.com), **Dharma Adventures** (www.dharmaadventures.com), **Earthbound Expeditions** (www.trektibet.com), **Explore Himalaya** (www.tibet-adventures.com, www.explorehimalaya.com) and **Tibet Travels** (www.tibettravels.com), though there are many more.

BUS
In 2005 Nepal's state bus company Sahja Yatayat started a weekly direct bus service

between Kathmandu and Lhasa. The service costs US$70 per person, plus US$60 for three nights accommodation and a service fee. Foreigners currently aren't allowed to take the bus due to Chinese visa and permit hassles, but this could change.

GETTING AROUND

Getting around Nepal can be a challenging business. The impossible terrain and extreme weather conditions, plus a high level of disorganisation, mean that trips rarely go exactly according to plan. On the other hand, Nepali ingenuity will usually get you to your destination in the end. Although travel can be frustrating, it also creates memorable moments by the score. Good humour, patience and snacks are essential prerequisites.

The whole gamut of transport options is available in Nepal, from hot-air balloons to elephants. Walking is still the most important, and the most reliable, method of getting from A to B and for moving cargo; more is carried by people in Nepal than by every other form of transport combined.

One of the major considerations when using any form of public transport is to avoid travelling during festival times (for details see p363), especially major ones such as Dasain and Tihar (Diwali). Buses and planes are booked solid, and forget flying if you haven't booked well in advance.

AIR

Nepal has a fairly extensive domestic air network, served by half a dozen airlines, though only the flights to Pokhara, Meghauli (for Chitwan), Lukla and Jomsom are much used by foreigners.

Residents and Nepali citizens pay approximately 35% of the tourist price for domestic air fares. Airlines will accept payment from visitors only in hard currency. See the Nepal Air Fares chart (p383) for details.

All travellers are charged an insurance surcharge of US$2 per leg. Air fares quoted in this book include this surcharge. At the time of research there was also a temporary fuel surcharge of between US$5 and US$9 per flight, which will continue as long as global fuel prices remain high.

The domestic terminal is the old Kathmandu airport, and its age shows. It can be a chaotic spot, particularly when flights are cancelled and crowds of stressed tourists generate an escalating atmosphere of fear and loathing.

Check in an hour early for domestic flights. Don't carry pocketknives, gas cigarette lighters, matches or even trekking poles in your carry-on luggage on any domestic flights. There is a Rs 170 domestic airport tax payable at check-in.

Airlines in Nepal

A number of private companies operate alongside the long-running, government-owned and chronically inefficient Royal

TRANSPORT

TRANSPORT

Airlines Corporation (RNAC). These airlines operate largely on the popular (ie economically viable and tourist-oriented) routes, although government regulations require that airlines devote 40% of their capacity to nontourist routes. The prices for the private airlines are slightly more than RNAC (by around US$10 per sector), but they offer better service and are much more reliable.

Most flights operate out of Kathmandu, but there are minor air hubs at Pokhara, Nepalganj in the southwest and Biratnagar in the southeast.

RNAC operates by far the most comprehensive range of scheduled flights around Nepal, with flights to Bhojpur, Biratnagar, Dhangadhi, Dolpo, Jomsom, Kathmandu, Lamidanda, Lukla, Manang, Nepalganj, Phaplu, Pokhara, Rajbiraj, Ramechhap, Rumjatar, Simikot, Surkhet, Taplejung and Tumlingtar, among others.

Buddha Air (☎ 01-5542494; www.buddhaair.com) has fast, modern aircraft; the trip to Pokhara from Kathmandu takes just 20 minutes, compared with up to 40 minutes with RNAC. Buddha Air has daily flights servicing Kathmandu, Pokhara, Biratnagar, Bhadrapur, Bhairawa, Nepalganj and Janakpur.

Cosmic Air (☎ 01-4427150; www.cosmicair.com) services Kathmandu, Bharatpur, Jomsom, Pokhara, Bhairawa, Simara, Biratnagar, Nepalganj and Tumlingtar.

The Sherpa-owned **Yeti Airlines** (☎ 01-4421215; www.yetiairlines.com) is one of the best domestic airlines and flies to Kathmandu,

Pokhara, Lukla, Phaplu, Manang, Bhairawa, Bhadrapur, Bharatpur, Biratnagar, Meghauli, Simara (for Birganj), Nepalganj, plus flights to Dolpa and Simikot from Nepalganj, and Jumla and Rara from Surkhet. You can book flights online.

Other airlines include **Skyline Airways** (www.skyair.com.np), **Shangri-La Air** (☎ 4439693; www.shangrilaair.com.np), **Gorkha Airlines** (☎ 4435121; gorkha@mos.com.np) and **Sita Air** (☎ 4445012).

Some flights, such as Kathmandu to Lukla (the main airstrip in the Everest region), are used mainly by trekkers. There are multiple daily flights during the trekking season but these do fill up in October so make a reservation in advance through a travel agency in Kathmandu or direct with an airline website. Flights from Kathmandu to Jomsom and Lukla can be plagued by bad-weather cancellations and a backlog of frustrated travellers, though this isn't the problem it was a few years ago. For flights in and out of Jomsom, Cosmic Air is the one to choose (US$63 plus US$7 surcharges); for Lukla, Yeti Airlines (US$97).

Maoist activity can temporarily close domestic airports in remote parts of the country. Check the state of play before basing your plans around remote airports, especially in the far west.

Try to book domestic flights a week in advance and, just as for flights out of Nepal, the most important rule is to reconfirm and reconfirm again. Names can 'fall off' the passenger list, particularly when there is pressure for seats. This is much more of a problem with RNAC than with the private operators.

There's generally no charge to change the date of a domestic air ticket. Cancellation charges vary but are generally free more than a day or two before departure.

BICYCLE

In Kathmandu and Pokhara there are many bicycle-rental outlets and this is a cheap and convenient way of getting around, particularly around the Kathmandu Valley. Regular bicycles cost around Rs 100 per day to rent, an Indian or Chinese made mountain bike costs from Rs 200 and an imported foreign bike costs around Rs 700. Children's bicycles can also be hired.

See p80 for detailed information on cycling in Nepal.

MOUNTAIN FLIGHTS

Every morning during the clear dry-season months (October to April), all the major private airlines offer mountain flights, with panoramic dawn views of the Himalaya and commentary on the passing peaks. Each passenger on six- to 30-seat turbo props is guaranteed a window seat and a visit to the cockpit.

The hour-long flight from Kathmandu costs US$124 (fuel charge included). If the weather is clear the views are stunning. Purists recommend Buddha Air as its planes are more spacious and fly you closer to Everest itself.

BUS

Buses are the main form of public transport in Nepal and in relative terms they're incredibly cheap. Very often they're also incredibly uncomfortable. They run pretty much everywhere and will stop for anyone. You can jump on local buses anywhere, but you'll find it much easier to get a seat if you catch a bus at its source rather than in mid-run. For longer-distance buses it's best to book a couple of days in advance.

The government bus company, known as Sajha Yatayat, has distinctive blue-and-white buses that service all the main routes except the far east and far west. Although marginally cheaper than private buses, these buses are generally very shabby, poorly maintained and rarely run to schedule; overall they are best avoided.

On popular tourist runs such as the Kathmandu–Pokhara, Kathmandu–Sunauli and Kathmandu–Nagarkot runs, there are a number of higher-grade, higher-priced and sometimes air-conditioned tourist buses aimed at the tourist market.

There are literally dozens of private bus companies – it seems all you need is one bus and you've got yourself a company. The condition of the buses range from reasonably comfortable minibuses to lumbering dinosaurs held together by little more than bits of wire and the combined hopes of the passengers. As with the Sajha buses, there is a booking office in each town where you can buy tickets for long-distance routes in advance.

On the longer routes there are 'express' minibuses, scheduled both by day and night. Day travel is generally preferable because you get to see the countryside (and there are some spectacular roads) and it's considerably safer. Night travel often involves a stop somewhere en route for a couple of hours sleep.

At the bottom of the heap are the local buses that run shorter routes, carry people, their luggage and often animals, and seem to stop more than they go. Travelling by local bus is no fun and should be kept to a minimum, although to reach many of the trekking roadheads there is little alternative.

Long-distance bus travel has slowed down recently due to the large number of tedious checkpoints set up by the Nepali military to counter potential Maoist activity. These gen-

AIR-CONDITIONING OF THE GODS

Though we don't particularly recommend it, many people – both locals and Westerners – prefer to ride on bus roofs. While this is officially banned in the Kathmandu Valley, it is common elsewhere, particularly during Dasain when pressure for seats is greatest. The arguments in favour are that you get an exhilarating ride with great views, the opportunity to watch your bags and, sometimes, room to stretch your legs.

If you do ride on the roof, make sure you are well wedged in, so you don't catapult off when the bus swerves, brakes or lurches. It's also best to sit facing forwards – that way you can see low-hanging wires and branches before you get swatted. Make sure you have sunscreen and appropriate clothing too, as it can be surprisingly cold up there.

erally involve everyone getting off the bus and walking through a checkpoint. Tourists are normally exempt and can stay on the bus. A couple of these checks can severely delay a trip, especially when buses start to back up. See p311 for details on the problems of road travel in far western Nepal.

Bus travel in Nepal poses a significant risk of accident. It's uncommon to drive for more than an hour on any stretch of road without passing the burnt-out shell of a public bus crushed like tin foil into the canyon below. Travelling on an overnight bus trip is probably the most dangerous thing you can do in Nepal, and is certainly a bigger risk than that currently posed by the Maoists and even more dangerous than the bungee jump (only kidding on that one). You are more than 30 times more likely to die in a road accident in Nepal than in most developed countries.

During the course of researching this guide we passed ten fatal bus crashes in one ten-day period, which between them killed over 200 people. Tourist buses are generally safer than public buses but still the message is clear; keep bus travel to a minimum.

CAR & MOTORCYCLE
Hire

There are no drive-yourself rental cars available in Nepal, but you can easily hire cars with drivers, or just a taxi. Expect to pay between US$50 and US$60 per day, including fuel, which at the time of research was set at Rs 67 per litre across the country.

It is quite popular to hire cars for return trips to both Pokhara and Royal Chitwan National Park from Kathmandu. A car from Kathmandu to Pokhara will probably cost around US$70 one way, or US$60 to Chitwan. A day's sightseeing around the Kathmandu Valley costs between US$20 and US$35. Remember that you'll have to pay for the driver's return trip whether or not you yourself return, as well as his food and accommodation for overnight trips.

Motorcycles can be rented in Kathmandu and Pokhara for around Rs 400 to 450 per day. See p158 and p265 for details.

Insurance

If you are planning to drive a motorbike in Nepal you should double check to see if your insurance coverage will cover you, as it may be excluded under 'dangerous activities'.

Road Rules

If you do drive be aware that left turns are allowed without stopping, even at controlled intersections with red lights. Also, traffic entering a roundabout has priority over traffic already on the roundabout. Almost no-one in Nepal signals and will pull out into traffic whether or not anyone is coming.

Finally, our best advice is to trust nothing and nobody. Expect kids, chickens, ducks, women, old men, babies, cows, dogs and almost anything else that can move to jump in front of you at any moment, without any kind of warning. Good luck.

Tours

A few Nepali travel companies, such as **Himalayan Offroad** (☎ 4700770; www.himalayanoffroad.com), run motorbike tours of Nepal and may be able to help with queries.

Himalayan Enfielders (☎ 4440462; www.enfielders.tk; Israeli Embassy, Lazimpat, Kathmandu) is an enthusiasts' touring club and service centre for Enfield Bullets.

Most foreign tour companies such as **Asia-Bike-Tours** (www.asiabiketours.com), **Ferris Wheels** (www.ferriswheels.com.au) and **Himalayan Roadrunners** (www.ridehigh.com) have suspended motorbike tours of Nepal until the security situation improves.

LOCAL TRANSPORTATION
Autorickshaw & Cycle-Rickshaw

Cycle-rickshaws are common in the old part of Kathmandu and can be a good way of making short trips through the crowded and narrow streets. They are also the most common form of short-distance public transport in towns throughout the Terai. Prices are highly negotiable.

Nepal's noxious three-wheeled autorickshaws are being phased out everywhere, but a few are still hanging on in a couple of Terai towns.

Taxi

Larger towns such as Kathmandu and Pokhara have taxis which, between a group of people, can be a good way to explore the Kathmandu Valley. Metered taxis have black licence plates; private cars often operate as taxis, particularly on long-distance routes or for extended periods, and have red plates.

Taxi meters are sometimes out of date (at the time of research they were OK), in which case tourists will be hard pushed to convince drivers to use them (with or without a surcharge) and will almost certainly have to negotiate the fare in advance. You will always pay more for a negotiated fare than a metered fare.

Tempo

A tempo is like an autorickshaw but bigger, and runs on fixed routes. In 2000, all diesel tempos were banned in the Kathmandu Valley, and have been replaced by electric and gas-powered *Safa* (clean) tempos and conventional petrol minibuses. This has made a noticeable difference to the levels of air pollution in the valley; the old Vikram tempos have all been relocated and can now be seen doing their smoke-belching best to clog the air between the Indian border and Nepal's border towns. Drivers pick up and drop off anywhere along the route; tap on the roof with a coin when you want to stop.

TOURS

There are few organised tours available in Kathmandu or to places of interest around the valley and further a field; see p162 for details. Normally it's just a matter of organising something through a travel agent, of which there are gazillions.

For organised rafting and mountain biking tours see p82 and p90; for organised treks see p327.

TRAIN

There are two train lines from Janakpur, but only the service east to Jaynagar over the Indian border carries passenger traffic. They're narrow-gauge trains and very slow, so they offer an interesting, if somewhat crowded, method of seeing the countryside. Note that tourists are not allowed to cross the border using the passenger train. See the boxed text, p316 for more details.

Health

CONTENTS

Nepal is a fantastic travel destination but many of the features that attract us, such as the topography and lack of modern infrastructure, may also pose particular risks to health. The vast majority of travellers to Nepal do so without medical problems. In those that become ill, the most common illnesses include traveller's diarrhoea and viral respiratory infections (colds). Far rarer but potentially more dangerous are accidents, injury and Acute Mountain Sickness.

Because of the remoteness of areas frequented by many visitors, sensible travellers will rely to some extent on their own medical knowledge and supplies when travelling to Nepal. As always, travellers who have pre-existing conditions, such as diabetes, should speak with their home medical practitioners before travel and bring adequate supplies of medications and necessary equipment.

BEFORE YOU GO

INSURANCE

Keep in mind that Nepal is a remote location, and if you become seriously injured or very sick you may need to be evacuated by air. Under these circumstances, you defi-

nitely don't want to be without adequate health insurance.

Prior to travel confirm your insurance particulars; certain activities may be classified as 'adventure' or 'extreme' sports, and these may require additional riders to the standard policy. Examples include insurance limitations upon activities above 4000m or specific sports such as paragliding or white-water rafting.

RECOMMENDED VACCINATIONS

Nepal does not officially require any immunisations for entry into the country, but the further off the beaten track you go, the more necessary it is to take precautions. Travellers who have come from an area infected with yellow fever are required to be vaccinated before entering the country. Record all vaccinations on an International Health Certificate, available from a doctor or government health department.

Plan ahead and schedule your vaccinations as some require more than one injection, while others should not be given together. Note that some vaccinations should not be given during pregnancy or to people with allergies.

It is recommended that you seek medical advice at least six weeks before travelling. Be aware that there is a greater risk of all kinds of disease for children and during pregnancy.

Discuss your requirements with your doctor, but vaccinations you should consider for this trip include the following:

Diphtheria & tetanus Vaccinations for these two diseases are usually combined and are recommended for everyone. After an initial course of three injections (usually given in childhood), boosters are necessary every 10 years.

Hepatitis A The vaccine for Hepatitis A (eg Avaxim, Havrix 1440 or VAQTA) provides long-term immunity (possibly lifelong) after an initial injection and a booster at six to 12 months.

Hepatitis B Vaccination involves three injections, the quickest course being over three weeks with a booster at 12 months.

Influenza 'Flu' is considered by many to be the most common vaccine-preventable illness in travellers. This vaccine is annual and based on the hemisphere of residence and travel destination.

Japanese B Encephalitis (JBE) JBE is a mosquito-borne viral encephalitis. At the time of writing there was a recent outbreak in the border areas of India. The risk of JBE is greatest in the Terai and during and after the monsoon. Like the rabies course, JBE vaccine is given as three injections over three to four weeks and boosted usually at three years. This vaccine is recommended for persons visiting high-risk areas and for prolonged stays.

Meningococcal Meningitis A single-dose vaccine boosted every three to five years is recommended for individuals at high risk and for extended stays.

Polio This serious, easily transmitted disease is still found in some developing countries, including Nepal. Everyone should keep up to date with this vaccination, which is normally given in childhood. A booster every 10 years maintains immunity.

Rabies Vaccination should be strongly considered for long-term or frequent travellers to countries with rabies, especially if you are engaged in activities such as running, trekking, cycling, caving, handling animals or travelling to remote areas, and for children (who may not report a bite). Pretravel rabies vaccination involves having three injections over 21 to 28 days. The vaccine obviates the need for rabies immunoglobulin, which may not be available in many areas (and is extremely expensive) and will also shorten the vaccine course: if someone who has been vaccinated is bitten or scratched by an animal they will require two vaccine booster injections, while those not vaccinated will require more. The booster for rabies vaccination is usually given after three years.

Tuberculosis The risk of tuberculosis (TB) to travellers is usually very low, unless you will be living with or closely associated with local people in high-risk areas. As most healthy adults do not develop symptoms, a skin test before and after travel to determine whether exposure has occurred may be considered. A vaccination (BCG) may be recommended for children and young adults living in these areas for three months or more.

Typhoid This vaccination is available either as an injection or oral capsules. A combined hepatitis A–typhoid vaccine was launched recently but its availability is still limited – check with your doctor to find out its status in your country.

Yellow fever This disease is not endemic in Nepal and a vaccine for yellow fever is required only if you are coming from an infected area. The record of this vaccine should be provided in a World Health Organization (WHO) Yellow Vaccination Booklet and is valid for 10 years.

MEDICAL CHECKLIST

Following is a list of items you should consider including in your medical kit – consult your pharmacist for brands available in your country.

- aspirin or paracetamol (acetaminophen in the USA) for pain or fever
- antihistamine for allergies, eg hay fever; to ease the itch from insect bites or stings; and to prevent motion sickness
- cold and flu tablets, throat lozenges and nasal decongestant
- multivitamins for long trips, when dietary vitamin intake may be inadequate
- antibiotics, particularly if you're travelling well off the beaten track; see your doctor, as antibiotics must be prescribed, and carry the prescription with you
- anti-inflammatory (ibuprofen) for muscle and joint overuse and pain; also for headache and fever
- loperamide or diphenoxylate 'blockers' for diarrhoea
- prochlorperazine or metoclopramide for nausea and vomiting
- rehydration mixture to prevent dehydration, which may occur, for example, during bouts of diarrhoea; particularly important when travelling with children
- insect repellent, sunscreen, lip balm and eye drops
- calamine lotion, sting-relief spray or aloe vera to ease irritation from sunburn and insect bites or stings
- antifungal cream or powder for fungal skin infections and thrush
- antiseptic (such as povidone-iodine) for cuts and grazes
- bandages, crepe wraps, Band-Aids (plasters) and other wound dressings
- water purification tablets or iodine
- scissors, tweezers and a thermometer, noting that mercury thermometers are prohibited by airlines
- sterile kit in case you need injections in a country with medical hygiene problems; discuss with your doctor

INTERNET RESOURCES

There are a number of excellent travel-health sites on the Internet. From the **Lonely Planet website** (www.lonelyplanet.com) there are links to the WHO and the US Centers for Disease Control & Prevention. Kathmandu's **CIWEC Clinic** (www.ciwec-clinic.com) has a very useful website providing medical advice relating specifically to travel in Nepal.

FURTHER READING

Lonely Planet's *Healthy Travel Asia & India* is a handy pocket size and is packed with useful information including pretrip planning, emergency first aid, immunisation and disease information, and what to do if you get sick on the road. *Travel with Children* from Lonely Planet also includes advice on travel health for younger children.

Other detailed health guides:

Complete Guide to Healthy Travel Recommendations for international travel from the US Centers for Disease Control & Prevention.

Staying Healthy in Asia, Africa & Latin America A detailed and well-organised guide by Dirk Schroeder.

Travellers' Health By Dr Richard Dawood. This is comprehensive, easy to read, authoritative and highly recommended, although it's rather large to lug around.

Where There Is No Doctor By David Werner. A very detailed guide intended for people going to work in a developing country.

OTHER PREPARATIONS

Make sure you're healthy before you start travelling. If you are going on a long trip make sure your teeth are OK. If you wear glasses, it's a good idea to take a spare pair and your prescription.

If you require a particular medication take a good supply, as it may not be available in Nepal. Necessary medications should be hand-carried aboard international flights. Also, take part of the packaging showing the generic name rather than the brand, which will make getting replacements easier. To avoid problems it's a good idea to have a legible prescription or letter from your doctor to show that you legally use the medication.

IN TRANSIT

DEEP VEIN THROMBOSIS (DVT)

Deep vein thrombosis occurs when blood clots form in the legs during plane flights, chiefly because of prolonged immobility. Although most blood clots are reabsorbed uneventfully, some may break off and travel through the blood vessels to the lungs, where they may cause life-threatening complications.

The chief symptom of DVT is swelling or pain in the foot, ankle or calf, usually but not always on just one side. When a blood clot travels to the lungs, it may cause chest pain and difficulty in breathing. Travellers with any of these symptoms should immediately seek medical attention.

To prevent the development of DVT on long flights you should walk about the cabin, perform isometric compressions of the leg muscles (ie contract the leg muscles while sitting), drink plenty of fluids, and avoid alcohol and tobacco.

MOTION SICKNESS

Eating lightly before and during a trip will reduce the chances of motion sickness. If you are prone to motion sickness try to find a place that minimises movement – near the wing on aircraft, near the centre on buses. Fresh air usually helps; reading and cigarette smoke don't. Commercial preparations for motion sickness, which can cause drowsiness, have to be taken before the trip commences. Ginger (available in capsule form) and peppermint (including mint-flavoured sweets) are natural preventatives.

IN NEPAL

AVAILABILITY & COST OF HEALTH CARE

Self-diagnosis and treatment can be risky, so you should always seek medical help. Although we do give drug dosages in this section, they are for emergency use only. Correct diagnosis is vital.

In Nepal the top-end hotels can usually recommend a good place to go for advice. In most places in Nepal standards of medical attention are so low that for some

---

EVERYDAY HEALTH

Normal body temperature is up to 37°C (98.6°F); more than 2°C (4°F) higher indicates a high fever. The normal adult pulse rate is 60 to 100 per minute (children 80 to 100, babies 100 to 140). As a general rule the pulse increases about 20 beats per minute for each 1°C (2°F) rise in fever.

Respiration (breathing) rate is also an indicator of illness. Count the number of breaths per minute: between 12 and 20 is normal for adults and older children (up to 30 for younger children, 40 for babies). People with a high fever or serious respiratory illness breathe more quickly than normal. More than 40 shallow breaths a minute may indicate pneumonia.

ailments the best advice is to go straight to Kathmandu.

Antibiotics should ideally be administered only under medical supervision. Take only the recommended dose at the prescribed intervals and use the whole course, even if the illness seems to be cured earlier. Stop immediately if there are any serious reactions and don't use the antibiotic at all if you are unsure that you have the correct one. Some people are allergic to commonly prescribed antibiotics such as penicillin; carry this information (eg on a bracelet) when travelling.

INFECTIOUS DISEASES
Hepatitis
A general term for inflammation of the liver, hepatitis is a common disease worldwide. There are several different viruses that cause hepatitis, and they differ in the way that they are transmitted. The symptoms are similar in all forms of the illness and include fever, chills, headache, fatigue, feelings of weakness as well as aches and pains, followed by loss of appetite, nausea, vomiting, abdominal pain, dark urine, light-coloured faeces, jaundiced (yellow) skin and yellowing of the whites of the eyes. People who have had hepatitis should avoid alcohol for some time after the illness, as the liver needs time to recover.

Hepatitis A is transmitted by contaminated drinking water and food. You should seek medical advice, but there is not much you can do apart from resting, drinking lots of fluids, eating lightly and avoiding fatty foods. Hygiene and habits may contribute to the virus' spread. In Nepal, the custom of sharing food from a single dish rather than using separate plates and a serving spoon may infect dinner companions. Hepatitis E is transmitted in the same way as hepatitis A; it can be particularly serious in pregnant women.

There are almost 300 million chronic carriers of hepatitis B in the world. It is spread through contact with infected blood, blood products or body fluids, for example through sexual contact, unsterilised needles and blood transfusions, or contact with blood via small breaks in the skin. Other risk situations include having a shave, tattoo or body piercing with contaminated equipment. The symptoms of hepatitis B may be more

severe than those for type A and the disease can lead to long-term problems such as chronic liver damage, liver cancer or a long-term carrier state. Hepatitis C and D are spread in the same way as hepatitis B and can also lead to long-term complications.

There are vaccines against hepatitis A and B, but there are currently no vaccines against the other types of hepatitis. Following the basic rules about food and water (hepatitis A and E) and avoiding risk situations (hepatitis B, C and D) are important preventative measures.

HIV & AIDS
Infection with HIV may lead to AIDS, which is a fatal disease. Any exposure to blood or body fluids may put the individual at risk. The disease is often transmitted through sexual contact or dirty needles – vaccinations, acupuncture, tattooing and body piercing can be potentially as dangerous as intravenous drug use. HIV/AIDS can also be spread through infected blood transfusions; some developing countries cannot afford to screen blood used for transfusions.

If you do need an injection, ask to see the syringe unwrapped in front of you, or take a needle and syringe pack with you. Fear of HIV infection should never preclude treatment for serious medical conditions.

Malaria
At the time of writing, there has been an outbreak of cerebral malaria in remote areas of the Terai. Most malaria in Nepal is the so-called benign vivax malaria and principally occurs in areas far from those frequented by tourists. Extremely small risk is present in some areas of Chitwan National Park during the monsoon; there is no risk in Kathmandu, Pokhara, or typical Himalayan trekking routes.

Long-term travellers and expat workers in high-risk areas should consider medication prophylaxis; all travellers should practise mosquito-bite avoidance (use of netting, repellents, etc) and engage in prompt evaluation if any fever develops after travel to such areas. Again, local knowledge regarding the current situation is essential.

Rabies
This fatal viral infection is found in many countries. Many animals can be infected

(such as dogs, cats, bats and monkeys) and it is their saliva that is infectious. Any bite, scratch or even lick from an animal should be cleaned immediately and thoroughly. Scrub with soap and running water, and then apply alcohol or iodine solution. Prompt medical help should be sought to receive a course of injections to prevent the onset of symptoms and death. Vaccination simplifies the treatment of animal bites.

Respiratory Infections
Upper-respiratory-tract infections (such as the common cold) are a common ailment in Nepal. Why are they such a serious problem? Respiratory infections are aggravated by high altitude, cold weather, pollution, chain-smoking and overcrowded conditions, which increase the opportunities for infection.

Symptoms include fever, weakness and sore throat. Any upper-respiratory-tract infection, including influenza, can lead to complications such as bronchitis and pneumonia, which may need to be treated with antibiotics. Seek medical help in this case.

No vaccine offers complete protection, but there are vaccines against influenza and pneumococcal pneumonia that might help. The influenza vaccine is good for no more than a year.

Sexually Transmitted Infections
While HIV/AIDS and hepatitis B can be transmitted through sexual contact, other sexually transmitted infections (STIs) include gonorrhoea, herpes and syphilis. Sores, blisters or rashes around the genitals and discharges or pain when urinating are common symptoms. In some STIs, such as wart virus or chlamydia, symptoms may be less marked or not observed at all, especially in women. Syphilis symptoms eventually disappear completely but the disease continues and can cause severe problems in later years. Although abstinence from sexual contact is the only 100% effective prevention, using condoms is also effective. Gonorrhoea and syphilis are treated with antibiotics. The different STIs each require specific antibiotics. There is no cure for herpes or AIDS.

TRAVELLER'S DIARRHOEA
Simple things such as a change of water, food or climate can cause a mild bout of diarrhoea, but a few rushed toilet trips with no other symptoms are not indicative of a major problem. Even Marco Polo got the runs.

Dehydration is the main danger with any diarrhoea, particularly in children, pregnant women or the elderly as it can occur quite quickly. Under all circumstances *fluid replacement* (at least equal to the volume being lost) is the most important thing to remember. Soda water, weak black tea with a little sugar, or soft drinks allowed to go flat and diluted 50% with clean water are all good. With severe diarrhoea a rehydrating solution is preferable to replace lost minerals and salts. Commercially available oral rehydration salts (ORS) are very useful; add them to boiled or bottled water. In an emergency you can make up a solution of six teaspoons of sugar and half a teaspoon of salt to a litre of boiled or bottled water. You need to drink at least the same volume of fluid that you are losing in bowel movements and vomiting. Urine is the best guide to the adequacy of replacement – if you have small amounts of concentrated urine, you need to drink more. Keep drinking small amounts often. Stick to a bland diet as you recover.

Loperamide or diphenoxylate can be used to bring relief from the symptoms, although they do not actually cure the problem. Only use these drugs if you do not have access to toilets, eg if you *must* travel. For children under 12 years these drugs are not recommended. Do not use these drugs if you have a high fever or are severely dehydrated.

In certain situations antibiotics may be required: diarrhoea with blood or mucus (dysentery), any diarrhoea with fever, profuse watery diarrhoea, persistent diarrhoea not improving after 48 hours and severe diarrhoea. These suggest a more serious cause, in which case gut-paralysing drugs should be avoided.

In these situations, a stool test may be necessary to diagnose what bug is causing your diarrhoea, so you should seek medical help urgently. Where this is not possible the recommended drugs for bacterial diarrhoea (the most likely cause of severe diarrhoea in travellers) are norfloxacin 400mg or ciprofloxacin 500mg twice daily for three days. These are not recommended for children or pregnant women. The drug of choice for children would be azithromycin with dosage dependent on weight. A three-day course is given. Alternative antibiotics may be given in pregnancy, but medical care is necessary.

Two other common causes of persistent diarrhoea in travellers are giardiasis and amoebic dysentery.

Amoebic Dysentery

Caused by the protozoan *Entamoeba histolytica,* amoebic dysentery is characterised by a gradual onset of low-grade diarrhoea, often with blood and mucus. Cramping, abdominal pain and vomiting are less likely than in other types of diarrhoea, and fever may not be present. Infection persists until treated and can recur and cause other health problems.

You should seek medical advice if you think you have giardiasis or amoebic dysentery, but where this is not possible, tindazole or metronidazole are the recommended drugs. Treatment is a 2g single dose of tindazole daily or 250mg of metronidazole three times daily for five to 10 days.

Both metronidazole and tindazole may be obtained in Nepal and are often sold in combination with other medications. If you are going to be travelling in high mountain areas, it might be a good idea to keep your own stock of these other medications with you.

Alcohol must not be consumed during the course of taking these medications; they may cause fatigue, nausea, abdominal discomfort and metallic taste.

Cyclospora

This intestinal parasite may cause significant fatigue and abdominal discomfort. Many expatriates avoid salads and uncooked vegetables, especially during and after the monsoon when this infection is most prevalent. The parasite may be diagnosed with stool examination and antibiotic treatment is for one week.

Giardiasis

Known as giardia, giardiasis is a type of diarrhoea that is relatively common in Nepal and is caused by a parasite, *Giardia lamblia.* Mountaineers often suffer from this problem. The parasite causing this intestinal disorder is present in contaminated water. Many kinds of mammals harbour this parasite, so you can get it easily from drinking 'pure mountain water' unless the area is devoid of animals. Simply brushing your teeth using contaminated water is sufficient to get giardiasis, or any other gut bug. Symptoms include stomach cramps, nausea, a bloated stomach, watery, foul-smelling diarrhoea and frequent gas. Giardiasis can appear several weeks after you have been exposed to the parasite. The symptoms may disappear for a few days and then return; this can go on for several months.

ENVIRONMENTAL HAZARDS
Acute Mountain Sickness

You should take care to acclimatise slowly and take things easy for the first couple of days in areas at high altitude. Lack of oxygen at altitudes over 2500m affects most people to some extent. The effect may be mild or severe and it occurs because less oxygen reaches the muscles and the brain at high altitude, requiring the heart and lungs to compensate by working harder. Acute Mountain Sickness (AMS) – altitude sickness – is common at high elevations; relevant factors are the rate of ascent and individual susceptibility. The major risk factor in AMS is the speed with which you make your ascent.

AMS is a notoriously fickle affliction and can also affect trekkers and walkers accustomed to walking at high altitudes. AMS has been fatal at 3000m, although 3500m to 4500m is the usual range.

ACCLIMATISATION

AMS is linked to the low oxygen content of air at high elevation. Those who travel up to Everest Base Camp, for instance, reach an altitude where the oxygen content of the air is about half of that at sea level.

With an increase in altitude, the human body needs time to develop physiological mechanisms to cope with the decreased oxygen. This process of acclimatisation is still not fully understood, but it is known to involve modifications in breathing patterns and heart rate induced by the autonomic nervous system, and an increase in the blood's oxygen-carrying capabilities. These compensatory mechanisms usually take about one to three days to develop at a particular altitude. Once you are acclimatised to a given height you are unlikely to get AMS at that height, but you can still get ill when you travel higher. If the ascent is too

HEALTH

high and too fast, these compensatory reactions may not kick into gear fast enough.

SYMPTOMS

Mild symptoms of AMS are very common in travellers visiting high altitudes, and usually develop during the first 24 hours at altitude. Most visitors to the mountains of Nepal suffer from some symptoms; these generally disappear through acclimatisation in several hours to several days.

Symptoms tend to be worse at night and include headache, dizziness, lethargy, loss of appetite, nausea, breathlessness and irritability. Difficulty sleeping is another common symptom.

AMS may become more serious without warning and can be fatal. Symptoms are caused by the accumulation of fluid in the lungs and brain, and include breathlessness at rest, a dry, irritative cough (which may progress to the production of pink, frothy sputum), severe headache, lack of coordination (typically leading to a 'drunken walk'), confusion, irrational behaviour, vomiting and eventually unconsciousness.

The symptoms of AMS, however mild, are a warning – be sure to take them seriously! Trekkers should keep an eye on each other as those experiencing symptoms, especially severe symptoms, may not be in a position to recognise them. One thing to note is that while the symptoms of mild AMS often precede those of severe AMS, this is not always the case. Severe AMS can strike with little or no warning.

PREVENTION

The best way to prevent AMS is to avoid rapid ascents to high altitudes. If you fly or bus into an area at high altitude, take it easy for at least three days – for most travellers this is long enough to get over any initial ill effects. At this point you might step up your programme by visiting a few sights around town. Within a week you should be ready for something a bit more adventurous, but do not push yourself to do anything that you are not comfortable with.

Steps to prevent Acute Mountain Sickness include:

■ Ascend slowly. Have frequent rest days, spending two to three nights at each rise of 1000m. If you reach a high altitude by trekking, acclimatisation takes place gradually and you are less likely to be affected than if you fly directly to high altitude.

■ Trekkers should bear in mind the climber's adage 'Climb high, sleep low'. It is always wise to sleep at a lower altitude than the greatest height reached during the day. High day climbs followed by a descent back to lower altitudes for the night are good preparation for high-altitude trekking. Also, once above 3000m, care should be taken not to increase the sleeping altitude by more than 400m per day. If the terrain won't allow for less than 400m of elevation gain, be ready to take an extra day off before tackling the climb.

■ Drink extra fluids. The mountain air is dry and cold, and moisture is lost as you breathe. Evaporation of sweat may occur unnoticed and result in dehydration.

■ Eat light, high-carbohydrate meals for more energy.

■ Avoid alcohol as it may increase the risk of dehydration, and don't smoke.

■ Avoid sedatives or sleeping pills.

■ When trekking, take a day off to rest and acclimatise if feeling overtired. If you or anyone else in your party is having a tough time make allowances for unscheduled stops.

■ Don't push yourself when climbing up to passes; rather, take plenty of breaks. You can usually get over the pass as easily tomorrow as you can today. Try to plan your itinerary so that long ascents can be divided into two or more days. Given the complexity and unknown variables involved with AMS and acclimatisation, trekkers should always err on the side of caution and ascend mountains slowly.

Persons prone to AMS or those required to make a rapid ascent (such as rescuers) may consider taking Diamox (acetazolamide); the usual dose is 125mg to 250mg twice daily. It is essential that this medication not be used as a substitute for slow ascent, or for descent and appropriate treatment if symptoms develop. The medication is a diuretic and possibly contributes to dehydration (extra fluid intake is necessary to compensate). Diamox may cause vision and taste changes and a tingling sensation in the fingers.

TREATMENT

Treat mild symptoms by resting at the same altitude until recovery, which usually takes a day or two. Take paracetamol or aspirin for headaches. If symptoms persist or become worse, however, *immediate descent* is necessary – even 500m can help.

The most effective treatment for severe AMS is to get down to a lower altitude as quickly as possible. In less severe cases the victim will be able to stagger down with some support; in other cases they may need to be carried down. Whatever the case, do not delay, as any delay could be fatal.

AMS victims may need to be flown out – make sure that you have adequate travel insurance.

Other treatments for AMS may include oxyen, acetazolamide (Diamox), nifedipine, dexamethasone and the Gamow bag. Drug treatments should never be used to avoid descent or to enable further ascent.

Cuts, Bites & Stings

CUTS & SCRATCHES

Wash any cut well and treat it with an antiseptic such as povidone-iodine or antibiotic ointment and sterile gauze dressing. Where possible avoid bandages and Band-Aids, which can keep wounds wet.

BEDBUGS, LICE & SCABIES

Bedbugs live in various places, but particularly in dirty mattresses and bedding, evidenced by spots of blood on bedclothes or on the wall. Bedbugs leave itchy bites in neat rows. Calamine lotion or a sting-relief spray may help.

All lice cause itching and discomfort. They make themselves at home in your hair (head lice), your clothing (body lice) or in your pubic hair (crabs). You catch lice through direct contact with infected people or by sharing combs, clothing and the like. Powder or shampoo treatment will kill the lice. Infected clothing should then be washed in very hot, soapy water and left in the sun to dry.

Like lice, scabies is spread by person-to-person contact and is relatively common in some schools and orphanages. Scabies is treated by specific medicated creams.

BITES & STINGS

Bee and wasp stings are usually painful rather than dangerous. However, people who are allergic to them may have severe breathing difficulties and require urgent medical care. Calamine lotion or a sting-relief spray will give relief and ice packs will reduce the pain and swelling.

LEECHES

In damp low-lying areas, leeches may be present; they attach themselves to your skin to suck your blood. Trekkers often get them on their legs or in their boots. Salt or a lighted match end will make them fall off. Do not pull them off, as the bite is then more likely to become infected. Clean and apply pressure if the point of attachment is bleeding. An insect repellent may help keep them away.

Food

There is an old colonial adage that says 'If you can cook it, boil it or peel it you can eat it…otherwise forget it'. Vegetables and fruit should be washed with purified or bottled water or peeled where possible. Beware of ice cream that is sold in the street or anywhere it might have melted and refrozen; if there's any doubt (eg a power cut in the last day or two) steer well clear. Undercooked meat should be avoided.

If a place looks clean and well run and the vendor also looks clean and healthy, then the food is probably safe. In general, places that are packed with travellers or locals will be fine, while empty restaurants are questionable.

Frostbite

This is the freezing of extremities, including fingers, toes and nose. Signs and symptoms include a whitish or waxy cast to the skin, or even crystals on the surface, plus itching, numbness and pain. Warm the affected areas by immersing them in warm (not hot) water or covering with blankets until the skin becomes flushed. Frostbitten parts should not be rubbed and should be protected from further damage with bulky gauze dressings. Avoid using the frostbitten limb. Pain and swelling are inevitable. Blisters should not be broken. Get medical attention right away. Antibiotics and anti-inflammatories are often prescribed.

Heat Exhaustion

Dehydration and salt deficiency can cause heat exhaustion. Take time to acclimatise to

HEALTH

high temperatures; drink sufficient liquids and do not do anything too physically demanding.

Salt deficiency is characterised by fatigue, lethargy, headaches, giddiness and muscle cramps; salt tablets may help, but adding extra salt to your food is better.

Hypothermia

Weather in Nepal is not to be taken lightly. Even in midsummer, passes and high areas can be hit without warning by sudden snowstorms. You should always be prepared for cold, wet or windy conditions, especially if you're out walking, hitching or trekking at high altitudes or even taking a long bus trip over mountains (particularly at night).

Hypothermia occurs when the body loses heat faster than it can produce it and the core temperature of the body falls. It is surprisingly easy to progress from very cold to dangerously cold through a combination of wind, wet clothing, fatigue and hunger, even if the air temperature is above freezing.

It is best to dress in layers; silk, wool and some of the new artificial fibres are all good insulating materials. A hat is important, as a lot of heat is lost through the head. A strong, waterproof outer layer and a 'space' blanket for emergencies are essential. Carry basic supplies, including food that contains simple sugars to generate heat quickly, and fluid to drink.

Symptoms of hypothermia are exhaustion, numb skin (particularly toes and fingers), shivering, slurred speech, irrational or violent behaviour, lethargy, stumbling, dizzy spells, muscle cramps and violent bursts of energy. Irrationality may take the form of sufferers claiming they are warm and trying to take off their clothes.

To treat mild hypothermia, first get the person out of the wind and rain, remove their clothing if it's wet and replace it with dry, warm clothing. Give them hot liquids (not alcohol) and some high-energy, easily digestible food. Do not rub victims; instead, allow them to slowly warm themselves. This should be enough to treat the early stages of hypothermia. The early recognition and treatment of mild hypothermia is the only way to prevent severe hypothermia, which is a critical condition.

Sunburn

It is very easy to get sunburnt in Nepal's high altitudes. Sunburn is more than just uncomfortable. Among the undesirable effects are premature skin ageing and possible skin cancer in later years. Sunscreen with a high sun protection factor (SPF), sunglasses and a wide-brimmed hat are good means of protection. Calamine lotion is good for treating mild sunburn.

Those with fair complexions should bring reflective sunscreen (containing zinc oxide or titanium oxide) with them. Apply the sunscreen to your nose and lips (and especially the tops of your ears if you are not wearing a hat).

Water

The number-one rule is *be careful of the water* and especially ice. If you don't know for certain that the water is safe you should assume the worst. In the country you should boil your own water or treat it with water-purification tablets. Milk should be treated with suspicion as it will be unpasteurised in the countryside, although boiled milk is fine if it is kept hygienically. Soft drinks and beer are always available wherever there is a shop, and these are always safe to drink, as is tea.

WATER PURIFICATION

The simplest way to purify water is to boil it thoroughly. In Nepal's higher-altitude areas water boils at a lower temperature and germs are less likely to be killed, so make sure you boil water for at least 10 minutes.

Consider purchasing a water filter for a long trip. There are two main kinds of filters. Total filters take out all parasites, bacteria and viruses, and make water safe to drink. They are often expensive, but they can be more cost-effective than buying bottled water. Simple filters (which can even be a nylon-mesh bag) take out dirt and larger foreign bodies from the water so that chemical solutions work much more effectively; if water is dirty, chemical solutions may not work at all. It's very important when buying a filter to read the specifications, so that you know exactly what it removes from the water and what it doesn't. Simple filtering will not remove all dangerous organisms, so if you cannot boil water it should be treated chemically.

Chlorine tablets (eg Puritabs or Steritabs) will kill many pathogens, but not giardia and amoebic cysts. Iodine is more effective for purifying water and is available in tablet form (eg Potable Aqua). Follow the directions carefully and remember that too much iodine can be harmful.

WOMEN'S HEALTH
Gynaecological Problems
Antibiotic use, synthetic underwear, sweating and contraceptive pills can lead to fungal vaginal infections, especially when travelling in hot climates. Fungal infections are characterised by a rash, itch and discharge. Nystatin, miconazole or clotrimazole pessaries or vaginal cream are the usual treatment, but some people use a more traditional remedy involving vinegar or lemon-juice douches, or yogurt. Maintaining good personal hygiene and wearing loose-fitting clothes and cotton underwear may help prevent these infections.

Sexually transmitted infections are a major cause of gynaecological problems. Symptoms include a smelly discharge, painful intercourse and sometimes a burning sensation when urinating. Medical attention should be sought and sexual partners must also be treated. Besides abstinence, the best thing is to practise safe sex using condoms.

Pregnancy
It is not advisable to travel to some places while pregnant as some vaccinations normally used to prevent serious diseases are not advisable during pregnancy. In addition, some diseases are much more serious for the mother (and may increase the risk of a stillborn child).

Most miscarriages occur during the first three months of pregnancy. Miscarriage is not uncommon and can occasionally lead to severe bleeding. The last three months should also be spent within reasonable distance of good medical care. Travel prior to 32 weeks is generally not a problem for pregnant women; airlines may restrict travel after this gestational time. Pregnant women should avoid all unnecessary medication, although vaccinations should still be taken where needed. Additional care should be taken to prevent illness and particular attention should be paid to diet and nutrition. Alcohol and nicotine, for example, should be avoided. Dehydration from diarrhoea is especially dangerous and prompt fluid intake is often important for pregnant women.

HEALTH

Language

CONTENTS

LANGUAGES OF NEPAL	
Language	**% of Total Population**
Nepali	50.3
Maithili	11.9
Bhojpuri	7.5
Tharu	5.4
Tamang	4.9
Newari	3.4
Rai	2.4
Magar	2.3
Abadhi	2.0
Limbu	1.4
Gurung	1.2
Sherpa	0.7
Other	8.6

Nepali is closely related to Hindi, and both languages belong to the Indo-European family. It's quite easy to get by with English in Nepal; most of the people visitors will have to deal with in the Kathmandu Valley and in Pokhara will speak some English. Along the main trekking trails, particularly the Annapurna Circuit, English is also widely understood.

Nonetheless, it's interesting to learn at least a little Nepali and it's quite an easy language to pick up. For a more comprehensive language guide, get a copy of Lonely Planet's *Nepali Phrasebook*, which includes Nepali script throughout.

Although Nepali is the national language and is used as a lingua franca (linking language) between all the country's ethnic groups, there are many other languages spoken. The Newars of the Kathmandu Valley, for example, speak Newari; other languages are spoken by the Tamangs, Sherpas, Rais, Limbus, Magars, Gurungs and other groups. In the Terai, bordering India, Hindi and Maithili, another Indian language of this region, are often spoken (see the table on this page for a breakdown of first languages spoken in Nepal).

Even if you learn no other Nepali, there is one word every visitor soon picks up – *namaste* (pronounced 'na-ma-stay'). Strictly translated it means 'I salute the god in you', but it's used as an everyday greeting that encompasses everything from 'Hello' to 'How are you?' and even 'See you again soon'. It should be accompanied with the hands held in a prayer-like position, the Nepali gesture equivalent to Westerners shaking hands.

STUDYING NEPALI

Peace Corps and other aid workers pick up a working knowledge of the language very quickly and there are language courses available that will enable you to get by with just four to eight weeks of intensive study. See Courses (p357) for details. In books, the best source for the serious language student is *Teach Yourself Nepali* by Michael Hutt and Abhi Sabedi, which concentrates on both written and spoken Nepali.

PRONUNCIATION
Vowels

a	as the 'u' in 'hut'
ā	as the 'ar' in 'garden' (no 'r' sound)
e	as the 'e' in 'best' but longer
i	as the 'i' in 'sister' but longer
o	as the 'o' in 'sold'
u	as the 'u' in 'put'
ai	as the 'i' in 'mine'
au	as the 'ow' in 'cow'

Consonants

Most Nepali consonants are quite similar to their English counterparts. The exceptions are the so-called retroflex consonants and the aspirated consonants. Retroflex sounds are made by curling the tongue tip back to touch the roof of the mouth as you make the sound; they are indicated in this guide by an underdot, eg **ṭ**, *Kaṭhmaṇḍu*.

Aspirated consonants are sounded more forcefully than they would be in English and are made with a short puff of air; they are indicated in this guide by h after the consonant, eg **kh**, *khānuhos* (please). You should ensure that you don't confuse the Nepali aspirated combinations **ph** and **th** with their English counterparts in words such as 'phone', 'this' and 'thin'. In Nepali, ph is pronounced as the 'p' in 'pit', and th is pronounced as the 't' in 'time'.

Both retroflex and aspirated consonants are best learned by having a native speaker demonstrate them for you. You could start with *Kaṭhmaṇḍu*, which contains both retroflex and aspirated consonants.

ACCOMMODATION

Where is a ...?	... kahā chha?
guesthouse	pāhuna ghar
hotel	hoṭel
camp site	shivir
lodge	laj

What is the address?
thegānā ke ho?
Please write down the address.
thegānā lekhunuhos
Can I get a place to stay here?
yahā bās paunchha?
May I look at the room?
kothā herna sakchhu?
How much is it per night?
ek rātko, kati paisā ho?
Does it include breakfast?
bihānako khāna samet ho?

room	kothā
clean	safā
dirty	mailo
fan	pankhā
hot water	tāto pāni

CONVERSATION & ESSENTIALS

Hello/Goodbye.	namaste
How are you?	tapāilai kasto chha?
Excuse me.	hajur
Please (give me).	dinuhos

Please (you have).	khānuhos
Thank you.	dhanyabad

Unlike in the West, verbal expressions of thanks are not the cultural norm in Nepal. Although neglecting to say 'Thank you' may make you feel a little uncomfortable, it is rarely necessary in a simple commercial transaction; foreigners going round saying dhanyabad all the time sounds distinctly odd to Nepalis.

I	ma
Yes. (I have)	chā
No. (I don't have)	chhaina
OK.	theekcha
Where?	kahā?
here	yahā
there	tyahā
good/pretty	ramro
I don't need it.	malai chahiṇa
I don't have it.	ma sanga chhaina
Wait a minute.	ek chhin parkhanos

EMERGENCIES

Help!	guhār!
It's an emergency!	āpaṭ paryo!
There's been an accident!	durghaṭanā bhayo!
Please call a doctor.	dākṭarlai bolāu-nuhos
Where is the (public) toilet?	shauchālaya kahā chha?
I'm lost.	ma harāye

HEALTH

Where can I find a good doctor?	rāmro dākṭar kaha pāincha?
Where is the nearest hospital?	yahā aspatāl kahā chha?
I don't feel well.	malāi sancho chhaina
I have diarrhoea.	dishā lāgyo
I have altitude sickness.	lekh lāgyo
I have a fever.	joro āyo
I'm having trouble breathing.	sās pherna sakdina
medicine	ausadhi
pharmacy	ausadhi pasal

I have ...	malāi ... lāgyo
asthma	damko byathā
diabetes	madhu meha
epilepsy	chāre rog

LANGUAGE DIFFICULTIES

Do you speak English?	*tapāi angreji bolna saknu hunchha?*
I only speak a little Nepali.	*ma ali nepāli bolchhu*
I understand.	*ma bujhchu*
I don't understand.	*maile bujhina*
Please say it again.	*pheri bhaṇuhos*
Please speak more slowly.	*tapāi bistārai bolnuhos*

NUMBERS

0	*sun·ya*	शून्य
1	*ek*	एक
2	*dui*	दइ
3	*tin*	तीन
4	*chār*	चार
5	*panch*	पाँच
6	*chha*	छ
7	*sāt*	सात
8	*āṭh*	आठ
9	*nau*	नौ
10	*das*	दस
11	*eghāra*	एघार
12	*bā-hra*	बाह्र
13	*te-hra*	तेह्र
14	*chau-dha*	चौध
15	*pan-dhra*	पन्ध्र
16	*so-hra*	सोह्र
17	*satra*	सत्र
18	*a-ṭhāra*	अठार
19	*un-nais*	उन्नाईस
20	*bis*	बीस
21	*ek kais*	एककाईस
22	*bais*	बाईस
23	*teis*	तेईस
24	*chau bis*	चौबीस
25	*pach-chis*	पच्चीस
26	*chhab-bis*	छब्बीस
27	*sat-tais*	सत्ताईस
28	*aṭ-ṭhais*	अट्ठाईस
29	*u-nan-tis*	उनन्तीस
30	*tis*	तीस
40	*chālis*	चालीस
50	*pachās*	पचास
60	*sā-ṭhi*	साठी
70	*sat-tari*	सत्तरी
80	*a-si*	असी
90	*nab-be*	नब्बे
100	*ek say*	एक सय
1,000	*ek hajār*	एक हजार
10,000	*das hajār*	दस हजार
100,000	*ek lākh*	एक लाख
200,000	*dui lākh*	दुइ लाख
1,000,000	*das lākh*	दस लाख

SHOPPING & SERVICES

Where is the market?	*bazār kata parchha?*
What is it made of?	*kele baneko?*
How much?	*kati?*
That's enough.	*pugyo*
I like this.	*malai yo ramro lagyo*
I don't like this.	*malai yo ramro lagena*

money	*paisa*
cheap	*sasto*
expensive	*mahango*
less	*kam*
more	*badhi*
little bit	*alikati*

bank	*baink*
... embassy	*... rājdutāvas*
museum	*samgrāhālaya*
police	*prahari*
post office	*post afis*
stamp	*tika*
envelope	*kham*
tourist office	*turist afis*

What time does it open/close?
  kati baje kholchha/banda garchha?
I want to change some money.
  paisā sātnu manlāgchha

SIGNS

खुला	Open
बन्द	Closed
प्रबेश	Entrance
निकास	Exit
प्रबेश निषेध	No Entry
धूम्रपान मनाही छ	No Smoking
मनाही/निषेध	Prohibited
शाचालय	Toilets
तातो	Hot
चिसो	Cold
खतरा	Danger
रोक्नुहोस	Stop
बाटो बन्द	Road Closed

Internet

Is there a local Internet cafe?
  ya·hā inṭarneṭ kyah·phe chha?
I'd like to get Internet access.
  ma·lai inṭarneṭ cha·hi·yo
I'd like to check my email.
  imel chek gar·nu·par·yo
I'd like to send an email.
  imel pa·ṭhau·nu·par·yo

TIME & DATES

What time is it?	*kati bajyo?*
It's one o'clock.	*ek bajyo*
minute	*minet*
hour	*ghantā*
day	*din*
today	*āja*
yesterday	*hijo*
tomorrow	*bholi*
now	*ahile*
week	*haptā*
month	*mahinā*

What day is it today?	*āja ke bār?*
Today is ...	*āja ... ho*

Monday	*som bār*
Tuesday	*mangal bār*
Wednesday	*budh bār*
Thursday	*bihi bār*
Friday	*sukra bār*
Saturday	*sani bār*
Sunday	*āita bār*

TRANSPORT

bus	*bus*
taxi	*taxi*
boat	*nāu*
ticket	*tikaṭ*

How can I get to ...?
 ... kolāgi kati paisā lāgchha?
Is it far from here?
 yahābata ke tādhā chha?
Can I walk there?
 hiḍera jāna sakinchhu?

I want to go to ...
 ma ... jānchhu
Where does this bus go?
 yo bus kahā jānchha?
How much is it to go to ...?
 ... jāna kati parchha?
I want a one-way/return ticket.
 jāne/jāne-āune tikaṭ dinuhos.
Does your taxi have a meter?
 tapāi ko taxi mā meter chha?

TREKKING

Which way is ...?
 ... jāne bato kata parchha?
Is there a village nearby?
 najikai gaun parchha?
How many hours/days to ...?
 ... kati ghaṇṭā/din?
Where is the porter?
 bhariya kata gayo?
I want to sleep.
 malai sutna man lagyo
I'm cold.
 malai jado lagyo
Please give me (water).
 malai (pani) dinuhos

way/trail	*sāno bāṭo*
bridge	*pul*
downhill	*orālo*
uphill	*ukālo*
left	*bāyā*
right	*dāyā*
cold	*jāḍo*
teahouse	*bhatti*

Also available from Lonely Planet:
Nepali Phrasebook

Glossary

Beware of the different methods of trans-
literating Nepali and the other languages
spoken in Nepal. There are many and
varied ways of spelling Nepali words. In
particular the letters 'b' and 'v' are often
interchanged.

ACAP – Annapurna Conservation Area Project
Aditya – ancient *Vedic* sun god, also known as Surya
Agni – ancient *Vedic god* of the hearth and fire
Agnipura – Buddhist symbol for fire
AMS – acute mountain sickness, also known as altitude
sickness
Ananda – the Buddha's chief disciple
Annapurna – the goddess of abundance and an
incarnation of *Mahadevi*
arna – water buffalo
Ashoka – Indian Buddhist emperor who spread Buddhism
throughout the subcontinent
Ashta Matrikas – the eight multi-armed mother
goddesses
aunsi – new moon
Avalokiteshvara – as *Gautama Buddha* is the Buddha of
our era, so Avalokiteshvara is the *Bodhisattva* of our era
avatar – incarnation of a deity living on Earth

bagh chal – traditional Nepali game
bahal – Buddhist monastery, usually two storeys high
and built around a courtyard
bahil – simpler version of a *bahal*
bajra – see *vajra*
ban – forest or jungle
bandar – langur monkeys
bandh – strike; see also *julus* and *chakka jam*
betel – mildly intoxicating concoction of areca nut and
lime, which is wrapped in betel leaf and chewed
Bhadrakali – Tantric goddess who is also a consort of
Bhairab
Bhagavad Gita – *Krishna*'s lessons to Arjuna, part of the
Mahabharata
Bhagwati – A form of *Durga,* and thus a form of the
goddess Parvati
Bhairab – the 'terrific' or fearsome Tantric form of *Shiva*
with 64 manifestations
bhalu – sloth bears
bhanjyang – mountain pass
bhatti – teahouse or village inn
Bhimsen – one of the Pandava brothers, from the
Mahabharata, seen as a god of tradesmen
bhojanalaya – basic Nepali restaurant or canteen

Bhote – high-altitude desert valleys north of the
Himalaya bordering Tibet; Nepali term for a Tibetan
bodhi tree – a pipal tree under which the Buddha was
sitting when he attained enlightenment, also known as
'bo tree'
Bodhisattva – a near-Buddha who renounces the
opportunity to attain *nirvana* in order to aid humankind
Bön – the pre-Buddhist animist religion of Tibet
Brahma – the creator god in the Hindu triad which
includes *Vishnu* and *Shiva*
Brahmin – the highest Hindu caste, said to originate
from *Brahma*'s head
Buddha – 'Awakened One'; the originator of Buddhism;
also regarded by Hindus as the ninth incarnation of *Vishnu*

chaitya – small *stupa,* which usually contains a *mantra*
rather than a Buddhist relic
chakka jam – literally 'jam the wheels', in which all
vehicles stay off the street during a strike; see also *bandh*
and *julus*
chakra – *Vishnu*'s disclike weapon, one of the four
symbols he holds
Chandra – moon god
charas – hashish
chautara – stone platforms around trees, which serve as
shady places for porters to rest
Chhetri – the second caste of Nepali Hindus, said to
originate from *Brahma*'s arms
chirag – ceremonial oil lamp
chituwa – leopards
Chomolangma – see *Qomolangma*
chörten – Tibetan Buddhist *stupa*
chowk – (pronounced 'choke') historically a courtyard
or marketplace; these days used more to refer to an
intersection or crossroads

daal – lentil soup; the main source of protein in the
Nepali diet
daal bhaat tarkari – staple meal of Hindu Nepalis,
consisting of lentil soup, rice and curried vegetables
Dalai Lama – spiritual leader of Tibetan Buddhist people
danda – hill
Dattatreya – deity who is thought of as a combination of
Brahma, Vishnu and *Shiva*
deval – temple
Devanagari – Sanskrit Nepali script
Devi – the short form of *Mahadevi,* the *shakti* to *Shiva*
dhaka – hand-woven cotton cloth
dharamsala – resthouse for pilgrims
dharma – Buddhist teachings

dhoka – door or gate
Dhyani Buddha – the original Adi Buddha created five Dhyani Buddhas, who in turn create the universe of each human era
doko – basket carried by porters
doonga – boat
dorje – see *vajra*
durbar – palace
Durga – fearsome manifestation of *Parvati, Shiva*'s consort
dyochen – a form of temple enshrining Tantric deities
dzopkyo – male cross between a *yak* and a cow; also zopkiok
dzum – female offspring of a *yak* and a cow; also zhum

ek – Nepali number one; a symbol of the unity of all life

freaks – 1960s term for young hippie travellers, from the overland era

gaagri – water ewer
gaida – rhinoceros
gaine – itinerant musician
ganas – *Shiva*'s companions
Ganesh – son of *Shiva* and *Parvati,* instantly recognisable by his elephant head
Ganga – goddess of the Ganges
ganja – marijuana
Garuda – the man-bird *vehicle* of *Vishnu*
Gautama Buddha – the Buddha of our era
Gelugpa – one of the four major schools of Tibetan Buddhism
ghanta – Tantric bell; the female equivalent of the *vajra*
ghat – steps beside a river; a 'burning ghat' is used for cremations
ghee – clarified butter
gompa – Tibetan Buddhist monastery
gopi – cowherd girl, companions of *Krishna*
gufa – cave
Gurkhas – Nepali soldiers who have long formed a part of the British army; the name comes from the region of Gorkha
Gurkhali – British army name for the Nepali language
Gurung – western hill people from around Gorkha and Pokhara

haat bajar – weekly bazaar
Hanuman – monkey god
harmika – square base on top of a *stupa*'s dome, upon which the eyes of the Buddha are painted
hathi – elephant
himal – range or massif with permanent snow
hiti – water conduit or tank with waterspouts
hookah – water pipe for smoking
howdah – riding platform for elephant passengers

incarnation – a particular life form; the form mortals assume is determined by *karma*
Indra – king of the *Vedic gods;* god of rain

Jagannath – *Krishna* as Lord of the Universe
Jambhala – god of wealth; look for his money bag and his attendant mongoose
janai – sacred thread, which high-caste Hindu men wear looped over their left shoulder
jatra – festival
jayanti – birthday
jhankri – faith healers who perform in a trance while beating drums
Jogini – mystical goddesses, counterparts to the 64 manifestations of *Bhairab*
jukha – leech
julus – a procession or demonstration; see also *bandh* and *chakka jam*

Kali – the most terrifying manifestation of *Parvati*
Kalki – *Vishnu*'s 10th and as yet unseen incarnation during which he will come riding a white horse and wielding a sword to destroy the world
Kalpa – day in the age of *Brahma*
Kam Dev – *Shiva*'s companion
Kamasutra – ancient Hindu text on erotic pleasures
karma – Buddhist and Hindu law of cause and effect, which continues from one life to another
Kartikkaya – god of war and son of *Shiva,* his *vehicle* is the cock or peacock; also known as Kumar or Skanda
Kaukala – *Shiva* in his fearsome aspect; he carries a trident with *Vishnu*'s gatekeeper's skeleton impaled upon it
KEEP – Kathmandu Environmental Education Project
Khas – Hindu hill people
khat – see *palanquin*
khata – Tibetan prayer scarf, presented to honoured guest or Buddhist *lama*
khola – stream or tributary
khukuri – traditional curved knife of the *Gurkhas*
kinkinimali – temple wind bells
kosi – river
kot – fort
Krishna – fun-loving eighth incarnation of *Vishnu*
Kumari – living goddess, a peaceful incarnation of *Kali*
kunda – water tank fed by springs
kutis – pilgrim hostels

la – mountain pass
lama – Tibetan Buddhist monk or priest
lathi – bamboo staves used by police during a protest
lingam – phallic symbol signifying *Shiva*'s creative powers

machan – a lookout tower used to view wildlife
Machhendranath – patron god of the Kathmandu Valley and an incarnation of *Avalokiteshvara*

Mahabharata – one of the major Hindu epics
Mahadeva – literally 'Great God'; Shiva
Mahadevi – literally 'Great Goddess', sometimes known as *Devi;* the *shakti* to *Shiva*
Mahayana – the 'greater-vehicle' of Buddhism; a later adaptation of the teaching which lays emphasis on the *Bodhisattva* ideal
mahseer – game fish of the Terai rivers
makara – mythical crocodile-like beast
Malla – royal dynasty of the Kathmandu Valley responsible for most of the important temples and palaces of the valley towns
mandala – geometrical and astrological representation of the path to enlightenment
mandir – temple
mani – stone carved with the Tibetan Buddhist chant *om mani padme hum*
Manjushri – Buddhist *Bodhisattva*
mantra – prayer formula or chant
Mara – Buddhist god of death; has three eyes and holds the *wheel of life*
math – Hindu priest's house
mela – country fair
misthan bhandar – Indian-style sweet house and snack bar

naga – serpent deity
Nagpura – Buddhist symbol for water
nak – female *yak*
namaste – traditional Hindu greeting (hello or goodbye), with the hands brought together at chest or head level, as a sign of respect
Nandi – *Shiva's vehicle,* the bull
Narayan – *Vishnu* as the sleeping figure on the cosmic ocean; from his navel *Brahma* appeared and went on to create the universe
Narsingha – man-lion incarnation of *Vishnu*
Newari – people of the Kathmandu Valley
nirvana – ultimate peace and cessation of rebirth (Buddhism)

om mani padme hum – sacred Buddhist *mantra,* which means 'hail to the jewel in the lotus'

padma – lotus flower
Padmapani – literally 'Lotus in Hand'; a manifestation of *Avalokiteshvara*
pagoda – multi-storeyed Nepali temple, whose design was exported across Asia
palanquin – portable covered bed usually shouldered by four men; also called a *khat*
Parvati – *Shiva's* consort
pashmina – goat wool blanket or shawl
Pashupati – *Shiva* as Lord of the Animals
path – small raised platform to shelter pilgrims

phanta – grass plains
pipal tree – see *bodhi tree*
pith – open shrine for a Tantric goddess
pokhari – large water tank, or small lake
prasad – food offering
prayer flag – square of cloth printed with a mantra and hung in a string as a prayer offering
prayer wheel – cylindrical wheel inscribed with a Buddhist prayer or *mantra* that is 'said' when the wheel spins
Prithvi – *Vedic* earth goddess
puja – religious offering or prayer
pujari – priest
puri – town
purnima – full moon

Qomolangma – Tibetan name for Mt Everest; literally 'Mother Goddess of the World' (also spelt Chomolangma)

rajpath – road or highway, literally 'king's road'
raksha bandhan – yellow thread worn on the wrist that is said to bring good fortune
Ramayana – Hindu epic
Rana –a line hereditary prime ministers who ruled Nepal from 1841 to 1951
rath – temple chariot in which the idol is conveyed in processions
Red Hats – name given collectively to adherents of the Nyingmapa, Kargyupa and Sakyapa schools of Tibetan Buddhism
rudraksha – dried seeds worn in necklaces by *sadhus*

SAARC – South Asian Association for Regional Cooperation; includes India, Nepal, Pakistan, Bangladesh and Sri Lanka
sadhu – wandering Hindu holy man
sagar – large sacred ponds
Sagarmatha – Nepali name for Mt Everest
sal – tree of the lower Himalayan foothills
saligram – a black ammonite fossil of a Jurassic-period sea creature which is also a symbol of *Shiva*
sankha – conch shell, one of *Vishnu's* four symbols
Saraswati – goddess of learning and creative arts, and consort of *Brahma*. She carries a lutelike instrument
seto – white
Shaivite – follower of *Shiva*
shakti – dynamic female element in male/female relationships; also a goddess
Sherpa – Buddhist hill people of Tibetan ancestry famed for work with mountaineering expeditions; with a lower case 's' means trek leader
Sherpani – female *Sherpa*
shikhara – Indian-style temple with tall corncoblike spire
Shitala Mai – ogress who became a protector of children
Shiva – the most powerful Hindu god, the creator and destroyer

sindur – red vermillion dust and mustard oil mixture used for offerings

sirdar – leader/organiser of a trekking party

sun – gold, or golden

STOL – short take off and landing aircraft used on mountain airstrips

stupa – bell-shaped Buddhist religious structure, originally designed to hold the relics of the *Buddha*

Sudra – the lowest Nepali caste, said to originate from *Brahma*'s feet

sundhara – fountain with golden spout

tabla – hand drum

tahr – wild mountain goat

tal – lake

Taleju Bhawani – Nepali goddess, an aspect of *Mahadevi* and the family deity of the *Malla* kings of the Kathmandu Valley

Tantric Buddhism – form of Buddhism that evolved in Tibet during the 10th to 15th centuries

tappu – island

Tara – White Tara is the consort of the *Dhyani Buddha* Vairocana; Green Tara is associated with Amoghasiddhi

teahouse trek – independent trekking between village inns (ie no camping)

tempo – three-wheeled, automated minivan commonly used in Nepal

Thakali – people of the Kali Gandaki Valley who specialise in running hotels

thali – literally a plate with compartments for different dishes; an all-you-can-eat set meal

thangka – Tibetan religious painting

third eye – symbolic eye on Buddha figures, used to indicate the Buddha's all-seeing wisdom and perception

thugpa – Tibetan noodle soup

tika – red sandalwood-paste spot marked on the forehead, particularly for religious occasions

tole – street or quarter of a town; sometimes used to refer to a square

tonga – horse carriage

topi – traditional Nepali cap

torana – carved pediment above temple doors

Tribhuvan – the king who in 1951 ended the *Rana* period and Nepal's long seclusion

trisul – trident weapon symbol of *Shiva*

tumpline – leather or cloth strip worn across the forehead or chest of a porter to support a load carried on the back

tunal – carved temple strut

tundikhel – parade ground

Uma Maheshwar – *Shiva* and *Parvati* in a pose where *Shiva* sits cross-legged and *Parvati* sits on his thigh and leans against him

Upanishads – ancient Vedic scripts, the last part of the *Vedas*

urna – the bump on the forehead of a *Buddha* or *Bodhisattva*

vahana – a god's animal mount or *vehicle*

Vaishnavite – follower of *Vishnu*

Vaisya – caste of merchants and farmers, said to originate from *Brahma*'s thighs

vajra – the 'thunderbolt' symbol of Buddhist power in Nepal; *dorje* in Tibetan

Vajra Jogini – a Tantric goddess, *shakti* to a *Bhairab*

Vasudhara – the wife of *Jambhala*, the god of wealth; she rides a chariot drawn by a pig

Vedas – ancient orthodox Hindu scriptures

Vedic gods – ancient Hindu gods described in the *Vedas*

vehicle – the animal with which a Hindu god is associated

vihara – Buddhist religious buildings and pilgrim accommodation

Vishnu – the preserver, one of the three main Hindu gods

wheel of life – representation of how humans are chained by desire to a life of suffering

yab-yum – Tibetan term for Tantric sexual union

yak – main Nepali beast of burden, a form of cattle found above 3000m

yaksha – attendant deity or nymph

Yama – *Vedic god* of death; his messenger is the crow

Yellow Hats – name sometimes given to adherents of the *Gelugpa* school of Tibetan Buddhism

yeti – abominable snowman

yogi – yoga master

yoni – female sexual symbol, equivalent of a *lingam*

zamindar – absentee landlord and/or moneylender

Behind the Scenes

THIS BOOK

This seventh edition of *Nepal* was written by Bradley Mayhew, Joe Bindloss and Stan Armington. Bradley, the coordinating author, also wrote the sixth edition with Lindsay Brown and Wanda Vivequin. The fifth edition was written by Hugh Finlay. This guidebook was commissioned in Lonely Planet's Melbourne office, and produced by the following:

Commissioning Editors Janine Eberle, Lucy Monie, Marg Toohey and Sam Trafford
Coordinating Editor Emma Gilmour
Coordinating Cartographer Natasha Velleley
Coordinating Layout Designer Wibowo Rusli
Managing Cartographer Shahara Ahmed
Assisting Editors David Carroll, John Hinman, Kate James
Assisting Cartographer David Connolly
Assisting Layout Designer Indra Kilfoyle
Cover Designer Wendy Wright
Colour Designer Pablo Gastar
Project Manager Eoin Dunlevy
Language Content Coordinator Quentin Frayne

Thanks to Imogen Bannister, Sally Darmody, Brigitte Ellemor, David Kraklau, Kate McDonald, Kim Noble, Trent Paton, Piers Pickard, Celia Wood

THANKS
BRADLEY MAYHEW
Foremost thanks go to Rajeev Shrestha, Megh Ale and Mukhiya Gurung for all kinds of help.

David Kraklau of the CIWEC Clinic was most helpful on all things medical and gave valuable input to the Health chapter. Götz Hägmuller, Ludmilla Hungerhuber and Susan Fowlds were generous with their time and giving me sneak preview of their Garden of Dreams.

Cheers to Joe and Stan for the beers in Kathmandu and for all their great help throughout the book. Cheers guys! The Sustainable Tourism Unit of the Nepal Tourism Board gave me a great introduction to their community tourism programmes.

Thanks to Andre and Alyson for superfine company on the trek up to Gokyo and Base Camp and to Phurba Sherpa and his wife Gyanu, who were the best Sherpa guides we could have hoped for.

As always, thanks to my wife Kelli, who had to put up with me being away for three months and then, even worse, had to put up with me being home for the next three months. Love you, honey.

JOE BINDLOSS
First up, I would like to credit my work on this title to my goddaughter Stella Benatar, and her sister Beatrice and brother Bart. Thanks also to my partner Linda for her constant support. In Kathmandu, thanks to Piers and Nikki Benatar for their ceaseless hospitality and to the various expats and NGOs who provided info on the security situation in the Terai. Thanks also to the staff of the Annupurna Conservation Area Project, the Nepal Tourism Board and the many travellers who provided tips and advice along the way. Thanks also to Bradley and Stan for advice and bringing the whole project together.

THE LONELY PLANET STORY

The story begins with a classic travel adventure: Tony and Maureen Wheeler's 1972 journey across Europe and Asia to Australia. There was no useful information about the overland trail then, so Tony and Maureen published the first Lonely Planet guidebook to meet a growing need.

From a kitchen table, Lonely Planet has grown to become the largest independent travel publisher in the world, with offices in Melbourne (Australia), Oakland (USA) and London (UK). Today Lonely Planet guidebooks cover the globe. There is an ever-growing list of books and information in a variety of media. Some things haven't changed. The main aim is still to make it possible for adventurous travellers to get out there – to explore and better understand the world.

At Lonely Planet we believe travellers can make a positive contribution to the countries they visit – if they respect their host communities and spend their money wisely. Every year 5% of company profit is donated to charities around the world.

OUR READERS

Many thanks to the travellers who used the last edition and wrote to us with helpful hints, useful advice and interesting anecdotes:

A Malgorzata Adamska, Sharifah Albukhary, Orson Alcocer, Federico & Miguel Aldasoro, Henk Allebosch, Mark Ambrose, William Arnemann, Harry Arnold **B** John Bachman, Meg Back, Gilles Bacon, Jon Baldwin, Lisa Ball, Terry Banks, David Barkshire, Bryony Bartlett, William Batten, Chris Beall, Rafe Benli, Danny Ben-Zvi, Scott Berry, Ron Bertram, Mark Bezodis, Haifeng Bi, Anna Bibby, Willem & Mieke Biezen, James Birrell, Nic Birrell, Mike & Liz Bissett, Sylwester Bizacki, Jay Blackhurst, Cathy Bond, Ian Boulton, Hugo Bouman, Ruth & Bart Boumans, Jo Boussemaere, Titus Brand, Josephine Brouard, James Brown, Leen Brugmans, Keith & Caryl Bryars, Robert Bugg, Corinne Burri, Amanda Buttitta **C** Jon Kepa Cabrera Guridi, Leah Campbell, Polly & Juliet Campbell, Bruce Carstairs, Pietro Catalano, H C Champion, Becky Chasey, Yee Cheng, Billy Clegg, Neil Cloake, David Coates, Alexei Collett, Cesar Colmenero, Sean Cordeiro, Carles Cufi **D** Roland Dahlman, Daphne Dakins, Steffen Damm, Geoffrey Davey, Alex & Kate Davis, Sonya Davis, Rimli & Sushil Dawka, Karsten Dax, Yigal Dayan, Koen de Boeck, Ronan de Lacy, Lucia de Toledo, Lucia de Vries, Simon de Young, James Delany, Wiel & Mien Derkx, Lynsey Devon, Marília Dias, Flor Diaz, Thomas Dobler, Poechmann Dominikus, William Donaldson, Anna Dowdall, Ray Dunn, Andrew Duy **E** Manny & Roni Elder, Usha Elderfield, Navyo Eller, Heiner Engellandt, Thomas Eriksson, Peter Evans, Tobias Evans **F** David Farmar, Magdalena & Krysztof Fedorowicz, Elinor Feldman, Vincke Filip, Nick Fletcher, Carl Flint, Eric Frankenmolen, Audire Franzen **G** Deborah Gan, Joao Garcia, Maike Gardner, Matthew Garfein, Mitchell Garlington, Sabine Gartner, Christina & Scott Gifford, Bhaju Ram Giri, Nuno Godinho, Peter & Claudia Goodridge, Jon Gourlay, Sara Gradwohl, Sara Grantham, Patty Greene, Jos Gremmen, Mark Griffiths, Chamsari Gurung **H** Miriam Hadcocks, Rebecca Haley, Julia Halford, Timothy Hallam, Fran Hamilton, Joe Hammond, Hillery Hanby, Manfred Hartmann, Sue Haviland, Tessa Haynes, Brian Hedley, Mark Heffernan, Triona Hensey, Els Hermans, Vicente Hernandez, Jacqueline Hewitt, Simon Heyes, Marike Hippe, Wiley Hoard, Louise Hogg, Max Hogg, Thomas Hohenberger, Ian Holdsworth **I** Daisuke Ikeda, Russell Inman, Barta Istvan, Rusch Ivo **J** Jane Jackman, Jennifer James, Simon Jeacock, Marjo Jenniskens, Loki Johnk, Stuart Johnston, Rowan & Anna Jones, Daran Joshi **K** Haemish Kane, Clara Karlsson Cassland, Noa Katz, Patricia Kelly, Ben Choo Chee Keong, Nawal Khattri, Magdalena Kijak, Rolaf Klapwijk, Roni & Ayala Klaus, Andy Klunder, Bettina Kocher, Dietrich Kohlschmidt, Jeroen Kok, Grazyna Krewin, Yvonne Kwakernaak **L** Niranjan Lamichhane, Barry Lane, Rein Langeland, Martin Langevoord, Nathalie Langlois, Iain Langridge, Magdalena Larraguibel, Fredrik Larsen, Josephine Lau, Bruno le Brize, Robert Leitz, Anne Leppert, Caroline Lewis, D Lintell-Smith, Richard Little, Karen Locke, Piers Locke, Erik Lohr, Jennifer Lonergan, Gabriella Lopez, Oriol Lopez-munte **M** Heather Macbeth, John Maclachlan, Martina Maelzig, Tamara Maerschalck, L Majdalinski, Andrew Manzardo, Caroline Martin,

SEND US YOUR FEEDBACK

We love to hear from travellers – your comments keep us on our toes and help make our books better. Our well-travelled team reads every word on what you loved or loathed about this book. Although we cannot reply individually to postal submissions, we always guarantee that your feedback goes straight to the appropriate authors, in time for the next edition. Each person who sends us information is thanked in the next edition – and the most useful submissions are rewarded with a free book.

To send us your updates – and find out about Lonely Planet events, newsletters and travel news – visit our award-winning website: **www.lonelyplanet.com/feedback**.

Note: We may edit, reproduce and incorporate your comments in Lonely Planet products such as guidebooks, websites and digital products, so let us know if you don't want your comments reproduced or your name acknowledged. For a copy of our privacy policy visit www.lonelyplanet.com/privacy.

Mylene Martinez, Greg Mason, Chris Matthew, Una McCormack, Fergus McGaugh, Laura McGuiness, Andrew & Christine McPherson, Sivan Megidish, Stefan Meivers, Jan Melisse, Janneke Michels, Emily Mitterhuemer, Bruce Moore, Garry Moore, Daniel Morgenstern, Silke Morkel, Susanna Mountcastle, Claudia Muecke, Henriette and Horst Müller, Neil Murdoch, Brian Murphy, Chris Murphy **N** Christiane Nepel, Hun Ng, Peter Ngan, Jean Nicolet, Verena Nobis, Mingma Norbu Sherpa, Lisa Norris, Chris Nunn **O** Richard Oakford, Nick O'Connor, Ivar Oiumshaugen, Ric Ostrower **P** Krupa Patel, A I Paulsen Petersen, Marianne Pedersen, Alexandra Peifer, Hanna Peseke, Daniela Peters, Morten Petersen, Brooke Pflasterer, Trisha Phelan, Bridget Phelps, Marijke Pielage, Jason Pilley, Roch-Alain Poirier, Emmanuelle Poncet, Vagelis Protopapas, Alice Purser **R** Eddie Racuobian, Wanda Radecka-Paryzek, Terrell Rafferty, Madeline Ravesloot, Brand Recht, Bronwyn Rees, Susanne Reiber, Perry Reid, Ina Ritzmann, Heather Rodgers, Margriet Roelands, Terry Rollins, Sushanta Roy-Choudhury, Gil Rozen, Mary Ryan, Diane Rydrych **S** Mischa Saleki, Elisabeth Samuelsson, Christine Sanders, Nicolas Saumart, John Saunders, Matthias Schermaier, Rainer Schlager, Simon Scholl, Matthias Schwarze, David Scott, Paul Scott, Katja Seifert, Gavin Sexton, Nitzan Shadmi, Adi Shaiak, Renu Sharma, PT Sherpa, SW Sherpa, Peter Sidgwick, Carolina Simpson, Emma Simpson, Malcolm Slater, Donald Slinger, Lucie Smidova, Alistair Smith, Emily Smith, Jason Smith, Mark Smith, Phil Smith, Bart Smits, Aity Soekidjo, Matthew Spruell, Lisa Steadman, Katja Stengler, Terry Stephenson, Douglas Stevens, Kristine Stevens, Linde Steverink, Maria Stewart, Chris Stolz, Viktor Streicher, Tom Stuart, Claudine Stuchell, Anders Svensson, Linda Swankie **T** Ricardo Tarifa, Ralph Teckenburg, Ritesh Thapa,

Joyce Thom, K R Tuladhar **V** Roel van de Wiel, Georges van den Bogaert, Thijs van den Burg, Piet van der Linden, Laurens van der Plaat, Donovan van Heuven, Peter van Nes, Meike van Tilburg, Davy & Kathleen Vanwijnsberghe, Clem Vetters, Yvonne & Michael Vintiner, Wanda Vivequin, Joris Vogels, Roman Vogt **W** Marcus Wagner, Philippe Walz-Balayn, SD Wangmo, Matt Ward, Natalie Ware, Mark Watson, Brian Weber, Paul Weller, Scott Wells, Pohsuan Weng, Karen Weston, Alison White, Bruno Widmer, Timothy Willis, Adela Willson, Katherine Wilson, Klaus Winterling, Patrick Witton, Gadi Wolach, Juergen Wolf, Isabel Wright **Y** Avishay Yarimi, Etsuko Yasunaga-Kenyon, Lawrence Yu, Nitzan Yudan **Z** Edme Zalinski, Wierd Zijlstra

ACKNOWLEDGMENTS

Many thanks to the following for the use of their content:

Globe on back cover ©Mountain High Maps 1993 Digital Wisdom, Inc.

Index

INDEX

INDEX

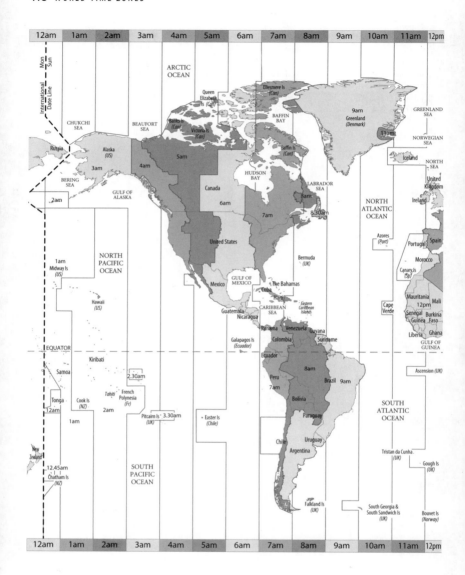

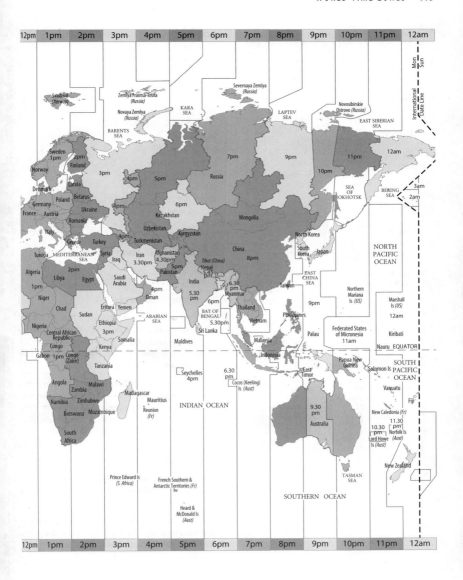

| 12pm | 1pm | 2pm | 3pm | 4pm | 5pm | 6pm | 7pm | 8pm | 9pm | 10pm | 11pm | 12am |

Mon
Sun
International Date Line

Svalbard (Norway)

Zemlya Frantsa-Iosifa (Russia)

Severnaya Zemlya (Russia)

Novosibirskie Ostrovo (Russia)

Novaya Zemlya (Russia)

KARA SEA

LAPTEV SEA

EAST SIBERIAN SEA

BARENTS SEA

Sweden
1pm
2pm
Finland

Norway

3pm

7pm

9pm

11pm

12am

Denmark
Latvia

10pm

Germany
Poland
Belarus

4pm

5pm

Russia

SEA OF OKHOTSK

3am

France
Austria
Ukraine

BERING SEA

2am

Italy
Romania

6pm

Kazakhstan

Mongolia

NORTH PACIFIC OCEAN

Greece
Turkey

Uzbekistan
Kyrgyzstan

North Korea

Tunisia
MEDITERRANEAN SEA
Syria
4pm
Turkmenistan

China
8pm

South Korea
Japan

Algeria
2pm
Libya
Egypt
Iran
3.30pm
Afghanistan
4.30pm
Iraq
Tibet (China)
Nepal
5pm
5.45
pm

EAST CHINA SEA

Northern Mariana Is (US)

Marshall Is (US)

1pm
Niger
Saudi Arabia
Pakistan
India
6.30
pm
Myanmar

Taiwan

9pm

12am

Chad
4pm
Oman
5.30
pm

Thailand

Philippines

Nigeria
Eritrea
Yemen

6pm

Vietnam

Palau

Federated States of Micronesia
11am

Kiribati

Central African Republic
Ethiopia
3pm
ARABIAN SEA

BAY OF BENGAL
5.30pm
Sri Lanka

Malaysia

Nauru EQUATOR

Congo
Somalia
Kenya
Maldives

Indonesia

Papua New Guinea
Solomon Is

SOUTH PACIFIC OCEAN

Gabon
1pm
Congo (Zaire)
Tanzania

Seychelles
4pm

East Timor

Vanuatu

Fiji

Angola
Malawi
Zambia
Zimbabwe
Madagascar
Mauritius

6.30
pm
Cocos (Keeling) Is (Aust)

New Caledonia (Fr)
11.30
pm

Namibia
Mozambique
Reunion (Fr)

INDIAN OCEAN

9.30
pm
Australia

10.30
pm
Norfolk Is (Aust)

Botswana

Lord Howe Is (Aust)

South Africa

New Zealand

Prince Edward Is (S. Africa)

French Southern & Antarctic Territories (Fr)
Iso

TASMAN SEA

SOUTHERN OCEAN

Heard & McDonald Is (Aust)

| 12pm | 1pm | 2pm | 3pm | 4pm | 5pm | 6pm | 7pm | 8pm | 9pm | 10pm | 11pm | 12am |

420

MAP LEGEND

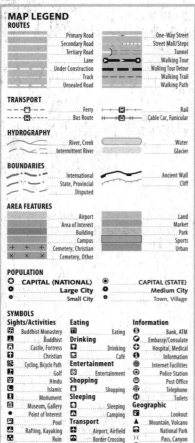

LONELY PLANET OFFICES

Australia
Head Office
Locked Bag 1, Footscray, Victoria 3011
☎ 03 8379 8000, fax 03 8379 8111
talk2us@lonelyplanet.com.au

USA
150 Linden St, Oakland, CA 94607
☎ 510 893 8555, toll free 800 275 8555
fax 510 893 8572
info@lonelyplanet.com

UK
72–82 Rosebery Ave,
Clerkenwell, London EC1R 4RW
☎ 020 7841 9000, fax 020 7841 9001
go@lonelyplanet.co.uk

Published by Lonely Planet Publications Pty Ltd
ABN 36 005 607 983

© Lonely Planet Publications Pty Ltd 2006

© photographers as indicated 2006

Cover photographs by Lonely Planet Images: Portrait of a sadhu in Bagmati, Kathmandu, Greg Elms (front); Mt Ama Dablan in Khumbu, Sagarmatha, Jeff Cantarutti (back). Many of the images in this guide are available for licensing from Lonely Planet Images: www.lonelyplanetimages.com.